THE

HISTORY OF NORMANDY

AND OF

ENGLAND,

BY

SIR FRANCIS PALGRAVE, K.H.

THE DEPUTY KEEPER OF HER MAJESTY'S
PUBLIC RECORDS

VOLUME I.

GENERAL RELATIONS OF MEDLÆVAL EUROPE;—
THE CARLOVINGIAN EMPIRE — THE DANISH
EXPEDITIONS IN THE GAULS — AND THE
ESTABLISHMENT OF ROLLO.

Narratione autem historica (ait Augustinus) cum præterita etiam hominum
instituta narrantur. non inter humana instituta ipsa historia numeranda
est; quia jam quæ transierunt, nec infecta fieri possunt, in ordine
temporum habenda sunt, quor im est conditor et administrator Deus.

LONDON.
JOHN W. PARKER AND SON,
WEST STRAND.

M DCCC LI

TO

HENRY HALLAM

THIS WORK IS

SUBMITTED AND INSCRIBED AS A TOKEN

OF THE AUTHOR'S LONG-CONTINUED AFFECTION,

RESPECT, AND HONOUR.

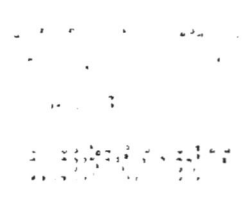

a 2

CONTENTS.

CHAPTER II.
THE ROMAN LANGUAGE.

CHAPTER III.

SCOPE AND OBJECT OF THE PRESENT HISTORY.

BOOK I.

CARLOVINGIAN NORMANDY.

CHAPTER I.

LOUIS-LE-DEBONNAIRE, HIS PREDECESSORS AND SUCCESSORS.

741—987.

Chapter II.

LOUIS-LE-DEBONNAIRE AND HIS SUCCESSORS, TO THE FINAL DETHRONEMENT OF THE CARLOVINGIAN DYNASTY.

824—987.

Events from the Death of Louis-le-Débonnaire and the Accession of Charles-le-Chauve to the Treaty of Mersen, 840—847.

A.D		PAGE
840	Death of Louis-le-Débonnaire . . .	309
840—841	Confusions ensuing thereupon	309-312
—	Lothair claims the paramount Sovereignty . . .	312, 313
—	Invades and occupies the dominions of Charles-le-Chauve	313, 314
—	And proposes terms to the latter	314
841	Charles-le-Chauve regains his territory and influence	314, 315
—	The regalia brought from Aquitaine . .	316, 317
—	Lothair's hatred against his brother Louis . . .	317, 318
—	Who defeats Lothair's troops	318
—	Junction of Louis and Charles at Châlons .	319
—	Great Danish invasion of Neustria	319
—	Their plans of warfare	320-322
—	Jarl Osker enters the Seine . . .	322, 323
—	Antient Rouen	323, 324
—	Rouen burned and plundered	324, 325
—	Jumièges and Fontenelle also	325, 326
—	Charles and Louis negociate with Lothair . .	327, 328
—	Nevertheless hostile movements continue .	328
—	Both armies take up positions near Auxerre . .	328, 329
—	Great battle of Fontenay	329-331
—	Lothair defeated	330
—	The victory's mournful morrow	332-334
—	Lothair renews negociations . . .	334
—	Further alliance of Charles and Louis-le-Germanique .	334, 335
—	Treaty and oaths of Strasburg	335
—	They advance against Lothair . . .	335
—	Lothair's flight—construed as an abdication .	336
—	His dominions shared between his brothers . .	336, 337
—	Lothair reassembles his forces	337
—	Negociations opened at Châlons . . .	337, 338
—	Saracen and Danish invasions	338, 339
—	Earthquakes—fires in the sky	339
—	Cosmical phenomena, their historical influence .	339, 340
843	Treaty of Verdun	341
—	Lothair's Imperial pre-eminence conceded . .	342
—	Lothair's kingdom	342, 343
—	Description and boundaries thereof . . .	343-345
—	East-Rhenane Territories assigned to Louis-le-Germanique	345
—	France to Charles-le-Chauve	345, 346

Summary of Carlovingian History.

CHAPTER III.

THE NORTHMEN DURING THE TIMES OF CHARLES-LE-CHAUVE AND ROBERT-LE-FORT, TO THE END OF THE REIGN.

840—877.

Chapter IV.

FLANDERS, FRANCE, AND THE NORTHMEN, TO THE DETHRONE-
MENT AND DEATH OF CHARLES-LE-CHAUVE, AND THE
FINAL DISMEMBERMENT OF THE CARLOVINGIAN EMPIRE.

862—888.

Chapter V.

DISMEMBERMENT OF THE EMPIRE : EUDES AND CHARLES-LE-
SIMPLE. ESTABLISHMENT OF ROLLO IN NORMANDY.

888—912.

NOTES.

INTRODUCTION.

CHAPTER I.

THE FOURTH MONARCHY.

CHAPTER II.

THE ROMAN LANGUAGE.

CHAPTER III.

BOOK I.
CARLOVINGIAN NORMANDY.

CHAPTER I.
LOUIS-LE-DEBONNAIRE, HIS PREDECESSORS AND SUCCESSORS.

A.D. 721—824.

Chapter II.

LOUIS-LE-DEBONNAIRE AND HIS SUCCESSORS, TO THE FINAL DETHRONEMENT OF THE CARLOVINGIAN DYNASTY.

CONCLUSION OF THE REIGN OF LOUIS-LE-DEBONNAIRE.

A.D. 824—840.

CHAPTER III.

THE NORTHMEN DURING THE TIMES OF CHARLES-LE-CHAUVE AND ROBERT-LE-FORT TO THE END OF THE REIGN.

A.D. 840—877.

Chapter IV.

FLANDERS, FRANCE, AND THE NORTHMEN, TO THE DETHRONE-
MENT AND DEATH OF CHARLES-LE-GRAS, AND THE FINAL
DISMEMBERMENT OF THE CARLOVINGIAN EMPIRE.

CHAPTER V.

DISMEMBERMENT OF THE EMPIRE.   EUDES AND CHARLES-LE-
SIMPLE.   ESTABLISHMENT OF ROLLO IN NORMANDY.

PREFACE.

THE circumstances leading me to undertake the present Work are fully explained in the third chapter of the Introduction. I have therein also given a summary of the different eras or periods which my design, as now modified, comprehends. The text of the fourth Book, or third Volume, containing the history of the Conqueror's three sons,—Robert, Rufus, and Henry,—in Normandy, in Palestine, and in England, is printed, and I am making every endeavour to complete the second, or intervening volume, as speedily as possible.

When I commenced, I did not contemplate a narrative history upon so extensive a scale as that which now appears; or rather, I proposed to myself a set of concurrent works (the History being one), so planned as that they should fit into each other,—mutually explanatory,—deducing and illustrating the mediæval history of England, not only as a Sovereign state, but also as a member of the Western Commonwealth, and exhibiting men and morals under different aspects, varying the treatment according to the subject-matter; yet all combining into one course of instruction with my other works more particularly devoted to our Constitutional History, or containing the original muniments or materials for the same.

The History of England, properly so called, the recital of English events and affairs, was first composed with the intent that it should continue the History of the Anglo-Saxons, in about six volumes of the same size.—Essays upon Literature, Science, the influence of the Church, the antagonism of the World, the Fine Arts, Guilds and Fraternities, Commerce, Literature, the Crusades, general views of the French Provinces more peculiarly connected with England, and the like, were sketched for the purpose of forming another work accompanying the History.—Useful information relating to legal or political institutions, (themes in themselves rather arid,) might, I thought, be popularly introduced through the medium of fictitious narrative.—Lastly, retaining a vivid recollection of the delight which, when younger, I had received from Southey's *Chronicle of the Cid*, I gratified myself by the supposition that there were passages in our English annals susceptible of being presented in a similar style; and I began a "Chronicle of John Lackland" accordingly.

None of these subsidiaries to the narrative history, however, satisfied me.—In order to mitigate the inherent dogmatism of disquisitions, I introduced in the Essays many historical anecdotes; but by plucking out the interesting characters and dramatic incidents, the History became impoverished for the enrichment of the Essays, and I therefore found that I could not afford to spend my means upon them.

Sir Walter Scott having exhausted his pleasurable stores in his *Tales of a Grandfather*, thus ruined his *History of Scotland*. He anticipated that both works would be equally read; but it may be doubted whether one in a hundred of the innumerable readers who, as children, were enraptured by the fascinating, yet most instructive passages of history collected for their amusement in the *Tales*, have, according to the author's expectation, "perused with advantage the graver publication designed for their use, when their appetite for knowledge should encrease with encreasing age."

In *The Merchant and the Friar*, I employ Roger Bacon as the expounder of Mediæval Science, but the action of the story is conceived for the purpose of explaining some important passages of our ancient Constitution. One principal object sought, was to depict the High Court of Parliament, during the period when service in the Upper House was deemed onerous, and the attendance in the Lower, though not altogether undesirable, was still reckoned a duty which many would shift off, just as we now endeavour to escape being put on juries, or becoming members of the Parish Vestry. The attributes of the Mediæval Parliament, moreover, require to be viewed under a different aspect to that which they now assume, (the Council being an integral organ thereof,) a Senate, and also a Supreme Court of Justice, to which the Subject could apply for actual redress of injuries—the poor man's Court, where the Englishman might sue in formâ pauperis without sustaining the poor man's degradation. It was the union of judicial and political characters in Parliament—the administration of remedial justice—which endeared that unparalleled Assembly to Old England: an attribute which has been completely ignored by foreigners, and never sufficiently acknowledged by ourselves. I therein also have attempted to correct the astounding misconceptions concerning trial by jury, and to substitute sober truth for the romantic fictions which exhibit a procedure— according to its present course and principles scarcely older than the Tudors—as a judgment by the Peers of the accused, the inheritance of Alfred's wisdom.

An unpublished work of the same class,—three generations of an imaginary Norfolk family,—elucidates the relative positions of landlord and tenant during the transition-period of military and villain tenures, Wat Tyler winding up the catastrophe. But when this tale was completed it became evident to the manufacturer that he had spoiled sound materials.—Moral or social discussions, grounded upon past or contemporary history, rarely, if ever, make any beneficial impression when clothed in a garb by which existences and inventions are confounded. Any incontestable misery pourtrayed in the Socialist Novel, which pricks the conscience of the Capitalist, he refuses as an invention ; and any invention which he can deflect so as to suit his own views, he adopts as a reality. Historical novels are mortal enemies to history.—*Ivanhoe* is all of a piece—language, characters, incidents, manners, thoughts, are out of time, out of place, out of season, out of reason, ideal or impossible.—When, on the waters of the gentle Don, there glided the Swan with *two* necks ; then Gurth, with the brass collar soldered round his *one*, so tight as to be incapable of being removed excepting by the use of the file, tended swine in the woodlands of Rotheram.

King John's mock black-letter Chronicle finally convinced me that modern antiques of every kind dispel all reverend notions of antiquity. The sensation of the sham is invincible. In the most perfect resuscitation of Henry the Third's " Early English," the tooling of the well-tempered town-made chisel inscribes "Victoria and Albert" upon every stone.

These adjuncts being discarded, I have absorbed any useful matter or reflections which they contained or suggested into this present history, thereby rendering it more diversified. Other considerations contributed to widen the field beyond the boundary I originally intended to occupy. Having in the history of the Anglo-Saxons introduced William the Bastard claiming as the heir-testamentary or expectant of the Confessor, I did not, according to my primary scheme, intend to deal with him in his earlier years : but when I worked upon the reign of William the Conqueror in England, I found I could not make out a satisfactory story otherwise than by presenting the same as a continuation of his previous life and fortunes. The like observation applied also to his advisers and companions, very particularly

to Lanfranc, the great restorer of the Church of
England; and therefore the necessity of a history of the Duchy of Normandy became apparent. Such a history has hitherto been a desi-
deratum in the English language; nor has this
subject been sufficiently treated by the French.
I would wish on all occasions to acknowledge the
deep obligations we owe to our French fellow-
labourers: but in Sismondi's history, Normandy
constitutes but a very small episode; and the
writers of less reputation, who have written
special histories of Normandy, however useful
they may be as pioneers, have not evinced the
merits characterizing the French school.

The richness of our Anglo-Norman history is
so exuberant that I could not bring myself to
compress the vintage into a juiceless residuum.
Therefore, renouncing the hope of prosecuting the
work to the Tudor era, I finally determined to
restrict myself to such a portion or portions as
my times would allow:—not stintedly, but upon
a scale commensurate with their value;—hence
the bulk which the work has acquired.

Arnold was blamed for the length of his
volumes. I would reply to the like objection,
should it be raised, in Arnold's words: "I am
"convinced by a tolerably large experience, that

" most readers find it almost impossible to impress
" on their memories a mere abridgment of history :
" the number of names and events crowded into
" a small space is overwhelming to them, and
" the absence of details in the narrative makes it
" impossible to communicate to it much of in-
" terest.   Neither characters nor events can be
" developed with that particularity which is the
" best help to the memory, because it attracts
" and engages us, and impresses images on the
" mind as well as facts."   Not merely are meagre
abridgments devoid of interest, but, under the
existing circumstances of society, they become
snares for the conscience, seducing men to content
themselves with a perfunctory notion of history,
and, when occasion calls, to act upon imperfect
knowledge.

Historical truth never can be elicited save by
comparison.   Particularly is this labour of comparison incumbent upon every one who, in his
sphere, may be called upon to legislate or influence the duty of legislation, a duty perhaps involving the most fearful responsibility which can
devolve upon any human being ; for the function
of the Lawgiver is the highest exercised by man.
Human institutions are rarely, perhaps never,
beneficial or mischievous, simply in themselves ;

they become beneficial or mischievous by their
relation to other institutions; and therefore when
presented to ratiocination without these concurrent
circumstances, they only mislead the judgment,
substituting words and phrases for real knowledge. No one book, however excellent, can teach
you singly and alone. History requires no less
study than Law. We cannot dabble in its practical application. Would you take upon yourself
to pay down your purchase-money for an acre
of land, upon your knowledge of conveyancing
derived from Blackstone's Commentaries?

The publication of a work which has occupied
the best part of my life is not unattended by
considerable anxiety. In every stage it has been
spoken: that is to say, written down by dictation, and transcribed from dictation. Advantages
and disadvantages, counterbalancing each other,
attend this mode of composition. The sound
of his own voice encourages the speaker to express his mind more fully than when he is
sitting before his desk.—The single amanuensis
represents a whole audience. But a speaker may
also be seduced into many liberties of speech,
and tempted to indulge in digressions and fancies which would not have occurred to him if
penning his silent thoughts in solitude.

I therefore appear somewhat in the character of a lecturer, who prints his lectures as they have been reported under his direction. He addresses pupils who belong to him, who interest him, whom he exerts himself to teach, trying to render his lessons intelligible and agreeable, varying his modes of expression according to the spur of the moment or the play of thought, and throwing in occasionally a word, when he judges by the aspect and manner of his hearers that an explanation, or modification, or an awakening of attention, is needed.—Hence the composition has acquired a species of familiar and colloquial character; and the Author trusts he shall obtain the indulgence granted to those whose position he assumes.—May he not hope to be excused as an instructor intent upon his duty, however imperfectly he may have succeeded?

Fully am I aware that I may be thought, on some occasions, to have neglected " the dignity of history."—But is any peculiar fashion of diction required for history? Wordsworth has for ever dispelled that notion with respect to poetry. Nor can history, otherwise than according to a remote analogy, be considered as a work of art, or subjected to normal rules. The notion of historical dignity may be as safely rejected as the

doctrine of dramatic unity. The more clearly the
story is told, the better it will be understood; the
more amusingly, the better it will be recollected.
The more the author has thought upon the subject, the more will he kindle congenial thoughts
in others. Trite truths are often the most weighty;
hackneyed incidents the most influential;—any
manner or device, any mode whereby you can
stamp them with a new form, renews their instructive value.—Tone, idiom, language, allusion
or illustration, whatever tends to rouse observation, to stimulate perception, or aid the memory,
adds to the power of instruction, in which consists the real dignity of history.

Any writer treating the dark or middle ages
has a much more delicate as well as difficult
task to perform than the historian engaged upon
the antecedent periods of classical antiquity.
His materials are more abounding, their compass
and variety greater, therefore the greater danger
of redundancy and confusion. The theme, and
every point connected therewith, has been made
painfully polemic and contentious.—The classical
historian is supported by general prepossessions
on his behalf: he has more than the old Prize-
fighter used to crave, a clear stage and no favour;
he has already got a clear stage and favour be-

sides. All his readers go with him, so far as the
subject is concerned. There may be great differences in historical theories, various estimates of
character, conflicting opinions respecting the tendencies of institutions, or the political lessons to
be derived therefrom : but, in essentials, opinions
are universally consentaneous—all worship in the
Parthenon, and crown the tomb of Leonidas ; all
agree in admiring Greece and Rome, their mythology, their literature, their poets, their heroes.
The unpleasant groupes of the picture are lightly
touched, depravity euphemized, vice condonated,
nay, rites and objects of worship, images of pollution which the archæologist dare not describe,
elicit a conciliatory apology as primeval symbols
of the powers of nature.

With respect to the mediæval era the case is
exactly reversed. A dead set has been made
against the middle ages, as periods immersed
in darkness, ignorance, and barbarity. But most
of all have these censures been directed against
mediæval Christianity,—" an abject superstition,
" tending only to the depression and debasement
" of the human mind."—According to the repre-
sentations promulgated by a celebrated authority
of the last century, who, in this Empire, has contributed more than any other, to direct public

opinion upon such subjects—" the barbarous na-
" tions, when converted to Christianity, changed
" the object, not the spirit of their religious wor-
" ship. They endeavoured to conciliate the favour
" of the true God, by means not unlike to those
" which they had employed in order to appease
" their false deities. Instead of aspiring to sanc-
" tity and virtue, which alone can render men
" accceptable to the great Author of order and
" of excellence, they imagined that they satisfied
" *every* obligation of duty by a scrupulous ob-
" servance of external ceremonies. Religion, ac-
" cording to their conception of it, comprehended
" *nothing* else ; and the rites, by which they per-
" suaded themselves that they should gain the
" favour of Heaven, were of such a nature as
" might have been expected from the rude ideas
" of the ages which devised and introduced them.
" They were either so unmeaning as to be alto-
" gether unworthy of the Being to whose honour
" they were consecrated, or so absurd as to be a
" disgrace to reason and humanity. Charlemagne
" in France, and Alfred the Great in England,
" endeavoured to dispel this darkness, and gave
" their subjects a short glimpse of light and know-
" ledge. But the ignorance of the age was too
" powerful for their efforts and institutions. The

" darkness returned, and settled over Europe more
" thick and heavy than before."

These calumnies,—which, if excused, are only
excusable by the plea of insuperable ignorance,—
not unfrequently exalted into fanatical hatred, have
been produced by various causes, some so subtle
that they escape us whilst we are recognizing them,
others discrepant amongst themselves, all nevertheless tending to the same conclusions. Sagacious
Fleury warns us that Christian antiquity was first
decried in Italy. He dates the sentiment from the
era of the revival of letters. The depreciation of
the dark ages originated, according to Fleury's
indication, from the disgust excited by the bar-
barisms of mediæval latinity:—the Scholar's enthusiasm, and the pedant's conceit, combining with
intellectual and moral tendencies adverse to religion. The agents he signalizes are a Politian, a
Valla, a Poggius, a Bembo : men of critical taste,
dubious faith and profligate lives, who cultivated
the elegances of literature amidst the atheism of
Padua, the paganism of Carregi, and the rank
debauchery of the Vatican. But Fleury stops
short in his deduction. In proportion as refinement advanced in modern Europe, so did most
good men participate in the same ethos, swayed
by that engouement for classical literature, which

rendered every name and thing connected with the mediæval periods baroque or absurd, whilst to heathenism, education and intellect yielded the deepest homage.

La Fable offre à l'esprit mille agrémens divers—
Là tous les noms heureux semblent nés pour les vers ;
Ulysse, Agamemnon, Oreste, Idomenée,
Helène, Menelaus, Paris, Hector, Enée.
O le plaisant projet d'un Poëte ignorant,
Qui de tant de héros va choisir Childebrand !
D'un seul nom quelquefois le son dur ou bizarre
Rend un poème entier, ou burlesque ou barbare.

All classes responded to these modish sentiments. Dom Rivet and Dom Clemencet, Dom Montfaucon and Dom Mabillon endeavoured to shew that they were not strangers to good company ; and, in order that they might not lose caste in the *Academie des Inscriptions,* or the *cercle,* spoke occasionally with fastidiousness of the dark ages.—Fenelon himself could find no better medium of inculcating the lessons of good government to the heir of the throne than through the adaptation of an Homeric fable.

Abstractedly from all the influences which we have sustained in common with the rest of the civilized commonwealth, our British disparagement of the middle ages has been exceedingly enhanced by our grizzled ecclesiastical or church-historians of the sixteenth and seventeenth centuries, men who instead of vindicating the Reformation, by the advocacy of reverence for holy things, obedience, love, charity, sought to establish righteousness through vengeance, and in all ways rendering evil for evil. " Hate your enemies" is with them the Law and the Prophets. These " standard works," accepted and received as Canonical Books, have tainted the nobility of our national mind. An adequate parallel to their bitterness, their shabbiness, their shirking, their habitual disregard of honour and veracity, is hardly afforded even by the so-called " Anti-Jacobin" press during the revolutionary and Imperial wars. The history of Napoleon, his Generals and the French nation, collected from these exaggerations of selfish loyalty, rabid aversion, and panic terror, would be the match of our popular and prevailing ideas concerning Hildebrand, or Anselm, or Becket, or Innocent III. or mediæval Catholicity in general, grounded upon our ancestorial traditionary " standard ecclesiastical authorities," such as Burnet's *Reformation*, or Fox's *Book of Martyrs*.—They are wrong when on the right side, false, when true.—The Judge drunken with party-fury, pronouncing the deserved sentence upon the guilty culprit, is equally a mur-

derer with the criminal whom he condemns:—
cruelty may be reprobated so as to generate
merciless malignity; idolatry, rebuked in a spirit
of blasphemy; superstition so derided as to blot
out belief in Omnipotence—never was any literature more calculated to derogate against the
glory of God and destroy good will towards man.

But the most wide pervading and influential
impulse to these sentiments emanated from philosophical France. The wit, the knowledge, all
the acquired talents and mental gifts bestowed
upon her men of letters, during the era of the
Encyclopédie, were devoted to their sincere vocation, their avowed object, their pride—the subversion of Christianity. Every branch of instruction, themes and subjects in themselves the most
innocent, the most agreeable, the most beneficial,
were thus consistently and unceasingly employed,
and none more successfully than mediæval history.

The scheme and intent of mediæval Catholicity was to render Faith the all-actuating and all-
controlling vitality. This high aspiration failed,
such a state of society being absolutely incompatible with the Kingdoms of the world. Nevertheless, so far as the system extended, it had
the effect of connecting every social element with

Christianity. And Christianity being thus wrought up into the mediæval system, every mediæval institution, character, or mode of thought afforded the means or vehicle for the vilification of Christianity. Never do these writers, or their School, whether in France or in Great Britain, Voltaire or Mably, Hume, Robertson, or Henry, treat the Clergy or the Church with fairness; not even with common honesty. If historical notoriety enforces the allowance of any merit to a Priest, the effect of this extorted acknowledgement is destroyed by a happy turn, a clever insinuation, or a coarse inuendo. Consult, for example, Hume when compelled to notice the Archbishop Hubert's exertions in procuring the concession of Magna Charta; and Henry, narrating the communications which passed between Gregory the Great and Saint Austin.

By a peculiar ingenuity of disingenuousness, they convert the efforts made by the mediæval Church for the repression of vice and immorality into accusations against her. The woful examples of profligacy, avarice, worldliness, corruption, and depravity, abounding during the middle ages (as they do amongst all men and in all ages), brought forward so prominently, occurring in a state of society offering far greater temptations

than our own, and affording far fewer opportunities of concealment, are recorded by the Pontiffs,
who warred against the delinquents—by the
Canons of the Councils legislating against the
iniquities, by the good and holy men who deplored the scandals and the sins of their times.
Those who adopt a similar plan act as a foreign
traveller might do, were he to gather from the
metropolitan Police reports, and the trials at
the Old Bailey, the peculiar characteristics of
the morals of England.

But about the period when the doctrines of
the French philosophical school were vigorously
propagated with all the charms of novelty in
England, the *rehabilitation* of the Middle Ages was
preparing by a young Fellow of St John's, and a
Collector of virtù, equally unconscious of each
other's proceedings, and of the great moral revolution they were destined to cause. The future
Bishop of Dromore, visiting at the house of a
country friend, saw, lying on the floor beneath
a bureau, an old, ragged, dirty, paper book, of
which the housemaid had torn away half for
the purpose of lighting her fires. Curiosity led
him to rescue the remaining leaves from destruction : and whilst the gentle antiquary was editing
the treasure of Minstrelsy he had acquired, the

Connoisseur was fitting up a tiny lath and plaster toyshop and raree-show in a suburban village :— Percy published the Reliques : Horace Walpole opened Strawberry Hill.————The term Gothic, in Addison's times the most intellectually degrading that could be applied, has become the symbol of admiration. The poetry of the Middle Ages is studied with delight ; some respect is paid to Mediæval Philosophy, more to Mediæval Divinity : Mediæval institutions, manners and customs, are favourite sources of popular literature. The overcharged and overwhelming imputations of gross ignorance have received the most complete refutation. Yet in the same manner as the opponents of the Middle Ages have condemned them for their virtues, so have their defenders extolled their faults, justified their sins—Chivalry, not unjustly stigmatized by Arnold as embodying the spirit of Antichrist—the atrocities of the Crusades,—even that most fatal error, the breach of the second commandment,—and elevated them to an ideal excellence which the world never saw, of universal piety, content, and happiness— " merrie old England."

May 2nd, 1851.

ERRATA AND CORRECTIONS.

Page 13, Marginal note, line 3, *for* Teutonic *read* historic.

69, line 8 from bottom, for *Julia bona* read *Insula bona.*

148, line 12, *for* Sithiu *read* St Quentin, and *dele* Saint Quentin line 12.

202, lines 6—9, *for* Roundhead or Cavalier, Papist or Protestant, &c., *read* " Roundhead" or " Cavalier," " Papist" or " Protestant," &c.

240, line 10 from bottom, *for* temptations *read* temptings

406, line 6 from bottom, *for* Henry the Fowler, son of Otho the Great, *read* son of Otho the Illustrious, and father of Otho the Great.

608, Marginal date line 2, *for* 862, *read* 885.

610, Marginal date line 2, *for* 885—896, *read* 885—886.

709, line 12 from bottom, *for* Charles-le-Gros, *read* Charles-le-Gras.

718, line 3, *for* and faithful expositors of traditions, *read* yet a faithful exposition of traditions.

INTRODUCTION.

GENERAL RELATIONS OF MEDIÆVAL HISTORY.

CHAPTER I.

THE FOURTH MONARCHY.

§ 1. FEW similes possess such truth as that most trite one—*the Stream of Time*—or rather the simile is the abstract idea of Time, presented to our sensuous perceptions, in the only form intelligible to the human mind. Every human being is only a bubble upon the surface of the water, conducted onwards, not according to his own choice, or in proportion to his own strength, but unconsciously, irresistibly, obeying the impulse given alike to him and to all others who have preceded him, even from the first Father of our race. Every event befalling the individual man or human society, every act and action produced by the instruments, often most strong when weakest, most subtilely instigative when most obscure, appointed to influence, direct, or govern the fortunes of their brethren, is comprehended in the eternal scheme, whereby the whole creation, Spiritual and Material, ever was, is, and will be an unity in course, object and destiny.

The events appearing to us consecutive, are essentially consentaneous : indistinct and transient disclosures of the decree, foredoomed before all Time, and not to be fulfilled until Time shall pass away :—dim glimpses of the changeless sky, caught between the vaporous margins of the driving clouds. Eternity is the perfect union,—utterly baffling to the human understanding,—of unceasing energy and absolute repose ; and the impossibility of conceiving this union compels us to make a deceitful distinction between efficient causes and final causes. The intentions we denominate final causes are eternally in operation: the beginning and the end are simultaneous in the designs of Him who is Alpha and Omega, the First and the Last.

But our intellect can only receive the idea of succession : no rest was intended for man : there can be none, till the power of Death shall be destroyed, and Heaven and Earth dissolved. No one generation can be severed from any preceding generation: we are all partners. Blessings and Curses are portions of our inheritance. The Father's sins are visited upon the Children; whilst again, the Children are benefited by graces not their own : the mercy as marvellous to us as the judgment.

History therefore becomes a continuous drama, wherein each scene conduces to the next, each act has its peculiar catastrophe, tangled into each other's chain, all inseparable. History is only another aspect of Time; and Time never stands still. Our grammar teaches us falsely: there is no such tense as the present, nor is the present tense admitted into the most philosophical of all languages; the only speech of man subsisting uncontaminated by any ideas resulting from the false worship of material idolatry, or the intellectual idolatry of false knowledge. To Man, all is either past or future : our mortal individuality has no other existence except in our recollections or by our anticipations. Before we think the thought, the Present, the indivisible moment has departed for ever, and merges in all precedent eternity.

But whilst the Stream, so truly depicting the sequence of mundane events, maintains the invincible downward course, it is otherwise with the agencies granted or permitted to Human Will—the consequences of the actions resulting from Man's responsibility. The current does not work alone : there are other forces which you must consider, — the forces originating in man's disobedience or obedience,—his seeking evil or good, his rebellion or his submission. You may reach the springs of the gushing waters, trace out the rills and rivulets as they swell and coalesce and fall into each other, delineate the feeders, map out the bights and bends, measure the banks and boundaries ; but you must do still more.

Mark the turning of the tide : a semblance, though an imperfect one, of the manner in which the opinions and secret operations of the human mind become manifest in the stream. First, a slender and scarcely perceptible thread ascends, quietly and gently, yet most steadily and undeviatingly, through the centre, occasioning the smallest counter-current, discernible merely by the slightest undulating ripples or the floating weeds.

But this thread speedily opens wider and wider, expanding, winning upon the main current, which narrows more and more, yielding to the intrusion, until the fluvial course is evident only in the diminishing currents on either brink, and these at last disappear, and the tide is wholly turned ; so that an Observer, who had never previously visited the river, or whose knowledge was limited to a portion of the banks, might well mistake the antagonistic counter-current for the regular stream.

Moreover, other causes may perplex him : the level of the stream, altered by the summer's drought or the winter's flood : the brackish or turbid springs rising from below, embittering or darkening the purer and clearer element, all may mislead him in his judgment ; yet still the river will flow on, in perennial strength, nou-

rished by the descending clouds, branching, eddy-
ing, spreading, dividing, until the waves return to
the ocean, hollowed by the Hand which separated
them from the waters above the firmament.

§ 2.   Even if the scheme of history deduced The Four Empires.
from the Four temporal Empires, as the pro-
gress of human events has been revealed by
the Prophetic Vision, possessed no other authority or recommendation than the character of a
technical or artificial system, calculated to assist
the Master in imparting the lesson and the Pupil
in retaining the instruction, none other so useful,
convenient and consistent, could be found.

Say rather, no other historical theory can be Revelation the found-ation of Universal History.
devised, enabling us to teach or study, however
erringly, the deeds, the institutions, and the unfolding destinies of mankind.   Indeed it is not
our knowledge, but our ignorance, which compels us to adopt this philosophy.   We have no
choice, save between the light and the darkness; for, with respect to the pristine ages of
the world, we know nothing historically true,
beyond the facts whereunto Holy Scriptures bear
their witness. The same Ineffable Wisdom, speaking in them, has also annihilated every other
authentic record of those remote eras, or covered
the memorials, if any exist, with an obscurity ·
which no acuteness can dispel.   If the Enquirers,
who, within the deserted temples of Misraim,
interrogate the dumb oracles, imagine that an

answer is returned, it is merely the echo of their own voice: the reply tells them only what they have told. If they fancy they see a living form amongst the monster idols, it is only the reverie of an opium-dream. The offering they have placed upon the altar is taken up again by them as their reward: they go out bearing the sacrifice they brought in, and nothing more.

Languages totally lost by the interruption of oral tradition. No language, and the mystic characters of Egypt are as a language, has ever been recovered after the interruption of oral tradition during one entire generation. Like the electric fire, transmitted through the living chain, hand grasping hand, if there be any break, the transmission ceases: let hand drop from hand, the ethereal energy is lost. In these latter days, all our conversance with ancient speech results mediately or immediately from living tradition. Each scholar has been an auditor . the living lips have spoken to the living ear: each learner has received the doctrine from a living teacher; and, teacher in his turn, there has never been a dead silence. No languages are so truly living as those which have been consecrated to prayer and praise. The Hebrew has never died; it is a living language: the Greek has never died; it is a living language: the Latin has never died; it is a living language. No hour has ever passed wherein their voices have not been heard; and, if this enquiry be pursued philologically, it will be found that

even when the continuous line of descent appears
to have failed, some other of the cognate dialects,
some other testimony derived from the Tower
of Confusion will still become the interpreter
which we require.

With the exception of those races governed
by a revealed or special providence, marked out
thereby as lessons or as warnings—none more
prominently amongst the uncovenanted, none
more instructively, than that wonderful people,
who, grounding their laws, their judgments, their
usages, their entire policy and entire faith upon
the first Commandment with promise, have been
rewarded by a national longevity unparalleled
in the world; for inasmuch as they amongst
the Gentile Empires alone have collectively deserved the blessing, by them alone has the blessing been earned;—all the history we know, all
we really need to know, all we can ever really
know, is inseparably bound in and wound up
with the spheres of Assyria, Persia, Greece and
Rome. In and by their successive developments,
every other power has been, or is preparing to
be, ruled, affected, or involved.

§ 3. Rome's cruelties, baffling conception by The Fourth
their infinity, her vices, so detestable that no continued
tongue can risk the pollution of holding them up ropean
to infamy, her absolute hatred against God, re- wealth.
ceived their chastisement; but her dominion was
not extinguished. Races the most adverse, who

divided her provinces amongst them as a spoil, who executed vengeance against her temples, who led her children into captivity, who insulted and loathed her imbecility and baseness, nevertheless humbly knelt before their Captive as the dispenser of their temporal power. Not of the blood of Rome, they claimed to be her heirs, engrafting their heroic ancestors upon the stem of the Cæsars.

Development of the Romano-Barbaric policy. This devolution of authority from Rome, this absorption of Roman authority by the Barbarians, this political, and more than political, this moral unity, this confirmation of a dominion which they seemed to subvert, this acknowledgment of the authority they defied, is the great truth upon which the whole history of European society, and more than European society, European civilization, depends

Rome, working in dark unconsciousness, prepared the nutriment for the Kings who were to arise out of her State. Claudius, by that harangue which we read deeply graven on brass, in the great Capital of Celtic Gaul, taught the soundest lessons of legislation. The ascription of the ancient Gaulish families into the Senatorial rank gave them an interest in their own country and in the Empire. The universal concession of Roman citizenship removed the badges of humiliation, the sources of grudge and jealousy; yet, as in all human institutions, there was a weakness counterbalancing the strength, an error neutralizing the wisdom. These privileges excited in the Provinces a tendency to separation, of which those bold, great, venturous, and often wise men, whom we too abusively call the Tyrants of the Lower Empire,—fully availed themselves. What possible reason have we to perpetuate the stigma unjustly conveyed by that term? Did the Empire offer any standard of legitimacy except success? Postumus was as legitimate in his great Empire of the Gauls as Aurelian. Can we deny that Carausius was the true Cæsar of Britain?—The provincial Emperors were in fact national Sovereigns; they founded the Thrones of Western Christendom.

The Romans had been gradually approximating to the Barbarians: the Barbarians, with even more alacrity and power, were wresting the dominion from the Empire. Were not the majority of the Emperors barbarians by name, by race, by lineage, by language, by character? These purple-clad Barbarians swayed the fortunes of the world. Long had this political commixture of races existed. The Romans taught their Vassals to become their Lords. They educated Goth and Celt and Teuton and Iberian for the Imperial throne, when they, the *Gens togata*, rejoiced in the submission voluntarily rendered by barbarian Sovereigns, who sought to encrease their own magnificence by accepting the Regal

The so-called Tyrants, the predecessors of the Dynasties of mediæval Europe

name and the Regal insignia from the Roman power. The first real king in Germany, Ariovistus, became King by the gratitude or favour of the first of the Cæsars.

Veneration command-ed by Rome.

We have all read how the Gaulish Warriors were stayed in silent awe before the Senate, assembled in that Forum which they were about to destroy. The columns rose in glory, again to fall; but the same veneration hovered amongst the ruins, continuing to hallow the cruelties, the depravities, the feebleness, the decrepitude of Rome. When the barbarian Sovereigns established themselves within the sacred boundaries of the Empire, when the Ostrogoth held his court at Verona, and the Frank encamped in Gaul, they honoured the very Sovereigns over whom they had usurped. Flushed with victory, the Barbarians scarcely dared to own, even to themselves, that they were rebels against the ancient Mistress of the World. Her fear was yet upon them.

There are appointed seasons of crisis, when it pleases Him through whom Kings reign and Princes decree justice, to withdraw the authority He has imparted. The commission by which they rule is cancelled. Then, all sovereignty collapses, obedience is gone, command utterly lost. Kings and Princes, crownless though crowned, naked though invested with the royal robe, shiver, powerless before the blast But except during these periods,—amongst which we reckon not

the established ascendancy of democracy, a regency the most despotic of all Monarchies, for
Monarchy is irrespective of the number who
may exercise the sovereignty, provided there be
a sufficient coercive unity and singleness of spirit
in the government — but except during these
periods, man inclines far more readily to obedience than to independence.   Yielding to the
natural law, the instinct of submission clings
to him.   He succumbs pleasurably to the feeling,
or rather the duty, of personal or hereditary
respect—Such is the moral force of historical
traditions, as they have been called by those
politicians and writers who weakly endeavour to
revive them by book antiquarianisms and æsthetic
artificialities.   And this duty honours him who
renders the service as much as, nay even more,
than the object to whom the duty is rendered.

Opinions and opportunities, war, policy, pride,
necessity, co-operated in the transmutations whereby the Fourth Monarchy was vested in the Kingdoms which sprung from Rome; transmutations
effected by simultaneous decomposition and consolidation.   The Barbarians had healthy minds,
rough, honest, devout.   Ancient traditions taught Supposed
kindred be-
the Franks to claim the Romans as their kins- tween the
Barba-
men.   The fair-haired Germans of the Rhine rians and
the Ro-
traced their ancestry to the banks of the Scaman- mans.
der and the fugitives of Troy.   Our Cymric tribes,
as is familiarly known, asserted the like origin.

The simple faith, accrediting such traditions, may have been fully as consonant to historical reasoning as the sceptical dogmatism of civilization, by which they are inexorably denied. An Anglo-Saxon Monk, deducing Cerdic's lineage from Noah through Woden, is, upon his theory, if you judge him merely by the logic of historical evidence, wiser than the philosophic historian, who commences his investigation by scorning at the common origin of mankind.

Traditional Genealogies, their truth and authenticity amongst primeval nations.

Amongst primitive races, whether flourishing in past ages, or lingering in our own, history is not distinguishable from genealogies. They reckon by generations, not by eras: man dealing with man, not deceiving himself with abstractions. It should seem that the literate mind is incompetent to judge fairly of the mind working through other instruments of thought. Our employment of writing, as the sole means of preserving knowledge, enfeebles the power of memory, and causes us to forget the powers of memory. Accustomed only to the cultivated plant, we do not sufficiently estimate the vigour of the natural growth. Could we penetrate into the inward mind of classes or races appearing to us the most stolid or degraded, we should know, that, vile as they are rendered in our sight by the squalor and stench of savage life, their capacities, perceptions and sensibilities, are identical with our own. The soul is not measured by the facial angle. The

Autochthon of Tasmania understood his law of real property and his canons of descent, as clearly as any English conveyancer; and his appreciation of his land's value was no less shrewd than that entertained by the Settler who cleared him off by gun, bloodhound, and poison. Genealogies entrusted to memory, known *by heart,*—that most forcible expression—are written in a living record, compared to which the Herald's Roll is chaff and straw. Flattery cannot interpolate a link in such pedigrees—not to be confounded with fabled dynastic lists :—ignorance cannot corrupt the manuscript : hostility cannot destroy the testimony, except by the total extirpation of the witnesses. Writing preserves ampler facts and transmits more accurate details ; yet, in these instances, without affording greater certainty.

A very singular concurrence enables us to estimate the comparative trustworthiness of lite- rate tradition, symbolical tradition, and oral tradition. Three remarkable migrations of the human race in these latter ages, have followed in close succession :—the settlement of the Northmen in Iceland and Greenland, and their occupation of America, so transient and so mysterious :—the Aztecs in their mighty march, descending to the plains of Anahuac ;—and the wave of population which spread to the farthest verge of Australasia.

The Northmen engraved the letters of the historic song on the Runic stave.—Mexico em-

Comparison between Teutonic facts preserved by letters, by symbols and by memory,—

—as exemplified amongst the Northmen, the Mexicans and the New Zealanders.

ployed conventional imagery.—The Maoris, aided only by the rudest contrivance, the notched stick, trusted to memory; and so accurately are these gentilitial facts recollected, that throughout their Island, the tribes, separated by distance and disjoined by enmity, agree completely in their tale. Here, however, we appeal to these national traditions simply as moral persuasives, acting upon Celts and Teutons, and becoming more peculiarly efficacious at the period when the Barbarians were amalgamating themselves with the Roman world. Every Leader of a Barbarian tribe, every Aspirant to dominion, every Barbarian who wore the diadem in a province of the Empire, consecrated his authority and legalized his sovereignty by the recognition of the Cæsars, and till he obtained that ratification, whether express or implied, he hardly relied upon his sword. These transactions colour the whole history of the Lower Empire. We quote not the examples proving the foregoing propositions, having done so elsewhere; neither can we here moot the contending arguments.

Barbarian Sovereignty legitimated by Roman authority.

There may have been double-dealing in such negociations; diplomatic skill, finesse, evasion: always the display of force, and frequently the direct exercise of force; but the territorial partition amongst the Barbarians had been long commencing. As is the case in all earthly dominions, the sentence of condemnation, though suspended

in execution, had been irrevocably passed upon
Rome during her period of resplendant prosperity and glory. All conquering, all colonizing
Empires,—colonization being only conquest disguised by a plausible name—increase by the appropriation of new elements, which, ultimately,
separate either by direct and outward impulse,
or through the inward fermentations and corpus-
cular attractions of human society.

The demarcations which the Romans assigned
to the local governments created by them, had
been regulated by the anterior organization of
the Gaulish States and Tribes; and the Tyrants
only obeyed the call of the Provinces, in which
a new nationality, partly grounded upon race,
was displaying itself The Provinces sought to
be independent, without ceasing to be Roman.
The Barbarians and Romans had long needed
each other, and had mutually abated their respective claims and pretensions. The Empire was
becoming Romano-Barbaric; each party tried to
profit by the other; neither was sincere. When
the Chieftains, Rome's mercenaries, Rome's colonists, Rome's enemies, sued for the dignity of
Consul or the title of Patrician, the Sacred Majesty of Byzantium might dread to refuse ; but
Byzantium could not do otherwise than grant,
and the Ostrogoth or the Frank knew the worth
of the distinction he craved. He honoured himself by the subserviency, protected himself by the

delegation; and this proud prostration of the strong before the weak, affords the clearest proof that the vassal fully understood the advantage which his obedience conferred.

Contemplate the heroic Chieftains of the Barbarian dynasties, each assuming the semblance of the Cæsars, and wise in that assumption. They profited by the provincial nationality which had been growing up during the tyrannic era. Postumus had been preparing the way for Tetricus, and Tetricus for Clovis—Clovis the Sicambrian,

Roman in signia and titles assumed by the Barbaric Sovereigns.

hailed as Consul, worshipped as Augustus. Thus did Leuvigild, the Visigoth, triumph in the Imperial policy; and in Britain the same principles spread over from the Gauls. Our Anglo-Saxons hastened into the communion of the Empire.—Ethelbert impressed the Roman wolf upon the rude Kentish coin—Edwin raised the Roman Standard—Athelstan is enthroned as the Basileus of Albion and the surrounding islands.

Import-ance of symbols of authority.

In the employment of these titles and symbols, sound political prudence guided the clear-sighted Barbarians. Pageantry is a portion of Royalty which cannot be safely discarded; and such pageantry, such adoption of Roman insignia and imagery became the constant assertion of their authority; for they thereby declared that they applied to themselves the doctrines of Imperial Sovereignty. To estimate the real importance of these proceedings, we need only advert to the feelings excited by analogous demonstrations in more recent times. The Cross-fleury and Martlets of the Confessor in the Howard bearing, cost the Earl of Surrey his life. Elizabeth never forgave the display of the English quarterings by her rival. France never liked the Lilies in our shield; not even when she had blotted them out from her own. Republican France, Consular France, inherited the sympathies of the Monarchy. The abandonment of the Fleurs-de-Lys, though indicating nought beyond the most obsolete of claims, was received as a message of kindness by the Great Nation: whilst at home, many politicians of no mean capacity doubted the prudence of maiming the Royal title, and discarding the honours for which Old England combated at Cressy and Poitiers.

But in truth any depreciation of these Roman titles and "trappings" is the expression of modern prejudice, rather than of antient feeling. Such regalia and regaline adornments were not the gays and gauds of a savage, aping civilization, but essential characteristics of the Monarch: the purple robe, transmitted by Anastasius to Clovis together with the diploma, gave him seizin of the consular dignity: the diadem, placed upon the head of the anointed Monarch, through the gift of the Emperor, conferred upon the Sicambrian the prerogative of Augustus.

§ 4. Amongst the most instructive lessons we

Rome never conquered by the Barbarians—A fact first brought forward by Guizot.

derive from the history of discoveries, is the tardiness of their revelation, the eye sightless, the ear without hearing, the nerve without tact, until the inward perception be roused. This condition of progress in practical art and physical science applies to all branches of human knowledge. We praise the patient skill which uncovers the strata of the palimpsest, and admire the strange enthusiast, who, braving the lethargic atmosphere of the Academic library, ventures in, and draws forth the precious Manuscript from the stagnant pools, whose silent waters engulph the untouched treasures collected by Bodley or Laud, Junius or Rawlinson, Gale or Moor or Parker: yet fully as new and important is the information obtained from the trite, well-known, and familiar authorities, which have only waited for the Interrogator, asking them to make the disclosure.

Facts pregnant with most signal truths have, until our own times, continued uninvestigated and unimproved; though plain and patent, presented to every reader, fruitlessly forcing themselves upon our notice, against which historians were previously constantly hitting their feet, and as constantly spurning out of their path.

Such is eminently the case with that due conception of the Eternal City's destiny, which the illustrious historical investigator, now the honour and the reproach of France, has presented

with equal modesty and emphasis. Rome never
was permanently conquered—never accepted the
Strangers' yoke—never became subjected to the
Barbarian. Rome alone continued purely Roman after the Imperial presence departed. Province after province was lost: plague, pestilence,
fire desolated the City, the habitations shrunk
away within the walls, a fierce and corrupt aristocracy, a depraved and cowardly populace, composed the community which defiled the Seven
Hills; but the succession was unbroken, and
Rome was Rome, and is Rome still. The glorious Degradation and
laurel-crowned phantasms of her ancient gran- baseness of
mediæval
deur hovered amongst her ruins. Combining with Rome.
her present degradation, the recollections of the
past imparted inspiration and bitterness to the
most polished Poet of the Anglo-Norman age.

> Par tibi Roma nihil, cum sis prope tota ruina:
> Quam magni fueris integra, fracta doces.—
> Non tamen annorum series, non flamma nec ensis
> Ad plenum potuit hoc abolere decus.—
> Urbs felix, si vel dominis urbs illa careret,
> Vel dominis esset turpe carere fide.

Rome's outward aspect, her form and feature,
vindicated her nationality. The Rome of the
first Gregory—of Honorius, of Saint Leo, of Hildebrand, displayed the continuous transmission
of ancient sentiment, living tradition, and proud
and haughty spirit.

The Fine Arts, as such, had perished: the
Sculptor's skill had been entirely repudiated by

C 2

primitive Faith. No majesty of expression, no loveliness of form, no magic of conception, no exquisiteness of taste, no delicacy of execution could in the firm minds of the early Christians atone for the impurity of the idols: they were without excuse.—Scarcely ever has there been an unmutilated statue of a Heathen deity excavated within the Roman territory. The effigies are ruined in the ruins. The fourteen fragments of Parian marble dug up in the baths of Nero, and now composing the Venus, the glory of the Medici, testify equally to the uncompromising zeal inculcated by the apostolic age, and the skill of the restoring artist, fostered by the patronage of those who, in the golden age of revival, derided the simplicity of the Apostles.

Nevertheless, the Romans clung to the memorials inherited from their forefathers: the Basilica repeated the forms of the Imperial structures: their architecture, however rudely, gave an outward testimony of the national sentiment. Traditional preservation of Roman architecture in Rome during the dark ages Such buildings declare that they are the productions of a people, who, fallen from their high estate, repelled the intrusion of a stranger. Mediæval Rome might be viewed as the palace of a decayed but noble family, retaining the tokens and symbols of ancestry, contrasting with naked walls and earthen floor. Of all the cities in Western Christendom, Rome was the only one in which Gothic architecture never obtained naturalization: that mystic and imaginative creation, so inseparably allied in popular opinion with mediæval Catholicism, was excluded from the Capital of the Christian world.

Thus also the palace of Crescentius, inhabited generations afterwards by Rienzi, strangely compacted of ancient fragments, and standing desolate upon the shores of the Tiber, still displays the anxiety which the "Brutus of the revived Republic" felt to shew that he dwelt as a Roman. His medals tell far more than the pages of history. Crescentius usurped the state and insignia of the Empire.—In like manner, with national, if not religious consistency, the national feeling overcoming the religious sentiment, the ancient ensigns, consecrated almost as the tutelary deities of the Legions, the Wolf, the Minotaur, the Dragon, the Eagle, came forth from the Capitol, and inaugurated the Teutonic successors of the Cæsars.

Like the other Italian Republics, municipal Rome sustained incessant changes in her communal organization; but dull darkness shrouds her rude, convulsive, and turbulent destinies. Obscurity of the municipal history of mediæval Rome.

How fortunate was fair Florence in her Chroniclers. their gifts, their talents, their industry, their knowledge: the tender affection of Malespini; the earnest pathos of Dino Compagni; the graphic inspiration of Villani, and the rich fund of information which renders him the second in order of the great European Historians of the mediæval period—England gave the first, Matthew Paris the Monk of Saint Alban's; and Flanders in her Froissart, the third—Rome had none like these amongst her sons. Uncouth diaries, meagre annalists, scattered and fragmentary muniments are the failing and imperfect sources of Rome's local and peculiar history. Few, indeed, comparatively, of the renowned names which have illustrated Italy, imperial Italy, mediæval Italy, or modern Italy, whether in literature, or poetry, or science, or arts, or arms, can really be assigned to that City which has given the intellectual impulse to the civilized world.

Antiquaries have painfully retrieved some indications of Rome's mediæval magistracy. Senators, Consuls, Patricians, glance and retreat before us The authority of the municipal rulers was continually disturbed by popular dissensions, and disgraced as well as enfeebled by the baseness, levity, avarice and venality which rendered the people—the dregs of the dregs of Romulus—the very proverb and bye-word of the nations. Nevertheless, mean and mendicant as Rome had become, the honour of opinion was continued to her; men bowed before the Community they despised, just as a Tiberius or a Caligula, brutalized by vice, was still an Emperor. Rome still enjoyed a preeminence which none could contest. The brazen Wolf dwelt in the Capitol, and the four

Moral pre-eminence of the City of Rome despite of her poverty and degradation.

letters, which, by an almost magic influence, convey the concrete idea of Rome's Empire, decked her monuments. Tattered and sordid and faded was her Imperial robe, still she triumphed —the Queen of Cities.

Unworthy of her trust, her trust was continued to her; and in the highest of her functions Rome retained her authority. Whether sincere or venal, whether prompted by veneration or suggested by faction, the Roman Municipality presented the Pontiff to the Primatial See of Christendom. That transcendent function, after many conflicts and contests and changes, became finally vested in the Cardinal hierarchy of the Roman Diocese; yet, whilst the popular concurrence subsisted, the postulation was the legal right of the Roman Commonwealth; nor did the demerits of the Patrons contaminate the Pontiff, unless he personally participated in them, or any how detract from his canonical authority as the consecrated successor of the Apostle. The foulnesses of the soil do not infect the fruit of the tree, which may ripen, sweet and nourishing, out of the impure earth by which the roots are surrounded.

§ 5. In physical Geography, the features of each district must be united to the rivers and mountain ranges beyond the square of the map. You must over-pass frontiers and artificial limits. Neither can the history of any particular State comprehended in the European Commonwealth

Charlemagne's history enters into the history of all the European States.

be studied profitably or properly, unless in connexion with the universal history of Western
Christendom. Hence the great difficulty of treating Modern History. The utmost expansion given
to the history of any particular State or Nation
must necessarily fail to include the general information, needful as the complement of the specialty. Perhaps there are few branches of human
knowledge concerning which it may be so truly
said, that the Learner must be his own Teacher:
and many portions of history, apparently the most
familiar, offer the greatest difficulty when you
attempt to grapple with them. Such is the
history of Charlemagne. Every State which
arose within the compass of his direct dominion
has been shaped through his influence, however
diversely, nay contradictorily, that influence may
have been modified; whilst his moral dominion
extended far beyond the geographical boundaries of his Empire. It was not arrested by Eyder
on the North or Ebro on the South, nor even by
the waves of the British Channel. The Anglo-
Saxon Empire ran parallel with the Carlovingian
Empire until the Norman Conquest, that junction
which completely let in all the principles appropriated by the Northmen, when they themselves
accepted the doctrines and policy proffered by
the Institutions of Roman France.

The ideal
Charle-
magne

It seems Charlemagne's fate that he should
always be in danger of shading into a mythic

Monarch—not a man of flesh and blood, but a personified theory. Turpin's Carolus Magnus, the Charlemagne of Roncesvalles; Ariosto's *Sacra Corona*, surrounded by Palatines and Doze-Piers, are scarcely more unlike the real rough, tough, shaggy old Monarch, than the conventional portraitures by which his real features have been supplanted.

It is an insuperable source of fallacy in human observation as well as in human judgment, that we never can sufficiently disjoin our own individuality from our estimates of moral nature. Admiring ourselves in others, we ascribe to those whom we love or admire the qualities we value in ourselves. We each see the landscape through our own stripe of the rainbow. A favourite hero by long-established prescription, few historical characters have been more disguised by fond adornment than Charlemagne. Each generation or school, has endeavoured to exhibit him as a normal model of excellence. Courtly Mezeray invests the son of Pepin with the faste of Louis-Quatorze; the polished Abbé Velly bestows upon the Frankish Emperor the abstract perfection of a dramatic hero; Boulainvilliers, the champion of the Noblesse, worships the founder of hereditary feudality; Mably discovers in the Capitulars the maxims of popular liberty; Montesquieu, the perfect philosophy of legislation. But, generally speaking, Charlemagne's historical aspect is derived from his patronage of literature. This notion of his literary character colours his political character, so that in the assumption of the Imperial authority, we are fain to consider him as a true romanticist—such as in our own days we have seen upon the Throne—seeking to appease hungry desires by playing with poetic fancies, to satisfy hard nature with pleasant words, to give substance and body to a dream.

The real Charlemagne

All these prestiges will vanish if we render to Charlemagne his well deserved encomium :—he was a great Warrior, a great Statesman, fitted for his own age.—It is a very ambiguous praise to say that a man is in advance of his age : if so, he is out of his place : he lives in a foreign country. Equally so if he lives in the past. No innovator so bold, so reckless and so crude, as he who makes the attempt (which never succeeds) to effect a resurrection of antiquity.

Charlemagne's practical character

We may put by the book, and study Charlemagne's achievements on the borders of the Rhine : better than in the book may the Traveller read Charlemagne's genuine character pictured upon the lovely unfolding landscape :—the huge Dom-Minsters, the fortresses of Religion : the yellow sunny rocks studded with the vine : the mulberry and the peach, ripening in the ruddy orchards ; the succulent pot-herbs and worts which stock the Bauer's garden,—these are the monuments and memorials of Charlemagne's mind.

The first health pledged when the flask is opened
at Johannisberg should be the Monarch's name
who gave the song-inspiring vintage. Charlemagne's superiority and ability consisted chiefly
in seeking and seizing the immediate advantages,
whatever they might be, which he could confer
upon others or obtain for himself. He was a
man of forethought, ready contrivance and useful
talent. He would employ every expedient, grasp
every opportunity, and provide for each day as it
was passing by.

The educational movement resulting from
Charlemagne's genius was practical. Two main
objects had he therein upon his conscience and his
mind. The first, was the support of the Christian
Faith: his Seven liberal Sciences circled round
Theology, the centre of the intellectual system.
No argument was needed as to the obligation of
uniting sacred and secular learning, because the
idea of disuniting them never was entertained.

His other object in patronizing learning and
instruction was the benefit of the State. He
sought to train good men of business: judges
well qualified, ready pen-men in his Chancery;
and this sage desire expanded into a wide in-
structional field. Charlemagne's exertions for Charle-
promoting the study of the Greek language— magne's
cultivation
his Greek professorships at Osnaburgh or Saltz- of the
Greek lan-
burgh—have been praised, doubted, discussed, as guage—
how mis-
understood
something very paradoxical, whereas his motives

were plain and his machinery simple.—Greek
was to all intents and purposes, the current language of an opulent and powerful nation, required
for the transaction of public affairs. A close
parallel, necessitated by the same causes, exists
in the capital of Charlemagne's successors. The
Oriental Academy at Vienna is constituted to
afford a supply of individuals qualified for the
diplomatic intercourse, arising out of the vicinity
and relations of the Austrian and Ottoman dominions, without any reference to the promotion
of philology—We find the same at home. If
the Persian language be taught at Haileybury, it
is to fit the future Writer for his Indian office.
He may study Ferdusi or Hafiz if he pleases, but
the cultivation of literature is not the intent with
which the learning is bestowed.

Theory of Char-lemagne's elevation to the Imperial authority.

Apply equivalent reasonings to the event common to all Europe, and in which all Europe is
concerned—the gathering-knot in the annals of
modern Europe. It has been said that the restoration of the Empire by Charlemagne was a great
idea; but his elevation to the Imperial dignity
is denaturalized by conventional historical phraseology —The erudite Jurist of Germany gives
you his treatise *de fictâ translatione Imperii*—
a title-page conveying a double misinterpretation
of the truth. No feigned or poetized pageant
was Charlemagne's Imperial elevation, not a fiction fostered by school-boy sentiment, or artistic

enthusiasm, or scholastic pedantry, but a reality of realities Neither was the transaction a translation of the Empire, for the seat of the Empire was still referred to Rome; nor a restoration of the Empire, for the Empire had never ceased. Strange that Historians should have encouraged each other in the error that the Empire, extinguished, as they say, in Augustulus, was now restored.—Restored '—never had it been suspended, either in principle, maxims, or feelings. The shattered, pillaged, dilapidated Empire was still one state, one community : the nations of Christendom were bound together by one common Faith : they accepted Religion, according to the etymology of the term, as the real connecting bond, tempted as they might be by the seductive error that the Church needed the protection of the Secular arm.

Distracted Christendom fell miserably short in practice, nevertheless the idea of religious unity was firmly inherent. This principle then subsisted like an instinct, upon which men acted unconsciously, without effort and without thought. But new thoughts were now awakened and new efforts roused : the usurpation of Irene endangered the very existence of the Empire : how could a female wear the Imperial diadem ? Moreover, Christendom had to dread a rival Empire,—the Empire of Islam, under one Chief, one Caliph uniting temporal and spiritual authority;

Charlemagne elevated to the Imperial authority for the purpose of continuing the Imperial succession.

and was not one Emperor equally needed for Christendom? Hence Charlemagne's call:—*Ne Pagani insultarent Christianis si Imperatoris nomen apud Christianos cessasset*—Pope and Clergy, Bishops and Abbots, Franks and Romans, advising, as they best might, with the people and communities of the West, acknowledged the Son of Pepin as the Cæsar, and invested him with the Imperial authority, bestowed by the Church, consecrated by the Church, but yet antagonistic to the Church of which the Emperor was the defender.

Charlemagne failed to perpetuate a dynasty. There was a deadly worm curling around his sceptre; but he fulfilled his vocation by imparting a new energy to the drooping genius of the Fourth Monarchy. Henceforward the Imperial principles of government, the doctrines, sentiments, jurisprudence and policy of Rome, became still more intimately kneaded into the Teutonism of the Western Commonwealth, causing the fermenting elements to enter into new combinations, and imparting that aspect and idiosyncrasy which distinguishes the civilized European from the other families of mankind.

Monarchical character of Modern Europe grounded upon Roman policy

§ 6. We, therefore, all live in the Roman world: the departed generations are not distinguishable in these reasonings from ourselves; the "dark ages" and the "middle ages" are merely bights and bends in the great stream of

Time, which we contemplate from the bridge by which the river is arched over. Rome conferred upon the Sovereigns of Modern Europe their principles of prerogative, their attributes of majesty. The powers of the State were concentrated in the Monarch by the *Lex Regia*, he the sole Legislator, though acting by advice; he the supreme Magistrate, delegating his powers. The Comites, the companions of Augustus, installed their successors in the palace of Clovis. European aristocracy is plumed by the stately nomenclature of the declining Empire. The Romans bestowed upon us that Institution so directly antagonistic to Teutonic ethos, nobility created by the Sovereign's grant. Every Duke and Dukedom, every Count and County, testifies to the Roman influence, and confesses the Barbarian's exulting appropriation of Roman spoils. No King of the Cherusci or of the old Saxons, no Marcomannic or Alemannic Sovereign, was ever the fountain of honour.

Policy of the Empire, how perpetuated in the European Commonwealth.

The titles, the dignities which adorned the Monarchy, participating in the splendour of the Throne, and adding to that splendour, are Roman in their origin : the civil hierarchy of Modern Europe, though quaintly gorgeous in heraldic glory, was grouped by Roman hands.

Dignities and Nobility.

Rome penned the oath of fealty, Rome trammelled her Conquerors by her doctrine of allegiance. The policy pursued by Rome towards

Feudality.

*

her dependents, who sought to avert her hostility or purchase her more dangerous aid, who sheltered themselves beneath her destructive power: the reception by Numidian or Parthian of the Crown, the Sceptre, the purple robe—that policy, conjoined to the territorial dotations of the Legions, and assimilating therewith the trusts and duties of the Leudes and the Vassi, prepared for mediæval Europe the inheritance of feudality.

Moreover, the Roman legislation, leaving undisturbed in the provinces all ancient customs of occupation and cultivation of land, readily entered into combination with Teutonic usages. The popular stigma of the Middle Ages, Villainage, was the universal law of the Roman Empire, nor did the barbarian invaders make much alteration, though they changed the forms; and, on the whole, diminished the oppressions and bondage which the coloni, the husbandmen, the servile peasantry of the Empire, sustained.

Villainage.

Whatever there be of system or consistency in mediæval feudality, whatever renders feudality a jurisprudence, chiefly results from the doctrines of the Empire. We read the history of Anglo-Norman England in Cisalpine Gaul. How does the expulsion of the English Thanes sink into insignificance compared with the feudality of Sulla!—*Veteres migrate Coloni.*—One hundred and fifty thousand land-holders expelled from their possessions to gratify the murderous Le-

Feudal jurisprudence mainly Roman.

gions. It is from the Imperial jurists, from Code and Pandect, that you recover the pristine maxims and principles of feudality : it is from the technical nomenclature of the Civilian that you enucleate the Feud's very name.

The jurisprudence of Rome had been res- *Influence and perpetuation of the Civil Laws* pected, and partially adopted by the Barbarians, even before they established themselves within the Empire. In many provinces the authority of the Roman law was never intermitted. As time advanced, the civil law gained even more rapidly upon the Teutonic legal forms, legal customs, legal principles ; upon " Dooms," and " Weissthumer, " upon " Morgen-gesprach " and " Sachsen Spiegel ;" so as to efface them in many States and Kingdoms, and to modify them in all. No *Municipalities, Guilds, and Corporations.* European Lawyer has failed to profit by Rome's written wisdom. The Roman municipalities and colleges of operatives and artificers, shooting forth their offsets, and consecrated by Christianity, covered Europe with those Guilds, Corporations and Communities, which fostered her social prosperity.

The Atlantic does not divide European so- *Great Councils, Parliaments, &c.* ciety—Rome presented to Europe the platform of her great Councils : but for the Imperial administration of the Empire combining with the Synods and Councils of the Church, never would the European Commonwealth have known her Diets, her States-General, her Cortes, her

Parliaments, her Congresses, her representative Assemblies.

When they built the Cloister and raised the Dungeon Tower, virtue was learned from Rome's lessons; her Sages heard as the revered teachers of temporal wisdom ; her Legends inspired the nation's fancy; her Warriors were contemplated as the bright examples of prowess and valour ; her Poets, her Historians, her Mythographers, her Fabulists furnished the Gothic Minstrel with the choicest subjects for geste and lay.—Alcides · the Fleece of Colchis : Alexander : the tale of Troy-divine. Amidst the ruins of Rome, Frank, and Goth, and Lombard listened to the awful tales of magic and enchantment, suggesting the very substance and character of Romance. In her annals, the Knight sought his pattern of courage, adventure, and strenuousness; and if there be such a sentiment as Chivalry, that sentiment in all the purer and nobler forms was nurtured and disciplined by Rome.

Roman taste gave the fashion to the garment ; Roman skill the models for the instruments of war. We have been told to seek in the Forests of Germany the origin of the feudal system and the conception of the Gothic aisle. We shall discover neither there. Architecture is the costume of society, and throughout European Christendom that costume was patterned from Rome. Unapt and unskilful pupils, she taught the Ostrogothic workman to plan the palace of Theodoric; the Frank, to decorate the Hall of Charlemagne; the Lombard, to vault the Duomo; the Norman, to design the Cathedral.

Above all, Rome imparted to our European civilization her luxury, her grandeur, her richness, her splendour, her exaltation of human reason, her spirit of free enquiry, her ready mutability, her unwearied activity, her expansive and devouring energy, her hardness of heart, her intellectual pride, her fierceness, her insatiate cruelty, that unrelenting cruelty which expels all other races out of the very pale of humanity: whilst our direction of thought, our literature, our languages, concur in uniting the Dominions, Kingdoms, States, Principalities and Powers, composing our Civilized Commonwealth in the Old Continent and the New, with the terrible People through whom that Civilized Commonwealth wields the thunderbolts of the dreadful Monarchy, diverse from all others which preceded amongst mankind.

Origin of Language not the subject of human philosophy.

§ 1. HE who breathed into Man's nostrils the breath of life, first opened the lips of Man. Adam first spake when he was solitary. No human ear but his own could hear the sound of the human voice; called into action under the immediate tuition of the Power from whom the faculty emanated.

No new mode of Language since the confusion of tongues.

Never since the Lord scattered mankind from the Plain of Shinar, has any distinct mode of Language been evolved. Or, if we place the same consideration under its subjective aspect, each nation and family, the progeny of the Preacher of righteousness, received a peculiar speech, the means and token of their division, but conformable to the talents lent to them for their Creator's service and glory.

Henceforward, until we pass far below the commencement of the period which Palætiologists denominate the *historical period*,—a period so well understood in the philosophical sense as to require no other definition—all enquiries concerning the formation of languages must cease. Excepting from Revelation, it is a thorough delusion to suppose that by our unassisted reason we can ascend to any more ancient condition than the

World now exhibits, or to any past state of the
World, for the purpose of discovering the causes
which produced the present order of things.—If
that knowledge be happiness, there is only One
who can bestow it upon man. The materials
for colligation possessed by Inductive Philosophy
consist only of the facts collected from actual
observation or verified experiment, (the latter
being in truth merely another expression for
observation), and these only admissible upon the
assumption that all laws of nature governing the
premises are taken into the argument,—that the
same laws have acted uniformly during the whole
process of operating causes,—and that all correla-
tions have continued unchanged.—The soul cumbered in her veil of flesh, can by her own powers
study nothing in material philosophy but the outward appearances, the phenomena which creation
now presents, and the working of the laws of
nature cognizable through sense, within the sphere
appointed for our sojourn. Her striving to know
more is rebellion All essences; all modes of
primordial production are completely beyond the
compass of human understanding, and utterly unattainable by the researches of human science.

We must not fret at the limit thus assigned to
scientific enquiry; Newton did not. Newton was
content to abide by it.—Do not call it a miserable
limit. It is the immovable limit of human intellect
designed by Infinite Wisdom, and to which intel-

No induc-
tions ad
missible in
science
except
grounded
upon ob-
servation
and ex-
perience.

lect must succumb. It is with the mind as with the body. You cannot add one hair to the finite number of the hairs of your head. You cannot increase by one molecule the bulk of your members beyond their measure written in the Book when as yet there was none of them.—We gain nothing by hypotheses of causation, or by speculations concerning the origins of planetary systems, or the former structures of our Globe, or the successive introductions during unnumbered ages of the Earth's vegetations or inhabitants, excepting the exercise and the sport. When we indulge in the pastime, we become like small children striving to gather fruit out of their reach or climb.—We jump and jump, and one of us may be a little taller than the other, or jump a little higher; but the height of the leap is predetermined for each of us by the length and strength of our little limbs. To rise above the mathematical line where the propulsive forces of nerve and muscle are finally conquered by the Earth's attraction is impossible. And clutching our little fists with nothing in them, down we all come again empty-handed to the ground.

Period during which human languages were more flexible than at present § 2. The phænomena of our Globe declare that the laws of nature, or the operations of secondary causes, physical or physiological, have not been invariably uniform or absolutely similar; some peculiar to the nascent world, all more intense; the collective life of all classes of animated beings endued with the vigour and flexibility of individual youth. Species and their varieties seem to have been produced by an inward nisus which decreased with the advancing age of the world. The like with respect to languages. The process of linguistic formation did not suddenly terminate. A certain degree of vitality in language, now lost to us, was still subsisting; somewhat also of the generative energy of speech, until about the era when the Canon of Holy Scripture was closed by the last mysterious Book of Prophecy.

The miraculous judgment dividing and confusing the human speech into its present alliances and families, working with continued though diminishing cogency, long permitted the diversified classes and orders to retain so much affinity, that words and roots, now seemingly most wide apart, were in their inception so proximate as to enable us, even now, to determine their cognate origin. Can any three languages, cursorily examined, appear more alien to each other than the Cymric, the Latin, and the German?—any three, in which three speakers could less understand each other? —any three groups of words which presented severally, and without interpretation, would look more unconnected than *gwraig, virago*, and *frau*? —Yet they are one and the same. Advert to a slight permutation of letters in the first, a softening in the second, and restore the original ortho-

Ancient identity of Language now dissonal, still perceptible.

graphy to the third ;—*frau* was first spelt *vrauch*, and their identity flashes on the mind.

No small portion of the pleasure accompanying Historical investigation, results from the stimulus afforded by the attempts to expound the dark riddles of past ages: the more difficult the problem, the greater the interest attending its solution. Imperfect are the data upon which the Etymologist investigates the early history of the great Teutonic and Celtic families, somewhat more extensive than the two words which include the whole pith of the Pictish controversy, but not very much more: he has to deal with scattered, scanty, and unsatisfactory materials, usually a name of town, mountain, or river, misheard by the stranger, mis-read by the author, or corrupted by the transcriber. *Bodenkos,* as we are told by Polybius, was the name given to the Po: *fundo carens,* is Pliny's interpretation. Metrodorus informs us that it was a Ligurian word. Is it not Celtic? for there was a town *Bodincomagus*—and we are asked whether *bodenkos* can be explained from the Celtic tongues? Read *bodenlos*—amend the penman's error, and you will have a pure German term.

Arnold's supposition that Βοδεγ-κος, given as the name of the Po, may be Celtic

Then we have inscriptions, so curious, so tempting as to be susceptible of almost any direction which the Philologist may choose. Take, for instance, the votive monuments buried beneath the Eucharistic Altar of Notre-Dame, and brought

Gaulish Altars found beneath the High Altar of Notre-Dame.

to light again as trophies of triumphant Christianity. These stones, with their rude imagery, are coeval records of the language, the faith, the nationality of Paris, when Tiberius ruled the Empire. You see on one the Ship, the symbol of the Waterman's Guild, adopted as the armorial bearing of Lutetia, retained by Paris in her shield notwithstanding every vicissitude, every change of people, religion, state, and monarchy, the heraldic emblem which has outlasted the banner of Saint Louis. On another, you observe three birds: you may count their number—so does the inscription, which also tells you their species, *trigaranus*. And of what race were the Parisian Gauls? *Tri* is what its sound suggests, *three* in the Teutonic dialects, *three* in the Celtic, and how far shall we pursue the numeral through every branch of the Caucasian family?—And the *garan* is first cousin if not brother to the crane of the German, the crane of the Cymri, the crane of the Greek, and how many more?—And when we hear of the Gaulish fane, which, from its iron portals, was called *Isarnodor*, the sounds, so intelligible to the English ear, do not impart any certain information concerning the nationality of the tribes to whom they belonged.

§ 3. Fourteen centuries have elapsed since the authority of the Roman Emperors ceased in Britain, yet scarcely does the farmer's ploughshare ever furrow the soil where a Roman City has flou-

Ambiguity of the linguistic evidence they afford.

Efforts made by the Romans for the purpose of compelling the nations to adopt the Latin

rished, or the stern Roman castramentation controlled the land,—whether the down or heath be still surrounded by the vallum, or the memory of the station preserved by the Notitia or the Itinerary,—without turning up the medals bearing the laurelled head, the weeping captive, the trophy, or the triumphal car, the tokens of Rome's sovereignty.—The husbandman's toil, the infant's busy hand, the excavator's pickaxe, the crumbling cliff, the rush of the rain, have constantly disclosed the Roman hoard during fourteen centuries; and yet that hoard seems as inexhaustible as if throughout the whole length and breadth of our Island the coin germinated in the ground. So vast are the quantities, that the imaginative Antiquary, baffled when he attempted to ascribe their multitude and dispersion to accident or chance, suggested the theory of design—the Romans, as our Archæologist tells us, purposely sowed and buried their mintage in the glebe, to the end that future ages might receive continual manifestations of their almost super-human power. Fanciful as the theory may be, accept it as an expression of the effect produced upon the mind by the irresistible instinct which impelled the Romans to build in all things for historical eternity.

Such have been the results of the endeavours made by the Romans to impose their language upon the vassal world. The mastery of language

Stukeley's supposition that the Romans buried their coins purposely as memorials

is the mastery of thought   They strove for that mastery, gained it, kept it, keep it: they, dead and gone, that Empire still is theirs. They would fain compel the subject nations to adopt their Latian speech; and the conquered obeyed, accepting the enjoined conformity as a high privilege, a bond of union, the creation of a new nationality.

The general submission of the Provinces is rendered the more conspicuous by the exceptions. The Semitic races resisted the Japhetian influence: perish they may, but they cannot change. Proconsuls and Prætors of Numidia might promulgate their decrees in Latin; but though Carthage was deleted, Thimiliga and Themetra retained their Suffetes, their Judges, who prided themselves upon their ancient patronymics, Hanno or Asdrubal, whilst the community retained their primeval tongue. Augustine acquired the Latin as the language of education; but when the peasantry of Hippo were interrogated who they were,—" Canaanites are we— *Canaani-anachnu*,"—was the reply—unchanged from their Punic ancestry.

The influence of the Latin language resisted by the Semitic races and the Greeks.

Beggarly starving Greece, cringing beneath the yoke, flexible as the reed, complied grudgingly, unwillingly, awkwardly, partially conforming when sustaining the pressure, but casting away the dialect of her Masters whom she dared not call Barbarians,—though she thought so in her heart—as soon as the pressure was removed.

—Greece testified her deep disgust by the rejection of Latin literature. Love of knowledge might tempt a Greek to consult the Latin Historian. Convenience, duty, interest, or the desire of advancement, compelled the Græculus to study the Roman Jurist; but he would have nothing to do with the language of Rome as the source of intellectual pleasure. It is more than doubtful whether any existing Latin manuscripts, excepting the magnificent volumes of the Pandects, exhibit the hand of a Greek Scribe. Stamboul does not know less or care less of or for Virgil and Horace, than Constantinople under the Comnenian family.

But the partial repulse which the Latin received from the Hellenic and Semitic provincials, to whom we must also add the sturdy Celtiberians and the Celts of Armorica, was far more than compensated by the success attending the Roman policy in all other portions of the Continental Empire. All the primitive dialects of Tuscany, Liguria, or Umbria, all national tongues of the Transpadane regions, all the linguistic memorials of the Boian and Insubrian were consumed by the dominant language. The Latin penetrated into the deepest recesses of the Cottian and Rhetian Alps, became naturalized in Dacia, firmly implanted amongst the rude Sards, and covered the Gauls. The Teutonic languages of the Barbarians who inherited the Imperial

authority melted away before the language
honoured by the purple—and the term *Latinitas*
was adopted as the synonym of Western Christendom.   The Ripuarian Franks assimilated
themselves to the Romans : the Salic judges who
administered the laws of Arbogast and Widogast
attempted to record the Doom of the Mallum,
like the Magistrate disciplined by the forensic
labours of the Roman Colony ; and the " Malberg
glosses," so perplexing to the philologist, rendered the national code intelligible to the Barbarian, who sustained a new subjection under his
native Sovereign.

Rarely, if ever, did the Barbarian Conqueror
dare, when acting as a Ruler, to speak his native
language . he endangered his Royal caste unless
he comported himself like a Roman on the throne ·
the very sound of the Latin language implied
supremacy and command.   The Latin was the
only recognized vehicle of official business in the
Romano-Barbarian States : the Sovereigns of
Teutonic blood promulgated their laws, asserted
their prerogative, bestowed their bounties, or rebuked their people in the language of the Cæsars.
Capitulars, Statutes, Rescripts, Charters, all public documents are written in Latin.   Until the
collapse of the Anglo-Saxon dynasty, no Chancellor of an Anglo-Saxon King or Basileus,
ever repudiated the precedent derived from the
Scribes and Notaries who had sat behind the

gilded barrier at the feet of the Emperor. With this exception, if it be one—for we may conjecture that the vernacular Charters are authentic versions of a Latin text, nor are we certain whether the Latin texts of our Anglo-Saxon laws may not have been the originals,—the Latin continued to be the living language of the State, the instrument of reasoning, the predominating vehicle of thought. When the Norman ruled in England and the Capetian in France, the Latin language constituted the educational test and token distinguishing the plebeian orders from the aristocracy of rank and talent.

The Romana Rustica

§ 4. Hitherto we have principally adverted to the effects produced by Sovereignty; but Rome was to be aided by auxiliaries more mighty than her wisdom. The Roman language was destined to conquer an intellectual Empire, through the medium and by the co-operation of the Peasant, the Colonus, the Freed-man, the Stranger, the Slave, the Jew, the Christian, the Bishop, the Priest, the Deacon, the Faithful, the Catechumen, the Confessor, the Martyr, invested moreover with varied forms, altered influences,—powers unpremeditated, unforeseen, unattainable by any device which human wit could have framed.

Whilst the *Urbane Latin*, the *Lingua Nobilis* of Quintilian, the Latin flourishing in the Augustan Age, was employed by all the cultivated classes, there existed by her side a sister, a rival, and yet a friend, constantly making inroads upon the classical territory. This was the Language known as the *Sermo pedestris*, the *Sermo simplex*, the *Lingua Rustica*, or *Ruralis*, severed into various cognate dialects, plainer in construction, not accentuated as in the tribune; some sounds elided, others exaggerated, divested of many inflections now found in the Latin language, as the latter became modelled by processes to us unknown, and fixed by the rules which the Grammarians laid down. A remarkable characteristic of the Latin language in the earlier age was its mutability. The hymns of the Salian priests became, after an interval of five hundred years, utterly unintelligible to the Romans; and, though in an opposite direction, ten times more distant from Cicero's language than the Norman dialect of Master Wace's *Roman du Rou* is from Cicero.

Some remains of the *Lingua Rustica* are extant in sepulchral inscriptions, which, however, exhibit this common parlance rather according to an amended or artificial form: that is to say, they shew an attempt to write Latin, but a Latin yielding to the pronunciation and idiom of the *Volgare* of the land. Not less remarkable is the existence of a Roman dialect in the parts of Dacia now constituting the modern Wallachia, where the language seems to have been perpe-

Idea of the Lingua Rustica, afforded by the inscriptions, and the Daco-Roman dialect of Wallachia

tuated from Trajan's Legions, settled as feudatories in the Kingdom of Decebalus. Strangely
disguised by Greek, Turkish and Sclavonian in-
termixtures, the Romanian or Daco-Roman,
nevertheless, still displays a close affinity to the
South-Appenine dialects of Modern Italy. When
cleared from these additions, the Daco-Roman
language approximates to the Roman *volgare*
spoken by Rienzi, soft and euphonic, though uncongenial to Dante's taste and dissonant to his
ears. Anyhow, the before-mentioned specimens
and fragments afford some notion of the Romana
Rustica during the Imperial Age. Dante reckoned fourteen principal dialects of the *Volgare*,
whilst, as he says, those of inferior consequence
were countless. The Bolognesi of the *Strada
Maggiore* spoke otherwise than those of the
Borgo San' Felice. Italy was unquestionably
circumstanced under the Roman domination
nearly as she is now: a variety of dialects flourishing in each locality, concurrent with one
predominating language, which, consecrated to
literature, afforded throughout the Peninsula the
means of common intercourse.

Influence of the servile and pro-letarian population upon lan-guage

§ 5. Whilst the Romans triumphed in all
the merciless insolence of baneful prosperity, another nation writhed in ceaseless anguish amongst
and beneath them, the vast nation of slaves, the
crime, the cancer, and ultimately the punishment
of Rome, constantly recruited by fresh captives,

hundreds, and thousands, and myriads, and chi-
liads, and millions.— The delicate matron and
tender damsel of Corinth, the grey-haired Senator
of Epirus, the athletic Goth, the blue-eyed Teuton,
the supple Sarmatian, the accomplished Lydian,
the Greek emparadised by luxury and intellect,
the Barbarian who had ranged in the free delights
of mountain and steppe, forest and wave, swept
away from every country which had been lacerated by the fangs of the Roman wolf, or torn
by the beak of the Roman eagle, fit symbols of
Roman power.

Each miserable importation, circumstanced like
the Africans in European settlements, could only
obtain an imperfect knowledge of the language
of their tyrants. Filling every employment, from
the lowest to the highest, swarming in every
villa, congregating in every atrium, chained to
every rich man's door, their modes of speech
accustomed every ear to their locution and infected the vernacular tongue. This servile talk
would readily combine with the vulgarisms of the
mob, the proletarian populace of the great cities,
but most especially of that foul Capital. the
vicious pronunciations, the clipt vocables, the sole-
cisms and blunders, the slang and cant, the obsce-
nity and ruffianism, the corruptions of language
corresponding to the debasement of the mind.

In the midst of this dinning tumult of tongues,
the Classical Latin, the Latin of the standard au-

thors, the Latin of literature, the Grammar Latin, retreating amongst the higher orders of society, struggled for existence. So actively pervading were the deteriorated dialects at Rome, that constant exertions were required to preserve the children of good families from the vernacular which constituted the language of the masses. Latin did not come by nature at Rome, any more than Greek. Both were languages of education; both required to be bought and taught.— To this effect are the instructions given by Saint Jerome, in his most curious letter to Læta, containing a complete system of education: his precautions for securing the infant against the colloquial language of the nurse, being scarcely less stringent than those which might be considered needful for Calcutta at the present day. Saint Jerome was any thing rather than a precisian in style, but he was anxious that Læta's daughter should speak honestly, as fitted her station, a Christian gentlewoman.

§ 6. A third powerful agency of mutation resulted from the employment of barbarian auxiliaries, half taught, well trained, very useful, though dangerous members of the Empire's military strength. The broken Greek of the Scythian Bow-bearer at Athens, was probably scarcely worse than the Latin mangled by the Illyrian or Tungrian Legionary. The promotion of their Chieftains to station and consequence did

Influence of these vulgar dialects at Rome. Latin taught to children of good families.

The military dialect of the Barbarian auxiliaries.

not necessitate any increase in liberal cultivation. Merobaudes, the Frank, who held so high a command in the Imperial army, inscribing his despatches upon his waxen tablets, (supposing he could write), would produce a Latin, rivalling in purity the French of Marshal Saxe. A military dialect must thus have been formed in and about the camps and stations of the Empire; the more readily, from the circumstance that the Romana Rustica prevailed amongst the armies. Though in regular Latin,—or at least corrected into Latin by the Historian,—the camp-song chanted by Aurelian's soldiery sounds exceedingly like the burden of a Mediæval popular ballad.

Nor are we without examples of similar medleys in more recent times. From the commixture of the Mahometan invaders with the Hindoos, arose the language which we call Hindoostanee, a name conveying no distinct idea; whereas its native denomination, *Ordoo Zabaun*, the speech of the Camp, the tongue of the Horde, commemorates its origin. In like manner, a military language, resulting from a rude and clumsy eclecticism, appeared in the *Grande Armée;* to which they gave the name of *Parler-soldat.* Its basis was the vernacular French of the Capital, but exceedingly deteriorated and amply vocabularized from the other languages of the mixed hosts whom Napoleon had assembled: this jargon became the medium of mutual communication

The Ordoo Zabaun of Hindostan such a military dialect, also the Parler-soldat of the Grande Armee

between Polish Lancer and Lombard Carabi-
neer, Swabian Boor and Parisian Garde.

§ 7. All the before-mentioned agencies and
impulses were, however, subordinate to the primum mobile, the orb in which they were universally involved. The subject of language, the
instrument, but also the restraint of thought,
is endless. The history of language, the mouth
speaking from the fulness of the heart, is the
history of human action, faith, art, policy, government, virtue, and crime. When society pro-
gresses, the language of the people necessarily
runs even with the line of society. You cannot
unite past and present; still less can you bring
back the past: moreover, the law of progress is
the law of storms; it is impossible to inscribe
an immutable statute of language on the peri-
phery of a vortex, whirling as it advances. Every
political development induces a concurrent alteration or expansion in conversation and composition. New principles are generated, new authorities introduced; new terms for the purpose
of explaining or concealing the conduct of public
men must be created: new responsibilities arise.
The evolution of new ideas renders the change
as easy as it is irresistible, being a natural change
indeed, like our own voice under varying emo-
tions, or in different periods of life: the boy
cannot speak like the baby, nor the man like the
boy: the wooer speaks otherwise than the hus-

Changes
produced
by pro-
gress of
Society.

Effect of
political
revolutions
upon lan-
guage

band; and every alteration in circumstances—
fortune or misfortune, health or sickness, prosperity or adversity, produces some corresponding
change of speech or inflexion of tone.

In French, the language of the *Ancien Re-* English Constitu-
gime has been revolutionized with the State. tional language cre-
Bossuet or Fenelon, Montesquieu, Helvetius, ated by the
Common-
and the Patriarch of Ferney all together, could wealth.
not have supplied *incivisme* or *tricolor*. Our
English Parliamentary or Constitutional language dates from the Commonwealth, since
which period our political vocabulary has continued enriching itself by every alternation of
party, or fluctuation of national feeling. We
have gained so much upon the old Heroes of
our language, that their panoply would be insufficient in the day of battle. Did we determine to
employ in political discussion no other words or
expressions than those warranted by judicious
Hooker or sagacious Verulam, we should be
utterly at fault. We might as well attempt to
make observations upon Jupiter's Satellites with
a Gorhambury astrolabe. The sonorous periods
of old Whitehall would so stiffen and starch a
despatch, that the subject-matter could never be
opened. Nay, were Burke to re-appear in the
House, and be restricted to the phraseology consecrated by his own oratory, he would feel himself no less ill at ease than if attired in his silk
coat, silk stockings, hair-bag, buckles, and sword.

Acquisitions of knowledge, improvements in science, commerce, manufactures, and arts, are still more creative . you must invent new words and phrases in sequence of every new invention. Let the Teachers who, with the best possible intentions advise us to draw exclusively from the well of English undefiled, try to follow their own counsel, and they will find the water utterly inadequate to supply the consumption of a single steam-engine boiler. No European people may seem better able to depend upon their own resources than the Germans, possessing in their language such treasures of words, and retaining the most unfettered powers of combination; yet so delicate are the shades of ideas, that in order to express the productions of English ingenuity and the fruits of English partizanship, they are driven to borrow from our own poor and comparatively unphilosophical compound:—*Locomotive, Conservative* and *Radical*, are all taken in bodily, and printed in German type as testimonies, that from us, the things, the ideas, and' the words have been derived.

Since the time of Royal Rome, Republican Rome had been seething with social and political revolutions. It is a mystery how the Latin settled into its present form between the dates of Numa and of Ennius. The grammatical cultivation of the language could not stop the utilitarian march of neology.—Old and successful practitioners always dislike new modes of treatment.—Cicero could not abide these innovations. He complains how rarely good Latin could be heard, especially amongst the Roman Ladies: not half a dozen, he says, of whom his wife's mother Lælia was one, spake correctly. In like manner the corruptions of colloquial language, even in the tribune, excite Quintilian's complaints: and truly, if Cicero believed that the standard of language was to be found in any past era, he must have sorrowed at contributing himself to the formation of a new tongue. It would have been impossible for Rome to keep out from her own territory, the influence of the foreign nations with whom she was connected by war or by peace; who resorted to the Capital for the purpose of profiting by her traffic, her splendour, her contamination. Had the Ager Romanus been surrounded by a wall of brass, each generation would have been compelled in old age to learn a new language unknown to youth.

Censures raised by Cicero and Quintilian upon the popular corruptions of the Latin.

All around was in mutation: the Roman machinery of government and administration had been in continued development. The whole frame and organization of the Empire was constructed and reconstructed. No one could or would mind Quintilian in common life: the physician, the rhetor, the jurisconsult, the artist, the trader, were constantly inviting new words into Roman citizenship. The stanch conservative

Mutations of the Latin during the Lower Empire.

Patriot might object and protest against this influx—but the people, having heard him in respectful silence, admitted, without discussion, the strangers to the civic freedom. Hence arose the eight or nine thousand words now banished *en masse* by the Lexicographer beyond the end of his alphabet, stigmatized and disgraced as barbarous, and against which the Student is warned. This so called barbarous nomenclature is, however, completely different in character from the matter which forms the staple of mediæval glossaries. Very few of the words are derived from Teutonic roots, being principally adaptations from the Greek, technological terms, names of plants and other natural objects, and Latin words applied in unclassical senses, and inflected or expanded in unclassical but useful and significant forms. But whoever considers this Vocabulary without reference to classical authority, will acknowledge that it contains a most valuable addition to the old store, evidently created by the alterations which Roman Society sustained.

Christianity most influential in altering the Latin language.

§ 8. And this leads us to the result, that, supposing the Roman Empire had continued to subsist in unbroken succession, untouched by Barbarian power, Rome still purely and prosperously Roman, the Cæsars still Cæsars, no otherwise altered by effluxion of time than the London of Queen Victoria is altered from the

London of Queen Anne, yet the introduction of Christianity would have given a new language to the Roman World. Faint as the national Faith of the Romans had become, yet it nevertheless was a constituent element of their language and literature. When the oracles were silenced, the intellectual power of Paganism was vanquished—her intellectual genius prepared to depart:—Heathen art, science, and literature, were smitten with slow but irremediable atrophy. Now began the diffusion of the Gospel, preached at Rome by the poor to the poor. Of the teachers, many were Orientals, to whom the Latin was in all respects a strange language, a disagreeable language : alien to their customs, opinions, and habits of thought. They were scarcely acquainted with Latin Grammar, certainly ignorant of its elegancies. The Christian Church turned away from all the liberal learning of the Heathen; it was included in their sphere of unmitigated antipathies. For Heathen learning was permeated by that Idolatry which they hated with a perfect hatred, a feeling unallayed so long as primitive purity and fervour prevailed.

Teachers of the Gospel hostile to Heathen learning.

The application of this historical fact to the dealings of the dark and middle ages with respect to Science and Literature and Art, must be reserved. We now advert to these sentiments merely with reference to their operation upon language. The Apostolical Constitutions prohi-

Books of the Gentiles prohibited by the Apostolic Constitutions.

bited all books of the Gentiles, and the works of the Classical Writers were generally neglected by the Christian Church during the decline of the Roman Empire, even when not absolutely condemned.

Individuals might not all be equally uncompromising. Some, inclining to the ways of the world, viewed Classical Literature with greater toleration; but on one point, Christendom was compelled to act uniformly and consistently. Urbane Latin, Classical Latin, was not convenient for ecclesiastical ministrations. The forms of speech prevailing amongst the early Christian congregations are partially evidenced by the Catacomb inscriptions—a frequent intermixture of bastardized Greek, exhibiting also the adoption of the Greek character for Latin words. For all composition in the higher sense, the Epistle, the Apology, the Commentary, the vocabulary of Pagan Rome was inadequate. Neither the doctrines nor the ceremonies nor the mysteries of Christianity could be taught, celebrated, or performed otherwise than through a complete modification of the Classical language. Christianity, for her own high duties, created her own language, breathing a new spirit into the tongue employed in Liturgical compositions, Prayer or Collect, Hymn or Psalm.

The rules of grammar were therefore relaxed, syntax disregarded, popular idioms introduced

Classical Latin inadequate to the wants of Christian Literature.

whenever custom or sense required them.—"It is our business," says Saint Augustine, "to be intelligible. What care I for the ferula of the Schoolmaster? I despise him."—Saint Augustine was quite right. Few folks have occasioned more injury to literature than the martinets of language: those who think correctly must often speak incorrectly. A noun, never before introduced into genteel company, will shine a gem if you are bold enough to set it in the Dictionary. The mind supplies the want of grammatical coherence · the language of feeling cannot follow injunctions or seek for precedents: an unauthorized phrase embodies your sentiments and becomes the vehicle of your meaning, with a strength and a logical precision which the code imposed by an Academy quenches and destroys. Whenever the era arrives in which artificial rules for style or language are accurately laid down and painfully obeyed, then literature is approaching her climacteric; the Doctor's prescriptions accelerate the Patient's decrepitude. Quintilian aided the decline of Latin genius, the *Cruscanti* condemned Tuscany to hopeless ineptitude.

Saint Augustine justifies his grammatical inaccuracies

§ 9. Classical Latin was peculiarly inapplicable to the most important literary labours of the Western Church during her earlier ages— the versions of the Holy Scriptures. As an exemplification, compare any passage of the Vulgate with the modern texts in which purity or

Translations of the Holy Scriptures, their influence upon language.

classical correctness has been attempted, Castellio or Beza—the Ten Commandments travestied in the style of the Twelve Tables. These translations exercised a most lively influence, not only upon the dogma, but the intellect of the Latins, and assisted in evolving many of the essential differences between them and the Orientals. To the Eastern Churches, Hellenic, Semitic, or mixed, the Holy Scriptures were readily accessible. They possessed the Septuagint, and also the ancient Aramean translations of the Old Testament; together with the original text of the New Testament, in the language of the majority. It was otherwise in the Latin Church: Greek was only understood by the educated minority, Hebrew and Chaldee hardly at all. Many translations of the Greek Scriptures were therefore made and circulated, but those of the Hebrew were innumerable. These productions, though prompted by sincere zeal, were inaccurate or imperfect; and the deficiencies of the current versions stimulated the Ezra of the Western Church to undertake his vast labour of love.

For obvious reasons, we here discuss the Vulgate merely as a literary monument. Translation, under any circumstances, is an intellectual process of considerable complexity. Trade hackwork is of course out of the question; but whenever the interpreter feels the obligation of throwing mind into mind, he must be able to give a true copy, though employing different pigments. Every language has its own mode of colouring thoughts, which cannot be transferred to another canvas, except by the substitution of equivalents; and this requires a peculiar talent, scarcely less rare than the endowments which qualify for original composition of a high order. Saint Jerome prepared himself for the task of interpretation, by his prayerful life-long application to Holy Writ. Without discarding the helps he could derive from his predecessors, he determined to work for himself and think for himself, making his Version honestly, substantially and completely from the originals. Hard and fast had Saint Jerome to labour. There were no Hebrew Dictionaries in those days, no Grammars, no Thesauri, none of the Desk and Closet-helps for philological study. No easy "Ladders to Learning," leaning against the library shelves. No well-stored cribs out of which you may pull the provender, all ready cut and dried for you, when you wish to cram and be filled. No wholesale warehouses where you can fit yourself out with erudition ready-made or second-hand. Saint Jerome had no means of acquiring the needful knowledge otherwise than by settling in Palestine, where, obtaining oral instruction, he learned the Hebrew, Arabic and Syrian or Chaldee tongues.

Saint Jerome acquires the Oriental languages by oral instruction.

In the whole compass of literary history, there is not a Chapter more interesting than that which could be made out of Jerome's correspondence concerning the Vulgate;—the criticisms which the Author sustained, disturbed even a Saint's temper. "If I had taken," says he, "to the making of mats or baskets, no one would have found fault with me." He had many troubles in journeys, in exertions for obtaining good manuscripts, and the like, but all such contrarieties weighed very little upon his mind, compared with the philological or literary difficulties he found in rendering the Word of God accessible to the multitude. He had to convey the truth, strength and simplicity of the Holy Scriptures, into a language, which, representing the original, would be so far conformable to the taste of the educated classes as not to offend by homeliness; but he could not help creating a new dialect: even the attention he paid to the collocation of words cut new channels for the Latin language.

Language of the Vulgate, its influence upon mediæval literature. Our translations of the Holy Scriptures effected a great change in the English language after the Reformation. The Vulgate acted upon the Classical and urbane Latin in the same sort, but far more energetically.- Not only did it become the main standard for ecclesiastical Latin, but for the general Latin of literature, inasmuch as the Holy Scriptures constituted the basis of all study. Scriptural Knowledge was transfused into the

" humanities" as the renovating life-blood. In the Catalogues of mediæval Libraries, the Books of the Holy Scriptures usually constitute the greater number of the volumes; and in their compositions the words and phrases of the Vulgate are so constantly interwoven as to shew that Saint Jerome's Latin was the language in which the writers thought.

§ 10. All the foregoing causes in their various stages, capacities, and developements, co-operated in diffusing the Roman dialects throughout the Empire. From the Latin, mediately or immediately, all the principal modern languages of the European Commonwealth, Cis-atlantic or Transatlantic,—excepting those of direct Sclavonian or Teutonic origin—are derived. All bore the Roman or Latin name . they never renounced their ancestry; never were considered otherwise than as subsidiary dialects. Four are the languages included in the Latin, said the Canon of St. Andrew's, "Church Latin, Italian, French, and Spanish."—*In lingua Latina continentur Ecclesiastica, Italica, Gallica et Hispanica*—or, if we adopt the slightly-differing classification which Dante has made, the *grammar* or *school Latin*, the " *Lingua del si*," the " *Lingua d'oc*," and the " *Lingua d'oil*," which last three denominations may fairly be assumed to represent the three great divisions of the Romance tongue.

We avoid the controversy of absolute pri-

Fordun's classification of the Latin dialects

ority : that is to say, which of these dialects first assumed a regular form. Were there no other reason, the absence of evidence must ever render the discussion, eminent as those writers are who have engaged in it, utterly unprofitable. Even the accessible materials have scarcely received a sufficient degree of philological care. As matters now stand, we actually want an edition of the *Divina Commedia*, representing the text according to the grammar and orthography which the Poet himself employed. It is sufficient for our purpose to know that almost all the Barbarians, —Visigoth, Frank, Burgundian, Mæsogoth, Lombard, who settled in the Italian and Iberian peninsulas and the Gauls, forgot or disused their original dialects about the conclusion of the ninth Century.

The Visigoths were probably amongst the earliest who abandoned their ancestral language. Pelayo, in the cavern of Covadonga spake the Romance of Toledo, which was, as it still is, amongst the least altered of the daughters of Rome. The Franks rushed into the adoption of the Roman language. The Merovingian Sovereigns were shamed out of Teutonic barbarity. German was the mother-tongue of Charlemagne and Louis le Debonnaire, but Latin was equally familiar to them. The Court of the Carlovingians afforded small protection to Teutonic feeling when the Sovereign held his state upon

813.
Canon of the Council of Tours, directing the Bishop

Gaulish or Belgic soil. The encreasing import- to preach in Romana ance of the Romance language is indicated by a Rustica, or in German. memorable Canon passed in the Council convened by Charlemagne at Tours, equally representing Eastern France and Western France, Austrasia and Neustria, Germany and the Gauls. The Bishops throughout the Transalpine Empire were enjoined to be diligent in preaching, and to take care that their discourses should be rendered either into *Romana Rustica*, or into *Theotisc* or *Deutsch*, to the end that all might understand. If there be any doubt as to the circumstances which suggested this regulation, they are soon removed. A singular combination of events and persons connected with a great European era, enables us to ascertain precisely the period when the chief body of the Frankish races, inhabiting the ter- ritory which afterwards became the kingdom of France, had in great measure, if not completely, abandoned their native Teutonic, so that the *Lingua Romana* ruled as their preponderating national language.

After the dreadful battle of Fontenai in 841 June 25. Burgundy, Fontenai near Vezelay, the field of Battle of Fontenai hatred where Charles-le-Chauve and Louis-le- between Charles-le- Germanique, combining against their brother Chauve and Louis- Lothar and their nephew, the adventurous, un- le-Ger- manique happy Pepin of Aquitaine, gained a victory more against Lothar and destructive to themselves than to the vanquished, Aquitaine. they held a Congress at Strasburg for the corro-

842.
Feb 14.
Conven-
tion of
Stras-
burg,
Roman
language
employed
in the di-
plomatic
proceed-
ings.

boration of the alliance. The proceedings were solemn : each monarch addressed his soldiery in his and their own tongue; that is to say, Charles in the *Lingua Romana*, Louis in the *Lingua Teudisca*, or *Deutsch*. The compact was then confirmed by mutual oaths; but in this stage of the transaction, the whole negociations being conducted with the most guarded diplomatic caution, the contracting sovereigns counterchanged. Charles swore in *Deutsch*, Louis in *Roman*. Lastly, when the armies concurred in the obligation, then the two nations severally made their declarations in their vernacular language, the army of Louis in *Deutsch*, the army of Charles in

Import-
ance ot
these docu-
ments, ex-
hibiting the
Romance
language
fully deve-
loped.

Roman. We know their very words, and we may equally discern in these pure and authentic specimens, respectively, the most intelligible High German, and the decided characteristics of the Roman language as exhibited in the translation of the Conqueror's Laws, which, though certainly not coeval, belongs to an early era of the Anglo-Norman dynasty.

Fontenai and Strasburg thus furnish one of the most important passages in Modern History : Germany and France arrayed against each other as severed states, distinct nations, the documents exemplifying each language fully formed, and transmitted to us, not casually or incorrectly, but by the best informed and most competent witness, nay, actor. The Chronicler who has preserved these precious evidences textually,—and so accurately, that, despite of the corruptions of transcribers which usually deform all similar fragments, scarcely a syllable is doubtful,—being Nithardus, grandson of Charlemagne through Bertha, his fair daughter, who contracted a clandestine marriage with Angelbert, the lay-abbot of St. Riquier, Count of Maritime France or Ponthieu, also a Chronicler. Nithardus, who succeeded to his father's dignities, was engaged in all the transactions and battles which he narrates. The history from which we transcribe is dedicated by him to King Charles, his cousin. Fresh dissensions arose: Nithardus vainly endeavoured to reconcile his kinsmen; and, unable to succeed, he quitted the Court in sorrow, and retired to his command, where a violent death—he was slain by the Northmen—prevented the completion of his most valuable annals. They end abruptly, and therefore without any colophon; but he notices an obscuration of the Sun (called by him an Eclipse) which happened whilst he was writing at Saint Cloud on the Loire—*dum hæc super Ligerim juxta Sanctum Chlodoaldum consistens scriberem*—on Sunday the fifteenth of the Kalends of November, whereby the date of the composition is fixed at about four years after the battle of Fontenai; this being the only concurrence of the same days between the battle and his death, so that he bears

Nithardus the Count of Maritime France, and grandson of Charlemagne—value of his historical testimony.

845 18 Oct Obscuration of the Sun noticed by Nithardus as having happened whilst he was writing.

F 2

witness to the events whilst they were quite fresh in his memory. Moreover, there is every reason to suppose that the addresses, oaths, and declarations, were prepared by Nithardus when fruitlessly endeavouring to tranquillize the fatal discord.

Modifications of the Roman dialects from pronunciation, &c.

§ 11. The propagation of language has been not unaptly pourtrayed by the Indian fig-tree: the branches dropping to the ground and taking root, the parent trunk surrounded by the progeny. The progress of the Romanesque languages was not entirely unobstructed; in some few spots the branches did not strike or vegetate, though we are unable to define the peculiarly uncongenial quality of the soil. How it happened that the *Sedici Communi* and the *Tredici Communi*, the neighbours of Verona and Vicenza, contrived to retain their Lombard-German, as they do to this very day—why they never would learn to talk Romance—no Philologist can tell; and this difficulty equally applies to some less noted Communities of the same blood, settled on the Italian side of the Monte Rosa. Moreover, many anomalies and unaccountabilities accompanied the growth, the flowering, and the fructification of the branches which flourished in the Empire. We can scarcely guess at the mental process leading to the general formation of the Romance vocabulary, rather from the oblique cases than the nominative: nor understand wherefore the Spaniard abbreviated *Do-*

minus into *Don'*, whilst *Domina* was decapitated into *'Na*, by the Provençal.

Physical differences of organization contributed largely to these changes; the susceptibility of the ear, the action of the tongue, agencies so obvious and yet so perplexing, not merely on account of their uniformity, but of their mutations—powers gained, altered, lost. As usual, ratiocination fails. Ask the Physiologist to explain why the modern Greek cannot follow his letter *Alpha* by a *Beta;* or why our Anglo-Saxon letter *Thorn*, once common to all the Teutonic nations, should now be rejected by all except the Icelanders and ourselves; nay, why the Dane, who could enunciate the letter *Thorn* or *Theta* before the Sceptre passed to the House of Oldenburg, should have lost the faculty with the new dynasty.

Mutations of the power of pronunciation.

With respect to the manner in which this cause operated, a familiar exposition may be afforded by the names of places. The Frank thickened the *Confluentes* of Rhine and Moselle into *Coblentz*, whilst perhaps before that Frank arrived on the borders of the Seine, *Julia bona* ran into *Lillebonne*.—The inhabitant of the Alpine valley elided *Augusta* into *Aosta;*—the Celtic Gaul condensed *Augustodunum* into *Autun;*— the Iberian amalgamated *Cæsarea-Augusta* into *Saragossa*. And thus the preference for one sound, the dislike of another, the rapidity or slovenliness of pronunciation, the slowness or

Examples of the alterations sustained by the Roman names of places.

liveliness of the speaker, helped to model each dialect of the Romance into its peculiar form. Yet never were the Latin words swamped by Teutonisms, or so altered or mutilated as to be undistinguishable. It is an easy *tour-de-force*, even now, to compose an Italian Sonnet or a Spanish Ode, in which every word should be purely Latin. All the languages thus developed continued true to their source. Some yet exist with scarcely any variation from their earliest age, such as the common dialect of the Sardinian peasantry. Others, more favoured, have expanded into richness, harmony, power. Science, art, and literature have only brought them nearer to their original parentage : the building has been enlarged with materials from the native quarry, and each addition has strengthened the pristine character.

Predominance of the Latin character in all the Neo-Latin Dialects.

The mutations distinguishing the Neo-Romane dialects from the ancient speech of Latium have been gradual and unintermitted, never concealing their identity. They have allied themselves to Rome's recollections, her poets, her historians, her laws. Vast as was the dominion of the Imperial Mother, they have exceeded that dominion. No longer bounded by the Ocean, they spread over the globe; and in Europe, Asia, and the New World an hundred million of those who profess the Christian faith, speak the languages derived from Rome.

Geographical diffusion of the Neo-Latin Dialects.

§ 12. The first amongst these dialects which became the language of literature, obtained an intellectual authority still retained by her, approaching to an œcumenical Empire. It is the language, concerning us most and nearest, as Anglo-Saxons, Anglo-Normans, or Englishmen, the language of our ancient jurisprudence and laws, the Romance, which, somewhat mistakenly called by the name of Norman, produced the French of the present age. Long before the Conqueror landed at Hastings, his language, the language of his fathers, the language of Roman Normandy, had prevailed in the Anglo-Saxon Court; so early that when Louis d'Outremer returned from England to ascend the Carlovingian throne, he could speak none other than that idiom furnishing the epithet indicating his fortunes. And the constant intercourse between Anglo-Saxon England and Normandy fostered the strange speech; the language of fashion, the language conciliating affections, introducing ideas, and clearing the way for the new dynasty.

Greeks and Romans marvelled at the strange and uncouth symbolical representation of the Gaulish Hercules, the Hercules Ogmius, the god of Eloquence, a decrepit old man, conquering without bodily strength, and leading the multitude by the chains of gold and silver fastened to their ears. The French have realized that symbol:—without exertion, without effort, but

Preponderating influence and power of the Langue d'Oïl, the basis of the modern French language.

Early cultivation of the French language by the Anglo-Saxons.

The charm of the Romane French

simply by the witchery of persuasion, the *Langue d'Oil* became pre-eminent over all her compeers, she won the love of the world, she well deserved it.—The German Ritterschaft of Otho the Great raised the war-cry in French, and the historians add, that they knew the language well. —"Son," is the address of the Norwegian Sage, who unfolds in his *Speculum Regale* the whole course of education and learning fitting the Merchant for his trade, the Priest for his ministry, the King for his duties; "learn Latin, learn French, for that is the widest speech of all."

937.
War-cry raised in French by the Germans.

1200—1300.
French cultivated in Norway.

Adopted by Brunetto Latini as the most popular vehicle for Literature.

The *Tesoro* of Brunetto Latini, almost identical with the *Speculum Regale* in design, and not very dissimilar in matter, was the wonder of the author's contemporaries, and his chiefest pride. Amidst the torments of the scorching plain, Dante hears the plaintive voice of his teacher still yearning after his earthly vanity:

"*Sieti racommandato il mio Tesoro*
Nel quale io vivo ancora—e più non chieggio"

But it was not in his own sweet *volgare* that Brunetto wrote the book of which the recollection touched his disembodied spirit—the ruling passion stronger than death—but in the dialect of the Trouveur, the most pleasureful to the reader, and affording the greatest means of circulation through its popularity. The brisk, active, industrious habits of the French aided this diffusion.—Amongst the Tartar hordes and in the encampment of Kublai Khan, the traveller was Diffusion of the Langue d Oil in Tartary, Greece, Syria. surprized by the artificer or the trader greeting him in the language of the Capetian capital. The Crusades spread the *Langue d'Oil* throughout the East; and Athens conversed with the fluency of Paris.

The poetic literature of mediæval Europe Influence of the Langue d'Oil upon the poetic literature of mediæval Europe received its most forcible and distinguishing impress from the Langue d'Oil, the language of Heraldry, the language of the Tournament, the language of the Geste, the language of Chivalry. The ancient and barbarous songs which delighted Charlemagne are forgotten: the traditions of Arthur might, in their pristine speech have still floated amongst the Cymric lineages; but without the aid of the Trouveur, never would the British lays have acquired their fascination: it was not until they became Romance that they were invested with their power. Teuton and Scandinavian yielded to the charms of France and the French tongue. Never, but for the model given by the Trouveurs of the *Langue d'Oil*, would the Germans have gained their national Epic. The title *Abenteuer*, prefixed to each song of the *Niebelungen Lied*, reveals the school in which the Suabian Minstrel was formed. Increasing moral influence of the French language as the language of civilization.

Great as the merits of the Teutonic forms of speech may be, and admirable as the talents they have employed, yet the languages of

Shakespeare and Milton and Schiller and Goethe, have failed to win the wreath belonging to the French tongue. National pride or national feeling must not be allowed to conceal this truth from us. The French language is our universal interpreter throughout the European Commonwealth. Justly may the French assert that their intellectual heroes constitute the advanced-guard of European progress. Their wit, their whim, their *verve*, their erudition, equally sparkling and profound, their grace, readiness, talent, their philosophy, their perfect trust in human reason, their complete emancipation from positive faith, all combine to give them that commanding station; and their language bestows the weapons wherewith they gain the victory. France created the emphatic name of *civilization*; and that language is amongst the most powerful of the efficient causes which promise or threaten to extend the Empire of civilization throughout the world

The Latin Language, its decline as a vernacular tongue

Latin retained in peculiar localities.

§ 13. Such has been the progress, the triumphant career of the Neo-Latin or Romance languages; yet the Classical Latin yielded slowly. There appear to have been peculiar localities, the opposite counterparts of the *Sedici* and *Tredici Communi*, in which the Latin subsisted with a certain degree of purity: a *volgare*, in the strict sense of the term. Race, habit, fancy, thus preserved the spirit in particular places and amongst peculiar classes, when it was yielding to the

Lingua Rustica elsewhere. Some few fragments of this familiar Latin are remarkable in philological history. The Latin seems to have been peculiarly affected by the military : the joyous song of Clothaire's triumphant soldiers arose in the strains of Latin popular verse; and the nightly hymn of the sentinels of Modena, pacing round their ramparts, resounded with a touching melody never known to classical Rome. We can therefore scarcely discern the boundary-line, or mark the exact era when the Urbane Latin ceased to be the vernacular tongue. The Church never employed any other. Whatever might be the origin of the Priest, whatever his race or blood, he lived *sub lege Romanâ* alone. Whenever Western Christendom came together in her representative form, no language but that of Rome was heard, no Council ever debated, no Canon was promulgated in any peculiar or vulgar tongue. In the State, the Latin retained the same pre-eminence: Latin still continued to be the language of all official communications, the language of respect, the language of courtesy, and, till the conclusion of the Hildebrandine era, or longer, the educational language of Knight and Baron, Count and Marquis, Duke and Prince, and Queen and King.

Latin, the language of Church and State.

From the plainness of language and simplicity of construction, the Bible presented to the people in Latin would read very readily into

Influence of the Vulgate upon the New Latin dialects.

Romanesque : certainly St. Jerome's pen and mind contributed materially to the formation of the Romance dialects. As amongst us in the times of the Commonwealth, Scripture language melted into the language of common life. The relative pronoun *che* or *que* has probably been introduced into the various Neo-Latin languages, mainly from the peculiar application of *quia* in the Vulgate. And for the etymology of the word of words, *parola, paraula, palabra,* we can scarcely find any source except the texts, in which the noun *parabola,* and the corresponding verb *parabolare,* are so emphatically employed.

Under these circumstances the Latin long continued intelligible amongst the common people, though they were unable to speak it correctly. An exact parallel to their condition in this respect may be found amongst the Italian or Provençal commonalty, by whom the discourse from the pulpit is fully understood, although the peasant who comprehends the preacher cannot speak a phrase in the language of the sermon. The era when Grammar-Latin became rather less accessible to the multitude can be ascertained with tolerable accuracy by the before-quoted decrees of the Gallican Councils, which direct the Bishop to homilize in the Vulgar tongue.

Latin retained to a consider-

§ 14. Subsequently to the Hildebrandine era the Romance languages swerved away more and more from their mother, growing up, full formed, able extent, notwith-standing the cultiva-tion of the Romance dialects. and handsomer, becoming better dressed, obtaining more regularity, more consistency, acquiring characteristics more pronounced, and at length a grammar of their own, systematic and well defined. They were now, to no inconsiderable extent, the languages of literature. Yet the Ecclesiastical or Grammar-Latin still commanded large provinces in the republic of letters and in the kingdoms of intellect : the decorous language of history and science, completely the language of philosophy ; and, as employed by the school-men, the vigour of these profound thinkers invested the homely cloister and refectory Latin with admirable conciseness and precision. But it is in the ecclesiastical Liturgies, the most devotional of uninspired compositions, that the Western Church speaks with unrivalled pathos, simplicity, and grandeur.

The revival of Letters rather checked than Dominion of the Latin Language checked by the preci-sion result-ing from the revival of Letters. enlarged the dominion of the Latin language. Classical correctness and the ethos of modern society are incompatible elements. The elegancies of Latin are destructive of its practical utility : there was no surer mode of stinting the capacities of thought than the pedantry which restricted that thought to Ciceronian phrase. A building in which the plan, the elevation, the chancel, the tower, every portion, every column, all the mullions, all the capitals, all the pinnacles, have been correctly copied from an ancient original, has assuredly earned the worst possible praise : convenience, applicability and truth all neglected and sacrificed. Nevertheless, even at the present moment, the Latin, despite the debilitating influences of Bembo and Valla, still flourishes amongst the Hierarchy of the Roman Church, composing a multitude which if assembled in one city would at least equal the population of Rome, when the Labarum shone on the Imperial Standard.

Upon the languages of Teutonic origin the Latin has exercised great influence, but most energetically upon our own. The very early admixture of the *Langue d'Oil*, the never interrupted employment of the French as the language of education, and the nomenclature created by the scientific and literary cultivation of advancing and civilized society, have Romanized our speech; the warp may be Anglo-Saxon, but the woof is Roman as well as the embroidery, and these foreign materials have so entered into the texture, that were they plucked out the web would be torn to rags, unravelled and destroyed.—July and August are monuments of Roman domination which will endure when the last vestiges of Roman splendour shall have perished from the face of the earth. They are inscribed upon the signs of the Zodiac, and will perpetuate the memory of the founders of the

Thorough incorporation of the Roman element in the English language.

Roman Empire in the regions now covered with the forests of the far West, and in the Plains of Australia, until the European or civilized Commonwealth, the great Fourth Empire, the Kingdom strong as iron, shall have fulfilled her appointed course, and be dissolved into the miry clay.

CHAPTER III.

SCOPE AND OBJECT OF THE PRESENT HISTORY.

Circum-
stances
under
which this
work ori-
ginated.

§ 1. THE work now presented to the public results from labours spread over many years of my life, labours commenced neither arbitrarily nor unwillingly, but whereto I was conducted as a duty. I mention this circumstance as an apology for undertaking a task already treated so often and repeatedly by writers who have acquired traditional and popular respect, that any further investigation of an apparently exhausted theme might seem superfluous. Imperfectly as my designs have been carried out, whether in skill, scheme or execution, such utility as my historical productions may possess will consist chiefly in their being considered as forming a course of instruction, which, begun more than a quarter of a century ago, I can now scarcely expect to complete; comprehending, according to my original conception, the whole mediæval history of the Anglo-Saxon, Anglo-Norman, Cymric and English races and nations, to the accession of the Tudor dynasty.

Value and importance of the English Records.

These designs originated out of an employment compelling me to concentrate my attention upon English history. Our English archives are unparalleled—none are equally ample, varied, and continuous; none have descended from remote times in equal preservation and regularity, not even the archives of the Vatican. In France, the most ancient consecutive records are the *Olim* registers, as they are called, commencing somewhat scantily under Saint Louis, whereas ours date from the Norman Conquest. The French never possessed any of greater antiquity, for the notion that the French records were captured or destroyed by the English is a mere fable. The proceedings of the *Etats-généraux* cannot, of course, begin sooner than the first Convocations of this imperfectly federal assembly under the House of Valois: the earliest and rather meagre registers of Royal Ordinances were not compiled till the reign of *Jean-le-Bon*; and although the conventions of the Provinces were held from an anterior date, yet none of their records preceding the fourteenth or fifteenth centuries exist with any degree of completeness.

The very circumstances which have protected and produced the title-deeds and evidences of the English constitution, are features of English history. The material conservation of our English Records results in the first instance from the signal mercy shown to our country, so singularly exempted, if we compare ourselves with other nations, from hostile devastation, whether occasioned by foreign foes or domestic dissensions. Never since the Conquest has London

Preservation of the English archives, partly owing to the exemption of this country from hostility.

heard the trumpet of a besieging army : never has an invader's standard floated upon that White Tower wherein our Records are contained.

Thus spared from the calamities which might have consumed or destroyed our public muniments, their preservation equally exemplifies other prerogative characteristics of our history. Such is the early incorporation of the States and territories anciently composing the Anglo-Saxon realm into one solid government, the Sovereign possessing the same substantive rights throughout his dominions,—notwithstanding some slight anomalies rather apparent than real,—and those dominions obeying the supremacy of one common legislature ; a process effected far more completely in England than in France, the kingdom whose circumstances, taken on the whole, were most analogous to our own.

Furthermore and in addition to this Imperial unity, are we distinguished amongst nations by the recognition of the principle that the national will should be ruled by the national law. Our high Court of Parliament was, from the beginning a remedial Court, a permanent tribunal, and not an accidental political assembly. English Our Constitution is not theoretically founded Constitution either upon Royal prerogative or upon popular grounded upon precedent and liberty, but upon justice, a reasonable submission practice to the authority of the past. This principle of justice necessitated a constant recurrence to precedent : *stare super vias antiquas,* the dead governing the living. What have our ancestors done ?—our predecessors in the like case, or under the like emergency ? In all our revolutionary conflicts, the main arguments employed by all contending parties were painfully and carefully adduced from the muniments of the Realm, —King or Clergy, Peers or Commons, Ministers or Parliaments appealing to the Roll, the Membrane, the Letter of the Law, upon which all their reasonings were to be grounded.

During the periods exhibiting the greatest turbulence, we therefore find an uniform system of interpellation, preferred in good faith to Record and to Charter. Widely as the interpreters of the texts may have differed, the text was reverenced by all. Hence, even in our own times, our oldest Records have never become obsolete : they were deposited in the Treasure-house of the State, not as archæological curiosities, but for their practical and living value. This, their material or bodily union and preservation, the effect of abstract constitutional principles, practically promoted and supported the same principles. Had a Castilian advocate in the reign of Philip the Fourth, wished, like a Selden, to quote the proceedings of the ancient Cortes, he could never have completed his constitutional pleadings. The protocols of the Spanish legislatures were dispersed throughout the Monasteries of the Kingdom, nor could they have been united by any exertion of research or labour.

Summary, indicating the succession of Constitutional Records

We take up our title from Domesday-book. There is not such another *Cadastre* existing, whether considered in relation to the era in which the Great Survey was compiled, or the historical, local or personal information which the volume contains.

The reign of Rufus is a blank as to Records, though the deficiency is supplied by store of Charters.—One great Roll of the Exchequer belonging to Henry Beauclerc, the first of our constitutional Kings, is extant.—A chasm ensues, probably occasioned by the destructive convulsions of King Stephen's reign; but upon the accession of Henry Plantagenet the series of these Records recommences, and continues uninterrupted till they ceased in consequence of the recent legislative enactments, which suppressed the Exchequer of Receipt, the most ancient financial establishment in Europe. These great Rolls furnish most curiously minute specifications of the Crown's territorial possessions, together with a vast variety of personal details.— Every Landholder in England, and every Englishman, was in danger of coming to the pay-table. Therein the sources and particulars of the revenue are fully set forth; and they incidentally elucidate almost every branch of our laws and policy during the transitional era of English history, when that system was maturing upon which our present Constitution is founded.

With the accession of Richard Cœur-de-Lion appear the Rolls of the Curia Regis, the proceedings before the Justiciars representing the person of the King. Modern legal enrolments are strictly formal, lifeless, and arid : not so the ancient records, formal, but not arid, strict, but not stereotyped narratives, exhibiting plaintiff and defendant, prosecutor and criminal, judges and suitors, in a lively and living form. Let me here remark that the interest of our judicial Records is not local, or confined to this our Country : they appertain not merely unto England but to the English people, now so commonly denominated the Anglo-Saxon race, wheresoever dispersed, for here we have, above all, the germs and elements of the Laws obtaining in the Imperial and triumphant Republic of America, expanding from the Atlantic to the Pacific; and whose States, together with our vast Colonies, seem appointed to cherish the institutions of England beneath other skies, when, yielding to the inevitable destiny of all human dominations, the power and splendour of the British Commonwealth shall have departed.

On the Feast-day of the Ascension, the twenty-seventh day of May, one thousand one hundred and ninety-nine, the day when John Duke of Nor-

1189.
Rolls of the Curia Regis, commencing upon the accession of Richard I

1199.
27th May.
Chancery enrolments beginning upon the day of King John's coronation.

mandy was crowned King of England, begin the
Rolls of the Chancery, the great Secretariat of
the realm, the Chancellor being Secretary of
State for all departments. Every instrument
authenticated by the Great Seal, whereby the
King declared his mind and will, was to be entered or enrolled upon these records. And here
again we read a deeper doctrine than is expressed
by the written words of the record. It is very
certain that no such enrolments were made
during the preceding reigns in England, nor do
we find the like in any coeval European State.
Now Hubert Archbishop of Canterbury, who was
appointed Chancellor on the day of King John's
Coronation, had been very active during the
interregnum which ensued between the death of
Cœur-de-Lion and the confirmation of John's
inchoate title. He was one of the Commissioners
or Justiciars deputed to England as soon as
Richard died; and the Archbishop, by causing
the English to become the men of John Duke
of Normandy, had secured the accession of the
new Sovereign. We therefore believe (as we
have stated elsewhere in this Work) that this
registration of State documents was connected
with the views entertained by the Prelate, who
declared how he anticipated that John would
bring Crown and Kingdom into the greatest confusion. Henceforward, all constitutional transactions between Crown and Subject are both

essentially and formally legal covenants, King and people alike obeying the supremacy of the law. The Coronation Oath is deposited in the Chancery, to be produced against the Sovereign, should the compact be infringed.

The Chancery-Rolls furnish us with the writs and other documents, demonstrating, not collaterally or inferentially, but directly and positively, the composition of the Great Council of the realm. In subsequent reigns, the records of the Legislature enlarge into the regular series of Parliament-Rolls, Statute-Rolls, and Bills or Petitions, still continued, and made up, so far as the Statute-Rolls are concerned, in the old form and fashion. And thus do we possess the muniments elucidating the whole course of our Constitution as it arose. The instruments exist, coeval and sincere, giving the required testimony, equally with respect to the acting parties and the transactions in which they were engaged, and exhibiting at the same time the whole process of formation, not effected by forethought or design, but by constant exertions, struggles, labour, fortuitous events, contending parties, contending passions: granted, persisted in, diverted, frustrated, or overruled, affording lessons, which, the evidence being lacking, cannot be taught by the history of any other country in the world.

§ 2. The unsupported industry of Prynne _{Circumstances} and Selden, and the other great constitutional _{under which the}

work en-
titled *The
Rise and
Progress
of the En-
glish Com-
monwealth
was com-
posed

lawyers of the preceding age, had been unable
to advance beyond the preliminary examinations
of the masses of documents absolutely needful for
the accurate and systematic investigation of our
constitutional history. Acting under public authority, I was entrusted with the formation of
collections intended to comprize all the extant
materials, elucidating the development and authority of the Legislature from the Conquest
to the accession of Henry the Eighth, when the
organization of the High Court of Parliament was
settled upon the scheme which still obtains.

Upon the details of these works and collections, this is not the occasion to speak. It is·
sufficient to observe that the volumes I was enabled to publish under the sanction of the House
of Commons, will, for the period which they include, afford an indispensable authority for the
solution of various important constitutional questions, as well as incontrovertible testimonies of
historical events, so that the general outline of
the constitutional periods therein comprized may
be traced in an authentic form

Engaged upon these public works, it appeared
to me that my official tasks would be insufficiently
executed, unless, acting in my private and individual capacity, I accompanied the collections
undertaken at the national expense, by what I
may term a preface and a perpetual commentary.
Ascending, therefore, to the earliest stages of

our history, I have, in the series of essays devoted to that object, endeavoured to elucidate the
rise and progress of the English Commonwealth
during the Anglo-Saxon period, proceeding by
synthesis ; examining in the first place, the duties,
rights, and privileges appertaining to the various
ranks and orders of society, the territorial organization which the country assumed in relation
to the people, and the attributes of the authorities
and tribunals federatively combined in our political Constitution.   In the Work comprehending
these enquiries, I have, therefore, attempted to
demonstrate, so to speak, the political anatomy of
the nation, and to connect that anatomy with the
national physiology, describing the organs of national vitality, and elucidating the laws of that
vitality.   Hence the disquisitions upon the legal
and social institutions of the Anglo-Saxons constitute the main portion of the Work, illustrated
by comparison with those of other nations.

Many important questions, which in this present composition are noticed briefly, and presented
rather as suggestions than as lessons, are in the
first-mentioned Work discussed minutely and
anxiously, supported by reference to the several
authorities upon which my opinions have been
formed.   Here I may be permitted to crave the
attention of the reader, in particular, to the five
chapters in which I explained the origin of feudality, the Carlovingian Institutions, and above

Chapters
10, 11, 17,
18,19,of the
*Rise and
Progress*,
to be read
in connex-
ion with the
present
Work

all, that doctrine upon which, as I believe, all
real conception of mediæval and modern history
depends, the deduction of authority from Rome:
and the continuity by which the States composing
the European or civilized Commonwealth (whatever may be their forms of government) are
Doctrine
of Imperial
succes-
sion —
Various
views of
Dubos,
Savigny,
Guizot,
Sismondi,
Allen,
Hallam,
Mitter-
meier, &c
united into the Fourth Great Empire. Those
who have attended to modern historical literature,
know full well how acutely and copiously the
Roman theory has been illustrated by foreign
enquirers, and also by our own. It has been sifted
and tried by discussion, by argument, and by contradiction; yet, perhaps, the most cogent proofs
establishing the Imperial or Roman doctrine are
found in the great diversity of principles prevailing amongst those who advocate the affirmative proposition. They have not combined for
any sectarian or party purpose: they have all
worked separately and independently, and, mainly
agreeing in the historical inductions, have employed the same inductions in support of very
different, nay, antagonistic sentiments. As for
myself, never would I have ventured to discuss a
question incidentally involving truths infinitely
higher than the theories of history, had I not de-
liberately considered the adverse arguments, not
merely those which have been offered, and particularly by that Friend whose opinions, knowledge, and judgment I prize in these subjects
above all others: but many further objections

which I clearly see could be cogently brought forward. If I have not attempted, as is often expedient, to remove the difficulties which might be raised by a hypothetical opponent, it is not, as far as I can judge, from having overlooked them. On this, and all other similar occasions, I have avoided any polemical or semi-polemical disputations, which, though they may confirm the writer in his own opinion, rarely have much effect except upon those who are predisposed in his favour.

§ 3. The object of my first-mentioned Work, the *Rise and Progress of the English Common-wealth*, enforced the absence of biographical portraiture and narrative detail. A constitutional History must be substantially confined to results. All the creative or poetical elements of History are necessarily excluded. I tried to supply that deficiency by a concurrent volume, containing a complete though familiar and concise history of English affairs from the acquisition of Britain by the Romans, and her first incorporation into the Fourth Empire, until the Norman Conquest. But that book, the *History of the Anglo-Saxons,* besides many blemishes and errors in execution, is incomplete in plan. The faults of workmanship are my own: the incompleteness of the plan I share with all my predecessors. English History is the joint graft of Anglo-Saxon history and Norman history. The history of

History of the Anglo-Saxons.

Necessity of connecting English history with the History of Normandy.

Normandy is as essential a section of English history as the history of \.'essex. We must adopt Rollo equally with Cerdic. The Norman dynasty is entirely ours.

I therefore now propose to reach the field of Hastings proceeding through another path, setting forth the history of Normandy from the first establishment of the *Terra Normannorum* as a settlement under the chieftains, who, indifferently denominated marquisses or counts, enlarged their dominions, encreasing and sustaining their authority, between and in spite of the two rival dynasties of France, the declining dynasty of Charlemagne, and the rising dynasty of the Capets, severally pursuing their course, wary and wise, bold and politic, improving every contingency, and singularly aided by good fortune. When the Capets finally established themselves upon the throne, the dominion founded by the Patrician Rollo expanded into the Norman Duchy, scarcely inferior in power to that Royal Crown to which the wearers of the Ducal Coronal rendered a nominal homage, whilst they exercised all the power of absolute sovereignty. It was not worth while even for the Conqueror to repudiate a bond unaccompanied by an obligation.

Family names employed by anticipation.

By anticipation I employ the term Capetian, for the purpose of designating Hugh Capet's family, as well in the ascending as the descending line, and I occasionally do the like with respect to the Plantagenets. There is much convenience and no incongruity attending this practice. The progenitors of a great man belong to him as well as his progeny. The ancestors and descendants of Hugh Capet, the ancestors and descendants of Geoffrey Plantagenet, equally exemplify that firm pursuit of power, that permanent individuality of character whereby they are respectively rendered so conspicuous. A division of the earlier Norman history into two periods, corresponding with the two French dynasties, is rendered advisable, not merely by the relations between the two States, but also by the internal affairs of the country. Normandy, during the Carlovingian era, was an arena of conflicting interests. The portion which remains unexpired of that era from Charles-le-Simple to Louis-le-Faineant, is nearly conterminous in extent with the domination of the three first Norman Sovereigns, *Rou, Raoul, Rollo,* or *Robert-Rollo, William Longue-épée,* and *Richard Sans-peur,* who, towards the conclusion of his long reign of forty-four years, witnessed the dethronement of the Carlovingian line and the accession of the third dynasty. The before-mentioned Norman Sovereigns had assimilated themselves to the general population of Neustria, they, the Clergy, and a large portion of the aristocracy, as well as the other earlier Danish settlers or their representatives, were thoroughly

Conflict in the early part of Norman history between the Romanized and the Danish interests.

Romanized. This was the stronger party. The Pagan or Danish party was the weaker, but being supported from Scandinavia, was sufficiently powerful to trouble the Christian or Romanized interest. In the Capetian era, the conflict ceases: Normandy under *Richard-le-Bon*,—whose reign commences in the same year with that of Robert the Second, the son and successor of Hugh Capet, had lost all Northern or Danish nationality. They were then only a provincial variety of the French nation, and the Duchy had grown definitively into a member of the French monarchy. The first and second Books therefore of this History, entitled *Carloringian Normandy* and *Capetian Normandy*, severally contain the before-mentioned eras, including other matters not strictly confined to Normandy, but needful for the connexion and illustration of the Norman story.

§ 4. Whoever now composes the early histories of such countries as France or England, histories, so generally recollected merely as half-forgotten school lessons, has to contend against great disadvantages : all the freshness of the subject is lost, whilst many of the perplexities remain to be solved. He has also to dispel many grave popular errors, not by direct contradiction, cavil, or criticism, but by the propagation of truth; information must be imparted without dogmatism, controversy carried on by silence. It is, therefore, most difficult for the historian to deter-

996
Normandy completely Romanized at the accession of Richard-le-Bon, or Richard II.

Observations upon the first two Books of this History 1. Carloringian Normandy 2 Capetian Normandy

mine between what should be said and what should be left untold.

Upon first consideration, it seems almost superfluous to multiply details of things popularly or vulgarly known, and equally objectionable to pass them over; yet whoever has endeavoured to realize in his own mind events, institutions, men, motives and things, will often find himself compelled to abridge what others have considered leading passages of history, and at the same time to invest with apparently disproportionate importance the topics which his predecessors have disregarded. If an edifice has one principal façade, the views taken by different artists will be pretty nearly the same; but this is not the case with the history of nations. They are vast and complex edifices, consisting of diversified and irregular portions, presenting many fronts, each claiming attention for their use, ornament, singularity, or grandeur. The aspect selected in one picture will be seen only in rapid perspective in another, and in a third quite cast into the shade.

Difficulty of treating historical subjects familiarly but imperfectly known

The Artist cannot change his position whilst he is working, or represent the same thing under two aspects at one time. Moreover, his picture will be affected by various casualties, a cloudy sky, or a bright sky, the leaves of his sketchbook turned over by the gust of wind, his colours dashed by the flying shower. But these out-

wardly permanent, or outwardly transitory circumstances, however influential, are all subordinate to, and overruled by, the Artist's inward
physical individuality and moral identity. No
person can see the same object in the same way;
and, from the spot where the Artist sketches, he
can only see the one aspect as *he* sees it. He can
only display to you his own mental or internal
view, resulting from the conformation or sensi-
bility of his eye, his appreciation of the comparative exigencies of form and of colour, his
ideas of harmony, his notions of effect, his conceptions of pictorial composition and art.

Therefore, instead of quarrelling with a writer
because his mode of treating history differs from
that which you would have preferred, you should
rather thank him for affording you the opportunity
of contemplating the Social Edifice from a position which you cannot reach, or in which you
would not like to place yourself. Historians can
never supersede each other: no one historian
can give you all you wish, no one can teach you
all you ought to learn, neither can comparisons
fairly be instituted between them; for no two
are identical in their views, no two possess
the same idiosyncrasies, the same opportunities,
the same opinions, the same intentions, the same
mind. History cannot be read off-hand, it must
be studied; studied by investigation and comparison—otherwise it profits no more—perhaps

less—than Palmerin of England or Amadis of Gaul.

§ 5. However fierce the mutual or internal dissensions of the Northmen or Danes —the terms are used as synonymous—they acted steadily in concert abroad. Properly compiled, a history of the *Gesta Danorum extra Daniam* would display a vast, and apparently systematic, scheme of spoliation and conquest: this is a task remaining to be satisfactorily performed. Could the expeditions, adventures, defeats and victories of the various nations who are fairly comprehended in this same Danish category,— Danes, Northmen, Frieselanders, Angles, Jutes, Saxons, all being shipmates,— be poetized in an Epic, the episodes would be as remarkable for their intricacy as the whole fable for its unity.—The first action in the Poem would be the maritime attacks made by the Saxon Pirates, during the reign (as it seems) of Honorius, upon the Roman Empire, and more especially that part of Armorica denominated the *Pagus Baiocassinus*, which, obtaining the name of the Saxon shore, afterwards merged in Normandy :—the catastrophe is furnished by the battle of Largs, when the bleached bones of Haco's army, defeated by Alexander of Scotland, were left as memorials of the last Norwegian invasion upon British ground.

In planning the present Work, it became needful to determine between a complete chro-

[margin note:] Unity of plan in the Danish expeditions.

nological history of the Norsk or Danish invasions in the British islands, the Baltic countries, Belgium, Aquitaine, Germany, nay, Italy
and Spain, and a history limited to a selection of
the principal incidents connected with the Nor-

The pre-
sent history
confined to
the Danes
in the Nor-
thern
Gauls.

thern Gauls. I have chosen the latter, and must
therefore refer to other works for the particulars needful to supply the deficiencies of the
narrative. Some contributions may be found
in my Anglo-Saxon History, which, though requiring correction and amplification, may be
consulted in parallel with the annals of the Danes
in Carlovingian and Capetian France. The mutual actions and reactions of the British islands
upon the Continent, and of the Continent upon
the British islands, will afford many subjects for
consideration.—The Anglo-Saxon Empire grew
only to perish and to be destroyed. Alfred himself gave the Dane more power to wield the battle-
axe by which that empire was to be cut down.

Extinction
of North-
ern or
Scandina-
vian na-
tionality
amongst
the North-
men.

Concerning the origin, migrations, ethnographical or ethical characteristics of the Scandinavians, I have said next to nothing : all are very
important subjects of enquiry, and have deservedly been treated with zealous and learned
diligence; but in the present instance their influences were evanescent. So far as concerns
the history of Normandy they may be safely
neglected ; for although the Danish national
spirit subsisted to a certain extent, and amongst

certain classes, until the reign of Richard-sans-peur, that spirit afterwards evaporated so completely, that when the *Terra Normannorum* became Normandy properly so called, the Normans scarcely retained any features of their Danish parentage. Normandy does not offer a vestige of Danish Paganism. The affectionate endeavours made by antiquaries to discover, even in popular superstitions, any reminiscences of the Asaheim myths, are distressingly unsuccessful. In manners, laws, customs, institutions, and above all, in language, the Normans thoroughly assimilated themselves to the other populations of Romanized France or Gaul.

They exulted in their ancestorial reminiscences, whether contributing to family pride, or the Duchy's fame and glory; but this was rather the artificial result of intellectual cultivation than a spontaneous natural feeling. Their antient story was first read in the compositions of the Clerk and the Trouveur. Dudo's Latin chronicle is the primary source of Norman History. Master Wace presented his *Roman du Rou* to Henry Plantagenet before the Skalld who penned the *Hrolfs Saga* was born. The uncontaminated Norskmen and Danskermen were, on their part, inimically estranged from their Romanized kinsmen. Unquestionably, they were proud of Rollo and his victories. They make their Hrolf the son of Raugnvalldur, Jarl or Earl of Mære. They tell

H 2

the tale of his conquests according to their own fancy, and call him *Rudo Jarl*, or the Earl of Rouen. Nevertheless they hated *li Duc Guillaume* as a Frenchman: Denmark and Norway would fain have delivered England from the foreign Conqueror.

Scandinavian traditions concerning Rollo,—reasons for neglecting them, and adopting the history of Dudon de St. Quentin. I abandon the Scandinavian encomiasts of Rollo with the less regret, on account of the discrepancy between their statements and the narrative we owe to Dudon de Saint-Quentin, who framed his history out of the family traditions as he received them from Richard-sans-peur the grandson of Rollo, Richard-le-Bon, Rollo's great-grandson, and Ralph Count of Ivrey Richard-sans-peur's half-brother: a sufficient reason for preferring his authority to that of writers, who are modern by comparison. The Sagas are not older than the twelfth century, and also irreconcileable amongst themselves.

French history, reasons for treating it fully in the present work. § 6. Whilst I have contracted my narrative concerning the Northmen, I have expanded upon the transactions illustrating the decline of the Carlovingian Empire, and the developement of the Capetian monarchy.

Throughout this History I have always looked forward, endeavouring steadily to consider the relations between the doctrines and events of the period upon which I am employed, and the doctrines and events of subsequent periods; and this, not merely for the purposes of English History, but also for the purposes of French History—studies equally necessary to Englishmen and Frenchmen,—each, indeed, to each, either to either : both nations counter-changed—to us and to them a common ground. This observation applies very forcibly to the history of the *Provinces,* or, as the French also call them, the *Grands Fiefs,* which, during the whole Anglo-Norman period, intimately connected England and France.

History of the French Provinces : their importance in English History.

Britanny and Maine the dependencies of Normandy,—the regal duchy of Armorica,—the energetic *Pagus Cœnomannorum,* dear to the Conqueror as his own paternal inheritance,—the magnificent Marquisate of Flanders,—the Counties of Boulogne and Ponthieu and the other Belgic or semi-Belgic Fiefs and dominions, from the Bresle, the boundary of Normandy, to the Scheldt —Blois and Chartres,—Anjou, whose dynasty renewed the splendour of the Conqueror's Empire,—Poitou and opulent Aquitaine, obeying the Plantagenet sceptre and extending the Anglo-Norman Empire even unto the Pyrenees.

All the fore-mentioned territories contributed ancestors to our aristocracy,—clergy to our Church,—rule and discipline to our Monasteries, —instructors to our architects,—teachers to our schools.—No history of Anglo-Norman England can approach to completeness, should we exclude ourselves from these sources of historic richness and variety. I have, therefore, interwoven as much of the anecdote connected with the French Provinces, as will be sufficient to embody the ideas of the reader concerning personages whose names otherwise pass away, without making sufficient impression upon the mind.

§ 7. In the *first Book*, I enter largely into the History of the Carlovingian Empire, until the partition effected between the three rival sons of Louis-le-Débonnaire by the treaties of Verdun and Mersen, the irreparable political schism of the Empire, severing France from Germany and from Italy—the starting-point of the modern European commonwealth. Hatred and ambition produced a jealous compromise; and the compromise, leaving ambition unsatisfied, rendered the hatred more inveterate, to be extinguished only by the extinction of the fated race.

In this first portion of the work I include a narrative genealogy or summary of Carlovingian history, according to the several branches of the family, deducing their descents until the reigning Houses expired in the male lines. This synopsis is to be taken as an outline-map on a small scale, intended for the purpose of shewing the relative positions of the portions which are afterwards given on a larger scale; an aid which will be found useful in rendering intelligible a narrative involved in great complexity. The Car-

[marginal notes:]
Book I. The Carlovingian Empire. The Danish expeditions in the Gauls till the establishment of Rollo, &c.

Genealogical summary of Carlovingian history. Book I. Chap. II. § 38—55, pp. 348—396.

lovingian era should be perfectly mastered by every historical student. We can scarcely discern any portion of European history wherein it does not enter as an element. Charlemagne's personal history is familiarly, if not accurately known. Historians have been repelled by the melancholy spectacle of his descendants' misfortunes; an inglorious narrative by comparison. They have hurried over the period with disgust. Yet misfortune furnishes the soundest commentary upon prosperity; and national humiliation is the retribution reserved for national glory. The "Age of Pericles"—might we not say the "Age of Aspasia?"—does not find its moral until we arrive at Greece degraded, Greece disgraced, Greece absorbed in the Roman Empire.

A history of the Danish expeditions in France is dislocated unless the concurrent events of national French history are included; for if they are omitted we can neither comprehend the causes which opened the country to the Pirates, nor appreciate the share taken by these enemies in breaking up the Empire. Normandy was planted when Osker sailed up the Seine, and left the terror of his name at Rouen. The Empire's fate was decided by the battle of Fontenay. Henceforward, the Northmen are constant participators in the fortunes of France.

A full illustration is given of the causes which advanced the Capets to their pre-eminent dignity.

Their history runs parallel with the history of the Northmen. Robert-le-Fort was courted by Charles-le-Chauve as the great opponent of the Danish power—an unsuccessful opponent; nevertheless, as time advanced, Normandy was worked into unison with the fabric of Capetian France. Charles the son of Louis-le-Bégue, so unfairly depreciated by the sobriquet of *le simple*, is universally known as the monarch who ceded Neustria to Rollo. King Charles toppled on his back by the rude soldier, and the blonde Gisella's marriage to the shaggy Dane, are incidents which we anticipate like the situations of a stock-play; but the transactions of Claire-sur-Epte only initiated the train of events tending to the ultimate stability of Normandy, in which Carlovingians, and Burgundians, and Capets, were equally efficient agents— willing or unwilling agents: and we shall find Rollo and his son Guillaume-longue-épée and his grandson Richard-sans-peur conspicuous in all the affairs of France—not yet premier Pairs of the Douze-pairs in style, but fully so by influence.

----

§ 8. RICHARD-SANS-PEUR, cruelly persecuted during his infancy by Louis-d'Outremer and his consort the proud Gerberga, lived to witness the extinction of the Carlovingian dynasty, and the accession of the "*Figliuol del Beccaio*." His reign, commenced in the first, and concluded in the

Book II.
Capetian
Normandy
Richard I.,
or Richard-
sans-peur,

second Book, corresponds with the transition era Richard II., or le-Bon.
equally of French history and of Norman his- Richard III
tory. When Richard was called to his father's Robert I, or Robert
succession, there was a chance that the Danishry, le-Diable, and Wil-
that is to say, the Northmen, who, retaining the liam the Bastard.
Danish spirit and settled in Normandy, were supported by fresh accessions from Scandinavia,
might have prevailed. But when, after a long
and prosperous rule, Richard-sans-peur was
borne to the grave, dug, according to his dying
request, without the walls of the great Abbey
Church of Fécamp, Normandy had wholly ceased
to be the Terra Normannorum,—it had become
the Duchy of Normandy, thoroughly Romanized,
thoroughly French,—as French as Paris.

Such is the position in which we shall find
Richard-le-Bon, the son of Richard-sans-peur.
The reign of Richard-le-Bon is peculiarly interesting by reason of those alliances and relations
with the Anglo-Saxon or Anglo-Danish Commonwealth, which, continuing under Richard's son,
Robert the First, or Robert-le-Diable, contributed
to Romanize the English mind, a moral subjugation, a conquest of England before the Conquest.

We are lastly introduced to William the Bastard as Duke of Normandy. The concluding
chapters of the second Book exhibit him wisely
and bravely contending against his enemies,
opposed in youth, toiling in manhood, and at
that time of life when men begin to think of rest,

entering upon a new career of labour, vexation, and disappointing prosperity.

In this second Book, as well as in the preceding portions of this history, I would particularly direct the attention of the reader to the constitutional processes by which the Duchy of Normandy was formed. The successive compacts between Carlovingians or Capetians on the one part, and Rollo and his descendants on the other part, constitute the grounds upon which Philippe-Auguste claimed jurisdiction over King John as his vassal, and confiscated the Duchy as forfeited by the vassal's felony. We shall see how far the Norman Patricians, Counts or Dukes, practically owned or testified obedience. The French Crown could produce no other evidence than the historical passages which will be quoted; and Saint Louis had some compunctions of conscience as to the legality of the jurisdiction which his father assumed.

Book III.
William
the Con-
queror.

§ 9. IN the *third* Book, we pass to the History of Duke William, as King of England. William's government was not so much a government of innovation, as one which prepared the way for a system, new equally to Normandy and to England. I do not believe that William the Conqueror attempted in the first instance to Normanize the vanquished :—such would appear to be the natural course of things; but if *le vrai n'est pas toujours le vraisemblable,* the apophthegm may be controlled by another, *le vraisemblable n'est pas toujours vrai.* However plausible the supposition that the Conqueror introduced Norman jurisprudence, Norman forms of government, and Norman tenures into this country, it is a supposition not supported by evidence, nay, contradicted by evidence; and inasmuch as we possess no monument whatever of Norman jurisprudence anterior to the Conquest, it is an inference drawn without premises.

Unquestionably, at a later period, a great similarity subsisted between the laws of Normandy and the laws of England; but England gave more to Normandy than she borrowed. The laws imposed by the Anglo-Norman dynasty upon the English were reflected back upon the victors. England was the more powerful and the more opulent territory. Institutions arose from the combination of the Anglo-Saxon laws with the measures needed for the restraint of a newly subjugated country, which imparted fresh vigour to the Sovereign authority. Duke William practised in Normandy the stern and orderly jurisprudence of the English King. The Anglo-Norman jurisprudence was matured by those who were trained in England. Learned men maintained that the *Grand Coutumier* of Normandy was originally Anglo-Saxon: the Normans were willing to believe that their wise usages were grounded upon the Confessor's laws. Nay, even after they became the immediate subjects of the Capetians, there were those who claimed Magna-Charta as the foundation of their franchises, and their safeguard against arbitrary power.

Book IV.
The Sons of the Conqueror, Courthose, Rufus, and Beauclerc.

§ 10. THE *fourth* Book contains the History of the Conqueror's three surviving Sons, Robert Courthose, William Rufus, and Henry Beauclerc. In relation to England, this Book might have been denominated, *The Reign of Rufus;* but I have avoided that title, in order to impress upon the reader the necessity of viewing all the transactions in which the three brethren were engaged, as being of equal importance in English History. We cannot disengage the History of Normandy from the History of England; and therefore I enter into the subject fully and completely, omitting nothing but mere local particulars and events, when they do not happen to be connected with persons eminent or known in English History. In this Book we follow Robert

History of the first Crusade, why introduced.

to the first Crusade: it is an event completely European, besides which, many incidents specially connected with England and Normandy are elucidated thereby. The disputes commonly called disputes between Church and State, the first personified in Anselm, the latter in Rufus, occupy a large portion of this Book; but I have both here and elsewhere avoided Church history, except when intermingled with the temporal concerns of the Commonwealth.

---

§ 11. THE history of the two surviving brothers, Robert Courthose and Henry Beauclerc is continued in the *fifth* Book; Henry reigning in England, Robert in Normandy, until the fratricidal battle of Tenchebrai gave the whole of the Conqueror's dominions to his youngest son, and consigned the elder to the dungeon in which he died. But a competitor arose, Robert's son, William the Clito, the Atheling,—an ill-conditioned and ill-fated young Prince :—much interest nevertheless attaches to his adventures and his misfortunes; the Clito's history also calls us into Flanders, a country which exercised so much personal as well as national influence in English affairs.

The conflicts between the two Swords, between Church and State, assumed a new aspect, Hildebrand's lessons and traditions directing the endeavours made by Anselm, to sustain, not only the conscientious independence of the Spirituality, but the soundness of the Commonwealth. Owing to the intimate commixture of Christian institutions and civil policy, the rights and interests of the community are concealed from us by the

Book V.
Robert
Courthose
and
Henry I.

technical phraseology whereby they are denominated the rights of the Church. We may have
a perception of the fact, but it is excluded from
our reasonings by our dispathies. A living and
active Policy is essential to Christianity—Christianity without a Policy is not a *Religion* but
a *Persuasion;* and the more intimate the co-
ordination or alliance of Church and State, the
greater the difficulty of harmonizing their energies.

The contests concerning investitures, so constantly presented to us in stereotyped phrases,
involved questions of extreme perplexity. The
canonical election of the Prelates appertained to
the clergy and laity of the " Civitas ;" a right
derived from the Primitive ages, but exercised
under various modifications, occasioned by personal privileges or local institutions, the various
ranks and orders, Princes, Nobles, People, having
a greater or lesser share in the choice or postulation. Direct authority as well as moral power
rendered the Bishop the " Defensor" or chief
Magistrate, the Father of the City. In his sacerdotal capacity he was a judge, having jurisdiction
over causes, which, though spiritual, involved
vast temporal interests and affected the most
intimate concerns of civil society. Called to the
Great Councils of the State, whether by reason
of his Episcopal office, or as a service due for his
temporalities, he nevertheless appeared in those
great Assemblies as the representative of the

Community by whose voice he had been placed in the Cathedra. Saint Ambrose was elected by acclamation and universal suffrage. Saint Ambrose could not have rebuked Theodosius had he not been the representative of Milan.

Of course the foregoing is, in a measure, a one-sided representation, but it is a side from which we have been accustomed to turn away. In respect of the Episcopacy, Hildebrand, labouring with all his heart and soul for the general reformation of Western Christendom, contended against two inveterate abuses, then equally destructive and disgraceful to Church and to State. The Sovereign was unquestionably entitled to a large share of influence in the selection of his Bishop; but the Sovereigns would not be content with less than the whole, and, by the operation of lay-investiture, they intruded their nominees into the Seat without any regard to the fitness of the individual or the opinions of the Church, that is to say the Community, Church and people being here convertible terms. The second abuse was simony.

Interpreting these acts according to modern ideas, the first exhibits the Crown forcing the Lord Mayor upon the Corporation of London, or nominating the Recorder; the other, a Jobber buying a Borough, or a legal Shark gravitating upon the Bench,—as in Stuart times,—by the weight of the purse slipped into the hands of the Lord of the Bedchamber. Both on the part of the clerks who purchased, and on the part of the patrons who sold, there prevailed the most scandalous corruption; and Hildebrand, sparing neither the bribed nor the bribers, incurred the inveterate odium of all the delinquents.

Hildebrand had no respect to persons in judgment. Sin levelled Emperors and beggars before him. The stigma attached to Hildebrand's name speaks the world's opinion of his inflexible zeal and impartial justice. Talleyrand designated history as a universal conspiracy against truth.—Never was this sarcasm more pungently appropriate than when applied to the treatment sustained by Becket, Anselm, and Hildebrand.

Books V. and VI. Blois and Plantagenet.

§ 12. BLOIS and Plantagenet afford the subjects of the fifth and sixth Books. The reigns of Stephen of Blois and Henry Plantagenet blend into one era—a transition era, when, yielding to the influence of circumstances and the cogency of positive legislation, the Anglo-Saxon usages and institutions were refashioned or rendered subordinate to new schemes and forms. The Saxon line is said to have been restored in the person of Henry the Second. Unquestionably a very strong popular sentiment existed, countenancing this expression; nevertheless it was during the reign of Henry the Second that the Anglo-Saxon

Commonwealth became the English Commonwealth. The greater number of the mutations ascribed to the Conqueror were not really effected till the reign of Henry the Second, when the common law of England was developed. With respect to what is called "Anglo-Norman jurisprudence," it is a system which existed under various modifications or grades of completeness in England, in Scotland, and in Normandy, being discernible also in Britanny; and it appears in all these countries to have arisen simultaneously or nearly so. If not absolutely invented by Henry Plantagenet or his advisers, this same system was unquestionably matured in the Anglo-Norman Chancery, and upon the Bench of the Anglo-Norman Justiciars.

§ 13. Mediæval writers and historians offer peculiar difficulties in their chronology:—we stumble at the very threshold. Our New Year's day was only New Year's day to a comparatively small fraction of the European community. Double-headed Janus maintained his station as ruler of the ecclesiastical calendars which followed the Roman computation; but the Clerk rejected that Calendar in secular affairs, and the practical *Caput anni* shifts about, so as to compel the student to be continually on his guard. Midwinter, Yule, or Christmas-day, was a popular era for the commencement of the solar year.

Mediæval chronology.

Uncertainties arising from the varying modes of computation.

A perplexing mode of computation prevailed extensively in France—a Paschal computation, according to which the new year began on Easter-Sunday—consequently the length of the Dominical solar year was extended or contracted in every year of the Paschal cycle; and inasmuch as the Paschal year may include thirteen lunar months, or parts of two Aprils, there are cases in which we cannot, otherwise than from internal evidence, determine whether the April belongs to the beginning or the end of the year.

The Feast of the Annunciation, or Lady-Day, was a favourite New Year's day, continued in England until the introduction of the new style. This enactment is an event of Parliamentary celebrity, nevertheless the need of adverting to the alteration has been repeatedly forgotten, even by our lawyers, when they have had to deal with documents now scarcely more than an hundred years old. We may therefore be excused, if we occasionally err with respect to a date of the ninth century.

To encrease the confusion, some Chroniclers, employing the Dominical year, advance upon their contemporaries by an entire year; and others are a year behind.

There are Chronicles in which dates are entirely omitted. Instead of expressing the year, some scribes contented themselves with repeating the word *annus*, on and on, without construction, note, or ordinal number, so that the date can only be supplied by comparison with other chronicles, or by conjecture. This mode of reckoning, or no-reckoning, occurs principally in the Cymric and Breton annals.

These external chronological difficulties, however, are surpassed by what we may term the internal chronological uncertainties; for, in the first case, namely the external difficulties, the computations go according to a rule, and when the canon has been ascertained, the supputation proceeds regularly; but in the second, they arise from the mode of making up the Records. A leaf of parchment was preserved in the study or library, and upon this memorandum-sheet the death of an important personage, or any other remarkable occurrence, was inscribed with a plummet, and afterwards incorporated in the Chronicle of the House. Annals exist, which are evidently transcripts from such memoranda in their simplest form, stating perhaps only one event for the year, and in some years none.

Uncertainties arising from the process of computation.

Occasionally the first notes were made upon waxen tablets; and these memoranda were from time to time amplified, being transcribed so as to constitute complete Chronographies. Subsequent compilers or annalists recast these texts: additions or interpolations were inserted just as the matter became available to each successive annalist, jotted in, here and there,—so as to fill up

the blank at the end of a short line,—or boustro-
phedon fashion, the insertion begun at the end of
the short line, being turned up into the blank
above, or down into the blank below, or inscribed
on the side margin, or at the top of the page, or
at the bottom. In the earlier stages of these
rifacciamenti, there are manuscripts in which
the differences of hand-writing, and the various
tints of the ink, shew how these Chronographies
were put together; but when re-transcribed, or
printed, such tokens are effaced, and we have
not any clue by which we can retrace our way.

Hence we never can be certain that the events
dated by any given dominical year, occurred
within such year; nor, if they did happen within
the year to which they are ascribed, whether
they did happen in the order according to
which they offer themselves, unless they be dated
in and within the text, that is to say, unless the
season, Lent, Summer, Harvest, or some kalendar
month, or Feast, or day of the month, be specified, or unless manifestly connected by natural
sequence or probability; for the style is often so
loose that even conjunctions do not necessarily
connect the phrases or their members.

Mediæval
authorities.
mode of
employing
them.

§ 14. Criticism may do somewhat towards
the rectification of historical difficulties, but let
her refrain from promising more than she can
perform. A spurious instrument may be detected:
if two dates are absolutely incongruous, you may

accept that which reason shews you to be most probable : amongst irreconcileable statements you may elect those most coherent with the series which you have formed. But an approximation to truth, except so far as concerns single and insulated facts, is the utmost we can obtain. We have absolute certainty that the battle of Trafalgar was fought; but there is so much variety in the accounts of the Logs, that we cannot ascertain with precision the hour when the battle commenced, nor the exact position or distance of the fleets from the shore.

Writing is an imperfect mode of communicating ideas. Writing is ever liable to suggest to the reader either more or less than the writer intended. It is only through your knowledge of your correspondent's sentiments that you thoroughly understand the letters even of the nearest and dearest—that you feel the weight of the trivial expression, or are enabled to construe the signification of silence. And yet, after all, the letter is unsatisfactory ; there is much that the nearest and dearest never can tell you, except face to face, side by side, hand in hand, arm in arm.

No written law is practically applicable or intelligible, unless speech comes in aid : the enigmas of obsolete jurisprudence are insoluble without the Advocate's pleading, or the Judge's decree. Through continued usage and tradition, the voices of Judge and Advocate live and are heard; but when those voices fail, then the old black-letter Reporter becomes as mysterious as the old black-letter Statute of which he is the expounder.

The " evidences of history " and the " witnesses of history" are expressions universally adopted; not absolutely incorrect, nevertheless, very illusory. We cannot deal with those "evidences" according to the rules of legal testimony; we cannot cross-examine our "witnesses," we cannot confront them. If insufficient, we cannot summon more than are to be had; if uninformed, we must not indoctrinate them; if silly, we cannot make them wise. When they stop short, we cannot extract an additional word. — Livy may be a credulous writer; but how shall we supply his place if we tell Livy to go down?

The forensic treatment of history—that is to say, by the rigid, logical, and quasi legal discussion of "historical evidence," is the application of a process entirely unsuitable to the materials, and therefore a detriment, not a support to truth,—an exercise of intellect, a clever argument, but an argument which may be disputed or refuted by a more clever enquirer. It is very painful to know how far this practice of straining to confirm History by "Undesigned coincidences" and "Trials of witnesses," and the like, has been carried. None are convinced, except those who are willing to be convinced; whilst the acute undergraduate, hesitating on the border of unbelief, smiles at Lardner's shallowness and Paley's cool ingenuity; and, if doubtful before, all his doubts are removed.

In studying such writers as the mediæval chroniclers, the first step is to acquire a thorough liking for them; so that, when we open the volume we should consider our employment not a fatigue, but a recreation, determining to read each writer in continuity. Indeed, it may be asserted that no History should, if profit be sought, be studied otherwise. Consulted in portions, dates may be verified and facts ascertained; but unless each whole be taken as a whole, it is impossible to grapple with the facts according to the spirit of the writer. — You cannot enjoy a landscape reflected in the fragments of a broken mirror. Excerpts, selections, pieces picked for quaintness or curiosity, pall the intellectual appetite. Elegant extracts, Anthologies, are sickly things: cut flowers have no vitality—the single growing violet lives sweetly, and lasts: the splendid bouquet decays into unsavoury trash, and as trash is thrown away; if the writer is weary, his yawning is contagious. There is no mental pleasure in receiving information collected from scraps and tatters, and consequently no mental pleasure in imparting it: the lesson you learn as a drudge will be repeated as a drudgery.

We should approach all inquiry with an obedient mind, more inclined to accept than to reject, to give faith than to disbelieve. Gratuitous falsehood is rare. Even Manetho's dynasties (as conjectured by a very learned man of the last century), may be misconceptions of truth — months called years—lists of concurrent Reguli tacked together, and made up into one roll or volumen. —As Manetho records them, so would our British dynasties appear—Picts, Scots and Cymri, East Saxons, South Saxons, West Saxons, Mercians, Northumbrians, Danes and Angles—were they arranged consecutively instead of being placed in parallel columns.

The mediæval chroniclers generally, but more especially those of the Merovingian and Carlovingian period, are authorities of high order: men well-informed, men known to the world, and knowing the world well: not a few amongst them are professed historians, entering upon their work with a full sense of its importance and of their own responsibility: others, biographers or autobiographers, who, commencing as historians or annalists, warm themselves as they proceed into memorialists of their own lives and times — statesmen, courtiers, ministers, prelates, soldiers, members of royal families—Gregory of Tours, Eginhard, Nithard, Prudentius, Hincmar, Rodolph of Fulda, Regino of Pruhm, Frodoard, conspicuous in their age—due allowance being made for circumstances—as Clarendon or Sully, Bishop

Burnet, Blaise de Montluc or Prince Eugene.
Yet, in productions emanating from actors or
participators in political events, the standard of
veracity is lowered by an inevitable alloy. The
more momentous the question, the greater the
difficulty of meeting with an unbiassed and competent relator. He who best knows the truth is
frequently the person most tempted to conceal or
distort his knowledge.—Can the soundest principles resist the malignant influence of names inseparably associated with hatred and contempt—
"Puritan" or "Papist"—or any other authorized
version of *Raca* in vernacular language?

Add to these textual and moral obstacles the
incurable debility of all human observation and
experience. Sir Walter Raleigh was as right in
estimating the impossibility of ascertaining perfect
truth, as he was wrong in the conclusion he drew
from his conviction. It is by our intention, and not
by the result of our labours, that we are to be
judged. If the knot cannot be opened, let us not
cut it, nor fret our tempers, nor wound our fingers
by trying to undo it, but be quite content to leave
it untied, and say so. We can do no more than
we are enabled: the crooked cannot be made
straight, nor the wanting numbered.—The preservation or destruction of historical materials is
as providential as the guidance of events. We are
not called to be the revealers of the hidden things:
it is not for us that the sea is to give up her dead.

In our conception of the historian's character, we are somewhat perplexed by the imperfect relation which his duties bear to other duties susceptible of accurate definition. He is, in a measure, an advocate, summing up before a tribunal; and yet an advocate who has not the wherewithal to make out a complete case, by the marshalling of unsatisfactory evidence.

Perhaps the modern historian of antiquity may also be considered as an interpreter, standing between two nations, and translating to the one, the annals of the other: a relator to his own people of the story which another nation has taught him. This comparison approaches, perhaps, somewhat closer to his proper functions: yet, if we confine ourselves even to mere and literal translation, the task offers no small difficulties: the Translator must have lived with both nations, and be familiarized, not merely with the foreign language, but with the foreign habits, customs, and thoughts of the foreign people.

The mode whereby the historian can best satisfy himself, and thus satisfy his readers, is to gain a tone of mind analogous to the result of living conversation and actual observation. You never understand a language so long as you have to make out the grammar, or look out the words in the dictionary: you do not really understand that language until the sight of the phrase suggests the meaning, until the knowledge comes to

you without an effort; becoming a part of yourself, without your knowing how you came by it,
like the good performer, who not only can play
at sight, but who, when he looks at the crotchets
and quavers, hears the sound of the notes through
the eye. You never can thoroughly realize a
locality till you have trodden the turf beneath
your feet, till you have breathed the air.

Laws, usages, habits, language, customs, en-
twine the bond which binds and bounds each
community. Those within the boundary possess
an instinctive sense of significations and realities,
which no foreigner can obtain. He may, however,
approximate to this sensation, by taking up his
residence in the country. Such was the course
adopted by the Father of History, and whereby he
attained that excellence which no one else perhaps
has equalled,—certainly none surpassed. Therefore we should treat the mediæval writers as we
ought to do if we were living amongst them, as
that foreign people with whom we wish to be
thoroughly acquainted,—an end we never can
accomplish unless we are perfectly on good terms
with them, unless we sincerely cultivate their
friendship, and try to win their good will—to
assimilate ourselves to their feelings, and become
one of themselves. We must not depreciate them
if they be dull, or revile them because we cannot
understand them, or be put out of humour with
their look, their accent, their garb.—Bear with

them, do not set yourself against them, do not pride yourselves in reckoning how much wiser or better you are · do not take offence at their imperfections, their simplicity, their rudeness, their ignorance, their ill-breeding, — or rather what you suppose to be ignorance or ill-breeding. You go to learn, to be instructed, and to make the best use you can for yourself and your own people, when you come home, of the knowledge you thus obtain.

The facts immediately before us are only portions of history, and we should accept the memorials of past ages for better and for worse,—taking them all in all. Throughout our studies we must receive the productions of our mediæval writers in a double character, not merely as records of facts, or supposed facts, but also monuments of literature, and memorials of mind. We should not in any wise content ourselves with being mere passive listeners to the story, but always strive to become acquainted with the narrator: we should endeavour to contemplate the book, identified with the writer, according to that truest maxim of friendship—*ama l'amico tuo, con il difetto suo*, —not simply tolerating your friend's faults, not loving him in spite of his faults, but loving him with his faults,—the faults inseparable from the man's individuality; you cannot have your friend without them—nor the book either.

Their writings contain much which may ap-

pear superfluous—useless in the present advanced
state of historical knowledge. Matthew of West-
minster, Marianus Scotus or Florence of Worcester, Godfrey of Viterbo and Eckhard of Urangen,
preface their histories with the annals of the
world, deduced through age and age, until they
reach the states of mediæval Christendom. If
these are neglected, still more if they are expunged; if we strike out the narrative founded
upon holy Writ, combined with Josephus and
Eusebius, Orosius and Justin, we obliterate the
memorials of their historical theory. The mediæval doctrine of history considered each race and
nation as exemplifying the decree imposed upon
the destinies of mankind.

These chronicles are strewed with texts, apt
to render us somewhat impatient, but they demonstrate the sedulous study of the Bible during
the dark and middle ages. They also testify that
spirit of humility which taught the wise to place
all human knowledge in subjection to the Divine
Word :—nay, even the apparently trivial employment of scriptural phraseology, sometimes sounding almost irreverent, resulted from their familiarity with the Scriptures. Like the Covenanters,
they thought in Scripture language.

The Monk Ordericus sermonizes occasionally;
dully, without doubt, yet we had better not sleep
during the Sermon: the proser instructs us according to the standard of his age; and perhaps

we shall be none the worse for the lessons we receive.

His quotations from the classics are very trite: the Preceptor thinks them only fit for the lowest form. This may be granted; but they reveal the extent of his classical knowledge: they shew you that the Norman Monks had a Sallust in Saint Evroul's library.—Sacred and profane are jumbled tastelessly: a text from Proverbs flanked by Lucan's verse; yet this quaint erudition realizes the writer's idiosyncrasy. Ordericus is thereby personified to us: we learn to know him as a living man, not merely as a name of nine letters. We see the Vulgate and the Latin poet upon his table: we learn how he was wont to study the classics for ornament, and to search the Scriptures for the perennial illustration of human nature.

Dudon de Saint-Quentin's turgid eloquence is occasionally fatiguing,—be patient—he will not tire us long; if we value valuable information, we shall be sorry when Dudon leaves off, and we listen with great profit to Dudon's style: he is addressing his patrons, the grandson and great grandson of Rollo: he is labouring to please them: he displays the tone of high-bred cultivation. His Latin is barbarous; nevertheless this rough kitchen-latin is a dialect to be learned by usage; and unless we can compare text with text, we shall never obtain materials for the glossary.

Superstition is laid to the charge of the Prelate : he deals in signs and portents, fire-drakes, bloody banners, armies fighting in the clouds, and stars streaming through the sky; yet these marvels are invaluable to the philosopher, the only recorded observations of natural phenomena, which otherwise would have been lost. The name of a *Mansus* or a *Pagus* occurring in some legend which we have been taught to despise as puerile, may furnish us with incontestable evidence of language, or fix a kingdom's landmark. And if our chronicler borrows largely from other chroniclers, we must not be wearied by such repetitions; for we thereby ascertain to what extent the writers so copied were diffused by publication, or received as standard authorities. If facts which other chroniclers tell clearly are related by him with slovenliness, or misunderstood, or distorted, we are furnished with a test whereby we can measure his judgment, accuracy and credibility.

Thus, habituating ourselves to treat bygone events as contemporaneous, living in the present world, yet striving to dwell with the past, we shall nevertheless be always more or less necessitated to deal with the history of those who are living in the unseen world, according to the process which we employ in our daily thoughts, discourse, or correspondence, concerning the beings we behold and the embodied souls we consort with, the society we encounter, the events within our observation, or presented to our eyes.

Past and present offer the same trials, and furnish the same discipline; or, rather past and present are one. After all our cogitations, we are coerced to acknowledge that blessings and judgments are equally inscrutable: that many failures are unaccountable, and many successes inexplicable; legitimate expectations of good sorely disappointed—good resulting from evil—large promises and small forthcomings; or the hap and the halfpenny turning to ten thousand pounds.— We are perplexed by secrets which we try to unravel, and fail: we try to account for human conduct, and believe we have thoroughly made out the character, and then are painfully convinced that we have been quite in the wrong. Inconsistencies grieve us in those we love and venerate: virtues vex us when we find them in those we hate or despise.—Driven to speak positively without the power of dismissing internal doubts; dogmatic though wavering; obeying our own judgment, and yet mistrusting our judgment; wearied by problems we cannot solve; egged on by curiosity never to be satisfied;—and compelled at last to humble ourselves, and chasten the desire for knowledge never here to be obtained.

BOOK I.

CARLOVINGIAN NORMANDY.

CHAPTER I.

LOUIS-LE-DEBONNAIRE, HIS PREDECESSORS AND SUCCESSORS

741—987.

§ 1. THE degeneracy of royal races has been frequently insisted on, almost invidiously, as affording an irrefragable argument against hereditary monarchy. Such at least is the sentiment raised by implication when the proposition is enounced; and amongst the examples of deterioration usually adduced, the Carlovingians stand forth most prominently.

The proposition is untrue in the abstract. Select any ancient regal family at a venture, and compare the members of that family with any others of lower degree, whose personal characters can be ascertained with equal precision.

For this branch of moral statistics, the plebeian or meaner classes do not afford the needful materials; but the rich genealogies of European aristocracy, the *Baronage*, the *Visitation*, the *Stammbuch*, the *Théatre d'Honneur*, the *Nobiliaro*,

741—987 will give you the means: crowned Dugdale, tabarded Vincent, cowled Anselme, or Imhoff, or Don Lope de Haro. Royalty may invoke the test: let it be honestly applied, and the investigation will fail to disclose any deduction from the accustomed averages of courage, ability or intellect. Indeed, the calculation would give an opposite result. Austria or Brunswick, Bourbon or Nassau absolutely gain, when paralleled with any known lineage in Germany, in England, or in France, whether anterior or coeval. Place them by the side of Dalberg, or of Truchsess, of Montmorency, or of Howard. It is a peculiar disadvantage attached to Royalty, that whilst princes are exposed to greater temptations than their subjects, their merits are brought more broadly into the blazing light, and construed inimically or deceitfully. Hard judges are we of those below us—harder when judging our superiors. Cruelly censured, more cruelly flattered, monarchs are the victims either way—their faults extenuated, except when combined with unpopular virtues, their virtues reviled if unpopular, their popular virtues soiled by vulgar praise. Mankind, by a re-action of rude contempt, compensate themselves for their own servility.

Untrue in the abstract, the imputation of degeneracy is equally untrue in this particular instance. Examine that wide-spreading imperial stem, rooted in Pepin of Heristal—much

noble fruit does that tree bear, noble though 741—987
bitter.—Charlemagne was one of those great men
whose talents concurring with their opportunities,
render them sole and single in the world. His
descendants are inferior by comparison, but not
positively. Few amongst them can be discovered
really deficient in the natural qualities or talents
needed for royal authority : some possessed these
qualities in a high degree—prudence, prowess,
contrivance, genius and energy. The fact rather
is, that, for their historical reputation, they had
overmuch talent. The rivals—sons and fathers,
fathers and sons. nephews and uncles, uncles and
nephews, brothers and brothers, were too equally
matched Had any one crushed his competitors,
so as to restore the ancestorial glory, all their
individual slips and weaknesses would have been
forgotten. But the whole family yielded to their
adverse Nemesis.

Clio has no toleration for the unprosperous :
the mirror in which she reflects their images mag-
nifies every blemish. She courses after the triumphal car, shouting like the crowd whom she
encourages and by whom she is encouraged:—woe
to the vanquished, woe to the weak, woe to the
oppressed, woe to the humble, woe to the poor,—
men, nations, kingdoms ! As in the world, so in
the page of history.

§ 2. Had it not been for their misfortunes, The ill-fortune attached to the Carlo-vingian Empire.
we should have heard nothing of·this supposed

K 2

degeneracy. Lodi does not afford stronger evidence of Napoleon's undaunted spirit, than is found in his open, avowed belief, that he, who created an Empire more vast and more transitory than Charlemagne's, owed his good fortune to a ruling Star, an inevitable Destiny. He did not fear that by this confession he lessened his own reputation, or detracted from his intellect, or humiliated his talent. We may dislike such terms as "ruling star" or "inevitable destiny," but the truth which the words convey is eternal. The whole system of the moral world depends on an Almighty Providence, ever present, ever active, directing or thwarting our own free agency.

How the Unchangeable counsel and human liberty can work concurrently, is utterly inconceivable to us. Nevertheless, insoluble as the problem must ever be, the consciousness of our own existence is not clearer than our innate perception that though Life and Death, Good and Evil, are set before us for our unrestrained choice, we all have had our course immutably defined for weal or woe . and, speaking in the common phrase with reference to worldly position, for good fortune, mediocrity or misfortune , for prosperity or misery. But Human Reason cannot abide that her divinations should be frustrated : the doctrines which we acknowledge practically we scarcely ever will recognize intellectually, and we strive to find any cause except the true one for

the unequal destinies of mankind. The perma- 741—987
nence of Charlemagne's Empire, even in his life-
time, though sustained by his wisdom and energy,
was nevertheless effected only through the con-
gruity of his exertions with a combination of circumstances which never could prevail again.—
When passed, the possibility was entirely lost.

Thick and lowering were the tempests gathering on the horizon, while the sun shone bright
and cheerful on the vaulted roofs of Aix-la-Chapelle; but as Charlemagne grew old, his good
fortune declined more rapidly than his declining
days Had his life been prolonged, he must have
yielded to the adversities which his own success
prepared. The conformation of his Empire invited external enemies, forbade internal peace.
He was taken away from the evil to come; even
like the merchant, who having toiled and fretted
to acquire great wealth, and succeeded in his
speculations by the contingencies of the mart or
the exchange, sickens and sinks when his Firm
is about to break, and is thus spared the humiliation of ruin.

Experience, charts, knowledge of sound- Partitions
of the Em-
ings, may enable the navigator to escape many pire unavoidable
dangers, but hurricanes will arise, rendering all
seamanship unavailing—*Afflavit Deus et dissi-
pantur.* The partitions of the Carlovingian
Empire were unavoidable. The system begun
under the Merovingians, the usage of the

74:—987 Frankish Realm, which could scarcely have been abandoned without difficulty by the son of Charles Martel, now became inevitable and destructive. Charlemagne's hand had grasped more sceptres than even that mighty hand could hold, and from the hands of his successors they could not but fall. The contests arising from these partitions were as irremediable as the partitions themselves.

The Fourth Monarchy not to be confounded with the Carlovingian Empire.

The Imperial authority, reinvigorated by Charlemagne, must be carefully distinguished from his personal Empire; though, viewed in the same line of sight, their images often blend into each other. As Emperor, Charlemagne represented the authority derived from Rome, Rome of the Eagle standard, Pagan Rome, Heathen Rome, the Rome of the Seven Hills, the Rome of Romulus, of Tarquin, of Brutus, the Rome of the Cæsars;— Rome drunken with the blood of Saints and Martyrs, the Rome who built the Coliseum and raised the triumphal arch, the Rome who crucified Saint Peter in the Forum of Nero, cast Saint Paul into the Mamertine dungeons, and plunged Saint John into the cauldron of boiling oil;—that Rome identified by ancient Fathers and interpreters with the Apocalyptic Babylon:—that Rome whose power was symbolized by the gothic imagery and rhyming epigraph of the Golden Bull, *Roma caput mundi, regit orbis frena rotundi.*— That Roman Empire, whose spirit transmigrated through Frederick of Hohenstauffen and Henry of Luxemburg and Joseph of Lorraine—That Imperial pre-eminence, which, placing its possessor at the honorary summit of the European Commonwealth, subsisted, however debilitated, till the end of the appointed season, when the portraiture of the last effete successor of Charlemagne filled the last vacant tablet in the Frankfort Rœmer Saal.

As the Representative of the Fourth Empire, Charlemagne was only a transitory instrument in her yet unaccomplished destiny. Our present concern lies with the political history of the Carlovingian Empire, composed of the Kingdoms descending to him by inheritance from an ancestor, who, but for success, would have been termed an usurper, united to the dominions so gloriously gained by his own successful talent, prowess, and energy.

Amongst other inherent germs of evil in the Carlovingian Empire, was the absence of any definite law of succession or heritable representation : the children acknowledged the parent's power of appointing or partitioning his dominions, but never obeyed that power practically or honestly unless under compulsion, or when it suited their own interest. No certain principle could be discovered, whether an appropriation once made to this or that son or nephew was or was not revocable or irrevocable. Some portions of the Empire had distinct constitutional rights; *Evils arising in the Carlovingian Empire from the absence of any certain law of succession.*

741—987 Aquitaine especially so . so also Armorica, so also Bavaria. Austrasia and Neustria were sometimes considered as united in one great national Assembly, and sometimes not. Popular assent to the succession was sometimes solicited and sometimes neglected : the throne was elective without election, hereditary without heirship. These excitements to jealousy and ambition were more than human nature could withstand, The dismemberments which ultimately distributed the Carlovingian Empire amongst Charlemagne's descendants, who shared them with the greater or lesser communities, with the princes or feudatories of mediæval Italy, Germany and France, were the natural cleavages of masses merely agglutinated by pressure   The races whom Charlemagne had subjugated, the ·countries over which he ruled, were centres of mutual repulsion.   The very essence of the Empire was the preparation for the impending disintegration.   No prudence could remedy the inherent malconformation of the Carlovingian Empire—the trouble was inseparably attached to the inheritance.

Carlovingian Empire. Its component parts mutually repulsive

Constantly assailed from within, the external enemies possessed a power of infestation which could not be quelled.   As I have observed on a former occasion, the Northmen, in particular, were like clouds of mosquitoes, which, dispersed by the hand passing through them, immediately gathered again.   In all their concerns,

Ill ends of the Carlovingians

the descendants of Charlemagne were beset by 741—987 untoward circumstances; events, which would have seemed indifferent or promising well, ending badly. The good wine turning sour: small hurts festering into ulcers . unhappy marriages; domestic dissensions, imprudencies of passion, infirmities, diseases; premature, violent and plebeian deaths, none in the field of battle; and these deaths occurring at junctures when the life of the Sovereign was of most importance for the welfare of the State.

§ 3. Mathematicians have felt aggrieved, because they often hear those who are usually called "sensible men," "educated men" and the like, assert that they do not doubt of "runs of luck," speaking in a tone which implies that the occurrences of such tides of success or adversity are occasioned by an unknown or mysterious cause. The Analyst calls this a superstition; but there is a superstition approaching to weakness, or worse, in being over afraid of superstition. Men do not doubt the fact of "luck," simply because the casual coincidences, which over-rule all theories of moral or mathematical probability, are matters of daily observation.

The theories of probabilities may be indisputably true according to mathematical reasoning, shewing that no one man can have a greater chance in the game than another; nevertheless, experience constantly contradicts the reasoning.

Doctrine of probabilities

741—987 Perhaps we may rather say, that both views of the question are true ; if so be we recollect that " chance," under every form or mode of existence, is predestinated in the universal plan of Providence. Matter, Life, Soul and Spirit are ruled by the One Maker of all things visible and invisible, the One Lord of infinity and eternity. Every permutation, every succession, every series and every combination of number, weight, or measure, is pre-ordained. Omnipresence cannot be absent. The Omnipotent cannot be limited, nor his Omniscience bounded. Upon that Earth which has been created for the habitation of man, accident is regulated with determined relations to the accountable beings who are affected by the events, fortuitous and yet designed. The Gamester is brought to the Casino when the faces of the die are to be turned uppermost which will make or mar his fortune. He is conducted thither to meet the pre-directed series of throws. By figures, and tables, and theorems we calculate ourselves out of these realities ; but activity, anxiety, above all, danger will surely bring them home " Every bullet has its billet," says the soldier, who falls into the contrary extreme, yielding to the dreary apathy of a blind fatality. Yet the soldier expresses himself truly, for the man who receives the mortal wound is driven by the destroying Angel before the mouth of the cannon whose discharge

is to cut him off.   And this involves the whole 741—987
bearing of casualties and apparent trifles upon
the mightiest affairs of collective mankind.
Universal History bears witness to the truth, yet
the Philosophy of History shrinks away from
the conclusions which she dares not deny.

Nor with respect to those events resulting
evidently from physical laws, is the need of
the acknowledgment less cogent; for we are
bound to reverence these laws as the emanations
of Almighty power, obeying His will.   When
the Sun's noon-day rays are made to fire the
meridian mortar, the explosion occasioned by the
unvaried rotation of the planetary sphere is effected by the workman whose adaptation of the lens
guided the concentrated beams.

Apply the same reasonings to all the operations of secondary causes developed in the
material or transitory world, when they are rendered directly and immediately subservient to the
government of the spiritual or eternal kingdom.
Very superficial and erroneous are the Teachers
who worry themselves to employ their Science,
the outward yet marvellous knowledge of the
works of God obtained through the senses, in
discrediting or denying the dispensation that the
particular events, occasioned by the regular and
orderly course of nature, do equally fulfil the
decree of special Providence.   The mist or the
blast may be condensed or dispersed, guided or

741—987 stayed by the general laws of electricity and heat, of air and moisture; and the fertility of the field certainly depends on the operation of the laws by which vegetation is promoted or retarded. But the husbandman, who acknowledges the abundance as a blessing, or who receives the failing crop as a punishment, has been allotted to that very field for his profit or his trial; and for *him*, each individual cloud has been wafted upon the wings of the wind, with the purposed intent that it may drop fatness on the glebe, or destroy the hopes of the harvest. No event can be disconnected from the First Cause of all events. It was one of the shallow gibes of Frederick "the Great," that, somehow or another, Providence always takes the side of the King who has the largest battalions. This dictum has not even the recommendation of historical truth—he himself falsified it. But even if it were true, it would not in any wise alter the highest truth, for the question would still remain to be answered, Who imparts the power by which the armies are raised?

Great perplexity of Carlovingian history. § 4. It is a hindrance to historical research that this Carlovingian era is the most confused in mediæval history; we approach it with distaste. The best informed amongst the French historians, while they expatiate upon the importance annexed to a period constituting the starting-point of our subsisting European system, express themselves strongly concerning the species of disgust excited by its perplexity. The investigator 741—987 feels entangled in a morass. The dissensions and dismemberments, divisions and subdivisions of the Carlovingians and the Carlovingian Empire, cannot be comprehended through any one consecutive recital. Each and every Emperor, King and Pretender, claims in his turn to be presented either as the principal or the subordinate agent. Austrasia, Neustria, Bavaria, Alemannia, Italy, Aquitaine, Lorraine, each kingdom or appanage has a special story, conflicting and conjoined with the story and stories of the others, and yet destitute of any unity sufficiently marked to present a decided prominence, round which the others may be satisfactorily grouped. Each narrative is twisted into loops, or darts off into abrupt zigzags: no one can be made to run in a straight path.

The materials which deter and invite the enquirer are most curious, copious and authentic. Five folio volumes are devoted by the Benedictines to Languedoc, the bulk of one such tome is filled with the history of Aquitaine during the Carlovingian reigns: the like proportion obtains in their equally extensive history of Burgundy, not a page too much in either. The Difficulties difficulties arising from this embarrassment of arising from copiousness of riches are enhanced by the frequent recurrence materials recurrence of the same family names; also by changes of of the same names, &c names; also by the plurality of names assigned to one and the same individual; also by the conversion of titles of dignity into proper names, the last peculiarly with females. These causes of confusion occur in other regions of mediæval history, particularly amongst the Cymric tribes; but then we are partially helped by patronymics, whereas the latter are absent amongst the nations who adopted the Romance tongues

Obscurity of historical Geography.   The historical Geography of the Carlovingian Empire is extremely obscure: denominations are given colloquially and loosely, names of nations or tribes confounded with names of countries, the name of a particular territory frequently translated to the whole dominion: just as we sometimes carelessly employ the name of "England," as equivalent to Great Britain, or to the United Kingdom, or even to the British Empire. Boundaries were changed, enlarged, contracted · thus the term Neustria is commonly but erroneously assigned to the district which afterwards became Normandy, though the Duchy was but a small portion of the Carlovingian Neustria. And inasmuch as this Carlovingian period is a transition period, the geographical nomenclature of later times is constantly blended by anticipation with more ancient designations. Systematic accuracy in the employment of the geographical names is scarcely obtainable; and when attainable, often inconsistent with intelligibility.

Summary of the Carlovingian   § 5. This first Chapter contains the argument of Norman history. The reign of Louis-le-débonnaire shattered the Carlovingian Empire and let the Northmen in; and as the shortest and clearest mode of explaining the future narrative, I shall also present the reader with a brief historical genealogy of the Carlovingians until their dethronement in Italy, Germany and France—their dethronement, not their extinction—summarily indicating the various partitions, divisions, and severances of the Empire, all with reference to transactions and events belonging to the history of Normandy, or to the provinces connected with Norman or Anglo-Norman history.

741—987 genealogies, presented as the argument of Norman story.

In compiling these genealogies, I have scarcely attempted to distinguish between the children called legitimate and those to whom legitimacy is denied. Opinion often made little difference between them: The "*Spurius*" is scarcely stigmatized—he was the child of the "*Amica*"—"*naturalis*" was taken adjectively, especially in England, equally to denote children born in lawful matrimony as well as those who were not: an ambiguity sometimes causing great mistakes. It is sometimes used to designate the child of a marriage voidable but not void: a *Nothus* was the offspring of adultery; yet the value of epithets in these matters was liable to great changes, and their meanings are very fluctuating: *Mamzer* was the most opprobrious, *e scorto natus*, but it did not disgrace Ebles of Poitou, or William the Conqueror.

Difficulty of distinguishing between legitimate and illegitimate children.

*

Illegitimate sons were evidently regarded with jealousy by the acknowledged heirs: some, thus branded, obtained the throne; the fact is, that it was often difficult to decide upon the *status* of the party. Concubinage was lawful according to the Teutonic usages, though condemned by the Church; but her jurisdiction in matrimonial causes was tardily acknowledged. We can scarcely discern the exact period when the benediction of the Priest became absolutely needful for the confirmation of a marriage already contracted according to the ancient customs and legal forms, taught by ancestorial tradition and recognized as binding amongst the Teutonic nations before they adopted Christianity. Or, to state the matter technically and in the language of our common law, the era had not yet arrived, when any proceeding like the Bishop's Certificate, *ne unques accoupli*, was received as conclusive evidence by the secular tribunal in questions of marriage. The terms *Regina* or *Amica*, *Uxor* or *Pellex*, are therefore not so scandalously apart from each other as they seem. If we try to sift the question,—which the French historians often do with more earnestness than profit, — the grounds of discrimination between the lawful or unlawful consort, the wife or the concubine, frequently become very vague and uncertain. Look at Charlemagne and the bevy of beauties who surround him—Himeltruda, Her-

mengarda, Bertha or Desiderata, Hildegarda, 741—987
Fastrada, Luitgarda, Mathelgarda, Adelinda, Ger-
suinda, Reguina, the unnamed damsel said to
have fascinated him by the talismanic ring :—
viewed as his Odalisks, they may all be reckoned
in nearly the same category.

The arrangement of this Chapter is not strictly
methodical : some sections are larger in proportion than others; but when compiling the synopsis, after having tried various plans to render the
subject useful and intelligible, I have acted as
if I were a teacher reading with a pupil.—In
that case, I would place before him the original
Chronicles, and underline, and also mark in the
margin those passages and particulars which
would either exemplify the ethos of the age, or
guide and help him in making out the subsequent
portions of Norman and Anglo-Norman history,
so much involved, first with the Carlovingians,
and next with the Capets.   The King of France
supporting or opposing a Duke of Normandy is a
character nearly as important to us as the Duke
of Normandy himself.   Names of persons and
names of places, men and localities, act upon
doctrines and incidents like the mordants which
fix the otherwise fugitive dye upon the memory;
and I would advise the student to peruse the following sections as if he were turning over my
marked and underlined volume.

The whole subject is most pregnant and fruit-

741—987 ful, not merely in relation to the events of this specific period, but from their connexion with the subsequent portions of French history. Even in the present contingencies and catastrophes distracting the European world, we are under the full play of the impulses given by the vicissitudes which the Carlovingian Empire sustained, and the principles then evolved.

Charles Martel and his issue

§ 6. CHARLES MARTEL had six sons; Carloman, Pepin-le-bref, Gripho, Remigius, Jerome, and Bernard.

741.

He divides Childeric's kingdom, and dies, Oct 24

Long-haired Childeric was still called King of the Franks; but the Major-domus thought no more about the descendant of Clovis at Soissons or wherever he might be, than the Governor General does of Aurungzebe's successor, Shah Allum, or whatever his name may be, at Delhi. When Charles Martel, prematurely old, felt the near approach of death, he apportioned amongst his three elder sons, Carloman, Pepin, and Gripho, the Kingdoms to which he had small right. Carloman shall rule Austrasia, Alemannia, the *Schwabenland*, and Thuringia. Let Pepin take Neustria, Burgundia, and the Provincia Romana. Gripho was to have a State, indicated as composed of counties or regions severed from the three Kingdoms of Burgundia, Neustria, and Austrasia. Ambition for the future glory of his family may have induced Charles Martel to stint the youngest of the three. In right of his mother Swanhilda,

Gripho was an *Agilolfing*, and might claim Ba- 741—987
varia, bold independent Bavaria, and his scantier
share would urge him on.—Aquitaine, not yet 741—768
reduced, was left to the valour of Carloman or
Pepin.

Upon the death of Charles Martel, a quarrel 741 748.
instantly arose in the family for their father's spoil. Dissensions between his sons
Carloman and Pepin combined against Gripho, to
deprive him of his modest appanage. Eginhard,
Charlemagne's son-in-law, represents Gripho as
the rebel. More impartial authorities shew the
contrary. Gripho dreaded his brothers, and with
his mother Swanhilda fled to a castle in the
Ardennes, and afterwards to Laon. We cannot
follow his wanderings : he fought bravely, and the
contests between him and his two brothers, but
ultimately only with Pepin the survivor, lasted
many years, during which he sustained great vicissitudes.—He conquered and lost Bavaria, extorted
from his brothers a Duchy containing twelve Counties, and lost them also. His struggles against
his enemies were unavailing, and he was miserably
slain. Carloman, troubled in conscience, grew 747
weary of the world, resigned his authority, be- Carloman abdicates
came a monk, and died happily at Monte-Casino. his children dispos-
Children he had : a son Drogo, and others whose sessed by their uncle
names we cannot ascertain. Thus abdicating, he Pepin
placed them under the wardship of his brother
Pepin. There was no hesitation on the part of
Pepin as to his proper course : he declared himself

741—987
741—768

the unlimited heir of Carloman's rights and realms, dispossessed his nephews completely, would not assign to them a county, not even a villa or domain; and causing them to be shorn, they died forgotten in some monastery.

Younger sons of Charles Martel.

With respect to the three younger sons of Charles Martel, they were all well provided for in the Church or by ecclesiastical preferments, and gave no trouble to their elder brother, Pepin. Remigius was elected to the see of Rouen: a good archbishop, and canonized. Jerome is said to have been Abbot of Sithiu, so well known in the times of Francis the First and Charles the Fifth as St. Quentin, a place of which we shall have much to say hereafter. Bernard, under the title of Comes or Count, was certainly Lay-abbot of that same great monastery. Bernard had five children— Adelhard, Wala or Wallach, Bernarius, Gundrada, and Theodrada. Adelhard and Wala were men who helped to change the whole fortunes of the Carlovingian Empire: unwitting of the results, they contributed most effectually to cause its downfall. They were half brothers: Wala's mother was a Saxon lady, and whether from his looks or some other token, this national descent was very conspicuous, though the son of a Frank and born in the Frankish land; and he was therefore usually called Wala the Saxon.

Bernard, Count or Lay-abbot of St.Quen- tin. his children

752
Accession of Pepin- le-bref.

§ 7. PEPIN-LE-BREF, possessing all royal pow- er, now assumed the title and state of a crowned

King, King of the Frankish monarchy. Childeric, 741—987
the last of the Merovingians, was deposed and
shorn. Carloman, a monk, was dead to the 741—814
world ; so also were his children—Gripho a
fugitive—the three younger brothers contented,
and the disposition of his dominions entirely in
Pepin's power.

Pepin-le-bref had two sons, David (for that Pepin-le-bref. divi-
really appears to have been his name) other- sion of his dominions.
wise Charles or Charlemagne, and Carloman.
Charlemagne obtained the western portion of
the Frankish Realm, extending in a somewhat
irregular line from Friezeland to the Pyrenees ;
Carloman had Austrasia, the ancient home of the
Franks, and long honoured as superior amongst
their kingdoms ; *la soveraine France ki est li
Royaumes de Austrasie*, as we find the same
denominated in the Chronicles of Saint Denis ;
moreover, the Kingdom of Burgundy, including
the Provincia Romana ; and Eastern Aquitaine, or
that region which was annexed to the Austrasian
Kingdom. Carloman died in the lifetime of his 771.
elder brother, leaving three sons, the canonized Carloman.
Bishop of Nice, Saint Sergius, and two others, the
elder named Pepin.

§ 8. CHARLEMAGNE took to himself the 768
whole of his father's realms : first his own share, Oct. 9.
and then his brother's. The issue of Carloman magne
were disinherited by their uncle. Saint Sergius
seems quietly to have abandoned all claims.

741—987 Gerberga, Carloman's widow, fled to Lombardy,
741—811 where she was received by her father King Desiderius, who attempted to assert the rights of her
young children his grandsons; but the *parvuli*,
as they are called by the Chroniclers, disappear
from history. If they lived, they fell into the
power of their uncle, and were probably shut up
and shorn in a monastery.

Charle-
magne's
children.
Charlemagne had seven sons who attained
maturity. Pepin-le-bossu, handsome in countenance, though marked by bodily deformity:
Charles, King of Neustria and Austrasia: Pepin,
(originally called Carloman,) King of Italy: Louis,
King of Aquitaine, in history denominated *Ludo-
ricus-pius*, or *Louis-le-débonnaire :* Drogo, Bishop of Metz, drowned whilst fishing, by a great
fish which drew him into the water: Hugh,
Abbot of Saint Quentin; and Clerk Thierry.
Pepin-le-bossu rebelled against Charlemagne,
seeking, as it is said, his father's life: he was par-
doned, but shut up in the monastery of Pruhm,
whose monks were then reclaiming the desolate
Eifeld.   In this and all similar cases, I anticipate
epithets, titles and dignities for the purpose of
identifying the parties. Charlemagne in his own
life-time never was addressed by his historic
name.   It was late before Charles, Pepin, and
Louis, received their Kingdoms.   Drogo and
Hugh did not acquire their preferments till after
Charlemagne's death.

Charlemagne divided his kingdom amongst 741—987
the second, third, and fourth—Charles, Pepin
and Louis—placing each son in the portion as- 741—814
806
signed to him, sharing the administration of his Division of
the Empire
between
Charles,
Pepin and
Louis.
dominions amongst his children during his life; a
division which he confirmed by Charter before the
prelates and nobles of the Gauls and Germany
at Thionville, six years after he received the Imperial Crown.   But they had all been actually in
possession of their authority many years before.

To Charles, he gave the head and heart of 806.
his realm.   Neustria, which may be considered Portion
assigned to
Charles,
Neustria,
Austrasia,
&c.
equivalent to modern France, north of the Seine,
and Austrasia, *Souveraine France*, now, thanks
to his conquests, extending from Meuse to Elbe :
Austrasia, whose ambit included the most primitive and unaltered of the Teutonic tribes, and
the most signal monuments of Roman domination and splendour,—Ostphalen, still swarming
with Heathendom ; free Friezeland, hardly conscious of the Imperial power, yet claiming her
liberties from the concessions of the majestic
Cæsar ; the red land of Westphalen, awed by
the mysterious Vehmgericht ; scarcely-subjugated
Taxandria, Menapia and the country of the Morini ; Brabant and Flanders, uncleared, covered
by the dark forests whose remnants yet subsist
in the woods of Soignies, all purely Teuton.   To
these were conjoined that rich and flourishing
Ripuarian country, whose sons had at so early

711—987 a period become the willing imitators or disciples
741—814 of Rome's legislation and policy,—Colonia Agrip-
pina, delighting in her Roman descent, whose
Senate and Republic long retained the municipal
ranks and orders which Rome had bestowed;—
Metz, whose citizens exulted that Metz was Metz ^v
before the Franks were known;—Treves, adorned
by the solid magnificence of Roman art, but
boasting that Treves had stood thirteen hundred
years ere Rome was founded.

Portion
assigned to
Pepin

Pepin had all Carlovingian Italy. Lombardy,
lost by Desiderius, from Alps to Appenines, the
Tuscan Marquisate, the Exarchate of Ravenna
and the Dukedom of Rome. Moreover, the wide-
extended land of Bavaria, as held by Tassilo,
opening down to Valtellina, conjoining Germany
with the Lombard marches. Thus his dominion,
bounded on the far North and East by the Her-
cynian forest and the Danube, descended to
Benevento, the extreme South of the Empire.

Portion
assigned to
Louis.

The portion assigned to Louis fully maintained his dignity amongst his brethren. He
was invested with the Kingdom of Aquitaine,
vastly enlarged by annexations and conquest:
Gascony, swarming with restless population :—the
Spanish marches, the marches of Gascony, the
marches of Gothia or Septimania,—the Tolosain
and Auvergne,—most also if not all the counties
and *pagi* within the great Archiepiscopal provinces of Bourges and Bourdeaux, composing

a state equally opulent and defensible.—Some
few margins excepted, Louis was acknowledged
in all the lands between Ebro, Rhone and Loire
and the Atlantic and Mediterranean, the seas
into which these three great rivers pour their
waters.

§ 9. Dangerous as the practice thus sanctioned by Charlemagne of dividing the Empire
may be pronounced, the transaction was dictated
by necessity. Infirmity of power resulted from
the ambition of power. It was physically impossible that such an Empire could continue to obey
a single Sovereign residing at Aix-la-Chapelle
or Ingleheim, Compiegne or Nimeguen. Charlemagne perceived that his Empire must fall to
pieces by its own weight, unless clamped together
by local governments possessing an unity of interest. Risk for risk, even with all hazards of
rivalry, who better than brethren? His institutions were carefully planned for maintaining an
unity of dominion. Yet anxious must have been
the retrospect, and more anxious the forebodings,
when Charlemagne, his heart trembling within
him, dictated the clauses, needful, as he deemed,
to secure the permanence of the dominion he had
founded. He declared that the younger branches
should be under the jurisdiction of the elder.—
The extent of the authority is obscurely indicated by its restrictions. Fathers or uncles were
not to inflict upon sons or nephews the punish-

711—987
741—814

Necessity
of the di-
vision of
the Carlo-
vingian
Empire.
Principles
of the par-
tition.
Gibbon's
censure ill-
founded

741—987

741—814

ments of death, mutilation, blinding, or perpetual imprisonment, the last so odiously accompanied by the enforced monastic vow. The Empire was governed as one State. A civil Hierarchy of Dukes or Counts, amovible perhaps by prerogative, but permanent in many cases by usage, or selected from the old enchorial lineages, satisfied to a certain extent the desire of nationality. Pepin he caused to be educated from his early youth in Lombardy. Louis was born in Aquitaine, and it is probable that the journey whereby his mother, Queen Hermengarda was brought to Cassenueil on the Lot, and which rendered him an Aquitanian by birth-place, did not result from accident. Moreover, the transmission of authority to his grandsons was, as it should seem, to depend upon a threefold title, the nomination of the parent, the election made by the people, and the assent of the surviving Monarchs, the uncles of the designated heir.

It is a mistaken supposition that the mediæval sovereigns were ignorant concerning the extent, value and situation of their dominions. This has been very confidently asserted with respect to the partitions of the Carlovingian Empire. But the system of administration was ably organized. The country was constantly traversed. They understood it from its own face. Travel and tramp are good teachers both of statistics and geography : much is learnt without maps or tables. Trust the farmer for knowing 741—987 every nook of his holding, though he may never 741—814 have seen a survey. Kings were thoroughly ac- quainted with the resources of their dominions ; —how much provisions a province would fur- nish, sheep or kine, oxen or swine ;—how much money could be collected, and whether the col- lection were easy or no ;—how many soldiers the land could raise, and whether, if raised, they were to be trusted or dreaded, stationed in the van or the rear. Charlemagne well knew the difficulties of dealing with the qualities and distinctions of race. In the tripartite division plotted out by him, his attention was peculiarly directed to these elements of strength and weak- ness.

Romanized Gauls, Romanized Franks, and the stern and half-reclaimed tribes retaining their ancient Teutonic spirit, were judiciously balanced in the kingdom given to Charles.—A similar equi- librium Charlemagne established in Pepin's por- tion, which included the extremes of refinement and barbarity.—Lastly, the solid kingdom of Aqui- taine, supporting the Spanish marches, opposed a needful bulwark against the Saracens, who pene- trating to the centre of the Provincia Romana, raised their towers upon the amphitheatre of Arles, the Arabs, checked, but not daunted, and yearning to avenge the shame they had sustained from Charles Martel's heavy hand.

§ 10. But the deep-thought schemes of Charlemagne's policy and political wisdom, his cares for the future, all came to nought. The black sails of the Northmen had been seen in the horizon hovering off the coasts of his Empire   the Saracens were renewing their attacks; the Slavonians attempted to regain their freedom, and the Carlovingian power received a check, indicating the approaching decline

Pepin, King of Italy, prepared to attack the rising republic of the Venetians. They had avoided acknowledging Pepin's authority and incurred Charlemagne's indignation : their merchants, already traders of note, had been expelled from Ravenna.   Pepin entered the Lagune with a mighty fleet.   The seat of government had been removed from Torcello to Malamocco : the vessels of Pepin, filled with the boldest soldiery, had successively occupied Chiozza, Palestrina, and Albiola.   Malamocco was indefensible; and by the advice of the Doge Angelo Participazio, the whole population took refuge in Rio Alto, unoccupied except by the fishermen whose hovels dotted its shores; and it was this migration, which, reducing the other isles to comparative insignificance, raised the Palace of the Adriatic Queen.   Entangled in the Lagune, the heavy drawing Lombard barks, surrounded by light Venetian boats, were pestered by the Greek fire. Many were burnt, some few escaped with the

741—987
741—814
Adverse contingencies disappointing the plans of Charlemagne.

809.
Pepin, King of Italy, attacks the Venetians in the Lagune, and is defeated by them.

rising tide. The engagement took place in or 741—987 about the Canale Orfano, which, according to the popular tradition, derived its name from this 814—840 battle: so many were the children rendered fatherless by the slaughter. A painting of the conflict still exists amongst the faded adornments of the dreary Sala del Scrutinio. Pepin retired 810 to Milan, sickened and died, leaving one son, Death of Pepin, King of Italy Bernard his successor.

This is the Pepin whose bounty raised at Verona the Basilica of San' Zeno, and whose sepulchral catacomb is excavated in the cemetery hard by.

Death had now grasped the family: within a 811. year, the death of Pepin was followed by the Death of Charles, King of Austrasia death of his brother Charles, King of Austrasia and Neustria. Charlemagne had been proud of Pepin; Louis was most promising, yet Charles was on the whole the son most dearly loved. The old Monarch was so afflicted and broken down, that his natural affection was almost imputed to him as a blame. His health failing, he put his affairs in order. All the Bishops, Abbots, Counts and Nobles, all the Senators of the Franks were convened at Aix-la-Chapelle. With their assent he directed Louis with his own hands, to 813 Septi Charle- magne in- augurates Louis-le- débonnaire as his suc- cessor lift up the crown from off the altar, and to place the diadem on his own head. *Vivat Imperator Ludovicus* resounded from the multitude. Then calling up Bernard the son of Pepin, Charlemagne invested his grandchild with Pepin's Kingdom of Italy, and caused him equally to be hailed as King: lastly, before the august assembly, he earnestly commended the children of his old age, his three young sons, Hugh, Drogo, and Thierry, to the care of the new Emperor: Louis swore that he would be their guardian and protector: no appanage did Charlemagne bestow upon them which might enfeeble the Empire—he entrusted them to their brother's love. In the gallery of the Basilica he had erected his marble throne, covered with plates of gold, studded with Greek cameos and astral gems from Nineveh or Babylon. Before that throne were the stairs, straight down

decending to the sepulchre which Charlemagne had already dug deep for himself in the holy ground, even when he raised that marble throne. Soon afterwards the huge broad flagstone which covers the vault was heaved up,—there they reverently deposited the embalmed corpse, surrounded by ghastly magnificence, sitting erect on his curule chair, clad in his silken robes, ponderous with broidery, pearls, and orfray, the imperial diadem on his head, his closed eyelids covered, his face swathed in the dead clothes, girt with his baldric, the ivory horn slung in his scarf, his good sword Joyeuse by his side, the Gospel-book open on his lap,—musk and amber, and sweet spices poured around,—his golden shield and golden sceptre pendant before him.

§ 11. Charlemagne's dissoluteness contrasts 741—987 painfully with the virtues of his mainly just and pious character. Haroun Alraschid's compeer, the 814—840 Charle- license of Bagdad luxuriated at Aix-la-Chapelle; magne's licentious- but the Moslem Caliph, far more excusable than ness the Christian Emperor, did not violate the law by which his conscience was bound.

Men hardly dared to blame the glorious Mo- Popular opinion re- narch, so bountiful, so brave, so charitable, so probating Charle- liberal to Priest and Poor, so equitable, so wise, magne. bright and active; in his genius both practical and poetical, so honest, affectionate and hearty, knowing his duty, so thoroughly following that duty in many points, sometimes even restraining his ambition, but never attempting to contend Evidence of the prevail- against the temptations of lust, becoming as he ing senti- ments in the grew older more doting in his folly. Great scan- Vision of Wettinus dal, but also great sorrow was occasioned by Char- lemagne's conduct, sorrow ending not with life. According to the doctrines of the age, prayer, penitence and charity connected the living with the departed: departed, not dead; living under punishment, but still within reach of help, asking for aid; hence the dead were perhaps more en- deared to the thoughts of those who loved them, even than when sustaining their earthly trial.

The subsistence of these dogmas in the largest portions of Christendom to the present day, very imperfectly represents the psychological influence which they possessed in the mediæval

741—987

814—840

era, when they were not opposed by any antagonistic habits of thought or philosophy.   In the
opinion, teaching that the supplications and good
works of those living in the valley of tears, refreshed the disembodied spirit, all were consentaneous.   However conflicting the forms of faith
might be, on this article of belief all substantially
agreed, Jew, Christian and Moslem.   All contemporary theology supported this credence, and no
one had contributed more to popularize the sentiment by connecting it with a literary or intellectual interest, than Gregory the Great, whose
dramatic dialogues contain so many legends of
visions and apparitions which now unfortunately
tempt us to irreverend scorn.   The state of the
dead was also constantly pourtrayed and realized
to the imagination by the rude precursors of
Orgagna and Michael Angelo,—corpses moulder-
ing in their sepulchres, the horrible conceptions
combining life and death, the half-fleshed skeleton, and the light of the eye glaring through the
hollow socket of the skull: Emperors, Kings,
Queens and Prelates, sinners and saints, writhing
in anguish or calm in beatitude, as seen in the
mosaics keenly glittering through the dark arches
of the Basilica, equally excited the fancy and
sustained the mourners' hopes and fears.

The cripple who had profited by Charlemagne's
bounty, the suitor whom he had graciously relieved, the criminal to whom he had shewn mercy,

the veteran who remembered his liberality, the
matron who in her blooming maiden days had
admired his noble features and stately form, the
monk secluded in the monastery which he had
endowed, would all seek to offer their suffrages
for the repose of his soul, his liberation from
expiatory flame.

Of the general opinion entertained concerning Charlemagne, the anxious grief prevailing
respecting the error, which more than any other,
has tarnished his transcendant reputation, we
possess a remarkable memorial.

Just where the Rhine rushes away with youthful vigour through the Lake of Constance, is the
Island of Reichenau, the *rich meadow*, thus called
from its great fertility, upon which, years ago, we
saw the portal, now demolished, the last mutilated
vestige of the monastery, in the Carlovingian era
one of the chief Colleges of the region, imparting
religion and instruction, light and knowledge to all
the nations and tribes around.   Faithful and prayerful were those at Reichenau, whose thoughts,
according to their conscience and doctrines, continued earnestly directed to the deceased Charlemagne's eternal welfare. Here was Heitto, who
had been confidentially employed by him in his
memorable embassy to Nicephorus the Byzantine
Emperor, Abbot and also Bishop of Bâle, not a
pluralist for profit or gain, but because the conjunction of the two offices rendered him the more

741—987

814—824
useful in the cause for which he so diligently laboured. It was Heitto who built that strangely-decorated Cathedral, in which the ornaments suggested by the timber fabrics of the Burgundians are combined with the mouldings and capitals roughly imitated from Roman art.—Here at Reichenau also was the monk Wettinus, the nephew of Grimoald, once also the friend of Charlemagne, and who, worn out by penances and devotional exercises, expired in the eleventh year after the accession of Louis-le-débonnaire.

824.
Oct 29, 30, and 31.
Trances and death of Wettinus, the Monk of Reichenau.
During three preceding days the sick man had fallen repeatedly into a state of syncope: tremendous shadows filled the cell: Demons armed with spears and shields, Saints sternly majestic appeared to aid and defend him, an Angel, as it seemed to the Sleeper, conducted him through the realms of chastisement, despair and glory. Wettinus passing beyond the first purgatorial Phlegethon, beheld the great Emperor punished by the direst torment, gnawed and lacerated by the hound of hell, yet not condemned to perdition— " *in sorte electorum ad vitam prædestinatus est* " — was the most comforting reply which the anxiously-enquiring Pilgrim received from his angelic guide.

At a later period of mediæval literature, it is often difficult to decide whether such visions are to be read as resulting from sincere impressions,

or as the vehicle of allegorical instruction, bold 741—987
reprehension or disguised satire. 814—824

The phantasms of Wettinus do not offer any such uncertainties. We cannot deny that they are authentic, and, so far as the intent of the narrators, true; and treating this very perplexed and awful enquiry simply as belonging to the history of the' human mind, we are enabled to trace— and not indistinctly—some of the causes suggesting the imagery, adapted to the conceptions of the percipient, thereby constituting, through him, a symbolical language, intelligible to the outward world.

However prevalent may have been the almost instinctive doctrine that an intermediate Hades of suffering is reserved for the justified sinner, the belief acquired greater force through the revelations recorded by Venerable Bede, which, sanctioned by his name, were disseminated throughout the Western Church. Visions of Fursæus (633) and Drithelm (696) included by Bede in his ecclesiastical history.

The Stranger, on the dank marshy shores of the oozy Yare, contemplating the lichen-encrusted ruins of the Roman castramentation,—Burgh Castle or Gariononum, scarcely supposes that those grey walls once enclosed the cell of an obscure anchorite, destined,—so strangely is the chain of causation involved,—to exercise a mighty influence equally upon the dogma and genius of Roman Christendom. This was the Milesian Scot Fursæus, who, received in East Anglia by

*   M 2

741—987

814—824

King Sigebert, there became enwrapped in the trances which disclosed to him the secrets of the world beyond the grave. Theologically, the development of these opinions concerns us not. But theology was as the sap flowing into all the branches of human literature; and Fursæus kindled the spark which, transmitted to the inharmonious Dante of a barbarous age, occasioned the first of the metrical compositions from whose combination the Divina Commedia arose.

Feast of
All Souls
—its origin.

Fursæus was followed by the Anglo-Saxon Drithelm, similarly gifted, similarly raised up, as was supposed, to convince the faithful that sin is a fearful reality. Sermon and Homily repeated these legends; and the curious archæologist still recovers from the walls of the East-Anglian churches, the fading traces of the grotesque designs by which the same lessons were imparted. The well-known festival for the dead, the Feast of All Souls, was not formally instituted till the eleventh century; but the dreams of the night, presented to the Celtic and Saxon recluses, had, long before, instigated the members of various monastic bodies, to agree upon periodical commemorations, enabling them to join in common prayer for the repose of the deceased, under chastisement, but not lost—and the earliest community who practised this work of faith and charity, were the monks assembled in the venerable sanctuary founded by the countryman of Fursæus the Scot, Saint Co-

lumbanus, the Monastery of Saint Gall. The 741–987
neighbouring House of Reichenau followed this
influential example. In the same year during 814—821
which Charlemagne received the Imperial Crown,
Saint Gall and Reichenau united themselves for
this pious observance into one sodality. And had
Wettinus lived till the fifteenth of November,
he would have joined in the annual Service appointed by mutual agreement for that day. In
preparation, without doubt, for this solemnity,
Wettinus had been subjecting himself to increased austerities, and applying himself to appropriate studies; and it was whilst reading
the Dialogues of Pope Gregory relating to the
apparitions of the dead, that the fainting fits had
come on.

The brethren had watched by the bed of Wet- The visions
of Wet-
tinus. As his strength failed he intreated them, tinus, taken
down by
before his tongue should be silenced, to bear Bishop
Heitto, and
record of his words. Detailing the substance of versified by
Walafrid
his visions, the narrative was taken down upon Strabo.
the waxen tablets. Heitto, on the following
morning, read these notes in the presence of four
other monks to the dying man, who confirmed
their accuracy: the Abbot-Bishop forthwith reduced them into a regular statement, plain and
unadorned. In order however to give greater
currency to the warnings which he deemed so
profitable, Heitto requested the celebrated Walafrid Strabo, who himself was afterwards Abbot

741—987
814—824

of Reichenau, to versify these disclosures—parables, if we choose so to accept them—of future retribution and mercy. The passage portraying Charlemagne is here inserted textually, being an indispensable graphic illustration. Consider it as an impression from an ancient block-engraving, the very reality itself, and therefore essentially better than the best fac-simile. No paraphrase, or summary, or translation, could convey any adequate idea of the uncouth, halting hexameters, or actually exhibit the acrostic device which conceals,and yet discloses the Monarch's name.

> Contemplatur item quemdam lustrante pupilla
> Ausoniæ quondam qui regna tenebat, et altæ
> Romanæ gentis, fixo consistere gressu,
> Oppositumque animal lacerare virilia stantis,
> Lætaque per reliquum corpus lùe membra carebant.
> Viderat hæc, magnoque stupens terrore profatur,
> Sortibus hic hominum, dum vitam in corpore gessit
> Iustitiæ nutritor erat, sæcloque moderno
> Maxima pro Domino fecit documenta vigere,
> Protexitque pio sacram tutamine plebem:
> Et velut in mundo sumpsit speciale cacumen
> Recta volens, dulcique volans per regna favore
> Ast hic quam sæva sub conditione tenetur,
> Tam tristique notam sustentat peste severam,
> Oro refer. Tum ductor. in his cruciatibus, inquit,
> Restat ob hoc, quando bona facta libidine turpi
> Fœdavit, ratus inlecebras sub mole bonorum
> Absumi, et vitam voluit finire suetis
> Sordibus. Ipse tamen vitam captabit opimam,
> Dispositum à Domino gaudens invadet honorem.

814.
Jan. 28
State of
affairs at
the death
of Charle-
magne.

§ 12. ON the day of Charlemagne's death, the fifth of the Kalends of February, still cele-

brated in some of the Gallican and German 741—987
churches as the Emperor's commemorative festival, Louis-le-débonnaire was at Doué in Anjou, 714—824
between Sablé and Angers, about ten miles from
the banks of the Loire. This was a favourite
hunting-seat or mansion which he had built, partly
formed out of a Roman Amphitheatre, portions
of whose walls are yet standing. Noble woods
and pleasant fishing-places surrounded Theo-
tuadum, as it was then called; and the locality,
thus rendered agreeable, was one of the four
principal Royal residences of the Aquitanian
King.

Louis had fully anticipated his father's death, 814 Feb.
and he must therefore have been prepared for Louis from
the journey to Aix-la-Chapelle. They retained a Anjou to
system of posting, less perfect than that which Chapelle.
previously prevailed under the Roman Empire,
yet regular; nevertheless, he did not reach his
destination until the thirtieth day after the event,
a particular worth noting, inasmuch as it affords
a tolerable estimate of the time required for communication between distant localities. Whilst
Louis was absent from the Austrasian Capital, the
affairs of government were carried on by the Imperial officers, who had assembled round the expiring Monarch at the Pfaltz of Aix-la-Chapelle—a
virtual interregnum, during which they possessed
great power. They had full opportunity of orga-
nizing any scheme of opposition or advancement,

741—987

763—814

if such were sought. According to the Frankish constitution, the Archicapellanus, or Chancellor— the Chancery being always held in the Royal Chapel—was chief or prime minister. At the period when Charlemagne died, his Seal, the signet gem displaying the bust of the Emperor crowned with the laurel wreath of Rome, was in the custody of Helisachar, Abbot of Saint Maximin, nigh Trèves. Confidence however is not necessarily annexed to official station. Helisachar enjoyed his dignity, but the Ministers whom Charlemagne trusted, who held the highest place in his favour, whom he considered as the proper guides, the protecting advisers of his children, and who had to receive the new Monarch, were two paternal relations, members of the royal family, the grandsons of Charles Martel, whose remarkable history commences during their early youth in the first years of Charlemagne's reign.

768—770.
The early
history of
Adelhard
and Wala,
the grand-
sons of
Charles
Martel, v
§ 6

§ 13. SUSPENDING our present narrative, and reverting to the genealogy given in a preceding Section, it will be found that the youngest of Charles Martel's six sons was Bernard, Lay-abbot or Count-abbot of Sithiu or St. Quentin. Upon Bernard's death, the Abbey was given to another Lay-abbot or Count-abbot. The name of the immediate successor is uncertain; but the principle of semi-secularization continued. Sithiu was again and again bestowed upon members of the Carlovingian family, and became the nucleus of the dominion out of which the great County of Vermandois was ultimately formed. Bernard's children, Adelhard and Wala, were received into the Imperial palace, an academy of elegance, good manners and sound learning, where, like the other noble youths fostered in the royal household, they experienced the Sovereign's graciousness and exercised his vigilance. Though useful and kind, yet Charlemagne's scheme of education was connected with State policy. Children thus nurtured, were hostages for the good behaviour of their kindred and connexions; and if the lads displayed any indications of becoming dangerous, means might be taken to prevent their being troublesome to others or themselves.

Popular traditions represent Bertha, Charlemagne's Mother, *Berthe-aux-grands-pieds*, as a mythic personification of simplicity and love— *il buon tempo quando Berta filava*,—that happy time when Bertha span, will it ever return in ours? Bertha had but one cause of grief with her son Charlemagne, he was not settled to her mind. But the Monarch having agreed to discard his beautiful Consort Himmeltruda, the Queen-mother now attempted the difficult task of providing him with a new Bride, supposing that if the new love were according to her heart, the damsel would be sure to be according to the heart of her son. A joyful season opened upon the Court of Aix-la-Chapelle when

741—987

768—814 —nurtured in Charlemagne's palace.

770. Marriage between the daughter of King Desiderius and Charlemagne brought about by Queen Bertha his mother.

741—987
768—814
the Queen-mother Bertha returned from Pavia,— the Palace of which the general form is still retraced in the massy quadrangle, flanked by the desolated Visconti towers,—conducting with her that fair one so anxiously sought, her name-√ sake, the young Bertha, daughter of Desiderius, King of Italy, the Lombard King.

The Princess had not been easily won. Scarcely covered at this period by a grudging friendship, the rivalry between the Franks and Lombards may have occasioned the obstacles; but Queen Bertha's persevering anxiety overcame them, and the Frankish nobles sanctioned and confirmed the marriage-compact by their oaths: a proceeding indicating some distrust on the part of

Name of the Lombard Princess changed to Desiderata.
Desiderius. When the Lombard Lady reached the dominions of her future husband, and the union was accomplished, the name of *Desiderata* was given to her, doubly appropriate, suggested equally by her father's name and by the sentiments which had brought her there.

This marriage began in wrong and ended in wrong. Himmeltruda his wife, the mother of his eldest son, Pepin-le-bossu, was discarded by Charlemagne's impetuous passions and volatile affection. The Frankish Chroniclers, some kinsmen like Eginhard his son-in-law, and all of them his favourites, his admirers or his friends, speak under their breath concerning these transactions: we get at them obscurely. No colourable pretence is alleged, no allusion made, even to a causeless divorce. Possibly Pepin's deformity was the reason why Charlemagne excluded him, the first-born, from the Throne; and his subsequent rebellion against his father may have been instigated by the injury he and his mother had sustained. A year had scarcely elapsed when Charlemagne, adding evil to evil, deeply grieving his mother and causing his nobles to violate their oaths, put away Desiderata, no longer desired. Childless, she found no favour in her husband's eyes, and Pope Stephen, as we are told, sanctioned the dissolution of the unhappy union. Charlemagne then took another wife, Hildegarda, mother of his three sons, Charles, Pepin King of Italy, and Louis, the Emperor now upon the throne.

741—987 768—814 771 Charlemagne repudiates Desiderata, and marries Hildegarda.

Charlemagne may have received some private rebukes from his Clergy, but never did they openly oppose his unbridled indulgence. There are seasons when popular sins are so universally condonated, so attractive, so recommended by national pride, so palliated by fashion, so fascinating to intellect, so intimately conducive to the material interests and resources of society, so thoroughly assimilated into the body politic, that it seems as if the Priesthood must, out of mere charity, yield to the universal hardness of heart: refraining from their duty lest rebuke should aggravate iniquity, by occasioning the worse

*

741—987
768—811

transgression, of sinning against warning and knowledge. Faith failing through irremovable ignorance, inveterate habit, or unsurmountable temptation, it appears impossible to correct the perceptions of the sinner, in whom a moral polarization of light has taken place—the black looks couleur-de-rose.

Take home instances, familiar instances, stale, vulgar instances, disagreeable instances, humiliating instances, they shew the truth more clearly. Can we conceive the possibility of any Parochial Minister gifted with the firmness, zeal, kindness, talent and earnestness, which fifty years ago, combining in due proportions, would have enabled him to exhort against wrecking on the Cornish Coast? Did any one incumbent of Newmarket or Epsom ever reprove the crowds who, to their temporal or eternal ruin, so thickly congregate upon the verdant turf of the Heath or the Downs : or chide the pestilential profligacy fostered by the race-course-stand, the betting-room and the roulette-table?—Influence and station may environ the offenders by circumstances which deter all but those who are raised up as special ministers of holiness. Whether a Charles, a James, or a William, listened or were supposed to listen in the Royal Closet, no voice was ever heard from the pulpit of Whitehall which could trouble the lovers of such charmers as Nell Gwynne or Mademoiselle de Querouaille, my Lady Cas-

tlemaine, Mistress Arabella Churchill, Miss Lucy 741—987
Walters or my Lady Orkney. Ward and Sheldon
were lulled into dutiful somnolence. Stilling- 768—814
fleet and Tillotson, waging an uncompromising
warfare against Socinian Heresy and Popish corruption, knew nothing whatever of the debauch-
eries perpetrated by King and Duke, which made
the Wapping sailors cry, Shame! The Revolution
did not diminish their mildness; and smiling
over their velvet cushions, they practised the
same toleration towards the phlegmatic amours
of him of the "glorious memory." Hoadly, gently
creeping up the Palace back-stairs in search of
the successive mitres of Bangor, Hereford, Salisbury, and Winchester, and fully impressed with
"the unreasonableness of nonconformity" to a
Monarch's liaison, never startled during his ascent
at the patched and painted Countesses of Yar-
mouth or of Suffolk, the bulky Baroness Kill-
mansegg, or the gawky Duchess of Kendal.—The
awe inspired by Charlemagne, the respect for
his active piety and zeal, his personal energy in
the good cause, the gratitude earned by his munificence, the prestige of his poetical grandeur,
subdued the Clergy into a practical connivance,
which would receive a harder name were it not
for the indulgence with which man is bound to
judge of human infirmity. Nor can we escape
from similar examples of moral debility in any
era.—Cranmer's docility reflects the accommo-

741—987 dation given by Pope Stephen. Desiderata is repeated in Anne of Cleves.

768—814
Adelhard
resents the
divorce of
Desiderata
—becomes
a monk at
Corbey. Adelhard, young, ardent, conscientious, was rendered indignant by Desiderata's wrongs. Was not Hildegarda an intrusive queen? Could he render to her that respect which his station in the Court required? He spoke loudly, honestly, boldly—spared not the Frankish nobles, reproached them with their flagrant untruth, till at length, sickened and disgusted with the world, he fled its trials and temptations and became a monk in the newly-founded Abbey of Corbey, afterwards called *vieux-Corbey*, near Amiens. You see the Abbey Towers from the parapet of Amiens Cathedral. During Adelhard's noviciate they put him to work in the garden; he became Abbot in course of time, and founded in Westphalia the Monastery called New Corbey, or Corvey, on the banks of the Weser.

774.
Desiderius
King of
Lombardy,
dethroned
by Charle-
magne, and
shorn as a
monk at
Corbey. About four years after Adelhard had professed, another fugitive, an unwilling fugitive, a prisoner, found refuge from trouble in the same sanctuary of Corbey. The repudiation of Desiderata had been followed by a war between the aggressive Franks and the yet warlike Lombards. Charlemagne invaded the dominions of Desiderius. The Alpine passes were well though unsuccessfully defended; but a series of victories gave to Charlemagne the Exarchate of Ravenna, the Venetian and Istrian provinces, Spoleto and Benevento,

Parma, Reggio, Mantua, finally Pavia and the 741—987
whole Lombard Kingdom. Yet it is said that
Desiderius was dethroned by treachery, and sur- 768—814
rendered by his lieges to Charlemagne, who transported him to France. He was shorn and placed
in custody at Corbey, where, after passing many
years in penitence and seclusion, he died. Some
of the Italian Chroniclers maintain that Charlemagne caused Desiderius to be blinded; but such
an unnecessary cruelty we would willingly disbelieve. Thus was the kingdom of Italy acquired,
of which, as before mentioned, Pepin had been
appointed King.

Wala the King's kinsman, continued in the
Pfaltz of Aix-la-Chapelle; encouraged and admired; and at the proper age, the Tyro—(we
must not commit the anachronism of calling
him an Esquire)—was invested with belt and
sword. Suddenly the young son of the Count- Wala
abbot Bernard roused Charlemagne's suspicion falls into
or anger. No reason is stated; but in the Mo- disgrace.
narch's estimation he had committed some grave
offence occasioning stern displeasure, yet tempered by consideration for his youth and merit.
Shall we suppose that Wala shared in his brother
Adelhard's sentiments, and continued to affront
the new Queen?—or another hypothesis may be
vaguely suggested. About this period Charlemagne was waging his cruel and exterminating
warfare against the old Saxons:—thousands of

741—987

768—814

captives made shorter by the head, as his admiring chroniclers relate, in the course of a day ; and the historian will scarcely exceed the permitted range of conjecture if he assumes that Wala the Saxon, unable to controul his national feeling, testified his horror against these aggressions. Might not Wala endeavour to raise again the Irminsule, which Charlemagne had cast down ?

Wala banished to a royal villa, and employed in servile labour.

Wala was banished to a distant Villa ; one of those royal domains, those vast farms which Charlemagne managed with so much prudent care : he was strictly watched, almost treated as a serf, a *theowe* according to the Anglo-Saxon law—a free-born man reduced to thraldom by legal judgment, employed in the meanest labours of husbandry. He had, however, preserved his insignia of dignity ; and he followed the plough and drove the wain, girt with belt and sword. While so employed, jolting in his vehicle drawn by bullocks, he chanced to meet a villein, clad in rustic gear. Wala entreated the peasant to exchange :—" Take the belt, take the sword— these decorations," said he, " no more befit me : mean have I become, mean and humble let me be."

Wala and Adelhard restored to Charlemagne's favour.

Here his personal history is suddenly broken off, until, after a chasm of many years, without any indication of intermediate adventures, we find Charles Martel's grandsons highest in Charlemagne's favour.

Count Wala, regaining the honours due to his 741—987 royal lineage, suddenly reappears as the husband of a noble damsel, daughter of William, Count of 768—814 Toulouse, that Count William sung and celebrated in minstrelsy and romance as *Guillaume Fierbras, Guillaume au Court-Nez,* or *Guillaume d'Orange,* whilst, in the ecclesiastical legends, he is discovered with somewhat more difficulty, under the name of *Guillaume-de-Gellone,* commemorating the monastery founded by him as a Prince, but wherein he died a recluse.

Favour flowing in, his utility fully recognized, Wala, stern, determined, pitiless, now continued actively engaged in various departments of the State, commanding Charlemagne's armies, warring against the Slavonians, ambassador to the Pagan Danes. It is interesting to observe the instinctive prescience which led Charlemagne to attempt the conciliation of these enemies. Count Wala was ultimately appointed chief of the royal household: "another Joseph," is the expression used by his Biographer,—*economus totius domus Augusti,*—a dreaded yet equitable judge, "Senator of the Senators, inferior only to Cæsar."

Adelhard appears to have been in great measure removed from his monastery; and, diverted from his proper charge to act as a confidential minister, he was much employed by Charlemagne in settling the affairs of Italy. First the fellow monk of Desiderius, and afterwards the Abbot

Adelhard much employed in Italy.

741—987
768—814 of Corbey, he, when Desiderius came within his care and custody, may have gained some useful information from the royal captive, qualifying him for the administration of the conquered territory. Pepin having assumed the government of Lombardy, Adelhard accompanied him as Chief Justiciar. Judgments given by him in that capacity are extant: his authority was so great that he may be considered as virtually associated to the King.

Wala employed also in Italy by Charlemagne. Wala was also often sent to Italy: he and Adelhard were successively or alternately entrusted with the guidance of Pepin's successor in the kingdom, his son Bernard, that grandchild whom Charlemagne peculiarly loved, assisting him by their advice, or more probably governing in his name. Wala resided with Bernard during the last year of Charlemagne's reign. A Saracen invasion then threatened Italy, and his aid and counsel were eminently needed, but he was recalled by the encreasing feebleness of the Emperor. Count Wala is one of the witnesses of Charlemagne's Will: he took charge of the palace when the Emperor expired, and it was there that the Senator of the Senators was found by Louis-le-débonnaire.

781—814
Louis King of Aquitaine. § 14. Louis had three sons by his first wife Hermengarda (she was the daughter of Ingelram Count of Hasbaye), Lothair, Pepin, and Louis: a fourth was afterwards born to him by a second

consort; he also had three daughters—Gisela, _{741—987}
married to Everard Count of Friuli, an Adelaide,
(perhaps also bearing some other name)—and _{768—814}
Hildegard. Count Everard was the father of King
Berengarius, *il Rè Berengario*, so well recollected at Monza and Milan, who acquired Italy,
when, upon the deposition of Charles-le-gros, that
realm was lost to the Carlovingian dynasty.

Louis, as King of Aquitaine, attained experience and wisdom, and earned universal love and
respect. Charlemagne's teaching and Charlemagne's care had turned to excellent account. An
Aquitanian by birth-place and nurtured in that
country, Louis, from his youth upwards, had
been the object of delight and admiration: he
had subdued the fiery Vascons by his grace, his
talent and adaptability, conforming himself to
their national customs, assuming their garb: a
gracious King and discreet withal, liberal in hand,
liberal in mind, but 'maintaining his authority by
intellect, strenuousness and justice.

He inherited his father's love for literature, Varied
and had eagerly profited by the education which talents of
Charlemagne bestowed. Louis was an excellent Louis-le-debonnaire.
Latin scholar, and well acquainted with the Greek
language. He delighted in the Poets and Rhetors
of the classical age;—the most humble, most
pleasantly-minded, most promising amongst Charlemagne's children, holy men had fondly designated him as fittest for the succession; the one

N 2

741—987 likeliest to flourish as a happy, and a happiness-
bestowing Sovereign.   Such expectations had
814—840 circled widely:—were talent, good intentions and
sincerity always sure to profit, his deeds would
Energy and have justified the anticipations.   King of Aqui-
wisdom
displayed taine, Louis assembled his Cour Plenière at
by Louis as
King of Toulouse; and the Capitol of that ancient mu-
Aquitaine.
nicipality, so noble amongst the adopted daughters of Rome, became his palace.   Three days
in each week he devoted to the administration
of the law, and his sage decisions were replete
with equity.   Louis was bold and energetic
as well as wise : no archer drew the bow with
greater strength, no huntsman chasing the tusked
boar could dart the Mozarabic *javalina*,—the
weapon still named from the animal against which
it was employed.—with more unerring skill.

Bravely did Louis encounter the wild and re-
sentful Avars.   Charlemagne subsequently placed
him at the head of the army destined to repel
the Infidels   the Saracens fled, Barcelona surrendered before him.   Those who recollected
Charlemagne at the same age of thirty-six years,
when the last bloom of youth had been succeeded
by the full fruit of manhood, might have said
that the son vied with the father in worth, cultivation, prowess and valour. Had he died King
of Aquitaine, he would have shone amongst the
best and most illustrious monarchs in French
history.

§ 15. Louis upon his accession to the Empire did not disappoint the promises given by
the pleasant manner, piety and conscientiousness
of the Aquitanian King. Imitating his predecessor Antoninus, the new Emperor accepted the
cognomen of *Pius*—perhaps bestowed upon him
by the Clergy or the Pope—and stamped the appellation upon his coins. The people called him
"*le débonnaire*," a name perpetuated by tradition;
for, so far as we have ascertained, this epithet of
le débonnaire never appears in writing until employed by the Monks of St. Denis, in their vernacular Chronicle. Archæologists may possibly
discover it lurking in some inedited *Chanson de
geste*, some Romance poem of the Trouveurs.

Earnest childlike faith was the peculiar characteristic of Louis-le-débonnaire. Commiserated
for this reason by historians, termed, rather in
disparagement than in praise, the Saint Louis of
the ninth century, his lot was cast in a dark and
troubled era, teeming with negligences and abuses.
History can only display the human economy of
the Spiritual Empire, therefore always full of
frailties and disorders, her ministers and members lingering, halting, yielding, flinching, failing,
falling off.—

— The Church, though no part of the world,
is included in the world   Her members, so long
as they are militant, must tread upon the world's
paths—aye, even in the desert of the Thebais—

741—987 live in the world's atmosphere, and breathe the
world's ambient air. Amongst the Great, the
811—840 garments of the Sainted Princess will be redolent
of her boudoir essences and cassolette perfumes:
amongst the Humble, the raiments of God's servants smell of the hovel's sordidness, the littered
stable, the smoky forge. The rich man, though
truly seeking heaven, will occasionally stumble
against his money-bags. The poor man, though
truly contrite, listens to the Pastor's exhortations
with unconscious selfishness and the asking glance
of hunger. Pervading faith dignifies the meanest
objects. Civilization imparts to the holiest her
admixture of utilitarianism and unreality. All
· communions partake of the taint.—Albertus Magnus is supposed by some to have been the in-
ventor of Gothic architecture. How grimly would
his ghost behold his Cologne Cathedral, completed
by the tributary fantasies of romantic æstheticism,
or the contributions coaxed from Teutonic belles
and beaux by the English-taught *Dombau-verein*
at the Bazaar and the Fancy Fair.—

In the Middle Ages, the Clergy were compelled
by their duties to engage actively in the rougher
concerns of the world, and these hard necessities
were constantly conflicting with the internal life
whence all their actions ought to spring. The
The eccle- inestimable temporal benefits bestowed by Reli-
siastical
reforms of gion upon mankind, often tempt even the right-
Louis-le-
débon- minded to consider the Church as approximating
naire

to an engine of State policy, not entirely a State 741—987
engine, but much of the same sort: a good help
to the Empire's wealth, credit, progress, security 814—840
and commercial prosperity. A discreet hint that
"Church extension" may co-operate in keeping
up the price of Consols occasionally breathes
amidst the appalling statistics of chartism and
"spiritual destitution" in the great manufacturing
towns: the concurrently-encreasing demand for
cotton goods and Christianity has been joyfully
proclaimed from the Missionary platform. The
gratitude due to Charlemagne's ample munificence, sometimes induced the conscientious
amongst the Sacerdotal Order to sad compromises
of principle : the patron and founder of so many
Abbeys and Bishopricks never scrupled to employ his foundations in his own way.

"Trovata la legge, trovato l'inganno:" says *The great abuse of*
the Italian proverb;—we would quote in Eng- *bestowing Abbeys as*
lish could we find a parallel adage; the good *lay bene-fices*
law immediately suggests the evasion: the
most salutary institutions are most susceptible
of malversations; and this was eminently the
case with the monastic institutions of the Middle
Ages. At the very period when, if sincerely
administered, their workings were so signally
and extensively useful and beneficent — calm
regions amidst the tumults of the world, homes
for the destitute, solaces to the poor, comforts to
the afflicted, schools of industry and learning—

741—987

814—840

they had to contend against the secular power which bestowed their possessions, honoured their position, and recognized their transcendant importance in society.

We can best exemplify the Carlovingian corruptions by contemplating a Great Commander on Blenheim field. If you ascended the rock of Chiusa, and reached the mysterious tower of San' Michele, where you passed between the ranged corpses, stationed as warders of the portal sculptured with zodiacal signs, and asked for the Abbot, the Monks informed you that you would find him in Marlborough's camp, for it was as *Monseigneur l'Abbé de Savoie* that Prince Eugène made his earliest campaigns, he being at that time Commendatory Abbot of that and another of the most venerable monasteries of ancient Lombardy, situated in the district to which, from its position, the name of "Piedmonte" was subsequently assigned. Such were the "Lay-Abbots" whom we have so often noticed, who held the most important monasteries in the Carlovingian Gauls,—a motley groupe,—stout soldiers, clever statesmen, delicate young princes, half-acknowledged husbands of princesses, or husbands fully declared, courtiers, most in favour with the monarch, partizans, who were to be conciliated by favours, or claimants who were to be pacified,—constituted the class who usually obtained these excellent pieces of preferment, which in many respects were more advan-

Prince Eugène Abbot of San' Michele in Chiusa, &c.

tageous than any secular domain. Sometimes 741—987
these Abbots Commendatory were in minor orders,
but very frequently mere laymen, like those we 814—810
have already noticed of Sithiu or Centulla. Outwardly the Abbey did not appear to be changed.
You heard of an Abbot as you now do of the noble
or reverend "Master" of this or that "Hospital,"
realizing the fines and rents according to the
valuations and currency of Queen Victoria, and
staving off the "Brethren," by tendering their
stipends in the nominal pence of Plantagenet.—
The Count was not in the Abbey, he might
be fighting against the Northmen, or enjoying
himself in the palace : truly there was a Prior
presiding in the refectory, and the monks were
chanting in the choir, but the real spirit of the
institution was of course fleeting away. How
earnestly the Church laboured to counteract these
monstrous misappropriations, by dauntless assertion of her lawful power, faith, energy, and diligence, cannot here be told. It may be a question
whether an ecclesiastical foundation given to a
secular man is more secularized than when held
by a Priest whose spirit is secular. There is
not much to choose; nevertheless, the evil was
enormous: amongst all the pious-minded the
practice excited great sorrow and scandal, whilst,
protected by so many interests, it was most inac-
cessible to reform.

A partial remedy, but satisfactory as far as

741—987
814—840

Classifi-
cation and
settlement
of Abbatial
tenures.

the measure extended, was applied by Louis. The duties annexed to the possessions and lands held by monastic communities, received an adjustment throughout a large portion of the Empire by the following distribution. Fourteen monasteries were to contribute to the *Dona* or gifts, and perform military service: sixteen were to be charged only with gifts; whilst the duty of praying for the welfare of the Emperor and his children and the Empire, was accepted by the State in full discharge of the obligations imposed upon the remainder. The division of Church-lands into lands held by Knight's service,—lands contributing to aids and subsidies,—and lands held in *frank almoigne*, prevailed subsequently in England as a portion of our constitutional Law. It was unquestionably recognized in the Anglo-Saxon Empire; but this is the earliest instance of a clear and definite legislation upon a subject which had great influence on the political position of the Clergy.

814—820
Good be-
ginning of
the reign
of Louis-
le-débon-
naire.

Heavy and vexatious taxes were remitted by Louis : he restrained the impudent gallantry of his beautiful sisters sternly but not unkindly. Obeying his father's earnest injunction, his three young brothers, Hugh, Drogo and Thierry, were cherished in the Palace, educated and cared for, as though they had been his own sons.

Economical in his household, but liberal and unsparing on all occasions when dignity required

expenditure and munificence, he appeared on the 741—987
throne in the full splendour of Imperial Majesty ⌣⌣
—all his garments were cloth of gold. So far as 814—840
depended upon his own intentions and exertions,
he maintained the civil and military dignity of the
Empire,—he numbered at one prosperous era more
vassals than his father. Nevertheless the heart of His aliena-
tion from
Louis became more and more alienated from the the world.
world : all about him were wont to remark, that
the example which he afforded rendered him a
true model for the Priesthood—perhaps a rebuke
to the ordinary character of a King.

Tastes, more stubborn than principles, less
susceptible of change, yielded to devotional feeling.—His fondness for that elegant literature
in which, thanks to his father's care, he was
so well versed, declined and ceased. The poets Louis-le-
débon-
and rhetors of classical antiquity were neglected, naire abandons clas-
and at length utterly cast aside for the study sical literature for the
of Holy Scripture. Even the heroic legends of study of
the Holy
the Frankish race, the ancient and barbarous Scriptures
lays which told the tales of Hildebrand or Hathu-
brand, the doughty deeds of primeval warriors
and fabled kings collected by Charlemagne, were
more than discarded by Louis; for he destroyed
the precious volume on account of the memorials of ancient heathenism perpetuated in the
national song. This proscription was not the
result of a blind or ignorant zeal: Louis appreciated the inestimable worth which poetry in-

741—987 volves; and whilst he laboured to extirpate the productions shunned by him as the vehicles of 811—840 evil, he sought to enlist the gift of verse and the endearing associations of national language in the service of the Lord.

Philology has been singularly enriched through this direction of his mind. It chanced that amongst the Continental Saxons a Husbandman exhibited a sudden development of poetic power, so high, so transcendant in the judgment of his own time and people, that the talent was ascribed to inspiration; another Cædmon in the Anglo-Saxon's ancient Fatherland.

Metrical version of the Holy Scriptures made under the dictation of Louis-le-débonnaire.

This Bard, this *Vates,* as he is termed by the contemporary writers, was invited by Louis to interpret the whole of the Old and New Testament in the Teutonic tongue; and the paraphrase which he composed in alliterative staves, —being, with the exception of one fragment, the only example existing in Germany of that ancient measure,—acquired the greatest praise and popularity from its clearness and elegance. A portion of this remarkable linguistic monument, comprehending a metrical harmony of the Gos-

Codex Cottonianus or Liber Aureus in the British Museum, a portion of such version.

pels, exists in the celebrated *Codex Cottonianus,* the *Liber Aureus,* once deemed the most valuable treasure of the renowned Collector to whom it formerly belonged, as well as of the national Repository in which the Manuscript is now contained.

§ 16.   Louis-le-débonnaire, humiliated before

the altar, is perhaps already prejudged by the ^{741—987}
historical student.—Let that judgment be rectified.
It is a happiness in our own British Empire ^{814—840}
possessed by no other nation, that the great
constitutional maxim, "The King can do no
wrong," has ceased to be a metaphor. Governing
according to Law, not merely the written Law,
but the equally binding unwritten law, resulting
from the usages and traditions of the British
Empire, the silent legislation effected by practice,
compromise, decorum, etiquette, official obedience
and official form, the Sovereign is released from
the performance of those public or political acts
of prerogative or government which involve moral
responsibility.

In our Empire, "the people are in no subjection, but such as they willingly have condescended
unto for their own behoof and security." The
wearer of the British Crown is "major singulis,
universis minor."—As Ruler of that British Empire, the person of the British Sovereign merges
in the person of the Ministers, and the moral responsibility of the Ruler, when executing such acts,
becomes the burthen of those Ministers, most
happily for the security of the commonwealth and
the peace of the Sovereign's mind : the liability
incurred by the nation is refracted through so
many media, that it is dispersed before reaching
the foot of the throne. To the voice, the influence,
the power of the people expressed or exercised in

British Constitution The Sovereign in all acts of Government exonerated from moral responsibility as a Sovereign.

741—987 Parliament, the Sovereign conforms. The law
enjoins such conformity. Should a British Sove-
814—840 reign ever dream of regaining the perilous prerogative abandoned by the last who wrote himself
"King of England"—the prerogative which William the Third possessed, exercised, and then
reluctantly surrendered for ever—the dangerous
venture of answering *Le Roi s'avisera*, in refusal
of the national demand, then the constitutional
monarchy would expire. But by our Sovereign's
obedience to the law, the responsibility is cast upon
the ranks and orders of the people, Archbishops,
Bishops, Dukes, Marquisses, Earls, Viscounts,
Barons, Knights, Citizens and Burgesses in Parliament assembled; and most of all, upon those whose
votes and voices sent the Commons there. If the
Rulers commit a wrong, it is instigated and sanctioned by the monarchy of the middle classes. If
any legislative act or proceeding offend against
our duties, the sin is lying at our own doors.

Greater
moral re-
sponsibility
of Mo-
narchs
in the
mediæval
period

But where this repartition and diffusion of
authority does not subsist, the Sovereign is exposed to grievous temptations: a hint may per-
vert justice, a smile wrest the laws for his own
gratification, a frown be the cause of hunting
down a State offender with implacable cruelty;
and in such a state of society as subsisted in the
mediæval period, the desire to remove a troublesome opponent may be expressed so emphatically,
that the ruffian courtier cannot fail to construe

the anticipation into a command. If roused to 741—987
repentance, should the King feel that he guided
the murderers, become convinced that he is ac- 814—840
countable for his own sin, and therefore impute
to himself his own rash words, is it his duty to
harden himself, or to testify penitence as open as
the crime, and to seek mercy?

Louis-le-débonnaire, accused by his own conscience, followed the dictate, and found comfort in
humiliation; faith solaced his misfortunes. Yet
these misfortunes have been perversely imputed
to his faith. Obedience to the dictates of religion was the predominating sentiment by which
Louis was actuated; and Historians, arguing
from his example, have been tempted to raise the
question, whether the piety of the man may not
be a pernicious debility in the Sovereign. The
fine gold destined for the vessels of the Sanctuary has not, as they say, hardness enough to
stand the wear and tear of human commerce : the
needful strength must be given by the baser alloy.

Dwelling, as we do, in twilight, always in the
shadow of death, it is often difficult to discriminate Faith and Superstition, or, in judging
others, to pronounce that their apparent conviction is a cover for delusion. Nevertheless, in the
case of Louis-le-débonnaire, we may convince
ourselves that it was not the excess of faith, but
the human accompaniment, inconsistency, which,
through this one individual, confirmed the ruin

741–987 of the great Carlovingian Empire; and this incon-
814—840 sistency was the result of one defect in his moral
or physical character, a minor failing, which
under other contingencies would have been
harmless, but in his political destiny became
over-ruling. Neither physiology nor psychology
can decide whether this defect be occasioned
through the body or through the mind; being

Nervous timidity the over- ruling defect in the charac- ter of Lou's- le-débon- naire. that which in ordinary and colloquial language
(the best exponent of social experience) is called
"nervous timidity." Louis never shrank from present danger; rarely, and perhaps but once, did he
allow his passive courage to submit to present
suffering; but the future appalled his imaginative mind. Shadows were his dread. Sometimes
he would support himself by the advice of his
counsellors, wholly throwing himself upon their
opinions; sometimes, and more dangerously, he
would be wholly guided by his own, and his very
irresolution urged him to acts of harshness, nay
cruelty, which his soul abhorred.

Contrast between the situa- tion of Louis King of Aqui- taine and Louis the Emperor. § 17. The circumstances of the Carlovingian
Empire, when the Imperial power devolved upon
Louis, were calculated to try him to the utmost,
to search his conscience, to prove his heart,
to discipline him by contrariety and affliction.
Humanly speaking, nothing but the heroic virtue
of unsparing firmness, reckless determination of
purpose screwed to the highest pitch, could have
resisted the combination of difficulties and dan-

gers and treasons against which the Sovereign had to contend.

741—987

Louis could not recollect the time when he had not been King of Aquitaine. Just turned two years of age, Pope Adrian baptized and crowned him upon the same day. Borne in his cradle from Rome to Aquitaine, the infant was exhibited to the people, held and steadied by the groom-nurse on the ambling steed. He had grown up as a King; and all the recollections of the Aquitanian reign were pleasurable—this exalted situation had brought out all his good qualities, restrained the development of his failings. Married young and happily to Hermengarda whom he loved and trusted, his conduct had, if tried by the ordinary standard of the era, been exemplarily correct· he enjoyed all the state and privileges annexed to royalty, exercised the most ennobling functions of a Sovereign, the administration of justice and mercy, and participated in all the excitements of war without sustaining any wearing anxieties. There was no rivalry between Charlemagne and Louis, no jealousy or grudge between father and son. Louis depended upon his father: submission to paternal authority was to him a privilege and a gain. Charlemagne's gigantic power and celebrity diffused protection throughout the Empire; and Louis, though ruling in his own territory as an independent and national King, was exalted by his

814—840
781.
Baptism and Coronation of Louis-le-débonnaire.

781—814
Prosperity of Louis when King of Aquitaine.

subjection to the Imperial Crown. Charlemagne's experience, opulence and armies, ever ready to succour or support him, guarded him from all apprehension of danger.

Far otherwise when Louis was thrown upon his own resources, himself the Emperor, supreme in dominion, seated upon a throne which invited retribution. The sword was never to depart from the House of Charles Martel, and Louis felt it piercing his heart. The exulting legend "*Renovatio Regni Francorum*," graced by the laurel-wreath of Rome, appears upon the imperial signet of Louis, but there was no youthful vitality. Brief had been the period of Carlovingian domination, yet the Imperial authority had reverted to the decrepitude of the Lower Empire, the debility of antiquity without its privileges. The Carlovingian Empire was utterly destitute of the consolidation resulting from long-practised constitutional usages, maxims admitted as self-evident truths, undiscussed cogencies, principles learnt without a teacher: the sanctity which time alone can impart, an element uncreateable by human intellect or power. On the contrary, the royal authority was infirm from the commencement: all the traditions of the past were hostile, whatever precedents memory could furnish were melancholy and painful, suggestive of disquiet, uncertainty, moral and political crime.

Louis-le-débonnaire was well versed in his-

Moral debility of the Frankish Empire.

tory; and if he consulted the chronicles of the 741—987
realm, such as were treasured at Tours or Saint
Denis, he would find them saturated with evil, 814—840
memorials of evil, lessons of evil; a faithless
nation, wild and profligate, fierce to others, fiercer
amongst themselves; loyalty an unknown sentiment, a people sharing and rejoicing in the
atrocities of their sovereigns.   The sovereigns, a
lineage void of natural affection: the name of their
traditionary ancestor, *Wahrmund*, "the mouth of
truth," being a constant satire against them:
false and fickle, love restrained them not nor consanguinity—some basely vicious, others wan-
toning in cruelty, indulged until that cruelty
became a morbid appetite or rather insanity;
children visited for their father's sins, and yet
unchastened by the punishment, and preparing,
by their own sins, the same inflictions for their
progeny.

§ 18.   DESTITUTE even of the conventional Crimes of
apologies for national iniquity are the Mero- vingians.
vingian annals, exhibiting, as they recede before
us, a weary display of wickedness without grandeur, dull and inglorious, unadorned by any of
the attributes through which splendid villany is
redeemed in history.   Glance merely at the succession:—Dagobert son of Sigebert murdered by   679.
the Austrasian nobles:—Childeric, the son of the   673.
second Clovis, his queen and children, slaughtered
in like manner by their aristocracy :—Dagobert,   638.

741—987 the first Dagobert, whose talent renders his stains
more visible, wallowing in outrageous profligacy,
814—840 murdering his nephew Chilperic the son of Cha-
613.
576—584. ribert to secure his spoil: — Brunhilda, sister,
mother and grandmother of Kings, torn to pieces
by wild horses, and her grandchildren slain by the
second Clothaire :—Chilperic concurring in the
575 assassination of his brother Sigebert :—encouraged by Fredegonda in those dire inflictions of
torture which caused him to be named the Nero
of the Franks, and perishing by the murderous
devices of that same Fredegonda:—Clothaire the
first and Childebert, brothers, incestuous, merciless, warring against each other, and then uniting
526. in the butchery of their nephews, the infant sons
of their brother Clodomir; he, Clothaire, stabbing
the imploring children, dashing them to the ground
as they shriek for mercy, causing his own son,
560. Chramnus, his wife and children, to be burnt
alive, and, stricken himself by death on the year
and the day after that day of horror.—Clovis, the
founder of the monarchy, pre-eminent in deceit
and ferocity ; consolidating his dominion by the
luxury of treachery and crime, planning the destruction of his own relations, like the hunstman
surrounding his prey, enjoying equally the sport
497—510. and the slaughter, causing the death of Sigebert by
the hands of his own son Cloderic, and entrapping
the parricide to destruction : King Chararic slain,
King Ragnacharius slain, King Richarius slain,

King Rignomer slain, Theodoric slain, Guntheric slain—all the members of the Merovingian race extirpated, until Clovis, standing alone amidst the corpses, becomes the sole representative of the lineage. All the previous long-haired Kings, all their kindred exterminated by him in whom the Franks exult as their glory.

§ 19. SMITTEN by their own iniquities, the Merovingians had passed away, they had received their chastisement; but, if turning from the contemplation of that race, Louis studied the deeds of his ancestors, weighed their own responsibilities, investigated his own title and judged his own claim to the throne, his conscience must have been equally grieved, and his mind even more disturbed.

Time was beginning to sanction the possession of authority: three generations had succeeded, yet each was saddened by remorse. If Louis recollected his brother Pepin, it was as a proclaimed rebel against their father Charlemagne, a prisoner who had wasted away in the Monastery of Pruhm, apparently a parricide in intent; and if Pepin was in any wise rendered excusable by their father's conduct towards the repudiated Himeltruda, this extenuation only inflicted another and additional pang. Furthermore, how had Charlemagne dealt with his own infant nephews, who could tell how the *parvuli* had disappeared?

741—987

814—840

When Louis consulted the great Charter by which Charlemagne had divided his Empire, the words read like a record of condemnation— *placuit nobis præcipere, ut nullus eorum per quaslibet occasiones, quemlibet ex illis apud se accusatum, sine justa discussione atque examinatione, aut occidere, aut membris mancare, aut excæcare, aut invitum tondere faciat*—Charlemagne and Carloman, and Pepin-le-bref had all transgressed the precepts of benignity and justice thus dictated. Charlemagne collected the future from the past: he anticipated that his descendants would commit the crimes of which he and his brother and his father had given them the precedents, vainly endeavouring to fence against evil by a phrase. So it fares with the Testator and his counsel, the memory of the speaker and his words effaced by his bequest, or, more affrontingly, remembered only as nullities—the delusions of the Tombstone and the Grave.

Ascend a grade higher in the family history: no resting-place of comfort could Louis find there—Carloman his uncle, and his own grandsire Pepin, cruelly persecuting their brother Gripho from youth to adolescence, from adolescence till death—Charles Martel, henceforward to be honoured as their heroic founder, how was he to be appreciated, according to conscience or to law?—Louis derived his authority through predecessors who gradually established themselves by a usurpation of the most odious 741—987 complexion; the sly dependant defrauding his patron; servants bearing rule over their masters; 814—840 ministers stealing away the confidence of the people from their Sovereign, a dominion grounded upon domestic treachery and disloyalty. Each Majordomus, each Mayor of the Palace, justified the improvement of his opportunities by the example of his predecessors. These Mayors of the Palace were not all of the same race, but they all pursued the same scheme, until the Merovingian dynasty was finally subverted by the people pronouncing sentence against a lineage, who, through their accumulated depravities, their sloth, their follies, had forfeited the throne.

§ 20. THEOLOGIANS have been accustomed to remark that there is no such thing as a new heresy: every erroneous doctrine, apparently new, say they, is only the repetition of an earlier error, brought forth under a new aspect, expressed more clearly or more obscurely, the venom enfeebled or more mortiferous, offered with some slight modification, or may be with none. In the main, the proposition is incontestable, yet incompletely enounced: it must not be confined to the dogmas of theology nor employed invidiously, but extended to all the doctrines and opinions, salutary or mischievous, sound or unsound, right or wrong, of the human mind. It is a universal intellectual proposition. Physiological science

Revolutionary opinions, their antiquity in France.

741—987 has ascertained, almost to the astonishment of
the observers, that notwithstanding all the varie-
814—840 ties of the children of Adam, their contrasts
of colour or differences in conformation, mould
of skull or shape of bone, or even in the texture
of tissues or membranes, their blood is identical. Amongst all the millions and millions of
mankind, the elements, proportions and magni-
tudes of serum and globule, the fluid and solid
composing the mysterious vehicle of life, present
an absolutely invariable and homogeneous unity;
the blood is one; and the life-blood is the type
of the living soul.

Whatever may be either the advantages which
the inbreathed spirit receives from physical causes
or moral relations, or the disadvantages resulting
from these bonds, our intellectual nature is also
invariable and homogeneous.   Whatever man
has thought, man will think: whatever he now
imagines he has imagined. Man's imaginations
may be translated into various dialects, but however multifarious in nomenclature they convey
the same meaning; there neither is nor can be
anything new under the sun. It is a hazardous
encomium to claim for any thought or invention
the merit of originality: a very uncertain mode
of bestowing praise; but far more hazardous to rail
at any political doctrine or dogma as an innovation. Oxford Convocation condemned as impious
the doctrine of the popular origin of royal autho-

rity. Did her Heads of houses recollect that the 741—987
political philosophy of Locke had been previously
taught by Hooker; and how much earlier?—Take 814—840
the following uncomplimentary portraiture of the
model King. It is not quoted from Mirabeau
or Lafayette, but from the *Roman de la Rose*.

> Lors convint que l'en esgardàt
> Aucun qui les loyes gardât,
> Et qui les maufeiteurs preist
> Et droit as plaintifz en feist,
> Ne nuls ne l'osast contredire,
> Lors s'assemblerent pour élire.
> Ung grant vilain entre eus eslurent
> Le plus ossu de quanqu'il furent,
> Le plus corsu et le greignor
> Si le firent prince et seignor.

§ 21. WHILST we assert the continuity of an- Doctrines of Divine
cient and modern principle, there is nevertheless right and popular
a wide diversity in modes of argument. Locke origin of Monarchy.
stands in the zone of intellectual progress which
connects and yet separates the ancient and the
modern reasoners: the former, however contradictory their doctrines or discrepant in their
Creeds, substantially agreed in supporting their
inductions by an appeal to Holy Scriptures. Too
often have the advocates of that doctrine, which,
in the language of our political philosophy is
termed the "Divine right of Kings," been swerved
by self-interested adulation: their opponents by
faction and self-will. Nevertheless, whilst admitting and deploring these wrestings of truth,
the greater part of the mutually antagonistic

741—987 advocates must be equally named with reverence :
814—840 few without respect. Nor should we harshly
censure those, who, enveloped in the calamities
of their times, boldly asserted their principles by
appealing to the sword.

Let us refrain from hard words against Roundhead or Cavalier, Papist or Protestant, Covenanter
or Royalist, Whigamore or Tory.—Piety, zeal,
intelligence, sincerity, employed in the investigation of questions so vitally important to human
society, courage exerted, suffering endured, death
faced on the field or welcomed on the scaffold,
torture, poverty, exile, contumely, all braved in
defence of loyalty or liberty, faith or nationality,
should have moderated even the rancour of an
enemy. Nor would it be difficult to allay the
miserable and besetting bitterness of political and
theological antipathies, an affliction to those who
entertain it and a snare to their consciences,
seducing them into worse errors than the mis-
deeds they reprobate, could we, but for once, cast
ourselves into the heart and mind of the men
whose destiny has compelled them to take a side
in any civil dissension, when the conflict becomes
practical in human society. How idle, how
thoughtless, how cruel, are then such bandied
terms as "base servility" or "unnatural treason."
Are the lacerations of feeling which the duty of
making a choice under such exigencies imposes,
adequately appreciated by the fortunate who are

spared the pangs?—Do we sufficiently feel the _{741—987}
blessing of not having been Englishmen when
the royal standard was unfurled at Nottingham— _{814—840}
not having been Scotsmen when Charles Edward
landed—not having been Irishmen of the Irish
after the battle of the Boyne?

§ 22.   THE DOCTRINE of the "Divine right of Kings," has been rendered, in a manner, odious from its illogical, and let us be permitted to add, erroneous connexion with the doctrine of uncon-ditional submission, whilst another misapprehen-sion, equally fruitful in rancour and discord, arises from the circumstance that the same truth may be so presented as to convey entirely contradictory meanings.   Supposing you wish to exemplify to a child the form of convexity, and for that purpose you trace a curved line on the paper before you, it will answer your intent; but you may equally employ the same curved line to suggest the idea of concavity : the curvature is concave or convex as you look to it on this side or on that side.   Point to the segment of the circle on the right side, it is convex, on the left it is concave.   It is one and the other, both or either—the truth of your assertion depends upon the position of your finger or the glance of your eye.   The apparently oppo-site doctrines of the derivation of monarchy from divine right, and the foundation of monarchy upon popular assent, are one and the same,— divine, if you look up to Heaven, earthly, if you

741—987 view the monarch amongst his equals before God,
from whose obedience, working out a counsel
814—810 which is not their own, royal authority obtains
its existence.

The mutual obligations of rulers and people
are taught in that Book which teaches all other
duties; but the precepts which require justice
and righteousness from the Sovereign, are no
less emphatic than the precepts enjoining reverence and obedience to the subject; equally
stringent on both. The tyrannical sovereign
shares the sin of the subject whom he provokes
to resistance; the perverse subject, the guilt of
the sovereign whom he tempts to illegal tyranny.
No fair reasoning can extort from Holy Writ
the condemnation of any of the various modes
through which government is exercised as an
ordinance. No exclusive sanction is given to
individual monarchy. However appointed or
constituted, the powers that be receive their
delegation from the same Source, a delegation
equally imparted to the ostentatious simplicity of
democracy and to the purple canopy and golden
crown. All govern by the grace of God, however
that grace may be misused, however obstinately
its very existence may be denied. Though you
expunge the acknowledgment from the Monarch's
style, it continues written in the eternal Charter.
But to designate any one form of civil government as the sole medium of Divine Right, thereby

refusing that sanction to all others, is a pre- 741—987
sumption which has disparaged Divine Truth,
and tempted the people to suspect that Faith 814—840
is invoked invidiously and craftily, for the purpose of aiding the policy of man. The teaching of our Churchmen has too often destroyed
the impressions of their sincerity. A Sextipartite
Homily against wilful rebellion, unbalanced by
a single text of warning to the rulers, betrays
the cause of lawful authority.

Nevertheless, it must be acknowledged that
monarchy, hereditary according to primogeniture,
the elder preferred before the younger, appears
more conformable to the spirit of the Divine
Law than democratic institutions. The pre-
eminences and rights given to the first-born, the
promise that, as a reward, dominion shall be
continued to children and children's children,
support this opinion. Moreover, strict hereditary
succession takes the nomination of the ruler
entirely out of man's hand; for this institution renders the agency of man subservient to the irrevocable past, leaving, as far as human will can be
said to possess the power of assent, the appointment to the Supreme Disposer of events. And,
practically, men feel it a mercy to be exonerated
from the labour of exercising such a power of
appointment. No theory can be more plausible
than that of election, yet, in the long run, this
theory always fails: nations are tired out by it,

741—987
814—819
they abandon the responsibility. As far as History is known, all democracies,—that is to say, the absolutism of the majority over the minority—all elective Sovereignties, with few apparent but no real exceptions, ultimately ruin the Commonwealth, or condense themselves into hereditary sovereignty.

Difficulties of the position of Louis upon his accession.

§ 23. CONTEMPLATING his affairs simply as a Statesman, putting conscience out of the question, the political difficulties encompassing Louis-le-débonnaire were manifold: they wrapped him round. Whatever precedents he could find in past history,—and more useful teachers than his Orosius and his Saint Augustine, no Monarch could have enjoyed—they only encreased his perplexity. The new and yet crumbling Carlovingian Empire was destitute of any constitutional principles to which you could appeal even in theoretical discussion. It was an untapestried Hall; the bowing walls freshly built with untempered mortar. There was no approximation to any code or canon, whereby the descent, transmission or acquisition of supreme authority could be regulated. Popular assent seemed to be almost the only principle definitely enounced. Try to discover any certainty from their annals.—

No Canon of inheritance established in the Carlovingian Empire.

Had any son the right to represent his father? Was there any privilege attached to primogeniture? any prerogative given to seniority? and if so, did the right or preference die with the party

or pass on to his progeny? And here Louis-le- _{741—987}
débonnaire was driven upon the practical question,
Could King Bernard, the son of Pepin, his elder _{814—819}
brother, be deprived of Pepin's rights?   Was not
Bernard the lawful successor to the supremacy,
either in right of seniority or as the ruler of Italy?
Was Rome to be subservient to Aix-la-Chapelle?
and to whom did Rome's sovereignty appertain?
Had the Duchy of Rome reverted to the Kingdom ^{Imperial}
of Italy, or was it annexed to the Imperial title? ^{Louis}
Louis took the Crown from off the Altar : the ^{dubious.}
Franks shouted *Vivat Imperator Ludovicus!*
but was he really Emperor?   Could Charlemagne
of his own authority empower Louis to assume
the Imperial diadem?   The very foundation of
the *Emperor* Charlemagne's authority was the
previous recognition of the *Patrician* Charlemagne by the Roman people; and when he received the diadem from the Pontiff, Leo spoke
equally as the representative of the *gens togata*,
the worthless, though legitimate inheritors of
the Eternal City, and as the spiritual head of
Western Christendom.

But there were deeper griefs and more
gnawing.   Could Louis prognosticate the destiny
preparing for his three sons? the eldest, Lothair,
a youth, the youngest, Louis, a mere child.   How
could he secure to them their share of dominion?
nay more, their liberty, their lives?   Louis-le-
débonnaire entertained a morbid anticipation of

741—987 early death, and were his children to be left to
their cousin King Bernard's mercies?

814—819   Whatever way Louis reasoned concerning himself, his family, or his sovereignty, he only argued
in a circle which brought him back to uncertainty.   If the Frankish Sovereign possessed an
indefeasible right, then his own ancestors were
usurpers; but if the Sovereigns were amenable
to the nation, then the proud, the versatile, the
treacherous Franks, the ruling and predominant
caste, might at any time, upon cause pretended
or found, make him share the fate of the last
Merovingians.   Charles Martel had been accepted
as the *gros vilain*, able to keep the peace; but
if he, Louis, failed, or was thought to fail, why
should not the Franks look out for another *gros
vilain*, whose thews and sinews would be more
adequate to the duty required; and those who
might organize the revolution were close at hand.
Upon the highest steps of the estrade, next to
the throne itself, there stood the Senator of the
Senators, the Administrator of the realm, another
Major-domus, a descendant of Charles Martel,
with Charles Martel's energy,—Count Wala; and
he, supported by his brother Adelhard, the rigid,
stern and inflexible enforcer of justice   Louis,
distrustful of his own judgment, always ended by
being at the disposal of his advisers, and his chief
adviser, Hermengarda, his wife, his Queen.

Without accusers, without witnesses, without

trial, without any definite charge, contrary to the
rights of the Frankish nobles, the privileges of
the Church or natural equity, Louis, yielding to
the counsellors who abused his confidence, caused
Abbot Adelhard to be arrested, and sent to the
island of Hero or Hermoutier, off the coast of
Poitou, below the estuary of the Loire, where he
was kept in vile captivity. Count Wala was seized,
compelled to become a monk, and thrust into
the cloister of Corbey, and his wife, the daughter
of Count William of Toulouse, from whom he
was thus separated, also confined in a monastery.
There is some difficulty in ascertaining her name,
but it seems that she was afterwards cruelly
drowned as a witch in the Saône. The other
members of the family were involved in the same
proscription; Bernard or Bernarius, the younger
brother, transported as a convict to the island
of Lerins in the Mediterranean, and their sister
Gundreda, a lady of the Royal Household, enforced to take the veil. The persecution of such
harmless individuals shows the panic fear by
which Louis-le-débonnaire was possessed.

§ 24. Sore repentance, sore punishment was
he preparing for himself; and whilst adopting
these measures, which accumulated sorrows instead of removing troubles, he began to take
counsel for the administration of the Empire.
Further perplexities. How was he to deal with
his sons? Lothair, audacious and hard, Pepin rest-

741—987

814—819
Banish-
ment of
Count
Wala and
his brother
Adelhard,
&c

814
First par-
tition of
the Empire
made by
Louis-le-
débon-
naire.

711—987
814—819

less, Louis scarcely formed : he feared them as future rivals, yet loved them tenderly. If he gave them authority, they might rise up against him ; if he did not, how was their succession to be confirmed? If he did not apportion their lots, they would quarrel for their share, and if he did, would they abide by his decision? The long-continued practice of the Frankish dynasties, as well as the absolute necessity of providing for local government, compelled him, however, to plan a partition, even as his father had done.

The Franks were very proud of their nationality, glorious in their Empire's unity and dignity. In their minds Charlemagne had become, and not unduly, the personification of the Commonwealth. "*L'Etat, c'est moi,*" is not a vain or insolent assertion of despotism, but simply the expressed consciousness of the mission bestowed upon the individual who obtains the mastery over society. The magic influence of Charlemagne maintained the unity of the Empire during his life, but the spell was breaking : the regalia of Charlemagne were amulets losing their charm under an adverse constellation.

Louis-le-débonnaire proceeded with caution. Italy belonged to the son of the elder Pepin, King Bernard, whose fealty he had received—the nephew, confirmed by his uncle's authority. He could therefore only deal with the territories on his side the Alps. Lothair received the ancient

Baier-land and its dependencies, extending from
Valtellina to the Northgau: Pepin repaired to
his father's kingdom of Aquitaine: the appanage
of Louis, the youngest, was postponed. Upon his
aspiring sons, Louis-le-débonnaire bestowed the
titles of Kings, yet scarcely intending to impart
any royal power. He contemplated that they
should be merely interposed between him and
the Counts or Dukes of the Empire as Imperial
Vicars; but in this position they had full opportunity of making friends, acquiring supporters,
forming parties. Prelates, nobles and people
courted the young Princes; and Lothair and
Pepin, thus prematurely advanced, while their
father was prematurely declining, never receded
from the vantage ground they had gained.

§ 25. According to the policy indicated by his
ancestors, Louis ought to have proceeded Rome-
wards : the fealty of the Roman people, rendered
to Pepin-le-bref and Charlemagne, was equally
required to testify their acceptance of Louis as
the legitimate successor of the Cæsars ; and their
acclamation needed to be confirmed by the Pontiff
bestowing the Imperial diadem. Louis-le-débonnaire was not really and fully acknowledged as
Emperor. Many studiously and stiffly spoke of
King Louis and Queen Hermengarda. The Romans had conspired against Pope Leo: the patricians rebelled against him : some say they sought
his death, threatening a repetition of the violences

Side notes:
741—987
814—819 Portions assigned to Lothair and to Pepin, being the first par-tition made by Louis-le-débon-naire.

Confirma-tion of the Imperial authority needed by Louis-le-débon-naire.

815—816 Transac-tions at Rome — rebellion against Pope Leo III.

P 2

from which he had been rescued by Charlemagne. There is scarcely any period during the middle ages wherein the aspirations of Rienzi do not appear. Temporal sovereignty in the modern sense, the Pope of Rome, hedged in by imperial authority and popular rights, did not possess, even fully admitting the grants of Saint Peter's patrimony; but he had the greatest pre-eminence in the Republic: not more than properly belonged to his functions and station, yet exciting recalcitrations and jealousies. Some of the conspirators

815. 816
Transac-
tions at
Rome —
Death of
Leo III.
Accession
of Stephen
IV
were condemned to death. The Romans invoked the protection of the proclaimed Emperor, so also the Pontiff: it was natural that he should seek to be helped by the son of his ancient patron Charlemagne.

The intervention of Louis-le-débonnaire, practically effected by King Bernard, restored tranquillity. Leo died in the course of the year—a very diligent, useful, and magnificent Pontiff. He employed the bountiful gifts received from Charlemagne in rebuilding and adorning many Churches: he surrounded the Sanctuary of St. Peter's with a balustrade of solid silver, and decorated the windows with variously-coloured glass, the first notice of this adornment, probably derived from Arabian art.

Leo was succeeded by Stephen the Fourth. Like his predecessor, Stephen had been educated from his earliest youth in the Lateran palace:

trained, in a manner, for the Popedom: and Leo 741—987 had designated him as most worthy of the dignity. The Clergy, Nobles and Citizens of 814—819 Rome accepted the recommendation of the departed Pontiff, and unanimously elected Stephen. Though well supported by their suffrages, he earnestly sought the friendship of Louis; and soon after his consecration, he induced the Roman people to acknowledge Louis as Emperor and render due allegiance. Legates appeared at the Frankish Court, the distant Aix-la-Chapelle, bearing a grateful message: the Pontiff would undertake a journey such as but one Pope had hitherto performed—he would cross the Alps, and invest the son of Charlemagne with the Imperial Crown.

816.
Pope Stephen
crosses the
Alps:—
Louis and
Hermengarda
crowned by
him at
Rheims.

At Rheims, where Clovis had been baptized, the highest dignity of Western Christendom was to be bestowed upon the representative of the lineage which had devoured the Merovingians. Stephen came accompanied by a large train of the Roman Clergy. The ceremony was performed in the great Basilica of Saint Remigius, before the Shrine now encircled by the Statues of the Dozepeers, the memorials of Charlemagne's legendary grandeur.

Stephen placed the imperial Crown on the head of Louis: this ratification of the inchoate dignity had been promised; but the affectionate pride of the husband received an unexpected

741—987 gratification. Hermengarda, kneeling before the
Pontiff, was also invested with the diadem: no
814—819 such honour had ever been bestowed upon a consort of Charlemagne. They were hailed as Augustus and Augusta;—Stephen gave his benediction
and departed; and Louis hastened to the forests
of Compiègne. The fame of his coronation spread.

Louis-le-débonnaire Ambassadors from the East, swarthy represen-
receives tatives of the Caliph Abdelrahman, renewing the
Embassies from the Caliph, the friendly intercourse begun by Haroun Alraschid,
Eastern Empire, the vied with the nations of the West in testifying
Slavi:— Danes seek that they acknowledged him as worthily suc-
his aid. ceeding to his father's honours. The Court
removed to the Pfaltz, the Palace of Aix-
la-Chapelle. Encreasing splendour environs the
Emperor:—a splendid embassy from Constantinople,—Nicephorus compliments his Imperial
brother:—the Dalmatian Slavi crave his aid:—
still more significant of his reputation, the very
Danes, whose vessels had threatened the Empire,
entreat his assistance and alliance.—The sons of
the Godfrey who contended against Charlemagne
had expelled Harold the King of Jutland: both
the competitors invoked the Imperial authority,
and the exile Harold—of whom we shall soon
hear more,—was supported by Louis-le-débon-

Further anxieties naire.
of Louis—
Church- § 26. In the conduct pursued by Louis
affairs — settlement against Adelhard and Wala we obtain an indica-
of the succession. tion of the developement which his character was

sustaining, exemplified affectingly and mourn- 741—987
fully throughout the subsequent course of his history : a conflict between an awakened conscience 814—819
and the duties and temptations of station, a
mind energetic in action, weak in deliberation,
fully appreciating the dignity and sanctity of
authority, but not always able to sustain that
dignity, thwarted, misled and betrayed by those
who surrounded him. Pure in morals, Louis was
unable to correct his licentious Court and dis-
orderly household. When he banished his sisters
and their lovers from the Palace, a domestic
insurrection ensued. Count Lambert, probably :
the Lambert who afterwards became Count of
the Armorican Marches, was wounded ; the para-
mours were driven away : one lost his eyes ; but
the punishment of the individuals did not ame-
liorate society.

Ecclesiastical affairs were in great disorder. Ecclesiastical affairs
As King, as Emperor, Louis-le-débonnaire was
fully bound to co-operate in their amendment;
for what Finance is in our days, Church-prin-
ciples were then—the mainspring in the general
policy of Christendom. Three hundred and
more years had elapsed since the institution of
monachism in the Western Church by Saint Benedict. The Order had spread widely during this
long period : their political importance and riches
had wonderfully encreased : the restraints were
slipping away, and they were degenerating ra-

741—987

814—819

Need at this period of Monastic reforms.

pidly from their primitive earnestness and simplicity. Destined to do great things, to preserve uncorrupted much of the salt of the earth, to promote the welfare of man and the glory of God, their decline was stayed, and amidst and through many trials, a season of revival at length ensued, distinguished by true wisdom and holy energy.

The Mediæval Church, a reforming Church.

The general healthiness of the mediæval Church is evinced by her unremitting endeavours to extirpate abuses. Every Council was a rebuke to the irregularities, laxities, vices and crimes of clergy and laity. It was essentially the character of the Latin or Western Church to be a reforming Church, never, during the middle ages, content to settle upon the lees. Not always acting wisely, not always temperately, not always consistently—sometimes slack, sometimes over-rigid ; never preventing backsliding ;—yet renewing her strength, and persevering in zeal and faithfulness ;—for even as it is with individuals, that the just man may fall seven times and rise again, so is it with Churches.

Though his power be not susceptible of any exact definition, Charlemagne virtually acted as the head or governor of the Gallican and German Churches ; his good sense and talent contributed to diminish the evils resulting from the confusion of temporal and spiritual power. He was the directing spirit of ecclesiastical legislation. Louis-le-débonnaire followed his example, and con-

sidered that in every way he was bound to take
as much upon himself as his father had done.
A rigid reformer had arisen, earnest and devout—
Saint Benedict of Aniana.   Louis sought to obtain
his co-operation in the restoration of monastic
discipline.   Many of the monks were assimilating
themselves to regular Canons, multiplying themselves into Congregations or Colleges, in which,
claiming the immunities of the regular Clergy,
they might indulge in pleasures and good cheer,
fare better in the Refectory, sport more freely
in the field.   Louis was very intent upon rectify-
ing these secularities; neither could he abide to
see his Bishops riding up and down with rich
gold belts and gem-decked daggers, splendid man-
tles flowing from their shoulders, and long gilt
spurs protruding from their heels.

There was another abuse, which may be considered either as social or ecclesiastical, against
which Louis strove.   It was truly the pride of
the Christian Church to repudiate any distinction
of rank or blood—all walls of separation broken
down,—all men, whatever might be their race or
descent, their rank or condition, bond or free,
equally eligible to her ministry, equally susceptible of a Priesthood, not inheritable in families,
but accessible to all mankind.

But when clerical privileges were recognized
and established by the State, it became needful
that in certain cases the State should inter-

741—987

814—819

Equality,
the privi-
lege of the
Church.
The Priest-
hood open
to all.

711—987

814—819

fere to prevent their perversion. A Clerk was exempted from all secular jurisdiction. Hence, according to the Imperial Constitutions, the magistrates of towns, the *Curiales*, could not, unless permitted to resign their office, take Holy Orders, because by so doing, they were released from the onerous obligations which their station imposed. —A *Miles*, for the like reason, could not receive Holy Orders, and thus discharge himself from the army:—a Crown debtor was under the like incapacity, until his debt was cleared, for as a member of the Hierarchy, he was no longer obnoxious to process:—neither could a serf, still less a slave, without the consent of the lord or master, because the services of the one and the person of the other belonged to that lord or master.

This was the legal theory; but in practice it was very much modified by the national conscience : Church and State co-operated in mitigating the harshness of such exclusions, and particularly with respect to servile Clerks. Sometimes the law provided that if a Serf was admitted into a monastery, his lord might be compensated by having two Serfs given him in the stead of the one who had been liberated by the tonsure. So also, if a Serf was shorn or entered a Monastery, the lord was barred by a year's non-claim; and the prevailing opinion set so strongly against these restrictions that they were little regarded. Holy orders conferred

upon a serf were only voidable, not void. The 741—987
serf-clerk continued a clerk till degraded by
canonical proceedings, and that upon a compe- 814—819
tent complaint preferred, within a limited period.
Charlemagne expressly encouraged the ordination
of the servile classes, and very large numbers
were received into the ranks of the hierarchy.—In
this lies the great fact of the disputes technically
called the disputes between the two swords, that
the French hierarchy had become, in the main,
a *roturier* hierarchy.

The Franks, whatever might be their Church- Jealousy
principles generally, entertained a haughty aris- against
tocratic aversion to the plebeian races, and the servile
better born Clergy cherished a great jealousy origin
against Clergy of servile origin. A priest or
monk of pure Frankish blood was often inclined
to look very scornfully upon the clerk whose
peasant parents were to be sought amongst the
Gaulish villainage. He approximated closely
in sentiment to a Philadelphia minister of any
religious denomination, who talks beautifully
about the love he bears towards his sable brother, his fellow-labourer in the vineyard, but
who will not allow the coloured preacher so
much as standing room in his church, chapel
or tabernacle. Louis-le-débonnaire was grieved Louis
at this prejudice: he testified constantly against gainst this
it. He did all in his power to encourage jealousy.
the " *wicked custom*," the "*pessima consuetudo*,"
of disregarding the stain of servitude A signal

711—987

814—819

example of his earnestness was presented in the case of his foster-brother Ebbo, who, being a thorough bred villein, *ex originalium servorum stirpe*, was through his influence promoted to the highest ecclesiastical dignity in the Gauls, the Archbishoprick of Rheims.

The appointment was most unexceptionable.— When Gislemar, who had been elected by the people of Rheims as their Archbishop, came to his book before the examining Bishops, he could scarcely read a line,—he was therefore rejected. Louis then proposed Ebbo, a man distinguished, notwithstanding his low birth, by his noble aspect and fine and well cultivated talent, and he was chosen upon this recommendation, without which it is probable that his merit would not have influenced the electors. In this instance the Sovereign did not exceed the powers which, as a member of the Church, he might fairly claim: his assistance turned the scale.

§ 27. The paucity and inaccuracy of observers, and still more the loss of observations, should teach us caution in our reasonings concerning the natural appearances of antiquity; nevertheless, taking into consideration those very circumstances by which our evidence is rendered so defective and scanty, it is indisputable that the cosmical phenomena occurring in the period commencing with the Fall of the Roman Empire and terminating about the period of the Crusades, were singularly remarkable and abundant.

Cosmical phæno- mena fre- quent dur- ing the dark ages, &c.

Great atmospheric and terrestrial commotions 741—987
prevailed during the reign of Louis-le-débonnaire,
accompanied by famines and epidemic diseases. 814—819
Showers of aerolithes, comets and upheavings
of the soil, perplexed and astounded the nations
The thermal springs of Aix-la-Chapelle which we
behold steaming, boiling, bursting through the
strata, indicate the volcanic energies below.—
These agencies were then more lively.—Earthquakes were frequent in that district —The whole
country adjoining was afflicted, and during this
generation the city of Aix-la-Chapelle was repeatedly disturbed and endangered by the concussions: so violent that the Palace was partly
ruined, and the golden globes adorning the Byzantine cupolas cast down, whilst the loud and
prolonged groanings which resounded from the
depths, increased the terror. Louis-le-débonnaire
was not appalled by omens: he considered the
servile or gentile dread of comet or star as for-
bidden by Holy Writ—nevertheless he was encouraged by Holy Writ to ponder upon such signs
and tokens as messages of wrath or warning.
They depressed his spirit, and they continued
many a year.

The Imperial Coronation at Rheims, the Anxieties
concerning
splendid pageantry, the obedience, apparently so the succession
willing and spontaneous, rendered to his Imperial
authority, had failed to restore comfort. Louis-
le-débonnaire continued to be harassed by trou-

741—987

814—819

bles; his family, his nobles, his people were all dissatisfied, and their grudges and anxieties reflected back upon him. The governments assigned to Lothair and Pepin looked precarious. Hermengarda might doubt whether any certain provision had been made for her sons: no lot was assigned by Louis to his namesake, his youngest boy, his *æquivocus*, as he called him. An irksome desire prevailed in the Imperial Court, not openly acknowledged, but certainly felt, to regain Italy. The Imperial succession still continued undetermined, and though Louis was under forty years of age, a universal apprehension prevailed, lest he might be cut off by sudden death.

§ 28. Louis preferred keeping Lent at Aixla-Chapelle. The site of the Pfaltz is still indicated by one picturesque fragment: a lofty wall, decorated at the summit by a graceful range of Gothic arcades, containing Statues of Emperors and Kings.

The approach to this palace from the Cathedral led through a long timber-gallery, such as we often see in ancient continental Castles, though rarely in England. It was on Good-

817.
April 10.

Louis-le-débonnaire in danger of losing his life by the fall of the palace gallery.

Friday when Louis and his train, returning from the offices of the solemn day, were passing along this corridor, that it gave way. The beams, it is said, were decayed; but this can hardly have been the case, for the building had been erected by Charlemagne, and it is most probable that the

collapse resulted from some previous disturbance 741—987
of the unstable soil. Many of the courtiers who
accompanied Louis were killed : all hurt, Louis 814—819
less grievously than others, yet very seriously.
Leech and chirurgeon took him in hand. Months
elapsed before his soundness was regained, and
though his corporeal recovery ensued, the shock
had deeply affected his mind. The accident
rendered the probability of death palpably sensible ; and he determined to settle the affairs of
his family and Empire on such a basis as might
ensure peace and tranquillity.

The Diet, the great Council of the Empire, 817
July
the Convention of Bishops and Abbots, Counts The Great
and Nobles, the Senate of the Franks, Clergy and Council at
Aix-la-
Laity, assembled at Aix-la-Chapelle in sunny July. Chapelle.
Solemn and joyous, these meetings, which par-
took equally of the nature of Parliaments and
Councils, were usually summoned at Whitsuntide,
so as to leave the summer vacation untouched
for such sports as the pleasant season afforded,
lake or river, garden or green-wood shade. The
Session therefore at this unusual period shows
the length of time which had elapsed before the
health of Louis was sufficiently restored. In this
Council various important Capitulars were enacted, some purely concerning ecclesiastical affairs,
others mixed : amongst them a complete and
very stringent code for the government, discipline
and correction of the canonical order.

741—987

814—819
817

Second partition of the Empire made by Louis-le-débonnaire Motion made in the Assembly for the settlement of the succession

However much the need of removing all uncertainties concerning the succession might press upon the mind of Louis, he shrunk from a decision, until the Council suddenly, and to him unexpectedly, demanded that he should follow the example of his progenitors, and provide for the succession of the realm. Louis, startled and disturbed, required time for deliberation; three days were employed in almsgiving and prayer. That the proposition so brought forward originated amongst the earnest partisans of the young princes, is as unquestionable, as it is impossible to ascertain which or who were the leaders in the movement.—By the unanimous voice and election of the Senate, Louis assenting, Lothair was declared his father's consort and successor in the Empire. Louis placed the Imperial Crown upon the head of his Son— " *Vivat Imperator Lotharius,*" shouted the joyous multitude, whilst Pepin and Louis, the first hitherto called king by courtesy, both received the Royal title by a decree of the assembly.

Lothair declared Emperor

Portion of the realm assigned to Pepin.

PEPIN continued to hold Aquitaine ; but the realm sustained various alterations in boundary : only a portion of Septimania, which had hitherto been conjoined with Aquitaine, was retained by him, namely the county of Carcassonne. On the north, the frontier was also somewhat contracted, but the loss was compensated by a dismemberment of Cisjurane Burgundy, three counties—

Autun, towering in Roman magnificence : smiling
Nevers, and dreary Avalon, where every stone
appears stamped with vestiges of once animated
nature.

Louis the younger obtained "Baioaria," taken 817.
Portions
from Lothair, and all her dependencies, annexed assigned to
Louis-le-
by alliance or conquest :—the fertile valleys of Germanique.
the Ems, the wide margraviates, the marches,
lands and kingdoms overspread by Sclavonian
tribes, Wilzians, Carinthians, Bohemians, and
Avars, were all subjected to his Crown. Such
was the compact and powerful Kingdom given
to Louis, whom the French historians usually
style *Louis-le-Germanique*, and whom we shall
so designate hereafter. His Kingdom, however,
may be best identified if we consider it as nearly
corresponding to the whole existing Austrian
Empire north of the Alps; together with modern
Bavaria, the Grisons, and a large portion of the
pristine Burgundian territories which now compose the Helvetic confederacy, and, pre-eminent
therein, that nursery of dynasties, the County of
Altorf.

Lothair, the firstborn, the Emperor, had not
any portion distinctly assigned to him. What his
brothers did not hold, would become his in
domain; but there is a special and stringent
direction that the Kingdom of Italy, Bernard's The
younger
Kingdom, was in all things to be obedient to him. brothers to
be depend-
Pepin and Louis once in each year were to ent on
the senior

741—987
814—819
appear before the throne of their elder brother, lovingly and fraternally, bearing the gifts, the acknowledgments of his superiority; but he, Lothair, is on his part exhorted to treat them with brotherly regard. The Kings were not to declare war or conclude peace otherwise than with the *senior's* assent. No further subdivision of the Empire was to ensue. In case of the death of any brother, such one of his sons alone was to succeed as the people should elect; should he die without issue, the Kingdom was to revert to the Empire. Thus the provisions asserted the great principle of Imperial unity, and implied that the Imperial diadem was to be hereditary in Lothair's line; three Kingdoms, Bavaria, Aquitaine, and Italy, being appendant to the Imperial dignity.

The *Charta Divisionis* was sealed by Louis to the foregoing effect,—his second partition of the Empire—a legislative as well as constitutional act, binding the parent and the children, and rendering the State the guardian equally of the rights of succession, and of the conditions upon which these rights were to be enjoyed.

817
The *Charta divisionis:*—its ambiguities

§ 29. This Charter, however, is neither clear nor complete. Some provisions are obscure: some important cases are not provided for, whether by accident or intent is uncertain—whilst the most important features, the extent, nature, and transmission of Lothair's supremacy, seem faintly sketched by a trembling hand. Read such clauses as the following:—" Pepinum et Hludowicum æquivocum nostrum, communi consilio placuit regiis insignire nominibus, et loca inferius denominata constituere, in quibus post decessum nostrum sub *seniore* fratre regali potestate potiantur. —Volumus ut semel in anno, tempore opportuno, de his quæ necessaria sunt, mutuo fraterno amore tractandi gratiâ, ad *seniorem fratrem* cum donis suis veniant.—Item volumus ut nec pacem nec bellum contra exteras nationes, absque consilio et consensu *senioris fratris* ullatenus suscipere præsumant.—Si absque legitimis liberis aliquis eorum decesserit, potestas illius ad *seniorem fratrem* revertatur,"—the word *senior* being employed in other chapters as absolutely designating the lord of a Vassal, without any reference to kindred or age.

Even in private life, if much importance be assigned to such precedencies or pre-eminences, an ill-defined headship in a family is singularly productive of ill-will and rancour. How much more fraught with evil in an Empire.—It is hardly possible, or rather it is impossible, in the passages above quoted from the charter, to distinguish between the relative duties resulting from *seniority* in the natural sense, and *seignory* in the legal sense. According to the fashion of writing then in use, the scribe could not help

2 2

741—987
814—819

out the construction of "*senior*" by the initial difference of a minuscule or a capital. Archicapellanus Hilduin and the Clerks of the Chapel might plausibly argue for either import, "*senior*" noun, or *senior* adjective, as they chose. This indistinct apprehension of the rights of blood and the rights of dominion, perplexed and confounded the Carlovingian Empire until its extinction.

General dissatisfaction: Pepin and Louis-le-Germanique jealous of Lothair.

The new scheme of government dissatisfied all parties. It purported to postpone the authority granted to the sons until their father's demise; but the reversion was immediately reduced by them into a litigious possession. Lothair could not understand how he was to be called his father's partner and sharer in the Empire, and yet continue subordinate to his father. When two are conjoined, one must take the lead, and Lothair determined that his father should become subject to him. Pepin and Louis-le-Germanique both bitterly envied Lothair's supremacy, whether as *Senior* or *Seigneur*. A King of the Obotrites, or of the Sorabians or the Avars, could not, despite of the smooth phrases, appear in a more humble capacity before the Imperial Throne.

§ 30. Bernard, King of Italy, was most offended of all : he, the representative of the elder line : he, who claimed Rome, the seat of the Empire. Bernard's submission to Charlemagne and to Louis was a personal duty , Charle-

magne he obeyed as his grandsire, Louis was 741—987
certainly Bernard's *senior*, the older man; but
he would in no wise concede that eldership to 814—819
817—818.
Lothair, the young son of the son. A powerful The revolt
of Bernard
King of
Italy
movement ensued in Bernard's favour. The
long-bearded Germans had become thoroughly
Romanized; and, to a great extent, the revolution which now broke out was an insurrection
of the Lombard-Italians against the Franks. Many
of the highest Clergy joined therein: Anselm
Archbishop of Milan, and Wulfphald, Bishop
of Cremona; on our side of the Alps, Theodulph, Bishop of Orleans.   This friend of Charlemagne and of Alcuin had been long settled
in Gaul, but he could not forget fair Italy.   In
Lombardy, the feeling was enthusiastic: the
municipal communities, always very powerful,
were unanimous on behalf of Bernard, and swore
to support his cause. King he was already .
therefore this renewed declaration was probably
intended to prepare the way for his assumption
of the Imperial dignity.   The Passes, the Alpine
Chiuse, were occupied by King Bernard's troops,
and the Empire of Louis threatened with imminent peril.

Louis received the intelligence when hunting
in the sport-abounding Vosges : a diplomatic
intrigue ensued, of which we only know the fatal
results. Generally speaking, the Franks hated
King Bernard.   His faithful counsellors, Wala
and Adelhard, had been taken from him, captives.

741—987 convicts, lingering in the cell of Corbey and the island of Hermoustiers. Hermengarda employed 814—819 817—818 King Bernard inveigled out of Italy — meetsLouis at Chalons. her wily emissaries: Bernard was inveigled out of Italy: the Frankish nobles, who brought the proposition which induced him to abandon the country where he was defended by his people and protected by the Alps, pledged themselves upon their oaths for his safety. He proceeded to seek a compromise with his uncle. A conference was held as far up as possible in the Gauls, and where the old Franks were strongest, at Châlons on the Saône. Bernard was appalled by his danger: he threw himself at the feet of Louis and implored forgiveness; but the inveterate Franks would not allow of mercy.

The subsequent transactions are related contradictorily and confusedly. None of the historians on this side the Alps liked to expatiate upon the subject; they were all imbued with the Frankish feeling. Hermengarda's share in the transactions would have been concealed from posterity but for 818 March, April. Bernard and his adherents tried and condemned at Aix-la-Chapelle. the Chronicle of one Andrew, a Milanese. Bernard and his adherents were brought to trial before the great Council at Aix-la-Chapelle. The safe-conduct went for nothing. The chief rebels, with the exception of the three Bishops, were condemned to death. Louis hesitated to confirm the sentence. A commutation of punishment was insidiously suggested. A confidential adviser,—was it not Hermengarda?—spoke or hinted to the following effect "Let Bernard and his three counsellors, Egidius, Reinhard, and ^{741—987} Rainier the son of that traitor Hardrath of Austrasia, who rebelled again and again against ^{814—819} your father, be blinded."—If Louis did not give a decided refusal, he did not prohibit: nay, his reply was interpreted into a direct assent. Perhaps he hardly understood the proposal. To an undecided and irresolute mind, the plainest words convey a sound of uncertainty.

Three days afterwards King Bernard was Bernard's dead. According to one version of the tragical miserable death. story, Bernard resisted desperately against the five executioners sent to tear out his eyes, and he was killed in the conflict. Some say that he and the other prisoners, after they had sustained the dreadful punishment, committed suicide in despair. The dungeon secrets were never distinctly disclosed; but, that the prisoners expired miserably, was certain. The corpse of King Bernard was conveyed to Milan: they buried him in Sant' Ambrogio, where his body lies. The epitaph tells nothing of his mode of death. One son he left, bearing the ancestorial name of Pepin, who remained obscurely in the power of Louis-le-débonnaire. The three Bishops were kept in custody, Theodulph at Angiers. The lives of the other parties implicated in Bernard's revolt were spared, but all their property was confiscated to the Crown. It was assumed in like manner that the infant Pepin had, through his father's delinquencies. forfeited all right t·

741—987 Italy. No advocate or friend spoke on his be-
814—819 half, and the kingdom was united in domain to the Imperial Crown.

Louis compels his brothers Drogo, Hugh, and Thierry to become monks.

§ 31. Hitherto the three young brothers of Louis-le-débonnaire, Drogo, Hugh, and Thierry, continuing in the palace, had experienced his cordial affection. At his father's behest, he swore to be their guardian : no jealousy, no ill-will appeared, and the oath had been conscientiously fulfilled. Threatening suspicions were now excited that some discontented party might raise up the Princes as his competitors. Apparently these apprehensions were causeless, but once excited and indulged, Louis could not dispel the dread. He determined to rid himself of his brothers. Monks they must be, a monastery their prison. He compelled them to be shorn against their will :—the foreboding anticipations of Charlemagne were realized. Louis-*le-débonnaire*, Ludovicus *Pius*, committed the harsh and unrighteous deed which his dying father forbade. The reluctant youths took the irrevocable vows against which their souls revolted, vows scarcely possible to be truly kept by them, and yet not to be violated without sin.

818.
July 3.
Death of Hermengarda.

§ 32. If Hermengarda instigated the cruel punishment and consequent death of Bernard, as is the prevailing opinion, she did not live to enjoy her success; she did not live to see Lothair, her favourite son, the crowned King of Italy—her own death speedily ensued   This loss fell

heavily upon Louis-le-débonnaire. He and Her- _{741—987}
mengarda had grown up together, and he loved
her tenderly. About this time he had been
engaged in active and fortunate military operations: he conducted a very successful expedition
against the Armoricans, the Celts were reduced
to submission; Benevento submitted without a
struggle; the Gascons were defeated, Lope Centulla, their Duke, accepted the boon of banishment; the Sclavonians yielded implicit obedience, and the authority of Louis seemed to per-
vade the whole Empire.

But the triumphant Emperor rejoiced not
in his prosperity. His mind was saddened: men
excused him, but his conscience smote him. Bernard's ghastly spectre haunted him; he could
not conceal from himself that his splendid Empire was insecure. Soon would his sons either
quarrel with him or amongst themselves. Harassed, depressed, self-reproached, he talked of
abdication: he would retire into a monastery—
a half wish, which the speaker could scarcely
have realized. Louis, warmly and fondly affectionate, was entirely unfitted for solitude: he
could not bear to sever himself from earthly ties;
moreover, he always felt that he ought not to
abandon the duties of government which had been
committed to him. Those about him, his counsellors, urged him to contract a second marriage.
Faithful to Hermengarda, Louis had not looked on

741—987 any other woman with eyes of desire ; nor would
he court by proxy, or take a wife upon report.
814—819 So they actually assembled at the palace the
819. Louis mar-daughters of his counts and nobles ; and from
ries his second wife the maidens presented to the Widower's choice,
Judith. he, before the year of mourning had expired,
selected a blooming, beautiful, brilliant, high-
spirited, accomplished and witty Princess, who,
besides her personal and mental gifts, had the
recommendation of appertaining to one of the
most powerful houses of the realm.

Guelph § 33. GUELPH the Agilolphing was her father:
Count of Altorf, Wilhelm Tell and the *Eidgenossenschaft* have
(died 820,) and his de-so dimmed the earlier eras of Swiss history, that
scendants. we rarely advert to the importance of Transjurane and Alpine Helvetia as constituting the
very core of Burgundy : the Dynasts who ruled
beneath Burgundian or Imperial Supremacy
are almost equally forgotten. Amongst a thousand travellers on the Lake of Lucerne, has one
of these tourists any reminiscence of Guelph
Count of Altorf, so illustrious by his descent, but
more illustrious through his progeny ? JUDITH,
the damsel selected by Louis-le-débonnaire, was
Guelph's eldest child.

Ethico founder of ETHICO, Conrad and Rodolph, his sons, are
the histo-each in their degree historically conspicuous.
rical Guel-phic family, Most particularly Ethico the eldest, the ancestor
(died 830). of Cunegunda or Cuniza, wife of Azzo Marquis
of Este, founder of our Guelphic family. From

Azzo came the Guelphic dukes of Bavaria and of 741—987
Saxony, and subsequently of Brunswick and of
Lunenburg, thus rendering Ethico the historical 814—819
stem of our own Imperial line.

CONRAD, the second son of Guelph of Altorf, Conrad I.
Abbot,
stands at the head of another lineage of great Count, and
Duke of
consequence : he married a daughter of Louis-le- Auxerre,
(died 862).
débonnaire, and therefore the step-daughter of
his sister Judith, who is called "Adelaide," which
denomination may be either a proper name or
an epithet. Conrad was Abbot of Saint Germain
of Auxerre, not to be confounded with Saint
Germain l'Auxerrois, and he bears the title of
Abbot, Count and Duke of Auxerre, accordingly ;
the Abbey of Auxerre narrowly escaped being
completely converted into an hereditary principality. Conrad was probably also Count of Paris.
This Conrad, distinguished dynastically as "Con- .. his children
rad the first," had three children, Guelph, Conrad
"the younger," and Hugh, two of whom succeeded somewhat irregularly to his dignities.

RODOLPH, the third son of Guelph of Altorf, Count Rodolph (died
held a high situation in the Court of France, but 866).
deeply suffering in the revolutions of the times :
he attained no higher station than the Comitial
honour.

GUELPH, grandson of Guelph of Altorf, and Guelph, the
grandson,
eldest son of Conrad, according to the Carlovin- Abbot of
Auxerre,
gian usage and his family pretensions, obtained &c (died
881).
his provision entirely from the Church.   Abbot

711—987 of Saint Riquier or Centulla, and, like his father,
819—830 Abbot of Auxerre, he died without known progeny.

Conrad the younger, Abbot of Sens, Count of Paris and Rhætia, (died 881). CONRAD, second son of Conrad, called *Conrad the younger*, Abbot of Sens, was also Count of Paris and of Rhætia, much engaged in wars with the Northmen. We shall resume his descendants in a subsequent paragraph.

Hugh, Abbot of Tours, &c. Count of Burgundy, &c. (died 887) HUGH, third son of Conrad, was as warlike as his brother. He was Abbot of Saint Martin of Tours, Saint Vedast of Arras, Saint Bertin at St. Omers, and, like his father and elder brother, Abbot of Saint Germain of Auxerre. Moreover he is called by historians Count of Burgundy, Count of Orleans, Count of Anjou, and Duke of Neustrian France; but the perplexing frequency of the name "Hugh" throws some difficulty upon his biography. He left one daughter,—PETRO-

Petronilla his daughter ancestress of the Plantagenets. NILLA, espoused to the bold Tertullus of the Gastinois,—the mother of the Plantagenets.

CONRAD "the younger," dynastically counted as "Conrad the second," to whom we must now revert, was the father of RAOUL or RODOLPH the

Rodolph I. (886—911.) Rodolph II. (911—937) Kings of Transjurane Burgundy, afterwards the Kingdom of Arles first, King of that portion of Transjurane Burgundy which under his son, RODOLPH the Second, subsequently expanded into the Kingdom of Arles. The erection of this Kingdom caused the severance of the countries on the left bank of the Rhone from the Crown of France till the close of the twelfth century. ADELAIDE, the daughter

of Conrad the second, who married RICHARD 741—987
Duke of Burgundy, surnamed *le Justicier*, was
by him, the mother of RAOUL (brother-in-law of 819—830
Hugh-le-grand) King of France. |

This meagre summary concerning a period
not obscure from want of historical evidence, yet
offering great difficulties in historical investigation, is most abundantly suggestive of thought.
It bespeaks more of the confusion prevailing
under the Carlovingians than a volume of disquisitions. In particular biographies, and in the
Origines of families, dull as they appear, the historian discovers the clearest clue to the destinies
of nations, the best corrective of dreamy gene-
ralizations, imaginations more arid than the driest
facts, results without premises, philosophications
meaningless as the melodious moanings of the
Æolian harp.

§ 34. The introduction of a step-mother
into a family, always a hazardous experiment,
was at this troubled and eventful era of fermenting discontent in a great Empire, rendered
aggravatedly perilous by the concourse of contrarieties and dangers besetting Louis-le-débonnaire until his dying day. Without doubt, Judith's
charms contributed to influence him in the first
instance ; but, apart from this consideration, there
were many reasons conducing to the preference
she obtained. The Romanized Franks and the
Germanic interests were beginning to oppose each

741—987 other. Louis-le-débonnaire seems now almost unconsciously to have felt a prescient confidence in
819—830 the German people, inclining his mind more to
Character
of the Em- them than during the earlier years of his life.
press Ju-
dith. Judith, cheerful, affectionate, noble, belonged to
a purely German and very distinguished House.
Like the other ladies of her era, she would have
been held unfit for her station had she not been
well versed in the Grammar-latin tongue, therefore her mere knowledge of the language implies
no extraordinary proficiency. But it was Judith's
encomium that she diligently cultivated her varied talents; and the learned men who inscribed
or dedicated their works to her, felt that in this
homage there was no unseemly flattery.

Court fa- § 35. Even if Louis-le-débonnaire, the wi-
vourites,— dowed father of three tall sons, had not really
reckoned somewhat above forty years of age, and
might have been reckoned above fifty, the prudence of his choice, would nevertheless have been
dubious. Under existing circumstances the position of a young and attractive Queen in such
a depraved coterie as the Court of Louis-le-
débonnaire was a domestic and national misfortune. Louis grieved at the evil, but he could not
destroy the contagion. The leprosy was in the
walls. The least reproachful designation appropriate to the Pfaltz was to call it a breeding nest
Abbot Hil- of political cabal and unprincipled treachery; the
duin the
Archicapel- main fomenters being the Monarch's sons. The

second marriage of Louis-le-débonnaire had been 741—987
urged on by a party, as a party measure: it is
impracticable to follow out these machinations 819—830
in their details; we can only guess at them from lanus, Bernard, son of William of
the consequences. Thus guessing, we can just Orange.
discern that the party who after Hermengarda's
death dissuaded Louis-le-débonnaire from continuing a widower, was in opposition to the party
of the sons.

Hilduin, the Archicapellanus, was now the Abbot Hilduin.
leading minister, a signal pluralist, holding three
Abbeys distinguished amongst the most venerated Sanctuaries in the Gauls, Saint Denis "in
France," Saint Germain des Prés, and Saint Médard at Soissons; the three yielding in rank to
none save Saint Martin of Tours, all most opulent, and Saint Médard, strong as any fortress in
the realm: not content with this accumulation,
he desired more. A new and powerful favourite
however had begun his slippery career : a new
object of homage and enmity, Bernard, son of
William of Orange, and godchild of Louis-le-
débonnaire.

§ 36. Count Bernard's rise is connected with 820.
a catastrophe, the mystery whereof is not dis- Bera, Count of Barcelona,
pelled by the minuteness with which the event appealed of treason
is narrated. Bera, Count of Barcelona, the by the Count Sa-
Emperor's intimate friend, was appealed of trea- nila
son by the Count Sanila; a case for battle-ordeal,
to be fought, if according to the Frankish tra-

741—987

819—830

ditions, nearly after the manner directed by our ancient English common law, justly compared to a rustic conflict—no sharp weapons allowed: appellor and appellee dismounted, wielding club and staff.

Bera and Sanila, however, were both Visigoths : to combat on horseback, with sword and spear, was their ancestorial right : that right they claimed, and the claim was allowed. In all things and above all things, the Mediæval Church dreaded the awful responsibility of venturing to impose limitations upon the power of Faith. National customs were inveterate; hence the Church had not yet been able to arrive at any clear and consistent decision concerning ordeals, or, as they were termed, "the judgments of God " These proceedings were not only excused, but even sanctioned by the clergy and laity; though occasionally individual judgment dissented, and some began to enquire whether the judicial combat and the trials by fire or water might not be rash temptations of Providence. According to its pristine application, the battle-trial was the ordeal least chargeable with presumptuous temerity, being simply a return to the law of nature. In some of the barbaric kingdoms, good policy diminished the inconveniences of these duels. Nevertheless the battle-trial was exceedingly perverted within the ambit of the ancient kingdom of Burgundy, where it was traditionally called the *Lex-Gundo-*

baldi, or *Loi-Gombette*, having received great extension from a constitution which King Gundobald had made.

741—987

819—830

Agobard, Archbishop of Lyons, a very learned Prelate, the strenuous opposer of image-worship, and possessing much influence, who had been often called to witness and deplore the mischief resulting from judicial combats, addressed a very earnest and well-reasoned letter to Louis-le-débonnaire, exhorting him to repress this objectionable usage.   The letter affords a spirited and interesting portraiture of society, and particularly displays the perplexities resulting from the diversified laws subsisting in the Frankish Empire.   Gundobald was an Arian, and Agobard considers his heresy as affording a strong presumption against his legislation.   But the main tenor of the argument is sound; and Agobard, as a theologian, argues that battle-trials were no longer warranted by the Scriptural examples usually adduced in their support.   Proceeding from Agobard, this testimony was the more irrecusable, inasmuch as his disposition was intolerant and fiery; and the prohibition of the water-ordeal by an Imperial Constitution promulgated in the Council of Worms, may be traced to Agobard's admonitions.

Battle-trial
condemned
by Ago-
bard,
Archbi-
shop of
Lyons

829

Water-
ordeal
prohibited

Louis-le-débonnaire could hardly avoid agreeing with Agobard: moreover he was persuaded that Sanila was a malicious accuser.—Therefore

741—987

819—830

820

Single combat at Toulouse between Bera and Sanila: the former defeated

he exerted himself to prevent the duel, acting sincerely but feebly. His mediation was ineffectual. Bera and Sanila galloped into the lists at Toulouse, their shields slung, their weapons in their hands, and the funeral bier stood before them ready in the field, prepared for the vanquished man; living or dead he must deck the gallows-tree. Face to face, Bera and Sanila reined in their coursers, awaiting the signal from the Emperor. Louis might have withheld the signal: he ought to have done so, but the people went with Count Sanila, and he dared not. The Count of Barcelona yielded to his enemy's skill, strength, or fortune, was bound in chains, cast upon the bier, and carried away from the scene of conflict, a disgraced and hooted traitor. Louis would not permit the sentence of death to be executed; he absolved Bera from guilt, and he therefore sent the defeated combatant to Rouen, where he remained at liberty. Though Louis-le-débonnaire grieved at the misfortune of the innocent, he could not resolve to act up to his own convictions, or perhaps was restrained by his advisers. Popular opinion branded Bera as a traitor . his

820.

Bera's county of Barcelona given to Bernard, together with Septimania.

honours and dignities were forfeited: the County of Barcelona was granted to Bernard of Orange —a suspicious transaction—and the County or Duchy of Septimania was added thereto.

Louis then bestowed upon Bernard in marriage a Princess who was either his sister or his half

sister, the excellent Doduana, who calls the Emperor her brother, and they were married in the
Pfaltz of Aix-la-Chapelle.—The manual of devotion still extant in the original Latin, and composed by Doduana for the use of her sons, from
whom she was separated by Bernard's profligacy
and harshness, is a most pleasant and touching
memorial of her maternal affection, acquirements,
scriptural knowledge and piety.   It is in this
work that she notices her relationship to Louis-
le-débonnaire.—As for Bernard, he insinuated
himself more and more into favour, was appointed Chamberlain, and became the Sovereign's most intimate confidant, to the extreme
detriment of the realm.

§ 37.   Louis-le-Germanique   was   born   to
Louis-le-débonnaire when King of Aquitaine, six
years before his accession to the Empire.   After
him, no more babes had been brought to the
Font.   It is very certain that so soon as the three
sons, Lothair, Pepin, and Louis were old enough
to speculate concerning the future enjoyment of
their father's dominions,—and at how early an
age were not such speculations entertained?—
they would scarcely have rejoiced very heartily
had they been summoned by the gossips into their
mother's darkened chamber, to welcome a fourth
brother.—Had such a brother been born subsequently to the promulgation of the *Charta Divi-*
sionis, when their three portions were definitively

741—087
819—830
The
Princess
Doduana
married
to Count
Bernard

The sons
of Louis-
le-débon-
naire
their en-
mity a-
gainst Ju-
dith.

ı ⸱

741—987
819—830 assigned, they would unquestionably have considered that fourth brother as an odious intruder. Their sordid feelings, however, were unawakened during Hermengarda's life-time, for she had ceased from child-bearing: but when the tender, blooming and luxuriant Judith became their father's wife, the contingency—whether near or remote—of an addition to the Imperial family rendered the second marriage doubly distasteful. Judith's merits only set her step-sons more against her. Her talent incensed them, her cheerfulness provoked them. She was immediately the object, as she afterwards became the persecuted victim, of their mean and unmanly hatred. They and all their numerous and encreasing partizans regarded the winning Beauty with unmitigated enmity and scorn. These sentiments became manifest; and whilst encircled by magnificence and outward prosperity, Louis sank into deeper melancholy. Reminiscences and forebodings, the absent and the present, the past and the future, the living and the dead, all troubled and grieved his soul.

Discontents pervaded large and influential classes. Notwithstanding his good intentions, the Clergy generally distrusted him. His sons, though divided by mutual grudges and envyings, united in jealousy against the Empress Judith: they pressed hard upon their father; and how were they to be conciliated? One year and another year had passed—the young Judith was still

childless; no chance, the world surmised, of her
ever being otherwise, unless by violating her mar-
riage-vows : rumours were rife—we have hints
concerning them.   Louis yearned for peace: and
in order to remove all uncertainty concerning
the succession of Lothair, Pepin and Louis-le-
Germanique, so that even were Judith to bear
him a fourth son, their wealth, their state, their
honours should remain undiminished, Louis-le-
débonnaire determined, by making further concessions, to ensure content and harmony.   A vain
project ; for, as the first step in his new scheme
of conciliation, he encreased the pre-eminence of
Lothair.

To this eldest Son, the Emperor designate,
he promised Italy in domain, negociated a marriage for him with Hementruda, daughter of
Hugh Count of Alsace, called the Poltroon, but
whose cowardice was rather a species of mo-
nomania than timidity in the proper sense, for
he was very able and very powerful.   Then ensued the merry Mayday of Nimeguen : the great
Council of the Empire assembled in Charlemagne's Burg.   Ecclesiastical buildings being the
usual places of convention, we may suppose that
they sat in the circular sanctuary—now the only
vestige of the sumptuous palace—whose form,
like Charlemagne's own Basilica at Aix-la-Chapelle, retraces the Churches of Helena at Jerusalem.   Here the nobles, prelates, and proceres

741—987

819—830
821.
Louis de-
termines
to make
further
concessions
to his sons

821
May 1,
Great
Council at
Nimeguen ·
confirma-
tion of the
Charta Di-
visionis.

741—987 of the Empire appeared—the *Charta Divisionis*
was read before them, paragraph by paragraph.
810—830 Confirmed again by the oaths of the assembly,
the establishment of the Imperial dignity in the
person of Lothair, and the partitions of the realms
and territories between Lothair, Pepin and Louis,
became the organic Law of the Empire, the defi-
nitive settlement by which all parties were bound.

821—822
Louis-le-
débon-
naire's
encreasing
melan-
choly. .

§ 38.   A restoration of tranquillity was seemingly effected, yet no relief ensued for the
desponding Louis-le-débonnaire. Hitherto there
was one recreation which always aided his bodily health and refreshed his anxious spirit,
the chase ; but hound and horn, and the darting
of the Moorish javelin in the wilds of the
Frankish Vosges, ceased to give him pleasure.
All the enjoyments of life sunk amidst his melancholy broodings upon the wrongs he had perpetrated or permitted.   He had profaned Holy
Orders : he had broken the solemn promise given
to his father : through his command were his
nearest of blood placed in a captivity painful to
their bodies and perilous to their souls, tempting
them to apostasy or despair : husbands separated
from their wives: the innocent branded with contumely or pining in banishment and poverty :
writhing in the grasp of the executioner : dying
in agonizing misery:—all through him.   His past
actions rose before him with scathing vividness,
and after struggling, he suddenly determined to

make compensation for the wrongs. He began ^{711—987}
by reparation and restitution. The prisoners
were released. Bernarius returned from Lerins : ^{819—830}
Adelhard was summoned from Hermoustier, and, recalls
invited to the Palace, took charge of the royal ^{Wala, &c., from banishment}
household: Wala came forth from his unwilling
seclusion at Corbey, and was received by the
people in triumph.—All the nobles banished for
their participation in King Bernard's insurrection
heard their sentence revoked by the Emperor's
free pardon, and repaired joyfully to their homes
and lands.

Hugh, Drogo, and Thierry beheld their bro- ^{821—822.}
ther a suppliant at their feet, beseeching for- ^{. . seeks to be recon-}
giveness. The reconciliation was cordial and en- ^{ciled to his brothers.}
during. Hugh was installed in three Abbeys, Saint ^{Hugh, Abbot of}
Bertin, Saint Quentin and Noailly, and appointed ^{three Abbeys, died}
to the office of Archicapellanus or Chancellor. He ^{844.}
is sometimes styled Count Hugh, and it is sup-
posed that some Burgundian district constituted
his County; but, as we have before observed, there
were several Counts bearing the name of Hugh
in Burgundy, and it is extremely difficult to distinguish amongst them. Hugh was honest, brave,
and true, but he lived quite as a layman: mention is made of his son Stephen : we may or may
not infer that he was married; for it is a rather
whimsical subterfuge of Père Anselm the geneal-
ogist, to assume that Stephen was called the son
of Hugh, as being a monk in some one of his
three Abbeys. However, be this as it may, Hugh

741—987 the Abbot was killed in battle, with many other Abbots of the same class as he.

819—830 Drogo, Bishop of Metz, died 855.

Drogo obtained a Canonry in the Cathedral of Metz, where he lived royally and merrily: nevertheless he was a sound and useful Churchman. Elected to the See of Metz, he proved a good Bishop, a comfort and support to his brother Louis-le-débonnaire. — Thierry appears to have been contented to continue as a Monk in his monastery.

Louis disturbed in conscience.

§ 39. Were these outward acts of equity and kindness a sufficient spiritual atonement for injustice, culpable negligence, or crime?—Louis had not silenced his conscience, and he therefore determined to ease his mind by appearing as a public penitent. Even as his sins had been committed before the world, so did he seek that his repentance should be shewn forth in the face of day. History presented to him one example of a Christian monarch who rose from his humiliation to greater honour. Before the gates of that Basilica where the murdered Bernard was entombed, had Theodosius cast himself at the feet of Saint Ambrose, submitting to reproof, entreating forgiveness, and accepting the conditions which the Church imposed. In the annals of the Empire was there any Cæsar whose authority had been more cheerfully obeyed than the triumphant, the glorious Theodosius, who united the grandeur of the old Roman to the virtues of the Christian hero? A

822 Council of Attigny.

great Council was convened at Attigny—Attigny

on the Aisne, not far from Soissons, an ancient
palace of the Merovingian kings, where the noble
Witikind had performed homage before Charlemagne, by whom so many thousands of his
countrymen had been slaughtered.

741—987
819—830

Here sat the prelates and princes of the
Empire, the people thronging in as witnesses of
their Sovereign's contrition. The uncrowned Louis
came forth in penitential garb, and made before
the assembled multitude a full and earnest acknowledgment: how he had sinned against Drogo, and
against Hugh, and against Thierry, and against
Adelhard, and against Wala, and against Bernarius, and against Bera, and against all whom he
had persecuted and despoiled, banished and put to
death; but chiefly against his murdered nephew
King Bernard; and many other sins did Louis
confess, of which no one had dared to accuse him.
And he had thought over and rehearsed all he
could recollect of his forefathers' sins and cruelties, and more particularly Charlemagne's, and
the trespasses which Charlemagne had committed
against the Church; and for all he asked pardon.
The prelates heard his confession, and declared
the penances, according to the principles then
prevailing, the tokens of sincerity and means of
grace, alms, prayers, bodily chastisement, stripes,
vigils, abstinence, such as were imposed upon
Edgar and sought by Plantagenet, the only
monarchs who, after Louis, are recorded to have

822.
Confession
made by
Louis be-
fore the
Council
submits to
penance.

741—987
819—830
openly testified their contrition for their sins; and, the burthen removed, he rebounded into activity, resuming the duties and trials of royalty with renewed vigour and energy.

817—829.

Era of Louis-le-debon-naire's outward prosperity

§ 40. Upon the accession of Louis-le-débonnaire, we have seen how cordially the authority of Charlemagne's son had been accepted. The nations rejoiced in his Empire. His marriage with Judith gave a new impulse to his apparent prosperity. Even when the penitent of Attigny had been most sorrowful, the Empire presented an aspect of cheerful dignity :—whilst the Master of the Feast knows the bitterness of his own heart, the world does not care to be disturbed in the banquet's enjoyment by knowing the sorrow; and an era of six or seven years ensued, characterized by activity, excitement, success and splendour.

Louis now principally resorted to the towering palaces in the Rhine-land, monuments of paternal magnificence. Ingelheim and Frankfort, when the Diets were assembled there, exhibited the temporal Head of the Western Commonwealth,—*Ludovicus divinâ propitiante clementiâ, Imperator Augustus*,—surrounded by every

Splendour of the Imperial Diets—Costume of the Counts.

attribute of majesty and honour. Prelates, nobles and people all convened—Austrasia and Neustria, Alemannia, Suabia, Bavaria, Burgundy, represented by their Bishops and their Abbots, the Dukes and the Counts wearing their golden

coronals and clad in the Roman chlamys, which 741—987
modern fashion only prevents us from discerning
in the Parliamentary robes of our Peers. In 819—830
this gorgeous senate Louis sat enthroned, Judith
by his side. Had Charlemagne ever thus presented a Consort with such imperial honour?

In the year subsequent to the Council of At- 823. July 15.
tigny, an event ensued at which the people mar- Birth of Charles-le-
velled and discussed; imparting the utmost joy to Chauve
Louis, and filling Lothair, Pepin and Louis-le-
Germanique, with spite and vexation—an unexpected event—Judith presented her husband with
his fourth son. The infant was named Charles,
after his Grandsire; and as he became older, his
fine lofty forehead exaggerating the absence of
the flowing locks which usually adorned the
Frankish noble, caused him to receive the name
of Charles-le-Chauve, by which he is universally
designated in French history.

The Borderers had given most trouble to
Charlemagne : his apprehension of the resulting
dangers instigated him to take more efficient
measures for restraining these semi-domestic
enemies. Louis continued the same policy with
extraordinary success, obtaining great influence
all around his varied empire. The Wends and 819—825
other Sclavonian tribes, so obstinately contending Sclavonians submit to
against Teutonic ascendency,—that stubborn Louis-le-débon-
battle of twelve centuries, still undecided,—ac- naire,
cepted the protection which the imperial Crown

bestowed. Their mutual hostilities induced them to claim the intervention of Louis-le-débonnaire ; —Sorabians, Obotrites, Bohemians, Wilzians, Moravians, Avars, obeyed his behests, and submitted to his decisions. Meligast and Celcadragus, rival brethren, sons of Liubi, implored his arbitration upon their claims—Ceadragus, the son of Thrasco, humbly testified his repentance for his insubordination, if not rebellion

Then appeared a legation from a Barbarian Chieftain, whose very name had hitherto been unknown—never hitherto subjected to the Carlovingian Crown—Omortag, King of the Bulgarians, imploring the friendship of Charlemagne's son. The Bulgarians were a people crushed between Greek and Teuton, and they therefore courted the guarantee of the Frankish Empire.

Michael, the treacherous friend and successor of Leo the Armenian, that Leo who, like Charlemagne, might glory in the epithet "Iconoclast," was fain to acknowledge a brother Emperor. A stately and solemn embassy appeared from the Blachernæ, the Ambassadors bearing with them as a grateful gift the works ascribed to the Athenian convert who believed upon the preaching of Saint Paul. Louis caused the manuscripts to be deposited in the Abbey of Saint Denis, where they were accepted as an inestimable treasure. Some years afterwards, Hilduin, imploring the pardon of Louis-le-débonnaire for his ingra-

titude, received from him the command to com- 741—987
pose the life of the Saint. An opinion had pre- ⌣⌣⌣
vailed that Dionysius the Areopagite, probably 819—830
Dionysius the first Bishop of Athens, and Dionysius, or Denis, certainly the first Bishop of
Paris, were not to be distinguished from each
other; and the affectionate though uncritical
labours of Hilduin, confounding hagiology and
apocryphal fable, completed the delusion.

From Rome Louis-le-débonnaire received due 817—824
homage.   Upon the death of Pope Stephen, Submission
Pascal, called to the Papal throne by the Roman of the Papal See to
clergy and people, had sought the confirmation Louis-le-
débon-
of his election from the Emperor.—So also naire.
Pascal's successor Eugenius; and the Diets of
the Empire were repeatedly graced by Pontifical
Legates—Benedict the Archdeacon, Quirinus the
Primicerius and Theophylact the Nomenclator;
Leo, the Magister Militum, and Sergius the Biblio-
thecary, reverently performing their obeisance,
acknowledged, on behalf of the Pontiff, the temporal supremacy possessed by the representative
of the Cæsars.

The Abbot of Mount Olivet comes from the The Abbot
of Mount
Holy Land, attracted by the munificence and Olivet.
kindness of Charlemagne's son.

The Republic of Venice, cautiously steering
between Byzantium and Rome, permits her acute
George the
representative, George the Presbyter, to follow Venetian
becomes a
as an attendant in the train of the Count of retainer of
the Count

741—987
———
819—830

Friuli. The individual in question was curiously distinguished by his skill. Equally versed in music and mechanics, he was able to construct "that delightful instrument called the Organ, producing the sound," as the Monk of Saint Gall carefully explains, "by the wind blown through pipes of brass." This George was employed to build the first Organ which ever pealed along the vaulting of Aix-la-Chapelle.

Occasional exertions of military power were needed to sustain this Imperial dignity. The ineffectual revolts of the distant March-lands gave Louis the gratification of success; just enough peril to dispel the monotony of opulent and pleasurable prosperity: thus the Sclavonians made a show of resistance, but were put down.

Other campaigns added still more to his reputation. Charlemagne himself had only reduced the Bretons into an impatient subjection. Morvan, the Celtic chieftain, refused his tribute: Louis-

818—822

Military expeditions conducted by Louis-le-débonnaire against the Bretons.

le-débonnaire advanced into the country. Morvan was slain, and his head brought to the Emperor. He was succeeded by Judicael, a Prince or *Mactiern*, also known—his name barbarised or corrupted by the Franks—as *Uidemaculus* or *Wiomarch*. Louis-le-débonnaire determined to break the strength of the Celts. Associating to himself his sons Pepin and Louis, he led his Imperial host into Armorica : Rennes

yielded, and Louis receiving the hostages given 741—987
by the Bretons, returned in triumph to Rouen.

§ 41.   Far more important in their relations 819—830
820.
to the future fortunes of France, of England, of Transac-
the World, were his transactions with Rollo's tions with
the Danes:
precursors : he gave the precedent which settled they attack
the coasts,
but are un-
the conquering Northman on Neustrian ground. able to
enter the
About the time when Louis-le-débonnaire was interior
engaged against the Sclavonians, the keen-eyed
Scandinavian and Cimbric pirates, always observ-
ant of opportunities and knowing how to seize
them, renewed their inroads upon the Belgic
shores. Louis, however, was fully prepared: he had
continued the precautions suggested by Charlemagne's forethought.   He knew the cities and
monasteries most likely to attract, and the estua-
ries most open to receive them.   From Seine to
Flanders the Frankish troops watched the coasts.
The Northmen effected a landing : they were
repelled by the Imperial forces, took to their
ships, sailed down the Channel and round into
the Atlantic, and compensated themselves by
plundering Aquitaine.   But notwithstanding the
daring of these greedy marauders, the Dansker-
men, as a nation, confessed the Imperial power ;
and an important Leader was bought off to be
a friend.

At the commencement of the reign of Louis-
le-débonnaire we noticed his interference between
two competitors, or rather parties, then con-

741—987 testing the superiority of Denmark—the sons of
Godfrey King of Lethra, and Harold King of
819—830 Jutland. Both belong to English history: from
826
Harold the lineage of Godfrey came "Eric of the bloody-
King of
Jutland axe," "King of the Pagans" in Northumbria, whilst
baptized at
Mayence Harold was grandfather to *Gorm-hin-rige*, Gorm
the mighty, the Gormund, Codrinus, Guthrun or
Guthrun-Athelstan, of our English historians,
who in King Alfred's time conquered East
Anglia, and settled the Danelaghe. Harold, when
he first sought the assistance of Louis-le-débonnaire, did homage to the Frankish crown; and
the imperial forces, Franks and Sclavonians,
crossing the Eyder, replaced him in a portion of
his dominions.

Again expelled, again Harold resorted to his
Suzerain; and so revered was the imperial authority, that the Dane determined to protect himself
by becoming to all intents and purposes a member of the Western Empire. The worshipper of
Thor and Odin could not decently claim admission
into the Latin Commonwealth: this impediment
was now removed. Harold, his wife, and his
son Godfrey, were baptized in the vast Dom of
Mayence. Louis stood as sponsor for King Harold;
Judith undertook the like office for his Consort;
Lothair accepted the same duty for Godfrey their
son, a future though transient feudatory on the
826 borders of the Seine. Louis invested Harold with
Investiture
of Harold, the purple robe of estate, girt him with his own

sword, dropped the golden coronal on his head. 711—987
Harold, kneeling before the Emperor, repeated
his homage, placing his hands between the hands 819—830
of the Emperor, and received from him a three- the homager of
fold grant;—a County or Graffschaft between county in
Rhine and Moselle, jocosely said to have been land, the
selected for the purpose of supplying the jovial Olden-
Danes with a store of good wine;—another, and the kingdom of
more important Fief or Benefice, Rustringia, a Denmark.
rich and extensive Gau or Pagus, included in the
ancient Frisick territory, and subsequently erected
into the Duchy of Oldenburg, to which was also
added the flourishing emporium of Doerstadt, now
almost obliterated from the map, nay even from
historical memory;—lastly, the kingdom of Denmark, which Harold acknowledged he would hold
of the Imperial Crown.

> Mox, manibus junctis, Regi se tradidit ultro,
>   Et secum regnum, quod sibi jure fuit.
> Suscipe, Cæsar, ait, me, necnon regna subacta:
>   Sponte tuis memet confero servitiis.
> Cæsar at ipse manus manibus suscepit honestis:
>   Junguntur Francis Danica regna piis.

Louis-le-débonnaire might boast that he had
accomplished greater things than his father could
have hoped for.   No longer was that fierce Dane
a dreaded enemy, but a feudatory and ally, whose
interest was united to the prosperity of his Sovereign: Harold was now lord of a rich and attractive domain, his own, though surrounded by the
Frankish territory—a Markgrave, whose private

741—987 interest would excite him to protect the Empire
——⏜—— from invasion—and, through the bounty of Char-
819—830 lemagne's son, an accepted member of that same
Empire, participating in its honours and glories.
In subsequent times, when the Heralds came
forth from the Frankfort Roemer Saal, and proclaimed the style of the successor of the Cæsars,
the epithet of *Mehrer des Reichs*, "Encreaser of
the Empire," called forth the loudest responding
shouts of the people—could not Louis-le-débonnaire most truly assert the title as his own?

Fatality of
misfortune
attending
Louis-le-
débon-
naire.

§ 42. In all these transactions there ought
to have been every element of stability: renown
abroad, good government, so far as the supreme
authority extended, at home, wise laws made,
the imperial judges dispatched upon their circuits to administer justice, the frontiers diligently
protected, enemies subdued, merit encouraged,
and a very earnest and sincere desire on the part
of the Monarch to do his duty—yet all in vain:
never were the boundaries of the Carlovingian
Empire so widely extended as at the juncture
immediately preceding that Empire's fall.

Nothing peculiar can be discerned in the
failings of Louis-le-débonnaire, or in the disappointments of his exertions. We observe him
constantly striving after more than he could
effect; never realizing his high aspirations, and
counteracting by transient weaknesses the permanent good which the excellence of his character

was calculated to bestow. All this is according 741—987
to the ordinary course of human nature : the
specialty in the history of Louis-le-débonnaire was 819—822
the destiny by which his inconsistencies have
been brought more into evidence than the analogous failings of any other mediæval or modern
monarch endued with equal piety and sincerity,
and his errors rendered more _fatally destructive. Sovereigns far less strenuous have resisted
adverse fortune and successfully opposed their
enemies ; but Louis was called to reign over
an Empire containing within itself the elements
of disintegration and ruin : his most bitter and
implacable enemies were his own sons.

His tenderness, his sweetness, his affection,
kept him halting between two opinions : whether
rigid or lax, stern or merciful, his conduct turned
against him. He began a comprehensive eccle- Inconsistencies of
siastical reform ; but the cunning "clerks of the Louis-le-
débon-
chapel," his ministry, continued to profit by the naire, so
severely
abuses which he had promised to restrain; and visited
upon him.
in these abuses he himself concurred, expecting
by his good temper and compliance to promote
peace and good-will. Could there be a stronger
testimony brought against Louis by the advocates of sound ecclesiastical discipline than the
example of his own brother Hugh, the stout warrior, holding the three Abbeys of Saint Quentin,
Saint Bertin, and Noailly? Such compromises of
principle, exaggerated by faction and discontent,
destroyed the confidence placed in his conscien-

741—987

819—822 tiousness : the Court grew worse and worse. The compensations he had made to the injured were imperfect. Bera was pining in degraded poverty at Rouen, whilst the fawning dissolute Count Bernard plumed himself as Count of Barcelona.

But the most grievous portion of his conduct related to Italy. Deeply had Louis deplored his culpable injustice against King Bernard, and on behalf of Bernard's adherents he had acted mercifully : they were recalled, and restored to their honours and lands. The restitution therefore of the Lombard kingdom to Bernard's son Pepin ought to have ensued as a necessary consequence; but the most subtle amongst the deceits by which the root of all evil tempts the righteous, the deceit imparting to selfishness the flavour of self-denial, and to covetousness the colour of liberality, the desire of family aggrandisement, the deceit which became the ruling passion of Louis, and from whence his most grievous punishments arose, the desire of encreasing his substance for his children, prevailed. Louis-le-débonnaire kept the rapine, and confirmed Lothair in the inheritance.

822—823
Lothan
sent to take
possession
of Lom-
bardy, ac-
companied
by Wala. Immediately after bewailing the death of King Bernard in the Council of Attigny, Louis despatched Lothair to take possession of Italy, selecting for him, as his minister and adviser, the very man whom he, Louis, had so terribly aggrieved. Yielding in the first instance to a panic suspicion, proceeding without law, punishing the hatred Wala . . . . arrested Wala,

equally untried, as the most faithful of subjects 741—987
and friends, placing him exactly in the position
where he would be most forcibly instigated to 819—822
revenge, and most able to do harm.

Lothair had been declared his father's consort
and successor in the Imperial dignity; but this 822—823
title was only inchoate: the benediction of the
Roman Pontiff had not been bestowed, the concurrence of the Roman people had not been
asked, nor was Lothair clearly acknowledged as
having a legal right to any practical share in the
Imperial Government. A burst of authority, a
coup d'état, might render him a pageant, not an
Emperor, or when confronted by his father, an
Emperor possessing less direct power than his
brethren, the kings of Bavaria and Aquitaine.
They had substantive domains, he had none. But
Italy was now given to him, a powerful and virtually independent kingdom: a fortress-kingdom;
and there Louis-le-débonnaire installed him, as
if he had sought to lend his selfish, deceitful son
the means of edging him off the throne.

Wala supported Lothair with the utmost
strenuousness, aided him by his astute counsel,
joined him in every thought, plan or scheme
which could weaken the authority of his father.
Against Louis, the stern, inflexible Wala entertained a mingled feeling of anger and contempt:
they crossed the Alps, and the way rapidly
opened for further enterprize.

741—987

822—823

817

The decree
by which
Louis-le-
débonnaire
enlarges
Saint
Peter's
patrimony,
and con-
firms the
elective
franchise of
the Roman
people.

§ 43. Upon the partition of the Empire decreed at Aix-la-Chapelle, Louis, with the consent. of his three sons, had resettled the affairs of Rome. The Imperial rescript, which Canonists and Legists were used to quote by its initial words, *Ego Ludovicus*, gave a new foundation to the Papal authority. The document exists in the form of a grant addressed to Pope Pascal, who had succeeded to the Apostolic Chair upon the death of Pope Stephen. Romanists and Protestants have agreed in endeavouring to eliminate this Charter as far as possible from ecclesiastical history, though constituting one of the most important passages in the mediæval annals of the Papal See till we reach the Hildebrandine age. Four copies are kept in the archives of the Vatican.—In addition to the various donations made by the Patrician Pepin and the Emperor Charlemagne, Louis, their successor, confirms to Saint Peter the city and duchy of Rome, Corsica and Sardinia, and very many other territories in Campania, Calabria, Apulia and elsewhere, of which the greater part art still comprized in the Pontifical States, or have been claimed by the Papal See.

The right of the Roman Clergy and people, and the Roman people alone, unmingled and uncontrolled, to elect the Pope, is acknowledged, renewed, and defended by the Cæsar. Without the confirmation of the Pontiff, the title of that Cæsar was incomplete ; and yet Louis inserts an

express and stringent reservation of the Imperial 741—987
Supremacy over the dominions which he cedes—
a most complicated combination of authorities, 822—825
being nevertheless perfectly intelligible when we
examine the principles, concurrent though antagonistic, by which the keys of Saint Peter and
the diadem of Augustus, the chair of the Pontiff
and the wolf of the Republic, the Church and
the Fourth Monarchy, were severally sustained.

Lothair advanced to Rome. Pope Pascal and April 5, 823.
the Romans came forth to meet him. On Easter- Lothair crowned as
day he received the Imperial crown before the altar Emperor at Rome
of Saint Peter, was hailed as Cæsar and Augustus, by Pope Pascal
and the Pope declared that henceforward he was His name associated
to possess all the rights of the pristine Emperors. to that of his father
Lothair assumed the government vigorously. His in public acts.
name was associated with that of his father in
public acts, *Ludovicus et Lotharius, divinâ
providentiâ Imperatores Augusti.* The Roman 825.
people shortly afterwards, Eugenius being Pon- Roman people
tiff, took the oaths of allegiance to Louis and take the oath of
Lothair jointly; and thus was effected a third fealty to him.
and complete partition of the Empire in this
miserable reign—a partition under the disguise
of an union—Louis-le-débonnaire, the father,
holding his splendid Court at Frankfort or Aix-
la-Chapelle, Lothair, the rival son, at Pavia,
having half and wanting all, preparing to deprive
his father of whatever remained to him of majesty
or power.

CHAPTER II.

LOUIS-LE-DEBONNAIRE AND HIS SUCCESSORS, TO THE FINAL DETHRONEMENT OF THE CARLOVINGIAN DYNASTY.

824—987.

French history, how studied, employed by the French for political advocacy. Thierry's views upon this tendency

§ 1. VERY diligently have the French studied their own History with reference to political discussion, and still more for the excitement, the extenuation or the advocacy of political action. They began even before the revival of literature. One of their most distinguished Historians has recently brought forward this tendency as a species of accusation against his fellow-countrymen : the spirit of their historical system, he complains, is only a reflection of the spirit of party.—If there be any guilt in such a partycourse, no culprit is more brilliant and successful than he.

From Gregory of Tours downwards, French history has been treated as a vast repository of texts—materials presented for improvement by the political enquirer. Contradictory as the assertion may appear, France, that land of Revolutions, has been fed by historical traditions. Close and clear reasoners are the French people, reasoners who endeavour to guide themselves by inductions from facts and realities, unlike the Germans, so prone to become absorbed in the

vastness of abstract speculation, mind brooding 824—987
upon mind. All ranks and orders, noblesse and
bourgeoisie, hierarchy and parliament, rochet and
longrobe, cloth of gold and cloth of frieze, have
laboured to establish the justice of their claims
by appeals to History. Speculative History has
been combined with the practical conflicts of the
State, and the evidences of History, supporting
or supposed to support each adverse pretension,
have been grouped into argumentative or systematic order.

Surely we need not quarrel with those who
have thus been incited to historical disquisition :
in such impulse there is no ground for blame.
The past instructs the present by the positive
application of historical facts, bestowing upon
them their highest value. If unused, where
is their worth?—hoarded coins, kept out of circulation, an armoury in which the weapons
embrowned by rust are hanging against the
damp, green wall. We do not say that an historian must necessarily be a politician, or that
he cannot be intelligently laborious except as
the expounder of a doctrine or a creed, or interesting without speaking as the organ of a
particular party; but it is a great help to him
if he be so. These feelings from within give
him a motive the more. No writer can narrate
impressively unless he feels forcibly; and there
is no influence which will impel any one who

824—987
824—829

really deserves the name of an Historian so energetically, as the earnest desire of propagating
opinions which he believes it to be his duty to
teach or proclaim.

Points of resem-
blance be-
tween the
revolutions
of the reign
of Louis-le-
débonnaire
and the
proceed-
ings of the
leaguers
and the re-
volutionists
of the re-
volution.

The Duchesse de Joyeuse sent her scissors
to Henri de Valois—a symbolical gift, a token,
a hieroglyphic,—to warn him how well he deserved the enforced seclusion of the long-haired
Kings. It was a chance that Henri was not shut
up in the Abbey at Soissons. The Revolution of
the ninth Century offers many analogies to the
troubles of the League, they breathe the same
spirit; but with respect to the results occasioned
by personal character, this Carlovingian revolution approaches closer to the Tricolor. Louis-
le-débonnaire was the *Louis-Seize*, Judith the
Marie-Antoinette of the Carlovingian era: the
most effective manœuvres of the party headed
by Wala and Lothair consisted in the able, pertinacious, and virulent attacks directed against
the reputation and honour of the Empress. The
corruption of the Court was inveterate—Louis
had utterly failed in his endeavours to begin well
at home. He had always feared to probe the
wound or apply the cautery. The profligacy of
the Palace passed from intrigue and gallantry
to assassination and murder — depravities and
crimes so often shading into one another, gar-
lands of roses round the drugged bowl. The
resplendent beauty of Judith, her wit, her spirit,

her free and open manners, were all so many snares to her, exposing her to censures and accusations, encouraging and embittering her malignant and unsparing enemies. Slanders and rumours soon settled into a definite accusation. Count Bernard of Septimania, the godson, the intimate friend and counsellor of Louis-le-débonnaire was universally reported to be the seducer of the Empress: she and her paramour were seeking to compass her husband's death : he, a degraded and passive wittol, and that young child, Charles, on whom he doated, the offspring of adultery.

§ 2. Open a mediæval *geste* at a venture: the chance is, that the plot turns upon a Queen's incontinence:—the bonhomme of a husband hears, shudders, and believes the denunciations received from the profligate courtier whose advances she has repelled, or the spiteful dwarf whipped for his insolence, or the wanton serving-wench seeking to win the easy Sovereign's heart, that his dear spouse, with whom he has lived years in peace and comfort and worshipped as a model of conjugal fidelity, is an adulteress. Without any further examination she is abandoned to the waves in a leaky boat, or driven into the desert to be devoured by lions, or chained to the stake amidst the pile of faggots where she is to be burned alive. Upon the same agreeable theme many pleasant variations are grounded. The

824—987
824—829

824—828
Approach
of the Re-
volutionary
period.

821—987 gentle Troubadour sought to vitiate woman's
824—828 chastity by his harmonious verse. The clever,
sarcastic, scurvy Trouveur delighted in woman's
degradation. The Minstrel represents the probability of female frailty as outweighing all moral
or physical improbabilities. The Queen-consort
is taken in labour; and the malignant hag, the
Queen-dowager, reports to her dutiful son that
her daughter-in-law has been delivered of a log
of wood, or a puppy dog, or seven puppy dogs,
as the case may be. The King translates these
preternatural births into portentous evidence of
his wife's crime, and condemnation then ensues
as before, the innocent Lady being however always
ultimately rescued.

False accu-
sations
against
female
chastity
a staple
theme in
mediæval
romances

The prototypes of these tales are unfortunately not rare in authentic mediæval history.
Very slight proofs, mere surmises, or incredible
accusations were accepted or employed by the
mediæval sovereigns for the purpose of ridding
themselves of their consorts. They constitute the
basis of the proceedings in the regal-divorce
causes, at all times the scandals and perils of
the throne. France and Germany in particular
offer instances of such calumnies carried to an
atrocious extent. The most magnanimous and
disinterested exertions of Pontifical power consist in the checks or corrections by which the
Church defended female innocence and restrained
the wild lasciviousness of kings. Such was the

protection given by Innocent the Third to the 824—987
friendless and desolate Ingeburga of Denmark.
Lothair, the second son of the Emperor Lothair, 824—828
second in birth, second in name, but the first
king of the kingdom of Lotharingia or Lorraine,
the persecutor of Theutberga, was a worthy pre-
cursor of Philip-Augustus. Philip-Augustus was
a worthy follower of Lothair. Each example,
however, offers peculiar features. Unquestionably many a royal-divorce suit which excites pain
or surprize was prosecuted groundlessly, yet in
good faith, by a corrupt husband, whose accusing
conscience led him to an easy belief of the mis-
conduct imputed to his wife: he judged her by
his own standard.

With Louis-le-débonnaire, the same process
of moral induction, often applied so fallaciously,
whether as the source of approbation or censure,
praise or blame, produced exactly the opposite
results. He, wavering in his opinions, and constitutionally prone to timid credulity, wholly put
aside all the calumnies by which Judith was
assailed. Not a single suspicion, from first to
last, ever disturbed the honest heart of Louis-le-
débonnaire: his fond delight in Judith continued unbounded. Indeed, from what we gather
concerning her, she very fully deserved his ten- Eucreasing
derness and love. To their young son, Charles, affection of
Louis clung with yearning affection. The boy débonnaire
was constantly with his parents, and the Emperor for Judith
and the Empress brought him forward as a Crown- Charles.

824—987

824—828

Prince in the Diets of the Empire. During that magnificent ceremonial, when Harold the Dane performed homage, Charles is described by an eye-witness as joyfully coursing along the marble pavement before them :—

> Ante patrem pulcher Carolus inclitus auro
> Lætus abit, plantis marmora pulsat ovans.
> Judith interea regali munere fulta
> Procedit ——

The unshaken confidence of Louis-le-débonnaire in Count Bernard we have already noticed. He was brought higher into trust, treated as the most intimate friend of the imperial family ; and the Count of Septimania was intruded as an imperial vicar into the dominions of Louis-le-Germanique, certainly trenching upon the privileges of that son.

Anxieties of Louis-le-débonnaire for the establishment and safety of Charles

§ 3. The paternal fondness of Louis-le-débonnaire for his young Charles was now darkening into the great trouble of his reign and life. The tripartite division of the Empire between Lothair, Pepin and Louis-le-Germanique was intended to be final and conclusive. Advisedly promulgating the grant upon the request of the States of the Empire, Louis had placed his sons in possession. Again, in the Placitum at Nimeguen, the Prelates and Nobles confirmed the compact, equally appertaining to the Sovereigns and the people. Consistently with this ratification, this act of settlement, what provision could be made for the young Charles? Louis-le-

débonnaire had scarcely anything left to him
worth acceptance which he could bestow: an
abbey, when one should become vacant, was the
only valuable appanage he could grant: the best
of these preferments were appropriated and the
Court filled with greedy expectants for the first
which should open to competition. But all doubts
and uncertainties must have merged in a more
fearful anticipative inquiry: how was Louis to
protect the freedom, the life of his child? How
would the Emperor Lothair, King Pepin and King
Louis act towards the son of the suspected, defamed and hated step-mother—a half-brother, excluded by the legislative entail? They, however,
did not allow him even this claim to consanguinity.
The sons of Hermengarda, or their partizans, asserted that "Charlot" was an adulterine bastard,
a *mamzer*, no brother at all. Perhaps, according
to family custom, they would cause him to be
degraded, or shorn in a monastery, like Hugh
and Drogo and Thierry, or condemn him to
death upon suspicion, and then pardoning him
like King Bernard, as a great mercy put out his
eyes.

In this strait, Judith unquestionably co-
operating, the hopes and plans of Louis turned
wholly to the one object of securing a Kingdom
for Charles : a desire which could not be effected
without a radical unsettlement of the Empire,
revoking the act declared to be irrevocable. He

824—987

824—828

828
Louis-le-
débonnaire
treats with
Lothair to
assent to
the endow-
ment of
Charles at
the expence
of Louis-le-
German-
ique.

824—987 might be encouraged in this dangerous attempt
by the discontents which the *Charta divisionis*
824—829 and the Treaty of Nimeguen had already occasioned amongst the benefitted parties. A political
schism had arisen between the three crowned
brothers: Pepin and Louis-le-Germanique groaned
at their *senior's* supremacy, and the *senior* because his *seniority* north of the Alps was imperfectly defined. Lothair, the Emperor, might
not have any objection to sanction a further subdivision of his brothers' portions in Germany and
the Gauls, by which process their powers would
be diminished.

Louis therefore treated with Lothair secretly,
and obtained his assent to the promotion and
endowment of Charles-le-Chauve. Louis-le-débonnaire proposed that the endowment should
be effected at the expence of Louis-le-Germanique, a fourth partition of the Empire. Louis-
le-débonnaire planned that this new kingdom
should be composed of the territories of which
Duke Bernard had assumed the government,—
"Alemannia, Rhætia and Transjurane Burgundy,"

829   a territory wholly of the German tongue. A
Council at
Worms,   Diet was convened at Worms, to which all the
fourth par-
tition of the sons were summoned. Pepin kept away. Lo-
Empire
Alemannia, thair retracted his dishonest consent, united
&c taken
from Louis- himself to Louis-le-Germanique: both were af-
le-Germa-
nique, and fronted and offended in the highest degree, and
given to
Charles-le- testified against the dismemberment. But Louis-
Chauve.

le-débonnaire persevered : the before-mentioned 824—987
dominions were given to Charles ; and the young
Prince, placed under Bernard's care, was sent to   829—830
take possession of the newly erected realm. This
was the *fourth* partition of the empire. The
education of Charles was entrusted to Bernard,
and, notwithstanding the troubles of the times,
pursued steadily.

Charles-le-Chauve became as well imbued Literary
with literature as his father and his grandsire. and talent
Important chronicles by which we now profit, le-Chauve
owe their origin to the liberal obedience which
his suggestions commanded. His court was the
resort of the learned, whom he encouraged by
munificence, but more efficiently by example and
generous rivalry.

An acute metaphysical theologian, he delighted in epistolary discussions, exercising the
ability of opponent and respondent.   Charlemagne gave to the Western Church the sublime
hymn *Veni Creator :* his grandson, instructed
by the example, cultivated the same noble talent, and his compositions were adopted in the
Gallican liturgics.—An expressive token of his
classical taste may be discerned in the name
Carlopolis, by which he sought to honour his
favourite palace—Compiègne, and the city he
there designed to found.

§ 4.   Louis-le-débonnaire, aware of the 829—830.
machinations forming against him and Judith, of the re-

824—987

829—830
volution ·
active
pait taken
by Wala trusted the more implicitly to Count Bernard, accumulating upon this minion every token of confidence. The attacks directed against the favourite were construed into evidences of his loyalty. This conduct accelerated the progress of the revolution. The rays of general discontent acquire their fiercest heat when concentrated upon the one hated head. No political change is so strenuously prosecuted, as when the propelling agents are vivified by their antipathy to the one man singled out for the sacrifice : the abstract sentiment concreted by individual feeling, national grievances exaggerated by particular jealousy. Or it may be asked whether any popular movement ever takes place until circumstances render some one man the visible and tangible mark of rancour, rightly or wrongly entertained. Laud swung down the monarchy in the person of Charles Stuart : Judge Jefferies Bernard
the object
of peculiar
enmity. determined the Revolution. Count Bernard was hated by the Emperor Lothair, by King Pepin and by King Louis-le-Germanique, as the efficient supporter of their detested pseudo-brother Charles Equally so by Archbishop Agobard, possibly on account of his immorality ; but worst of all was Bernard hated by his own brother-in-law Wala, his loudest, most inveterate, most cogent and dogged accuser. It is a strange moral insanity that kindred can rarely see the absurdity of befouling their own nest. The close connexion

between Wala and Bernard increased the acer- _{824—987}
bity of the feud.   Wala encouraged in every way
the odium cast upon guiltless Judith's supposed _{820—830}
paramour.   Every effort was made throughout
the now-commencing revolution to irritate and
excite the public mind.

§ 5.   A libel and pamphlet literature arose, Libel lite-
the crest of the foaming waves, a nationally ^{rature of} the ninth
characteristic literature, re-appearing in the sub- century
sequently corresponding crises of the ancient
monarchy.   The *pièces justificatives* of the *Mémoires de Louis-le-débonnaire* should be bound
up with the *Mémoires de la Ligue;* the *Mémoires de la Ligue* introduce the *Mémoires de
la Fronde*, and all should be numbered consecutively and made into one set, as introductory to the *Mémoires de la Révolution
Française.*

In such a collection we should find Archbishop Agobard's addresses to the people, and
also the reply to Agobard's addresses—the *Con-
questio Domini Ludovici Imperatoris*,—the pa-
thetic lament in which the dethroned Louis, like
another Charles Stuart, narrates the indignities
he sustained   The collection would also include
a very curious political Biography of Wala, the
source supplying the materials for our narrative
of his youthful adventures.   This work consists of
a series of conversations, in which the several
individuals concerned are designated by fictitious

824—987 names—a plan instigated equally by the desire
829—830 of concealment and the lurid drollery often accompanying the most fatal intrigues, the morbid merriment elicited by intense anxiety. The interlocutors apply the most vituperative language in disparagement of Count Bernard. They call him *Naso*, a name ludicrously contrasting with the personal epithet characterising the Count of Orange his father, *Guillaume-au-court-nez*. Louis-le-débonnaire and Judith are scorned under the appellations of Justinian and Justina: Pepin is Melanius: Lothair, Honorius; and Louis, Gratian;—but the hero is Wala, under the more euphonic denomination of Arsenius.

The *Epitaphium Arsenii* a vindication of Wala

Indeed the *Epitaphium Arsenii*, a title given to the biography in consequence of the addition of a second and concluding part, made after Wala's death, is completely devoted to the justification of his public and private conduct throughout the Revolution. But Paschasius Radbertus the apologist, his disciple at Corbey and afterwards Abbot, has performed an unlucky service to his friend's memory. His vindication displays the extreme bitterness of Wala's character. We learn the extent of Wala's hostility against Louis-le-débonnaire by the attempted extenuation. — Antiquaries would have been sorely puzzled by this extraordinary composition, had not the Hercules of archæologists, Dom Mabillon, who unearthed the single existing manuscript, also in-

geniously discovered the key which decyphered 824—987
the mystery.

829—830

It may be remarked, that the literary fancy
of employing fictitious names, which amused an
Alcuin and a Charlemagne, was common during
the Middle Ages. Belonging to this particular
era, we have a threnody upon the death of Abbot
Adelhard, also due to Paschasius, an eclogue in
which the *Vieille Corbey,* the mother monastery
in Picardy, and young Corbey the daughter on
the Weser, alternate their lamentations as Phyllis
and Galatea.

The Councils, considered as ecclesiastical, often
oscillated in character between synods and secular
parliaments. The Bishops were virtually or actually the elected representatives of their diocesan
cities; and matters, in our estimation purely secular, were therein treated and discussed. This
commixture of spiritual and temporal affairs resulted from the pervading authority of the Church
exercised through the Hierarchy—an authority,
the blessing of the mediæval era, notwithstanding
its inevitably concomitant human defects, aber-
rations and abuses. Wala led the opposition,
his loud harangues declaring that the decline of
the Empire was occasioned by the incompetence
of Louis-le-débonnaire. All the mischiefs en- Wala takes
suing from the parricidal ambition of his sons, the lead in
the Coun-
the selfish partizanship of the nobles, the people's cils—attacking
Louis-le-
faithlessness, were attributed to the Sovereign, débonnaire.
the sufferer; and his participation in the govern-

821—987

829—830

ment of the Church, such as had been excused or applauded in Charlemagne, was imputed to him as an unjustifiable usurpation. Wala was a lover of truth and a lover of justice; but exaggerated virtues may prove more deceitful and mischievous than acknowledged vices. Wala's dramatic biography affords some conception of his ungovernable impetuosity, and enables us to form a vague hypothesis concerning the motives which instigated him.—Did not Judith tease him by her clever and sarcastic tongue?—Against Count Bernard, vain and profligate, Wala was spurred by contempt, family bickerings and political jealousy; and, exulting in his own firm and iron character, he despised the pliability and indecision of Louis-le-débonnaire.

830.

Feb. 8.

Expedition against the Bretons.

§ 6. At this juncture, Louis-le-débonnaire undertook another raid-royal against Armorica, now governed by Nominoé, a prince literally taken from the plough, and who had been confirmed in his dominion by the Carlovingian crown. Lambert commanded at Nantes as Count of the Breton Marches, where the Romanised Franks settled in considerable numbers. Louis-le-débonnaire set his army in motion during Lent, that holy time when, according to the precepts of the Church, the truce of God ought to have been most strictly observed,—so urgent was the supposed exigency, the alleged revolt of the Celtic King,—an unfounded allegation, say the Breton Historians who maintain that Nominoé con-

tinued faithful to Louis-le-débonnaire, but that
Bernard and Count Lambert the traitor suggested
the inroad to forward some scheme of their own.

824—987
829—830

Anyhow, the expedition was most unfortunate. Such was the general state of affairs, that
every shrewd and clearsighted waiter upon opportunities began to plan how he could profit
by the revolution, which all, save the Sovereign,
knew was impending. Louis might have had a
sufficient token of his own debility when he
marshalled, or rather endeavoured to marshal,
his army against the Bretons. A starved array :—
the larger number of the nobles and troops who
ought to have obeyed his summons, refused.
Some, as we infer from subsequent proceedings,
professed scruples about the Lenten season: nevertheless no scruples of any kind prevented their
mustering with determined hostility against Louis-
le-débonnaire in that city, which, after centuries
of obscurity, rarely varied by any important event,
was now destined to become the *primum mobile*
of France, may be of the civilized world.

The Mili-
tary Sum-
mons of
Louis dis-
obeyed.

§ 7. French writers, French historians, French
ecclesiastics, all Frenchmen, whatever may be
their principles or views, are unanimous in
asserting that the royal decree of the Merovingian Clovis rendered Paris the capital of
France. This is an article of national faith ;—
but rarely has there been a more signal example of faith yielding to authority, without
evidence and against probability. When Pope

Paris not
the actual
capital of
the French
monarchy
till the ac-
cession of
the Capets.

1622.

824—987
825—830
Paris not an archiepiscopal See until the reign of Louis Treize.

Gregory the Fifteenth, at the request of Louis son of Henri-quatre, erected the See of Paris into an Archbishoprick, he assigns the antient preeminence of Paris as a reason for the promotion in the Gallican hierarchy given to her Prelate, then Jean-François de Gondy, brother of the Cardinal de Retz, whom he succeeded. If the validity of the concession depended upon the truth of the recital, the Papal Bull would be void; for nothing is more certain than that Paris never became the capital of France until after the accession of the third dynasty.—Paris made the Capets, the Capets made Paris.—A mere archæological question thus acquires the greatest value in French history.

Paris, a city of inferior order under the Romans, Merovingians and Carlovingians.

Julian's affection for Lutetia was kindled by the rustic plainness and simplicity gracing the island and its pleasant vicinity. Lutetia, under the Roman domination, continued unhonoured by those privileges and institutions which distinguished the great cities of the Gauls, enabling Toulouse and Tournay and Nîmes, and so many others, to deduce their municipal genealogy in uninterrupted line from the Republic or the Roman Empire. The vigorous defence which the inhabitants had maintained against Cæsar earned the displeasure of the conquerors, and Paris is placed in the lowest rank, amongst the Vectigales of the Empire. Compared with the cities distinguished by their traditionary reputation or as seats of government, Rheims, where Clovis was baptized,

Soissons, where he was installed in royalty, Or- 821—987
leans the erudite, Metz, proud of her immemorial
antiquity,—the *bonne ville de Paris*, however 829—830
proud she might be in after times, dwindles into
a provincial town.

Clovis, it is true, occasionally held his Court
in the Imperial Palace of the Cæsars, which,
though at some distance from the shores of the
island-city, was connected therewith. Some of
his immediate successors, Clodomir, Childebert
and Chilperic, also dwelt there, but they were
frequently attracted away by halls and towers
affording the enjoyment of wood and wold. The
palace of a Merovingian or Carlovingian Sovereign
was worth nothing without a hunting-ground.
Paris was neglected more and more during the
concluding periods of the first dynasty; and
Charlemagne, excepting perhaps when Paris might
be on his road, never resided there at all.

But though destitute of royal favour, Paris
had within her from the first foundation of the
Frankish monarchy, aye, and long before the
foundation of the Frankish monarchy, the elements of that importance which she afterwards
acquired.

As a Christian city, though her Bishop was
only a suffragan of Sens, yet great veneration
was rendered to the memory of her first prelate
Dionysius, enhanced by the legendary traditions
of the Areopagite, whilst the great Monastery of
which Saint Denis was the patron, and the other

Importance
of the Isle
of Paris
derived
from the
command
of the river
Seine:

824—987
829—830
powerful and opulent foundations, Saint Germain
des Près, Saint Germain l'Auxerrois, Sainte Geneviève, and Saint Laurent, rendered the vicinity
one of the most interesting ecclesiastical districts
in the kingdom.

But the influential cause which elevated mediæval Paris into a metropolis of permanently
national pre-eminence, whatever other claims she
might possess upon moral feeling, will be best
understood if we consult the map and consider
the position of the island-city,—look upon her
armorial bearing, the Bark and expound her
symbolical heraldry.—Down to Mantes the Seine,
then much broader than at present, was called
"the Water of Paris ;" and, from the Gaulish
times, Paris was held by the Navicularii or
Bargemen, who, subsequently incorporated as a
Collegium according to the Roman law, became,
by virtue of royal ordinances, the municipality of
the Hôtel de Ville. The Prevôt des Marchands
rose to the station of her chief magistrate : her
political influence sprung out of her mercantile
Paris occu-
pied by the
revolution-
ary party. activity and opulence. Whoever held Paris commanded the Seine ; and Paris, hitherto almost un-
observed in the Carlovingian Empire, now bursts
into notice. The City of Revolutions begins her
real history by the first French Revolution.
Paris, where the influence, whether personal or
constitutional of the Sovereign was then at its
minimum, which owed nothing to his favour or
his bounty, where he was neither respected nor

feared, and where the shadows of the Merovingian kings interred at Sainte Geneviève might seem to threaten the usurping lineage, was appointed as the place of muster for the Revolutionists. There the whole hostile party, the clergy, the troops, the nobles, assembled.

§ 8.   Pepin of Aquitaine came forward as the Leader of the insurrection. As soon as the banner was raised, Lothair and Louis-le-Germanique joined the king of Aquitaine. Noble objects, according to their proclamation, incited the insurgent sons—love for their parent, love for their King, love for their country. Louis was held in thraldom by an adulterous consort and her insidious paramour : they sought to deliver the Emperor from the domestic conspiracy which threatened his throne and life. Louis-le-débonnaire was completely without support : Count Bernard fled, Judith took refuge in Laon, the hill-fortress of the Frankish kings.

Louis repaired to Compiègne, was seized by his sons, and subjected to shameful violence, not a priest or soldier, councillor or comforter, stood by him. Judith they pursued to the rock of Laon. Dragged out of Saint Mary's Monastery, no sanctuary, no manly feeling, protected the helpless Empress. They reviled her, ill-treated her, threatened her with death : they held out that she had no hope of mercy unless she could induce her husband to become a monk, and vacate the throne—the last Merovingian

824—987
830

830.
March—
May.
Outbreak
of the re-
volution.
The Royal
Family
taken pri-
soners.

Louis sub-
jected to
personal
violence.

824—987 had done so. Louis had once sought to be a monk: he was already a monk in heart—why 829—830 not become one in habit, and be happy in a monastery? But Louis resisted. Called to perform the duties of a Sovereign, he would not abandon these duties. The menaces against Judith became fiercer. In order that she might save her life, Judith, Louis advised her to put on the veil. As for cruelly treated by himself, he required time for consideration. Con- her step- rad and Rodolph, the brothers of the Empress, sons. were seized, shorn, and placed in custody in separate monasteries. Count Bernard escaped his enemies: not so his brother Herbert, who was caught and blinded. The sons harassed their father by lacerating his feelings. Judith was hurried from monastery to monastery, and at last imprisoned at Poitiers, in the monastery of Saint Radegund, of which the desecrated Church still exists, unroofed, but otherwise a perfect Carlovingian monument.

830—831. § 9. Louis-le-débonnaire, however, was still Counter- supported by a powerful party. He, his friends revolution begins and adherents had been taken by surprize: had he fallen back at once upon the great independent cities towards the Rhine, they would have enabled him to withstand the power of Paris. He was loved and pitied, nor would the sound Germanic portions of the Empire easily renounce their Sovereign. The jailer-sons were compelled to relax in the custody of their prisoner, venerable through his sorrows. He promised to reform the

abuses of government, principally in relation to 821—987
Church-affairs, and the counter-revolution was
now rapidly maturing. Lothair nevertheless as- 830—831
Disunion
between
Lothair
sumed the supreme authority, treating his father
as a dethroned monarch and his brothers Pepin and his
brothers.
and Louis as his vassals, to their great indig-
nation. They suspected that they had been over-
reached:—had they not been playing Lothair's
game?

The confidants of Louis-le-débonnaire craftily Schemes
employed
by Louis
for the
purpose of
promoting
fresh dis-
union—a
fifth parti-
tion of the
empire
proposed.
suggested to him that he might detach Pepin and
Louis-le-Germanique from their elder brother,
and employ the faithless against the disobedient:
an item of degrading policy added to the family
account and encreasing the sum total of wrong.
Gundobald, a monk, ambitious and unconscien-
tious (afterwards Archbishop of Rouen) was the
negotiator. A *fifth* partition of the Empire was
proposed.—Lothair to be restricted to Italy, the
kingdoms of Pepin and Louis-le-Germanique to
be encreased and a competent endowment given
to Charles-le-Chauve. The revulsion of feeling in
favour of Louis, became impetuous amongst the
northern and eastern populations of the Em-
pire. It was agreed that a general Placitum The cause
of the
restoration
prospers
should be summoned for the purpose of a paci-
fication. Lothair proposed that the Assembly
should be held somewhere in Romanized Gaul;
but Louis, knowing where his own strength
was to be found, convened the Placitum at Nime-

824—987

830—831
Louis-le-
débonnaire
replaced
in his
authority

guen, amongst or nigh his peculiar adherents.
The Germans generally felt deeply for the humiliation which the son of Charlemagne had sustained, and rose enthusiastically in his favour.
Lothair was urged by his partizans to give battle
to his father, but he dared not. Louis-le-débonnaire was replaced upon the Imperial throne, and,
reinaugurated, he reassumed the exercise of his
power. The leaders of the revolt were tried, and
found guilty of high treason; Louis-le-débonnaire's mercy remitted the sentence of capital
punishment. Wala was ordered to return to his
monastery at Corbey and live according to rule,
but he would not acknowledge that he had been
in the wrong; and his obstinacy was punished by
imprisonment in a cavern near the lake of Geneva.

Submission
of Lothair
and his
brothers.

Judith
clears her-
self of the
charges
brought
against her
by wager
of law,
and Ber-
nard by
wager of
battle

Judith, restored to her husband, the vows she
had taken upon compulsion were pronounced to
be null. Proclamation was made that any one
who could prefer any charge against the Empress,
still stigmatized by report as an adulteress, should
come forward. No witness appeared: nevertheless, according to the antient usages of the Franks,
she cleared herself by compurgation or wager of
law—she declared her innocence upon oath, and
the compurgators swore that they believed in the
truth of her asseveration. The compurgatory
process, common under various modifications to
all the antient nations, could never be otherwise
than an uncertain mode of trial, yet wisely

adapted to the imperfection of human judgment 824—987
and the exigencies of human society. The legist
will find it impracticable to suggest any more 832—833
eligible mode for repelling a grave accusation
positively preferred, though grounded only upon
common fame—*troth* undistinguishable from *truth.*
—affirmative evidence unattainable, and negative
evidence unavailable.—Bernard vindicated himself against the imputation by wager of battle.
He challenged his accusers, but no accuser dared
to meet him in the lists. Lothair was deprived
of the Imperial authority, and returned to Italy,
Pepin to Aquitaine, and Louis-le-Germanique to
his diminished kingdom, Alemannia being administered on behalf of Charles-le-Chauve; and
Louis-le-débonnaire hastened to Remiremont in
the Vosges, resorting again to the scenes which
had delighted him in his bright youthful days,
the streams swarming with fish and the forests
stocked with game and deer.

§ 10. It must be accepted as an incontro- Reanima-
vertible axiom, that a restoration never places a tion of the
revolution-
monarch exactly in the situation which he held ary party
before : he comes in by a new title. Louis can
scarcely be said to have been restored: the violence which ejected him was transient, his case
was not the resumption of an authority which
had ceased, but rather the triumph of a party
over a faction. Louis had defeated Lothair : the
North-German interest had prevailed over Ro-

824—987 manized France. Much as Louis deserved the
love of his subjects, he failed to retain their con-
832—833 fidence. The Lothairians, as we may call them,
Agobard being their chief intellectual leader,
maintained that the conduct of Louis was wholly
illegal:—by disturbing the settlement of the
kingdom, violating the compact upon which the
primary partition of the Empire was founded
and the *Charta divisionis* confirmed by oath,
he was an instigator of perjury, a delinquent
against the state.—All these motives are expressed in Agobard's manifesto. *Audite omnes
gentes*, are the words by which Agobard begins
his address: sternly and solemnly energetic, he
fulminates his political anathema, and the sentiments were universally adopted by the Revolutionists.

832
The sons
revolt
again

　A period of distracting anxiety ensued. Louis,
mistrustful of his sons, yet not daring to shew his
suspicions: the sons only waiting an opportunity
for commencing hostilities. Louis soon gave them
that opportunity. Pepin behaved discourteously
and ungraciously, refused to attend a general
Placitum, and disturbed the Christmas festivities
by an abrupt departure from the Court. Louis
construed this conduct into a revolt, and prepared
to act accordingly. Louis-le-Germanique, from
whom so large a portion of his dominion had been
wrested for the benefit of Charles, made a general
levy of all his subjects, Germans and Sclavonians,

bond and free, and prepared to recover Aleman- 824—987
nia, the old Suabian land.   Yet Louis-le-débonnaire, undismayed and uninstructed by adversity, 833
and never abandoning his ruling idea, only sought
to turn all the circumstances to the advantage
of his darling Charles, and proposed a *sixth*
division of his empire.   He adjudicated that Louis attempts to
Aquitaine was forfeited by Pepin : this kingdom gain
Lothair, by
he would give to Charles, and Lothair should sacrificing
Pepin and
receive the remaining portions of the Empire. Louis-le-
German-
The proceeding was equally harsh and un- ique. He
proposes a
constitutional : the Aquitanians claimed to have *sixth* partition of the
a voice in the election of their sovereign : no one Empire.
knew the right better than Louis-le-débonnaire,
but his doting fondness for Charles blinded him.

If the Aquitanians made a show of assent
to the transfer, their consent was extorted ; and
amongst the many errors of Louis-le-débonnaire,
none was more conducive to calamity.   All the
enemies of Louis recovered their transiently depressed energy.   Wala was delivered from his
cavern   The alliance between Lothair, Pepin
and Louis-le-Germanique was renewed, and they
declared open war against their father.   Hostilities were recommenced by them, considerately
and vindictively.   Lothair marched from Italy 828.
Pope Gre-
accompanied by Pope Gregory the Fourth, who gory IV.
conse-
had succeeded to the Pontificate, a Roman by crated.
birth, and to whom Rome owed many monuments of magnificence.   The Pontiff had been

824—987 persuaded to sanction by his presence the parricidal invasion.

833.
833—June
The Luegenfeld or Field of Falsehood

§ 11. Near Colmar, in the heart of that noble undulating plain of fertile Alsace, between the Rhine and the lengthening ranges of the Vosges, the region so cherished by Louis-le-débonnaire, is a hill then known and reverenced as the *Siegberg*, the "mountain of victory;" the champagne country below being denominated the "bloody field," the *Roth-feld*,—names transmitted by oral tradition, and bearing record of some desperate conflict, which, fought there in the pristine ages of the Teutons, had left no other trace upon human memory. Here the armies encamped, host against host, tents ranged opposite to tents,

Louis betrayed into the power of his sons.

the sons against the father. A neutral ground separated the camps: on either side the blow was delayed. Faint and lingering feelings of decency and duty restrained the unnatural children: earnest affection induced the father to proffer peace and forgiveness. Pope Gregory had associated himself to Lothair, ostensibly as a mediator. Louis treated and parleyed, but ineffectually : thus whilst the old Emperor wasted the valuable time, his cunning sons improved the delay, and they now warred by seduction and treachery. An unrestrained communication and intercourse subsisted between the two camps, troops and chieftains mixed and mingled as friends: this Bishop or that Count was bribed to retreat from the failing cause, others were flattered away or warned against the folly of adhering to a crazy old man, and thus incurring the vengeance of the young Sovereigns.

824—987
833

A cruel defection ensued: Counts, Bishops, Abbots, Commanders, all deserted Louis: hardly any one even tried to resist the contagious treason. The two armies became one army, the combined army of the allied brethren. A very few hesitated, as if they thought of continuing faithful, but Louis would not allow his friends to share in his misfortunes.—"Do not abide with me,"—said he; " do not peril life or limb for my sake: go over to my sons." When the abandonment was completed, when priests, nobles, soldiers, servants, even to the meanest, had departed from him, Louis-le-débonnaire came forth from his tent, accompanied by the Empress Judith, holding their boy Charles by the hand, and the old man, the matron and the child became captives in the power of the foe.

Louis deserted by his followers, &c.

Louis, Judith, and Charles made prisoners

The victorious sons seemed somewhat moved: greeting their father they embraced him; yet this token of affection or respect was a mockery, for they treated their parent as a degraded and contemptible enemy. They had promised Louis that Judith should not be separated from him, but they immediately violated that promise, and subjected her to rigid detention. Louis and the young Charles continued under arrest in Lothair's tent

824—987 till they were removed to their respective places
of confinement.

833.

Thus ended the present conflict. The glorious
visions of the primeval heroes, hitherto hovering over hill and plain, were henceforward dispelled by the hard reality of modern felony. So
shameful was the falsity displayed, that from this
time forth the *Roth-feld* lost its ancient name.
No longer the *Roth-feld*, the encrimsoned field of
ancestral victory, but the *Luegen-feld*, the "Field
of Lies :" the honest German soil was perennially
branded by the treachery. On the *Luegen-feld*
the trust and the faith and the power and the
spirit of the Frankish race passed for ever away.

Persecu-
tions in-
flicted upon
the Impe-
rial Family

§ 12.   Lothair, Pepin and Louis-le-Germanique immediately began to consider the partition
of the Empire; but first they had to dispose of
their prisoners.   Judith was sent across the Alps

Louis-le-
débonnaire
imprisoned
in the
Abbey of
Saint Mé-
dard.

to Tortona. At Pruhm, now an established State-
prison, a cell was prepared for Charlot. Louis-
le-débonnaire, who had been kept in close custody
by Lothair, was transferred to Soissons. Humiliated, despised, a willing penitent and yet an
indignant monarch, they incarcerated him in that
tower, which, together with the sepulchral crypt
of Chlothaire and Sigebert, alone remains to
mark the site of the magnificent Abbey. Abbot
Hilduin was well contented to turn the key upon
his benefactor and master. All parties during
this revolution appealed to the passions of the

people—the sons of Louis, to justify their wrongs against their father, the father, to obtain compassion, if not vengeance, for his wrongs.—" They placed me here," says Louis himself in the *Con-questio*, the Complaint in which he details his misfortunes, "striving to drive me to an abdica-
" tion, being well aware how I honour the sanc-
" tuary and how I venerate the memory of Saint
" Médard and Saint Sebastian. They continually
" perplexed me by false intelligence : sometimes
" they told me that my wife had become a nun ;
" sometimes that she was dead ; sometimes that
" my innocent Charles, whom they knew I loved
" above all things, was shorn as a monk ; and in-
" asmuch as I, deprived of my kingdom, my wife,
" my child, could not bear these griefs, I passed
" my days and nights in tears and sorrow."—

Louis still steadily refused the surrender of his Crown, but his enemies persevered in assailing him with ingenious and inexorable consistency. They worked upon his truly tender conscience. He knew his own sins : he appeared again as a penitent before the altar, clad in sackcloth and deprived of his sword.

And now ensued the catastrophe to which all the preceding transactions had been tending, the deposition of Louis-le-débonnaire—not the first example in the middle ages, yet nevertheless most memorable in the series of lessons afforded equally to people and to kings, those lessons

821—987

833.

Extract from the *Complaint* of Louis-le-débonnaire.

833.
Deposition of Louis-le-débonnaire.

824—987 which all must take, though they may refuse to
profit by them.   The power of deposing kings
833—834 is inevitably deduced from the Divine right of
kings.   Their high office is vicarial and delegated.   The dominion given to Sovereigns by
the King of kings is not inherent or indefeasible,
but conditional on their governing according to
law and justice.

The doc-
trine of
royal re-
sponsibility
as laid
down in
Hooker's
Ecclesiasti-
cal Polity.

Solemnly and truly has an enlightened conscience pronounced that " on earth there should
" not be any alive altogether without standing in
" awe of some by whom they are to be con-
" trolled and bridled."   " The good estate of a
" commonwealth within itself is thought on no-
" thing to depend more than upon these two
" special affections, fear and love : fear in the
" highest governor himself, and love in the sub-
" jects which live under him.   The subjects' love
" for the most part continueth, as long as the
" righteousness of kings doth last ; in whom
" virtue decayeth not, as long as they fear to do
" that which may alienate the loving hearts of
" their subjects from them."   " In the mighty
" upon earth, (which are not always so virtuous
" and holy that their own good minds will bridle
" them), what may we look for, considering the
" fraility of man's nature, if the world do once
" hold it for a maxim that kings ought to live in
" no subjection : that how grievous disorders
" soever they fall into, none may have coercive

" power over them ?"—The eternal law of God, 824—987
irrespective of any humanly devised policy or
legislation, creates the original compact between 833—834
King and people: and the dethronement of
the Sovereign who violates the bond is the deserved penalty. The Divine displeasure chas-
tises the monarch through His appointed ministers of righteousness or wrath, even though
those ministers may be His enemies.

But in this particular case the violent and The pro-ceedings by which Louis-le-débonnaire was deposed, irregular.
irregular proceedings which professed to deprive
Louis-le-débonnaire of his regal authority, are
not to be vindicated by the general doctrines
which authorize the exercise of this transcen-
dently exceptional power. The tribunal was
altogether incompetent: an irregular convention
of certain Bishops of the Gauls, assembled without proper sanction, and destitute of any jurisdiction over the Head of the Empire: a conven-
ticle, a conciliabulum, good for nothing. The
charges to which we have before alluded were
futile, the arguments irrelevant, and the ceremonies and doctrines of the Church prostituted
and perverted for the purpose of forwarding the
parricidal projects entertained by Lothair and his
brethren.—The pretended judgment was the
worst of all social crimes, an act of force cloaked
in the garb of justice, and therefore bringing
justice into disrepute, and casting obloquy upon
the very principles by which justice is sustained.

824—987

835—836
The second
counter-re-
volution.
Louis-le-
débonnaire
again
restored.

§ 13. But the phases of this Revolution succeeded each other with national rapidity. A very large and influential party continued faithful to the monarch, though they had neglectfully surrendered him to his fate. The shame of the *Luegen-feld* was upon them : they were appalled by the disclosure of their own corruptions. The more unmixed portions of the Franks, as well as the purely Teutonic dominions, rose in arms to deliver the Emperor. The three brothers quarrelled. Lothair was now the reigning Emperor, Cæsar and Augustus, without a partner in his dignity : Louis and Pepin found that they had worked to give him an undivided supremacy. Louis-le-Germanique began to testify an apparent sense of duty towards his father : Pepin, open hostility to both his brothers. Lothair astutely evaded the contest. The old Emperor and the young Charles were severally released and brought to Paris.

Conferences ensued between Lothair on the one part, and a powerful deputation proceeding from the German realms on the other part. The threatening aspect of the Germans aided their arguments. They demanded the liberation of their old Emperor : Pepin was advancing with his army ; Lothair retreated. Louis-le-débonnaire entered the Abbey of Saint-Denis : the Bishops absolved him. Girt again with his sword, the symbol of power, his re-accession was announced

by the people's cheerful acclaim. Wife and child 824—987
were restored to him. No disobedience, no rebellion could harden the heart of Louis : the guilty 835—836
sons were too happy to avail themselves of his
facile tenderness ; and after some incidental movements of partial and receding hostility, we behold
him re-established on his throne.

Lothair was ultimately settled in Lombardy,
holding his court at Pavia. With him resided
Wala ; and it was an effective conducement to
the present transient respite, that he, the old
man, once the fomenter of the revolution, the
cause of such bitter dissension between father and
son, was now most desirous to promote peace ;—
the best component qualities of his energetic
character were revived during the brief space of
life which remained to him.

There was great reason indeed that the Em- 835—836. Renewed Incursions of the Northmen.
pire should be united : the Danes, the Northmen,
had been re-appearing in great strength, embold-
ened to more incessant depredations than at any
previous period, circling round and round the
Gauls, but particularly directing their attacks to
the Belgic coasts. The great commercial city of
Dœrstadt was again ravaged. In this city alone
they burnt and destroyed fifty-four churches, and
they settled in Walcheren, then a portion of
the Delta of the Scheldt, subsequently broken by
the raging floods into the five *Zee-land* islands.
They were also evidently directing themselves

824—987
835.
towards the estuary of the Seine. Could they gain possession of the islands embraced by the meandering river, each would be a Danish fortress in Gaul.

Louis-le-débonnaire was fully attentive to the defence of the realm; but the realm was not so dear to him as his child, Charles; and he and Judith were more and more wrapt up in that son. They were both dissatisfied with the portion assigned to Charles; and although Louis had suffered so bitterly from his previous endeavours on behalf of the boy, he actually planned a *seventh* partition of the empire.

835 —June
A *seventh*
partition
of the Em-
pire pro-
posed, in
the Placi-
tum at Cré-
mieux
He accordingly summoned a great diet at Crémieux, on the Rhone, near Lyons, where he proposed his scheme. No inconveniences, no obstacles, no dangers, restrained him from the attempt. Italy, all the territory south of the Alps, should continue to be ruled by Lothair. Aquitaine, the kingdom of Pepin, received a considerable extension—the whole territory between Seine and Loire, and thence also beyond the Seine up to the confines of the Belgic tongue. Louis was to lose Alemannia, but large cessions were made to him on the north—the whole tract between Scheldt and Rhine—by which he would gain Aix-la-Chapelle as his capital; and Charles, in addition to Alemannia, taken from Louis, was to rule Provence, the greater part of Burgundy, the dioceses of Rheims, Laon and

Treves, and other adjoining or interspersed dominions.

The proposition, a complete dislocation of
the Empire, was however, for the present, abandoned.   Louis-le-Germanique, who would on no
account part with any territory of the German
tongue, rejected the overture with great indignation.   Lothair also was grievously dissatisfied:
he would never surrender Aix-la-Chapelle, so consecrated by the remembrances of Charlemagne—
Charlemagne's palace, Charlemagne's tomb.

Old Wala undertook the laborious journey
from Bobbio, for the purpose of negotiating some
pacific settlement.   Louis and Judith received
Wala with entire heartiness and goodwill, in which
he fully participated.   All mutual wrongs and
grudges were forgiven, and expectations raised
that Lothair and Louis-le-Germanique would
yield.   It was agreed that a Diet should be convened at Worms, where Lothair would attend, and
conform to his father's injunctions.   The appointed
time arrived: no Lothair at the Diet.   Contagious fevers were prevailing in Italy: Wala died
at Bobbio.   His sincerity as well as his influence
over Lothair now became manifest; for Lothair,
no longer tempered by Wala's advice, evaded the
meeting at Worms, and again began to machinate
against his father.   Whether the pestilence in
Italy extended to France, or whether, like trees
coevally planted in an avenue, they were all

284—987
837.
wearing out concurrently, it so happened that
the greater number of the individuals who had
distinguished themselves most in the Revolution
died about this time. Many of them had been
the enemies, the bitter enemies of Louis, but
they were men of renown: he had been reconciled to them, he mourned their loss as losses
to the State, and he also received the fate of
his contemporaries as a warning to himself.
Whilst a general depression prevailed throughout
the realm, the Franks lamented their declining
fortunes, and laid all the blame upon their gover-
nors.—Foolish people, smitten people: their own
faithlessness, their own cowardice aggravated the
evils they sustained.

Louis meditated a pilgrimage to Rome, partly
for political reasons, partly for devotional purposes; but he was arrested in his progress. The
Northmen were again plundering and ravaging
the Belgic shores. A comet glaring in the sky,
a globe of fire as it is described, added to the
contagious dismay. Louis summoned his host to
meet at Nimeguen, where Charlemagne's Burg,
as yet unassailed by the Scandinavian, still maintained the pristine imperial splendour. He had
determined to take the command in person, and
to conduct his army against the enemy, but the
Northmen did not wait his approach: they returned to their ships unscathed, laden with booty.
Years before the death of Charlemagne provision

Further
ravages of
the North-
men.

had been made for the guarding of the coast. 824—987
The loss and disgrace were bitterly felt, but the
success of the inroad was entirely owing to the   837
pusillanimity and treachery of the Franks, who
neglected the directions which had been given
for watching the shores.

§ 14.   During these calamities Judith con-   837.
tinued her misguided endeavours to procure a Placitum at Aix.
more ample establishment for the young Charles. Eighth division of
Amidst all the dangers of the times she urged the Empire in favour of
Louis-le-débonnaire to the determination of try- Charles-le-Chauve.
ing an *eighth* partition of the Empire.   A Diet
was held at Aix-la-Chapelle, where so many
reminiscences of sorrow, trouble and disappointment were accumulating; and in this assembly
he bestowed upon Charles the largest, finest, and
most commanding portion of his northern dominions   In the description which the Chroniclers afford of these territories, we encounter
the usual uncertainties arising from a vague
enumeration; but the boundaries are stated with
sufficient clearness to shew that the cessions
extended from the Saxon lands to the Atlantic,
and as far South as the borders of Aquitaine.

Charles-le-Chauve was solemnly inaugurated. Inaugura-
In the presence of Louis-le-débonnaire, the pre- Charles-le-
lates and nobles of the newly-erected Kingdom Chauve.
were required to take the oaths to the Sovereign
and to become his vassals.   All who held royal
Benefices or Feuds commended themselves to the

824—987
838
young King at the behest of the Emperor, and
became his men —The ceremony was distinguished by a significant novelty. When the
clergy advanced to the throne for the purpose
of performing their fealty, Hilduin, Abbot of
Saint-Denis, appeared as premier Prelate, the
Archbishop of Rheims being set aside; and the
first amongst the laity was Gerard, the first
recorded Count of Paris. The recent transactions
had manifested the importance of the island-city,
and the station assigned to Count Gerard, answering as the premier peer of the new kingdom,
denotes the pre-eminence Paris began to assume.

This great political transaction was a desperate venture, which again brought the whole
Empire to the verge of ruin. The three sons of
Hermengarda were wholly opposed to this magnificent endowment of Judith's intruding son.
For the benefit of Charles-le-Chauve, and without
any other reason, the best parts of western and
southern Germany had been swept into his net—
an outrageous confiscation. But Louis-le-Germanique, true to his name and supported by his
people, was determined not to part with a single
Gau which spake the German tongue; and he
prepared for resistance. The usual vacillation of
Louis-le-débonnaire was provoked into firm determination : acting as a soldier, he determined
to regain a once deserved reputation, to shew
that he, Charlemagne's son, had fought under

Discontent
of the
three elder
brothers

the standard of the Great Emperor of the West. 824—987
He summoned his Host to meet at Mayence.

Lothair avoided any conflict, and Louis-le-
débonnaire proceeded in prosecuting the establishment of Charles upon the throne. A Diet was
held at Cérisy, or Kiersey, on the Oise. The more
he had given to Charles the more he sought to
give; and, with doting infatuation, a further partition was now tried by the old Emperor for
the *ninth* time. He decreed that Louis-le-Germanique had forfeited all his dominions except
Baioaria—Alsace, Saxony, Thuringia, Austrasia,
Alemannia, all taken away. Charles-le-Chauve,
now fifteen years of age, was solemnly pronounced
to be out of wardship, and his father girt him
with the sword of manhood. Hitherto Charles
had been too young to rule in the Kingdoms
assigned to him: henceforward he was to reign.
For the purpose of effacing the still subsisting recollections of his reputedly-dubious origin by the
prestige of historical traditions, he was crowned
"King of Neustria," like his illustrious namesake
and grandsire.

§ 15. At this juncture, Pepin, the most
affectionate of Hermengarda's sons, (and yet he
had rebelled three or four times against his
father) died, leaving two children, Pepin the
second of that name in Aquitaine, and Charles.
The Aquitanians determined to have the boy
Pepin as their King. Emeno, Count of Poitiers,

839—840
838.
September.
Council of
Kiersey on
the Oise —
Further
partition of
the empire
(being the
ninth) pro-
posed in
favour of
Charles-le-
Chauve

839—840.
Mutations
in Aqui-
taine —
Death of
Pepin

824—987

839.
The Aqui-
tanians
proclaim
the young-
er Pepin,
but his
grand-
father ex-
cludes him
from the
succession.

and Bernard his brother, were the leaders of the national insurrection. From this family descended *Guillaume tête d'étoupe*, or Shaggy-poll, Count of Poitiers, Count of Auvergne, and Duke of Aquitaine, who married the Adela or Princess Gerloc, also called Heloisa, daughter of Rollo. It is always very interesting to observe such lineages clearing themselves out of the darkness.

The election of the younger Pepin was not however carried unanimously. Certain nobles and others declared that the Aquitanians were bound to wait for the sanction of his grandfather the Emperor. Louis-le-débonnaire refused his assent, and gave his reasons —The young Pepin was wild, boisterous, and required good training. He would remove his grandson from Aquitaine, and educate him in his own palace, for the Aquitanians would ruin him—a most ungracious declaration from Louis-le-débonnaire, born in Aquitaine, educated in Aquitaine, and thoroughly assimilated to Aquitaine from his earliest youth.

Pepin, as he grew up, became equally distinguished by his beauty and his turbulence : headstrong, bold, irascible, debauched, fearless, the very prototype of a ballad-hero. The national privileges of the Aquitanians enabled them to share in the selection of their sovereigns : the spirit, if not the letter of the *Charta divisionis*, promised to the younger Pepin his father's kingdom. It is very possible that the boy Pepin, already

manifested some of the faults which marred his 824—987
talent and energy after he had been rendered
reckless by injustice and misfortune; and an easy 839
self-delusion convinced Louis-le-débonnaire that
the wayward grandson he wished to disinherit
was absolutely irreclaimable. Young Pepin's pretensions or rights must yield to the welfare of
the Empire—another and more eligible successor
must be found. Louis revived the sentence of
forfeiture which he had pronounced against Pepin the father. Lothair had an ample provision :
the undutiful Louis-le-Germanique was unworthy
of favour. Who then ought to rule Aquitaine?
Who so deserving as Charles King of Neustria?—
upon him accordingly was the realm bestowed.

§ 16. And yet there were those about Renewal
of the civil
Louis-le-débonnaire who lauded him for his pru- wars—attacks of the
dence and kindness.—This wonderful infatuation Northmen.
put an end to all hesitation on the part of Louis-
le-Germanique. Levying all his forces, Germans
and Sclavonians, he invaded Alemannia and recovered the territories which had been usurped
from him. The Aquitanians rose in revolt on
behalf of the boy Pepin. Earth and heaven appeared in confusion. Another comet became visible
in the sign of Aries, pendant over the nether
world with threatening fire. Streams of asteroids
were again seen, and the Northmen renewed their
dreadful ravages. Nevertheless, striving against
errors and calamities, Louis-le-débonnaire, though

821—987

839

suffering from infirmities which had brought on a premature old age, was stirred to greater vigour. Even Lothair found it expedient to temporize, and he repaired to his father at Worms.

A great Placitum was held nigh the Garden of Roses, and Lothair, kneeling before his father, entreated pardon for his repeated acts of ingratitude and disobedience. But this apparent contrition was directed to a cunning scheme of aggrandizement : Lothair complained that he, the Emperor, the firstborn, was still deprived of a fair and equitable proportion of the great Carlovingian inheritance : so many of the arching circles had been broken away from the Imperial crown, that the mutilated diadem was a crown of dishonour. True to his ruling desire, the advantage of Charles-le-Chauve, the basis of the treaty was easily settled by Louis-le-débonnaire.—The younger Pepin to be wholly excluded, Louis-le-Germanique restricted to Baoiaria proper, without any appurtenances or appendages—nothing but Baoiaria. Grandson and son, brother and nephew, thus excluded and despoiled, Louis-le-débonnaire concluded the *tenth*, the last proposed partition of the Empire, offering to Lothair —either that he (Lothair) should plan out the division and leave the choice to Charles,—or that he (Louis) should make the division. Lothair accepted the latter suggestion. To him, as Em-

Proceedings at Worms between Louis-le-débonnaire and Lothair.

Tenth partition of the empire made by Louis

peror, were assigned the Eastern territories
(Bavaria excepted)—all the lands beyond Meuse
and Rhine—various Burgundian districts, chiefly
in modern Switzerland—modern Provence and
all beyond to Italy.—The residue was given to
Charles-le-Chauve, who, by anticipation, we may
call king of France, though as yet the name of
"Francia" appertained only to a particular portion of his territory on the western side of the
Rhine.

824—987

839—840

But this partition required to be enforced
by the sword. The young Pepin, the boy
Pepin, was still in Aquitaine. Emeno and the
national party, by a sudden and successful movement, had gained possession of the country, and
caused the boy to be crowned as their king.
Louis-le-débonnaire was immediately in action :
with Judith to comfort him, and the young
Charles to delight him, he crossed the Loire.
His promptitude produced delusive obedience.—
Convened at Clermont, the magnates of Aquitaine performed homage to Charles-le-Chauve :
provoked to unusual sternness, Louis-le-débonnaire testified a vindictive sense of justice de-
priving Emeno of the County of Poitiers, and
condemning to death numerous offenders; who,
as it is said, conjoined the offences of rapine and
rebellion.

839—840.
Aquitanian
insurrec-
tion—the
insurgents
reduced by
Louis-le-
débon-
naire.

§ 17. Compelled to be satisfied with Aquitaine's uneasy and enforced submission, Louis-

X 2

824—987 le-débonnaire was speedily called away to renew his unhappy warfare. Louis-le-Germanique
840
March—
April.
Revolt of
Louis-le-
German-
ique—he
is defeated
by his
father
bursting out from Bavaria, and heartily supported by his people, had reoccupied Alemannia.
Louis-le-débonnaire buckled on his burnished
hawberk,—and leaving Judith and Charles at
Poitiers, marched against his contumacious son.
So energetic was the old father's rally, that
Louis-le-Germanique was compelled to retreat
into Bavaria; and Louis-le-débonnaire, victor in
this deplorable conflict, summoned a Diet of the
Empire to be held at Worms on the Feast of
Saint Rumbold, the first day of July then next
ensuing.—Lothair was commanded to attend for
the purpose of advising on very important affairs, probably the complete subjugation of his
German brother.

But the end was nigh—Louis-le-débonnaire
never saw any of his children again. At Frankfort on the Maine he stayed his progress: it
was springtime, past Whitsuntide.—The season
had been rendered awful: on the eve of the
Ascension the sun was totally eclipsed, and the
stars shone with nocturnal brightness. His sto-
mach refused nourishment, weakness and languor
gained upon him. Uneasy and seeking rest, the
sick man fancied that he would pass the approaching summer upon the island which, dividing the heavily gushing Rhine, is now covered
by the picturesque towers of the Pfaltz; and

840.
May.
Eve of the
Ascension.
Great
eclipse

he desired that a thatched lodge or leafy hut 824—987
should be there prepared, such as had served
for him when hunting in the forest or as a   840
soldier in the field—lying on his couch, he longed
for the soothing music of the gurgling waters, and
the freshness of the waving wind. Thither was he
conveyed, his bark floating down from stream to
stream. Many of the clergy were in attendance—
amongst others, his brother, Archbishop Drogo,
who at this time held the office of Archicapellanus: and Drogo received the last injunctions
which the son of Charlemagne had to impart.

His imperial crown and sword he sent to Lothair, with the earnest request that he would be
kind and true to Judith the widowed empress,
and keep his word and promise to his brother
Charles. Dying of inanition, the bed of the humble and contrite sinner was surrounded by the
priests who continued in prayer with him and   840.
for him till he expired. He died on the third   June 20.
Sunday in June; and his corpse was removed to   Death of
Metz, and buried in the Basilica of Saint Ar-   Louis-le-
nolph, without the walls of the city.   débon-
                                                    naire.

> Imperit fulmen, Francorum nobile culmen,
> Erutus à seculo conditur hoc tumulo.
> Rex Hludovicus pietatis tantus amicus;
> Quod pius a populo, dicitur et titulo.

---

§ 18. EMPIRE, tomb, epitaph, basilica, have   840, 841
all disappeared . all are nullities.—A dislocated   Confusion
                                                    occasioned

824—987

840—841
by the
death of
Louis-le-
débon-
naire.

arch is sometimes held together by a single shrivelled tendril of withered ivy : when the decayed stalk breaks, the stones separate, and the fabric falls.—So long as Louis-le-débonnaire lived, the presence of the old man, his name, his title, the habitual respect he still commanded, imparted to the Carlovingian Empire an aspect of constitutional unity; but with his death terminated the slight coherence which until then the dominion had retained.

The political relations and affairs of the Empire had become so complicated and involved by the repeated partitions and by the transactions attendant upon the partitions—promises accepted and promises rescinded, charters granted and charters annulled—that Lothair, Louis-le-Germanique, Charles-le-Chauve and Pepin, had each a quarrel against one or the other or others of them. Humanly speaking, no one could be decidedly blamed, no one clearly justified: every one amongst them could urge some *grief* which was more or less well founded.—None were absolutely in the right, none absolutely in the wrong, and yet each had some plausible reason to offer in support of his own claim, or against the claim of his adversary. Lothair designated as Emperor by the Charter, accepted as Emperor by the Magnates, crowned as Emperor by the Pontiff, hailed as Emperor by the Roman people, asserted a paramount sovereignty. Monarch of monarchs,

Seigneur as well as *Senior*, his vassal brothers 824—987 were not to reign otherwise than in subordination to the Imperial diadem. Louis-le-Germanique 840—841 had been deprived of the largest portion of his dominions in favour of Lothair and Charles-le-Chauve, and Lothair and Charles-le-Chauve would not restore them. Louis-le-Germanique insisted that the stipulations in the *Charta divisionis* were in his favour : Lothair, the like : Charles-le-Chauve was no party to a compact executed before he was born. Pepin, deprived of Aquitaine, struggled for his very existence. Though scarcely more than sixteen years of age, this young Prince—one of the many who have missed celebrity for want of a minstrel—obtained singular importance through his spirit, his indomitability, and his hold upon the uncertain loyalty of the people, whether during the brief seasons when he ruled as King, or when he wandered as a pretender. Pepin, the embodied personification of Gascon pugnacity and versatility, became a principal personage in the conflict which ensued and a plague to Charles-le-Chauve, until being finally secured by his uncle, he expired in dreary captivity.

There were large classes and influential individuals who yearned for peace. However unfortunately some of the higher clergy had been involved in the political dissensions, still the main body had been diligently working in the

Impracticability of maintaining peace.

824—987
840—841
obscurity which best ensures a conscientious discharge of duty: whilst the sounder members of
the hierarchy and laity, keenly sensible of the
Empire's misfortune, deplored the national sins.
But the bitter passions between the brethren
opposed any pacification. Each was surrounded
by advisers who expected to profit by dissension.
Neither could the Sovereigns or their advisers
resist the encreasingly energetic sense of nationality, the fresh life arising amongst the races,
which in the first instance severed the nations
of the German tongue from the nations of the
Roman tongue, and subsequently aided in producing the other States and Powers composing
the Latin or European Commonwealth.

None of the sons had followed their father's
body to the grave. None mourned or made a
show of mourning: the trumpet was the Emperor's dirge, and the shout of armies his requiem.
Lothair upon receiving the tidings of his father's
Lothair claims the paramount imperial sovereign- ty. death, immediately caused his own accession to
be proclaimed throughout the Empire, declaring
the extent of the authority he assumed. He
threatened the infliction of capital punishment
upon all who might refuse to take the oaths of
fealty: at the same time he promised not only
to confirm, but to encrease the grants made by
his father. A sufficient degree of uncertainty
attended the tenure of a *Benefice* or a *Lehn* (I
avoid using the term *Feud* as long as I can), to

occasion some degree of expectation and anxiety 824—987
upon the accession of a new Sovereign. He
might refuse a renewal, or ask an exorbitant price   840
for the concession; and the conduct adopted by
Lothair would work upon the nobles both by
interest and by fear.

§ 19.   Three brothers, and a nephew the son Lothair
of a brother, four bitter and inveterate enemies, hostility.
stung and stimulated by long-continued contests,
successes and defeats, hopes inspired and hopes
destroyed, wrongs inflicted and wrongs sustained
—it was obvious that some two or some three
must coalesce, and equally was it obvious that
the contest could not terminate unless or until
some one or more of them should be completely
put down.   Lothair, crossing the Alps, attacked
Louis without even a challenge or declaration of
hostilities: none was needed.   The Bavarian king
opposed a stout resistance.   Lothair therefore He gains
desisted from his operations in the East of the Charles-le-
Empire and attacked Charles-le-Chauve.   The
young king of Neustria was in considerable perplexity,—his realm was in a state of insurrection.
Armorica threw off his supremacy: the Aquitanians had risen for the support of Pepin.   Lothair
advanced far into France, modern France; and
the two greatest personages in that part of the
kingdom, Hilduin Abbot of Saint-Denis and
Gerard Count of Paris, the first who had sworn
allegiance to Charles, were the first to break

824—987 their oaths, and transfer their worthless faith to Lothair.

840

All the territory north of the Loire was in a manner lost to Charles, and all south on the point of being so ; therefore he solicited peace. Lothair was willing to treat ; for Louis-le-Germanique, cordially aided by his Germans, was pressing hard against him on the Eastern side of the Empire. Lothair sought to gain time, and sug- Lothair gested terms. A conference was appointed to proposes terms to be held at Attigny, the scene of their father's Charles-le- Chauve. penitence, and a new partition of the Empire was proposed. Lothair was quite ready to sacrifice his nephew, consequently he offered Charles the dominions of Pepin,—Aquitaine, together with Septimania, Provence and ten counties between Seine and Loire. The latter proposal, obscure to us, was perhaps intended to convey all Neustria except Armorica.

Charles demurred, but requested Lothair to spare their brother, Louis-le-Germanique, who now was in distress. Whilst he was uniting the Germans under his banner, the Sclavonians were rising against him, and the Northmen, hovering round the coasts, and filling the channel with their vessels, encreased the dread and confusion.

841

Charles-le- Chauve encreases in influ- ence.

But Charles was young, conciliating, accom- plished, gentle, and yet possessing great firmness. He had prospered under his adversities, he gained over the affections of many of the nobility and

chieftains, was successful in conciliating the fickle
Aquitanians, withdrawing a portion of the wavering chieftains from Pepin, and compelling the
submission of the worthless Bernard, Count of
Septimania, who had latterly revolted from his
old patron and master Louis-le-débonnaire, and
supported the adverse party.—Not long afterwards this faithless and depraved man, who had
caused so much evil to his country, being involved in some further treason, was put to death
by Charles-le-Chauve.

§ 20.   Louis-le-Germanique now desired to
ally himself to his brother Charles: the latter
had gained and inspired confidence. Having well
considered his plan of campaign, he prepared to
cross the Seine, and establish his authority in
Paris, a position of which the importance was
now fully appreciated by all parties. The passage
of the river was disputed by Lothair's adherents
amongst the nobles, but the Merchants, the
Corporation, as we should say, of Paris, assisted
Charles. By their advice he marched to Rouen,
and took possession of a fleet of vessels lying
off the city in the ample Seine, and probably
intended to co-operate with the coast-guard of
the estuary below. He then occupied Paris and
the adjoining country, lodged himself in the
Palais des Thermes, and celebrated the Paschal
feast before the altars of Saint-Germain and
Saint-Denis.

824—987

840

841.
Successful
campaign
of Charles.
He occu-
pies Paris.

Charles-le-
Chauve at
Paris.

824—987

840
The
regalia
brought to
him from
Aquitaine.

Splendour, show and finery distinguished the Franks, priests, warriors or kings. In after life no monarch delighted himself more in magnificence than Charles-le-Chauve; but he was now unwillingly reduced to a state of squalid simplicity. So hasty had been the march of Charles and his troop, that the young General-King had brought nothing with him on his horse save his armour, and the single suit of clothes all dusty and sordid which he wore. Beggarly apparel ill befitted *Pâque-fleurie*, the joyous vernal festival; but there was no wardrobe, and thus on Easter Eve, having risen from the bath—for these delicate and luxurious Roman customs prevailed, and long continued to prevail in the Gauls,—he could only prepare to put on again the soiled and faded clothing he had put off, when at the very moment there came up, unbidden and unexpectedly, a small detachment, a *manipulus* from Aquitaine, bearing crown, sceptre, mantle; and the noble young king appeared before the Parisians and the Army in the full paraphernalia of royalty.

Such an unexpected change in outward circumstances excited equal wonder and delight. A reassumption of royal state, contrived and premeditated, would not have had much moral effect; but the unforeseen accident, accepted as a happy omen, gave new courage to the adherents of the young King.

This incident is minutely related by one who was present, Charlemagne's grandson, the historian Count Nithard; and inasmuch as he deemed the matter of great importance, it becomes so to us; we must accept the wares at the market-price of the day. That the regalia should have been conveyed so speedily and safely to Paris from such a "vast distance" *per tot terrarum spatia*—they probably had been deposited at Toulouse—excites Nithard's peculiar thankfulness and astonishment, and not without reason The transit was really very difficult. They had to traverse central France, over and amongst the crags and lava-streams and mounds of fresh scoria, intersecting mountainous Vivarais and Auvergne, ejected during the tremendous eruptions which, in the fifth century, had encreased the terrors of the Gothic invasions Even in the reign of Louis-Quatorze so imperfect were the means of communication, that during a season of scarcity north of the Loire, it was found impracticable to supply Paris from the harvests of the fertile Limagne.

§ 21. Lothair's policy was always peculiarly tortuous.—Availing himself of the paltry passions and inclinations of men, he was fully bent on the destruction of his brother Louis, so earnestly and determinately, that he, whilome a parricide in intent, was now in heart a fratricide. Adalbert Count of Metz bore a deadly hatred against

824—987

841

Lothair's hatred against Louis.

Louis-le-Germanique. Much favoured by Lothair, Adalbert had been recently incapacitated by illness, but he unexpectedly recovered, so as to promise the means of assisting Lothair's fell designs. Lothair having promoted Adalbert to the royal Dukedom of Austrasia, secretly treated with the troops of Louis : they abandoned their Sovereign, and, utterly destitute of support, he retreated to faithful Baioaria, his own land.

The frustration of any coalition, moral, political, or military, between Charles and Louis, was in Lothair's mind, at this juncture, the most important object he could attain, and he stationed a large body of troops under Duke Adalbert's command in Rhætia, for the purpose of preventing the union of the allies. But communications had been opened between Charles and Louis ; and Charles moving westward, Louis in concert with him advanced consentaneously from Baioaria, and encountered the imperial troops. They were thoroughly routed and with great loss, and Adalbert was slain, to the extreme gratification of Louis. The junction so dreaded by Lothair ensued at Châlons : the triumph which the two brothers had gained over the third brother and their fellow-countrymen excited the greatest rejoicings.

In the encampment of the combined armies there was an universal jubilee ; but there were others rejoicing more deeply—those who had

May 13, 841.
Louis defeats the troops of Lothair.

Triumphant junction of Louis and Charles at Châlons.

watched every movement of the inveterate 824– 987
brethren, who had entered as heartily as themselves into the interest excited by the suicidal 841
conflict.—

Whilst Franks and Germans, Austrasians
and Neustrians are exterminating each other, the
Northmen have begun to gather the rich harvest
which, for them, Charlemagne's son and Charlemagne's grandsons have so diligently prepared.

§ 22.   England was at this period pestered by *The great Danish in-vasion of Neustria.*
the Danish marauders.   Ethelwolf, King Alfred's
father, whose reign is concurrent with the conclusion of the reign of Louis-le-débonnaire and
the first seventeen years of the reign of Charles,
was just able to keep the Danes in check; nevertheless the Heathens became bolder and bolder;
never daunted, never dispirited.   London, Canterbury, Rochester, were stormed and pillaged,
and our southern coasts and ports seem to have
been constantly annoyed or occupied by them.

The unity which pervaded the achievements *Unity ex-hibited by the general conception of the Danish or Scandina-vian inva-sions*
of the pirate-warriors sustained them in all their
enterprizes until their mission was fulfilled.
Whatever may have been their internal dissensions and enmities, they conducted their enterprizes as one people,—one nation actuated by
one spirit, having one object in which they all
concurred; and, encouraged by their success in
Britain, they now pursued their enterprises more
fiercely in the Gauls.

824—987
841
Henceforward, and until their conflagrations were extinguished, the Gauls and the British islands, the North Sea, the Channel and the Atlantic coasts, nay, even the Mediterranean, may be considered as included in one vast scheme of predatory yet consistent invasion; and their systematic assaults, descents, and expeditions, whether consecutive or simultaneous, accelerated or delayed, almost indicate a grand design of rendering Latin Europe their Empire.

Their plan of invasion.
The Northern fleets and vessels, however dispersed in action, were always in communication with each other, so that the several Hosts and Bands might assist in their mutual exigencies, or best profit by their mutual good fortunes. In the British islands as well as on the Continent their operations were uniform. Fleet after fleet, squadron after squadron, vessel after vessel, they sought to crush the country between river and river or between river and sea, a *battue* encircling the prey.

Alterations in the levels, &c. of the coasts, &c.
The *littoral* has sustained many alterations, —cliff and beach, length and level, height and depth, have changed and interchanged. Estimated according to a general average, we may assert that, bordering on the North sea and the Channel, and as far as the Scheldt, the land has gained and the sea has lost: beyond the Scheldt, the land has lost and the sea has gained. The bays on the coasts of France and England were

generally much deeper than they are at present, 824—987
and the rivers more abundant in water, whether
flowing in the stream, spreading in the sheeted 841
Alterations
broad, or stagnating in the marsh. It is very of the
course of
important to notice these facts : such physical rivers, &c
mutations, rarely recollected by historians, have
been almost universally neglected in historical
geography, a branch of science yet imperfectly
pursued. We have (for example) never seen a
single map of Roman Britain whose delineator
has not joined the isle of Thanet to the Kentish
land. On the Gaulish coasts, the tides, particularly in the Seine, rose much higher up than
at present ; and many of the existing peninsulas which cause the river's sinuous course, encreasing the landscape's beauty, were then not
presqu'isles, but completely eyots and islands.—
The French academicians, who have investigated
these questions with the most conscientious
diligence, leave us in doubt whether the isle
d'Oisselle, a very important and celebrated military post during the northern invasions, has not
been obliterated by alluvion.

The facilities thus afforded for penetrating
into the country encouraged the Northmen's desperate pertinacity—the seas, the blue billows, the
bolgen-blaa of the Danish ballads, were their home.
Beaten off from the Belgic or Neustrian coast,
they would ply the oar and hoist the black sail
for Essex or Kent, East Anglia or Northumbria.

824—987
841 Discomfited on the northern shores, they darted southwards in search of refuge or of spoil. If they lost their booty in England, Italy offered more: if the field were covered with the dead, Jutland, Denmark, Norway, would send off their berserkers to replace the slain; and the slain were quaffing mead in Valhalla.

841.
May 12.
The Danish
fleet, com-
manded by
Jarl Osker,
enters the
Seine. Hitherto, however much the Northmen had troubled the Frankish Empire, their depredations were confined to the coasts. The precautions adopted by Louis-le-débonnaire, ill-served and neglected as he had been by the Franks, were not fully adequate to repel the Pirates; but he had sufficiently protected the inland territory. Never yet had the Pirate vessels floated on the fresh waters: never had their crews seen the land on either side.

But immediately after Charles had withdrawn the Frankish squadron from Rouen, the acute and active Northmen, who had been watching their opportunity, occupied the estuary of the Seine.

Osker, hitherto undistinguishable amongst the Danish captains of the Channel fleet, conducted the expedition: an unusually high tide facilitated the invasion.—On the eve preceding the very day when Louis cut up and dispersed the Frankish army under the Duke of Austrasia's command, did Osker's fleet enter the brimful river. The Seine flood-tides were then accompanied by a

sudden head or rise of waters, the sea conflicting
with the river, similar to the *Eager* or *eau-guerre*,
so remarkable in the mouth of the Severn : the
roar could be heard five leagues off. As their
vessels rowed upwards, and the crews contemplated the unfolding of the winding shores, how
the prospect must have delighted the Northmen
during this their first navigation of the Seine :
the fruitful fields, thick orchards, the bright,
cheerful, and healthy cliffs, and the succession of
villas, burghs and monasteries, basking securely
in the enjoyment of undisturbed opulence. Generations had elapsed since the country had been
visited by any calamity, the Northmen had been
kept off, and commerce and agriculture equally
contributed to the people's prosperity. But the
Danish fleet never slackened oar or sail, the
crews never touched the land : they had a great
object in view, they would not halt to plunder
now,—lose the tide, not they !

Osker was seeking to secure the booty of
Rouen by a *coup-de-main*.—Gallo-roman Rothomagus, and the various suburbs and villages included in its modern municipal *octroi*, constituted
a congeries of islands, another Venice upon
Seine. The ground-plot of the present flourishing Position of ancient Rouen.
city was either partly occupied or much inter-
sected by the ramifying channels of the river,
as well as by various rivulets, the Renelle, the
Aubette and the Robec, the *Roth-bach*, or *red-*

824—987
841
beck, the red stream—a name of which the ety-mology perplexes the ethnographist, uncertain whether the Teutonic roots should be claimed for the Gaulish indwellers, or the Scandinavian invader.—The bed of the Seine came very nigh the Cathedral; the Church of *Saint Martin de la Roquette* was so called in consequence of its being built upon a small rock in the middle of the waters, and the parishes of Saint-Clement, Saint-Eloi, and Saint-Etienne were insular likewise. The city was fired and plundered. Defence was wholly impracticable, and great slaughter ensued: it was reported that the arch-bishop was killed. This, however, was not the case: Gundobald, the Prelate, escaped like the monks of Saint Ouen, who fled, bearing with them the relics of the Saint; but the Monastery, then standing beyond the city precinct, was sacked, and the buildings exceedingly damaged. It is thought, however, by some architectural antiquaries that the *Tour des Clercs*, the Ro-manesque fragment now incorporated with the exquisitely delicate Flamboyant structure, is a portion of the apse belonging to the original Basilica. Of the Cathedral, hardly one stone remained upon another; nor were the injuries which the sacred structures of Rouen received during this invasion effectually repaired, until the piety of Rollo and the Normans restored the fabrics their forefathers had destroyed.

14—16
May
Rouen
burned and
plundered.

Osker's three days' occupation of Rouen was remuneratingly successful. Their vessels loaded with spoil and captives, gentle and simple, clerks, merchants, citizens, soldiers, peasants, nuns, dames, damsels, the Danes dropped down the Seine, to complete their devastation on the shores. They had struck the first blow at the Provincial capital, and were now comparatively at leisure.

Dagobert and Clothaire's foundation, Jumièges, preeminent for sanctity, was surrounded by a large and populous bourgade, which had grown up under the fostering protection of the Abbey. The monks dispersed themselves, after burying a portion of their treasure. So complete was the scatteraway, that one of the brethren never stopped till he reached Saint-Gâll. This incident furnishes an anecdote for the history of melody. The fugitive bore with him an antiphonarium, containing various *sequences*, a rhythmical and cadenced Church-song, then much in use in the Northern Gauls. Now, at Saint-Gâll, there was a young monk named Notker, possessing a singular talent for music : this science he studied deeply ; and the Neustrian sequences, a style of composition hitherto unknown there, suggested to him the composition of others, which produced a great effect upon the liturgical chant prevailing during the middle ages.

Below Jumièges the Danish fleet came opposite to another monastery dedicated to the

824—987

841

24, 25 May.
The Danes at Jumièges and Fontenelle.

824—987
———
841

founder, Saint Wandregisilius, whose harsh and uncouth name has been supplanted by the pleasanter sounding denomination derived from the adjoining fountain. Fontenelle was then as flourishing as Jumièges : there were seven churches clustering together, the monastery was environed by vineyards and gardens ; and the monks, who had cleared away the woods, were diligent in every branch of their calling : their library was amongst the richest in Neustria. Warned by the example of Jumièges, the community offered money to the Danes, and the accepted gift purchased for them a perilous respite.—We become acquainted with the devastations inflicted upon the monasteries, because they possessed historians to commemorate them ; but every locality on the shores of the Seine as well as the adjoining country, suffered equally from the Danish fury. Most probably it was during this invasion that Juliabona, the modern Lillebonne, proud in her temples and amphitheatre, her marble and gilded statues, was destroyed, and ruins covered the remains of magnificence, now brought to light again by antiquarian zeal. The Danes then quitted the Seine, having formed their plans for renewing the encouraging enterprize,—another time they would do more.—Normandy dates from Osker's three days' occupation of Rouen.

Charles and
Louis nego-
ciate for
peace

§ 23. This terrible and terrifying visitation, though we trace its influence upon the conduct

of the contending brothers, could not check their
hostilities. Whether the Pagus Rothomagensis
and the other dioceses and provinces ravaged by
Osker, belonged at this juncture to Charles or to
Lothair, neither could give any help or spare any
force for the defence of the country against the
invaders. Charles, however, felt the calamity
keenly. Rouen he claimed, as included in his
own Neustrian realm : compared also with Lothair, he was conscientiously desirous of effecting
a restoration of peace, and entertained a more
lively appreciation of the transgression which
these unnatural dissensions involved. His youth,
instead of being a disadvantage, encreased his
influence; and however subsequently depressed
by vicissitudes, lapses and misfortunes, he often
retraced some of the noble characteristics which
had adorned his grandsire.

Louis allowed his brother to take the lead
in the transactions which ensued. Charles and
Lothair were contending less for territory than
for sovereignty, and negociations were commenced, prosecuted in good faith by Charles, but
astutely by Lothair : the younger brothers seeking
to obtain a speedy and satisfactory pacification,
the elder, by procrastination, to encrease his
forces and profit by the pressure Charles was sustaining. Louis and Charles humbled themselves
before Lothair, but he interpreted their offers into
symptoms of artifice or terror. Each succeeding

[margin:] 824—987
841

[margin:] Proposal made them to avert hostilities

824—987

841

proposal they made was rejected or evaded. Would Lothair accept all they had in their camp? money, gold, jewels, tents, equipments, stores, all except their horses and arms?—or, as we should say, allow them to retreat with the honours of war? Would he be satisfied with a large encrease of territory, to be ceded by Louis and Charles, extending from the Ardennes to the Rhine? If this was unsatisfactory, let the whole of "France" be divided, and he should choose his share.— Any reasonable concession to obtain quiet for Church and State, and prevent the shedding of Christian blood.

Hostile
movements
continued
by both
parties

§ 24. Lothair had been concentrating his forces. The Burgundians from Jura to Rhone supported him cordially. He relied much upon the Aquitanians, and the boy Pepin was rapidly advancing at their head to aid his Emperor-uncle : Charles had been equally active. To-

841
21—23
June
Position of
the armies
in the vi-
cinity of
Auxerre.

wards the end of June the armies both took their positions in the vicinity of Auxerre : Charles and Louis at Tauriac, Lothair about Fontenay, and anxiously, for though Pepin and his con-tingent were momentarily expected, they had not come up. Lothair pitched his imperial tent upon a rising ground, "*la montagne des alouettes.*" Marshes, copses, and the valley of a small river, then called the rivulet of the Burgundians, sepa-rated the armies. Hostilities were suspended by the negociations, which continued during three

days. On the third, the mystic eve of Saint John 824—987
the Baptist, Charles and Louis renewed their
848
offers. Lothair required a delay till the morrow: 23 June
for no other reason, as he asserted, than that he The parley.
might be able to form such a determination as
should be for the common profit and blessing of
them all. This asseveration was solemnly confirmed by oath—oaths cost him nothing,—all
Lothair wanted was to gain a day. Pepin, he
knew, was advancing rapidly, and in the course
of a few hours the tramp of the Aquitanian
cavalry was heard, and the forces joined.

On the Feast of Saint John the Baptist Pepin 24 June.
appeared in the camp at Tauriac, but he had no The challenge
answer to give on the part of Lothair; and the
brothers then, seeing that there was no hope of
determining the great controversy otherwise than
by force of arms, solemnly summoned Lothair to
abide by the judgment of God. They and their
Host would meet him and his Host in the valley
on the following day, at two hours after midnight, when the dark twilight contends with the
dawn :—they defied him.

Lothair received the message with insolent
contempt, but gladly accepted the challenge ; and
on the morrow of Saint John the Baptist, the long 25 June.
bright merry summer-day, ensued the direful The great
battle of
battle-strife, kings, nobles, kinsmen, each smiting Fontenay—
defeat of
against kings, nobles, and kinsmen, with infu- the Emperor Lo-
riated antipathy. Louis-le-Germanique directed thair.

824—987   the onslaught against Lothair: a second division
841   was commanded by Charles-le-Chauve, the third
          by Count Adelhard.   Count Nithardus, the his-
torian who relates the tale we tell, fought in
this division, and he speaks with soldier-like pride
of the service which his sword then rendered,
whilst Angelbert, Count Nithard's brother, was
ranged under the standard of Lothair.

Never since that tremendous battle in the
Catalaunian fields, when Hun and Ostrogoth contended for the mastery, had the Gauls witnessed
equal slaughter.   What the Roncesvalles "dolo-
rous rout" appears in romance, Fontenay becomes
in authentic history.

The tradi-   National traditions deplored the loss of an
tions of the
slaughter   hundred thousand combatants.   Moreover, the
of Fonte-
nay   custom of Champagne was ever afterwards appealed to, like the gavel-kind custom of Kent,
as the living record of a boon obtained, though
from a very different cause, the concession made
to affliction, not the reward of steadfastness and
bravery.   Champagne possessed a peculiar privilege derogating from the otherwise universal
maxim of the French law, the doctrine which forbade the derivation of nobility from the distaff,
whereas in Champagne, nobility was transmitted
by maternal descent, irrespective of the father's
blood; and this privilege was supposed to have
been bestowed for the purpose of preventing the
otherwise imminent extinction of the aristocracy.

The loss was proportionally severe in both 824—987 armies: in both the ranks were equally mown ⌣⌣⌣ down by the mutual energy of destruction. Lo- 841 thair's army was, however, thoroughly routed: the Emperor and his troops fled in confusion, and the corpse-encumbered greensward was left in the power of the Neustrian and German kings.

Listen to the wail which rises from the field The la- ment of of Fontenay—the rude and barbarous rhythm of Angelbert, the brother the warrior, who, fighting to the death against of Count Nithard. his brethren, encreased the carnage which he escaped and deplored.

Bella clamant hinc et inde,
Pugna gravis oritur:
Frater fratri mortem parat,
Nepoti avunculus;
Filius nec patri suo
Exhibet quod meruit.

Laude pugna non est digna
Nec canatur melode:
Oriens, meridianus
Occidens vel aquilo
Plangent illos qui fuerunt
Illo casu mortui.

Gramen illud ros et imber
Nec humectet pluvia·
In quo fortes ceciderunt
Prælio doctissimi·
Plangent illos qui fuerunt
Illo casu mortui.

Maledicta dies illa
Nec in anni circulis
Numeretur, sed radatur
Ab omni memoria:
Jubar solis illi desit,
Aurora crepusculo.

Hoc autem scelus peractum,
Quod descripsi rytmicè,
Angelbertus ego vidi
Pugnansque cum aliis,
Solus de multis remansi
Prima frontis acie.

Noxque illa, nox amara,
Noxque dura nimium,
In qua fortes ceciderunt
Prælio doctissimi,
Pater, mater, soror, frater,
Quos amici fleverant.

§ 25. Success, even when most joyful, the attainment of any hope however lawful, is always

followed by heaviness, frequently by sadness; but this was a victory without success, a day altogether of horror and of mourning. Charles and Louis and the chieftains who had survived, assembled themselves in deliberation. Some of the commanders, hot and embittered, clamoured for revenge, urging the Kings to chase the retreating foe, and end the feud by condign vengeance. Piety and pity prevailed; and it was agreed that they should sheathe their swords and await the better thoughts which the following day, the Lord's day, might suggest. They employed themselves in comforting and tending the wounded;—and after Mass had been sung they gave burial to the dead, the last of the seven works of mercy.

Kings and people now sought the instruction of their Pastors. War, the vengeance of God upon nations, is an essential condition in the present captivity of the Church, for war and bloodshed cannot cease upon earth until the Church is triumphant—Her duty is to abide in patience and faith whilst the Vials of wrath are pouring out, until the time of times, when all the kingdoms of the World shall come to an end and the kingdom of God prevail, when the great and dreadful Advent shall ensue, and the bow be broken, and the spear snapped in sunder. So long as the lusts of man call down the chastisement of wars and fightings, so long must that chastisement be humbly endured. In the present 824—987 case, the Bishops, conforming to the prevailing theology, considered that an appeal having been 841 made to the Lord of Hosts, though none of the combatants might be guiltless, yet much extenuation could be found for those who had sincerely waged the war in defence of right and justice. Each man was therefore to examine his own conscience, and repent if he had been in any wise actuated by vain glory, covetousness or revenge.—Three days of humiliation, fasting and prayer were enjoined; and the injunction thus given was devoutly obeyed.

Three days of fasting and penitence after the battle.

The decree of retribution against the descendants of Charles Martel was now manifest—Henceforward the existence of the Carlovingian Empire was but a continued agony. The glory of the Franks was lost, their strength taken from them, their power consumed. They became the jest and scorn of their enemies, and, more bitter, of themselves. Nevertheless there was left amongst them the seed of national regeneration: they were gifted with the most rare of all national virtues—nay, that virtue without which no other national virtue can avail, national self-knowledge, leading to national repentance—they neither flattered themselves nor deceived themselves: they never sought to conceal the extent of their misfortunes, nor tried to excuse or palliate their national transgressions and sins, but acknow-

824—987 ledged that, low as they had been brought, they
deserved their humiliation.

842
Lothair's
cause de-
clining, he
renews ne-
gociations
with
Charles.

§ 26. The Northmen recommenced their attacks with aggravated fury. That the Royal brothers should unite against the common enemy had become an impossible idea. All the endeav-ours of the contending parties continued absorbed in the one main object of mutual harm and de-struction; and, however weakened by the slaugh-ter of Fontenay, their forces continued for the present nearly as equally balanced as before. Charles concentrated his troops about Paris: Lothair began to treat   Political ambition was mingled in him with perverseness, and the most uncharitable dislike of his second brother. Lo-thair had been strenuously assisted by his nephew Pepin, but he was quite willing to sacrifice the young Prince and to abandon him. to Charles, provided Charles would equally abandon Louis. —All France, excepting Provence and Septima-nia, should belong to Charles.

842
Feb. 14.
Treaty and
oath of
Strasburgh
(see p 66)

The offer was rejected. Charles strengthened his alliance with Louis, and the compact of Strasburgh, that memorable testimony of the formation of language and the separation of races, confirmed the bond. The cause of Lothair on the whole, was declining :—none of the bre-thren had been guiltless towards their father, and he, the most guilty, prospered the least. The contest had become well defined, Lothair

seeking a full and entire supremacy over the 824—987
Empire, his brothers striving to confirm themselves as independent Sovereigns. Lothair had 842
by his own acts irreparably damaged the very
authority he now sought—he was snared in his
own devices. Constantly opposing his imperial
father, he had taught the lesson of a more stubborn resistance against himself. Why should
Charles and Louis-le-Germanique render more
obedience to the Emperor Lothair than Lothair
had done to Louis-le-débonnaire ?

The greater portion of the German nations, March,—
April, 842
those in whom the Teutonic sentiment was most Louis and
vivid, identified themselves with Louis. Power- Charles
advance
ful forces, Bavarians, Suabians, poured in to join against
Lothair
him, mustering at Mayence. Lothair was in the
Pfaltz of Aix-la-Chapelle, still rich with the
treasures of Charlemagne, precious metals and
jewels and wonders of Byzantine and Syrian and
Arabian art.   Harold the Dane the Count of Rustringia, Count Hatto and Otgar Archbishop of
Mayence, were stationed near the Moselle, for the
purpose of defending the passage of the river;
but the combined armies of Louis and Charles
advanced rapidly and powerfully both by land
and by water. On their approach, the Arch-
bishop and his fellow-commanders fled ; and when Flight of
Lothair.
Lothair heard that the enemy had penetrated as
far as Sintzig, he, seized with terror, abandoned
Aix-la-Chapelle, clearing the Palace of all its

824—987
842—843
treasures; and, for the purpose of satisfying his soldiery, breaking in pieces even the wonderful planisphere, the memorial of Charlemagne's opulence and science.

842.
Council at Aix-la-Chapelle, Lothair's flight construed as an act of abdication.
§ 27. Louis and Charles took possession of the pillaged and deserted Pfaltz. Bishops and Clergy were convened in Council at Aix-la-Chapelle. The Kings moved the hierarchy to deliver their judgment.—All the offences which Lothair had committed were adduced against him. The Prelates declared that his disobedience, his perjuries, his implacable hostility, the evils he had brought upon the people, rendered him unworthy of authority.—He had agreed to abide the Battle-ordeal, and was condemned: he had ratified the condemnation by his flight, his throne was vacant; how could order be best taken for the welfare of Church and State?

Their decision was uncompromising, the Bishops unanimously determined that Lothair's royal authority having ceased, his French and German dominions should be shared between his two brothers. Louis and Charles respectively chose twelve arbitrators: Count Nithardus was one of them, and here unfortunately occurs an hiatus in Nithard's manuscript. His most interesting memoir suggested by Charles-le-Chauve, when they were on their journey to Châlons, as after mentioned, is left unfinished. He composed the history at intervals, waiting to complete the work for leisure, which never came. The fourth and concluding book is fragmentary, and the particulars of the proposed partition are lost; but subsequent proceedings sufficiently denote, that, generally speaking, the Rhine and Meuse indicated the boundaries—from Rhine and Meuse to the West, the kingdom of Charles, from Rhine and Meuse to the East, the kingdom of Louis.— With the countries on the other side of the Alps, the Synod did not deal: Italy was beyond their jurisdiction, that Kingdom appertained to the Emperor. The Carlovingian Empire was beginning to be disentangled from the Roman Empire, and the Prelates at Aix dared not venture to assume any authority over the Crown which the Pontiff and the Roman people had bestowed.— "Lothair has lost his rights over us, but we do not touch Augustus Cæsar."

824—987
842—843
Partition between Louis and Charles-le-Chauve proposed by the Aix-la-Chapelle decree.

§ 28. The Aix-la-Chapelle decree, however, though a very powerful demonstration, was, for the present, only an abortive project: Septimania and Burgundy did not concur: Rome and Italy ignored the transaction altogether. Lothair reassembled his troops, and stationed himself with an imposing degree of force towards the Rhone. Negotiations were opened at Châlons—fancy King Charles and Nithard riding thither side by side, talking over the classical composition of the Count's history—A new partition was proposed by Lothair: Italy, Bavaria and Aquitaine were

842—843.
Transactions and events until the conclusion of the treaty of Verdun

842.
Negotiations opened at Châlons

824—987
812

respectively to be treated as indivisible kingdoms : he, Lothair, to have Italy—Louis, Baioaria, and Charles, Aquitaine : Pepin's rights were completely abandoned—the residue of the Empire to be divided between the brothers. With caution however and courteous discretion, Lothair suggested that the honour of his Imperial Crown might entitle him to the largest portion of territory; whilst, somewhat less explicitly, he intimated that he was not unwilling to acknowledge the independence of his brothers' realms.

Wearisome delays ensued. National troubles, affecting all parties, encreased.—The approach (as men believed) of Attila's resuscitated Horde, the Hungarians, the Mogers, two hundred and sixteen thousand monsters who ate human flesh and drank human blood, and who were hungry and thirsty for their cannibal feast and food, might perhaps be heard as a far distant roar.—Flanders, Armorica, and Aquitaine were terribly ravaged by the Scandinavians, and domestic treachery aided the pirates. Bordeaux, Xaintes and Nantes were pillaged, the latter city desolated, the inhabitants dispersed or massacred, and the surrounding country rendered waste unto the borders of Anjou. These expeditions profited so well to the Vikingars that they henceforward afflicted the Loire as much as the Seine.

Invasions of Saracens and Northmen

The Moslem forces occupied Benevento, Bari, great part of the Kingdom of Naples, and ultimately profaned Saint Peter's shrine and sacked

and plundered Imperial Rome.   Other turbaned
hosts from the opposite coast of Africa, imitating
the Baltic tactics, sailed up the Rhone.   Charles
Martel had expelled the Saracens from Arles,
but the progeny of Charles Martel could not
wield his weapon.   The miscreants stormed the
city; and the amphitheatre circuit, converted by
them into a fortress, is still crowned by their
Mauresque towers.

§ 29.   The cosmical phenomena, so physically 824—987
and morally important during the mediæval era,
continued and encreased.   The heavens throbbed
with blue and red and yellow fires : comets and
cometary beams traversed the sky—tremendous
earthquakes encreased the alarm—The volcanic
Rhine region was particularly disturbed, but the
concussions were not confined to this locality.
Commencing with earth-thunder, the shocks prevailed seven days throughout the Gauls, the sub-
terraneous "bellowings," as they are described,
recurring periodically at certain ascertained
watches and hours of night and day.   To these
were added keen famine and dire pestilence.

Taken in the wider sense, every physical
phenomenon is an historical incident, whether
affecting the material condition of man or his
mind—the pestilence-breathing blast not more so
than the Aurora's innocuous beams.   Feebly and
faintheartedly would Livy, the rebuker of a corrupt and apostate generation, have fulfilled his

Cosmical phenomena, earthquakes, fires in the sky, &c.

Physical phenomena, to be considered as historical incidents.

824—987

842—*

high mission, had he not constantly and faithfully borne witness to the prodigies whilome received by his forefathers, as testifying the active presence of the Deity, teaching them to nourish their strength by confessing their weakness, and to acknowledge that their power was a free gift, which the Gods, the Divine warnings contemned, would take away.

Science cannot dispel this lurking belief, so flippantly denominated "superstition"—it is innate and unconquerable. If the weather be coarse during the national Fête, the tricolor is gloomy. The Parisian crowds are dispirited by the darkened heavens, and they loudly give utter-

Pyschological reality of omens and prognostics.

ance to their heaviness. That a bright gleam of sunshine should suddenly illuminate the House of Peers and dart down upon the Lords Commissioners when they declared the Royal assent to the Reform Bill, was joyfully accepted by the hardheaded unimaginative Radical as a happy foreboding.—Tokens, predictions, prognostics, possess a psychological reality. All events are but the consummation of preceding causes, distinctly felt though not clearly apprehended until the accomplishment ensues. Whilst the strain is sounding, the pre-established harmony of atmosphere, of nerve and of soul reveals to the most untutored listener that the tune will end with the key-note, though he cannot explain why each succeeding bar leads to the concluding chord.

§ 30. The notables and nobles from and in all parts of the Empire called for a pacification, and the call was obeyed. At Coblentz, the three envious brothers, the three grudging and hostile Kings, were convened in stately Congress, their nobles, their prelates and one hundred and ten delegates or commissioners,—a special Parliament. They held their Sessions in that edifice still appearing as the principal feature in the sunny and cheerful city, the twin-towered Church of Saint Castor. Apart from the mutual jealousies which would have embarrassed a plain question, great practical and political difficulties attended the negotiations. The negotiators were doing far more than they knew about: they began the plotting out of the future European community. Upon what principles were the divisions to be appropriated? Extent, fertility, opulence, laws, customs, all required consideration. Schemes were proposed and canvassed, dismissed and resumed, until the kings and diplomatists again assembled. 824—987 842—843 842—813 Proceedings leading to the treaty of Verdun

Three years after the death of Louis-le-débonnaire, the treaty was concluded, which, assuming the Carlovingian Empire to be the first, became the second stage in the organization of Western or Latin Europe.—The history of modern Europe is an exposition of the treaty of Verdun. 843 Aug. Treaty of Verdun, Carlovingian inheritance divided.

§ 31. A precedency quite unchallenged as to rank, though entirely undefined as to jurisdiction, Lothair's precedency acknowledged by all parties

824—987
843
belonged to Lothair: "*Seigneur*" or "*Senior*," all questions concerning his authority were left undetermined. Whether the junior brothers were to acknowledge the natural right of the first-born or the political supremacy of the Emperor, no one can tell; yet in the opinion of the German jurists, the treaty of Verdun contains the invisible *punctum saliens* of the public law, which ruled, or professed to rule, the Romano-Germanic Empire.

The principle which connected the provinces and regions allotted to Lothair, was the average preponderance of some one or more of the Roman elements, either in the races or the laws, or the languages, or the institutions, or the traditions, or the opinions of the people. Italy became the territorial basis of the opulent and dignified endowments assigned to Augustus, who, crowned by the Pontiff, confirmed that Pontiff on his throne. In Rome, as all then admitted, none can rightly rule except the Emperor. Lothair's kingdom was therefore built upon Italy: but the name of Charlemagne, and the long-continued usages of government entitled Lothair to demand Aix-la-Chapelle, the constitutional Austrasian metropolis. These two Imperial residences, each the Cæsar's palace, each adding dignity to the other, the centres of the two great Cisalpine and Transalpine Crown-lands, were conjoined by an unbroken and continuous territory, including all the varieties of soil, climate and

Lothair's
portion of
the Empire.

production offered by the richest and most active portions of Europe, the wine and the oil of the South, the harvests and pastures of the North.

824—987

843

From the teeming floods of the German Ocean and the sands and denes of Frisia, Lothair's Imperial kingdom extended to the luxuriant regions of Capua, the olives and chestnut-groves of the Abruzzi, and the ¨emerald and sapphire waves of the Mediterranean and Tyrrhene seas. The Cisalpine Eastern and Western boundaries were indicated or formed by the Scheldt, the Meuse and the two great rivers so kindred in the etymology of their names, so contrary to each other in their course, the Rhine and the Rhone. Not in all cases did the frontier reach quite up to the banks of the several rivers, yet that frontier was rarely, if ever, removed beyond a short day's journey from the river or the river-valley boundaries.

Boundaries of Lothair's kingdom.

The compact and solid conformation of this realm, so scanty in average latitude but so ample in longitude, renders its chorography singularly conspicuous on the historical map; and we trace the demarcations imposed by the treaty of Verdun in the peculiar character of the architectural monuments still subsisting within the compass of Lothair's realm. The coincidence is indisputable; the particular cause of the coincidence is concealed amongst the mysteries of architectural development. The scenery of Rhine

Peculiar character of the Lotharingian ecclesiastical architecture.

and Moselle will always be associated in our re-collection with the venerable ecclesiastical buildings adorning the landscape, and spreading over the adjoining districts in stately splendour. Their normal features are most distinctly pronounced in the church of Saint Castor, where the conferences were held: the tall, square, many-storied and compartmented bell-towers, the apse crowned by open galleries, and the other details which the eye impresses so clearly on the memory and the pencil delineates with so much facility, whilst the pen fails in pourtraying them.

Cologne may first present these combined peculiarities to the stranger ; but all ancient Lotharingia abounds with them. When the traveller, pursuing his journey towards Lotharingian Italy, traverses the Alps through either of the *Chiuse*, the accustomed Lotharingian passes of Mont Cenis or Saint Gothard, the same models still appear; and had not the reverend Abbey Church of Saint Gall yielded in the last age to modern taste, that structure would have exhibited the type in vast magnificence   The Lotharingian style flourishes throughout the whole of Lotharingian Lombardy, which, besides the modern province so called, includes the Venetian Terra firma, Tyrol and Trent, Ticino, Piedmont, Parma, Piacenza and Modena. In Tuscany the Lotharingian style contends with the productions of another school, displaying more accurate reminiscences of Roman

art.—The City of the Cæsars proudly rejected 824—987
ultramontane taste; but the usage of the bell
enforced her priesthood to admit the Teutonic 843
" Glocken-thurm:" the Basilica of " San Giovanni
e Paolo," originally raised by the Roman Patrician Pammachius, the husband of Paulina, Saint
Jerome's sister, was, during the subsistence of the
Carlovingian domination, rebuilt by an architect
taught in the barbarian colonies of Germany or
Belgic Gaul. And the Lotharingian normal design lastly meets and abandons us at Rome.

Lothair's Kingdom on the North of the Alps The lots assigned to Louis and Charles.
is a grand Imperial highway athwart the Cisal-
pine Continent.—The territories on the East and
on the West of this kingdom (West of the Rhone
and East of the Rhine) naturally became the
lots of Louis and of Charles, aggregating themselves respectively to the undivided kingdoms of
Baioaria and of Aquitaine. Louis took as far
North and East as Charlemagne's power had
extended, Charles as far South as the Marches
of Spain; and this division created territorial
France. With the exception of Provence and
some few portions of Lotharingia, there is not
any where the value of fifty miles difference in
frontier between the kingdom of France in the
reign of Louis-Quatorze, and the kingdom given
to Charles-le-Chauve by the treaty of Verdun.
Some four years afterwards, Northmen and Saracens pressing harder, this Verdun compact (cer-

824—987

847

847. Feb. Treaty of Mersen.

tain arrondissemens being completed by the sup-plementary treaty of Thionville) received a final ratification pursuant to a third treaty concluded at Mersen nigh Maestricht, when the kingdoms of the three brothers were respectively declared to be hereditary, provided the nephews consented to be obedient to their uncles, *si tamen ipsi ne-potes patruis obedientes esse consenserint,* and various other additional articles and covenants, deceptively promising a permanent pacification, were engrossed in the tripartite chirograph which each monarch signed with his own hand.

Relations between particular history and universal history.

§ 32. THE COMPLEXITIES, the intricacies, the alliances, the feuds, the dissensions, the distrac-tions attending the dissolution of the Carlovingian Empire, render the historian dizzy in attempting to relate them: he is a traveller bewildered among confusing tracks in a driving snow-storm. But during this storm the states of modern Europe are rising: the storm is a spring-tide storm, a storm which breaks up the soil and stimulates germination : the buds begin to burst amidst the turmoil of the elements, and the silver lilies of France, and the gay genista of Anjou, nay, even the bright roses of England, are springing.

The instruction derived from the particular history of any one nation or state encreases in geometrical ratio to the student's knowledge of

universal history. No state, no population, not 824—987
even the smallest or most inconsiderable, is absolutely inert in the macrocosm of humanity. Each
state constitutes a system, involved or affected
by other systems, orbs gyrating about other orbs,
whirling in cycles and epicycles, sometimes obeying mutual attractions or yielding to mutual
repulsions, fighting in their courses; and the
utmost perfection of historical knowledge which
any human capacity can attain must be imperfection—not knowledge, but a diminution of
ignorance. This indeed must be affirmed concerning all human knowledge: there is no encrease of such knowledge, only a removal of
obstructions, a picture faintly brought out by
rubbing off the soil. The study of history ought
to be a labour of love, but it is nevertheless a
hard labour. Your hand cannot be aided by
machinery. There is no "history for the million."
In this branch of science, no small book can
really teach you great things: your philosophy
of universal history is a ghost, your epitome of
universal history a skeleton: if you try to em-
brace the spectre, your arms go through and
hug the dry bones, bones which no flesh will
ever cover.

Nevertheless the richest narrator must occasionally epitomize, and the most barren epito-
mizer will of necessity be sometimes stimulated
into abstract or general reasoning; yet since men

824—987 have begun to indite books, we cannot recollect more than one writer of history who has succeeded in effecting the symmetrical combination of condensation and expansion, text and comment blended in due proportion—he of the most admirable and most debased talent—the author of the *Decline and Fall*

Carlovingian genealogies. § 33. For the purpose of conducting my reader through this era of consternation, and in order that he may better comprehend the course of European events in connexion with those of France, Normandy and England, I shall resume the narrative genealogies of the Carlovingian families until they become extinguished in the male line. I include in this, and in a subsequent chapter, some notices of the three rival Kingdoms, *Italy*, *Provence*, and *Burgundy* (the last two afterwards united into the Kingdom of *Arles*), which arose upon Carlovingian ground during the subsistence of the Carlovingian dynasty. I shall also indicate the partitions and divisions of the Carlovingian Empire, which were effected or sustained after the death of Louis-le-débonnaire: fragments shivering into fragments. Excepting in the Iberian peninsula south of the Ebro, every European power, living or defunct, sovereign or subordinate, speaking the Roman, Tudesque or Sclavonian tongues, has been either

mediately or immediately shaped out of these 824—987
partitions. The reader must make for himself an
universal history of Europe, seeking the comple-
mentary histories, determining according to his
own views which histories he will consider as
principal, and which as accessories.—It is my
wish to help others as I have been helped myself, and to teach as I have been taught.

Most assuredly, no period of modern history The difficulties of
is so fundamentally important to the student as Carlovingian geo-
the Carlovingian era, or so difficult to compre- graphy,
onomastic
hend—States independent yet conjoined, their nomenclature and
geography repulsively difficult, territorial divi- textual
arrange-
sions marbled, spotted, or clouded and contorted ment.
into each other, complicated and broken,—no
ordinary sized map of the Empire can exhibit
the details with any approximation to clearness.
Special maps are therefore required. A map can
only exhibit one scheme of political boundaries,
as existing at one given period of time: those
professing to do more are so blurred as to be
nearly useless. Large and small, general and
particular, fifty maps would be needful to complete the Carlovingian Atlas.

Not the least of the obscurities arises from
repetitions of names. "Charles" occurs eleven
times in the Carlovingian genealogies, "Louis"
nine times : there are six "Pepins," five "Carlo-
mans" and four "Lothairs"; and the nobles draw
only from the most scanty family onomastic
nomenclatures. The epithets "Martel" and the

824—987 like, by which the Sovereigns are now distinguished, are never affixed to their names in the coeval histories. Even Charlemagne is merely "Carolus;" and during the later periods of the Empire there are so many homonyms as to confuse the most attentive investigator.

The concurrency of the several lines and branches adds exceedingly to the difficulty: their histories are not successive but synchronous, and the arrangement of the text in parallel columns (practised by some of my predecessors, of whose labours I thankfully avail myself), and which at first would be thought most natural, cannot be executed neatly or conveniently : the plan becomes unmanageable and wearisome; and the learned and eminent modern historians of France

The Carlovingian portions of Sismondi and Luden unsatisfactory and of Germany, who have respectively combined the more prominent or leading Carlovingian incidents in one narrative, fail to extricate themselves from its labyrinthine perplexity. I therefore shall proceed according to lineages and individuals, rendering each section, as far as is practicable, a self-contained statement; yet, re-

See I. § 5 p. 145. ferring the reader to my former explanations, I must remind him that the plan pursued is not strictly methodical, but freely varied according to the bearing and nature of the matter. All the synchronous sections should be severally compared with each other, and thus placed parallel in the reader's mind.

The people who live in the pages of the

historian, who speak through his books, are to 824—987
be the reader's companions. He takes more
kindly to them, if, occasionally looking behind, he
is prepared for their approach, or, looking onwards, espies them on the road before him. It Genealogies, their
is not well for the personages of the historical value in
historical
drama to rise on the stage through the trap- enquiries.
doors. They should first appear entering in between the side scenes. Their play will be better
understood then. We are puzzled when a King
or Count suddenly lands upon our historical
ground like a collier winched up through a shaft.
Many genealogical details are given in the course
of this history. When in common life we are introduced to any new acquaintance, we instinctively
endeavour to render our ideas concerning him
precise, by enquiring into his family and connections—where did he 'come from,—whom does he
belong to—whom did he marry—how many
children has he got—how are they settled? Nor
is it an impertinent curiosity which prompts such
questions: never do we thoroughly know the
stranger until these particulars are ascertained.
Historical characters present themselves to us as
new acquaintances, new even when their names
are familiar, for generally we only suppose we
know them; and they should be treated after the
same guise.—Genealogies are as important in the
general, as they are in the special. It is a thoroughly vulgar error to sneer at the Herald be-

824—987 cause he is grotesquely clad, or to deride genealogical studies as vain enquiries because they may minister to vanity.

Utility of family histories.
The history of any one noble or private family—would that we had more of them composed with conscientious discretion,—is often an essential portion of national history, and always a perpetual commentary upon the national history. Such a family history gives you a vertical section of the strata, presented at one view. No other process affords an equally distinct disclosure of the chronological progress of human society. Inductive philosophy flourishes according to the copiousness and accuracy of the experimental observations upon which the science is founded. So far therefore as there can be any historical science, the observations made upon man, separately and individually, are the only legitimate sources of induction. Collective society displays the consequences and not the impulses.

Mediæval history is in danger of becoming either a weary task or a feeble romance, a dogmatic truism or a fantastic illusion. We are all of us apt to be tempted by the queer, the quaint, the æsthetic; and somewhat more attention than is needful is bestowed upon the mea-

Mediæval history, unnecessarily invested with a controversial character.
surements of high head-dresses and long-peaked shoes. Mediæval history has also been invested with a controversial character. Historians have insensibly become defenders or assailants: hence

on the one part somewhat too much marvel and 824—987
cry of wonder, and on the other part somewhat
too much contempt and depreciation. The corrective is to be sought in those details which
unite themselves to our ordinary sympathies,
without misleading the imagination.

In the course of this work I have never
shunned repetitions of any sort or kind, when I
have found repetitions needful. Repetitions are
not superfluities; nor is it surplussage to reiterate
the same thought or fact under diverse combinations. The present generation can only commence
the task of correcting the prevailing notions respecting the formation and policy, whether civil
or ecclesiastical, of the mediæval European communities; and there is and will be a mighty conflict of opinions, right and wrong against right
and wrong, to accomplish this end. In some provinces the rank weeds should be plucked up, in
others the tangled forest felled. All we can expect from each historian is that he should stam-
mer a few imperfect developments of truth : each
enquirer partially elucidating some obscure passages in the progress of society: dispelling favourite
or deluding visions or dreams: cutting, when practicable, the conventional pictures out of their
frames, and replacing them by portraits taken
from the life; but, above all, uncramping or shat-
tering the pedestals supporting the idols which
have won the false worship of the multitude, so

824—987 that they may nod in their niches or topple down.
—My object, first and last, is to know the individuals and to make them known. Our Mother-
tongue has played us a sorry trick in separating
the meanings of "history" and of "story." "History" and "story" are one word in etymology, in
fact, and in deed. The distinction imposed upon
our minds by usage of speech causes us to forget
that, in both, the subject is the same,—man and
man's actions. What would a story be unless the
tale-teller took the utmost pains to bring his personages before you?

Carlo-
vingian
lineages.
Lombard,
§ 35.
*Aquita-
nian,* § 36
*Lotharin-
gian,* § 37-
44.
German,
§ 45-52
French,
§ 53-55.

§ 34. THE CARLOVINGIAN FAMILY must be
considered as divided into five Lines or Houses.
The *Lombard* line descended from PEPIN, the son
of Charlemagne: the *Aquitanian* from PEPIN,
the son of Louis-le-débonnaire: the *Lotharingian*
from the Emperor LOTHAIR: the *German* from
LOUIS-LE-GERMANIQUE; and the *French* from
CHARLES-LE-CHAUVE. We have arranged the
several Houses according to the duration of their
several sovereignties. The rival royal lineages of
Italy (when that realm was lost to the Carlovingians), *Provence, Burgundy* and *Arles,* have their
places at the most convenient points of insertion
after the reign of Charles-le-Chauve, and we will
now take them in due order.

§ 35. THE LOMBARD LINE of the Carlovingian family, though deprived of royal honours, acquired subsequently great importance both in France and in Normandy, where Charlemagne's descendants long retained the respect due to their mighty ancestor's name. PEPIN, son of the miserable Bernard king of Lombardy, whom we left under his uncle's dubious protection, obtained an inadequate but tranquil appanage—the rich Abbey of Saint Quentin, and also Peronne, "Peronne la pucelle," castle and seigneury. This Pepin of Peronne had three sons,—BERNARD,—HERBERT —and PEPIN.

824—987

840—1080
The Lombard line—origin of the House of Vermandois.

Pepin, son of King Bernard, Abbot and Seigneur of St Quentin and Peronne, died after 840.

BERNARD, the eldest son of Pepin of Peronne, probably died in his father's lifetime: some writers connect him by alliance with the Guelphs of Bavaria.

HERBERT, the second son of Pepin of Peronne, succeeded both to the Abbey and the Seigneury, holding them conjointly; and, widely extending his power, he acquired the illustrious historical title of Count of Vermandois—noble, royal, imperial Vermandois,—from the Gallo-Roman name of the district.—A hamlet or village called *Vermandois* still exists; but antiquaries dispute much whether Saint Quentin be or be not the ancient Augusta-Veromanduorum. The dominion annexed thereto included the cities and territories of Rheims, Soissons, Meaux and Senlis.

Herbert the First, count of Vermandois, died 902.

824—987
840—1080

The aforesaid Herbert, the *second* son of Pepin of Peronne, is dynastically, or amongst the Counts of Vermandois, reckoned Herbert *the First*. He had an only son Herbert (of whom we speak in a subsequent paragraph) and two daughters, the eldest, whose name is not known, married to Otho Count of Franconia, and BEA-TRICE, married to Robert Duke of France, son of Robert-le-Fort.

Pepin Count of Senlis and Valois, died after 893: his family.

PEPIN, the third son of Pepin of Peronne, became Count of Senlis and Valois, leaving a son or grandson BERNARD, the *Bernard-de-Senlis* of the Norman chroniclers. A sister or half sister of Bernard-de-Senlis, whose name is unknown, was the *poppet*, the *bonne-amie* of Rollo, and mother of his son and successor, Guillaume-Longue-épée. The great families of Valois, Saint-Simon and Hamme, all come from Vermandois.

902—943.
Herbert II.

HERBERT, the only son of Herbert the first, dynastically reckoned Herbert *the Second,* was Count of Vermandois and also of Troyes, one of the most powerful feudatories of northern France. Well was he able to avenge himself upon the Carlovingians for the wrongs which his ancestor had sustained.

See § 59.

Sons of Herbert II.

This Herbert the Second, had by his wife Hilde-branda (according to some authorities daughter of Robert Duke of France, and if so, his own niece) five sons, to wit,—EUDES Count of Amiens,—ALBERT the First, Count of Vermandois,—Ro-

BERT Count of Troyes,—another HERBERT, who, 824—987
upon the death of his brother Robert, became
Count of Troyes,—and HUGH who at the age of 840—1080
five years was intruded by his Father Herbert
into the Archbishoprick of Rheims—This absurdly
indecent nomination was opposed, and Hugh ultimately deprived, but the disputes occasioned
thereby were scandalously violent. Frodoardus of
Rheims, the most valuable historian of his era,
was persecuted and imprisoned for supporting
the cause of Artaldus, the canonical competitor.

Herbert the Second also had two daughters— Daughters
of Herbert
to wit, ALICE or ADELAIDE wife of ARNOLPH II.
Count of Flanders,—LUITGARDA married to her
kinsman GUILLAUME-LONGUE-ÉPÉE, and after his
death to THIBAUT-LE-VIEUX, or Thibaut-le-Tri-
cheur, Count of Blois and Chartres; this Thibaut
being the son of Gerlo the Dane, the near relation
of Rollo.

ALBERT, surnamed the "Pious," and dynas- 943—983.
tically reckoned Albert the First, married Ger- Albert I.
Count of
berga, daughter of Louis d'Outremer.—We are Vermandois.
under great obligations to Albert of Vermandois, for he introduced the first historian of
Normandy, Dudo, Dean of Saint-Quentin, her
Herodotus, to the patronage of Richard-sans-peur.

The Fiefs of Vermandois and Valois were Herbert
IV, died
reunited in the person of Herbert the Fourth 1080, his
daughter
(the lineal descendant of Count Albert), whose Adela,
married to
only child Adela brought them to Hugh-le-Grand, Hugh, son
of Henry I.

824—987 the Crusader, second son of Henry the First King of France—from Hugh and Adela came the 840—1050 second line of Vermandois and Valois.

The Aqui-
tanian line
speedily
extin-
guished.

§ 36. AQUITANIA'S unfortunate line was speedily extinguished.—PEPIN King of Aquitaine, second son of Louis-le-débonnaire, left two sons,

Pepin II.
died about
855   See
Chap. III.

the despoiled PEPIN the Second, king, pretender, monk and pirate, married (as is supposed) to the sister of Robert-le-Fort, but who died in prison, childless; and CHARLES, whom his uncle Charles-le-Chauve persecuted into holy orders. Unwilling to submit, the young prince escaped from Corbey, attempting to regain his secular rights; but misfortune humbled his spirit, and he ultimately accepted the obligations against which he had rebelled: an exemplary priest, Archbishop of

Charles,
Abp. of
Mayence,
died 863.

Mayence, chosen to the see by clergy and people, he worthily fulfilled the duties to which he was called.

840—855.

Lothair and
his lineage.
Disobe-
dience of
his sons.

§ 37. LOTHAIR the Emperor, eldest son of Louis-le-débonnaire, left three sons, LOUIS, LOTHAIR and CHARLES. The lessons he, the father, had taught, were ill-calculated for the training of dutiful children. Avenging Nemesis compelled him to take a hearty drink from the self-same cup of bitterness: Louis, his eldest son, deprived him of the proudest portion of his Empire.

The election of Pope Sergius, made without 824—987
Lothair's assent, excited his anger : he despatched
a large army to Rome, commanded by Louis, 840—855.
for the purpose of enforcing obedience. Louis
was thus placed in the same relative situation
towards his father Lothair, as he, Lothair, had
been placed with respect to his father Louis-le-
débonnaire—entrusted with the like mission, exposed to the like temptation, furnished with the
like opportunity. Pope Sergius and the Romans   844
consistently acted in like manner as Pope Pascal (see § 38, 44)
and the Romans had formerly done. When Louis King of Lombardy
and the Frankish army approached the city, by Pope Sergius.
the Roman clergy and senators received the
Emperor's son with royal honours.   The Pope
crowned Louis as King of Lombardy before Saint
Peter's Altar.   A second journey to Rome, a   Dec. 2.
850.
second *Rom-fahrt*, procured for Louis the Im- Louis II.
crowned as
perial Crown.   It was not worth while to ask Emperor
by Pope
Lothair's consent : a species of mocking apology Leo.
was made to him.   Henceforward, though "*Lotharius Imperator*" might appear in Charter or
Diploma, and the fealty-form be preserved to
him, his sovereignty in Italy was gone. The prey
Lothair tore from his father was snatched from
him by his son.

Lothair's life wasted away obscurely and ig-
nobly, his coasts grievously troubled by the Northmen, to whom he was compelled to cede large
districts, no honour or respect rendered to his

824—987
840—869
Imperial title, his health declining, his heart broken, the Pfaltz of Aix-la-chapelle, his ancestorial hall, became a wretchedness. He quitted the Palace once and for all, and, traversing the Ardennes repaired to Pruhm, the prison-house of so many of his family. Renouncing the world which was leaving him, he shrouded his head in the cowl, and died a professed monk in the Abbey. Yet posthumous vanity followed him there, and the monks adorned his tomb with a glorious epitaph.

Sept. 29 855.
Death of Lothair.

844—875
Louis II.
eldest son
of Lothair:
see § 44.
§ 38. LOUIS the Emperor, the eldest son of Lothair, married the clever and intriguing Engelburga, supposed to be a daughter of the Duke of Spoleto, by whom he had two sons, who both died infants, and two daughters, one a professed nun, Abbess of Santa Giulia at Brescia, and HER-MENGARDA, married to Boso, son either of Bovo Count of the Ardennes, or of Theodorick Count of Autun, and brother or half-brother of Richard-le-Justicier Count or Duke of Burgundy.

Hermen-
garda, see
§ 44, and
chap. IV.
§ 2.

855—869
Lothair II.
second son
of the
Emperor
Lothair,
and his
lineage
See § 39—
42.
LOTHAIR the second son, his father's namesake (also dynastically styled Lothair the Second), was betrothed to Waldrada, sister of Gunther, Archbishop of Cologne, but married to Thiutberga, sister of Hubert, Count, under Carlovingian supremacy, of Transjurane Burgundy, the Valais, Geneva and Chablais and the rest of modern Switzerland as far as the Reuss, moreover Abbot of three Abbeys, the royal Saint Maurice in the

Valais, Saint Martin of Tours and Luxeuil. He _{824 987} was killed in battle.

840—856

Lothair's conduct towards Thiutberga was detestably malevolent; and, seeking a divorce, he preferred the most foul and incredible accusations against her. The transactions connected with this repudiation do not belong to us, but they tended, far more than any political disaster could have done, to the degradation of the Carlovingian name. No children were born to Lothair the Second by Thiutberga, but by Waldrada he had one son, the unfortunate HUGH, Count or Hugh of Alsace. See § 43, and Chap. IV. Duke of Alsace, and several daughters, two of whom must be noticed.—BERTHA, twice married, first to Thibaut Count of Arles, and secondly to Adelhard Marquis of Ivrea; and GISELLA married to Godfrey the Dane, who became a Carlovingian feudatory. Our attention must be directed to this Princess from the parallelism between her and Gisella, the daughter of Charles the Simple and wife of our Norman Rollo.

CHARLES King of Provence, the third and 855—863 Charles of Provence. See § 41. youngest son of the Emperor Lothair, died childless.

---

§ 39. UPON the death of the Emperor Lo- 855—856 Partition of Lothair's Empire amongst his sons: their dissensions. thair his share of the Carlovingian inheritance, the Kingdom acquired by disobedience, violence, deceit and fraud, sustained further partitions: Lothair's piece of the rent garment was clutched

824—987
835—856.

and tattered again and again by his nearest of kin, his three sons, and their two uncles, and the sons and the sons' sons of his sons and uncles, till the lineage ended.

The process of political self-destruction which severed the Empire upon the death of Louis-le-débonnaire, continued after the death of Lothair, on a smaller scale, but with undiminished bitterness and virulence. The Emperor Lothair had directed and confirmed the partition of his third of the Carlovingian Empire, appointed to him by the treaty of Verdun. With respect to Italy, there was little to say; Louis, his eldest son, was in possession, Louis the Emperor, second of the name. But such confirmation as could be imparted by Lothair's declaration—for Louis-le-Germanique might contest his nephew's rights —was willingly bestowed.

Louis II. takes Italy. See § 44.

Lothair II. takes various Austrasian, Burgundian and other territories, constituting the Kingdom of Lotharingia or Lorrain.

To his namesake, his second son, designated dynastically in the Carlovingian annals as LOTHAIR the Second, the Emperor Lothair gave the ancient and venerable seat of government, Aix-la-Chapelle, those portions of the pristine Austrasia which had not passed to Charles-le-Chauve and Louis-le-Germanique, and Transjurane Burgundy. This Kingdom did not correspond exactly with any of the former constitutional divisions of the Empire. It included many races and many tongues, the Tudesque, the Belgic and the Romance, in various dialects. The possession of Aix-

la-Chapelle might have entitled the elder Lothair 824—987
to adopt the style of King of Austrasia. But the
associations connected with the *ancien régime* 855—856.
were fretted out by the multiplied divisions, subdivisions and changes which the Empire had sustained, and the *Regnum Lotharii* assumed, at a
very early period after its erection, the denomination of *Lotharingia, Lothier-regne,* or *Lorraine.*

The extent and importance of this realm will
be best understood by adopting a description
given in the terms of more modern geography.—
Lothair inherited from his father the thirteen Can-
tons of Switzerland with their allies and tribu-
taries, East or Free Friesland, Oldenburgh, the
whole of the United Netherlands, and all other
territories included in the Archbishopric of
Utrecht, the *Trois Evéchés,* Metz, Toul and Verdun, the electorates of Trèves and of Cologne, the
Palatine Bishoprick of Liège, Alsace and Franche-
Comté, Hainault and the Cambresis, Brabant
(known in intermediate stages as Basse-Lorraine,
or the Duchy of Lohier), Namur, Juliers and
Cleves, Luxemburgh and Limburg, the Duchy of
Bar and the Duchy which retained the name of
Lorraine, the only memorial of the antient and
dissolved kingdom.

CHARLES, the youngest son, received the re- Charles,
mainder of Lothair's dominions, the counties of King of
Provence.
Ussez and the Vivarais on the right bank of the See § 41.
Rhone, various Burgundian provinces, including

824—987
855—856

the duchy of Lyons, and generally the territories adjoining or bounded by the Jura, the Alps, Cottian or Penine, the Rhone and the Durance.

. The finest portions of the Troubadour fatherland belonged to Charles. He held his Court at Lyons; but Provence proper, the land between the perennial rushing Rhone and the stony bed of the torrent Durance, was the most attractive portion of his dominions, and gave her name to the new kingdom.

856
Conference
at Orbe:
the two
elder bro-
thers en-
deavour to
despoil the
younger.

§ 40. In the year following their father's death, the three sons of Lothair came together at Orbe in the Burgundian Jura. The circular watch-tower of the castle where they assembled, a structure of very singular character, existed within our recollection, the last token of the dignity once possessed by the present obscure and insignificant town. As a matter of course, the three brothers met as rivals; and a quarrel ensued concerning the division of their inheritance. Louis, the Emperor, claiming all his father's dominions equally by pre-eminence and right of primogeniture, had a particular demand against Charles for the districts connected with the Alpine passes. Lothair for the same reason; whilst Charles also desired an extension towards the Alps or the Jura : so violently did they dispute that they came to blows in the Council-chamber. The scuffle being quieted, the two elder brothers, Louis and Lothair, though each was involved in sword-point

litigation against the other, agreed nevertheless 824—987
cordially upon one proposition, that according to
family precedent they would join in despoiling 856
the younger and weaker.   Lothair seized his
brother Charles, and would have compelled him
to be tonsured, but the nobles rescued the young
prince from the hands of his brothers, and the
design was frustrated.

The three sons of Lothair thus in conflict, their Louis-le-
Germaniqueand
two uncles Louis-le-Germanique and Charles- Charles-le-
le-Chauve prepared to assert their pretensions. Chauve
enter into
They assumed that the treaties of Verdun, Thion- the quarrel.
ville and Mersen conferred upon Lothair only
a life-interest in his dominions, and that he being
deceased, his sons had no right thereto.—Charles
King of Provence, the youngest son of the Em- See § 41,
42, 44.
peror Lothair, was the first who died, then King
Lothair : the Emperor Louis, the eldest son, died
last, and their several histories must therefore be
related in corresponding sequence.   But so long
as they lived, they and their two uncles, Louis-
le-Germanique and Charles-le-Chauve, and their See § 45-52.
cousins, Carloman, Louis and Charles, the sons of
Louis-le-Germanique, and their second cousins
Carloman and Louis the sons of Louis-le-Bégue
and grandsons of Charles-le-Chauve, and the survivors and survivor of them, were worrying or
warring for the dominions which had belonged to
the cowl-clad corpse decaying beneath the con-
vent-vault in the Ardennes.

855—863
854—863.
Charles
King of
Provence,
summary of
his history.

§ 41. CHARLES, King of Provence, possessed much talent, ability and goodness of disposition; but he was afflicted by epilepsy, and he therefore continued unmarried and childless. Brothers and uncles, all hungry for his dominions, looked on in longing expectation for the dropping of that frail life which stood in their way. Charles-le-

861.
Charles-le-
Chauve
invades the
Kingdom
of Charles
of Pro-
vence.

Chauve was the most impatient. A favourable opportunity occurred in consequence of the encreasing infirmities of the king of Provence, who being unable to manage the affairs of government, acted by a noble who was appointed as a lieutenant or administrator. This inconvenient though needful arrangement displeased certain of the nobles, and they invited Charles-le-Chauve. France, at this period, was overrun by the ma-

See Ch.III rauding Danes, but Charles-le-Chauve was neither restrained by principle nor deterred by danger, and he invaded the territories of his helpless nephew. The subjects of that nephew were true men, and the rapacious uncle was driven back with disgrace. King Lothair was more prudent: he courted the sickly brother, who gratefully

Charles,
king of
Provence,
died 863

appointed him to be his heir. Charles died in a fit, and was buried in the Church of Saint Pierre at Lyons. This is not the Cathedral, but an abbatial Church, on the other side of the Saône.

§ 42. LOTHAIR prepared immediately to take possession of his brother's bequest, provoking at once a family contest; but Charles-le-Chauve, extremely perplexed by the Northmen, could not participate in the fray, so the Emperor Louis and Lothair, the two surviving brothers of king Charles of Provence, had to fight the matter out. The Danes were in very great force in the north of Germany: they had twice entered the Rhine, and as far as Cologne, and below, the river and its banks were occupied by their fleets and troops; yet Lothair, abandoning the defence of his own country, attacked his late brother's dominions: the Emperor Louis also. Troubles and difficulties induced them to agree upon a pacification: Lothair took the Lyonnais, the Duchy of Vienne, afterwards the *Delphinat*, or *Dauphinée*, the Vivarais and the county of Ussez; but the country relapsed into great disorder, and ere long was severed from the Carlovingian crown.

The dishonourable disputes arising out of Lothair's divorce occupied him during the whole of his reign. The Danes also continually troubled his dominions. Discredited and disgraced, he died of apoplexy at Piacenza. His wretched Queens, Thiutberga and Waldrada, both retired into monasteries.

824—987

863—869
Conclusion of the reign of Lothair II.

864
Contest between his brothers for the Lotharingian kingdom, which they agree to divide.

Lothair II. died 8 Aug. 869.

824—987

860—888

Lotharin-
gia, from
the death
of Lothair
to Charles-
le-Gras

§ 43. AFTER King Lothair's death nine family competitors successively came into the field for that much-coveted Lotharingia, as well as for the remainder of Lothair's possessions, the domains which had devolved upon him by the death of his brother Charles—a crowd of competitors; for every dispute in this distracted family was necessarily a European war. First of all Lothair's son, Waldrada's son, the bold Hugh Count of Alsace; next his brother, the Emperor Louis; then his senior uncle Louis-le-Germanique and his junior uncle Charles-le-Chauve; subsequently his cousins Carloman and Louis, the sons of Louis-le-Germanique; moreover, their namesakes, the other Carloman and the other Louis, sons of Louis-le-Bégue; and after the deaths of Charles-le-Chauve and of Louis-le-Bégue, Charles-le-Gras.

Hugh, Waldrada's son, the son of a crowned Queen, might adduce strong and plausible reasons for maintaining that he was legitimate; but the power and influence of his opponents, all having an equally adverse interest against this Prince, caused him to be pronounced a bastard.—If Count Hugh was not his father's heir, then, according to treaties, the kingdom belonged to the Emperor Louis, and if he was removed, Louis-le-Germanique, the *Senior* of the family, was the heir. Such rights as Charles-le-Chauve might possess would place him fourth in order; but Charles who, amongst the nearest of kin had least claim—if

any principle held good in these disputes,—was the _{824—987}
first who made a seizure of the prize. Louis-le- _{869—888}
Germanique was very ill, thought to be in danger
of death, Louis the Emperor opposing the Saracens, the inveterate foes of Christendom, Charles-
le-Chauve himself, extremely driven by the Danes,
who were then ravaging the north of France ; but
the opportunity was too tempting to be neglected.
Charles-le-Chauve occupied Lotharingia ; and, _{Sept 9, 869.}
Hincmar of Rheims officiating, was very solemnly _{Charles-le Chauve}
crowned and anointed king, according to the forms _{crowned king of}
and ceremonies which had hallowed the accession _{Lotharin-gia.}
of the Merovingian and Carlovingian Sovereigns.

But this usurped Kingdom vanished, to the
great depreciation of Carlovingian royalty. Whilst
Charles-le-Chauve was triumphing in the acquisition of the Lotharingian Crown, the Northmen
were levying contributions in Touraine and Anjou,
and uniting themselves with the Bretons. Louis-
le-Germanique recovered his health and assembled
his forces. Pope Adrian solemnly censured Charles
for his rapacity ; and the monarch, however ambitious, had a tender concern upon his mind, his
amours with Richilda, which occupied him as much
as a Kingdom. The consequence was a mutual _{Aug. 8, 870.}
compromise of claims between the King of France _{Partition}
and Louis-le-Germanique. They agreed to share _{of Lothair's dominions.}
Lotharingia. The lot of Charles consisted of Bur-
gundy and Provence, and most of those Lotharingian dominions where the French or Walloon

824—987
855—875
tongue was and yet is spoken: the boundary-lines of the language not having sustained any material variation since the Carlovingian age; but he also took some purely Belgic territories, especially that very important district successively known as Basse-Lorraine, the duchy of Lohier, and Brabant. Modern history is dawning fast upon us. Louis-le-Germanique received Aix-la-Chapelle, Cologne, Treves, Utrecht, Strasburgh, Metz,—indeed, nearly all the territories of the Belgic and German tongues,—and by the award of the arbitrators, he was considerably the gainer.

This division was settled with cautious minuteness; and the schedule enumerates all the *parcels*, as a conveyancer would say. Language seems to have exercised considerable influence in determining the apportionment. The unknown compiler of the ancient vernacular history which has acquired traditional celebrity under the conventional title of the " Chronicles of Saint Denis," was so much puzzled by the uncouth Tudesque names that he left most of them out—he could not Frenchify them—*maintes autres villes et citez ne sont pas ici nommées, pour ce que le noms sont en langue Thyoyse, ou l'on ne peut assigner propre François.* A special disquisition would be required to elucidate this transaction, and the investigation would be well bestowed, for it was in Lotharingia that the antient Teutonic organization of the *gau* was first obliterated by

mediæval Feudality in the strict and legal sense 824—987
of the term; and the dismembered states were
amongst the most important in France and the 855—875
Germanic Empire.

Treaties, however, were completely illusory: 876.
Charles-le-
when Louis-le-Germanique was on his death- Chauve
contests the
bed, and Charles-le-Chauve nearly in the same whole of
Lotharin-
state, the latter attempted to usurp the dominion gia.
he had ceded to his brother; but he was shamefully defeated.   The continuation of this section,
and the fate of Lothair's wretched son, Count
Hugh, whose eyes were torn out by Charles-le- See Chap-
ters III. IV.
Gras, will be found in subsequent chapters.

§ 44.   Louis the Emperor and King, who Louis II.
Emperor
survived his brothers and all their lineage— and King.
See § 37,
except Hugh of Alsace,—being engaged in the 38.
dissensions before narrated, reigned in a constant
state of arduous, adventurous and varied conflict.
The meteoric brilliancy of the Italian republicks
has thrown the less popular, though not less instructive eras of her history under her Kings and
Emperors, into comparative dimness.   Mediæval
Italy is, for the greater part, as an unenclosed
waste—yet waste only because the land has been
neglected, waiting for some historian to cultivate
her fertility.

Calabria, Benevento, Apulia, swarmed with
Saracen armies, threatening the whole of Italy.

824—987 At this period the Hesperian Peninsula was the
bulwark of Latin Christendom against the com-
855—875 mon enemy. The jealousies of the Christians
menaced the Empire with the subjugation sustained by Spain. The Counts and Dukes of Lombard
blood never ceased to hate the house of Charlemagne, and the people of the south participated
in those feelings. Adalgisius Count of Benevento,
and another Count, Adalferius, yielding to the
instigation of the citizens, rebelled against the
Emperor. Combining with the Moslems, they
basely and treacherously seized the Sovereign,
whom they confined in the Castle. The names or
titles of the Saracens who aided Adalgisius must
be guessed at, under the disguises of *Saducto*,

871. *Sado* or *Sadoan*, *Sogden* or *Sugdan*. Powerfully
Louis II.
traitorously supported, however, by the Duke of Friuli and
seized at
Benevento· the Frankish soldiery, Louis was liberated; and
coeval
ballad a popular ballad is extant, written in alphabetical
upon his
liberation. stanzas, commemorating the plot and the plot's
frustration. This rhythm, which must have originated in some of the localities, where, however
corrupted, the vernacular Latin had not yet been
superseded by the lingua rustica or Romance, is
a very remarkable monument of the grammatical confusion which disintegrated the classical
tongue.

Audite omnes fines terræ errore cum tristitia,
Quale scelus fuid factum Benevento Civitas.
Lhuduicum comprenderunt sancto, pio Augusto.

Beneventani se adunarunt ad unum consilium,
Adalferio loquebatur, et dicebant Principi :
' Si nos eum vivum dimitemus, certe nos peribimus.

' Celus magnum preparavit in istam Provintiam,
' Regnum nostrum nobis tollit : nos habet pro nihilum.
' Plures mala nobis fecit. Rectum est, ut monad.'

Deposuerunt sancto pio de suo palatio ;
Adalferio illum ducebat usque ad pretorium :
Ille verò gaude visum tamquam ad martirium.

Exierunt Sado et Saducto, inoviabant imperio.
Et ipse sanctè pius incipiebat dicere :
' Tamquam ad latronem venistis cum gladiis et fustibus.'

824—987

855—875

Speedily did the tidings cross the Alps—the
Emperor Louis is slain !—Joyful news this for
his junior uncle Charles-le-Chauve, who had been
eagerly coveting his nephew's inheritance; and
he marched rapidly towards Mont-Cenis. Joyful
news equally to his senior uncle Louis-le-Germanique, who immediately despatched his third and
youngest son Charles to secure the Burgundian
passes.—Was there any concert between these
uncles and the Beneventine patriots ? Had bruit
or message from Adalgisius or Adalferius the
Lombard Counts, or from Saracen Cid or Saracen Soldan, prepared the Kings of France and
Germany for the intelligence ?—But the expectations of both these kinsmen were disappointed :
the safety of Louis became known, and moreover
how completely he had been rescued from his
enemies. Charles-le-Chauve, who had left France
in prey to the Danes, halted at Besançon and

871
Louis-le-
German-
ique and
Charles-le-
chauve
prepare to
seize Italy.

824—987
855—875 turned back; and the expedition headed by the younger Charles was abandoned.

Both retraced their journeys, but without retracting their designs. There was no period during the reign of the Emperor Louis in which he and his brothers and uncles were otherwise than unfriendly or inimical—always grudging, envying or fighting.

The Carlovingians exhausted all their bad passions on their nearest kinsmen, and reserved their amiabilities for strangers, a species of favouritism not very uncommon. Louis the Emperor was mild, charitable, merciful, generous and brave · under more auspicious circumstances he might have been another Trajan. He nobly asserted his imperial dignity against the cavils of the Constantinopolitan Emperor. Had not his strength been wasted in family dissensions, the Franks might have renovated the prosperity of the Peninsula, and emulated the glory of the Roman Empire. Prosecuting an undaunted warfare against the infidels, nine thousand (as it is said) fell, when opposed to the Imperial army, in the battle of Capua, one amongst a series of successful conflicts. Crowned with the laurel in the Capitol by the Pope, amidst the salutations of the Roman Senate and Roman people, and going forth in stately procession to the Lateran Palace, the triumphal honours of the ancient Cæsars, the testimony of national gratitude, were

872
Louis successful against the Saracens— his Roman triumph.

fitly revived in favour of the victorious Emperor. 824—987
But his fortune suddenly declined: a comet, fearfully resplendent,—"a torch," they called the 855—875
blazing star,—alarmed Italy. The Saracens returned and burned Benevento;—Louis, who was Aug 13, 875
then in the neighbourhood of Brescia, died on Death of Emperor
the following day, and his corpse was tempora- Louis II.
rily deposited in the Duomo of Saint Philaster.
There congregated the Bishops and Clergy of
Lombardy with hymn and psalm, and the lamentations of the crowds conjoining, they bore the
body to Milan. Andrea the priest, our Chronicler,
was one of the supporters of the bier : they buried
Louis in Sant' Ambrogio.

The Lombard magnates assembled at Pavia
to deliberate concerning the succession. Hermengarda, the high-minded daughter of Louis, his only
child, had been betrothed to Constantine, son of
the Emperor Basil. Another Irene, she might
have been thought worthy of the Imperial Crown ;
but the Lombard nobles wished to weaken the
Royal authority by dividing the Monarchy. They
proposed that the government should be exercised by two Sovereigns, the one to be a check
upon the other, and they invited both Louis-le- 875
Germanique and Charles-le-Chauve to share the Louis-le-Germa-nique and
Kingdom. Louis-le-Germanique was detained Charles-le-Chauve
at Frankfort by troublous affairs, and therefore both in-vited by
he sent his youngest son Charles, his third son, the Lom-bard
the stripling whom the Italians called by the nobles.
affectionate diminutive, Caroletto.

824—987
855—857
Hermen-
garda's
aspirations
See Chap.
IV. § 2
Charles-le-Chauve came in person : Berengarius his nephew, the son of Everard Duke of
Friuli by Gisella the daughter of Louis-le-débonnaire, assisted him powerfully; and Charles-
le-Chauve obtained the Crown, but not to keep
it——" I will not live,' said the maiden Hermengarda, "if I, the daughter of an Emperor and the
betrothed of an Emperor, do not make my husband a king." Boso won the blooming heroine,
and when she had a husband, she succeeded in
gaining for him a kingdom (though not in Italy),
which, more than any other usurpation, accelerated the downfall of the Carlovingian dynasty.

826—876
Louis-le-
German-
ique.
§ 45 LOUIS-LE-GERMANIQUE, the third son
of Louis-le-débonnaire, considered himself, after
the death of his brother Lothair, as the head
of the family. He was not Emperor: that dignity
belonged to Louis his nephew ; but the Imperial
title was, in his estimation, irrelevant :—the law
of nature and the directions of the *Charta
Divisionis* rendered the Senior's right indefeasible. The talent of Louis-le-Germanique was
great, his disposition generous : deservedly was
Louis loved by the Germans as their first national
king. But the Carlovingian curse neutralized all
his virtues. We have seen how he had violated
every natural feeling towards his father. The
slaughter of the battle of Fontenay did not mitigate his enmity against his brothers. Louis was

an excellent ally to the fiercest enemies of the 824—987
Empire: his strifes and bickerings with his nephews, the sons of Lothair, have been already 826—876
noticed, but he did much worse. Accepting the
invitation offered by certain discontented nobles,
the treaties of Verdun and Mersen vanished into
smoke; and at the very time when Charles-le- 858—859
Louis-le-
Chauve was enveloped by the Danes and dis- Germanique at-
tracted by his children and his nephews, Louis-le- tempts to
dethrone
Germanique invaded France, and nearly succeeded Charles-le-
Chauve.
in expelling Judith's son from the kingdom. See Chap.
III.

A rapid turn of affairs replaced Charles-le-
Chauve, but the German and French branches of
the Carlovingian family were henceforth permanently separated and frequently hostile: families
foreign to each other, antagonistic kingdoms, co-
operating only for mutual destruction. Louis-le-
Germanique married an "Emma," a noble lady
of doubtful lineage, but known by this name or
epithet, and the better commemoration of goodness, virtue and great piety. He had three sons
by her, CARLOMAN, LOUIS and CHARLES: Carlo- His troubles with
man, magnanimous in disposition, distinguished by his children § 47,
beauty and vigour, pleasant in speech, mild and 48, 49.
gentle: Louis affectionate, wise, learned: Charles,
the youngest, the Caroletto of the Italians, apparently energetic, prescient and qualified for his
high station. But in none of these sons had their
father any comfort: there was no antidote for the
hereditary Carlovingian contagion of disobedience;
and the disobedient father received his due reward.

§ 46. No subjects were so troublesome to the Carlovingians as the Sclavonians, and with sorrowful reason on both sides, savage revenge being kindled by savage oppression, and the oppressors avenging the revenge. The Teutonic nations treated the Sclavonians as we view " natives," or " aborigines," a genus somewhat inferior to man and not so valuable as the beast, to be left alive only when they could not be exterminated —to be cleared off, to be evicted or improved from the face of the earth : creatures not having any right to be fed at the great table of Him by whom the fulness is bestowed ; in short, a race " doomed " according to the stereotyped phrase, " to be extinguished by the progress of civilization."

The history of the transactions between the Sclavonians and their cognate races and the Germans, is a hideous page in the dark book of human calamity.——Join not in abetting prosperous crime by the most pernicious of deceptions, the sophistry which encourages wickedness by the cant vocabulary of praise, the pretence of faith, or the promise of renown : the spirit which adopts for heroes Cromwell in Ireland or Cœur-de-Lion in Palestine. When the Grand Master of the Livonian Knights received investiture, the Prelate of the Order pronounced the following words :——*Das Schwerdt empfang durch meine hand—Zum Schutze Gottes und Marien land.*—— The slaughter of the Lithuanians is scarcely so

---

824—987

826—876

Oppressions sustained by the Sclavonian nations.

fearful as the moral delusion which fell upon the priestly-soldier or soldier-priest by whom the benediction was bestowed or received.

821—987

876

At the commencement of the Carlovingian era, the Elbe separated the great Teutonic and Slavo-Wendish families.—The Sclavonians combined Oriental aptness with European firmness: a patriarchal nation, simple and primitive, clinging together by those strong ties of affection which peculiarly belong to that state of society. A strange tradition floated amongst them, telling how Alexander the Great, out of love for Roxolana, had granted his Empire to them by charter. Subdued by the Carlovingians, reduced to galling bondage in some parts of the German North, and rendered tributary in others, their spirit was unbroken, and whenever opportunity served they rose against their tyrants. They fought for all that can be dear to mankind—land and liberty, language and nationality.

Both parties were wild, both ferocious, both treacherous, both merciless; but the Germans the most condemnable, for they made the higher profession. The violence exercised towards these unhappy people is not so odious as the insolent arrogance by which the Teutons asserted their ascendancy, scarcely effaced in our own times. In the last century, no workman of Slavo-Wendish blood could be admitted into the trading guilds: *Vetter Michel*, the unwashed cobbler, would not bear the smell of a Wend.—Even more signi-

824—987 ficant is the fact, that the term *Sclave*, according
826—876 to its own meaning, *Glory*, should have been converted by the Germanic nations into the degrading sense which the word now conveys, the perversion testifying the burning brand of contempt
stamped by the Germans upon the nation to
whom the name belonged.

In relating these deeds, the Germans are tran-
quilly complacent. Literature perpetuates all
national injustices. Clio cannot tell truth : she
cannot help being a false thing, it is her nature :
it is the inherent deceit of history, the subtle
deceit, the irremediable deceit, to be essentially
subjective, and therefore inevitably selfish. For
want of an history written by an Helot, how little
do we know of Sparta.—But this by the way.

Annoy-
ance. given
to Louis by
his sons.
Carloman
See § 49

Arnolph
son of Car-
loman. See
§ 52.

§ 47. CARLOMAN had been invested by his
father with the Sclavonian duchy of Carinthia.
The mother of his children was Lituinda, a Ca-
rinthian damsel of royal or noble race, to whom
the designation of wife is refused by the French
and German chroniclers. Their son ARNOLPH,
wise and prudent, was very remarkable for his
beauty; and his cheerful spirit corresponded with
his aspect : their daughter GISELLA was married
to Zwentibold King of the Moravians. The first
instances known in history of any alliances between Teuton and Sclavonic blood are furnished
by the family of Carloman. This connection

made Carloman more akin to the Sclavonians: he
leagued himself with Rastiz King of the Wends,
and usurped a large portion of the Sclavonian
and Pannonian territories, which Louis-le-Germanique had inherited or acquired. The enmities
and dissensions with his father continued many
years: Carloman was deprived of his duchy, reconciled, put in arrest, escaped, revolted over and
over again, and never settled into any satisfactory
relations with his father so long as they lived.

824—987
826—876

LOUIS-LE-JEUNE, or LOUIS THE SAXON, was
equally troublesome. Affronted, because certain
benefices had been given to Carloman, he excited
the Thuringians and Saxons to insurrection, took
under his protection various rebellious noblemen
whom his father had deprived of their lands, and
did not scruple to deceive his father by false
oaths and false declarations: Louis-le-Jeune, like
his elder brother, was engaged in fierce hostility
against his uncle Charles-le-Chauve.

Louis-le-
Jeune or
Louis the
Saxon See
§ 50.

See Chap.
III.

CHARLES, Caroletto, the youngest son of Louis-
le-Germanique, was insolently disobedient to his
father, and indeed imitated his brothers in their
unkindness.—Yet now and then there were short,
bright intervals in the lives of the sons, when
they were useful, kind and affectionate to their
father,—touches of sweetness in his weary life,
more weary towards its close.

Charles,
§ 51.

The successful enlargement of his Kingdom,
and the still greater success of earning the affection

Other
troubles
sustained

824—987

826—876
by Louis-
le-Ger-
manique.

of his subjects, gave Louis-le-Germanique no joy. Sclavonians and Northmen troubled him again and again. Germany was visited by an extraordinary plague—swarms of locusts producing famine by their ravages, pestilence by their corruption—winters of uncommon severity. It was when Germany was thus afflicted, that the Sclavonians renewed their efforts to recover their freedom. Threescore and ten years had passed over the head of Louis, but he could not rest. He made a fruitless attempt to win Italy, and only reaped disappointment. Emma died, to her husband's inconsolable grief; yet, amidst all these

876
28 Aug.
Death
of Louis-
le-Ger-
manique.

troubles, he directed another expedition against his brother Charles-le-Chauve, when death, and death alone, ended their discord.—All the children of Louis-le-débonnaire were enemies from cradle to grave.

876—877
Dissen-
sions of the
sons of
Louis-le-
German-
ique.

§ 48. Upon the death of Louis-le-Germanique, his dominions, so well governed by him, were, according to inveterate custom, divided, giving a further impulse to the dissolution of the Carlovingian Empire. Louis-le-Germanique made an apportionment during his life-time, which the coheirs prepared to contest. In the congress held at Swalifeld they settled the matter with somewhat less bickering than usual, but still continuing that severance of the Teutonic nations which forbids the unity of their " Vaterland."

§ 49.   CARLOMAN took Baioaria, Bohemia, Carinthia, dominions including the mediæval Duchy of Austria, and a portion of those Pannonian plains to which the terrible Hungarians, the Mcgors, commanded by their Seven Hetumogors, the chieftains wary and fierce, Arpad, and Zcbolsu, and Curzan, and Ete, and Lelu, and Zemera, and Horcu, were marching.   But a higher fortune was preparing for Carloman. Upon the death of the Emperor Louis, he challenged Italy.   This involved him in sharp and successful competition with his uncle Charles-le-Chauve.   Graceful, courteous, energetic, Carloman won the favour of the Italian nobles and was saluted Emperor.   With singular generosity he exhibited the rare example of kindness to a brother, surrendering to Louis the Saxon the portions of Lotharingia which had devolved to him.   Yet it is quite consistent with Carloman's character to suppose that sound policy supplied the place of principle—his prudence restrained the appetite of dominion; and he felt the inexpediency of retaining a territory so far distant from the Imperial Kingdom which he now ruled.   Carloman's youth, bodily and mental power and talent, promised to revive the waning glories of the Carlovingian Crown; but having entered the second year of his reign, Carloman, the strong man, fell, smitten by the palsy.   Speech was restored in a very slight degree to the sufferer, who was immediately beset by his anxious bro-

824—987

877—880.

Carloman's share and reign

877

Carloman obtains the kingdom of Italy and the Imperial dignity.

879.

Carloman struck by the palsy.

824—987 thers. Louis determined to obtain the Baioarian and Sclavonian dominions, and prevailing upon
876—882 the nobles to support him and none other, he compelled the poor helpless hopeless Carloman to sign an instrument by which he surrendered himself, his wife and his son, into his brother's guardianship. Charles established himself in Italy. The two committees of person and estate
22 March, 880 (the technical terms of our practical jurispru-
Death of Carloman. dence are not inappropriate) had the decency to wait for the absolute assumption of royal autho- rity till the breath was out of the dying man's body—but their patience was not tried long.— Carloman died in the course of the next year; Louis annexed the German and Sclavonian do- minions of Carloman to his own, bestowing how-
881. ever the Duchy of Carinthia upon his nephew
Charles, King of Arnolph:—Charles (to whom we soon return)
Italy, &c. See §52 and was invested with the iron Crown at Pavia.
Chap. IV.

876—882   § 50. LOUIS THE SAXON had the country
Louis the Saxon. which gave him his denomination; moreover Franconia, Friezeland, Thuringia, and, by the bounty of his brother Carloman, Basse-Lorraine. He was twice married—his first consort, the daughter of Count Adelard, he espoused against the wishes of his father. From her he separated; possibly they were only betrothed, possibly also she was the mother of his son Hugh, considered to be illegitimate By Luitgarda, the daughter of

Ludolph Duke of Saxony, he had one son, whom 824—987 he christened by his own name,—a precious life was this infant Louis to his father;—and, Hugh 876—882 being excluded, the child was his designated heir. As soon as Louis had in the manner before mentioned acquired Basse-Lorraine, Charles-le-Chauve, without any warning, invaded the country for the purpose of annexing the province to the dominions which the Northmen were wresting from See Chap III. him. Louis the Saxon, on his part, fought bravely and with exasperation : Charles-le-Chauve was compelled to retreat disgracefully, and in anguish of mind.

Louis the Saxon hated the French branch See § 54 &c. Chap. IV. of his family. When his cousins in the second degree, Carloman and Louis, sons of Louis-le-Bégue and grandsons of Charles-le-Chauve, were almost ruined by the northern invasions, he profited by their distress, extorted from them the residue of that much-coveted Lorraine country, and subsequently endeavoured to dispossess them of the whole kingdom of France.

The dexterous management adopted by Louis, and the death of Carloman, gave him Baioaria and Baioaria's dependencies; but whilst he was taking possession of the fine German kingdom, he sustained the most grievous loss, — his child, his fondling namesake, who accompanied him to 880. Ratisbon to witness his inauguration, fell from Unfortunate death of the child Louis. the palace-window and was deplorably killed.

824—987 The dominions of Louis were repeatedly ravaged
by the Northmen.   He gained a complete victory
876—882 over them in the Ardennes, but their impetus
did not sustain any check ; and the death of the
880—881 young prince Hugh, a brave and honest son, was
Battles
with the
Northmen a loss scantily compensated to Louis by the victory.   In the subsequent battle at Ebsdorf, his
troops were totally defeated by King Eric and
the Northmen.   His brother-in-law Bruno, two
882 Bishops, twelve Counts and eighteen Palatine
Death of
Louis the
Saxon. officers, were slain.   Louis sickened and sunk
under his trials and troubles, and died of vexation and sorrow.

876—888.
Charles-le-
Gras and
his acqu-
sitions. § 51. CHARLES, the Caroletto of the Italians, the
third and youngest son of Louis-le-Germanique,
received Alemannia or Suabia.   He once was
visited by a strange and sudden horror, crying
out that he was pursued by a Demon.   Popular
opinion attributed this attack to distress of mind,
remorse for the great trouble he had occasioned
to his father.   His mental faculties were never
afterwards affected, but excessive corpulence gave
him an unseemly appearance, approximating to
infirmity.   *Caroletto,* as he grew older, waxed
into *Carlone,* his unwieldy obesity suggested the
half-ludicrous popular epithet by which he is so
unhappily recognized,—"Karl der dicke," " Carolus Crassus," Charles-le-Gras.—

He seems to have been twice married : the name of his first wife is not known—during this period of confusion chronicles become scanty. His second wife was Richarda, defamed as an adulteress, a crime of which she offered to clear herself by the ordeal; but Charles never cohabited with her. One only son he had by an unmarried mother, Bernard the *mamzer*, whom he laboured to establish as his successor. Towards the close of his life, Charles launched suddenly into a brilliant career of success, promising a splendid future. Charles having attached himself in the first instance to his brother Carloman, obtained Lombardy by that brother's opportune demise. He then advanced rapidly to Rome : Nobles and Pope yielded, and on the Feast of the Epiphany he received the Imperial crown from the hands of the Pontiff.

Thus suddenly placed in the highest dignity of the West, another great promotion opened to him upon the death of Louis the Saxon. Charles the Emperor, King of Lombardy, King of Alemannia, was unanimously invoked by the Germans as their protector and defender.—Let him proceed in re-establishing the integrity of the Empire : let Italy and Germany again be protected by the might of one supreme Sovereign.—The Lombards joined his standard with alacrity.

Equally successful was Charles north of the Alps.—Kaiser Karl is coming '—he was greeted

Marginal notes:
824—987
876—888
880
Charles-le-Gras, King of Italy,
6 Jan 881, receives the Imperial Crown
882
He acquires Bavaria upon the death of Louis the Saxon.

CC 2

824—987 at Worms with exuberant joy.—Kaiser Karl is
coming! Bavarians, Saxons, Franks, Thuringians
884 and Alemanni mustered to his support, and all
Germany gladly obeyed him.

Charles-le-
Gras King
of France
See § 53,
54.
Emperor Charles was pursuing a consistent
scheme, he was seeking to reunite the dominions
of his great ancestor. the premature deaths of
the childless Louis and Carloman, the sons of
Louis-le-Bégue, accelerated the accomplishment
of his plans. The infant Charles-le-Simple, the
posthumous son of Louis-le-Bégue, being rejected,
the Emperor Charles-le-Gras, King of Lombardy
and King of Germany, became King of France,
and Charlemagne's supremacy seemed to be re-
888 stored. But for how long?—Charles-le-Gras was
His misera-
ble death. deposed, begged his bread, and is supposed to
have been strangled. His son, the favoured
Bernard, died in obscurity and misery.

887—921 § 52. ARNOLPH, the Sclavo-Teuton, the noble,
Arnolph
and his
lineage.
the honest, the sturdy son of Carloman and Liut-
winda, now acquired the kingdom of Germany.
Shortly afterwards he was elevated to the Empire
by the unanimous voice of the nobles. His ability
fully justified their choice, and his talents and
virtues promised an era of national prosperity;
899 but after obtaining the dignity, three years only of
Death of
Arnolph. life were allotted to him, and he died leaving
two sons, ZWENTIBOLD and LOUIS, whom the Ger-

mans call *Ludwig das Kind*, "Louis the child," 824—987
also three daughters—HADWISA, married to Otho
duke of Saxony—GLISMONDA, married to Conrad 899
of Fritzlar, Count of Franconia and Wetteravia—
and BERTHA, married to Luithard, Count of Cleves.

In the meanwhile the Carlovingian Empire See § 54, 59.
was rapidly dissolving. EUDES, Count of Paris,
ascended the throne of France. BOSO, Hermengarda's husband, founded the Kingdom of Provence. BERENGER, a most energetic and renowned
Sovereign, "*il Re Berengario*," was made King
of Italy and Emperor, the Lombard nobles the
Roman people and the Papal sanction all concurring; but the German nobles would only re- 899
cognize LUDWIG DAS KIND, who, being seven Ludwig das Kind (Louis III. or IV.) his son, called to the Throne.
years of age, was inaugurated as king of Ger-
many in the Diet of Forscheim. Zwentibold
was appointed to Lorraine by his father; his
harshness offended the influential leaders, they
excited his brother Ludwig, or rather his partisans, to dethrone him; and Zwentibold was slain.

Misfortunes thickened upon Germany. The
" Feud of Babenburgh" plunged Suabia and Alemannia into all the miseries of civil war: the
Magyars spread themselves far and wide into See chap. III. § 2.
Thuringia and Saxony and beyond. Amidst these
calamities, the young Emperor Ludwig suddenly Died 21 Jan 911.
died, being about fifteen years of age. The
chronicles, usually so ample in obituary details
concerning monarchs, scarcely notice his death:

824—987 even the place where the event happened is not
known.   It should seem as if there were some
reason for their reticence.   The male lineage of
911—917 Charlemagne in this branch being thus extin-
Conrad I
King of the guished, CONRAD, the son of Glismonda and Con-
Germans. rad of Franconia, quietly established himself upon
the Throne.   The country was in such a state of
exhaustion, that clergy, nobles and people in general cared not either to assent or to dissent when
Extinction Conrad was proposed by his partizans.   The Car-
of the Car-
lovingian lovingian supremacy in Germany expired; and,
Imperial
dignity after many vicissitudes, the Imperial dignity was
re-settled into the new form of that organization
whose style involves an irreconcileable contradiction in terms, the so called "Holy Roman Empire."

840—877   § 53. We now revert to the youngest branch
Charles-le-
Chauve and of the dying Carlovingian race, in which the
his chil-
dren. struggle for existence was longest maintained.

The first wife of CHARLES-LE-CHAUVE, the
first king of France, was Ermentruda, the daughter of Eudo Count of Orleans, pious and affectionate, seeking to be a peacemaker, but unre-
quited by her husband's love.   Charles longed
for her death, and that death enabled him to
espouse RICHILDA, with whom he had previously
cohabited.   This lady, concubine and Queen, was
sister or half-sister of Boso (the husband of Her-

mengarda), who by this marriage therefore be- 824—987 came brother-in-law to the King. 840—877

Unhappy in his kingdom, more unhappy in his family, scarcely able to defend himself against the perfidious attacks of his brother Louis, Charles-le-Chauve was the assailant, in his turn, of all his nephews and great nephews, being also involved in harassing dissensions with his own children. He had eight sons, four by Ermentruda, four by Richilda,—all sons of bitterness or sorrow.

LOUIS-LE-BÉGUE, the eldest son, stammered Louis-le-Bégue died 879. exceedingly, a great hinderance, the faculty of addressing his warriors being no less needful to a King than the power of vaulting on his steed. Charles interfered with the affections of Louis, provoking him to disobedience; and Louis became a discontented and grudging son, crossing his father's intentions, and courting and supporting his father's enemies.

The second son, CHARLES, was appointed King of Aquitaine by his father. Bold, ambitious and able, he, during his short life, repeatedly rebelled against his parent, and brought on his own death by an idle frolic. Returning late in Charles King of Aquitaine died 868. the evening from a hunting party, heated perhaps by the cups of Bordeaux wine, he boyishly entered into a scuffle with his companions, youths like himself, one of whom, Alboin, not recognizing him in the dark, angrily struck him on the head

*C C 4

824—987 with a sword. The blow was not immediately fatal; but Charles became insane, and lingered painfully during two years before he died.

LOTHAIR, the third son, was born lame and unhealthy: humble, affectionate, diligent and pious, his disposition was excellent. Nominated Abbot Lothair died 886. of Saint Germain l'Auxerrois, he died at an early age.

851—873. Carloman died 866. CARLOMAN, the fourth son, was also compelled by his father to take Orders. Very ample preferment was bestowed upon him: the Abbey of Saint Médard, Saint Riquier or Centulla, Lombes and many others: thereby exciting great scandal. This misappropriation was most unfortunate to all parties. Carloman would not be contented: he teased his father, cheated him, conspired, rebelled, and, being tried for his treasons, was condemned to lose his eyes. Charles-le-Chauve sanctioned the execution of his sentence, and it was so far mercifully carried into effect as not to kill the victim. The poor blinded wretch was harboured by his uncle Louis-le-Germanique, and maintained in a monastery out of charity. He died childless.

The four above mentioned were Ermentruda's sons. By Richilda, that loved Richilda, Charles-le-Chauve had four more—Pepin, Drogo, a second Louis and a second Charles, all of whom died young or infants: the last, when his parents were in great distress.—Charles-le-Chauve had

several daughters: all became Abbesses except ^{824—987}
Judith, an undutiful girl of ungovernable passions,
whose first husband was Ethelwulf, king Alfred's ⁸⁴¹
father. After his death, she contracted a scandalous marriage with her step-son king Ethelbald.
Of her third husband, Baldwin the Forester, we Judith.
shall speak fully hereafter. (see Chap. IV. § 1.)

§ 54. LOUIS-LE-BÉGUE inherited his father's 877—929
dominions : in early life he had been much at- Louis-le-
Bégue and
tached to Ansgarda, sister of a Burgundian Count, his children
Eudes or Odo. Charles-le-Chauve refused his IV.)
(see Chap.
assent to this union, wishing to effect a State-
alliance between Louis and a Breton (or *Breyzad*)
princess. Louis, therefore, espoused Ansgarda
clandestinely, but was compelled by his father
to divorce her, and she was defamed as a concubine. The projected match with the betrothed
daughter of the Armorican king Herispoë failed,
and Louis then married an *Adeliza* or princess,
named JUDITH, whose lineage cannot be determined: this marriage was also of doubtful validity.

LOUIS-LE-BÉGUE, sickening about the time of 10 April,
879.
his accession, never recovered his health, but Louis-le-
Bégue died.
lingered and died before he had attained the
age of thirty-four years, or completed the second
of his reign. By Ansgarda he had two children, LOUIS and CARLOMAN, who succeeded to
their father's dominions, and reigned jointly—
both most promising youths, singularly affec-

824—987
936—987

Louis III.
died 882,
Carloman
died 884.

Charles-le-
Simple
excluded
in the first
instance by
Charles-le-
Gras. (see
Chap IV.
§ 21.)

(See § 59.)

tionate to each other, both valiant, both bitterly assailed by their cousin Louis the Saxon, who contested their title, and both died childless; Louis, the eldest, first, and Carloman two years after, cut off by violent deaths, caused through their own rashness or imprudence—they threw their lives away.

CHARLES, whose honesty earned for him the epithet of " LE-SIMPLE," son of Louis-le-Bégue by the Adeliza Judith, a posthumous child, struggled bravely, but unsuccessfully against treachery and misfortune. Excluded in the first instance from the succession by his ambitious uncle Charles-le-Gras, he was compelled to yield to EUDES CAPET, who assumed the royal title. Charles had also to contest the throne with ROBERT Duke of France the brother of Eudes. Supposed to have been thrice married, Charles had two children. Historical theory cannot decide whether the first consort was wife or concubine, and there is much obscurity concerning Frederuna, the second. The third was Elfgiva, or Eadgiva, the daughter of our Edward the Elder. By the unknown companion of his bed, Charles had the daughter who was given to Rollo,—GISELLA, a name not unfrequent in the Frankish genealogies, yet somewhat perplexing, inasmuch as it may possibly be only an epithet or a by-name—perhaps *Gesellin*, a companion, or perhaps *Gisle*, or *Gisla*, a hostage, or pledge of friendship or love.

By Elfgiva he had one son, LOUIS, afterwards surnamed LOUIS-D'OUTREMER.

Finally deposed by RAOUL or RODOLPH King of Burgundy the son of Richard-le-Justicier, Charles-le-Simple died in captivity.

824—987

893
Charles-le-Simple finally de-throned 923, died 929.

---

§ 55. LOUIS-D'OUTREMER, son of Charles-le-Simple by Elfgiva, obtained the throne upon the death of Raoul: a fugitive in his childhood, a fugitive in maturer age, he was killed by a strange mischance, either caused by or connected with insanity.

936—987
Descend-ants of Charles-le-Simple. Louis-d'Outremer died 954.

Louis was married to Gerberga, daughter of Henry the Fowler, duke of Saxony and afterwards king of Germany, by whom he had three children who attained man's estate, LOTHAIR, CARLOMAN and CHARLES.—LOTHAIR succeeded Louis in his kingdom. CARLOMAN, given as an hostage to the Normans, died in captivity. CHARLES was invested with the dukedom of Lorraine by his cousin the Emperor Otho. This Charles Duke of Lorraine was married to Agnes, daughter of Herbert Count of Troyes, by whom he had two sons, Louis and Charles. From this family came the Dukes of Lohier or Brabant, the house of Guise, and, amongst numerous illustrious descendants, Godfrey of Boulogne. The Duke Charles endeavoured to vindicate his rights to the Crown of France, and partially succeeded;

824—987 but, basely betrayed into the power of his enemies, he died in captivity.

987
Charles,
Duke of
Lorraine,
died 1101.
Lothair
died 986.

LOTHAIR died of poison, the crime being
imputed to his adulterous wife Emma. He left
one son, LOUIS-LE-FAINÉANT, who also died childless, poisoned (as is supposed) by his wife Blanche,

Louis-le-
Fainéant
died 987

the daughter of an Aquitanian nobleman,—and
the third dynasty obtained the Throne.

Moral and
political
failure of
Carlovin-
gian Em-
pire

The descendants of one *gros-vilain* gave place
to another *gros-vilain*—the lineage was worried
out, worn out, stricken and consumed. As the
Carlovingians began, so they closed. Force and
fraud raised them up : force and fraud put them
down.

§ 56. NEVERTHELESS the transcendant dignity
of Charlemagne, steeped in fiction, and encreasing
in splendour as his form receded into the mists
of antiquity, perpetuated his empire upon popular
imagination, more powerful than reason. Admiring nations bowed before the majestic Phantom.
Whilst his real laws, his codes and institutions,
were wholly effaced, the fabled Doze-peers rose as
living beings before the world : centuries elapsed
before the noble families, who boasted the blood
of Charlemagne, entirely renounced the hope
which their ancestry inspired.

But these dazzling though undefined visions
received their tremendous realization in our own

age, when the Oriflamme's folds floated over the façade of Notre-Dame, and the Pontiff placed the Imperial Crown upon the brow of Napoleon, his throne surrounded by fantastic feudalism. Both Emperors, prototype, antitype, and also types of futurity, entered upon equivalent missions : both failed in gaining their hearts' desires.

824—987

987
Compari-
son be-
tween the
Empires of
Charle-
magne and
of Napo-
leon.

Self-deceived, Charlemagne would have sunk in confusion could he have comprehended how he performed not the good he sought, and did the evil he abhorred. Dimly conscious of his own intentions, unable to construe his own contending thoughts, Charlemagne's scheme of imperial sovereignty amounted to the erection of a Christian Caliphate. Emperor-Pontiff, head of the Catholic Commonwealth, head of the Church, head of the State, supreme in temporals, supreme in spirituals, *Emir-ul-Moslemin*, Commander of the Faithful, Christianity propagated and defended by the sword, Religion, fully acknowledged to be all-pervading and paramount, yet practically treated as a portion of human policy and entirely subordinate to human policy, — Such were the principles animating this phase of the Fourth Monarchy, emphatically symbolized by the heraldic crown of the "Holy Roman Empire," the mitre within and included by the diadem.

Napoleon sought the creation of an antichristian Imperial Pontificate, the Caliphate of Positive Civilization : his aspiration was the establishment of absolute dominion, corporeal and intellectual,

824—987
———
987

the mastery over body and soul, Faith respected only as an influential and venerable delusion: the aiding powers of Religion accepted until she should be chilled out and the unfed flame expire, and Positive Philosophy complete her task of emancipating the matured intellect from the remaining swathing bands which had been needful during the infancy of human society. And the theories of Charlemagne and of Napoleon, though irreconcilably antagonistic in their conception, would, were either fully developed, become identical in their results, notwithstanding their contrarieties. They start in opposite directions, but circling round, their courses would—were it permitted that they should persevere continuously and consistently—meet at the same point of convergence and attain the same end.

Moreover the territorial Empires of Napoleon and of Charlemagne had their organically fatal characteristic in common. Each Founder attempted to accomplish political impossibilities, to conjoin communities unsusceptible of amalgamation, to harmonize the discordant elements which could only be kept together by external force, whilst their internal forces sprung them asunder—a unity without internal union. But even as the wonderful agencies revealed to modern chemistry effect in a short hour the processes which nature silently elaborates during a long growth of time, so in like manner did the energies of civilization effect in three years that dissolution, for which, in the analogous precedent, seven generations were required.

824—987

987
Extinction of the Carlovingian legislation and constitution.

The devastations, the insatiate appetite of domination, the hereditary and contagious disobediences, the crimes, dissensions, hatreds which devoured the Carlovingian dynasty, had produced political destruction long before the actual subversion of the Carlovingian thrones. Charlemagne's great glory was his legislation, the wisdom speaking in his institutions, the activity and diligence which rendered words realities. But the descendants of Charlemagne trampled his Capitulars to rags in their battles and turmoils. After the reign of Charles-le-Chauve, these ordinances, enacted by the Sovereign in the general Diets of the realm, cease. The few occasional statutes which occur scarcely deserve the name of Capitulars, and even these soon terminate entirely. No longer was any general legislation exercised by the State: no attempt made to reform abuses or to enforce the vigour of the laws.

According to the Carlovingian Constitution, justice was brought home to every man's door by the *Missi Dominici*, the Judges travelling their circuits and representing the Sovereign, the centre and source of remedial power: the Emperor was to afford redress when every other authority failed. Unless by the mandate or in the presence of these Judges, or of the Imperial Counts, the local legis-

824—987
897

lature, the Mallum, the Shire-moot, could not be convened. Counts were no longer regularly appointed. Those in office, whether holding for life, during pleasure, or hereditary, withdrew obedience from the Sovereign, and the regular administration of justice expired.

It was the law, that, upon the accession of a new Senior or Sovereign, or upon every mutation of a Lord, the vassals or tenants of Benefices had to renew their oaths of fealty as well as their homage. We have seen how feebly these solemn compacts were binding either upon honour or upon conscience, and the ceremonies were probably generally neglected. We gather this information from the great emphasis with which the performance of homage is noticed in certain particular instances, shewing that such an acknowledgement had become the exception and not the rule: these circumstances dissolved the bonds of political authority.

The subsequent situation of France testifies how completely the Carlovingian legislation was obliterated.—Contrast France and England. The Norman Conquest left the English nation possessed of the laws and usages of their Anglo-Saxon ancestors; but when the third dynasty ascended the French throne, not a vestige of the earlier jurisprudence remained—the Salic Judges, Arbogast, Widogast, Bodogast and Salogast were utterly forgotten: Legists would have been scared by their very names. The dooms of the Salic and Ripuarian Franks and of the Burgundian and Gothic kings had all completely passed away. The antient laws were neither upheld by practice nor honoured by tradition; and hence the Carlovingian system of legislation has, in the main, become a guess and a mystery.

The Northmen broke down the hallowed tomb of Charlemagne, and stabled their horses upon his grave; and the Jews bury their dead where stood the marble-paved and porphyry-columned Palace of Ingleheim.—Charlemagne left nothing enduring except a name and a fable, an ivory horn, and the fag end of an old song.

§ 57. It might be expected that this utter *Social order pre-*collapse, this fainting-fit of civil government *served by the Hier-*during the decline and fall of the Carlovingian *archy.* dynasty, would have produced complete extinction.—Not at all : France was nursing herself into future strength, and maturing the elements of national stability.

Families might decay, kings be deposed, nobles slaughtered, the Courts of Justice disused, laws and lawgivers silenced, but there was a magistracy invested with a power not dependant upon kings, tribunals permeated by indestructible vitality. During this dark and dismal period, Carlovingian France, almost a sacerdotal Commonwealth, was sustained by the Hierarchy. The French bishopricks, more than any other north

821—987

987
of the Alps, conformed to the civil, political and ethnographical repartitions of the country. The *Gallia Christiana* furnishes the best topographical commentary upon Cæsar's Commentaries. It is there that you find the principal data for the maps of *Gallia Romana* or *Gallia Antiqua*. Sanson and D'Anville, in making out the Ædui or the Bituriges, or the Carnutes, or the Cenomani, have had no sure guides except the episcopal circumscriptions. When these fail, as they sometimes do, topographer and geographer are at fault, and fight the fierce battle of archæological controversy. The Romans, wise people, avoided disturbing the Gaulish populations more than was absolutely necessary. The Gaulish civitates, their boundaries unchanged, became the Roman governments; and the Christian dioceses of the earlier periods were always conterminous with the civil governments.

Bishops representatives of the people. This territorial coincidence of the temporal and spiritual magistracies was extremely potential in the policy of the Gauls. In each diocese the Bishop was originally either virtually or literally elected by clergy and people. The liberty of elections had been restored by Louis-le-débonnaire; and although the Crown still continued to exercise considerable influence in the appointment of the pastors, and that influence was susceptible of abuse, yet the royal malversations in episcopal preferments, partially repressed by

the energy of the Church, never became so 824—987
mischievous and unprincipled as in the case of
987
the Abbeys; and, very generally, the pervading
spirit of the hierarchy corrected the individual
unhealthiness, so that even royal nominees were
converted into the most firm defenders of ecclesiastical liberty against the encroachments of the
Crown. Therefore, generally speaking, each Diocese had a chief magistrate, a governor of the
people representing the people; and the ecclesiastical synods, composed of these representatives,
aided the debility or supplied the non-existence of
the legislative or judicial powers, preserved good
order, watched over public morals, and supported
the dilapidated fabric of society. No hereditary
senate, no delegated lay-assembly could possess
equal independence, dare to speak so loudly or
rebuke so sternly, none so efficiently protect the
weak or be so bold against the strong. Kings
quailed in the presence of the Priesthood; and
the meanest were not beneath their care.

Yet Faith alone could never have resuscitated The "Grands fiefs" of France
the State . the aid of the world's weapons is
needed for the world's human government: the
kingdoms of the earth are earthly. It is a great
misfortune for any country to be visited by a
revolution, but far greater when no heroes are
engendered qualified to ride upon the storm—a
human help afforded only by God's providence.
The demand does not necessarily create the supply.

D D 2

821—987

987

Political crises occur when opportunity and temptation, the poignancy of suffering, the courageous cowardice of extreme danger or the highest call of patriotism, may all fail to elicit the bold, the honest, the prudent, the wise, or the greatly bad, to reconstitute the Commonwealth, or even to subdue anarchy by the tranquillity of despotism.

The new lineages.

§ 58. It was otherwise with France.—Whilst the Carlovingians are perishing off the land, we gradually discern the forefathers of those stately lineages, the Dukes, the Marquisses, the Counts, the Viscounts, the Châtelains, the Vîdames, prototypes of the fabled Paladins, paragons, if ever there were, of gallantry, spirit, gentleness, courage, courtesy and honour. The genealogists working in their vocation, the grateful monk, the obsequious herald, and the loyally laborious historian, have thought it their duty to discover for most or all of these lineages princely or royal ancestors, losing themselves in primitive eld. Some of the "great feudatories" were unquestionably saplings growing from the old roots, or grafts upon the old trunks; but the majority neither talked nor cared nor knew about such pedigrees. Virtue, in the Roman sense of the term, had been granted to them, their virtue raised them to their power.

Robert-le-Fort

Exalted amidst the throng of the new men, the *gros-vilains*, the men whose now time-honoured names had then no yesterday, was the Founder of that fated family, bearing in irregular succession the various titles of Abbots, Counts, Dukes, Marquisses, Kings, working their bark through the wreckage of the Carlovingian Empire,—vassals, rivals, competitors, allies, ministers, masters of the doomed Carlovingian race—their fortunes chequered yet consistent, varied yet uniform— appearing to lose but gaining, rising and sinking, waxing and waning but never totally eclipsed, never dipping below the horizon,—retreating yet advancing—every discomfiture the step back before the leap, every adversity the forerunner of prosperity. Which amongst our European dynasties, taken all in all, can compete with the progeny of Robert-le-Fort, that lineage whose unbroken descent from man to man during a thousand years, the male heir never wanting, has been marked out for preservation through chance and change, peril and trial, triumph and degradation, virtue and vice, sanctity and sin, wisdom and folly, by a peculiar Providence, unparalleled in history?

824—987
987

§ 59. ROBERT-LE-FORT married Adelaide, widow of a Conrad, Count of Paris, probably the nephew of the Empress Judith. By her he had two sons, EUDES and ROBERT, both dukes of France, both kings of France, and RICHILDA, wife of Richard Count of Troyes.

867—987.
Robert-le-Fort and his lineage. See Chap. III. § 35.

824—987
807—987
Eudes died
898
Robert II.
died 923.
See § 35

EUDES, the good and brave, died childless. The second son, ROBERT, allied himself to the inimical lineage of Vermandois, espousing Beatrice, daughter of Herbert the first, Count of Vermandois, by whom he had three children, EMMA, wife and Queen of Raoul duke of Burgundy and King of France,—HILDEBRANDA, who added strength and influence to her mother's kindred by marrying Herbert the second, Count of Vermandois;—and HUGH, " Hugh-le-Grand," "Hugh-le-blanc," or "Hugh-l'Abbé;" the first epithet bespeaking his consequence, the second his complexion, and the third, the vast prefer- ments which he held. Robert's second wife was Rothilda. This lady was closely but dubiously connected with Charles-le-Simple.

Hugh-le-
Grand died
956
Hugh Ca-
pet.

HUGH-LE-GRAND was thrice married: his first wife, Eadhilda, connected him with the royalty of England and of France, for she was daughter of Edward the Elder, sister of Queen Edgiva, and therefore aunt of Louis d'Outremer, the son of Edgiva by Charles-le-Simple. His second wife was Hadwisa, also called Edith, daughter of the Emperor Henry the Fowler, son of Otho the Great. His third wife, who died childless, is said to have been a niece of Charles-le-Simple. Hadwisa bore him several children, amongst whom two only need be here noticed, EMMA, wife of Richard-sans-peur, the grandson of Rollo, and HUGH CAPET

Such was the lineage of ROBERT-LE-FORT in the descending grades, but whom do we encounter in the ascending?—"*Pipinus Rotberto comiti et Britonibus sociatur.*"—This phrase is absolutely the first distinct notice we find concerning Robert-le-Fort in authentic history : no preface, no designation, not the slightest explanation of the commanding position which he had obtained. During two centuries subsequent to the death of Robert-le-Fort nothing whatever was recollected respecting his ancestry, except certain reports that his father was one Witikind, a Saxon stranger, a poor man probably, an humble man, but may be a stalwart soldier endued with energy and strength. In proportion as the Capetian Crown increased in brilliancy, so was more light reflected back upon the progenitors of the monarch, and you have half-a-dozen contradictory theories concerning the origin of the Capetian family.—Conradus Urspergensis Abbot of Lichtenau proves that Witikind was no other than the great and heroic chieftain of the Saxon race.—Chifflet the erudite deduces Robert-le-Fort from Guelph the Agilolphing.—Père Tournemine branches Robert off from Charlemagne ; and Legendre from Ansprandus, king of Lombardy.—Zampini takes Childebert as the stem,—and Monsieur le duc d'Epernay discerns a misty Nibelung.—In each of these conflicting pedigrees, and they are spread before us, there is not as you read them a hitch or a

824—987

867—987
Robert-le-Fort · obscurity of his ancestry.

824—987 chasm, all runs smooth and clear; but still we
867—987 fall back upon the fact that they did not enjoy a
crumb of coeval credence. The early traditions
of France were uniform in their import that the
humble origin of the Capets was their glory. The
old Romance tells us that Hugh Capet was once
a butcher; for albeit born of gentle blood, yet
having mortgaged his land, he took to the trade
in frolickry;—and somehow or another, or in
some stage or another of the pedigree, be sure
that the symbolical kernel of the truth is unquestionably enclosed in Dante's rhyme:

> "*Chiamato fui di là Ugo Ciappetta:*
> *Di me son nati i Filippi e i Luigi*
> *Per cui novellamente è Francia retta.*
> *Figluol fui d'un beccaio di Parigi.*"—

Chapter III.

840—877.

§ 1. INTERNAL enemies and external ene- 840—877

mies, enemies known, enemies unknown, enemies The enemies of the
provoked, enemies unprovoked, enemies from the Empire
East, enemies from the West, enemies from the
South, enemies from the North, from the seas,
the rivers and the hills.—Our sailors box the
compass, improving Charlemagne's lessons. Charlemagne began to give the compound names by
which the rhombs of the mariner's card are known;
and from every circling point of the horizon the
wind wafted an enemy. Christians and half-
Christians, Mahometans and idolaters, diverse
races, and diverse tongues,—worshippers of Thor
and Odin, Promo, Chrodo, Jutebog, Zernebog,
Belbog, Zutebor, and lion-visaged Radegast, Swan-
towit with four heads, triple-headed Triglaw,
and genial Siewa, the many-breasted teeming
Siewa with the bunch of grapes in her hand,—
Gascon, Vascon or Escalduanac, Celt or Breyzad,
Jute, Norsk and Dansker; Ishmaelite, Moor, Saracen; Sorb, Wend and Obotrite; Lech, Zech and
Magyar,—all conjoined with the infatuated Carlovingian Princes and their more infatuated subjects
in effecting the Empire's destruction.

810—877 Alas ! for Charlemagne's victories, Charlemagne's conquests, Charlemagne's wisdom, cultivation and knowledge — all come to naught, turned to confusion. Aquitania, a festering ulcer, rebellious, and tempting the offspring of the throne to disobedience and rebellion, Armorica no longer merely an insurgent province, but a kingdom striving for independence and liberty, the Sclavonians breaking up the borders of the Empire. Worse than all, the extinction of natural affection, truth, faith, honesty and loyalty : the hand of each brother, not figuratively but literally lifted against each other, every father distrustful, every son disobedient. Certain obscure ejaculatory English-Saxon verses are extant, describing a country in utter misery, which, partially divested of their archaic orthography, run as follows :—" *Land-king wilful, dooms-man nimmand, rich-man niggard, poor-man proud, gaveloc broken, child unbuxom, churl unthewed, fool reckless, old-man loveless, woman shameless, land lawless, better be lifeless."* — These rapid lines, of which there are many more, sounding as having been transmitted from remote antiquity, truly characterize the wretchedness of the Empire—the whole one vast Luegen-feld, flooded by falsehood, without comfort, without rest.

862—897
The Hungarian
invasions.
§ 2. The troubles on the Eastern side of the Empire animated and encouraged the fiercest and most recent assailants, the Hungarians :

plague upon plagues, misery upon miseries— 840—877
unexpected, unintelligible, the uncouthness of
the visitation encreasing the horror. The face of 862—897
the sun-burnt Saracen was well known to the
Romanized Teutons and Romanized Gauls: an
old acquaintance, an infidel certainly, but a man
like other men, who lived in a house, could read
and write, and was attired in silk and satin. The
fair and blue-eyed Scandinavian, though fierce,
was comparatively a neighbour, whose barks
and barges were dreaded, yet accustomed. But
these uncouth fur-clad hordes had nothing in
common with any foe whom the Christian had
seen, against whom he had fought, or by whom
he had been subdued. Learned men traced the
Hungarians indeed from history: the history was
appalling, and history and tradition conjoined in
exciting insuperable terror. Attila's bones were
imprisoned in his secret sepulchre, but the
scourge of God was raised to chastise the Christian with increased severity.

The language spoken by these Scythians,
distinguished by some unique peculiarities of
construction, and offering only the faintest similarity to any other known speech, refuses to aid
the Ethnographist's speculations. According to
their own primitive traditions, the ruling caste,
the main body of the nation, were the children
of Mogor the son of Magog. The Hebrew name
Mogor signifies "Terror;" and slightly varied by

840—877 the Orientals into "Magyar" became the rallying
cry of the once-splendid Hungarian nationality.
897—950 But the denomination of Hungarian was equally
retained by the Mogors: it is as Hungarians
that they are admitted into European history.

The Hun-
gaiian
invasions
ot Italy,
Germany
and the
Gauls

However acquired or transmitted, the knowledge which the Hungarians possessed concerning
the countries once the scenes of Attila's victories,
was neither inaccurate nor inconsiderable. The
aspirations of Almus, supreme among the seven
Hetumogors, and of his son and grandson, Arpad
and Zulta, display a grandeur, disproportionate
perhaps to their forces, yet worthy of their predecessor's renown.

Early in young Zulta's reign, three chief
Hetumogors, Lelu the son of Tosu, Ver-Bulsu, or
" Bulsu the bloody," the son of Bogat, and Bou-
ton the son of Culpun—King Bela's Chancellor
must warrant our orthography—marched through
Carinthia and Friuli and entered Italy, which
they contemplated as an appendage of their
encreasing realm.   Imperial Pavia burnt and destroyed, the Scythian locusts devoured the Lombard plains. Germany they devastated from side
to side. Their Parthian cavalry crossed the
Rhine—Lotharingia and Burgundy, Brabant and
Vermandois, the Counties and Dioceses of Louvaine and Cambray, Laôn, Rheims and Châlons,
were traversed and penetrated by their armies.
They spread over central and Southern France to

Nîmes and Toulouse, through Provence and Aqui- 840—877
taine, till they came down to the Mediterranean
shores. Berenger King of Italy is said to have 897—950
invited them. Arnolph once sought their deadly
aid. There was a short season of libration,when the
Hungarians by alliance, junction, or coalition with
the Carlovingian rivals, or with the other domestic
or foreign enemies of the Empire, might have
effected a permanent conquest. Their chivalry
however failed : diseases, the result of unwonted
food and an unaccustomed climate, thinned their
squadrons. Thick flew the arrows from their
bows of elastic horn; but, in close conflict, the
light-armed Tartar horsemen were unequally
matched against the steadier ranks of the French
and the Germans. Zulta had wisely organized
and fortified the rising Kingdom of Hungary;
they were proud of their fertile conquest, to
them a new father-land; and the Hetumogors
and their hordes returned home, trains of captives
and bales of plunder rewarding their prowess.

Briefly and dolefully do the Chroniclers of
France, Germany and Italy, describe and lament
the vast fury of the Hungarian ravages. Tradition and poetry impart life and colour to these
meagre narratives. The German Boor still points
at the haunted Cairn, as covering the uneasy
bed or the troubled grave of the restless Huns
whose swords are heard to clash beneath the soil.
Throughout fair France the grinning, boar-tusked,

840—877
———
897—950

ensanguined, child-devouring Ogres appalled the doubtingly incredulous delighted tremblers round the blazing hearth. And we yet possess the solemn chaunt by which the centinel of Modena, pacing along the rampart, cheered his companions and beguiled the weary watches of the night —the floating melody which the half-awakened sleeper can scarcely distinguish from a dream :

> " O Tu qui servas armis ista mœnia,
> Noli dormire, moneo, sed vigila.
> Dum Hector vigil extitit in Troïa,
> Non eam cepit fraudulenta Græcia.
> Primâ quiete dormiente Troia,
> Laxavit Sinon fallax claustra perfida.
> Per funem lapsa occultata agmina
> Invadunt Urbem, et incendunt Pergama.
> Fortis juventus, virtus audax bellica,
> Vestra per muros audiantur carmina :
> Et sit in armis alterna vigilia,
> Ne fraus hostilis hæc invadat mœnia.
> Resultet Echo comes : eja vigila!
> Per muros eja, dicat Echo, vigila!"

714—900.
The Sara-
cen inva-
sions.

§ 3. Far more destructive during the hateful succession of divisions and jealousies, feuds, frauds and treacheries, were the Saracens and the Northmen, hacking and hewing, cutting and carving, making their partitions also, here with Danish battle-axe, there with Damascus blade.

The Saracen expeditions continued the formidable warfare by which they had won the Iberian peninsula, and previously assailed the Gauls. Nothing daunted by the defeats received

from Charles-Martel, they treated the Aqui- 840—877
tanian and Narbonensic Gauls as a country to
which they possessed a natural claim : in sultry 714—900
Saracen
Provence you feel to breathe the Zahara air. invasions
of Italy and
The Aquitanians were well inclined to fraternize Provence
with the Mahometans. No thanks either to
Adalgisius and Adalferius and the Beneventine
Lombards, that the Carlovingian Emperor had
not been supplanted by a Sultan of Naples, whose
Emirs would have extended their conquests
round to the realm of the Ommiades. Antioch,
Alexandria, Jerusalem, bowed humbly before the
Arab, and it seemed more than once uncertain
whether Rome would not be equally reduced to
servitude. The Western Pontiff was threatened
by the captivity inflicted upon the oriental Pa-
triarchs : Saint Peter's successor might groan in
bondage, like the successors of Saint Ignatius,
Saint James or Saint Mark. The great Mediterranean lake appeared destined to become a Moslem
lake; and why not? An Emperor of Morocco,
according to the reasoning so irrefutable when
supported by the arguments of civilization, would
have as good a right as an Emperor of France.

Few early Provençal or Aquitanian Chronicles have been preserved, consequently the
history of the country is very obscure. We have
evidence however that the Saracens came over
in great numbers. Their attacks and partial
successes are not unfrequently noticed, but the

840—877

714—900
Saracen
settlement
and influ-
ence in
Provence.
larger and more continuous immigrations are only incidentally recorded. Fraxinet, a castle or fortress on the coast, somewhere nigh Fréjus, became the nucleus of a Saracen colony midway between Italy and Spain, and readily reached from Africa. This position offered great advantages. The Saracens expanded themselves over the country. They mastered the passes of the Cottian and Penine Alps, following the footsteps of Hannibal. Various localities have received their denomination from these invaders. The *forêt des Maures* on the Fréjus coast, *Puy-Maure*, and *Mont-Maure* near Gap, the *Col de Maure* near Château Dauphin, and the whole County of *Maurienne*, testify their occupancy; and it is considered that the Saracen blood has left deep traces in the aspect as well as the character of the Provençals.

With the Saracens probably came also a large proportion of Jews, who subsequently acquired considerable influence, rivalling their Spanish brethren, the Sephardim, in literature and intellectual cultivation. But the Moslems were as much at variance amongst themselves as the Christians:—a divided Caliphate in the presence of a divided Empire. The Musnud of Bagdad has fallen like the Throne of Aix-la-Chapelle. Power had the Saracens given to them for accelerating the ruin of Carlovingian domination, but no power to build up for themselves out of the

ruins. How casual and fantastic are the ele- 840—877
ments of popular celebrity! Turpin and Ariosto
contribute the most enduring memorials of 714—900
Charlemagne's renown; and Haroun Alraschid
reigns throughout Frangistaun by the lips of
Sheherazade.

Notwithstanding their ultimate expulsion from
Italy and the Gauls, the Mahometans kept up
their continual claim.—Dragutte and Barbarossa
infested the Mediterranean shores with undiminished pertinacity. The harems of Tunis and
Tripoli were adorned by the flowers of beauty
rudely plucked from the cottages and the villas,
the chateaux and the palaces of Liguria or
Tuscany, Romagna or the Abruzzi, Languedoc
or Provence, who under a more fortunate or a
more adverse star would have furnished models
for Titian or Raphael, heightened the licentious
revelry of a Borgia, or graced the courts of
Henri-quatre or François-premier. The best
names of the French noblesse and gentry might
have answered the roll-call of the Algerine galley,
whose bench levelled all distinctions, the captive
peasant chained by the side of his captive seigneur.
Even now, the frequent towers, adding romance
to the lovely Riviera, anxiously commanding the
promontories and protecting the gleaming bays,
attest the harass so long inflicted by the infidel,
and the vicinity of Africa's hostile shore.

§ 4. Elsewhere have we alluded to the

840—877
815—1013
The
Scandi-
navian
invasions.

European extent of Scandinavian piracy. It was, according to common expression, a chance, but in truth a wonderful ruling of Providence, that the pure Scandinavian and Jutish races had not prevented Cortes, Cabot and Columbus, colonizing and conquering broad America. Human sagacity cannot discern any adequate reason why the Northmen, whose energy established the once flourishing republic of Iceland, braved the eternal snows of Greenland, and explored the shores of the Pilgrim Fathers, should not in all respects have anticipated their successors of Visigothic, Roman, Gaulish, or "Anglo-Saxon" blood, and spread themselves over the forest-clad continent, then scarcely tenanted by the tribes who have since been exterminated by the poison-blast of civilization. What voice directed Leif Ericson and Thorfind to abandon the fertile Vinland? and who can explain wherefore that incipient domination was crushed, through which, had it been permitted, the whole course of the world's future history would have been changed?

Our discoursings in this work concerning the Scandinavian invasions are cursory and partial : we only contemplate them in Belgium, the Gauls and the borders. A general notion of the Danish inroads in these countries, so far as they are known —and very imperfectly known—from history, may be obtained by employing an easy process. Take the map, and colour with vermilion the provinces, districts and shores which the Northmen visited, as the record of each invasion. The colouring will have to be repeated more than ninety times successively before you arrive at the conclusion of the Carlovingian dynasty. Furthermore, mark by the usual symbol of war, two crossed swords, the localities where battles were fought by or against the pirates : where they were defeated or triumphant, or where they pillaged, burned or destroyed; and the valleys and banks of Elbe, Rhine and Moselle, Scheldt, Meuse, Somme and Seine, Loire, Garonne and Adour, the inland Allier, and all the coasts and coast-lands between estuary and estuary and the countries between the river-streams, will appear bristling as with chevaux-de-frise.

840—877

815—1013
Historical map of the Scandinavian, Saracen and Hungarian invasions.

The strongly-fenced Roman cities, the venerated Abbeys and their dependent bourgades, often more flourishing and extensive than the ancient seats of government, the opulent sea-ports and trading towns, were all equally exposed to the Danish attacks, stunned by the Northmen's approach, subjugated by their fury. Aix-la-chapelle, Nimeguen and Treves, Cologne, Bonn, Coblentz, Worms, Hamburgh, Metz, Toul and Verdun, Tolbiac, Tournay, Terouenne and Tongres, Doerstadt and Quantowick, Arras, Amiens, Cambray, Ghent, Louvaine, Maestricht, Stavelo and Deventer, Fleury, Hasbey and Corbey, Nuys and Malmedi, Marmoutier and Noirmoutier, Pruhm,

840—877
815—1013
Condé, Sithiu and Centulla, Saint-Denis, Saint-Omer, Saint-Riquier and Saint-Quentin, Saint-Florent, Luçon, Lillebonne, Fontenelle, Jumièges, Evreux, Baieux, Rouen, Paris and Orleans, Auxerre and Troyes, Angers, Nantes and Rennes, Amboise, Blois, Beauvais and Tours, Noyon, Lisledieu and Grand-lieu, Chartres, Méaux, Melun, Autun, Clermont, Bourges, Valence, Périgueux, Poitiers, Angoulême, Bourdeaux, Xaintes, Toulouse, Melle, Limoges, Auches, Tarbes, Dax, Leictoure;—an enumeration collected almost at haphazard, exhibits a very incomplete indication of the places which the Northmen occupied, plundered or ruined, in some instances so thoroughly that even episcopal sees never recovered their prosperity.—Such a specific catalogue of ravages, could it be rendered perfect, would only supply scanty data for calculating the heaviness of the sufferings which the Empire sustained. Each City, Town or Abbey, must be taken as synonymous with a Pagus, a Province, a Diocese; and all the countries, not merely on the line of march, but all around, were involved in the desolation. Then if you think fit, denote the Saracen and Hungarian invasions by darker-ensanguined tints, by crossed assagays, scimitars or arrows, and apply the same reasoning to them, and you will approximate to a notion of the misery, and understand how rare and dispersed were the favoured regions spared from the actual presence of the enemy.

§ 5. But the whole annals of the Northmen in the Gauls are rendered irremediably defective through the insufficiency of coeval historical testimony. The Chroniclers naturally gave prominence to the events concerning them most, or which occurred in their vicinity: the facts relating to remote localities were not mentioned or not known; and the evidences of one inroad were often destroyed by a subsequent devastation. We have scarcely any chronicles originating in the places enumerated in the preceding summary, except such as started again when the Northern incursions slackened or ceased. We are tantalized by a single fragment of the chronicle of Fontenelle, which without doubt would have removed many annoying difficulties. The chronicles of Jumièges are entirely lost. Of Nantes, there are only confused fragments, probably rewritten from recollection. The chronicles of all the monasteries in the diocese of Paris have perished: nothing from Saint Germain-des-près, or Saint-Germain-l'Auxerrois, or Sainte-Généviève—nothing Carlovingian from Saint-Denis

Anterior to Abbot Suger we do not possess any chronicle, properly so called, appertaining to that renowned Monastery. The sumptuous black-letter folios, the pride of Verard's press, so prized by the bibliomaniac, and not destitute of importance to the collector as curious specimens of typography, have no intrinsic connexion what-

[marginal notes]
840—877
815—1013
Historical evidence of the Danish invasions.

Destruction of Chronicles.

810—877
815—1013

ever with the Abbey, excepting that the sources employed by the compiler may have been consulted in the library. They profess to be the "Chroniques de France *selon* qu'elles sont conservées à Saint-Denis."—We have really no means of ascertaining their composer—may be the author was a monk, may be not : a plausible conjecture has been hazarded, that a household minstrel of Alphonso Count of Poitiers began to indite the work in the reign of Saint-Louis. At all events this vernacular Romane text does not contain a single line from any chronicle excepting those still extant in the original Latin. As an historical monument the Chronicle is valueless, which negative quality may, *primâ facie,* be predicated respecting any similar black-letter book : two to one, rubbish—either superseded by more correct or complete editions, or not multiplied by subsequent editors, because not worth multiplying.

In the conflagrations of Saint-Riquier, Centulla of the hundred towers, that most venerated and most important sanctuary, all ancient records perished; and the circumstances connected with Nithardus singularly exemplify the absence of accurate information regarding the Danish invasions. Nithardus, a cultivator of literature, a real historian, a statesman, a soldier high in rank, Count of Ponthieu or the Maritime shore, conversant with public affairs, would have been the man to furnish us with full details of the events

of his times; but, with the fragment of his own 840—877
history, Nithardus completely disappears. We
know nothing beyond the asterisks with which 815—1013
the published fragment ends. About a hundred
and fifty years after the reign of Charles-le-
Chauve, the Church having been rebuilt, search
was made amongst the tombs by Gervinus the
Abbot and Hariulphus a fellow-monk, the writer
who recommenced the annals of his community.
Lying by the side of Angelbertus his father, they
discovered the rudely-embalmed corpse of Count
Nithard. The skull, fractured by the Danish
battle-axe, told the story of his last exploit:
he had unquestionably fallen in the defence of
Ponthieu. But even when Hariulphus wrote,
they had not the slightest knowledge of the time
or circumstances of Nithard's death; nor have
we any account, till a later period, of the invasions which the province sustained.

The historical materials relating to the Gauls
south of the Loire are exceedingly scanty: concerning Orleans, Blois, Tours, Perigord, Bordeaux, Toulouse, nothing is left but a few jejune
annals. The vast archiepiscopal province of
Bourges, comprising the Dioceses of Clermont,
Limoges, Tulle, le Puys and Sainte-Flour, including, according to more modern geography,
the Limousin, Périgord, Auvergne, Vellay, Vivarais, indeed the whole of central France and the
Dauphinois and a great deal of the Rhone coun-

840—877 try, is nearly a blank. Excepting when we
815—1013 enjoy the lively company of Sidonius Apollinaris,
the last individual representing the gentleman-
bishop of the Roman age, and gain a glimpse
of pious Avitus, we are in almost unvaried
solitude.

Our texts for Carlovingian history are mainly
derived from the northern dioceses of France and
Germany, principally from the ecclesiastical province of Rheims. So far as the records extend,
they are exceedingly valuable and authentic,
many of them having been compiled by persons
high in authority and enjoying the confidence
of the sovereigns, but whose notices of events
happening in distant places are only collateral
and casual. Where the chronicles fail, our materials must be drawn from the legends of Saints,
accounts of the translation of relics and the like;
veracious as far as the intentions of the writers
were concerned, but usually put together or
composed long subsequently to the sufferings,
and rendered inaccurate by the excitements of
maundering transmission, re-echoing the sounds
of confusion and terror. Generally speaking, the
Gauls south of the Loire were much severed both
by interest and feelings from the northern provinces: their history can only be scantily gathered
from the Chroniclers belonging to the Langue-
d'oil, or the Belgic or Tudesque countries. So
deficient are these memorials, that the only know-

ledge we possess concerning the destruction of 840—877
the six episcopal sees of Gascony, arises from an
incidental allusion in a charter.   815—1013

§ 6.   If we compare the preceding summary General
of the Danish invasions with the proposed co- the naval
loured and symbolized map, it will be observed tary opera-
that they constitute three principal schemes of the North-
naval and military operations, respectively go- Gauls, and
verned and guided by the great rivers and the Germany.
intervening sea-shores.   In or adjoining the valleys of the rivers, these schemes may sometimes
blend into each other, but on the whole they are
well defined.

The first scheme of operations includes the The North
territories between Rhine and Scheldt, and ditions.
Scheldt and Elbe: the furthest southern point
reached by the Northmen in this direction
was somewhere between the Rhine and the
Neckar.   Eastward, the Scandinavians scattered
as far as Russia; but we must not follow them
there.

The second scheme of operations affected the The Seine
countries between Seine and Loire, and again expedi-
from the Seine eastward towards the Somme
and Oise.   These operations were connected with
those of the Rhine Northmen.

The third scheme of operations was prose- The Loire
cuted in the countries between Loire and Garonne ronne ex-
and Garonne and Adour, frequently flashing towards Spain, and expanding inland as far as the

840—877 Allier and central France, nay, to the very centre, to Bourges.

815—1013 When the Spaniards were regaining their own country from the Ishmaelites, each Hidalgo appropriated to himself in prospect his *Conquista*, the territory he intended to settle and win; and no other Hidalgo was to interfere therewith. Somewhat of the same understanding subsisted amongst the Anglo-Norman subjugators of the Cymri, the March-lords of Wales. Strongbow and his followers did the like in persecuted· Ireland. The Danes conducted their piracies according to a similar system, though less perfectly regulated. Instances of discord however occur occasionally amongst the marauders: they brought with them a proportion of their internal dissensions. Dane was occasionally bribed to fight against Dane, for they were exceedingly fond of money; but on the whole these quarrels and betrayals did not affect the habitual unity of the great enterprize.

Danish Fiefs or benefices in Lotharingia. Lotharingia suffered dreadfully during the Rhine and Scheldt invasions. They were peculiarly fierce, and the facts afford much historical instruction. Anterior to Rollo, the cessions made in Lotharingia furnish memorable examples of benefices or feuds, granted to the Danish chieftains for the purpose of purchasing a suspension of hostilities, or employing them as defenders of the Marches against their own countrymen.

The Loire expeditions produced very impor- tant consequences; but they are obscurely nar- rated. The Danish conquests are rather to be collected from inferences and results than from direct and substantial narratives.

840—877
815—1013

The Northmen established themselves not only in the neighbourhood of the river, but inland. The Breton Marches harboured and encouraged them as enemies or as friends. Their settlements in these countries were probably scarcely less ex- tensive than those effected by Rollo in Normandy. Hastings held the County of Chartres. Blois, won by Gerlo the Dane, kinsman of Rollo, became the seat of a Danish dynasty, but the Northmen of the Loire had no Dudon de Saint-Quentin; and the absence of any national historian has con- cealed the progress of their fortunes.

The North-men ot the Loire.

The Seine expeditions concern us most nearly : it is therefore to this series of inroads that we principally apply ourselves, adverting neverthe- less to the others so far as may be needful for the general elucidation of our story, and connect- ing the Norman narrative with the principal events of Carlovingian France and Capetian France—Normandy rising, as the Carlovingian dynasty declined, and fully flourishing when the Capets won the crown.

§ 7. During Louis-le-débonnaire's calamitous reign, the Danish attacks had been formidable, and yet in a measure experimental. The Northmen,

Sequence of Danish attacks after the battle of Fontenay.

840—877
815—1013 acutely and warily observing the opportunities of success, were biding their time.   They united the spirit and adaptability of the British sailor with the Buccaneer's ferocity. But these pirates shaded also into traders. In either capacity they received copious intelligence concerning the events of the empire : all the Carlovingian treacheries, dissensions and cruelties were gain for the Danish cause.   Every crime or folly of the Carlovingian Sovereigns enured to the benefit of the Northmen : every Frank or German who fell in the civil wars was an enemy removed.

Whilst the sons of Louis-le-débonnaire were pursuing their warfare, the inherent instinct of the Northmen taught them that the marching troops would soon lie dead as carrion.—"Hurrah!" —cried the Danes at Rouen, when King Louis and King Charles were rejoicing at the defeat of Emperor Lothair's army. Well therefore were they prepared for a battle of Fontenay ; and the news of the direful slaughter rebounded throughout the North and all the Baltic and North Sea shores. The attacks upon " Romerige," as they called the Empire, hitherto tentative, were now continued systematically. From the Belt to the Dardanelles the Danes familiarized themselves with the navigation : their fleets covered the seas, their sturdy and active warriors overspread the land. Not unfrequently, historical evidence combining with popular tradition enables us to recognize the

chieftains who appear as the heroes of these long- 840—877
protracted conflicts : whilst they dart and flicker
athwart the waves, we may follow their track 815—1013
from their own old countries Scandinavia and the
North, or their newer settlements in the British
islands.

Regner-Lodbrok, and Biorn-Ironside, Lod- Danish invaders of
brok's son, become conspicuous, their inroads in the Gauls identified
France being only digressions from their achieve- by their acts on the
ments beyond the channel. It was not the British islands, &c.
armour of Biorn which gave him the name of
Ironside: no shield hung on Biorn's arm, no helmet covered his brow, no hauberk protected his
breast.—Such defences were rendered needless
by his Sorceress-mother, whose magical liniments
had hardened the tender body of her babe.
Sigurd son of King Ingiald the Ost-man, king of
Waterford, and Sydroc the younger, and another
Sydroc, King Ivar's son, conqueror of Dublin,
appear in succession,—moreover, Welland, the
father of Vidric the sturdy *Kœmpe*, who slew the
Langbeen Rise, that " longshanked giant," whose
proper name has merged in this descriptive portraiture. And Hastings, who stalks forward as
the persecutor of the Gauls, he, may be, who set
fire to thatch-roofed Cirencester by letting loose
a flight of sparrows with lighted coals tied beneath their wings.

§ 8. During eleven years after the pillage of 842—844
Rouen, Osker continued afloat, incessantly occu- Great Danish expeditions
pied in devastation. An *Osker-Saga* is wanting

840—877

842—844
on the
coasts of
the Chan-
nel, Loire,
&c.
to detail the particulars of his enterprizes; but he was probably the leader who conducted a bold and successful expedition on the northern coasts, much about the time that Lothair, Louis, and Charles were engaged in the battles and negotiations which produced the treaty of Verdun. The merchant-guilds of Exeter and London mourned with fellow-feeling the pillage of opulent Quantowick, the chief mint of the Gauls, to which was necessarily annexed the chief table or bank of exchange. The calamity is specially recorded in our Saxon chronicle: never but once afterwards is Quantowick mentioned in history. Natural causes, however, co-operated with the calamities of war in extinguishing this once-celebrated commercial city; the haven is completely concealed by the encreasing sands. Topographers can only guess that Quantowick was situated somewhere near Etaples in Picardy.

Loire and the Garonne were filled with the black-sailed squadrons: Nantes burned and plundered, the inhabitants scattered like silly sheep: noble Toulouse, equally cowardly, Counts and Senators fleeing from their Capitol: Treves and Cologne as yet unstruck, but trembling. Encouraged by success, the Northmen varied the indulgences of rapine. The Danes attacked Lusitania and Spain, spoiling the Saracens, their competitors in the work of affliction.

The ravages which the Northmen were committing in England alarmed the Carlovingians, without impressing them. Belief, unaccompanied by conviction, is an ever-enduring moral pheno-menon. The very presence of the invaders within the Empire scarcely enabled Sovereigns or people to realize their danger. Amidst family quarrels and national dissensions and the seductions of insatiate ambition, the trouble given by the Northmen appeared a small matter, so intent were the brothers on their rivalry.

840—877
⌣
842—844

Some precautions however were adopted. Eric the Red, the son of Godfrey, the ancient rival and enemy of Harold, was now acknow-ledged as the *Over-King* or supreme monarch of Denmark, though probably without much power of enforcing obedience. However, he enjoyed the honour; and the Carlovingian monarchs treated the "Over-King" as a responsible sove-reign. They threatened King Eric with reprisals —small account did he make of their warnings. From time to time various means of defence were concerted. Charles-le-Chauve acted firmly, but the ground he stood upon was rotten. The Sovereigns tormented each other, the people be-trayed the Sovereigns, and the Empire lingered in spasmodic misery.

§ 9. France was heavily afflicted: a fearfully cold year was followed by another still colder and more inclement. The North wind blew inces-santly all through the Winter, all through the pale and leafless Spring. The roots of the vines

844—845.
The cold
years—
Regner
Lodbrok
(845) en-
ters the
Seine.

840—877

844—845

were perished by the frost—the wolves starved out of their forests, even in Aquitaine. The cunning animals, wer-wolves, *loups-garoux*, invaded the villages and towns, foraging for human flesh, marshalling themselves in troops, occupying the roads, conducting their operations with military skill, emulating man in the tactics of destruction.

Meanwhile the Danish hosts were in bright activity. Regner Lodbrok and his fellows fitted out their fleet, ten times twelve dragons of the sea. Early in the bleak Spring they sailed, and the stout-built vessels ploughed cheerily through the crashing ice on the heaving Seine. Regner Lodbrok defied the piercing blast in his shaggy garments—Osker's example had instructed his countrymen where they could find sport, where the game was to be sought; and Regner prepared to strike a heavy blow.

Amidst all misfortunes France retained an irrepressible elasticity. The monks, huddling themselves together in their desolated habitations, had resettled at Fontenelle and Jumièges, and the country-folks diligently tilled the fields. But the Danes spared Fontenelle and Jumièges for the nonce, that monks and peasants might be better worth plundering another time. Rouen dared not offer any opposition. The Northmen quietly occupied the City: we apprehend that some knots or bands of the Northmen began even now to domicile themselves there, it being scarcely

Rouen occupied again by the Danes.

possible to account for the condition of Normandy under Rollo otherwise than by the supposition, that the country had long previously received a considerable Danish population. 840—877 842—845

§ 10. Paris, the point to which the North- Carlovin-gian Paris. men were advancing by land and water, was the key of France, properly so called. Paris taken, the Seine would become a Danish river: Paris defended, the Danes might be restrained, perhaps expelled. The Capetian "Duchy of France," not yet created by any act of State, was beginning to be formed through the encreasing influence of the future Capital.

Antient cities are in the nature of palimpsests,—each generation erasing the writing of the preceding generation, and superimposing layers of other writings and newer-formed characters, line upon line; each successively superinduced line teaching a more modern lesson, telling a more recent tale.

In the page presented by the Paris of the nineteenth century, a paragraph occasionally remains, exhibiting the fine Valois-Orleans "lettres gothiques," imparting dignity to the tomes of chivalry: here and there, deeper, you may still discern scattered specimens of the quaintly-elegant calligraphy which delighted Saint-Louis: below these, some scanty vestiges of the stately Carlovingian uncials: and lastly, piercing through all the strata, a few firm majuscules inscribed by

840—877
842—845 Roman power, a syllable or two and no more ;— but the whole text restamped by the neat, monotonous, well-cut fount, cast in the matrices of civilization.   It is very difficult therefore to read the enchorial characters of Paris as the city existed in the reign of Charles-le-Chauve, though in some degree we are able to retrace their tenor.

Alterations in the bed and level of the Seine   The Seine, as we have before remarked, was very much wider than at the present day.   The whole level of the city and of all the adjoining fauxbourgs has been considerably raised, and the bed of the river has evidently sustained much elevation also.   The antient fluviatile spread of surface is distinctly shewn by the inundations which occurred early in the course of the last century, about a hundred and thirty years ago, when the Champs-Elysées were deeply inundated: the water came up also to the very front of the Hôtel-des-Invalides and surrounded the Palais-Bourbon.

Two bridges afforded access to the city-island. On the north, the Pont-du-change ; the Petit-pont on the south.   The Grand-Châtelet includes within the thickness of the walls a Carlovingian, or perhaps a Roman fortress, the station of the Parisian Navicularii under the Roman Empire. It is doubtful whether, properly speaking, there was more than one city-gate, the Petit-Châtelet being probably in the nature of an outwork or postern.   Within the island there was only one church of importance, namely, Saint-Etienne, afterwards Notre-Dame.

On either bank of the ample Seine the cul- 840—877
tivated and populous country was dotted with
flourishing bourgades and splendid structures: 842—845
the present remains of the Palais-des-Thermes
attest the antient strength of the edifice, then
towering in Babylonian altitude. This architectural magnificence was peculiarly manifested by
a very lofty vaulted hall, not demolished till the
reign of Louis-quinze; and in the other surviving portions the steady Roman arches may yet
be seen, contrasting with the florid pinnacles and
canopies and flamboyant tracery of the Hotel-de-
Clugny. The terre-plain over the hall was formed
into a terraced garden.

Saint-Germain-l'Auxerrois, Saint-Germain-des- Architec-
tural cha-
près, Sainte-Généviève, and Saint-Victor, all pos- racter of
the Great
sessed a castellated aspect. We have evidence Monaste-
ries of Paris.
of the robustness of these ancient monasteries in
the prison of the Abbaye, the only remaining
fragment of conventual Saint-Germain-des-près,
and which obtained such fatal celebrity during
the Revolution. The great tower of the church
is attributed to Childebert: the porch, now mutilated, was a monument to the honour of the
Merovingian dynasty. Against the slender pillars
were the effigies of the kings and queens,—Clovis,
venerable, gaunt and grave, according to the
sculptor's realization,—holy Clotilda, her long-
flowing tresses woven and braided with bands
of orfray.

F F 2

840—877
842—845

The interior of the building is Carlovingian : the ample Corinthianized capitals are unaltered, and if instead of the more recent vaulting we substitute the open roof and tyebeams of a Roman Basilica, and imagine the shrines richly decorated with the jaspers and precious marbles which have long since disappeared, we may obtain a tolerably correct idea of Saint-Germain-des-près when the vessels of Regner Lodbrok sailed up the Seine. Saint-Victor was splendidly adorned, but not a trace or recollection of the structure remains. The walls of Sainte-Géneviève shone with gilded mosaics patterned from Rome or Byzantium.

Charles-le-Chauve stations himself at Saint-Denis.

Saint-Denis had already become the nucleus of an important bourgade : the monks had taken the relics out of their depositories, and were preparing to escape. They were however well protected : Charles-le-Chauve had stationed himself with his troops before the Abbey. Expecting the approach of the Northmen, he had done his utmost to concentrate his forces Opposite to his position an island divided the Seine. Ilis troops were neither numerous nor hearty, yet the Danes dared not attack him. They made their way along the river by the off channel, spread themselves also over the adjoining country, ravaging like furies. A large detachment landed at Charlevanne, near Saint-Germain-en-laye, on the spot where Louis-quatorze afterwards built the machine of Marli.

Eleven corpses swinging from gibbets planted 840—877
on an eyot, announced to the French the punishment by which any resistance would be 845
visited ; and, in all the villages about Paris, the
same ghastly spectacle, rigid carcasses suspended
to the bare and naked boughs, repeated the warning. The river also gave the like stern monition,
the dead-men drifting in the water or stranded
on the shores.

Fierce as the Northmen generally were, they
exceeded their usual ferocity, whether instigated
by the inhumanity of Regner Lodbrok and Ironside, or whether the cruelties were aggravated by
the Vikingar, not in rage but upon cold-blooded
calculation, for the purpose of exciting greater
terror. Any how, the result was the same. With
such panic were the Franks stricken, that they
gave themselves up for lost. Paris island, Paris
river, Paris bridges, Paris towers were singularly
defensible :—the Palais-des-Thermes, the monasteries were as so many castles. Had the inhabitants, for their own sakes, co-operated with
Charles-le-Chauve, the retreat of the Danes
would have been entirely cut off; but they were
palsied in mind and body, neither thought of
resistance nor attempted resistance, and abandoned themselves to despair. 28 March, 845.

§ 11. On Easter Eve the Danes entered Paris. Regner Lodbrok and the Danes en- ter Paris
Joyless did the austere season render the vernal
festival of the Resurrection throughout the Gauls.

840—877 *Pâques-fleurie*—but spring denied her early gar-

845 lands; hepatica, primrose, violet and snowdrop were nipped in their clemmed buds, and the altars unadorned by flowers. At Paris they need them not: no tapers are lighted, no mass is read, no anthems sung.—Bishop Erchenrad setting the example, the priests and clerks deserted their churches: the monks fled, bearing with them their shrines: soldiers, citizens and sailors, abandoned their fortresses, dwellings and vessels: the great gate was left open, Paris emptied of her inhabitants, the city a solitude. The Danes hied at once to the untenanted monasteries: all valuable objects had been removed or concealed, but the Northmen employed themselves after their fashion. In the church of Saint-Germain-des-

Damage done to Saint-Germain-des-près prés they swarmed up the pillars and galleries, and pulled the roof to pieces: the larchen beams being sought as excellent ship-timber. In the city, generally, they did not commit much devastation. They lodged themselves in the empty houses, and plundered all the moveables. Silver and gold were hidden, but baser metals were worth carrying away, and the iron-work of Paris gate added to the freight of the Danish barks and barges: without doubt, also, the Danes found ample stores of provision in the city and in the monasteries.

The Danes retire from Paris The Franks did not make any attempt to attack or dislodge the enemy, but a more efficient power compelled the Danes to retire from the city: disease raged among them, dysentery—a complaint frequently noticed, probably occasioned by their inordinate potations of the country-wine. Their own well-brewed strong ale was far healthier.

Regner Lodbrok was equally astute and bold, his craft is conspicuous in his legendary story. Had Charles-le-Chauve advanced from Saint-Denis and attacked the Danes, few if any could have escaped. Regner therefore made proposals to the King, promising to evacuate Paris upon receiving a competent subsidy. Charles himself was in great difficulty. His efforts for the defence of his country were disappointed. Troops he had assembled, but the cowards would neither move nor act: the king was powerless. In this strait he therefore offered an enormous subsidy, seven Danegeld paid by thousand pounds of silver:—a sum calculated by Charles-le-Chauve the Academicians, whose researches guide us in elucidating this perplexed portion of French history, at five hundred and twenty thousand livres. This was the first Danegeld paid by France, an unhappy precedent, and yet unavoidable: the pusillanimity of his subjects compelled Charles to adopt this disgraceful compromise. The money was levied upon the inhabitants of Paris and the adjoining provinces,—right that they should bear the burthen brought upon themselves by their self-desertion.

Regner returned joyfully to Denmark: he

840—877 repaired to Eric the Red, boasting of his exploits
and their profit—how he and his Danes had ren-
845—849 dered the Rœmerige tributary, the money he had
received, the booty he had carried away. His bravery of speech affronted the Over-king, who
openly told the grim Sea-rover he did not believe
him. Regner came again before his scoffing sovereign, followed by gangs of his crew, some carrying the big iron bar of the Paris gate, the others
laden with a carved larchen beam, plucked from
the roof of Saint-Germain-des-près. These trophies, laid before King Eric's throne, were the
silent but irrecusable testimonies of Regner's victory.

§ 12 The display of prize and plunder excited Eric the Red to try his fortune : the reports
which Regner brought of the abject cowardice
manifested by the Carlovingian subjects, rendered the temptation the stronger. A remunerative
venture upon the easiest terms was thus offered
to the Northmen, an inducement more attractive
than glory. Six hundred vessels composed Eric's
fleet · none so well equipped had hitherto invaded
Germany or the Gauls, and they entered the
promising Elbe.

On the banks of that river a new city had
arisen under the auspices of Charlemagne,—the
845. future flourishing emporium of the North, wisely
Hamburgh
plundered planned for the purpose of connecting Scandinavia
by King
Eric. and Germany, and at the same time assisting in

the defence of the Empire. Pagan Wends and Obotrites, Saxons still yearning for their pristine independence and the Baltic pirates, were all to be held in check by Hamburgh. The City, an archiepiscopal See, the Patriarchate of Scandinavia, Cathedral, Castle, Church and Monastery, shone fresh and strong from the builder's hands. Suddenly was Hamburgh surrounded by the yelling Northmen : the stout Carlovingian warriors, real Germans of the Germans, fled away—no great shame therefore that Archbishop Anscharius should scurry for his life, stripped of his garments, " nudus," says Adam of Bremen—a figure of speech, but as near the truth as well may be. Anscharius fled to Bremen, where envious Bishop Luderic refused to receive his brother. Anscharius ultimately returned to Hamburgh, and was restored, not merely to his dignity, but to peace and comfort with the Danes. He was a kind and good man, and laid the foundation of the Scandinavian mission by redeeming captive children and educating them in Christian doctrines. Eric, his persecutor, became his affectionate protector and friend, and may be said to have met his death in the battle of Flensburgh for the sake of Anscharius.

§ 13. Conflicts again in the Aquitanian rivers:—the Danes in great force, Osker their commander : Charles drove them off from Bourdeaux, but the discontented Aquitanians were plotting

840—877

845—849

846—849.
Danish
expeditions
in Aquitaine
and Spain.

840—877
846—850 and machinating to separate themselves from the Frankish Crown. Many supported Pepin, others looked towards Germany: the rich city was surrendered to the Danes. The French laid the treason to the charge of the Jews—hard upon the Jews to stigmatize them as the betrayers: hard upon Ganelone di Maganza to shew him up in romaunt and poesy as the very Coryphæus of felonry, when the whole Carlovingian Empire was infected with universal treachery.

The Northern fleets quitting the Loire, again visited the Spanish coasts. The gold of Spain, her warmth, her wines, attracted the invaders: indeed, they were only following the course of their brethren, if not their forefathers. The Visigoths were the last amongst the kindred nations who departed from the Euxine shores and the Eastern Asgard. Destiny guided them far from the regions which thenceforward constituted the chief domain of the Asi, yet there were poetical recollections in the North of these wanderings and peregrinations. Well might the Norwegian damsels sing in their ballads of heroism and love, how *Myklagard and the land of Spain, lie wide away o'er the lee :*

"Myklagard ok Spanialand
Thad liggur so langt af leidi."

Seville was plundered, and though the fleet of Abdelrahman ultimately chased the Danes from the coasts, their cruise was successful, and their booty safely transported to Scandinavia and the Baltic islands. Many a tumulus, many a mound under the cold sky, when opened by the groping antiquary or the honest boor, still presents the happy excavator with the golden denars which the Vikingar had hoarded at home.

840—877

850

Blazing hostility again in the North.—Frieze-land, close and nigh to the Jutland shores, was a favourite and successful field of enterprize. Roric, the nephew of Harold, occupied the country : Lothair endeavoured to expel the Dane, but he had not the power of prosecuting any effectual warfare. His untrustworthy forces were employed either in watching or opposing his own brothers. The Emperor therefore attempted the perilous compromise previously tried with Harold. Rustringia was granted to Count Roric, as a benefice ; and the Imperial Diet confirmed the donation. Roric,—a Count, a Markgrave,—performed homage, placed his hands between the hands of Lothair, and covenanted to protect the Empire against his unbeneficed countrymen and kinsmen.—The transaction was acutely planned : an instinctive antipathy subsists between those who have and those who have not, which, as the world goes, often withstands the sympathies of affinity or consanguinity. Lothair calculated that he might thus rely upon estranging Roric from the Danish people ; and another precedent was afforded for Rollo's future establishment in Normandy.

850.

Roric's expedition—Rustringia granted to him as a benefice.

840—877

850
850.
Godfrey
the son of
Harold
enters the
Seine.

§ 14. Circumstances continued to promote this system of infeudation. Concurrently with Roric's expedition, Godfrey the son of Harold king of Denmark, the Atheling who with his parents had been baptized at Mayence, sailed up the Seine, he and his crews levying contributions on the country, according to their wont. The Franks vituperated Godfrey as a faithless Pagan; but it was not fair to censure the Northmen for violences which the Franks were committing amongst themselves and upon themselves. Charles-le-Chauve was very vigilant, but his people were nerveless, and he invoked the assistance of his brother Lothair, bound to him by treaties, bound to him by feeling.

Having done so, Charles immediately felt that he had preferred an imprudent request. A brother introduced into Neustria might be far more dangerous than a Dane: therefore Charles desisted from urging Lothair, and determined to acquire Benefices granted to Godfrey Godfrey's alliance by a competent cession of territory. The Benefice was in the vicinity of the Seine, the grant not being made simply to Godfrey, but also to his followers:—*terram eis ad inhabitandum delegavit.* This obscure though important settlement afterwards merged in the Norman Duchy.—The repetitions and similarities of the Scandinavian names are no less confusing than those which occur in Carlovingian history. It is therefore necessary to remark that Godfrey, the son of King Harold, must not be confounded with Godfrey son of Harold, Jarl of Jutland, also a beneficiary of the empire, who married Gisella King Lothair's daughter.

§ 15. The foemen thus fixed and planted in the Gauls, others appear and re-appear with un-diminished ferocity. Jarl Osker, having pillaged Bourdeaux, established a military station near the city,—probably consisting of entrenchments or earth-works which could be protected by his vessels in the Garonne, and likewise command the country. Osker then sailed northwards, and returned to the well-known Seine. During two hundred and eighty-seven days did his vessels continue in the river, whether cruising or moored —an aquatic colony, the Danes dispersing themselves when they thought fit on the land. They ruined the ruins of Fontenelle, burnt Saint-Bavon at Ghent, burnt Beauvais, and desolated the whole intervening tract. The Franks, plucking up heart of grace, attacked a body of straggling Northmen at a village now called Ouarde, situate on the river Epte, a boundary of future Normandy : some few Danes were slain, the remainder re-treated into a wood : they did not concern themselves anxiously about points of honour. The average insignificance of the conflicts, and the evident exaggerations of Danish defeats and Frankish victories, emphatically testify the pre-ponderance which the Northmen had obtained.

840—877

850—855

850—851

Osker's re-turn to the Seine.

840—877 When the Franks actually fought the Danes, the
852
Chroniclers relate the rally as an event much out
of the common course—a wonder:—they remind
us, in more ways than one, of the despatches
in the Pekin gazette, relating the successes
gained over the barbarians.

851—855   § 16.   The pirate-empire was rapidly widen-
Concurrent
operations
of the
Danes in
the British
Islands and
in the
Gauls.
ing: the Danes spreading their warfare throughout the British Islands, unhappy Ireland experi-
encing ample measure of their fury: Armagh was
dreadfully devastated, and the most encouraging
successes obtained by them in England.   About
this time they established themselves in Kent, win-
tering in Thanet: their vessels swept the narrow
seas, the English Channel was becoming a Danish
channel.   This command of the English coast
gave them a fulcrum of greater power against
France and Belgium.   Friezeland and all the
adjoining parts were completely subdued, and their
attacks upon France became more pertinacious.

9 Oct 852.
Sidroc and
Godfrev
enter the
Seine.
Sidroc, the Irish-Dane, accompanied by a third
Godfrey, who must be distinguished from the two
previously mentioned, entered the Seine.   Acting
according to a more definite project of settling
themselves throughout Neustria than they had
hitherto entertained, they fortified themselves
in a position which afterwards acquired great cele-
The Danes
establish
themselves
at Jeu-
fosse
brity during the Danish and Norman wars—
Givoldi-fossa is the name given to the place by
the Chroniclers: the exact situation has been

much debated by the French historians; how- 851—854
ever, it appears to have been at or near a village
now called Jeu-fosse, just above the confluence 853—855
of the Epte and the Seine, not far from Vernon,
about half-way between Rouen and Paris. The
Chroniclers speak of *Giroldi-fossa* as an island,
whereas Jeu-fosse is situated upon the main land ;
but in all probability the channels which then
insulated the Danish entrenchments—they are
said to be yet discernible—have been filled up
by alluvion. From this stronghold the Danes
sent forth their destructive expeditions, ravaging
the country far and wide, doing much harm and
threatening to inflict more.

The imminent peril produced a transitory concord between Charles and his brother Lothair;
but Lothair could give no help even if he had
been true, for he was sickening and declining,
soon about to be laid in his sepulchre at Pruhm. (See II § 37, p 360)
The Franks refused to face the enemy : the Danes
therefore continued in this part of Neustria
throughout the winter, the spring and part of
the next summer; then, sailing out of the Seine 853—854.
they coasted round to the Loire, plundered Nantes, Danes having quitted
Angers and Blois again, burned Tours, and greatly the Seine,
attack and
plunder the
damaged the Church of Saint-Martin—the Glas- shores of
the Loire
tonbury of the Gauls. The Danes, determined
to gain the mastery of the Seine, were proceeding
consistently. Near the point where the Andelle
and the Eure fall into that river, was situated a

851—854

853—854

very favourite residence of Charlemagne, an antient palace called Pistres, about five leagues from
Rouen. The Carlovingian Sovereigns were accustomed to hold their great councils in this royal
mansion, and some noted ordinances were there
promulgated, quoted by historians as the Capitulars of Pistres, just as we speak of the Statutes

18 July, 855.

Sidroc re-enters the Seine

of Kenilworth or Merton. Pistres had hitherto
escaped; but the Irish-Dane Sidroc had marked
the place, and re-entering the Seine with a very
large fleet, he accomplished his intent, and temporarily occupied palace, river and territory.
Meanwhile Blois and Orleans were captured, and
further devastations perpetrated on the Loire,
yet Charles-le-Chauve, albeit grievously troubled
by his own flesh and blood, was not despairing:
he employed every exertion to oppose them; and
by an unexpected contingency this revival of
energy received encouragement from the Danes
themselves.

854—855

Civil war amongst the Danes: battle of Flensburgh and death of Eric the Red.

Eric the Red, the former persecutor of Anscharius, though not professedly a Christian, was
now most favourably inclined towards Christianity, won over by the goodness and kindness of the
Archbishop. Through this conduct, the monarch
provoked the inveterate hatred of the Northmen.
The malcontents at home communicated with
their countrymen abroad: the pirate-kings, dispersed as they were, agreed unanimously to forego
their free-bootery, and, returning home, avenge

their national institutions, their gods, and their laws —Guthrun, Eric's nephew, commanded the insurgents. The armies met nigh Flensburgh in Jutland: during three days, the battle raged so fiercely that all the chieftains—Eric, Guthrun and a cohort (so to speak) of Kings and Jarls— perished in the conflict. Equally tremendous was the slaughter in every rank and degree—Norsk- men, Danes, Swedes, Jutes, champions and churls. Loudly did the Franks exult in the real or imaginary results of Flensburgh fight, the pirates who had devastated them during twenty years self-punished by a Danish Fontenay, all the nobility of the Vikingar exterminated, the royal lineages, as they believed, extirpated : the report prevailed that only one little child was left, and the Franks expected they would be for ever relieved from their tormenting enemies.— But few were the months during which they were permitted to enjoy the pleasing delusion.

§ 17. Dreadful adversaries again arose, the Piratical Hosts visiting and revisiting the Gauls with invigorated desperation. Biorn-Ironside, the invulnerable Biorn, his fleet joining Sidroc, again entered the persecuted Seine. They landed im- mediately, and marched westward, slaying all who resisted. Charles-le-Chauve, however, was in the field, and having succeeded in keeping his dastardly troops together, the Danes sustained some loss and retreated to the river; but they

(margin notes:) 851—854 855

855 Sep. Biorn-Iron- side's expe- dition.

851—854 derided their enemies : the foray had paid
them.

855

Sidroc sailed for the Loire. In the meanwhile
another Danish squadron of Northmen had occupied Nantes. Herispoë, the Armorican king, purchased Sidroc's alliance, and retained him to
attack his countrymen. But the pirates were
men of business : the Danes occupying Nantes
opened a bargain with Sidroc and overbid He-
rispoe, and Sidroc sailed away. Biorn-Ironside

Biorn occu-
pies the
island of
Oscelles

continuing in the Seine, had examined the country and occupied the island of Oscelles, the *crux*
of French topography. Academicians and Archæologists, Dom Duplessis and Dom Mabillon, Dom
Felibien and Dom Sirmond, Père Daniel and Père
Dubois, Baluze and Valois, Le-Bœuf and Bonamy,
attest by their disputations the contending opinions respecting a position, considered as the
most important during the war. These diligent
and learned men, well conversant with the country, have not been able to decide on the locality,
some bringing the place within a league of Paris,
and others within three of Rouen.

This controversy must not be considered as
an idle display of antiquarian pertinacity, for it
shews, more clearly than any mere argument
could do, the extent of the variations which the
Seine's course and channels have sustained, casting the greatest obscurity upon a question of
home topography in a well-known region, and

where difficulties would appear to be most easily 851—854 susceptible of solution.—All things considered, however, we are inclined to place Oscelles in the 855 vicinity of Pont-de-l'Arche, just below the confluence of Seine and Eure. Here Biorn raised an entrenchment or camp, which became the Danish head-quarters: here they established themselves whenever they chose. Oscelles gave them the complete command of the river; hence they sent forth their detachments by land or by water, helping themselves to what they needed, and keeping Paris in constant anxiety.

§ 18. It is evident that the Danes who had *The Northern invasions facilitated by the domestic disunion of the Royal family.* thus obtained the virtual mastery of France were not numerous. In England, not only the ancient Danelaghe, but many other districts retain and retained the records of their preponderance in the names of places and the aspect of the people. Our institutions also recall their memory; but in France, even in the countries where they settled and naturalized themselves, nigh the Loire where they colonized, in Normandy where they ruled, they were completely absorbed amongst the Romanized population. Like a stage-procession winding in and out, disappearing and returning, their numbers were magnified by their activity. If it so happened that they were in danger of being hit, they evaded the blow: when their stores were exhausted, they departed till the next harvest, or sought a harvest elsewhere. They consi-

dered themselves as Landlords to whom a periodical rent ought to be rendered :—when the rent
was due they came and distrained.

Charles
troubled by
his chil-
dren.

Charles, during the whole of his reign, was
perplexed and entangled by difficulties—a cloud
of enemies surrounded him, the Northmen perhaps
the least inveterate: his own people, his own kinsmen, his own children, were vigilant, constant
and intimate foes. Visitations fell heavily upon
Charles, and, as all men do, he often invited
the scourge. Trials and punishments, afflictions
sent and chastisements deserved, the tribulations
constituting the mysterious discipline of human
existence, are perhaps more instructive in the
cases of exalted personages than in private life,
because they are less invidiously quotable and
more clearly shewn, and history therefore should
disclose them. Amongst his numerous children
only one could have given him comfort—lame
Lothair, who died young. All the others were
troubles, or objects of care and sorrow.

The King's own conduct contributed to poison
the minds of his household. His marriage with
his noble concubine Richilda, Count Boso's
beautiful sister, the fifth day after Ermentruda's
death, raises a strong presumption that his criminal passion enhanced the misfortunes which he
sustained. Louis, his eldest son, Louis-le-Bégue,
became discontented, a fomenter of mischief,
amounting to rebellion and treason. Charles

was not blameless in his conduct towards this 851—854
son : the endeavours which he made for the pur- 843—857
pose of compelling Louis to discard the betrothed,
if not the consort, whom he loved, in order that
he might contract a state-marriage, encreased
the disunion.

Louis-le-Bégue was urgent for an appanage— Jealousies between Charles-le-Chauve and Louis-le-Bégue.
abbeys, counties, dukedoms, or a kingdom. Fa-
mily precedents warranted such demands, but
Charles-le-Chauve was cautious, distrustful, loath
to bestow any donation which might encrease his
son's influence and power. Very significant of the
schism between the father and the son is the
list of forests in which Charles wholly prohibits
his son from sporting : a long list of preserves,
including Compiègne. As to the other forests,
Louis only received a very qualified licence : he
may chase a deer whilst passing through, let slip
a hound or spear a wild boar, but nothing else.—
This Capitular is an amusing and memorable
example of the hunter's jealousy. To the young
prince, such a prohibition must have been almost
as annoying as the refusal of a kingdom.

§ 19. Aquitanian affairs are singularly com- 843—857
plicated with the Northern invasions. The de- The affairs of Aquitaine.
ficiency of local chronicles concerning central
France and the other countries south of the Loire,
and indeed the general absence of information
respecting this region—half France—precludes us
from forming any accurate idea of the outrage-

854—855 ous revolutions which the Aquitanian kingdom
sustained.   Amongst the acts of injustice committed by Louis-le-débonnaire, perhaps the least
excusable was his conduct towards his grandson
Pepin. He robbed the child solely for the purpose
of aggrandizing his favourite Charles; and upon
Charles he bestowed an inheritance of confusion.
Putting the morality of the act out of the question, the exclusion of the younger Pepin was
a grave political error. The Vasques or Gascons,
a distinct race, fiery, fickle, haughty, jealous of
their privileges, and as proud of their privileges,
franchises and nationality as their Iberian brethren,
could not be slighted with impunity: they disliked
and dreaded the union of the French and Aquitanian Crowns. All Pepin's uncles were adverse,
all combined against him, all betrayed him in
their turns; but he defied them all.   The Aquitanians refused to acknowledge his dethronement:
during many years they supported him heartily.
He surprized the troops of Charles near Angoulême, put them to flight, and completely defeated
them.

844.
Pepin de-
feats the
forces of
Charles-le-
Chauve in
the battle of
Angou-
lême.

In this battle, Abbot Hugh, the son of Charlemagne, was killed. Charles-le-Chauve was compelled to accept of a compromise: he knew the
full extent of his danger. Nominoe and his
Bretons, probably in concert with Pepin, had
passed beyond their confines and invaded Maine,
which Louis-le-Bégue desired as an appanage.

Charles must have been equally apprehensive that if the hostility of the Aquitanians continued unmitigated, their discontent would interfere with the defence of the country—nay, possibly induce them to aid the enemy.

854—855

844

This last anticipation was realized. The Danes menaced, and menacing made their assault. They entered the Dordogne, Charles repelled them; but they were not deterred, and their defeat in the river was followed by the most profitable acquisition of Bourdeaux. He therefore compromised with his adversary, consenting that Pepin should resume the government of Aquitaine, excepting Saintonge, the Angoumois, and Poitou : the two first-mentioned Counties, Charles reserved for himself, the last he granted to Rainulph or Ramnulf, son of Gerard Count of Auvergne. Concurrently with this restoration, the three brothers held a congress, enjoining Pepin to obey King Charles, as a nephew ought to obey an uncle : a very ambiguous precept, involving that pregnant principle of discord,—the confusion of family subordination and state-authority which had proved the bane of the Empire ; and, in their hollow recognition, they all avoided giving the royal title to the Aquitanian king.

845

Charles cedes a portion of Aquitaine to Pepin.

What was the "obedience" which Pepin was bound to render? was he undutiful, or his uncle harsh and exacting?—we know not ;—but Pepin concerted plans for making himself entirely inde-

848

Pepin preparing to render himself independent, treats with the Saracens and Northmen.

854—855
848

pendent; and Charles re-entered Aquitaine with the declared intention of subduing the rebel. Pepin prepared actively for defence. There were three inveterate foes of the Franks who would co-operate with him—the Saracen, the Northman, and the Breton. The Aquitanians were not unfriendly towards the Moslems. William of Toulouse, son of the notorious Bernard Count of Septimania by his wife, the accomplished and affectionate Doduana, entered willingly into the plot. Abdelrahman was invited from Cordova. The Saracens occupied the Spanish marches; and the Northmen were courted. Hence the invasion before mentioned, when they captured Toulouse.

Charles-le-Chauve's expedition began favourably: a faction amongst the unstable Aquitanians had already discarded their chosen Pepin and joined Charles. Pepin was ousted, and Charles

Charles-le-
Chauve
marches
against
Pepin, and
is crowned
King of
Aquitaine.

solemnly crowned as king of the country. Pepin, however, made a stubborn resistance. Sancho Sanchion, Count or Duke of the Gascons, supported Pepin: a fierce war continued in the southern parts of Aquitaine, which exposed the rest of the Gauls the more to the Danish ravages; —the Franks seeming totally insensible to their own folly.

852
Pepin be-
trayed by
Sancho
Sanchion,
and im-
prisoned
in Saint-
Médard.

About this time Bourdeaux was taken by Osker. Charles, the younger brother of Pepin, emerged from his obscurity, and fought against the persecuting uncle. He was captured by treach-

ery, delivered to Charles-le-Chauve, and compelled 854—855
to take Orders: it is he who afterwards became 853—856
the good Archbishop at Mayence. Treacheries
were involved in treacheries. Sancho Sanchion,
who encouraged Pepin and acted as his most
earnest friend, concluded a base bargain with
Charles-le-Chauve, surprized Pepin at a feast—an
aggravation of perfidy—and delivered him into
the hands of his uncle. Pepin was sent to Saint-
Médard. Here he was treated equally as an
unwilling novice and as a prisoner: an oath of
fealty to Charles-le-Chauve was also extorted
from him,—an absurd aggravation of harshness,
and laying further snares for his conscience.
Obligations accepted under duresse, oaths imposed by duresse, discredited all the principles
of religion and honour.

§ 20. Charles-le-Chauve now ruled in Aqui- Further revolutions in
Aquitaine,
Louis-le-
Germanique solicit-
ed to aid—
he sends
Louis the
Saxon
taine, or seemed to do so, for the Aquitanians
withdrew their obedience, became extremely discontented, and sought to rid themselves of his
authority. The contagious turbulence spread
with encreasing virulence amongst the French
chieftains. Louis-le-Germanique, who fomented
the disaffection whilst pretending reluctance, was
invited as the deliverer of the country.

In Germany there prevailed an inveterate
hatred of Charles: his usual appellation was
Sennacherib, or *the Tyrant.*—Free us from our
oppressor—was the supplication of the Aquita-

854—855 nians; to this cry his brother responded; but
Louis was unable to quit Germany. Carloman
854 and Rastiz, the Wends and Carinthians, gave him
sufficient employment: he therefore sent his son
Louis the Saxon in his stead; and a singular
rumour has been transmitted to us, that the
Armoricans accepted the younger Louis as Count
or King of "Cornouailles."

854

Louis the
Saxon is
abandoned
by the
Aquita-
nians

Louis the Saxon hastened from Baioaria; but
when, after his long march, he had crossed the
Loire, the Aquitanians who sought him so earnestly just before, had changed their minds. Louis
the Saxon was there, but they would have none
of Louis. One Count alone came forward to join
the German Prince. Pepin tried to escape from
Saint-Médard by the connivance of some of the
inmates, but he was intercepted: his abettors
were punished, and he was compelled to kneel
down and be shorn, take the vows, put on the
cowl and become a Benedictine, as far as shaven
crown, vows and cowl, could make him such.
But the active adventurer renewed his attempt

Pepin es-
capes from
Saint-Mé-
dard.

and got off clear, cast away his hateful garb,
reached Aquitaine all shaven and shorn, and
appeared again as a warrior and as a king.

There were now three competitors for Aquitaine—the German Louis, Charles-le-Chauve, and
Pepin—all virtually (and Pepin ultimately actually) helping the Northmen. Charles-le-Chauve
was the most successful, Louis the Saxon fled,

Pepin's partizans fell off: he had no money. 854—855
Charles-le-Chauve prospered, and caused his son
Charles, the thoughtless boy, to be acknowledged 857
15 Oct.
855.
king of Aquitaine; he was solemnly anointed
and crowned at Limoges. After a few months The young
Charles
crowned
of nominal reign, the young Charles was deposed, King of
Aquitaine.
and Pepin re-acknowledged; but, before the year
closed, the Aquitanians repudiated Pepin and 856
Charles de-
re-deposed him, and re-acknowledged the young posed by
the Aqui-
Charles. Pepin, desolate and reckless, now allied tanians, and
Pepin re-
himself with the Northmen. Poitou, Aquitaine acknow-
ledged.
and the Counties of Blois and Chartres, were Pepin de-
posed, and
all invaded and pillaged. Orleans was encour- Charles
acknow-
ledged
aged to resistance by her Bishop, and the Danes again.
retreated; but the apathy and treachery of the
nobles enabled the Pirates to regain the city. The
Northmen were peculiarly inveterate against the
Bishops; and the Bishop of Chartres, Frodbaldus,
who like another Wulstan encouraged his people
to defend the houses of God and their own, was
so fiercely hunted by the Danes, that, attempting
to swim across the Eure, he was drowned.

§ 21. The Seine as well as the future Duchy
of France being laid open to the Northmen, Paris,
partially recovered from Regner Lodbrok's invasion, was assailed with more fell intent.

The surrounding districts were ravaged, and 857
the great monasteries, heretofore sacked, were Paris
attacked
now destroyed. Only three Churches were found again by
the North-
standing — Saint-Denis, Saint-Germain-des-près, men.

854–855
848
and Saint-Etienne or Notre-Dame—these having redeemed themselves by contributions to the enemy; but Saint-Denis made a bad bargain. The Northmen did not hold to their contract, or another company of pirates did not consider it as binding: the Monastery was burnt to a shell, and a most heavy ransom paid for the liberation of Abbot Louis, Charlemagne's grandson by his daughter Rothaida. Sainte-Généviève suffered most severely amongst all; and the pristine beauty of the structure rendered the calamity more conspicuous and the distress more poignant. During three centuries, the desolated grandeur of the shattered ruins continued to excite sorrow and dread, the fragments and particles of the gilt mosaics glistering upon the fire-scathed vaultings.

Such were the apprehensions excited by the visitations of the Northmen, that a new supplication,—*A furore Normannorum libera nos*, was introduced into the Gallican liturgies. They broke open the sepulchres, plundered the tombs of the Merovingian Sovereigns, and scattered the bones of Clovis and Clotilda.

So keenly was the wound which they had inflicted at Sainte-Généviève still felt in after times, that the same petition,—"*A furore Normannorum libera nos*"—continued to be intoned in the Abbey Choir even till the era of Louistreize: it is not impossible but that the dread inspired by the Lion of the North may have

Destruction of the antient Basilica of Généviève.

imparted a new reality to the archaic ritual. 854—855
Moreover, besides the commemoration thus kept
up in prayer, the community steadily observed a 857
statute which forbade the admission of any monk
of Danish blood The prohibition, inscribed on
stone, was shewn to the visitor when he entered
the Cloister, and testified their determination
never to receive a Dansker-man within their
walls.

The relics of Sainte-Généviève had been carried away by the monks. Until the reign of
Philippe-Auguste the Church remained desolate,
uncovered and open to the sky. Abbot Stephen
(afterwards Bishop of Tournay) then began the
restoration. Another sanctuary was erected, containing the renewed shrine of the patroness of
Paris, vast and gloomy, and inspiring religious
awe : pendant over the portal, hung the iron sanctuary ring which, touched by the fugitive, protected him from the avenger.

Such was the traditionary respect rendered
to the dark Gothic Basilica, that the building was
preserved when the new edifice arose—Corinthian
portico and mathematically balanced cupola—
equally testifying the encrease of architectural
skill and the decline of religious sentiment.—The
last fragments of the ancient consecrated fabric
were not uprooted until after the restoration of
the Bourbons. We well recollect the belfry-
tower, standing, when we first saw Paris, upon

840—877 the dusty and desolate plot : the Church had been
857 previously demolished by the *Bande-noire*, and
the empty stone-coffins of the Merovingian kings
were found as they had been left by the Scandinavian grave-robbers, plundered, broken open
and in confusion.

The shrine of Sainte-Généviève has been put
aside in a neglected corner of an adjoining parochial Church, and every vestige of Christianity
is obliterated from the Pantheon—*Aux grands
hommes la Patrie reconnoissante*—the Sanctuary
dedicated to the revilers of the Most High ; and
the altar trodden down by the star-crowned statue
symbolising Immortality,—their immortality—
stars glaring with the Unquenchable fire—the
immortality of the never-dying Worm.

Cowardice
of the
Franks.

§ 22. Amongst the calamities of the times,
the destruction of the Parisian monasteries seems
to have worked peculiarly on the imagination.
Paschasius Radbertus, the biographer of Wala,
expatiates upon this misery when writing his
Commentary on Jeremiah.   The general discontent was vented by the people in vituperations
against Charles-le-Chauve, whom they accused as
the cause of their misfortunes.   This was the
accustomed subterfuge of self-reproach : their
panic-cowardice was shameful and almost inexplicable.   The Counts had full power to summon
the lieges for the defence of the country : the
Franks were strong men, well armed, well trained,

the country abounded with resources; and if the Counts neglected their duty, the Franks were fully able to combine and defend themselves, to fight for their vineyards, their harvests, and their homes. Yet instead of making any resistance, the recreants scarcely ever attempted to oppose the enemy, even in the strongest fortified cities; the few occasions when they held out were so exceptional, that the raising of a siege is most usually ascribed to a miracle.

854—855
853—859

Charles-le-Chauve did not lose heart. Entangled, embarrassed, yet undeterred, he formed a grand strategic plan for recovering the Seine and securing Paris, and, through Paris, central and southern France. The first movement now needed against the Danes would necessarily be the dispersion of their nest in the Isle d'Oscelles. He summoned his Arrièreban, and blockaded the Northmen. Affairs in Aquitaine had become more adverse; Charles the boy was again expelled; and so intricately variable and contradictory were the political tergiversations of those times, that Pepin was equally a fugitive, seeking protection from his uncle. Amidst all these disturbances Charles conducted his operations vigorously. He intended to establish a complete line of fortifications and fortified posts, calculated, if the French could be roused from their fatal apathy, to frustrate the Pagan designs. After his death, though the works were only partially

Plans of Charles-le-Chauve for the expulsion of the Northmen: he blockades them in Oscelles.

854—855 executed, Paris was saved by his military pre-
853—859 science. The blockade of Oscelles therefore
interested not merely Charles-le-Chauve or
France, but the whole Carlovingian Empire.

853—859.

Conspiracy for the dethronement of Charles-le-Chauve, and the substitution of Louis-le-Germanique.

§ 23. During five years the discontented nobles and popular leaders of France had been plotting to depose Charles-le-Chauve, through the instrumentality of his brother Louis-le-Germanique. In the rapid and imperfect narratives of the Chroniclers a few names of the disaffected *meneurs* are mentioned, whom we cannot easily identify—a Gunzeline, a Gosfrid, or an Hervey;— others somewhat better known, such as the son of Bernard of Septimania; but the name of the most celebrated amongst them all, the most illustrious in France, he who holds a paramount station in European history, is not disclosed until after the explosion.

Louis was apprehensive, as he declared, lest he should be accused of ambition. Dangers and conscientious scruples might combine to restrain him: his disobedient sons, Louis the younger, Carloman, and Charles, were digging pitfalls for their father. The Sclavonians were disturbing the German realm, the Czechs or Bohemians revolting, the Daleminzians recalcitrating against the imposed tributes. But, at length, the opportune moment arrived: the Northmen were defending themselves vigorously in Oscelles, levying contributions upon the country, feeding themselves from the stores of Paris; and when Charles-le-Chauve was exerting himself manfully to clear the Empire from these insatiate enemies, his own brother, his pledged and sworn ally, casting off all reserve, moved towards France at the head of a powerful army, animated by personal, political, and national antipathy. 851—855
858

The Luegen-feld treachery was acted over again. The first notice which Charles received of his brother's hostile approach was the uproar in his own camp, the camp before Oscelles. His army broke up. Counts, vassals, soldiers abandoned their liege Sovereign, for the purpose of supporting the fratricidal Louis. A cowardly stratagem was practised against Charles by his own people when he was reconnoitring the enemy, exposing him to the hazard either of death or capture by the Northmen. Still Charles bore up—constant adversity had steeled him against adversity; and re-assembling such scanty forces as he could yet command, he advanced to resist the invasion.

Louis-le-Germanique, raising his banner at Worms, began his march triumphantly from Chrimhilda's Garden of Roses. The Germans were exasperated against Charles " the Tyrant," the subjects of Charles equally inveterate against their sovereign. Aug.-Dec. 858.
Louis-le-Germanique invades France.

The Nobles, generally, were adverse to a Sovereign who disregarded the exclusive privileges

851—855
858

claimed by noble birth, and considered *virtue* as equivalent to ancestry.—There was a strong party amongst the Clergy against him. His dilapidations of Church-property had given great offence, and not without sufficient reason. Abuses are sometimes partially restrained by the modesty of power; yet appetite comes by eating—as the French phrase has it,—and the spurious bashfulness of indulged irresponsibility rarely lasts. Hitherto it had been understood that certain Abbeys were always to be treated as real ecclesiastical benefices, and bestowed only upon unmarried clerks. Charles-le-Chauve, yielding to State necessity, now, without any hesitation, granted the Clergy-reserves indiscriminately as lay-fees. It seems that he was also suspected of sympathy with Godeschalck, whose opinions upon predestination had been condemned by the Gallican Church.—Wenilo, Archbishop of Sens, was prominently active amongst the insurrectionists. —"*Wenilo*" and "*Ganelone*" are only linguistic varieties of the same name; and a commentator upon the cycle of Carlovingian fictions may be tempted to suppose that the appellation of Ariosto's poetical arch-traitor was suggested by this ecclesiastical delinquent.

858.
Nov. 12.
Charles-le-Chauve betrayed by his troops.

Aquitanians, Bretons, Counts from all parts of France, promised help to Louis-le-Germanique, or joined his standard; yet Charles persevered, and, with such few troops as still adhered to him,

resolved to encounter the advancing enemy. The 851—855
armies came in sight of each other near Brienne
on the Aube, the nursery school of Napoleon. 858—859
The stand which Charles had made, enabled him
to commence negotiations with Louis; but discontent was encreasing amongst his own soldiery,
and he anticipated their defection by retreating to
Burgundy, where he still relied on finding support
from the partizans who remained to him.

Louis-le-Germanique, advancing as a deliverer Louis-le-Germanique acknowledged as King of France. Charles deposed by a Conciliabulum.
and a conqueror, held his Court at Troyes, as-
suming the royal authority, welcoming and guer-
doning all who had deserted from his brother.
Counties, abbeys and domains were granted pro-
fusely. —Wenilo convened a Conciliabulum at
Attigny, wherein a sentence of deposition was
pronounced against the fugitive King.

Louis, now king of Germany France and Aquitaine, surprized at his own successes, considered
himself entirely secure. Disbanding his forces, he
dismissed all care from his mind, and enjoyed
his unexpected good fortune; but treachery was
so kneaded into the character of the Franks, that
their recognition of the new Sovereign was the
transition to his abandonment. Charles recovered his strength and influence, Louis-le-Ger-
manique was universally discarded; and without 859. Louis-le-Germanique expelled, and Charles-le-Chauve restored.
even attempting to maintain his position, he sur-
rendered the kingdom of France. His retreat
was a flight, and the pursuit was so hot, that

851—855
859 Charles, had he chosen, might have captured the fugitive. It was full time indeed that Louis should repair to his own country. The Eastern Marches were all in commotion. The Sorbs were striving to rid themselves of the German yoke, and had slain their Duke, Cziztebor, the feudatory of Louis. The other Sclavonian tribes prepared for revolt. With triumph had Louis set out from Chrimhilda's Garden of Roses: he returned to the Garden of Roses covered with disgrace and shame.

859.
Fresh dis-
turbances
in Aqui-
taine and in
Armorica.
Pepin joins
Robert-le-
Fort (see
II. § 59) and
the Bre-
tons

§ 24. In the meanwhile, Northmen and Aquitanians were incessant in their disturbances. The Franks between Seine and Loire made an unsuccessful endeavour to expel the Danes. A peace had been concluded between Charles and Pepin, and the latter was reinstated in a portion of Aquitaine; but hostilities again arose between the uncle and that nephew whom he dreaded more than Lodbrok, Biorn-Ironside, Sidroc or Oscar. The Aquitanians, who had rejoiced in the return of Pepin, rejoiced as much when they cashiered him. The boy Charles was replaced upon the Aquitanian throne, and Pepin expelled for the fourth or fifth time—we are baffled in attempting a correct account of these changes—but, inexhaustible in resources, and endued with the wisdom of desperation, Pepin knew the point where the kingdom of Charles was peculiarly vulnerable, a country open to his worst enemies, the Northmen, a country peopled by a race still burning with national vengeance against the Franks, a race now 851—855 supported by the alliance of a Chieftain who had 859 acquired the highest reputation, "another Judas Maccabæus" in popular estimation, a stranger or the son of a stranger, under whom the Armoricans had rallied, who had been the head and front of the confederation against Charles, ROBERT-LE-FORT, the first of the Capets,—"*Pipinus Rotberto Comiti et Britonibus sociatur*"—is the brief announcement of the change coming upon the Monarchy's destiny.

§ 25. It is a marvellous history, that of Armorica, reminiscences of truth and traditions of fable inextricably intermingled. The huge rocks piled on the borders of the gloomy Morbihan will not answer your interrogatories. Celtic history, so interesting, so affecting, so noble, has been rendered the meaningless vacuity of literature, by the unbounded speculations of the learned. When will Druidical archæologists be convinced that menzhir and peul-ven, cromlech and kistvaen tell us nothing; and from nothing nothing comes. You can no more judge of their age than the eye can estimate the height of the clouds: these shapeless masses impart but one lesson, the impossibility of recovering by induction any knowledge of the speechless past. Waste not your oil. Give it up, that speechless past; whether fact or chronology, doctrine or mythology; whether in Europe or Asia, Africa or

History of Britanny: its close connexion with the history of England.

851—855 America;—at Thebes or Palenque, on Lycian
shore or Salisbury plain: lost is lost: gone, is
818   gone for ever.

Yet close by that inexplicable Morbihan memorial are the excavated walls of the Roman
station, replacing the Celtic city, whose people,
impelled to the South and deserting their habitations, established the Adriatic's island queen.
Even as the Galatians of the Narbonnensic
Gaul became the Asiatic Galatians, so did the
Gaulish Veneti become the Veneti of Italy.

The seat of the Veneti was subsequently occupied by the immigration proceeding from the
greater Britain, the second Celtic colony:—such
has been the process according to which the pilgrimage of races has been usually conducted—
families attracted by the kindred families which
have preceded them. When the Arabs conquered Carthage, they were but the followers
of the Canaanites who had fled to Carthage
before Joshua's devouring sword. And thus,
in the lesser Britanny, the Loegrians introduced their language and their laws, settling
another Cornouaille opposite our Cornwall, and
another Gwynneth retracing the Gwynneth of
Siluria, and appointing another local habitation
for Tristran and the Morholt, symbolized in the
fable of Saint Michael's guarded Mount, surrounded by the submerged shore.

Britanny was an integral portion of the Con-

queror's empire, and the histories of Normandy ^{851—855}
and the history of England are interwoven with
Armorica's destinies. From the earliest period ^{843—844}
when the events of Armorica become known
with any degree of certitude, they are combined
with the annals of our own island.

Riche-mont, Mont-aigue and Mont-gomery are
three proud memorials of the Conquest; but the
proudest is Alan Fergant's tower on the ver-
dantly shadowed Swale, ruling the inheritance
of the Anglo-Saxon Edwin;—a monument of the
retributive Nemesis, avenging on those Saxons
their expulsion of Alan's ancestors from their
aboriginal island.

§ 26. Charlemagne's supremacy over the Important subjugation of Armorica by the Carlovingians.
Armoricans may be compared to the dominion
exercised by Imperial Russia amongst the Caucasian tribes—periods during which the vassals
dare not claim the rights of independence, intercalated amongst the converse periods when the
Emperor cannot assert the rights of authority;
yet the Frank would not abandon the prerogative
of the Cæsars, whilst the mutual antipathy between the races inflamed the desire of dominion
on the one part, and the determination of resistance on the other. Britanny is divided into
Bretagne Bretonnante and *Bretagne Gallicante*,
according to the predominance of the Breyzad
and the Romane languages respectively. The
latter constituted the march-lands, and here the

851—855 Counts-marchers were placed by Charlemagne
and his successors, Franks mostly by lineage;
818—833 yet one Breyzad, Nominoë, was trusted by Louis-
le-débonnaire with a delegated authority.

818
Nominoë
accepts the
protection
of Louis-le-
débon-
naire.

Nominoë deserved his power : he was one of
the new men of the era, literally taken from the
plough. Inimical traditions tell how the tyrant's
ploughshare discovered a treasure, the gold which
enabled the usurper to win the crown. Those
who favoured Nominoë, or were his favourites,
complimented him by a lineage ascending to the
fabled chieftains of King Arthur's days; but the
Monasteries he had plundered revenged themselves by proclaiming his ignoble origin. The
dissensions among the Franks enabled Nominoë
to increase his authority. Could there be any
adversary of the empire so stupid as not to
profit by the battle of Fontenay ?—During the
dreadful devastations which the Normans were
committing in the Carlovingian march-land or
County of Nantes, Nominoë attacked and occupied the march-land of Rennes; and then he
and Count Lambert, whom we recollect in the
Pfaltz of Aix-la-Chapelle in the very beginning
of Louis-le-débonnaire's reign, turned their weapons against France. Nominoë assumed the
royal title, vindicated the independence of his
antient people, and enabled them, in the time
of Rollo, to assert with incorrect grandiloquence,
pardonable in political argument, that the Frank

had never reigned within the proper Armorican 851—855 boundaries.

§ 27. Five expeditions, five raids-royal, con- 843—850
843—844 ducted by Charles-le-Chauve in person, succes- First expedition of sively entered Armorica: he encamped around Charles-le-Chauve Rennes: the severe season and the insufficiency into Britanny. of his forces compelled him to retreat. Baffled, but not dispirited, he resumed the conflict in the following year. Charles inherited Charlemagne's genius. Inferior in opportunity, inferior in fortune, he possessed the spirit and talent, which, unmarred by fate, might have enrolled him in the rank of conquerors. Again he advanced boldly 845 into Armorica. But Charles was unacquainted Second expedition of with the country: his ardour rendered him in- Charles-le-Chauve cautious. The artifices of Nominoë enticed the against the Bretons. royal general and the Frankish army into a marshy tract between the Oult and the Villaine, the river giving a name to one of the Departments which have obliterated Britanny from the map of France.—It was a celebrated Field where the armies thus encountered, the field of Balaon: the Field famed or defamed by a battle fought long ago in the dismal times, in the times of Chilperic and Fredegonda, between Guerech and Beppolin, a desperate and bloody strife between kinsman and kinsmen, the strifes which constitute the sorrow of Celtic history.

The hardy Saxons, from the " Otlingua Saxonica " near Bayeux, that Teutonic settlement

851—855
858

which had preceded the establishment of their brethren in our insular Britain, were marshalled as the vanguard of the Frankish army. They fought desperately, but ineffectually; the light and active Breton cavalry pierced through and broke the ranks of the enemy. Battle-axe and sword yielded to javelin and the spear. Two days did the conflict continue, till at length Charles, retreating before Nominoë, took refuge in Mans; and the victorious chief, who had already assumed the title of King, obtained, after long negotiations with the successor of Saint Peter, the golden crown.

850
Third expedition of Charles-le-Chauve into Brittanny.

So earnest was Charles-le-Chauve for the subjugation of Britanny, that amidst the turmoils of the Danish invasions, and the enmity of his brothers, he recommenced hostilities. Upon the borders of Armorica, the Romanized population, more especially the citizens, longed for reunion with the Franks, and invited Charles to resume his authority, the Count, his lieutenant, having been expelled from the borders of the Loire. Charles therefore invaded Armorica, and placed garrisons in Rennes and amidst the ruins of Nantes. But the energetic Nominoë was in the height of his power: he occupied and subjugated Anjou and Maine. Nominoë's army, conjoined with the insurgent Lambert, then entered the Pays-Chartrain. Fortune seemed to promise that, Arthur's fabled glories restored, the Gauls be-

tween the Seine, the Loire and the sea, should 851—855
be ruled by a Celtic dynasty; but sudden death
stayed the progress of the Hero :—he left three 861—862
children by his Queen Argantael, the eldest Herispoë.

Charles acknowledged the rights of Herispoë,
confirmed him in his authority, and received the
proud vassal's homage. Vassalage did not practically imply obedience Violent dissensions arose
between France and Armorica. Charles led a 851—852.
fourth and a fifth expedition into Herispoë's do- Fourth and fifth expe-ditions of Charles a-gainst the Bretons.
minions. Herispoë opposed a stout resistance,
obtained his own terms, and accepting a fresh
investiture from Charles, he assumed the royal
title by his Suzerain's authority. Herispoë was
inclining towards the Franks, and willing to assimilate himself, like his successors, to the prevailing ethos of the Empire. A family alliance
was projected: hitherto had the proud Franks
disdained the Celtic race, and the Celts loathed
their oppressors; but the interests and inclinations of the Sovereigns prevailed over national
antagonisms, and it was agreed that Louis-le- Marriage proposed
Bégue, the heir-apparent of Charles, should be- between Louis-le-
come the husband of Herispoë's daughter. The Bégue and the daugh-
affections of Louis were fixed upon Ansgarda, his ter of He-rispoe
first love: the promise however of an ample
appanage, Maine—a State almost independent,
though claimed equally by Franks and Armoricans—Le Perche, and all the Counties lying

851—855 around and between Chartres, Orleans, and Tours,
‾‾‾‾ procured a reluctant compliance ; and the policy
861   which in a subsequent age united the fleur-de-lis
of France and the ermines of Britanny was near
to have succeeded.

858   § 28.   Armorica repudiated the antinational
Discontent
excited   policy of her ruler : the alliance with the Franks
thereby in
Armorica·   deeply incensed the Breyzad race.   A conspiracy
Herispoe
killed by   was matured against Herispoë by a rival, his
Solomon,
who suc-   nephew Solomon.   This chieftain, claiming the
ceeds
supreme dignity, and hitherto protected and
trusted by Charles-le-Chauve, had already obtained the county of Rennes, one third of Armorica.   Herispoë sought refuge in a Church,
but his foemen killed him before the altar.

861—862   The Danes were pouring into France : Charles,
The great
Danish in-   however, assembled his forces, and prepared to
vasions un-
der Wel-   avenge the disappointment of his hopes; but the
land, &c.
new Armorican King was the stronger.   French
affairs were becoming more and more troubled :
the conspiracy for the deposition of Charles and
the substitution of Louis-le-Germanique had ramified into this distant region.   Robert-le-Fort was
in Britanny, heading the confederacy; and it was
at this juncture that Pepin of Aquitaine, joining
Robert-le-Fort and the Bretons, turned the scale.

§ 29.   Anglo-Saxon England must be read
in parallel with the history of France.   Early
in Ethelbert's reign Winchester was sacked and
burned to the ground by the Danes   A mis-

chance followed their success. — Returning to their vessels, merry and spoil-encumbered, they were attacked by the Hampshire-men, command- ed by Ethelwolf and Osric, and some of their detachments were dispersed; but they recoiled with greater force on the other side of the Chan- nel. Half a day, or a day, landed them on the opposite coast, and they infested the whole of the shores from Scheldt to Seine; Amiens was taken, so also Nimeguen, the Bishop put on board ship in chains, Bayeux taken and the Bishop killed: Terouenne, the ancient capital of the Morini, burnt—the once opulent Terouenne— Wolsey's Terouenne, Henry the Eighth's Terou- enne, Francis the First's Terouenne, which, after rising again to exuberant prosperity, was ruined for the gratification of her burgher-rival's jealousies.

Up the Seine sailed Jarl Welland with a fleet of two hundred ships—towns, villages and villas burning on every side. Notwithstanding their repeated warnings, the Parisians neglected every means of defence: they dared not, or cared not, cowardice combining with apathy. The Danes, as they were wont to do in England, horsed themselves, and the general tenor of events tends to shew that gaining influence by inspiring terror or acquiring friendships, they received assistance from the people.

On Easter morn, a sad anniversary, they sur- rounded and entered the city. The Monks of

851—855
861

Saint-Germain-des-près were surprized whilst singing matins, the monastery plundered, the buildings set on fire; the various merchants who attempted to rescue their property by boating up the Seine, intercepted and their goods and wares captured and despoiled.

861
Measures of defence adopted by Charles-le-Chauve.

§ 30. Consternation filled the country. Charles-le-Chauve was at Senlis, harassed, unsupported, unassisted; nevertheless he immediately actively resumed his offensive and defensive warfare against the Danes. Forts and entrenchments were raised at the place now called Pont-de-l'Arche. The bridge was built by him also, the admiration which the strength of the fabric excited, was testified by the antient popular name — le-Pont-du-diable : preparations were made for defending the shores of the Marne, and above all for strengthening Paris and Paris island.

Charles perplexes the North-men.

Leaving Louis-le-Bégue at Senlis as Regent, aided by competent advisers, and imposing upon Bishop Erpuin the anxious guardianship of his blooming daughter the ardent Judith, the twice widowed widow of sixteen, Charles marched to the field of action, perplexing the Northmen by devices, policy, energy. Bribes were very useful —he set the Danes at variance amongst themselves: their progress was checked by the intrenched armaments stationed on the banks of the Marne. Jarl Welland settled in the Gauls,

became the homager of King Charles, accepted a 851—855
Benefice or Fief, and was baptized, together with
his family and followers. 861

But these advantageous results of policy are Robert-le-Fort aban-
trivial, compared to his success in gaining over the dons the confede-
chief of the adverse conspiracy. By some nego- racy, and enters the
tiations, which the Chroniclers neither explain service of Charles.
nor attempt to explain, Charles-le-Chauve at-
tracted Robert-le-Fort once and for all into his
service. Henceforward Robert lived and died as
the most exalted and most energetic amongst the
lieges of the Carlovingian crown. This remarkable transaction seems to be shunned by the contemporary annalists. A paragraph, inserted in
the confused narrative belonging to a subsequent
year, merely discloses that a defection had taken
place amongst the confederates, begun by the
intriguing and doubly faithless Guntfrid and
Gozeline, through whose intervention Robert-le-
Fort was reconciled to his Sovereign. No praises
are bestowed upon Robert-le-Fort for his newly-
awakened loyalty: no blame imputed to the partizan, who, deserting his associates, leaves them
to their fate, and earns the most proud and ample
reward.

Solomon and the Armoricans, and all the 861
Prelates and Counts with whom he had co-ope- Robert-le-Fort be-
rated being abandoned, we behold ROBERT-LE- comes the homager of
FORT kneeling before Charles-le-Chauve at Melun, Charles-le-Chauve

851—855   becoming his homager, greeted and honoured.

862

Soon after, a Placitum or Great Council was held at Compiègne. In this assembly, and by the assent of the *Optimates*, the Seine and its islands, and that most important island Paris,

861   and all the country between Seine and Loire,

Marquisate of France and Anjou granted to Robert-le-Fort.

were granted to Robert, the Duchy of France, though not yet so called, morever the Angevine Marches, or County of Outre-Maine, all to be held by Robert-le-Fort as barriers against North-men and Bretons, and by which cessions the realm was to be defended. Only a portion of this dominion owned the obedience of Charles: the Bretons were in their own country, the North-men in the country they were making their own: the grant therefore was a license to Robert to win as much as he could, and to keep his acqui-sitions should he succeed.

Influence of the Danes upon the Frankish population.

§ 31. A very alarming symptom attending the Danish invasions was the encreasing moral and material power which the Northmen were acquiring in the Gauls. The left bank of the Seine was nearly abandoned by the inhabitants, and consequently such of the invaders as chose to remain had ample room to colonize; neither does it appear that the people, especially the peasantry, were always averse to them. The Northmen plundered and ravaged; but there are always a great many who have nothing to lose by being plundered and ravaged, and who are much inclined to ask the question put by the horse in the fable,—can the new master ride me harder than my old master has done?

Three of the fiercest Pirates who assailed the Gauls are respectively called " Hastings" or "Alsting" in the Chronicles; and one of the three was a peasant from the neighbourhood of Tours, who, enlisting amongst the Pirates, distinguished himself lamentably by his renegade ferocity. A monk who joined the Danes was captured and hanged; but Pepin of Aquitaine, by adopting the Danish rites and customs, afforded the most illustrious or most disgraceful example. It may not be necessary to infer that Pepin ate horseflesh or swore by the holy bracelet, nevertheless he united himself thoroughly with the Northmen.

The abdication of his own national usages caused Pepin to be detested as a Pagan. Sancho Sanchion's cruel treachery had not destroyed Pepin's confidence in his friends : betrayed into his uncle's power by the enticement of Count Rainulph, Pepin was condemned to death—a sentence scarcely mitigated when commuted into perpetual imprisonment. Pepin's apostasy, political if not religious, was punished by perfidy, and perfidy was rewarded by sacrilege; for Count Rainulph received, as a guerdon for his good services, the noble Abbey of Saint-Hilary at Poitiers, which he united to his lay honour and dignity. The young king Charles, on his part,

Pepin of Aquitaine having joined the Danes, condemned to perpetual imprisonment.

851—877
862—864
Charles
king of
Aquitaine,
his disobe-
dience and
rebellion.

868.
His death
Chap. II.
§ 53. p 391

862.
Louis-le-
Bégue re-
bels against
his father.

had occasioned great vexation to his father. He, at the age of seventeen, married the widow of a Count Humbert. Charles-le-Chauve was very strict in asserting his paternal rights, and this marriage, possibly connected with some political intrigue, deeply offended him. The quarrel became so serious that Charles-le-Chauve marched an army against his son. Charles of Aquitaine submitted to his father: displaying much courage, he defeated the Northmen, and gave good promise,—when his death ensued miserably in consequence of his half-drunken scuffle with Alboin.

As for Robert-le-Fort, his adhesion to Charles-le-Chauve was unqualified and complete. He devoted himself entirely to the king's service, without scruple, without hesitation and without reserve. Robert's military talent and fortitude materially retarded the Northmens progress. Whilst Charles pressed them hard by land, Robert dispersed the Danish squadron in the Loire, bribed away other of the marauders; and the Breton confederacy was on the point of dissolution.

§ 32. A dangerous enemy thus converted into a firm and useful ally, the adversaries of the Crown and Kingdom humbled, the rebellion headed by his brother suppressed, Charles might expect to rid France of the Danish marauders. However another enemy arose exactly where an enemy might have been anticipated, from the bosom of his own family. Louis-le-Bégue's grudges against his father encreased. Charles 851—877 dealt with the abbeys exactly as they did in Scotland when John Knox was preparing to pull 862—864 them down. The Abbey of Saint-Martin of Tours, that most sacred sanctuary, was granted to Louis-le-Bégue as an appanage; but this concession did not satisfy him. Judith, through the aid and connivance of Louis, eloped from Senlis with the sturdy, handsome forester. We shall have more to say about this amour, so fraught with political consequences. The Counts Guntfrid and Gozeline, who betrayed the associated Frankish and Armorican chieftains, now reverted to the party they had deceived, and machinated against Charles—and by their persuasions Louis deserted his Regency, evaded from the Court, joined the Breton alliance, and carried on the warfare against his father with unmitigated pertinacity.

Louis-le-Bégue took the command of a host of Bretons, with which he invaded Anjou, wasting the country as much as any Northman could have done. Robert-le-Fort advanced unhesitatingly, He is defeated by and completely defeated the rebel heir-apparent. Robert-le-Fort. After this, Louis-le-Bégue returned to his obedience, and a surly reconciliation ensued. When Louis absconded, Charles had granted the Abbey of Saint-Martin to Count Hubert, Hermentruda's brother, also abbot of the royal Abbey of Saint-Maurice in the Valais, so that this preferment

851—877
862—864

could not now be restored to Louis; but, as a compensation, he received the county of Méaux and the abbeys of Saint-Crispin and Marmoutier; and with respect to the title of King of Neustria, which Louis had assumed, the assumption (in the first instance prohibited) was neither acknowledged nor denied. The kingdom of Aquitaine was subsequently bestowed upon him. But Charles-le-Chauve compelled Louis to divorce his Ansgarda, the mother of two sons, and family concord was imperfectly restored. Carloman his brother, who for many years had been in revolt against Charles-le-Chauve, sometimes in open hostility, sometimes secretly conspiring, persevered

Carloman's punishment and death. See p. 392.

in his evil course, until, as before noticed, he sustained a dreadful punishment, and died, a blinded fugitive and mendicant.

863—864
The Northmen continue their invasions.

§ 33.   Danes and Northmen continued their invasions : the young Rollo was about to embark, and commence that adventurous and devious course which, when twelve years had elapsed, brought him to the Seine.   The attacks which crippled, and ultimately ruined the Anglo-Saxon Empire continued against England, though the crisis was long retarded by Alfred's wisdom.

The Northmen encreased in numbers and in confidence, and their devastations extended wider and wider.   Charles-le-Chauve employed active and intelligent exertions for the defence of the kingdom. It was decreed that fortifications should

be erected throughout the country, but entrenchments and walls cannot make loyal hearts.

851—877

863—864

Charles-le-Chauve trifled too much with the
conscience of his subjects. The dilapidations of
Church-property contributed to the discouragement and prostration of the national feeling.
Church-fees were granted universally to the nobles
and soldiery, and the people believed that the
gift brought misfortune upon the lay intruders.
Count Hubert, the lay Abbot of Saint Maurice
in the Valais, was wretchedly killed within a
short time after he obtained Saint-Martin-de-
Tours. Saint-Hilary at Poitiers, the Abbey profaned by the secular misappropriation, was burned,
and the conflagration construed as the punishment of the profanation. But this did not concern Count Rainulph, the stout soldier Abbot.
If the monks were dispersed, the charges of the
establishment were saved, and he fattened upon
the Abbey's lands. The citizens paid a Danegeld: the city was spared for the nonce, and
the Danes laughed in their sleeves when they
touched the money.

Scandal ex-
cited by the
grants of
Abbeys as
lay-fees

Robert kept the Northmen in check, yet only
by incessant exertion. He inured the future kings
of France, his two young sons, Eudes and Robert,
to the tug of war, making them his companions
in his enterprises. The banks of the Loire were
particularly guarded by him, for here the principal attacks were directed. Two battles ensued.

Robert-le-
Fort and
his sons.

851—877 In the first he defeated the Northmen; but the

864—865 defeat called for a reinforcement, and the call was answered. In their turn they assailed Robert, who was wounded and compelled to retreat.—Neither Count, Duke, Marquis or King, nor the whole force of France, could clear the Loire country of the Danes.

Northmen again in the Seine and Loire, defeated by Robert.

§ 34. During all these transactions the Seine country continued much harassed, Paris put under contribution, the casks rolled out of the cellars into the Danish barges, and the monks of Saint-Denis groaned whilst the roistering Danish men were living at free quarters in the Monastery. A fierce battle raged in central France. Bourges and Clermont were occupied by the Danes, the littoral of the Loire again and again devastated, Fleury burned, Orleans burned, Poitiers burned. The citizens who had seen Saint-Hilary on fire now took their share in the common calamity.

865. Robert's triumph.

Robert concentrated his forces, encountered the Danes in battle, defeated them, and sent their raven-banners and arms to Charles-le-Chauve as trophies of victory: an act performed with a degree of emphasis and display unusual in that age, when war was a dull and bloody business, rarely attended by pomp and pride, the main excitements of the warrior being the expectation of plunder or the dread of danger. But Robert was, in fact, pursuing the war on his own account; and it was the policy of Charles-le-Chauve to give the first of the Capets a greater stake in the game. More dignities and territories were bestowed upon him, the Counties of Auxerre and Nevers.

851—877

864—865

Confidence being partially revived, the government of Charles-le-Chauve displayed considerable vigour. Amongst the marchings and traversings of the Northmen, one particular region, nearly corresponding with the antient kingdom of Soissons, had chanced more than any other to be exempted from their devastations. Here the Northmen were out of sight and in a measure out of mind. It was the lurid tranquillity enjoyed by the quarter of a besieged town beyond the range of the shells. Here alone Charles-le-Chauve can be properly said to have ruled : here he diligently pursued his favourite studies, corresponded with the learned and penned his verse, here his Court retained an antique brilliancy, whether that Court was held in forest-encircled Compiègne, salubrious Senlis, pleasant Epernay on the Marne, or in the magnificent tower which crowned the rock of Lâon.

Government as exercised by Charles-le-Chauve.

Portion of the kingdom exempted from the Danish invasions.

Charles-le-Chauve attempted to exemplify the principles of his namesake and grandsire. A dignified and friendly intercourse with the Saracens was renewed. Mahomet of Cordova presented his tokens of respect, perfumes and aromatics and silken pavilions. The Counts who failed to discharge their duty against the Northmen were

851—877 degraded, and their benefices forfeited. Good
laws were enacted, and Capitulars promulgated
864—865 worthy of Charlemagne, wise, well-considered
and practical, if the state of the kingdom had
allowed them to be put into practice.

But that one condition was wanting: the
incurable unsoundness of the state frustrated all
efforts to avert the evil. Treachery was on every
side. Bernard, Count of Auvergne, the son of the
too-celebrated Bernard by the affectionate Doduana, conspired against Charles, lying in ambush to
slay him, thus seeking to avenge the death of his
own father. Bernard was also inveterate against
the two commanders in whom the king placed the
greatest confidence, Rainulph Count of Poitiers,
and Robert-le-Fort. The plot being discovered,
Bernard fled from justice, and his county was
given to Robert, henceforward a Prince ruling
on both sides of the Loire : moreover the Duke
or Marquis of France received the Abbey of
Saint-Martin, still the most coveted piece of preferment in the Gauls, and which was now treated
by Charles-le-Chauve without any reminiscence
of its ecclesiastical character.

Conspiracy of Bernard of Septi- mania.

865
Robert-le-
Fort de-
feated by
the North-
men

§ 35. Robert's exertions were more needed
than ever; but his fortunes began to decline: the
Northmen rose refreshed after the chastisement
they had received. Robert had stationed himself
at Melun : he assembled the Frankish forces : with
him was vigorous Eudes—Eudes the first-born

and disciple of the matured warrior; but on this 831—877
occasion the father and the son, the Duke of
France and the defender of Paris, her future King, 864—865
were eminently unfortunate. The Northmen landed and offered battle. Robert and Eudes fled, and
the Northmen re-embarked upon their vessels,
carrying off their prey:—the Danes had won
trophies in their turn. Great consternation ensued. '
Charles was compelled to submit to a Dane-geld.
The money was raised by an impost partly in the
nature of a land-tax, fairly assessed, and not so
heavy as on previous occasions, but the tribute
was accompanied by degrading conditions. The
captives taken by the Danes and who had escaped
from them were to be restored, or their value
compensated; and in like manner the Franks
were to pay the were or blood-fine for every
Dane who had been killed; a strange stipulation,
explicable only upon the supposition that troth
plighted to the Northmen had been broken by
the Franks, who now sustained the penalty.

§ 36. Robert's mischance was followed by 865—866
the necessity of competing with a very formid- Hastings in the Loire.
able individual enemy—Hastings or Alsting, one War be-tween him and Robert.
of the three who bear this dreaded name. It is
a doubtful point whether this renowned chieftain
can be the Hastings who held the County of
Chartres in the time of Rollo; for, as previously
noticed, three pirate chieftains answer to the
appellation of Hastings; and though the com-

851—877
865—866 mencement and the conclusion of Rollo's career are precisely ascertained, much uncertainty attends the intermediate chronology.

Hastings had already for many years infested the Gauls: he pillaged Rouen, and his activity perhaps obtained for him the repute of devastations committed by others; or he may have been confounded with his namesakes.—Rouen, Nantes, Angers, Tours, Orleans, Beauvais, Nimeguen, Poitou, Saintonge, Perigord, Limoges, Artois and Auvergne, are all enumerated amongst the places and countries which Hastings ravaged. Like Cromwell in Ireland, Hastings became a semi-mythic character, accumulating upon himself the current anecdotes of cunning, skill and ferocity, so as to gain the reputation of the most destructive amongst the invaders.

The Dane-geld, and the concessions paid and rendered to the Northmen, incited them to pursue their attacks with more alacrity: co-operating with the Armoricans, they again pillaged Mans. Hastings re-entered the Loire, and whilst the Danishmens fleet, their floating camp, occupied the broad estuary, they ravaged the Armorican Marches, Nantes, Anjou, Poitou and Tours, devastating Robert-le-Fort's country on either side of the river. Robert took his station about fourteen miles from Angers, in a species of peninsula formed by the confluence of Maine and Sarthe, where he was joined by Rainulph

Count of Poitou. Both had increased in power, but their followers were discouraged by the popular sentiment prevailing against their usurpations of the ecclesiastical possessions. Bad luck was augured:—it was a shame and a scandal that the Abbot of Saint-Martin and the Abbot of Saint-Hilary should be heading the soldiery in the field.—Robert and Rainulph determined to be the assailants. The Danes were inferior in numbers, and also were in danger of being cut off from their ships; and therefore retreating, they fell back upon the town, now a small village, of Pont-sur-Sarthe, then called *Brise-Sarthe*— the Brig of Sarthe.

851—877

866

866
Count-Abbot Robert and Count-Abbot Rainulph advance against the Northmen.

The Franks gained ground so rapidly upon the Northmen, that the latter could not avoid a battle. Hastings prepared for defence as readily as he had attempted to escape fighting, and he immediately availed himself of the capabilities which the site afforded. The Church was large, built strongly of stone—massy walls, offering no other openings except tall narrow loop-hole windows, and these only on one side; as appears from an unaltered portion of the still-existing nave. The "Basilica,"—thus it is termed by the Chronicler,—was, from its construction, a strong hold, having possibly been intended for that purpose, as is frequently the case in border countries. Hastings with his picked men threw themselves into the Church: the remaining Danes, not so

The fatal affair of Pont-sur-Sarthe.

851—877
866—870
protected, were cut down and slaughtered by the Franks. A good day's work—thought Robert-le-Fort;—but the work was not half done. The Church was filled with its fearless garrison, quiet, defying the enemy by their silence. Robert commanded his men to pitch their tents, and prepare the artillery for the assault on the following day.

The then present day had been a day of great exertion and trial. Count Robert, Abbot Robert, heated, excited, exhausted, doffed his armour, threw helmet here and hauberk there, and stretched his stalwart body and sinewy limbs on the grass. Count Rainulph, Abbot Rainulph, stood further off, carefully examining the Church: he had a foreboding of danger. Both commanders forgot that keen eyes were marking them, and keen weapons pointed at them from behind the unglazed loop-hole windows. Forth darted the Arbalest-bolt, mortally wounding the Count of Poitou: the doors of the Church opened, the Northmen rushed out, shouting and yelling, slew the Marquis of France, and dragged his dying corpse into the Church. Rainulph lingered three days, the Frankish forces dispersed, and the swaggering Northmen returned safely to their ships, and sailed away.—Thus died the first of the Capets.

866
25 July.
Robert-le-
Fort killed
at Brise-
Sarthe.

866—870
Transient
improve-
ment in the
State of
France.
§ 37. Whilst Robert-le-Fort had guarded the Loire, Charles was co-operating quite as effi-

ciently in the defence of the Seine.   Although 851—877
the Northmen who had quitted their free quarters at Saint-Denis were still cruising in the 866—870
river, Charles kept the command at Pistres, super-
intending the works which he proposed to construct, wains and wagons arriving with materials.
These works were continued at different periods,
the most enduring as well as the most useful
being the pier-bridge or break-water which he
built across the Seine for the defence of Paris, and
which entirely answered the purpose of closing
the river against the Northmen.

Many circumstances contributed to encourage
Charles.   The Danes relaxed in their attacks
upon the Gauls, for they were concentrating
their forces in England.   Northumbria, East
Anglia, Mercia, tell the story,—colonized, conquered, and becoming the Danelaghe.   The chief
Vikingar were drawn off upon this great enterprize : they were posting their armies across our
island, and occupying the best situations on the
sea-coast ; and until they had accomplished their
intent, they could not spare many of their vessels
or men for France.   When they had completed
the conquest of Mercia, and deposed Ceolwulf,
their mock King, they still had much to do, therefore the Gauls enjoyed somewhat longer intervals
of rest, the attacks were less continuous, yet very
sharp when they came, and encreasing towards
the conclusion of the reign.

851—877

866—870
Robert-le-
Fort s hon-
ors and be-
nefices
treated as
escheats,
andgranted
to Hugh
l'Abbé.

§ 38. Robert-le-Fort's death was an astounding state-event. Charles-le-Chauve seemed to be endowed with new power. From Witikind the stranger, Robert-le-Fort had not inherited honours or possessions, counties or benefices, land or fee. So far as depended upon Charles-le-Chauve's wishes and intentions, the sons of Robert-le-Fort, Eudes and Robert, would have shared their Grandfather's poverty, and the family have relapsed into primitive obscurity. The law of beneficiary or feudal succession fluctuated rather undeterminately between favour and equity, the Senior's gratitude or inclination supporting the claim which justice might unimpeachably but ungraciously deny. A Sovereign could always delay, and not unfrequently withhold, the expectancies of the heir, more especially an infant heir.

To constitute a strictly legal right, descent during three generations was required. Had Charles-le-Chauve entertained any love for the memory of Robert-le-Fort, owned to owning any thanks for Robert's services, the sons would have received their father's domains, instead of which he treated the whole as lapsed or escheated. The church-fees and the lay-fees, the dukedoms, marquisates and counties held by Robert-le-Fort, were all resumed by the Crown.

Robert-le-Fort, dead, was in a manner completely forgotten—a dead man out of mind : no memorial was ever raised to celebrate his fame :

no monument records his death except the frag- 851—877 ment of Brise-Sarthe church-wall: not even an *obit* founded at Brise-Sarthe for Robert's soul's Robert's honours granted to Hugh the Count-Abbot. See p. 236. repose. His place was taken by a new favourite, a new Commander-in-Chief, a new Prime Minister, one whom Charles could well trust—his cousin Hugh, third son of the Guelphic Conrad, the Empress Judith's brother, the lay-clerk, the soldier-priest, the Abbot-Count, Duke and Commendatory of Auxerre. Count Hugh obtained all the possessions which Robert-le-Fort had enjoyed, abusively or rightfully, according to law, or against law, and he now appears as Abbot of Saint-Martin of Tours, Abbot of Saint-Vedast of Arras, Abbot of Saint-Bertin, Count of Burgundy, Count of Anjou, Duke or Marquis of Neustrian France—titles accompanied by solid power.

§ 39. Charles-le-Chauve prosecuted his at- 861—874. Affairs of Armorica or Britanny. tacks upon Armorica. His interferences—hostile and pacific—ultimately amalgamated the political existence of the Celtic provinces and the fortunes of Capetian France. Britanny was engrafted upon Normandy, and Normandy linked Britanny to England. The Danes also are actively and passively involved in the Breton affairs, which become elemental in French history.

From this period our knowledge of Britanny, Obscurity of early Armorican history though still vague and imperfect, begins to emerge from obscurity. Armorican historical au-

851—877
864—874 thorities, in the proper sense of the term, exist only in hagiological narratives, and a few fragmentary monastic annals. Some information has been very recently gathered from ballads and legends preserved amongst the Breyzad peasantry; but the knowledge thus proffered cannot be accepted with much satisfaction or confidence. Oral traditions have been irretrievably denaturalized by the machine-manufactory of modern romantic literature. Copy-right spoils the native aroma of the popular tale; Border Minstrelsies and Waverley novels have soiled the lustre and quenched the spirit of national poesy and patrimonial story. Where charms and incantations are practised, it is said that a Spell never works if learned out of a book : the living tongue must address the living ear : the disciple's eye must meet the master's glance, and his hand be touched by the teacher's hand : the words of power are powerless, unless the embodied soul has communed with the embodied soul. Legendary lore becomes lifeless when laid on the drawing-room table. It is the sincerity of the narrator, the honest credence of credulity, which alone imparts worthiness to the narration. The æsthetic garb, the affectation of belief, the patronizing condescension of superior knowledge, the kind allowances made for superstition, or the philosophic sneer, are all equally stifling to tradition's true vitality.

The history of the Breyzad race must be ex- 851—877
tracted from the evidence of their opponents. 864—876
Grievous dissensions subsisted between the Frankish and Celtic clergy, Dôl, contesting the Primacy
with Tours, rival Metropolitans and rival Bishops
frowning upon each other with the jealousy of
Kings. More Christian charity might assuredly
have been displayed; yet such unhappy contests
were neither ambitious nor trivial. Upon jurisdiction depends discipline, and upon discipline
the welfare of the Church and her spiritual
prosperity. Angry excitement in such a cause
deserves excuse, though it be unsusceptible of
justification. The Armoricans wavered in their
antipathies : hard pressed occasionally by the
Franks, the Breyzads were sometimes inclined to
coalesce with the Danes. Their king, Solomon,
made peace with the Northmen, and helped them
to gather in the vintages of Anjou. But Charles-
le-Chauve and the Franks acted more vigorously
than heretofore. The Roman fortifications of
Le Mans, still so perfect, were energetically
defended—Tours equally so.—Hugh the Abbot
routed the Northmen. Charles-le-Chauve and
the Armorican Sovereign were conjoined, notwithstanding their enmities, by a common interest
and exposed to common dangers ; and the Bretons
concluded an alliance with the Franks. Maine,
afterwards the pride of the Norman Conqueror,
was fully recovered from the Danes through So-

851—877

848—1390

lomon's energy, Anjou, cleared of the enemy. In return, Charles sanctioned the royal title assumed by the Celtic monarch; and the Breton historians believe, or relate, how Solomon sent his golden statue to the Roman Pontiff, how he wore a golden crown and coined golden money.—No specimen of this mintage has however been recovered by the most diligent numismatic collector.

874
Solomon
killed by
Pasquitain
and Gur-
vand.

§ 40. Solomon had murdered Herispoë his kinsman: the crime was visited upon the criminal in similar guise. A cousin and a nephew, Pasquitain and Gurvand, conspired against him. As Herispoë had taken refuge in a Church, so did Solomon. He anticipated the Sanctuary's desecration by a voluntary surrender; but his victorious kinsmen caused him to be blinded. The king was cast into prison, where he lingered and died; and Breyzad recollections have canonized his memory.

Gurvand
and Pasqui-
tain died
874.

877—907
Alain-le-
Grand.

These successful chieftains shared Armorica. Mutual enmity was fostered by good fortune. Gurvand, sinking under a grievous malady, was borne to the battle-field in a litter: his troops gained the victory, but their royal general died of exhaustion. Pasquitain was murdered before the end of the same year. Alain, brother of Pasquitain, obtaining the supremacy of Armorica, recovered Nantes from the Northmen: his exploits earned for him the epithet of "the Great," "Alain-le-Grand." But the Danes returned again and again; and his daughter's son, Alain-barbe-torte, 851—877 no unworthy competitor of Guillaume-longue-épée, acknowledged the second Norman Duke as his lawful Suzerain.

912—1390
937—952
Alain-
barbe-
torte

§ 41. Considerable enlargement of dominion was obtained by Solomon:—he gained the March-lands, inhabited by a mixed population, much Romanized, especially in the cities, where the powers of government had been contested by or divided between the Carlovingian and Armorican Sovereigns. 912—1390
Territorial
organiza-
tion of Brit-
anny The
Counts of
Britanny,
Earls of
Richmond
in England. These territories were, during the reign of Charles-le-Chauve, unequivocally placed under Solomon's national authority, and permanently united to Britanny. Cession or force gave him also various districts in Maine and Anjou, and in future Normandy, the Avranchin, and the whole County of the Côtentin. Charles-le-Simple authorized Rollo to conquer these last-mentioned territories: Rollo would have done so without permission; and they became integral portions of his Duchy. Historical Britanny settled into four great counties, which also absorbed the Carlovingian march-lands, Rennes, Nantes, Vannes and Cornouailles, rivalling and jealousing, snarling and warring against each other for the royal or ducal dignity, until the supremacy was permanently established in Alan Fergant's line, the ally, the opponent, the son-in-law of William the Bastard. But the suzerainty or superiority of all Britanny was vested in the Conqueror's and the

851—877 Plantagenet's lineage, till the forfeiture incurred
840—870 by King John, an unjust exercise of justice.

Nevertheless the loss of Normandy did not
sever Britanny from England. Breton Dukes continued Earls and Peers of this realm : the royal
house of Dreux, the sons of France, rejoiced in this
1390 conjunction of honours; nor was the connexion
14 Rich. II. finally dissolved, until Richard of Bourdeaux's
Parliament inflicted a statutory deprivation upon
the valiant Jean de Montfort. Few historical
symbols are more suggestive than the single
shield over the Altar table of the Yorkshire
Richmond, the pane corroded and darkened by
the blast, the shower and the sunbeam, displaying
in obscurely-transparent tints the chequée of gold
and azure with the bordure of gules and the
canton ermine—the token of that union.

876, &c.
Transac-
tions in the
Loire
country

§ 42. Many important dispositions were
effected by Charles in the Loire country. It was
the policy of this unfairly depreciated Sovereign,
to recruit the failing ranks of the false and dege-
nerate Frankish aristocracy, by calling up to his
Peerage the wise, the able, the honest and the
bold of ignoble birth. It is a moot point to what
extent the aristocratic principle originally extended amongst the antient Franks; but Charles-
le-Chauve was very obviously inclined against the
exclusiveness claimed by the noble lineages. We
know that Louis-le-débonnaire incurred much
odium by equalizing gentle and simple through

the medium of the Church; and we believe that 851—877
Charles-le-Chauve attempted a similar levelling in ⸺
the civil hierarchy. The implacable opposition 840—888
raised against him, the slanders and vituperations
heaped upon him by the Chroniclers, most probably result from this cause. He sought to surround himself with new men, the men without
ancestry; and the earliest historian of the House
of Anjou both describes this system, and affords
the most splendid example of the theory adopted
by the king.

Pre-eminent amongst these parvenus was Origin of
the Planta-
Torquatus or Tortulfus, an Armorican peasant, a genets.
very rustic, a backwoodsman, who lived by hunting and such like occupations, almost in solitude,
cultivating his " quillets," his *cueillettes* of land,
and driving his own oxen, harnessed to his
plough.

Torquatus entered or was invited into the Torquatus
the Fo-
service of Charles-le-Chauve, and rose high in his rester.
Sovereign's confidence: a prudent, a bold, and a
good man. Charles appointed him Forester of
the forest called "the Blackbird's Nest," the *nid
du merle*, a pleasant name, not the less pleasant
for its familiarity. This happened during the
conflicts with the Northmen. Torquatus served
Charles strenuously in the wars, and obtained
great authority: another Cincinnatus, according
to the old-fashioned classical comparisons much
employed by the monkish Chroniclers.

851—877

870—877
Tertullus,
son of Tor-
quatus,
married
Petronilla,
daughter of
Hugh
l'Abbé.

Tertullus, son of Torquatus, inherited his father's energies, quick and acute, patient of fatigue, ambitious and aspiring; he became the liege-man of Charles; and his marriage with Petronilla the King's cousin, Count Hugh the Abbot's daughter, introduced him into the very circle of the royal family. Château-Landon and other Benefices in the Gastinois were acquired by him, possibly as the lady's dowry. Seneschal also was Tertullus of the same ample Gastinois territory.

870—888
Ingelger,
son of Ter-
tullus, the
first here-
ditary
Count of
Anjou.

Ingelger, son of Tertullus and Petronilla, appears as the first hereditary Count of Anjou Outre-Maine,—Marquis, Consul or Count of Anjou,—for all these titles are assigned to him. Yet the ploughman Torquatus must be reckoned as the primary Plantagenet : the rustic Torquatus founded that brilliant family, who, encreasing in dignity, influence, and power, afford a most remarkable exemplification of ancestorial talent, perpetuated from generation to generation. When the monk of Marmoutier dedicates his *Gesta Consulum Andegavensium* to king Henry, who ruled from the furthest border of Scotland to the Pyrennees, he invites his royal patron to exult in his plebeian progenitor's original humility. That such an appeal could be made to Henry Fitz-Empress, affords a noble proof of his intellectual grandeur.

§ 43. Thus arose one of the greatest *Grands-fiefs* of Capetian France. Chartres, afterwards united to Blois, was created by an analogous though not identical process: the builder was compelled to deal with such materials as he found, and Charles-le-Chauve sought to profit equally by the Northmens depression and by the removal of Robert-le-Fort. The occasional national apostasy of those Franks who conformed to the ethos, if not the religion, of the Northmen, enrolling themselves in the pirate ranks, was much more than compensated by the influence which the Romanized Franks and Gauls,—French men in fact,—exercised upon the invaders. Many of the Northmen were wearied of their piracy. The Romane tongue fascinated the Northmen: the comforts of France attracted them, religion subdued them. Their disposition was pliable, adaptable, cheerful, and though fierce, not inherently blood-thirsty. However dilapidated the old venerable Rœmerige might be, that effete Empire held a station in dignity and honour, higher beyond all compare than the more vigorous Jarldoms, Isles, and Kingdoms of the North. Rome perpetuated her monarchy by vanquishing her conquerors: the gift was not withdrawn from her.

A considerable portion of the Danes, consenting to be baptized, settled themselves in the land; and these converts, multiplying in the Northern parts of the Empire, and stigmatized as "pseudo-christians," were viewed with more anxiety than edification. Facts and presumptions support the

851—877

870—888
Pacific settlement of the Northmen encouraged by Charles-le-Chauve.

851—877
875—877
inference that they married with the French women,—they could scarcely find any others, for it was impossible that their vessels could bring over many female passengers. From the beginning, Rollo and his kinsmen always took consorts or companions from French families, or those Danish families who had received a thoroughly French education. Such alliances are evidences of the general usage; and the rapid extinction of the Norsk or Danish language, must be accepted as the consequence and cause of the intermixture of races, by which the Scandinavians were so speedily absorbed in the general mass of population. Hastings, otherwise Alstingus, obtained from Charles-le-Chauve the county of Chartres. He did not, however, remain there; for not having any children, and being otherwise troubled, he returned to Denmark, having sold

890

Gerlo, otherwise Thibaut, Count of Blois and Chartres, died about 918.

his Benefice to Gerlo, also called Thibaut, Rollo's kinsman, father of Thibaut the centenarian, Thibaut Count of Blois, who is moreover sometimes called " le Vieux," but whose conduct earned for him the more odiously characteristic epithets of " le Tricheur," or " le Fourbe," by which he is generally known in history; though his father, if we are to judge from the only anecdote preserved concerning him, deserved them quite as well.

875—876
Transactions in Italy. Assumption

§ 44. In Charlemagne's lineage gifts became snares, talents were unprofitable, noble tendencies refracted from their right direction, and

designs, laudable in the world's opinion, rendered
the means of worldly degradation and shame.
Charles-le-Chauve, sapient, energetic, his mind
strongly tending towards good, was involved
during his life in encreasing disappointment,
trouble and misery.

851—877

875—877
of the Im-
perial dig-
nity by
Charles-le-
Chauve

His ambition of renown and dominion, his
earnest seeking to imitate the prowess of Rome's
heroes, and to emulate the fame of that grandsire whose name he bore, could only be gratified
at the expence of his nearest relations. Indeed,
the Carlovingians were absorbed in a Serbonian
bog of destructive discords. All were correspondingly insatiate: their constant enmities, open
violences, secret treacheries, almost justified them
respectively in their mutual aggressions—each
might plead the necessity of self-defence—self-
defence, the most insidious temptation to self-
deceit; and thus Charles, in particular, disguised
to himself the odious features of the desires in
which he indulged.

We have seen how each death, each misfortune which befel his brethren or his nephews,
had been eagerly seized for profit; but now
there was presented to him the highest prize.
Louis the Emperor buried in Sant' Ambrogio,
the imperial dignity fell into abeyance—and to
whom now belonged the most exalted station in
Western Christendom?

Prospects
opened to
Charles by
the death of
the Em-
peror Louis
(Chap. II §
49,) p. 345.

Had the Carlovingian theory been fully developed, a Cæsar always installed in the lifetime of Augustus, there never would have been an interregnum. Had the yet maiden Hermengarda been married, the husband of the Emperor's daughter would unquestionably have been the presumptive successor; but the postulation made by the Lombard nobles sought to divide the realm between Louis-le-Germanique and Charles-le-Chauve, both being invited to share the Kingdom of Italy, the porch conducting to the Imperial throne. Louis-le-Germanique appeared by his sons, Charles, or Caroletto, and the bold Carloman. Charles-le-Chauve came in person: Charles Fitz-Louis was deluded by him, and Carloman induced to desert his father's and his own cause by his uncle's bribes.

Charles proceeded triumphantly to Rome, welcomed as Charlemagne's successor,—the successor of Augustus. Senate and people, the *Gens togata*, opening their itching palms, legitimate successors of a venerable name, not the less legitimate on account of their degeneracy, inheriting the baseness inseparably combined with their ancestorial and national glories, saluted him as Cæsar; and the Pontiff placed upon his brows the Imperial diadem. The venal city, tainted to the core, never even sought the concealment of her shame, patent, as of old, throughout the Roman world. Learned men extracted from Sallust the apt commentary upon the events of

their current day, scoffing at Charles as Jugurtha's 851—877
imitator: the Franks sneered; and the affronted and
yet envious Germans contemplated the transac- 875—877
tions with feigned disgust and unconcealed enmity.

The Lombard aristocracy had offered their _{Charles ac-cepted as}
kingdom to Louis-le-Germanique and Charles-le- _{Emperor by Lombardy}
Chauve conjointly. Berenger, his nephew, son of _{and the Gauls.}
his sister Gisella and the Friulian Count Eve-
rard, co-operating with Boso, induced prelates,
nobles, and people, to renounce the scheme of di-
midiated authorities and accept Charles, now the
Roman Emperor, without a partner on the throne.
A Diet was held at Pavia, unequalled for solemnity and splendour. Charles was invested with
the iron crown, whilst Boso, Richilda's brother,
the newly-created Duke of Lombardy or Milan,
sat below, wearing on his brows a golden coronal,
the proud insignia bestowed by the unsuspecting
bounty of his brother-in-law.

A third confirmation was needed. Charles-
le-Chauve returned to the Gauls, accompanied
by the Papal Legate : a synod assembled at Pontyon in Champagne—sometimes mistaken for the
more familiar Pont-sur-yonne. France, Burgundy
and Aquitaine, Neustria, Septimania and Provence, represented in the assembly by their
Bishops, and unanimously consenting, acknowledged the glorious Emperor "Carolus Augustus"
as their protector and defender. Charles, with
the title of Emperor, assumed the state apper-

851—877

876—877

taining to that transcendant dignity, the arched diadem, the eagle-crowned sceptre, the golden belt and purple buskins, the ample dalmatica, the habit of Imperial royalty, permitted only to an anointed Sovereign. Unquestionably such grave magnificence delighted his imagination; nor can we condemn the policy which induced him to adopt the pageantry proclaiming the authority legitimately his own; but his Frankish subjects in some degree, and the Germans even more, were inclined to take offence. Reports were spread that he threatened to depose his brother Louis.—"My armies shall drink up the Rhine,"—was the speech attributed to him,—"and we will cross as on dry land."

Wars between Charles-le-Chauve and Louis-le-German-ique's family. (See Chap. II. § 43, 47, 48, 50, pp. 371, 382, 385.)

§ 45. Louis-le-Germanique, the old man, never having resigned his precedence as *Senior* of the family, resented any pretensions which the Imperial dignity might inspire. The antipathy between the Germans and the French continued unmitigated. In Louis, personally, encreasing age enhanced the bitterness of animosity: his mild and benign disposition irretrievably perverted, strife was more grateful than peace, and he prepared to advance with his army against his brother, the step-mother's son whom he had hated from the day that the babe was born; but

28 Aug. 876 Death of Louis-le-Germa-nique.

he dropped into the grave before the commencement of hostilities.

Yet these demonstrations on the part of Louis

were not unnecessary. Charles had no feeling
whatever of good faith, he never pretended to
have any—the sentiment was unknown in the
Carlovingian breast. Events immediately testified that the plans of aggrandizement entertained
by him, were entitled to all the praise or all the
blame which a conqueror can expect or deserve.
The Emperor assembled a numerous army, the
Northmen not more apt or eager for plunder.
He claimed all German Lotharingia, and all the
other German dominions on the left bank of the
Rhine. The antient Frankish Sovereign fully
asserted the pretension, that France was entitled
to the free German stream as her natural boundary. Richilda, great with child, accompanying
him, he set out from Compiègne, intending to
receive the Lotharingian homages at Metz; and,
once in Lotharingia, he might be aided by Franco
Bishop of Tongres, who had assisted in his coronation, an able and most influential friend.

But unpleasant reports circulated: Danish
squadrons, heretofore well known on the English
coast, were disturbing the Empire; and Charles
directed his route to Cologne.

Court and army there received alarming but
not unexpected intelligence. On the Feast-day of
Saint Cornelius, the Northmen, after plundering
the Scheldt country, again entered the Seine.
They committed their usual mischiefs in Belgium,
carrying off prey and captives; and an hundred

831—877

876—877

16 Sept
876
The North-
men, com-
manded by
Rollo, enter
the Seine.

851—877 of their largest barks—"quas nostrates *bargas* vocant," says Archbishop Hincmar—filled the

876—877 Neustrian river. Their forces landed, and the country was desolated far and near and around. All the troops Charles could muster would not have been over many to match these invaders.— If during any period of the Danish wars his presence was needed to encourage and direct the soldiery, it was now, for the Danish commander was Rollo.

Sept — Oct. 876.

Louis occupies Andernach. Charles endeavours to circumvent him.

But Charles could not desist—reputation, desire, heart and soul, were engaged in the enterprize: he continued his hostile progress. Louis the Saxon (who had succeeded to his father) was alarmed at his uncle's approach, and, proposing terms, solicited grace and favour; nevertheless Louis the supplicant was undismayed, and crossing the Rhine during the night, he reached Andernach, whose fortifications still testify its pristine strength. Charles-le-Chauve planned to conquer his enemy by deceit. The Carlovingian princes were deadened to any consciousness of conscience, honesty or honour in political affairs, however good and worthy they might be in other social relations : not by any means a singular case, whether individually or in the "masses."—Has King, Prince of the Blood-royal, President of the Republic, or President du Conseil, Ministre d'état, Member of the Chamber, Legitimist, Doctrinaire or Red Republican, Partiprêtre or Socialist, ever suspected any injustice or cruelty in the captivity of Abdel-Kader, the hecatombs of Zaatcha, or the holocausts of Ouled-el-Dahra?

851—877
876—877

Burthened Richilda was sent to that antiently honoured Carlovingian palace, Heristal on the Meuse, under Bishop Franco's care. Charles entertained the offers made by Louis the Saxon, and sent envoys to him, ostensibly for the purpose of negotiating a truce, but really in order to throw him off his guard.

On the very day when the Emperor despatched these pacific negotiators, he was preparing to resume his march. At midnight the trumpets sounded, and the Imperial army was in motion, followed and accompanied by a vast train of suttlers, camp-attendants and baggage. The heavy, misty autumn rain came down in torrents, and continued pouring incessantly all through the night and the following day; the tracks, miscalled roads, were trampled into deep mire. In this condition the Imperial army drew nigh Andernach, when the intelligence of their advance was conveyed to King Louis. He and his army immediately sallied out, and charged the Imperialists. Dismayed, fatigued, wet through and through, the soldiers and their equipments were so drenched that their swords clung in the soaked scabbards, and the jaded horses stood stock-still when the spurs were struck into their

8 Oct 876.
The army of Charles-le-Chauve routed at Andernach.

851—877
876—877

steaming sides. They were thrown into irretriev-
able disorder : the rout was complete, and the
flight shameful. The fugitives blocked up the
ways. Some few escaped, saving their lives at
the expence of their reputation, but the majority
were taken prisoners. A knot of the principal
commanders, amongst them Gauzeline, Abbot of
Saint-Denis, and afterwards Bishop of Paris,
ineffectually endeavoured to conceal themselves
in the woods. They sustained the disgrace of
falling into the power of the peasantry, who
plundered their plunderers—arms, armour, garments, all became the Villein's prize. Counts,
Abbots. Bishops and Knights, were stripped stark
naked, so that for decency's sake they tried to
cover themselves with wisps of herbage or hay.

Richilda fled from Heristal, and, in the very
course of her most distressing journey, early in the
dawning, when the cocks were crowing, she was
delivered of her child. No sister-woman had the
labouring Empress to serve or aid her in her
hour of anguish : a groom carried the newborn
babe, afterwards baptized "Charles:"—the infant
lived till the following year, when its feeble life
was closed ; but the parents honoured the little
child's memory by causing its body to be interred at Saint-Denis. Charles-le-Chauve rejoined
Richilda at Attigny: had Louis the Saxon continued the war, the Emperor would have been
wholly lost.

§ 46. During these disastrous conflicts, the Empire's forces wasted, and the Sovereigns and their people consumed by exasperation, Rollo and his Northmen, uninterrupted or feebly opposed, were continuing their coast-devastations and occupying the Seine-country. Charles-le-Chauve, harassed, and declining in health, was compelled to temporize and adopt the expedients, which, under similar urgencies, had previously procured a transient respite. He despatched certain Magnates to treat with the invaders. Count Conrad is named as the head of this legation:— the consequent proceedings indicate that the well-trusted Franco, Bishop of Tongres, was also included in the embassy. They were empowered to conclude a pacification with the Northmen upon any terms — peace at any price; the result to be reported to the Sovereign and his legislature in the great Placitum summoned to be held at Samoucy — a royal residence near the rock of Laon.

851—877

876—877
876

Negotiations with the Northmen attempted by Charles-le-Chauve.

§ 47. We are now fairly confronted with ROLLO, and adopting the words or verse of the Norman Trouveur, we shall begin, and, in beginning, shorten the lengthened story.

Rollo, his history grounded upon family traditions, corrected by the Frankish Chroniclers.

A Rou sommes venu, et de Rou vous dirons
La commence l'istoire, que nous dire derons.
Mais pour l'œvre esploitier, li vers abrigerons ;
La voie est longue et grief, et li labour creignons.

851—877
876—877

The Northern Sagas concerning Rudo-Jarl, and Hrolf-ganger, however fondly we may once have listened to them, we here renounce:— no injustice will such rejection inflict upon the inventive talents of the Scalds, or upon Rollo's honour.

Three generations elapsed before any portion of Rollo's personal history was committed to writing in Normandy. The recollection of his deeds and exploits was vividly impressed upon the memory of his grandchildren and great grandchildren, through whom we learn them; but the details were rendered involuntarily inaccurate, equally by knowledge and by want of knowledge. It is a constant error in the conversational narrator, thoroughly imbued with his subject, to presuppose in his hearers the information which he himself possesses. The most truthful general reminiscences concerning an ancestor, are quite compatible with very defective perceptions, of the attendant circumstances,— times and places, friends or enemies.

Rollo's career was prolonged through the reigns of a first, a second and a third Charles— Charles-le-Chauve, Charles-le-Gras, and Charles-le-Simple. Five or six Counts Bernard and Counts Berenger flourished during the same era. Two prelates, each bearing the somewhat unfrequent name of Franco, were successively empowered or necessitated to treat with or for the Northmen.

Rollo's exploits in England connected him with an Anglo-Saxon Athelstan and a Danish Athelstan—that is to say Guthrun, King Alfred's foster-son, so called upon his baptism. Nor can we be surprized if the Pirates who landed upon the North-sea coast, failed to distinguish between a Regulus or a King actually domineering over Bernicia or East-Anglia, with whom they were immediately in relation, and the distant Basileus of Britain.

These circumstances involved the order of events, as detailed by Dudon de Saint-Quentin, the family historian, in a confusion which can only be rectified by comparison with the Frankish chroniclers. But their notices are scanty and grudging . the subject was unpleasant to them. If Archbishop Hincmar, whose annals (soon about to be cut short by the Northmen) furnish the basis of French history during this period, had heard of Rollo, he hated the odious name; and, to the last, amongst the Carlovingians, the Normans were only known as the Pirates. Necessity might compel the Frankish monarch to recognize the Northman as a Count or "Patrician;" but the Franks secretly protested against their own acts, and were always prepared to treat the same Northman as an intruding enemy. Nevertheless a tolerably satisfactory chronological adjustment of the main incidents, is not impracticable; for the unquestionable facts of French history

851—877

876—877

Dudon de Saint-Quentin Confusion of his family narrative.

L L 2

851—877 enable us to moor the floating traditions near the proper points of the shore.

876—877
Adventures
of Rollo,
previously
to his ap-
pearance in
France.
Rollo, the son of a Chieftain, a Norwegian Jarl may be, whose name, however, was forgotten in the family, and his brother Gorm, quarrelled with their King or "Over-king;" and, the younger brother being slain, the elder embarked as a Viking-chief for England—an ordinary and an accustomed voyage, yet it was reported that he had been directed thither by a dream. Much were the Northmen influenced by visions of the night. Rollo, it is said, sought the advice of some Christian priest, who counselled him to obey the warning. The English could only see an enemy in Rollo: sharp conflicts took place, but he was ultimately received into the *Grith* or peace of the English, who assisted him in refitting his vessels. The usual fortunes of the seas impelled or conducted Rollo to the Belgic coast. Walcheren was attacked by the young hero, about the period when the Lotharingian war between Charles-le-Chauve and Louis the Saxon was breaking out: an auspicious moment for the invaders. The coasts and ports of Belgium and France were now thoroughly familiar to the Dansker-men; and Rollo, following the career suggested to every Northman who chose to adopt the guidance of Osker and Lodbrok and Biorn and Sidroc and Godfrey, sailed up the oft-visited Seine. Rollo

stayed his fleet at Jumièges : humanity or inci- 851—877
pient devotion induced him to spare the dilapidated monastery, where remnants of the dispersed 876—877
flock had reassembled.   He landed hard by the
chapel of Saint-Vedast, and, entering the deserted
sanctuary, reverently deposited before the Altar
the relics of Saint-Himeltruda, removed from a
Belgian Shrine.

In the meanwhile Bishop Franco arrived at 16 Sept.
876
Rouen.   John the archbishop, first of this name Rollo sails
up the
in the ecclesiastical Fasti of the City, was away. Seine.
The fortifications had been dismantled, the sacred
edifices ruined; and the Archbishop's absence
denotes that the other influential personages
had equally abandoned their charge.   The impoverished and defenceless inhabitants were extremely alarmed, more particularly the traders,
the bargemen, whose small commerce was stopped by the hostile occupation of the river.   The
citizens determined to capitulate, and Bishop
Franco—whom the Northmen erroneously believed to be the local Prelate—consenting and
aiding, Rollo was invited to a peaceful occupation of Rouen, terra firma and islands.   He Rollo
lands at
stayed his vessel's course at the foot of the rock Rouen.
upon which he beheld the insular Church of
Saint-Martin, and according to tradition he there
anchored his bark.   The fertile country, devastated and thinly peopled, invited a new inhabit-
ancy : encouraging examples had previously been

851—877

876—877
Rollo occu-
pies Rouen
and the ad-
joining
country,
and de-
mands a
Danegeld.

afforded to the Northmen, Godfrey's followers were already quietly naturalized there, and Rollo may then have formed the plan of substituting permanent colonization for periodical plunder.— His Host, his Men, his "Baronage" ultimately took possession of the country, measuring and dividing their lots, according to the Danish custom, by the rope.—Bishop Franco negotiated, and a Danegeld of five thousand pounds was demanded by Rollo as the price of forbearance from hostilities.

876—877
Charles-le-
Chauve
submits to
the terms,
and pre-
pares to re-
sume ope-
rations in
Italy.

§ 48. Hard terms;—but Charles, intent upon the consolidation of his Imperial authority whilst he was losing his Kingdom, dared not resist Rollo. The intelligence of the treaty was conveyed to the Emperor-King at Samoucy, and he prepared to fulfil the conditions; nevertheless he despatched troops for the purpose of presenting a respectable front against the Northmen. Anxiety, labour, exertion, were wearing him out and destroying his constitution; and though only fifty-four years old, he was yielding to premature decay. Pleurisy attacked him : despairing of his life, the discouragement of mind encreased the danger. His favourite and trusty body-physician was the celebrated Zedechias the Jew, who had been so successful in his practice, that the beneficial results produced by Arabian science and the energetic medicaments which the East supplied, were represented by his competitors as the effect of magic—nay, that the apparent cures were only portentous delusions; but if the leech-craft of Zedechias failed, then Zedechias was a wilful murderer, his pharmacy was poison.

851—877
867—877

The royal patient did recover, and opportunely: exertion was called for, and his energies responded to the call. The Danegeld must be paid: the Saracens had resumed their invasions of Italy.

877.
April to June.

Salerno, Gaeta, Amalfi and Naples, after maintaining a treacherous neutrality, combined with the Moslems; and the presence of Charles was required at Rome, equally for the defence of Christendom's capital, and the ratification of his own imperial dignity. The clergy had not yet fully concurred in synod, neither had the beloved Richilda received the imperial Crown.

The Imperial authority recognized in the Gauls. Charles-le-Chauve proceeds to Italy

The Clergy and laity of "France" and of "Burgundy," thus distinguished in the acts and proceedings, were convened, separately and afterwards conjointly; and all ranks and orders bore their share in contributing the subsidy to Rollo. Two very important capitulars of manifold tenor were enacted at Kiersy. Various regulations are made for the purpose of protecting the tenant-right of the beneficiary or feudal vassals; amongst others the clause so often quoted,—and misunderstood almost as often as quoted,—for preventing the usurpation of an "honour" during the minority of the customary heir—the abuse by which Robert-le-Fort's children,

877
14 and 16 June.
The Capitulars of Kiersy.

851—877 Eudes and Robert, had been deprived of their
inheritance.—Charles appointed a Council of Re-

876—877 gency to assist Louis-le-Bégue in his govern-
Louis-le-
Bégue ap- ment.   The councillors are to take their turns in
pointed
Regent attendance : first amongst the Counts is named
Theodoric of Autun, the High Chamberlain of
the kingdom.   The Statutes were read and proclaimed to the people by Gauzelin, the learned
and warlike Abbot of Saint-Germain, the prisoner
of Andernach, who, upon his liberation, had been
appointed to the office of Chancellor.   These
urgent affairs completed, Charles-le-Chauve and
his Consort departed, accompanied by trains of
horses and mules laden with treasure.   Boso,
the duke of Lombardy, Hugh the Abbot, Bernard
Planta-Pilosa, or Plante-velue, Count of Auvergne,
and Bernard Marquis of Septimania, were to join
him with reinforcements.   The Roman synod had
been convened, their approbation given, and the
Pontiff met the Sovereign in the Lombard Palace
of Pavia —Was the maiden Hermengarda present,
she who had declared that she would not live
otherwise than as the spouse of a crowned King?

Defection   Unwelcome rumours disturbed the Court fes-
of the no-
bles. tivities. Charles-le-Chauve knew that he was surrounded by danger and treachery; therefore, quitting Pavia, the Imperial Court progressed home-
wards to Tortona, the scene of his mother's
humiliation The hurried and anxious ceremony
of Richilda's coronation was performed by the

Pope, but uneasiness increased. Charles sent the Empress across the Mont-Cenis with the treasure —nor was she thought in safety till, reaching Maurienne, she awaited the bursting storm.

851—877

876—877
Charles-le-
Chauve and
Richilda fly
from Italy.

Charles expected the aid of his brother-in-law the new duke of Lombardy, Hugh the Abbot, Bernard Plante-velue and Bernard Marquis of Septimania, but none came; each had his own selfish or separate concerns and plans, but all conjoined against Charles and his authority.— Hermengarda must answer for the absence of Boso.

The panic became intense—Carloman approached, heading a large army of dreaded Baioarians, and more dreaded Sclavonians. The Pope retreated to Rome, and Charles abandoned Italy, hastening after the loved and fugitive Richilda. Fever seized him, and he could not continue his journey beyond the foot of the Pass. The prescriptions of Zedechias availed no further, and the hand of death was upon him. He had not much need to take thought for the succession to the Empire. The brilliant Charles of Aquitaine was dead: the pious and affectionate Lothair was dead: the blinded Carloman was dead: all his children by Richilda, Pepin, and Drogo, and the second Louis, and the poor hunted babe Charles, were dead:—none left except Louis-le-Bègue. He therefore delivered to Richilda the Writ empowering her step-son to take possession of the king-

851—877
876—877
6 Oct. 877.
Death of
Charles-le
Chauve.

dom, together with the time-honoured symbols of sovereignty, sceptre, robe and royal crown, and the sword of state, known by the name of Saint Peter's sword; and he expired, Richilda by his bedside, in a wretched hovel. They would have borne his corpse to France, but the loathsome decay which ensued prevented the removal of his remains, and seven years elapsed ere his bones were deposited at Saint-Denis.

CHAPTER IV.

862—888.

§ 1. IT is anything rather than a vulgar
error or a fondness for paradox to trace great
events from causes, which, in common parlance
we denominate "small"—"small," merely because
the human intellect is utterly incompetent to
grasp the truth, that all secondary or occasional
causes are equally essential in the series decreed
by Eternal Providence. If any one appear greater
than another to our imperfect sight, this comparative difference in magnitude is only a decep-
tion, occasioned by the larger visual angle which
they subtend in consequence of our position upon
this sublunary sphere. When the Lights were
set in the firmament of the heavens to divide the
light from the darkness, then and thenceforth
each future beat of the second became as necessary to complete our time-reckoned centuries as
the minute, the hour, the day, the month and the
year : not one could be wanting. The relations
of the events composing man's universal destiny,
have, by the Eternal Will, been rendered as un-
alterable as the laws of numbers, each and all
compose the immutable aggregate. Collective
humanity is governed through the laws imposed

862—888

862—919
Great
events pro-
duced by
small
causes

862—888 upon individual humanity; you can no more ima-
862—919 gine away any one pulsation of your heart, or
any one thought you have entertained, or any one
feeling you have felt, or any one thing during
the whole course of your life, within memory, or
beyond memory, in which you have been active
or passive, than you can fancy that two and two
minus one make four.

No leaf could have developed but from its
specific spray, no spray could have been propelled
but from its specific branch, no branch could have
ramified but from its specific stem. Nor could
the stem have attained its organic growth except
upon the specific spot where the seed-fruit was
cast—planted on the soil where the root could
strike and the waters nourish—where the tender
germ breaking through the ground should be
defended from harm, the canker-worm curl
away, and the cattle forbear to browse, the
treading foot of man be averted and his hand
restrained, where the wind should not wither,
and the sun should shine.—From the day when
the earth brought forth the tree yielding fruit,
not a single tree upon the face of that earth could
have been according to his kind, or yielded fruit
according to his kind, otherwise than through
the concurrence of the appointed conditions, physical, vital, and spiritual, all immutably necessary
—numbers without number.

One unerring Justice, unbounded Love, and infinite Wisdom pervades all worlds, material and

spiritual. Had not each and every one of your ancestors, from the first created out of the dust of the earth, been conceived and born, breathing, living, and dying, as they were conceived and born, and breathed and lived and died, your present existence, as you now exist, would have been impossible. All the co-operating destinies of all your parents have produced yours, they have entered into your flesh and blood, they were chosen for you : you cannot repudiate any one of them : all have made you what you are—their haps and their hazards, their healths and diseases, their virtues and vices, their rewards and inflictions, their weal and their woe. The rock is a combination of atoms, and human society's whole contexture results from individual fate, individual responsibility, individual obedience, individual disobedience, individual necessity, and individual free will.——

862—888
862—919

MARRIAGE opens many chapters in the world's history. As in the most humble families, so in the most exalted, as in the families of the hearth, so in the families of nations—the Novel's catastrophe is the commencement of the reality. The world's government is carried on through human passions and affections. Science cannot analyze nor philosophy reach them in their commencement, manifest as they become in their course, and potent in their close.

Political consequences of Marriage.

That "Love is Lord of all" must be received

862—888
862—919
as an aphorism not the less incontrovertible on account of the phrase's poetical inanity. The most important political changes and revolutions have resulted from marriage—or what ought to have been marriage—the bond, its neglect, or violation. When the rights or traditions of royalty are deduced through the *spindleside*, marriages accomplish the most radical of revolutions: that is to say, the introduction of a dynasty subjecting the nation to a new Sovereign-line. The people are then conquered by the marriage-ring—often happily; nevertheless they are conquered. The fortunes of the State are included in the nativity of the State's Founder, and in the nativities of all his ancestors. the fall of the Empire is determined by the Conqueror's horoscope, and the horoscopes of all his progenitors. Let alone Rowena's wassail-cup, fair Helen and the siege of Troy town — Arletta's pretty feet twinkling in the brook made her the mother of William the Bastard. Employing astrological dialect, the planetary aspects ruling Hubert the tanner's natal hour, designated him to be the grandsire of a King. But for the tanner of Falaise, Arletta's father, Harold would not have fallen at Hastings, no Anglo-Norman dynasty could have arisen, no British Empire.—

Charles-le-Chauve attempted a deep, but unsuccessful policy. Generally, the Carlovingian princes selected their consorts under the influence

of fancy or affection, seeking to please the eye 862—888
or the heart, without reference to the collateral
advantages resulting from family alliances : Louis- 862—919
le-Débonnaire chose Judith, like a Sultan throwing down his handkerchief before an Odalisk.
Had more provident caution been exercised, we
should not find so many Queens and Empresses
whose lineage remained unknown till the latter
days, when heraldic decorum suggested the expe-
diency of providing them with fitting ancestry.
Charles-le-Chauve, sensitively alive to the advantages attainable through matrimonial policy, made
it his design to aggrandize his family by marriages of state ; but it was his destiny to have those
designs crossed by marriages of inclination.   Indeed, he set but an indifferent example of prudence ; for his scandalous second marriage accelerated the great calamities of his reign.   Louis-
le-Bégue disappointed him : Charles of Aquitaine
disappointed him ; but with his daughter, "Madame Judith,"—we take a pleasure in calling her
as we find her denominated by the worthy Pieter
Van Oudegherst, the Lieutenant-bailli of Tournay, in whose history her adventures are most
amusingly, if not most veraciously told—there
appeared every prospect of success.

Ever since Charlemagne's days a respectful,
friendly, and not unfrequent intercourse had subsisted between the Western Emperor and the
Basileus of Britain. Charlemagne addressed Offa

862—888
862—919

856.
Judith,
daughter of
Charles-le-
Chauve,
married to
King Eth-
elwulf.

upon equal terms Britain gave the Gauls the great teacher Alcuin; and, notwithstanding the devastations of the Northmen, their common enemy, England still excelled in opulence, and retained a most distinguished station in the Western Commonwealth. An alliance between England and France might enable both countries to resist the Danes; and the opportunity arose for cementing such a union. Ethelwulf, journeying with his son, the child Alfred, from Rome, was splendidly received by Charles-le-Chauve at his palace of Verberie. A royal visit thus paid, presupposes a royal invitation; and, for a purpose. Betrothed in July, the grey-headed Ethelwulf and the precocious Judith, then perhaps fourteen years of age, were married in October. Archbishop Hincmar pronounced the benediction, not entirely identical with the modern Roman usage; and this antient ritual, some portions whereof may be heard in our Liturgy, possesses singular dignity and impressive solemnity. Moreover, Judith was crowned as Queen, gifts and guerdons were bestowed with unsparing kindness; and Ethelwulf and his bride repaired to England.

858.
Judith
after the
death of
Ethelwulf,
marries her
step-son
Ethelbald.

The nuptial rejoicings speedily shaded into discomfort, unhappiness and sin. Judith is the Frenchwoman concerning whom our Anglo-Saxon chroniclers speak so sullenly and despitefully. Ethelwulf, in order to make way for her, had repudiated Osburga, Alfred's mother. Judith's

coronation affronted the English. Queen Ed- _{862—888}
burga's crimes had brought the dignity of Queen
into disrepute: no consort of an English Sove- _{862—863}
reign had subsequently assumed that title, or sat
as Queen by her husband's side. Judith's conduct confirmed the antipathies entertained against
her. After Ethelwulf's death, she contracted an
incestuous and disgusting marriage, espousing
Ethelbald, her step-son;—an action contemplated
by the English with unmitigated aversion and
horror.—Instructive warnings against national
prejudices are afforded by the calumnies of the
French chronicler, who assumes that the mis-
deed which the English nation universally detested was quite indifferent to them, and quotes
their apathy as a proof of England's spiritual
darkness and moral contamination. Ethelbald's
inglorious reign being speedily terminated by his
death, Judith sold her English possessions, and
returned to her father.

Previously to her marriage with Ethelwulf,
Judith had been courted by Baudouin Bras-de-fer,
or *Boudewyn-den-Yzeren*, one of her father's   ₈₆₂
foresters:—strenuous, as his name imports, fair, _{After Eth-elbald's}
well-favoured in countenance, pleasant in speech, _{death, Ju-dith re-}
prudent and wise. That such a tender, though _{turns to France}
twice-married, widow would be easily accessible
to a third admirer might be anticipated; and
Charles-le-Chauve was prepared to give her away
again, but in due time, and when a fitting suitor

862—883
862—863

should offer. Judith was therefore entrusted to Bishop Erpuin, at Senlis, that pleasant and healthy abode, the royal nursery, where the kings of France were accustomed to send their children : some Romane arches of their palace, inclosing a wild fragrant garden, were standing a few years ago.

Widows were peculiarly protected against violence, actual or constructive, rude force or gentle persuasion, by Saint Gregory's canon,—" *Si quis viduam in uxorem furatus fuerit, ipse et consentientes ei. anathema sint.*"—It was a Crown prerogative amongst the Franks that no female of the royal family could marry without her parents' assent ; and Judith was to remain under the *Mundbyrd* or wardship of Church and State, till she should either resign herself to widowhood, or relieve her guardians by the imposition of their anxiety upon a third husband. We have seen how Charles-le-Chauve, when called away to oppose the Danes, delegated his authority to Louis-le-Bégue as Regent. The brother made common cause with his sister, and becoming, according to the plain-spoken Archbishop Hincmar, the go-between, she eloped in disguise with her first love, the Forester.

862
Judith elopes from Senlis with Baldwin the Forester.

And who was this Baldwin the Forester?— Toison d'or, King-at-arms, would read out Baldwin's history most currently from the shields in the choir of Bruges, or the canopied imagery decking the delicately-traceried Town-hall. The

Legendary history of the Foresters of Flanders.

founder of the family, as many said, was Lyderic 862—877
of Harlebec in Charles Martel's reign ; and this
Lyderic, marrying the Princess Flandrina, became 862—863
Lord of the Country, in whose geographical denomination she has been commemorated. The
Dean of Saint Donat's might perhaps demur, and
maintain that Flanders was so called from Flanbertus, expelled with his brother Flaminius from
Beauvais by Andromedes king of the Belgians,
which same Flanbertus and Flaminius, afterwards
founding the once splendid city of Bailleul, established the new colony; the names of the founders
being perpetually commemorated in the appellations of the country and the people.   Flanders
took her name from *Flanbertus ;* and from *Flaminius* were the Flemings called.

Some, however, were rather inclined to be- Prince Lyderic and
lieve that the real progenitor of this truly illus- the Princess Er-
trious family was another Prince Lyderic, who mengarda.
flourished in King Dagobert's days. His father
was the noble Salvaert, a Burgundian prince, who,
married to the Princess Ermengarda, daughter of Gerard de Roussillon, and fleeing from
the Franks, took refuge in the forest of Harlebec
near Lisle, very unfortunately, for there they fell
into the power of a most ill-conditioned tyrant,
the gigantic Phinaert, who murdered Prince Salvaert and drove the Princess into the forest, where,
according to custom, she was delivered of her
child Lyderic, so called from the good anchorite

862—888 who became his godfather. Lyderic, coming to
862—863 man's estate, after many adventures—including a voyage to England, where he married the Princess Gratiana—released his mother from captivity, and was installed in the dignity and honour of first Count-Forester.

Historians, who are contented to leave the earlier traditions of Flemish history undetailed, insert Baldwin in their genealogies as the son of Count Odoacre, son of Count Ingelram, both hereditary Counts-Foresters, whose epitaphs were to be seen in the last century cut on stone at Bruges. An Ingelram, the *Missus*, the Justice in Eyre of Charles-le-Chauve, had certainly authority over some of the Districts constituting Flanders. Making, however, every allowance for archaeological uncertainties, it is impossible to find a place in history for Baldwin's assumed father. They sculptured his effigy on the façade of Bruges' Stadthuys, but cotemporary chronicles and unaccommodating charters leave no room for him. Hence erudite and honest Vredius, chief amongst the critical genealogists of Flanders, has converted "Odoacre" into a word of command— "*Houd-u-wacker*"—*Hold thyself stoutly* — the admonition which, as he conjectures, either Ingelram or Baldwin, or both or either of them, would diligently address to the soldiery employed in guarding their shores.

Historical pyrrhonism may become more detri-

Ingelram and Odoacre, ancestors ascribed to Baldwin.

mental to historical truth than historical credulity. 802—883
We may reject and reject till we attenuate history
into sapless meagreness,—like the king of France, 862—863
who, refusing all food lest he should be poisoned,
brought himself to death's door by starvation.

In the present instance, however, we are relieved from the difficulties which often embarrass
such enquiries. The fanciful tales we have
noticed are palpably recent, not older than the
thirteenth century, if so old: they must be
ascribed to the *Menestrels* who flourished during
the golden age of romance poetry. The Walloon
Trouveurs were excellently fluent and skilful:
French poetry, the poetry of the Langue d'oil,
was nurtured in the Border Provinces of France;
and the successors of Rollo and of Baudouin fostered the talent, which, in maturer growth, illustrated the Romane tongue. Some *Chanson-de
Geste*, perhaps still to be recovered amongst the
piles of manuscripts, the treasured yet neglected
stores constituting the pride and the lumber of
museums and public libraries, may reveal the
primary source of the adventures narrated by
the standard historian denominated the Flemish
Livy.—Yet these legends, though unquestionably
fictitious, are very convincing, when contrasted
with more genuine evidence, in bringing out the
truth. All the antient and authentic chroniclers
now extant maintain an unbroken silence as
to Baudouin's ancestry. They do not pretend to
discover his father.—Baudouin Bras-de-fer was

862—888
862—863
another Robert-le-Fort, a *novus homo*, a man without ancestors, triumphing by talent, prowess and energy.

Under ordinary circumstances, Baudouin was calculated to deserve the utmost encouragement from Charles-le-Chauve, even as he protected and exalted Torquatus the Forester, promoting him out of the Blackbird's nest to dignity and honour; but Baudouin thwarted the Royal Father's will, and Charles-le-Chauve was exceedingly Resentment of Charles-le-Chauve. offended by the Forester's presumption. Charles fiercely resented this domestic rebellion. Parental authority, Papal decrees, royal prerogative, the laws of Church and State and his own plans and inclinations, were all equally infringed and opposed. He summoned a council at Soissons, declared to his prelates and nobles how his daughter had absconded with an adulterer and a thief; and Baudouin was outlawed. Furthermore, convening an ecclesiastical council, Saint Gregory's Canon *Si quis furatus fuerit*, and so forth, being duly propounded, excommunication was fulminated against the ravisher and the consenting Judith: King Lothair was urged to concur in the proceedings. Lastly, in a great council or Placitum held at Pistres on the Seine, the civil and ecclesiastical sentences were confirmed, and the lieges generally enjoined against affording any harbour, countenance, or support to the delinquents.

Charles-le-Chauve's anger was more natural

than wise. Could Judith have been recovered
from Baudouin, she would have left her character
behind her: there would have been no help but
to confine the wanton in a monastery. If she
continued with the Forester, he, provoked by the
father's conduct, had it in his power to become
a very dangerous enemy. The forests of Flanders
extended over Lotharingian ground : the coasts
were open to the Northmen; and there soon
became reason to apprehend that he might make
common cause with the enemy. But Baudouin
though venturesome, was neither obdurate nor
perverse. He and Judith sought the mediation
of the Holy See. Pope Nicholas interceded
earnestly both with Charles-le-Chauve and Hermentruda. To the king, he pointed out the
political dangers which might ensue, were reconciliation refused; his appeal to the mother's
affection was grounded upon the contrition of
the delinquents. Baudouin and Judith repaired
to Charles-le-Chauve at Soissons. They were
restored to favour, and by his consent they were
married at Auxerre; yet he emphatically testified
his opinion of their conduct by refusing to be
present at the nuptials.

Flanders hitherto had no political existence.
Previously to Baudouin's era, Flanders or "Flan-
.dria" is a designation belonging, as learned men
conjecture, to a Gau or Pagus, afterwards known
as the *Franc de Bruges*, and noticed only in a

862—888
862—863

863
Oct
Baldwin
and Judith
married
after their
elopement.

Antient
state of the
territory of
Flanders.

862—888 single charter. Popularly, the name of Flanders
had obtained with respect to a much larger sur-
862—863 rounding Belgic country, an extensive district,
whose boundaries were indicated by natural or
peculiar characters, rather than constituted by
precise demarcations : other examples occur of
this habitual and intelligible though somewhat
indeterminate chorography—Take for instance,
Le Bocage in France, or the *Weald, High-Suffolk*,
Flanders, a or the *Fen Country* in England. The name of
forest and
marsh- "Flanders" was thus given to the wide, and in a
country
degree indefinite tract, of which the Forester Baudouin and his predecessors had the official range
or care. According to the idiom of the Middle
Ages, the term "Forest" did not exactly convey
the idea which the word now suggests, not being
applied exclusively to wood-land, but to any wild
and unreclaimed region ; and Flanders, though
containing fine and noble wood-lands, also included vast extents of moors and downs and
plashes and marshes, bordered by the Ocean on
the North and by the Ardennes on the South, ⸕
of which large portions remained uncleared.

Excellent commencements had however been
made. Saint Audomerus, Saint Amandus, Saint
Bavon, and their companions and disciples, guided
and directed those agricultural colonists, who,
labouring in the service of their Divine Master,
and converting the sentence of toil into a perennial blessing, gave the first impulse to that

industry which has rendered the Netherlands the
Garden of the North.   But the inhabitants always
needed to struggle against the waters; and any
etymology of the name of Flamingia, or Flanders,
which we can guess at, seems intended to designate that the land was so called from being half-
drowned.   Thirty-five inundations, which afflicted
the country at various intervals from the tenth
to the sixteenth century, have entirely altered
the coast-line; and the interior features of the
country, though less affected, have been much
changed by the diversions which the river-courses
have sustained: fertile pastures on the sea-bord
severed and channelled into islands, islands worn
into sand-banks, and the sand-banks ultimately
submerged by the invincible element.

These physical catastrophes produced remarkable political and moral consequences in other
countries not touched by the waves.   Numbers
of the sturdy natives emigrated, seeking new
homes, working their way and fighting their
way.   Some were driven back into Germany,
others forward into the British islands.   They
principally sought or were invited into the territories of the Celtic races, whom they consumed.
Scotland, Wales and Ireland bear testimony to
the Flemish energy.   The plough, speeded by
mammon, may become an engine of human destruction, desolating as the sword.

Whatever had been the original amplitude of

862—888
862—863

Inunda-
tions of
Flanders,
and their
conse-
quences.

877—888 the districts over which Baudouin had any controul or authority, the boundaries were now
862
Flanders
granted to enlarged and defined. Kneeling before Charles-
le-Chauve, placing his hands between the hands
Baudouin
as an here- of the Sovereign, he received his "honour:"—
ditary
County or the Forester of Flanders was created Count or
Marqui-
sate. Marquis. All the countries between the Scheldt,
the Somme and the sea, became his Benefice;
so that only a narrow and contested tract divided
Baudouin's Flanders from Normandy. According
to an antient nomenclature, ten Counties, to wit,
Theerenburch, Arras, Boulogne, Guisnes, Saint-
Paul, Hesdin, Blandemont, Bruges, Harlebec and
Tournay, were comprehended in the noble grant
which Baudouin obtained from his father-in-law.
The development of Flanders and her feudal
dependencies is an integral portion of European
history, requiring the labours of those competent
to perform the neglected task.

Children of   Baudouin and Judith's first child was named
Baudouin
and Judith. Charles; but the infant died.   Judith sorrowed
Charles
died an in- much at his death, which she attributed to the
fant.
want of mother's milk; and she therefore determined herself to give suck to the next babe,
named Baudouin after his father.   The Licu-
tenant-bailli of Tournay expatiates upon the
maternal conduct of "Madame Judith," a reproach to the matronly luxury and self-indulg-
ence of his times.
877—919
Baudouin-   Baudouin the Second's manly vigour did
le-Chauve

credit to his mother's tenderness. When he 877—888
grew up to man's estate, he assumed the epithet
of *le-Chauve*, in honour of his Imperial Grand- 877—919
father, though his locks were abundant as those
adorning any Merovingian King. Judith's first
two husbands had in a manner connected Flanders with England. Baudouin-le-Chauve renew- ʻ
ed the connexion more creditably, by marrying
Elfreda or Elftruda, king Alfred's daughter.

Baudouin Bras-de-fer, once settled in his
dominion, almost disappears from notice. His
renown may have scared the Northman—at
all events, so long as he lived, no important
invasions of his honours or territories are recorded. Subsequently to his marriage hardly
anything is commemorated concerning him, except useful works and good works, towns and
fortresses improved, monasteries endowed, charity
abundantly bestowed. In the centre of Ghent
we may yet see the dark battered towers surrounding the *'Sgravesteen* or *Petra Comitis*, the
castellated palace of Baudouin-Bras-de-fer: the
Second Baudouin added the fortifications which
defended the birthplace of Charles-Quint.

The eldest son and successor of Baudouin-le- Arnoul-le-Vieux, son of Baudouin-le-Chauve.
Chauve was Arnoul, who obtained the epithet of
le-Vieux. Fourth in descent from this Arnoul
was Baudouin-de-Lisle, father of the Conqueror's
faithful and affectionate Matilda. All these matters are of great interest to us: Normandy scarcely

877—888
862—888

proved more influential in the formation of the Anglo-Norman Commonwealth than Flanders, encreasing in prosperity rapidly yet steadily.

Feudal relations of Flanders.

The Count of Flanders took his seat as one of the twelve Peers—the Duke of Normandy premier amongst the Dukes, the Count of Flanders premier amongst the Counts, rejoicing in the honour of bearing the sword before the king. Yet the Count or Marquis of Flanders was only imperfectly dependent upon the French Suzerain. In respect of Ghent, and the very important *Ambachten* and other districts known as *Rijks-Vlaenderen,* the Count was a Prince of the Holy Roman Empire. Baudouin's Castle of Ghent was built on Imperial ground. The feudal relations between the Count of Flanders and France were scarcely more than parchment-texts, efficient enough when the sword's point could engross the commentary, but very inert otherwise. Like the Normandy-Duke, he litigated the question whether his homage should be homage simple, or homage liege. Sometimes he assisted the Capets with his contingent for forty days, and sometimes refused his contingent, and approached so nearly to the condition of an independent Sovereign, that, according to the opinion of Flemish Jurists, Flanders might be truly styled a Monarchy.

877—888

§ 2. Louis-le-Bégue was placed by his father's death under circumstances of peculiar

difficulty: Baudouin Bras-de-fer, from whom he 877—888
had good reason to expect support, gave him no
assistance, and remained aloof, perhaps impeded 877—879
877
by bodily infirmity, pending the short but very July—Dec.
important contest which ensued. The maxim— Transac-
tions upon
the acces-
le mort saisit le vif,—the King never dies, was sion of
Louis-le-
not then accepted as embodying an incontro- Bégue
vertible dogma ; on the contrary, we doubt if
the doctrine was recognized theoretically in any
European Kingdom before the sixteenth century:
the royal dignity was in abeyance unless a successor was or had been constitutionally acknowledged Consequently, during two months after
the death of Charles-le-Chauve, France was without a King, although Louis-le-Bégue endeavoured
to exercise the royal prerogative, granting Abbeys
and Counties, or assuming that he could make
such grants: scarcely benefitting those whom he
favoured, and encreasing the number of his ill-
wishers and opponents

Richilda, with a step-mother's enmity, was Party op-
posed to
much averse to his succession; and through and Louis-le-
Bégue.
with her, a very powerful party was organized
against Louis-le-Bégue It will be recollected
that none of the nobles, whose aid Charles had
expected when in Italy, came to him according to
their promise. Boso, ambitious, acute and enter- Boso mar-
ried to
prizing, was maturing important designs. About Hermen-
garda,
this time, or perhaps somewhat sooner, Hermen- daughter of
the Empe-
garda, the Maiden, the daughter of the Emperor ror Louis
(p 376).

877—888
877—879 Louis, eloped with him, and became his consort. Boso, according to common fame, had poisoned his wife Engeltruda, in order to make room in his bed for this Princess; but whether he did or did not commit the crime,—whether he carried off Hermengarda, or whether she consented, or whether the future King of Italy, Berengarius, helped the lovers, as Louis-le-Bégue had done, are matters about which historians are at variance. Engeltruda was a woman of bad character. True or false, the facts and the rumours exemplify the popular and prevailing standard of morality.

Clergy and Nobility, intriguers and soundly-minded being equally unanimous in this respect, determined that Louis should not ascend the throne with the power which his father had enjoyed. It was their intention to demand a reform of the real or supposed abuses prevailing under the preceding reign.

877
30 Nov.
Royal in-
signia, &c,
delivered
by Richilda
to Louis-le-
Bégue On Saint Andrew's Day, Richilda, repairing to Compiègne, reluctantly delivered to Louis the testamentary writ, whereby Charles-le-Chauve had designated him as his successor, together with the tokens of authority, purple robe and arched crown, Saint Peter's sword and the rod of justice, shining with gems and gold. But these were put aside: the Frankish clergy and nobles paid no attention to seal and monogram or royal insignia, hallowed though they might be by the associations of antiquity: they em-

phatically ignored the existence of hereditary right; and Louis-le-Bégue came in as a constitutional, we may almost say as a revolutionary king. Hincmar, another Hubert, conducted the transaction. The Bishops, representatives of the people, interrogated Louis whether he would observe law and justice. Upon his assent, homage was performed . the homagers professed fealty and allegiance to their Senior and King, "Louis, son of Charles and Hermentruda;" and the son of Charles and Hermentruda then signed and subscribed with his own hand the declaration confessing himself King by the choice of the people,—"Ego Ludovicus misericordiâ Domini Dei nostri et electione populi Rex constitutus,"—promising to preserve those national franchises and privileges which, in the phraseology of the times, so misinterpreted by modern ideas, were called the rights of the Church; and to govern by the common council of the lieges the people committed to his care. The engagement thus ratified, Hincmar completed the ceremonies of coronation and consecration. Let it be observed how carefully and specifically hereditary right is denied; for though the *Seigneur-Roi* is denominated the son of Charles and Hermentruda, yet this description amounts to nothing more than a personal designation. Acting under the same impression and with the same intent, Napoleon's Senate,

877—888

877—879

Louis-le-Bégue receives the homages, and subscribes the Declaration.

·

6 Dec.
Louis-le-Bégue crowned.

877—888
877—879
when they recalled the Bourbon, as carefully endeavoured to protect themselves against the acknowledgment of any hereditary or inchoate title, by drily accepting "Louis-Stanislaus-Xavier." With equal carefulness " Louis-Stanislaus-Xavier" strove to rebut the inference by reckoning on from his predecessors, and taking the style of Louis-Dixhuit.

Louis-le-
Bégue un-
fairly dis-
paraged

All this was but mournful vanity. A Celtic Seer would have beheld Louis-le-Bégue ascending the throne, arrayed for his funeral, the winding-sheet's white folds wrapping themselves around him: he was afflicted with an incurable disease. After Louis-le-Bégue's death, when it served people's interest to disparage his memory, they called him *le Fainéant—Nihil faciens—qui nihil fecit*—but he had no time to do anything; and during his short reign, his earnestly-intended exertions were clogged by his subjects' coldness and traversed by adverse destiny. The Northmen were ravaging the Seine-country to such an extent, that stout Hugh the Abbot requested aid. Emeno, a Count in Poitou, rebelled: so also Gosfried, son of Roric Count of Maine. Louis-le-Bégue marched immediately to the troubled country; but at Tours he became so ill that he could not advance any further. His life was despaired of; but having unexpectedly rallied, he negotiated with the Bretons and obtained their homages; and upon his invitation the Pope—Pope John—

crossed the Alps, and after holding a Council at 862—888
Troyes, bestowed upon him, for the second time,
the royal crown. 877—878

This transaction affords much matter for 878.
consideration. Some suppose that the coro- Louis
nation was an Imperial coronation. Others, that again by
the new King sought to establish an absolute VIII
authority; but a more obvious explanation can be
suggested. Very serious doubts existed, whether
the marriage of Louis with Judith the Adeliza
could be a lawful marriage. She was a veiled
recluse whom he carried off from the Royal
Monastery of Cala, or Chelles on the Marne.
Founded by Clotilda, this Convent acquired great
celebrity, as a normal school and general educational establishment for damsels of Royal blood,—
a female College. Here the Anglo-Saxon kings
were accustomed to send their daughters. Saint
Milburga, Abbess of Wenlock, daughter of the
Mercian Merwald, was trained at Cala.—Charles-
le-Chauve not only sanctioned but instigated this
irregular or even scandalous matrimony, and
possibly the Adeliza was (as her title imports)
recommended by her relationship to some influential Royal Family. If the Adeliza had taken
the claustral vows, her nuptial vow was null :
Ansgarda, first espoused by Louis-le-Bégue and
the mother of his sons Louis and Carloman, was
also still living. We are most imperfectly informed concerning these marriages : according

862—888
877—878
to a widely-spread impression, either might be considered void, and Louis sustained the humiliating mortification of ascertaining, that such was the Supreme Pontiff's opinion with respect to the Adeliza.

Pope John refused to recognize the fair fugitive of Chelles, pupil, novice or nun, as the wife of Louis-le-Bégue. Thrice betrothed, Louis-le-Bégue, according to the average of opinions, never had a lawful consort; and consequently, upon the same average, never any legitimate progeny.

Four Sovereigns ruling in the Carlovingian empire

(See p. 337).

§ 3.   An ill-combined and unharmonious Tetrarchy ruled the Carlovingian Empire.   Three Sovereigns, descended from the Emperor Lothair, by Louis-le-Germanique, represented the German or Senior line.   Carloman, Louis-le-Germanique's eldest son, held the Baioarian and Sclavonian States, King also of Italy.   Louis the Saxon, the second son, retained the best parts of Northern Germany, Saxony, including the red land of Westphalia, Franconia, Friezeland and much of Lotharingia.   Charles, or Caroletto, "Charles-le-Gras" in popular history, the third son, was restricted to a dotation or apanage in Suabia, but aspiring to more extensive authority, and qualified to win, if not to retain, exalted power.—Louis-le-Bégue represented the French or Junior line.

These were the possessors of thrones, but who were to reign when thrones should become vacant ?   Pepin King of Italy's descendants, the now prosperous house of Lombardy-Vermandois, had tacitly waived their legitimate pretensions. When any one of the four regnant Sovereigns should die, the Seniors or Senior, the survivors and survivor might contend for the inheritance; but, looking beyond Carloman of Baioaria, Louis the Saxon, Charles of Suabia, and Louis-le-Bégue, to whom did the reversion appertain? 862—888
877—878

This was the perplexity clouding the mind of every thoughtful man:—although there might be many claimants, yet there was only one clearly-acknowledged legitimate heir, or *throne-capable* representative of Charlemagne, and this representative was an infant child, Louis the Saxon's sprightly boy. Doctrine and sentiment had much changed upon the subject of connubial legitimacy, since the Merovingian era. Lax in practice, the Franks had improved in theoretical consistency concerning marriage · the teaching of the Church had imparted greater sanctity to the union. Ecclesiastical Canons were prevailing over national customs:—the progeny born of connexions unconsecrated by the Priest were more decidedly lowered in position than before; and, except Louis the Saxon's boy, all the next of kin to the ruling Sovereigns, the Carlovingian princes Louis and Carloman of France, Hugh of Alsace, Arnolph of Carinthia, and Hugh the Saxon, were *mamzers*, either by reputation or undeniably. Only one uncon-
tested
legitimate
heir to the
four Sove-
reigns.

862—888
877—878
The five reputed bastards, viz. Louis and Carloman.

A large and influential party stigmatized Louis and Carloman, the sons of Louis-le-Bégue, as illegitimate : their mother Ansgarda was defamed as a concubine, the living witness of their disqualification. We cannot pronounce upon the validity of the reasons, possibly insufficient, which sustained this conclusion; but the adverse opinion subsisted permanently, and a personal dislike was nourished against these princes, strengthening any plausible arguments, if such there were, branding their birth with disgrace.

Hugh of Alsace.

Hugh, titular Count of Alsace, Lothair and Waldrada's son, stood in the same painfully ambiguous station. Waldrada had claimed to be reckoned a lawful wife; but her son, denied the rights of royal birth, was equally deprived of the respectability resulting from a recognized position in society.

Arnolph of Carinthia

Arnolph, Duke of Carinthia, the brilliant son of the heroic Carloman, by the left-handed Sclavonian consort, was prominently known as a bastard: his half-caste rendered the circumstances of his origin the more conspicuous.

Hugh the Saxon.

Lastly, Hugh, eldest son of Louis the Saxon, though dearly loved by his father, and deserving and returning that love, never forgot or concealed his illegitimacy.

Louis and Carloman were however the least blemished, their inchoate title to royalty, though not absolutely unchallenged, was not strenuously

contested. Their father, and all about the court ^{862—888}
and the royal family, treated Ansgarda's sons as
heirs apparent; but Hugh of Alsace, Arnolph of ^{877—878}
Carinthia, and Hugh of Saxony, were classed in
a definite category—all three marked out as
base-born Carlovingians—not one of the three
deemed to be genuine, or entitled by descent to
a Carlovingian crown.

So far as external enemies were concerned, ^{Presenti-ment of dangers in the Em-pire}
it chanced that the present moment was one of
comparative tranquillity:—the Gauls somewhat
spared from Danish invasions: the Danes having
enough to do in England:—Alfred driven into
Athelney, meekly submitting to his well-known
chiding from the Neat-herd's wife;—and the conflict in our island at its fiercest.—The Danish
moveable forces were therefore transiently diminished upon the Continent, and the coasts were
less disturbed.   But France was broken up by
the troubles; and there was a general feeling of
insecurity, a presentiment of impending danger.
Every man knew his neighbour's untruth: every
man acted upon the conviction that no trust or
confidence could be reposed either in individuals
or in general society.   The Four Kings were all
jealous of each other, each yearning for the dominions of cousin or brother—none of the Four
aged, yet each hungry for the other's death.
Nevertheless two of the Four, Louis the Saxon
and Louis-le-Bégue, whose dominions bordered,

862—888

878—879

were drawn closer by surrounding pressures, and sought to dissemble their animosity. Parental love was strong in both. Louis the Saxon was earnestly anxious that his namesake, his sprightly child, should succeed to the German kingdom— Louis-le-Bégue equally desired to secure his royal rights for Louis and Carloman, the sons of his first love.

878
1 Nov.
Treaty of
Foron
Louis-le-
Bégue and
Louis the
Saxon mu-
tually
guarantee
the rights
of their
children.

Whatever opinions might have been fostered, no contradiction had, until the death of Charles-le-Chauve, been given to the doctrine that the Sovereignty was inherently and exclusively vested in the Carlovingian family, but the rights of the individuals composing that family were not definitely ascertained. It still continued to be a vexed question whether a Senior or a Senior's representative might not demand the dominion of a Junior or Junior's representative, in preference to the issue of such Junior—the son postponed to an elder collateral. This leaven of discord had fermented from the beginning, but now other causes of trouble had arisen, for the hitherto indefeasible supremacy of the collective Carlovingian lineage had been impugned by implication. Louis-le-Bégue confessed that he received his throne from the nation's choice. There also subsisted, what must be unfortunately termed a natural antipathy between the German line and the French; both were, however, now compelled to seek co-operating aid.

The sovereigns, Louis-le-Bégue and Louis the Saxon, met at Foron in Lotharingia, not far from Maestricht, and concluded the articles of a treaty to be thereafter confirmed in a solemn Diet, Carloman and Caroletto being summoned to attend. The object which both parents had most at heart, a mutual guarantee for their children's security, they effected in words. Louis-le-Bégue covenanted and swore to defend the hereditary right of the infant Louis. Louis the Saxon on his part covenanted, should he survive, to defend the sons of Louis-le-Bégue and any other children whom he might have, in the secure and quiet possession of their paternal kingdom, as their counsellor and protector. Never were the antagonistic theories and consequences of self-subsisting legitimacy and elective or constitutional monarchy, more distinctly contemplated and understood by any political reasoners, than by these kings.—The compact concluded, each departed to his own dominions.

The illness of Louis encreased: his bodily strength declined rapidly. In the wilds of the Ardennes there was a renowned monastery dedicated to the hunter's legendary patron; there Saint Hubert's votary lingered. No longer stinted in his sport by a father's grudging behest, the jealously preserved forest was his own; but the poor beasts were now very effectually protected against their tormentor, by the feebleness

862—888

878—879

878—879
Nov.—Feb.
Louis-le-Bégue detained by encreasing illness in the Ardennes.

862—888
878—9

of the royal huntsman's nerves and the anxiety of his mind :—no power had Louis to slip the hound, no care to dart the spear. A rebellion broke out in Burgundy. Bernard, Count of Autun, had been recently deprived of all his honours, which were divided between his name-sake Bernard Plante-velue, and the High Chamberlain, Theodorick, the great intriguer. Some authorities assert that Theodorick was the father of Boso, or may be father-in-law, or may be his step-father, anyhow closely allied to Boso, and a prime mover in the little world of agitation disturbing the Gauls.

879
Feb Mar.
Revolts in
Burgundy

The deposed count Bernard insurrectionized the country Louis-le-Bégue, in nowise content to compromise his rights, determined to march against the revolters, and would have headed his troops, but at Troyes he sunk into a state of hopeless debility. His eldest son, the young Louis, was sent away under the care of Hugh the Abbot, Count Boso, and Bernard Plante-velue. Theodorick the High-Chamberlain was to have continued with them, but the narrative is much confused; and when the obscurity dissipates, we find that Theodorick had separated himself from the rest—and for a reason.

Louis crept on, and with great difficulty reached the humble monastery of Jouarre, near Compiègne. He was now thoroughly exhausted, and feeling himself at the last gasp, he entrusted to Odo, bishop of Beauvais and Count Alboin, the crown and robe, the sceptre of mercy and rod of justice. The expiring Monarch charged these friends and ministers that they should deliver the royal insignia to his son Louis, together with a Writ, or precept, addressed to the council of regency, directing the inauguration and consecration of the boy as his successor. On the following day the winding-sheet shrouded over the king's closed eyes. He died on Good Friday, and on Easter Eve they buried him.

§ 4. Great constitutional importance was attached, by usage and custom, to the regalia. According to ancient traditions, the delivery of these symbols actually conveyed the royal authority. Analogies may be found to this opinion. The Lord High Treasurer of England, were there one, would receive his appointment by delivery of the Staff. The Lord Chancellor, as is well-known, is created by the delivery of the Seals. Bishop Odo and Count Alboin took leave of their dying master, and set out upon their journey, with the full intention of retarding or defeating the Will which he had declared; for as soon as they heard of the King's death, they, instead of executing their commission, surrendered the tokens of sovereignty to the High Chamberlain Theodorick, investing him with whatever influence might result from possession of the insignia; and a revolutionary interregnum ensued.

862—888
879

10 April,
879
Death of
Louis-le-
Bégue

879
Interreg-
num after
the death
of Louis-
le-Bégue

862—888
———
879
17 Sep. 879.
Birth of
Charles-le-
Simple.

Besides Louis and Carloman, another heir might be expected. The Adeliza Judith was pregnant. She brought forth her babe (whom the mother called Charles, in honour of his ancestors) on Saint Lambert's feast day, five months after the death of Louis-le-Bégue. We do not hear anything more concerning the Adeliza: perhaps the Nun of Chelles, repenting her broken vows, returned to monastic seclusion. The child was first protected by Hugh the Abbot: he then disappears, until we ascertain that he had passed under the care of Rainulph the second, the son of Bernard of Septimania, Count of Poitiers; but anyhow the political existence of "Charles-le-Simple" was ignored during his early infancy, and when he afterwards was produced on the scene, uncharitable doubts were raised concerning his status, extending beyond the questions occasioned by the circumstances of his mother's marriage.

Parties or
factions
supporting
or opposing
the children
of Louis-le-
Bégue.

§ 5. Three parties, or factions, now arose, by or through whose exertions or persuasions the succession was to be determined. All the great men, clergy and nobles, had been fully preparing themselves for the vacancy of the throne, and all had determined to improve the contingency for their own advantage. Hugh the Abbot was pre-eminent in the party which supported the claims of the young princes Louis and Carloman. Others spurned the "concubine's sons." Gauzeline, the

brave Abbot of Saint-Denis, subsequently Bishop 862—888
of Paris, who had persuaded the distinguished and
experienced Count Conrad the Guelph to join 879
him, laboured to bring in Louis the Saxon. Taken
prisoner, cuffed and stripped at Andernach, the
Royal victor could not help pitying Gauzeline's
rueful plight and treated him kindly; and an Parties
favouring
intimate friendship then arose between them Louis the
Saxon.
which now fructified. The benefices Louis the
Saxon could bestow offered strong temptations;
yet amongst his partizans some may have been
influenced by less selfish motives. The divisions
and morcellings of the Carlovingian territories
among so many disputing *Roitelets,* or Reguli,
were destructive of national strength; and the
encreasing misfortunes of the empire enhanced
the unavailing regrets entertained by those who, Parties
favouring
through their faithlessness, had aggravated the Boso.
prevailing evils. There were many who were
ready to adopt any measure for the purpose of
restoring the antient unity; and the reconsolida-
tion of the Carlovingian empire under one Sovereign, appertaining to the Senior line, would be
a glorious consummation. Chief amongst these,
in learning, dignity and station, was—as subsequent events disclosed,—Archbishop Hincmar,
embued with the traditions of the old time; but
he does not appear openly amongst the *Meneurs,*
though we discern his intentions just visible
through the turbid narratives.

862—888
879—880

A third party would have been willing to discard the Carlovingian line completely, and to introduce Count Boso; but he rejected the proposition, possibly having already considered how he might establish himself more securely by adopting another scheme. Theodorick the Chamberlain transferred the County of Autun to Boso, who in exchange surrendered certain abbeys held as lay fees; and Boso, Count of Autun and Provence, and Duke of Lombardy, advocated the children of the late Sovereign.

The Gauzeline party therefore acted resolutely, and addressed their invitation to Louis the Saxon and his wife, proud Luitgarda, who ruled with her husband, and ruled him also; for historians speak of the masterful Queen as being highly influential in public affairs

Louis the
Saxon in-
vades the
territories
of Louis
and Carlo-
man.

There seemed no conception amongst these Carlovingian princes that any promise was made to be kept. Louis the Saxon, anticipating the invitation, had determined to seize the French dominions. As soon as the death of Louis-le-Bégue occurred, the Saxon Louis marched his army and prepared to gain Lotharingia and then win the whole kingdom. What had become of the treaty of Foron? Six months had scarcely elapsed since Louis the Saxon had solemnly covenanted and sworn to the dying Louis-le-Bégue, that he would support and defend the young children in the quiet possession of their paternal kingdoms,

he their counsellor and protector; and now he did 862—888
not give a thought to his engagement. Covenant
and oath signed and sworn in winter, oath and 879—880
covenant broken and violated in the spring. The
German army reached Metz and Verdun, perpe-
trating as much mischief as the Pagan Danes
could have done. The German chroniclers excuse their disorders by alleging that the people
refused to supply provisions at a fair price to
the soldiers, so they helped themselves.

There was full room for the play of parties; Louis is bought off by the cession of Lotharin-gia.
and Theodorick, the practised politician, Hugh
the Abbot, and Count Boso disconcerted their
adversaries' game, inducing Louis the Saxon to
retreat, which plan they effected by surrendering to him that portion of Lotharingia recently
ceded to Charles-le-Chauve, also the abbey of
Saint-Vedast, or Arras, as a make-weight : the
abbatial demesne and abbatial seigneuries of Saint
Vedast, would, as in other abusive examples, be
annexed to the King-Abbot's crown-lands. Louis
agreed without consulting his supporters, Abbot
Gauzeline and Count Conrad, and returned to
Frankfort, where he had to bear with Queen
Luitgarda's extreme disgust. " Had I been with
you, Sir King, you would have got and kept the
whole kingdom."—But Louis the Saxon had sufficient reason for the conduct he pursued. The 879
news reached him how his brother Carloman was Louis the Saxon ob-tains the administra-
stricken with the palsy, and that his death,

862—888
879—880
tion of his
brother
Carloman's
German
dominions
(see p. 383).
though the event might be somewhat protracted, was certain, whilst the Duke of Carinthia, Arnolph the Bastard, would probably endeavour to assume the supreme authority.   Therefore Louis hastened to Baioaria, where he compelled his almost speechless brother to admit him as Regent or Administrator of the Kingdom, the actual dominion being only postponed till death should release the sufferer.

879—880
Louis and
Carloman
called to
the throne
jointly—
they divide
their
father's
kingdom.

§ 6.   Louis the Saxon having thus suspended his pretensions upon France,—for he had not abandoned them, —Hugh the Abbot and his party obtained the ascendancy.   We have seen how Louis-le-Bégue appointed his eldest son, reckoned by historians as "Louis the Third," to be his successor; but without pronouncing upon the rights of Carloman or of any future children he might have.   Hugh the Abbot and those who acted with him, construed the late king's bequest into a recommendation which they would neither rudely reject nor implicitly obey.   They therefore bestowed the distracted, diminished and divided kingdom, from which some of the most important provinces had just been detached, upon Louis and Carloman conjointly.   The boys were inaugurated, but with maimed rites.   Hincmar, to whom, as Archbishop of Rheims, the high office of bestowing the benediction appertained,

879
Louis IV
and Carlo-

did not assist.

It is not certain whether any other Metro-

politan gave the sanction of his presence, by 862—888
which substitution the irregularity could have 879—880
been palliated. An obscure monastery in the Gas- man crowned at Ferrieres
tinois was the place selected for the undignified
ceremony, a transaction involved in doubt and
obscurity. Some short time afterwards, the young
kings, meeting at Amiens, amicably divided their
dominions, Louis taking Neustria and the Marches,
Carloman, Aquitaine and Burgundy and their
Marches, and so much as he could regain.

§ 7. "So much as he could regain"—for, 879—880 Boso founds the new king-dom of Provence, afterwards the king-dom of Arles.
during the preceding events, the finest portion of
la belle France had been torn away.—"I will not
live," said the maiden Hermengarda, "if I, an
Emperor's betrothed and an Emperor's daughter,
do not make my husband a king."—No aspiration
could have been more congenial to the ambitious
spirit of Count Boso, the crowned duke of Lombardy, who won her : no contingency more inviting than the present confusion of affairs : no
season more favourable than the disturbed interregnum : no era more cognate than this, when
the doctrine, teaching that the Crown is bestowed
by the choice of the people for the wealth and
safeguard of the people, had been so recently
and emphatically acknowledged, and Louis-le-
Bégue the son of Charles-le-Chauve, the son of
Louis-le-Débonnaire, the son of Charlemagne, his
hereditary authority disclaimed, inaugurated by
the people's will.

862—888

879—880

Leaving contending kings to their chances, and other partizans to their own devices, Boso repaired to Provence, where the country. extremely exhausted by the incursions of Saracens and Northmen, needed a defender. Six metropolitans, Besançon, Lyons, Vienne, Arles, Aix and Tarantaise, eighteen Bishops. and the chief nobles of the respective provinces, assembled in Council on the plain before the royal Castle of Mantaille, nigh the rushing Rhone.

15 Oct. 879.

Boso elected king in and by the Synod of Mantaille.

The Prelates, taking up the speech as Princes of the Church and representatives of the people, declared that the countries committed to their charge were without a king or protecting chief, and by unanimous consent they raised the "serene prince, the Lord Boso," to the royal authority— recording their motives in the constitutional Act they subscribed. No specific territory is assigned, no boundary named; and it should seem that Boso might rule as king wherever he could command obedience. The realm which actually obeyed him was sufficiently noble and extensive. All the countries which then had, or subsequently obtained, the denominations of Provence, Dauphiné, Savoy, the Lyonnais, and Bresse, and some other districts of Burgundy, accepted Hermengarda's husband as their Sovereign, and he was anointed and crowned, with the ceremonies appertaining to an ancient monarchy. Thus arose the kingdom called, under Boso's successors, the

kingdom of Arles and Burgundy, and afterwards 862—888
subdivided into Counties and Dukedoms, which
exercised the most powerful influence in France 879—880
and the Empire.

§ 8.   The affront resulting to the Carlovin- Great poli-
tical detri-
gians damaged them more than the loss of ment occa-
sioned to
cities and provinces. Boso's successful usurpation the Carlo-
vingian
dispelled the prestige hitherto consecrating the interests by
Boso's ele-
Carlovingian Crown. We use the term "Crown," vation
because all the Franks and Germans, and even
all the inhabitants of Gaul who had been ruled
by the great Emperor, maintained, notwithstanding their enmities and divisions, a union of
political sympathy, priding themselves upon the
importance the Empire possessed in the Christian
commonwealth, and therefore resenting any diminution of that importance. Since the Lombard
dynasty expired in the person of Desiderius, no
crowned and anointed kings had ruled within
the Carlovingian Empire or its dependencies,
save and except the sovereigns of Carlovingian
blood. It was an unheard presumption, that a
stranger should aspire to such a dignity. Boso's
elevation destroyed the exclusive family mono-
poly, and renewed the recollections of the times
when Pepin-le-Bref was only a noble example
of the *gros vilain*. All the Carlovingian sovereigns and princes, and all who in any degree
identified themselves with the Carlovingians, were
therefore direfully offended; whilst their per-

862—888
879—880

sonal enemies, severed from the Carlovingian interests like Hugh the son of Waldrada, or the Slavi, were correspondingly gratified.

Whatever pacifications were simulated with Boso, his Carlovingian cotemporaries only sought the intruder's destruction. Endued with extraordinary talent, activity and ingenuity, and supported and comforted by Hermengarda's valour and love, Boso defeated his opponents, and was as constantly employed in assailing them.

Boso's merits and talents.

After his accession, of which the full and authentic protocols are extant—and very interesting they are—we hardly know anything concerning Boso directly and personally, except what we collect from two or three Charters, in which he serves himself heir to his Carlovingian predecessors, and the help afforded to the imagination by the characteristic groupe, believed to have been copied from an antient painting in Vienne Cathedral, representing him and his crouching lion, held by a silken bridle. Nevertheless, we have every reason to conjecture that Boso, concurrently with his own success, encouraged the most dangerous enemies of the Empire, the Northmen, and that he acted conjointly with Hugh, Waldrada's son.—Humiliated as a bastard, any birthright denied, the arguments in favour of Hugh's legitimacy might almost compete with those adduced in favour of Louis and Carloman. But all the Carlovingians had been inveterate

Hugh, the son of Waldrada, heads an insurrection in Lotharingia.

against Hugh, and he rejected them in his turn. 862—888
Prosecuting a Robin-Hood insurrectionary warfare in Lotharingia, he was contriving to act 879—880
against Louis the Saxon, or Louis the Saxon's
brothers the Baioarian Carloman and Suabian
Charles, or against Louis and Carloman of France,
with any who might assist him, whether Christians or pseudo-Christians, pirates or pagans.

§ 9. Since Charlemagne's death, never had Renewal of
the Danish
circumstances been so opportune, or offering the invasions
upon a
like encouragement to the Danes, or they so more extensive
competent to avail themselves of the opening. scale.
Wisely and energetically as Alfred had defended
his realms and people, he was nevertheless glad
to purchase tranquillity by presenting Guthrun
at the font, and legalizing his rough-hewn godson
as King of the East-Anglian Danelaghe. Hastings
commanded the Loire-country, and the dreaded
and half-converted Danes, dispersed as colonists
in various regions of Northern Gaul, were ready
to join in the hurrah. Rollo was preparing to re-
visit Rouen ; and the whole body of the Northern
nations, encouraged by their British triumphs,
were busily fitting out a series of expeditions,
armada following armada, clearly displaying
their projects of effecting a territorial conquest.
Hitherto the Northmen had rather avoided the
genuine Teutonic countries on the Continent,
where they encountered purer races than the
Romanized Franks and more like themselves.

862—888
879—880

The English acquisitions, though laboriously won, taught them that they need not dread any kindred enemy. Combining naval and military operations, their attacks again extended on either side of the Elbe, and westward and southward from Elbe to Meuse, from Meuse to Somme, from Somme to Seine, from Seine to Loire, the Danish settlers in the Gauls co-operating with the new comers, their old friends.

Danish Commanders fierceness and continuity of their invasions.

Fierce, bold and experienced were the chieftains who now simultaneously or successively assaulted the Carlovingian Empire. Sigfried or Sigurd, King of South Jutland and son or grandson of Regner Lodbrok, Godfrey, son of Harold, Gorm or Orm or Worm, Hardacnute's son, King of Lethra, and Oskytel or Auscatil or Ketil, probably he who had desolated Croyland and murdered good Abbot Theodore, whose slaughter called for vengeance; and Gormund, Hals and Rollo, and Rollo's wily kinsman Gerlo, and Botho, afterwards Constable of Rollo's host, well provided with artillery, animated by a new spirit, bringing all their wit and weight to bear on the regions they ravaged. The attacks, movements, sieges and engagements, by and with or between the Northmen and the Carlovingians, now became so incessant, that any period when the Gauls, Belgium or Northern Germany were free from the Danish ravages, was merely exceptional. The Northmen might be defeated, but the very shed-

ding of their blood made the fire blaze more 862—888
fiercely. The multitudes of troops they raised,
fully evince that they intended to establish 879—881
their dominion within the Empire's boundaries,
according to the plans which they were accom-
plishing in England. Had they subdued the
Frisic and Saxon coasts, together with Belgium
and the Picardy of modern times, they would have
created a "Danelaghe" corresponding to East
Anglia and Northumbria, rendering the German
Ocean a Danish ocean, their territory extending round and round, and from land to land.

§ 10. Sovereigns so young as Louis and Car- Louis and Carloman
loman had never heretofore reigned;—boys, lite- —amiabi-lity of
rally,—unsupported, slandered, betrayed, nay, their cha-racters.
worse than betrayed, abandoned to their own wild
energies. But in other respects the situation of
the Kingdom was also unexampled : though the
royal authority might be divided, Louis and Carloman were conjoined in affection.—For the first
and the last time in the sad Carlovingian annals,
—from the hero Charles-Martel to the Fainéant
in whom the line expired,—the family exhibited
two brethren sincerely loving each other—free
from envy, jealousy, — co-operating as loving
friends, between whom not the slightest quarrel
or dissension is recorded.

These lads were the only Carlovingian Sovereigns who appreciated the simple truth, that
concord is strength : Louis and Carloman never

862—888
879—881

entertained the idea of profiting by enmity. Their mutual confidence they extended to their cousins, the German Princes, scheming, treacherous, always working underhand. Moreover, Louis and Carloman were handsome, vigorous and healthy, warriors in body and mind: had there been any loyalty left amongst the Franks, they might have cherished these last blossoms of the cankered stem as giving hope of the Empire's revival.

The conference of Orbe.

The same cause which diverted Louis the Saxon from his attacks upon France, Carloman's illness—the opportunity of profiting by a brother's affliction—sent Caroletto or Charles of Suabia to Lombardy. Orbe, where the sons of Lothair whilome assembled in angry discussion, again became the scene of a congress, but a peaceful one: even had there been no better motives, self-interest dictated union. Here the Kings of France, Louis and Carloman, met their cousin:

880—881
Charles-le-Gras King of Italy and Emperor
(v. p. 387.)

measures, which proved unavailing, were concerted for suppressing the Provence revolution. Louis promised that he would abstain from occupying any territory which might revert to Charles: the latter proceeded to Lombardy, and obtained the Iron and Imperial crowns. The Frankish Sovereigns returned to their kingdom, where the Northmen had savagely resumed their warfare.

Another atmospheric cycle of inclemency was in course, the rivers frozen, the earth parched with cold, the season impeding military opera-

tions. Young Louis nevertheless marched to the 862—888
Loire and attacked the Northmen, who were
extending their settlements and ravaging the 879—881
879.
30 Nov.
country. Loud was the triumph of the Franks Battle of
the Vi-
on Saint Andrew's mass-day—the young Warrior, genne
leading on his troops, completely routed the
Danes, whose carcases choked the shallow Vi-
genne. But this victory was only an incident
in the great campaign, now commencing with
raging violence in the North.

§ 11. Baldwin's iron arm rested in the coffin, 880—881
Danish in-
and the whole Northern coast was covered by vasions
proceed
the Danes, whose combined forces had landed,— with en-
creased
national and individual hostility or rather treach- vigour.
ery, co-operating amongst the Franks in their
favour. Strong suspicions support the accusation that King Boso and Count Hugh had concerted their schemes with the Northmen. But
amongst the meisné of domestic traitors, Isembard, the Seigneur of La Ferté in Ponthieu,
obtained the pre-eminence. Isembard's castle- Louis the
Saxon in-
garth now constitutes a suburb of Saint Valery. vited again
by Abbot
He was also Avoué of Centulla or Saint-Riquier. Gauzeline
and Con-
We have full notice that the parties which dis- rad against
Louis III.
tracted France were malignantly active. Gau- and Carlo-
man
zeline and Conrad invited Louis the Saxon again
to Lorraine : he advanced a second time with
his Bellona, in the full purpose of extending his
conquests over the whole Frankish kingdom.
But these designs received signal frustration :

862—888
880
the Danes, excited to the highest pitch by the Carlovingian dissensions, overspread the North-sea and channel territories with their forces. Godfrey, entering the Elbe, landed and advanced to the Somme country, which he overwhelmed by his multitude. Abbot Gauzeline and Count Conrad could not afford to Louis the Saxon the support they expected: their insurrectionary power was below their will.

Louis the Saxon, Queen Liutgarda consenting, made peace with Louis and Carloman; and he might well rejoice in the pacification, for his kingdom was in the greatest danger. Saxons and Thuringians fought desperately: they had good reason, they were fighting for their lives. The Northmen occupied Ghent, where they wintered. Louis the Saxon was perplexed by the encreasing perils; nevertheless he placed himself at the head of his army, assisted by Hugh, his brave and affectionate

880
Battle of
the Ar-
dennes.
Danes de-
feated, but
Hugh, son
of Louis
the Saxon,
killed.
son. The first battle was the battle of the Ardennes, a desperate conflict. The Danes began to give way: Hugh, yielding to his ardour, was lost among the Northmen. Louis the Saxon immediately stayed his troops: could he but save his child, what mattered renouncing the advantage? he hoped that Hugh had been taken prisoner, and that a ransom might be accepted,—he would give any sum of money to redeem the captive; but Hugh never reappeared alive, Godfrey had slain him. The battle was over: five thousand North-

men are said to have fallen,—a victory gained by
Louis at the price of an irreparable loss! The
Northmen retreated to their vessels, having previously burnt their dead : the last known instance
of funeral cremation. The King sought his son's
body : the corpse was found and buried at Laures-
heim.

§ 12.   Then followed the most calamitous
battle of Luneburg Heath, otherwise the battle of
Ebbsdorf, wherein the Danes avenged, and more
than avenged, their disgrace in the Ardennes.
Godfrey is supposed to have been again the conquering leader.   The Germans were thoroughly
routed and cut to pieces.   Bruno Duke of
Saxony, Queen Liutgarda's brother, the Bishops
of Minden and Hildesheim, Theodorick and Mar-
quard, eleven Counts and eighteen other of the
King's chief Barons or vassals, were killed, and
nearly all the survivors captured and swept away
as prisoners by the Northmen.   The slain had
perished gloriously:—defending their country and
faith they died the martyrs' death, and received
the martyrs' honours; and their commemoration
was celebrated in the Sachsen-land churches till
comparatively recent times.

An unexampled sorrow was created throughout Saxony by this calamity, which, for a time,
exhausted the country;—Scandinavia and Jutland and the Baltic isles resounded with exultation.   But there were others who rejoiced in the

862—883

880—881

880
Feb 2,
Battle of
Ebbsdorf.
The Ger-
mans de-
feated by
the Danes
—greatness
of their
loss.

862—888
880—881 retribution which afflicts an enemy through the means of an enemy: nations who hated the Danes hailed the Danish victory: the oppressed and enthralled Sclavonians, Daleminzians, Bohemians, Sorbs, who immediately retaliated upon their tyrants, and wasted Thuringia and Saxony with fire and sword.

Sorrows, vexations and misfortunes accumulated upon the head of Louis the Saxon, each succeeding year more dreary. Yet one consolation remained to him, his lively boy; and for the child's sake as well as his own, his despondency was cheered by a great accession of good fortune, the pleasurable zest being heightened by the patience with which he had waited during nearly three years for the full enjoyment of the inheritance. Carloman, upon whom the Germans and Italians had fixed their hopes neither presumptuously nor unworthily—the courteous, the brave, the learned Carloman, in whom, the moment before the stroke had fallen upon him, no bodily or mental talent required for the defence and honour of the throne was wanting,— after lingering so long in distressful languor— now expired. Carloman's talents were inherited by the Sclavonian concubine's son, who had been named Arnolph by his father in honour of Arnolph of Metz, the patriarch of the Carlovingian dynasty. Probably Carloman had bestowed the appellation with some hope of designating the

Death of Carloman of Bavaria —Louis the Saxon obtains the kingdom.

22 March, 880.

Prince as his successor, but the bold and popular 862—888
youth was not yet able to assert his claim,—
he must content himself a while with his Carin- 880—881
thian Duchy.

Upon receiving the intelligence of his brother's death, the sufferer's happy release, Louis,
with his Queen and only child, his heir, hastened
to Ratisbon.   Arnolph secured himself in his
castle of Mosaburch, surrounded by impassable
marshes.   The Baioarian nobles hailed the arrival
of King Louis and the boy Louis, submitting themselves with extreme alacrity to his sovereignty.
Arnolph also became a homager, and thereby
maintained his position, being confirmed by Louis
in the Duchy of Carinthia.   And thus Louis had
obtained his heart's desire, his brother's kingdom 880
Death of
Louis the
Saxon's
child.
(see p 385.)
for himself and his child; but the active child,
brought to witness his father's inauguration, fell
from the palace-window, his skull was fractured,
his brains were dashed out.—Never afterwards
had Louis the Saxon a gleam of brightness; and
his cheerless life was soon brought to a close.

§ 13.   It was the constant complaint of the Treachery
and disloy-
alty of the
Franks.
Romane Franks, that they had no chieftain around
whom they could rally.   An idle and factious pretence,—chieftains they possessed, fully competent
to have enabled them to concentrate their national forces and energies; but the one thing was
wanting—truth.   Louis and Carloman the young
royal brothers,—very young,—were endued with

862—888 remarkable gifts and talents, both of body and
880—881 mind : unshaken, energetic, active, faithful to each
other, faithful to all with whom they were concerned; and they were guided and aided by the
most experienced surviving warrior of the era,
Hugh the Abbot. In the experience of this military counsellor, the Franks ought to have placed
full confidence. Loyalty should have bound them
to their young Sovereigns; but that sanctifying
gift, that unselfish, natural affection,—which,
after all, is the truest support of monarchy, as
well as the source of the greatest comfort and
ennoblement to a people,—was taken away.

The Tetrarchy was re-established : there were
now again four reigning Carlovingian Sovereigns.
How long could or ought this Tetrarchy to endure ? Charles the Emperor, the exalted representative of the Senior or German line, had won
universal confidence.—His reputation increased
in proportion to his successes :—Louis the Saxon
was evidently drawing nigh his end, and all the
countries of the Teutonic tongue would naturally
seek for Kaiser Karl as their sovereign : Louis
and Carloman, the representatives of the French
line, might be considered as minors,—were they
reduced to dependance, France would once more
be incorporated with the Empire ?—These considerations revived Archbishop Hincmar's political
enthusiasm for the restoration of Carlovingian
unity ; and he exhorted and advised the Emperor

The Em-
peror
Charles,
his en-
creasing
influence.

to treat the two young French kings as his wards, 862—888
and to take order for the due and regular government of their kingdom—in other words, to de- 880—881
throne them, the preparation for captivity and
death.

The advice was bestowed exactly at the time
when the Brothers were displaying extraordinary boldness, merit, and talent and giving
the greatest promise of excellence. Archbishop
Hincmar was a sound theologian, upright in his
conduct, a wise man and a good man : but political casuistry stupifies the conscience of the wise
and the good. Hincmar's conduct towards the
grandsons of Charles-le-Chauve was, from the
beginning, equivalent to a prophecy of evil:
therefore he tried hard to make his words
come true. No immediate step was taken by
the Emperor to follow the Archbishop's suggestions; but the influence of Louis and Carloman was sensibly diminished, and their subjects
continued to betray their kings, their country
and themselves, by apathy and treachery.

§ 14. The Danish invasions, the exploits of 880—881
Louis of
France, his
operations
against the
Danes
Sigfried and Godfrey, excited the apprehensions
and energies of the young French Sovereigns.
The Northmen continued stretching and speeding
over the country. Corbey and Amiens had been
pillaged, Cambray taken, Arras occupied and the
Northmen stationed in the Abbey of Saint-Vedast.
They burnt the city but spared the Churches:

862—838
880—881
in other respects their devastations were merciless. Plunder, which they had reaped so abundantly, no longer satisfied the bloody Danes; they
slew the inhabitants indiscriminately. Whether
the people submitted or not, they sustained the
same fate. All about Courtrai, where they established their winter-quarters, they exterminated
the inhabitants.

Evidently calculating upon subduing the country by terror, they succeeded to a considerable
extent. Abbot Gauzeline summoned his troops,
but when they had to face the Danes they ran
away, and the people generally gave themselves
up to passive despair. Carloman could not withdraw from Burgundy, and Louis, returning to
Neustria, had to fight the battle singlehanded.
Unexperienced in the art of war, the youth's
acuteness and daring compensated for his deficiencies. Nay more, so far as his dastardly and
unprincipled subjects were susceptible of the
inspiration, he excited them to quit themselves
like men.

The Danes were masters of the Seine and
Loire districts. Gormund and his companions
commenced movements for the purpose of gain-
ing a tract offering a very strong position, adjoin-
ing the future Norman Duchy. This is the
Vimeux constituting subsequently a bailliage of
Ponthieu, a compact peninsula, enclosed by the
Somme on the North-East, and on the South-

West by the river Bresle,—which river Bresle, 862—888
skirting the walls of Eu, falls into the sea at
the well-known Tréport, and subsequently con- 880—881
stituted the boundary between Ponthieu and
Normandy. A classical land is the Vimeux in
our English history. The Vimeux contains Azin- The Vimeux
territory—
court's battle-field : on this coast was Harold its connexion with
shipwrecked : here is Saint-Valery, the embark- English
history.
ation port of the Conqueror.

Gormund and his Danes, the recreant Isembard guiding them, having plundered Beauvais
and all around, advanced sea-ward and encamped
in the Vimeux, readily accessible to their vessels
on the extended coast. Isembard's castle of la 881
Feb
Ferté gave them cover when needed on the sea- Gormund
and the
side, whilst on the opposite frontier they were Danes
occupy the
protected by the expanded estuary of the Somme, Vimeux.
rendering the whole territory unusually defensible. Laden with booty, they halted between Eu
and the locality where Abbeville now stands,—
for, as yet, the *Abbatis-Villa* was not built,—in
and about the hamlet of Saulcourt. Louis, whose
spies had diligently marked their movements, here
surprized them. The Danes, probably feasting Battle of
Saulcourt.
and getting drunk, expecting any thing rather Louis defeats the
than the onslaught, were put to flight. Gormund Danes.
and Isembard were killed, the latter, according to
tradition, fell by the sword of Louis. A tumulus
still called the *Tombe-d'Isembard* marks the spot
where the traitor perished ; but the sepulchral

862—888 mound wastes away beneath the ploughshare, which turns up the relics of the conflict.

880—881

Far and wide spread the intelligence of the victory, the numbers of the slain encreasing in proportion as the fame receded from the scene of slaughter. Popular lays transmitted to posterity false Isembard's felony and the Pagans' chastisement; and the battle of Saulcourt was equally commemorated in a song constituting a remarkable specimen of German poetry—being amongst the earliest examples of Teutonic rhyme. The versification is inharmonious, lacking the dulcet rhythmic melody which sounds in the ballads of Scotland, or in the parents of the Scottish ballads, the marvellous *Kiæmpe-viser* of the Dane, but spirited, and breathing life and power; telling how " Ludwig " takes shield and spear, and leads on his troops, chaunting *Kyrie eleison*,—and how the blood rose in the cheeks of the Frankish soldiers, enjoying the sport of war.

Antient Teutonic song commemorating the victory.

Bad conduct of the Frankish troops after the victory.

The folly, however, of the Franks,—vain-glorious cowards,—neutralized the success. They relapsed into disreputable disorder, emulating the Danish debauchery without possessing the Danish sturdiness and Danish sagacity. A body of Northmen who escaped the general dispersion sallied forth, and attacked these rascally troops. The Franks scattered and gave way—many were killed : had not young Louis alighted from his horse and rallied them, fighting furiously and exerting himself beyond his bodily strength, they would have sustained the disgrace of a total defeat from a defeated enemy.

862—888
881—882

The Vimeux slaughter did not produce any perceptible effect upon the general fortunes of the war.—Reckless of loss, the Northman's resources seemed inexhaustible. All the Scandinavian and cognate nations were enthusiastic for conquest, and they re-entered France. Louis, on his part, was worked up to corresponding energy: the young hero fully prepared himself for all emergencies, and determined to repel the enemy. Abbot Hugh still continued to be a trusty adviser in counsel, a wise and fearless warrior in the field; but the young King was virtually deserted by his subjects, who, whenever they could, displayed their incorrigible recreancy. He was constantly spurring them on; and they, as constantly, falling back. They acted as though they were seeking occasions to degrade themselves. About two miles from Arras, at Estreuns or Etrun, above the confluence of the Scarpe and the Ugy, is a *Camp de César*, one of those numerous antient fortifications, circled and guarded by deep trenches and grassy ramparts, which, scattered throughout the Gauls, are universally ascribed by popular tradition to the Roman conqueror, thus rendered memorials of his might and the lasting domination bestowed upon his Empire.

881
Louis adds additional fortifications to the Camp of Cæsar at Estreuns nigh Arras.

Louis strengthened this fortress by outworks

862—888

881—882

and stoccades. If not Cæsar's, the camp is worthy of Cæsar. So advantageous is the position, and so firm and fresh the foss and rampire, that Marshal Villars availed himself of the protection the station afforded, when Marlborough marched to invest Bouchain. But the strategic talents of the young Louis were rendered wholly unprofit-

Cowardice of his nobles. able by the cowardly baseness of the Franks. The fortifications being completed, he could neither persuade nor compel any of his nobles to undertake the perilous command of the Post— shame they had none, all sense of honour was bartered or scared away ; and then they raised the cry that the measures Louis adopted were burthensome to the Franks, and advantageous only to the enemy.

20 Jan 882. Death of Louis the Saxon. § 15. At this juncture the heart-broken, childless Louis the Saxon, died, brought to the grave by grief. Whilst the Romanized Franks were despising their young King, the Germans had been favouring him, planning to raise him to the throne. The Teutonic song of Vimeux, the Song of Victory, as the lay was designated by learned

Louis of France refuses the offer of Lotharingia. Dom Mabillon, is not unreasonably conjectured to be a political ballad : a specimen of party minstrelsy, prompted or purchased by those who had sought to array the young hero Louis, the Frankish Louis, against their decayed unprosperous Sovereign. The idiom of the composition supports this conjecture—such a pure Franco-

Theotisk language as the song exhibits, was no 862—888 longer spoken in any portion of the dominions which the son of Louis-le-Bégue then actually 881—882 ruled.

The nobles of German Lotharingia therefore immediately turned to Louis, and offered homage. According to the prevailing usages, they were justified in making the proposal. Louis, on his part, had he adapted his conscience to the standard of public morals sanctioned by his kinsmen and progenitors, would have been fully authorized in accepting the proffered kingdom. But, unlike any other Carlovingian Sovereign who had hitherto reigned, Louis remembered the oath he had sworn at Orbe to his cousin Charles the Emperor, and the sincere and honest youth refused the homages. Nevertheless he was willing to give all the aid in his power, and he despatched detachments to resist the Northmen then harassing the country.

Affairs summoned Louis to the Outre-Seine district. He presented himself to receive the submission of the Armorican Sovereigns, and then advanced to Tours. Hastings and his Danes were commencing hostilities, but Louis pacified them by display of force and employment of policy; and it is possible that at this time Hastings was confirmed in the county of Chartres.

His successes in treating with the Armoricans and the Danes.

If any were now rightminded amongst the Franks, the most joyful anticipations ought to

862—888 have prevailed. Thankfulness might be well in-
882 spired by the bright character of the two young
Kings.   Sincere affection conjoined them, living
examples of boldness and courage, faith and truth.
But no renovation could be imparted to Charlemagne's blighted race.   Louis met with his death
ingloriously, casually, and in a manner, foolishly,
—a frolic killed him.   Pursuing in dalliance a
fair damsel, probably of Danish lineage, Gur-
mund's daughter, she fled into her father's house.
His horse dashed him through the low, narrow
portal, gallopping merrily after the girl.   Bowing forward to save his forehead from the blow,
the eager rider gave himself the harm he tried to
avoid; he could not stoop enough to clear the
transom, which crushed him against the pommel
of the saddle; and the severe bruises he received,
concurring with an inward injury occasioned by
his desperate exertions in the Vimeux battle,
5 Aug. 882. became mortal.   Dying, Louis was removed to
Death of
Louis III. Saint-Denis, where he expired.

Attempts seem to have been made to conceal the cause of his death, the accounts of the
circumstances being perplexed, and contradictory.
Those who loved Louis, deplored the loss of the
kingdom's hope: his enemies slandered him as
a young ruffian, distinguished only by vice and
absurdity, employing language so coarse and
uncharitable that the charges refute themselves:
the character given by his revilers could scarcely

have been merited during a long life of inveterate profligacy. 862—888

§ 16. Carloman, at the age of sixteen, succeeded to his brother's dominions, troubles, courage and fatal destiny. Louis the Saxon's death, followed by the death of his namesake the young French King and the encreasing confusion of the Empire, imparted a fresh impulse to the pertinacious activity of the Danes : the country literally burning from Rhine to Scheldt, from Scheldt to Seine, and far in the interior, where they had never hitherto penetrated. 881—882
882
Carloman succeeds to the entire kingdom.

These renewed attacks had commenced during the last months of Louis the Saxon's reign, when the Northmen established themselves in Charlemagne's imperial fortress at Nimeguen. They were temporarily subsidized away, but they re-entered the city, and continued afterwards in possession for many years, and burned Charlemagne's Roman palace, second only, if second, to Ingleheim. The circular Church, the "Capella" or "Cupola," alone escaped, and still exists : the name borne by that remarkable structure, the *Heiden Kapelle*, bears record to the occupation of the sanctuary by the Pagans. The devastation spread extensively into Lotharingia and Rhenane Germany. The whole of the Hespen-gau, or Hasbay, was ravaged, and all as far as the Moselle ; and the antient Roman cities, hitherto spared, and the Burghs, which flourished round the Monaste- 881-882
The great Danish invasion of the Rhine, Scheldt and Meuse country

862—888
881—882
ries, were involved in the same destruction. Carloman, at the time of his brother's death, was employed in besieging Vienne, where he was energetically attacking Boso; but the sound of the Danish hurrah reached him there, and the Neustrian nobles earnestly invited the young King to meet them, receive their homage, and undertake the defence of the country. The boy rejoiced in the war, and assumed the command with determinate energy.

The ravages of the Northmen had indeed been desperate. Trèves burnt, Cologne burnt, Maestricht burnt, Tolbiac burnt, Liege burnt, Tongres burnt, Cambray burnt, Coblentz burnt, Bonn burnt, Juliers burnt, Cornelien-Munster burnt, Malmedi burnt, Aix-la-chapelle burnt. Metz was defended by her Roman fortifications and the valour of Bishop Wala; but Wala was afterwards killed in a chance skirmish, having fought bravely. The Netherlandish country suffered dreadfully. Aldenburgh, Rodenburgh, Furnes, Alost, Oudenarde, Comines, Bailleul, Harlebec, Torholt, Antwerp, Poperingues, Cassel, Nuys, and very many other opulent towns, whose names are first commemorated by their calamities, were ravaged and destroyed. Thus did the Danes pollute, pillage and ruin the great Roman cities of the North, the strongest, the richest, the most honoured by tradition and piety—schools of learning, monuments of art, seats of luxury, imperial grandeur, some dating from the earliest periods, but many more which had arisen silently under the genial protection of the monastic communities, and whose healthy and prosperous existence we ascertain from their misfortunes.

§ 17. Germany, like France, was filled with consternation : Franconians, Thuringians, Bavarians, Saxons, Frisons, now all conjoined in imploring Kaiser Karl to sustain the falling Empire. A grand Diet was held at Worms— Here the homages were rendered. All the lieges of the late kingdom of Louis the Saxon, and all the lieges of the Baioarian kingdom and the appurtenances thereof, became the Kaiser's men. Arnolph, confirmed in his Duchy of Carinthia by the Kaiser, submitted with the rest. If Arnolph, coming forth from Mosaburch, unwillingly saw his father's realm bestowed upon his uncle, if his jealousy had been suspected, means were taken to obtain a greater hold upon his conscience : he was either required to give a stronger and more binding pledge than the ordinary ceremonies—now mere forms—afforded, or he proffered a more solemn adjuration. And upon the holiest relic, a particle of the true cross, he took the oath, which, if violated, might bring upon his head the direst vengeance.

The German nations thoroughly confided in the Emperor's prowess. Placing themselves willingly and gladly under his protection, they be-

862—888

882—883

882
The Emperor Charles invited by the Germanic nations.

862—888 lieved that Kaiser Karl had inherited Charle-
882—888 magne's valour; and, when guided by such a
commander, never would they fear an enemy. On
either side of the Alps equal enthusiasm prevailed.
Troops from Lombardy joined the musters which
flocked in from Alemannia and Saxony, Franconia, Suabia and Frisia: a most imposing army
assembled, and a splendid muster at Andernach
promised transcendant victory to the Emperor.

Oct 882.
Battle of
Condé be-
tween Car-
loman and
the Danes.

Carloman, on his part, fully took his share
in the perils and exertions of the war. The
Northmen established themselves in modern
Picardy, near Condé, a name so familiar to us
from the title which it imparted. Carloman gave
them battle, the Danes were worsted, upwards
of a thousand were killed; but the Pagans
quitted Condé, nothing daunted, pursuing their
hostilities beyond the Oise. For the thousand
Northmen killed, thousands re-entered the country: corpses strewed the roads and highways,
clerks and laymen, nobles and peasants, women
and children and infants at the breast.

As usual, no trust, no honour.—The nobles
who invited young Carloman to defend them
refused to participate in his dangers: he had
scarcely any means of opposing the invaders
except through his own courage and personal

Districts
hitherto
spared,
Soissons,
&c.ravaged
by the
Danes.

exertions. The antient kingdom of Soissons had
been hitherto singularly spared, an oasis of tranquillity;—possibly owing some portion of that

tranquillity to the awe which the veneration ren- 862—888
dered to the patron saints inspired even amongst 882—883
the Danes. But the protecting influences now
failed, and the exempted regions tasted the
scourge. For the first time, the rock of Lâon
was insulted: the Pagans occupied Soissons and
invested hallowed Rheims. Bearing with him Nov 882.
Saint-Remi's relics, Archbishop Hincmar fled by Flight and death of Arch- bishop Hincmar.
night. He died soon after: with the year, his
chronicle suddenly ends: it is supposed that he
dictated the last paragraphs; and we henceforth
lose the coeval testimony afforded by the ablest
and best-informed witness of this doleful era.

Hincmar, the chiefest statesman, knew more
of the events connected with the leading partizans than any other chronicler; had he continued
his task he might possibly have instructed us how
and in what manner Eudes, the son of Robert-
le-Fort, Eudes Capet, Count of Paris, attained
his great celebrity. All memorials concerning
Eudes are lost until we come upon him by sur-
prise, when, supported by Abbot Gauzeline, who
during these transactions became Bishop of Paris,
we find the hero defending the future Capital
against the Northmen, and turning the fortunes
of France.

§ 18. Kaiser Karl began gloriously; but diffi- The Empe- ror Charles Difficulties of his situa- tion.
culties thronged rapidly round him, and the cry
of jubilee, so loud at Worms, and swelling louder
at Andernach, suddenly dropped and became faint

862—883
882—883

and fainter. Italy was disturbed, dissensions prevailed in the Western borders, wasting the national strength. Poppo Count of the Suabian Marches and Egino quarrelled—Saxons against Thuringians. These local feuds occasioned great trouble; but Henry, Poppo's brother, who held a county or benefice in the Rhine country, remained faithful to Charles, a ready and earnest partizan. Few names of North-German chieftains are mentioned during the present crisis of Carlovingian history: so many were felled down on Luneburg Heath, that the old aristocracy seems to have been nearly extirpated: the Danes cleared the soil for the growth of new families. Moreover, the Emperor Charles was not treated honestly: Liutward, Bishop of Vercelli, the Emperor's prime minister in Italy, enjoyed his master's confidence; but heavy charges are preferred against the Prelate. He was accused of undue familiarity with the Empress Richarda. This noble lady, said to be daughter of a Scottish king, held the station of consort, but Charles did not cohabit with her.—Charles lived with an obscure concubine, by whom he had Bernard, the child upon whom he doted, his only child.

882
The Emperor Charles baffled by the Danes, compelled to make peace upon disadvantageous terms.

Charles became depressed :—probably the morbid affection, whatever the disease may have been, which rendered his aspect so woefully conspicuous,—was gaining upon him. *Caroletto*, the name the Italians gave him, implies delicacy

of form: and we may therefore conclude that 862—888
his youthful appearance had suggested the endearing diminutive, and his general conduct until 882—883
this campaign displays much activity as well as
talent; but henceforward, we observe his spirit
declining, and the malady occasioning more distress.

§ 19.   Sigfried, Godfrey, Worm or Orm, and Unsuccess-ful blockade of Esloo— Friesland ceded to Godfrey, and Dane-gelt paid to Sigfried.
Hals, the four wary and sturdy chieftains, en-
trenched themselves at Esloo on the Meuse.
The Danes had acquired sound experience in war:
ingenious handicraftsmen, they profited by the
arts and contrivances of the Romanized nations
amongst whom they were thrown.   They carried
their skill to Normandy, they did not learn it
there.   Esloo was a strong fort, and ably defended: an assault being impracticable, Charles
commenced a regular blockade.   The Northmen
were straitened by deficiency of provisions, and
considered themselves in peril; yet the Emperor's
operations did not prosper: the sultry weather
set in, the locality was insalubrious, an epidemic
broke out in his camp.   The heart of Charles sunk
within him, his discouragement was manifest;
and, agreeing to the terms proposed, he accepted
a very disadvantageous compromise, through the
faithless bishop's evil counsel, as the Franks asserted,—false Liutward, bribed by Danish money.

Godfrey demanded all the benefices whilome
held by his Danish predecessors on the North Sea

862—888 coast, and more than they had held, all Friezeland, Friezeland East, and Friezeland West, from
883—884 Weser to Meuse, and all the islands, a territory
so extensive and important, that the cession was
considered as rendering him the Emperor's partner, a compeer in the realm.

Gisella
daughter of
King Lo-
thair, mar-
ried to
Godfrey
the Dane.
(See p. 394.) Other conditions accompanying the treaty
gave him a still further claim to such a designation. Godfrey was baptized; and, at the neophyte's request, Charles bestowed upon the Dane
in marriage his kinswoman Gisella, the outlaw
Hugh's own sister, daughter of the late king
Lothair and Waldrada. She was no longer in
the bloom of youth, five and thirty years old
at least. Gisella seems to have been an affectionate wife to Godfrey during the brief term
of their marriage; yet unless that marriage had
been suggested to the brave Dane, he could
scarcely have sued for the mature Princess of his
own accord; and we are left to conjecture who
may have been his adviser. This marriage between
Godfrey and Gisella bears upon one of the most
perplexing points in Norman history: it has been
alleged, and not without ingenious plausibility,
that Rollo's marriage with Gisella, Charles-le-
Simple's daughter, is only a mistaken traditionary
version of the transactions we are now recording.
But the name-coincidence must be considered as
merely accidental, or, to speak more precisely,
resulting from the circumstance that *Gisla* or

Gesellin might be either a baptismal name, or a 862—883 conventional or family-circle appellation.

Sigfried had no objection to baptism, he was 883—884 Sigfried baptized, and tri- bute paid to him also bought off, and receiving gifts in gold and silver to the amount of somewhat more than two thousand and eighty pounds or livres—"we reckon the pound at twenty sols," says the annalist—he departed for Paris.

§ 20. Carloman was not included in this The Danes re-enter the Somme country armistice : the Northmen had not touched his money, therefore after the Esloo proceedings they crossed the Meuse, no one daring to raise a finger against them, spread themselves over the country, and occupied Amiens as their winter-quarters. The Frankish nobles, instead of supporting their valiant young king, abandoned all plans of defence ; and holding a great council at Compiègne, opened negotiations with the Danes. The Primores treated in Carloman's name, but without consulting him : their counsel, to have pleased the young warrior, would have been of another sort.

It might be thought that the Franks could not render themselves more vile than by such cowardice, yet they contrived to place themselves a stage lower than mere cowards : they exhibited an utter want of common sense. Needing a negotiator fit to manage a treaty with the The Frank- ish nobles negotiate with the Danes. cunning, greedy Danish chieftains, they, for this purpose chose a fellow-Dane, a born enemy, an

862—888
883—884

enemy who knew their weakness, who had profited by their dissensions and their disloyalty, Sigfried, the pseudo-Christian. Whilst the Danes were merry-making at Amiens, and the Frankish nobles in anxious session at Compiègne, Sigfried journeyed backwards and forwards, hither and thither, as the mediator, bearing and returning demands and replies, proposals and answers, spinning out the tedious negotiation, the Danes however, not staying proceedings, but marauding or levying black-mail all the while.

884
Feb. 2
Tribute
imposed
by the
Danes.

At length came Candlemas-day : a dark day for the Franks, when the Danes declared the amount of the geld they imposed—twelve thousand pounds, at twenty sols to the livre—for which they would grant a truce till October. The money was raised with extreme difficulty : shrines stripped of their gold and jewels and pillaged sacristies, furnished some portion of the funds. Between Danes and Franks, Pagans and Christians, enemies and friends, the Church fared miserably; all drew upon her, all spoiled her.

At length the last geld-instalment was paid ; but the Franks did not thereby purchase any exemption from disquietude. Beyond the Scheldt, in Lotharingia, the Danes continued plundering ; nor were the Franks by any means certain that after the Danes received the money, they would keep to their bargain. However, they evacuated Amiens, and marched and boated towards the

coast, the Frankish troops following them quietly 862—888
and at a respectful distance. The Franks could
884—885
not be sure that the Danes would not turn back
again; nor were they relieved from their apprehensions until they heard how the Pagans had
fairly embarked at Boulogne. As usual, however, the compromise was ineffectual, some of the
Danes may have crossed over to England, but the
greater part cruised in the Channel : their carni-
vorous instinct taught them that they would soon
be able to fall again upon their prey.

Carloman, the immediate pressure removed, 884
Dec. 6.
rode for pastime to the forest of Baisieux in the Death of
Carloman.
Corbiois, between Arras and Amiens, still recog-
nizable in the scrubby woodlands crossed by the
chaussée. The sportsman never seems to be
deterred by the Nemesis so frequently avenging
the wantonly causeless destruction of God's creatures, the answer to their call of agony. Carloman having chased a wild boar, the animal
in self-defence turned round and attacked his
unprovoked enemy : Berthold, the king's companion, trying to save his master's life, ended it.
His spear pierced Carloman's thigh, the wound
festered and became incurable : they buried the
king at Saint-Denis. As soon as the hovering
Northmen, bought off from the Somme, heard of
Carloman's death, their raven banners pounced
again upon the French territory. They had well
chosen their time : Hugh the Abbot, hitherto so

862—888 stout, lost his wits: the French were without
government, courage or wisdom.

884—885

Yet, could Hugh the Abbot and the Primores who composed a species of irregular Regency have broken the spell of terror, they were fully competent to defend the country; but instead of resisting the enemy, the Frankish nobles tried to reason and argue him away, remonstrating with the Northmen against the breach of the treaty.—Had not twelve thousand pounds, at twenty sols to the livre, been paid to them within the year to withdraw their forces? and now they were there again.

885
The Danes renew their invasions on Carloman's death, and demand another Danegelt.

Not so, quoth the Dane—According to the beneficiary or feudal system, a *gersum* was rendered to the Seigneur upon the Vassal's death, but also in some cases upon the death of the Lord—a life-bargain. This principle the Northmen applied to their transactions with the French: their engagement expired with Carloman's life, they had concluded their bargain with him, and not with the kingdom. If Carloman's successor or the French, wished to renew the treaty, the Danes must have the same amount of tribute repeated, sol for sol, livre for livre, the same in weight or the same in tale—on no other terms would they allow the kingdom peace or rest.

885
The Emperor Charles, invited to the Throne of France.

§ 21. Who was to succeed Carloman?—the child of the Adeliza Judith, of whom she was delivered five months after Louis-le-Bégue's death : from whose birthday, the feast of Saint 862—888 Lambert, the foul-mouthed gossips reckoned 885 back to the season when Louis was sinking under mortal illness, and spitefully whispered their conclusions? The child probably continued under the care of Rainulph the second, Count of Poitiers; but had any party been inclined to think of such an infant, a regency must have been appointed to govern in his name; and he was silently passed over.—Kaiser Karl, at this time in Italy, was therefore the only competent legitimate successor to the kingdom. Notwithstanding the reverses he had sustained, his reputation still stood high,—if they excluded the Kaiser, whom could they elect, unless they repudiated the Imperial lineage, and elected the half-caste Arnolph, or some gros-vilain, some stranger?

Theodorick, the High Chamberlain, was, for the fourth time within seven years, called upon to perform the duty of inviting a Sovereign to ascend the throne. Destiny seemed to have accomplished the end which patriots sought. The injurious severances might be terminated, Apparent reunion of the rents closed, the dissensions healed, no longer the divided Empire a divided, but a united Empire. Charles, king of Germany, Charles, king of Italy, Charles, king of France, Charles the Emperor—Charlemagne's magnificent inheritance again subjected to a Charles, under whose auspices all the former prosperity of the Franks might be restored.

862—888
~~~~
885
TheFrench
tender
their ho-
mages, and
immedi-
ately neg-
lect their
duty.

Yet this was a mere delusion, the Carlovingian empire was an effigy destitute of a soul: the organic spirit had for ever departed. Emperor Charles hastened from Italy, and on his arrival in France, the French with corresponding alacrity hastened to greet their Sovereign. Kneeling before him, they placed their hands between his hands, and became his men.—It is a weariness to be constantly remarking upon the perfect faithlessness of these generations, yet it is right to recollect, that whenever the solemn oaths and engagements binding Seigneur and Vassal by mutual promises of protection, trust and truth, were violated by either party, the delinquents set at nought religion, honour and morality.

French allegiance was not more lasting than the familiar notion of the lover's vow. The Emperor, accepting the Crown, undertook an anxious task : the Northmen were ravaging Lotharingia desperately: they entered and held the strong cities : amongst others they thus occupied Louvaine. Charles summoned his army for the purpose of expelling the enemy: ruefully scanty was the reluctant arrière-ban, Hugh the Abbot had the gout, and sent his essoign. The besieging army dispersed disgracefully—the jolly Northmen, as the Franks retreated, crowded on the Louvaine walls and shouted out their jeers, scoffing against the dastards.

§ 22. Dangers gathered apace on the further

confines. The cession made by Charles to Godfrey 862—888
the Dane was a transaction of dubious import,
a refined and wily policy, and therefore liable to 885
Friezeland
be defeated by contingencies, so nicely weighted and Lotha-
ringia,
in the balance of argument, that the scales were Godfrey,
and Hugh.
as nearly as possible in equilibrium. Godfrey's
County of Friezeland extended from the æstuary
and æstuary islands of the Meuse unto the Weser:
a territory which, according to more recent political demarcations, contained Holland and the
largest portion of the Dutch Netherlands, the Godfrey's
County of
Duchy of Oldenburgh, the Duchy of East Frieze- Friezeland
its extent.
land, and very many Seigneuries and Commu-
nities.—Here were the seven Sea-lands, the Commonwealth whose representatives assembled under
the oaks of Opstal-boom. Here were and are the
Theel-lands, amongst whose happy and contented
indwellers the Agrarian law, elsewhere a phantom
either lovely or terrific according to the spectator's
mind, has been fully recognized, even to the present age. Hence, according to the traditions of
the country, came Hengist and Rowena;—a valuable and opulent territory, but constantly exposed
to the raging ocean as well as to the pirate.

Therefore it was the duty of each Frison to
raise and strengthen the doughty dyke, which, in
the words of their antient doom-book, "encircles
the land like a golden ring; and the Frison was
to defend his dear Father-land against the sea The Fri-
sons.
with the spade and with the fork and with the Their love
of liberty.

862—888
885

Difficulty
of reducing
the Frisons
to subjec-
tion

hod; and against the Southern Saxon and the Northman, against the tall helmet and the red shield and the unrighteous might, with the point of the lance and the edge of the sword and the brown coat of mail.—And thus shall we Frisons defend our land within and without, if they will help us, God and Saint Peter!"

So spake this energetic race, when they fully asserted the patriarchal liberties which rendered their commonwealth as truly illustrious as the fondly favoured republics of Italy, though denied the capriciously bestowed reward of historic fame. But the Frisons had to endure many trying vicissitudes: they were repeatedly attacked and partially vanquished by the Northmen: they were compelled to shelter themselves under the Imperial eagle. Thrice had the Carlovingian Monarchs, in the assertion of their supremacy, granted Friezeland as a Benefice to Danish chieftains, but none of these Counts had remained in the country; and one cause, without doubt, which obstructed the establishment of Danish supremacy, had been the sturdy independence of the native tribes.—"The men," says an English writer of the fifteenth century, "be high of body, strong of virtue, stern and fierce of heart: they be free, and not subject to lordship of other nations, and they put themselves in peril of death by cause of freedom, and they had liever die than be under the yoke of thraldom."

Such was the character which the Frisons earned when they had vindicated their independence; and the Emperor Charles effected, politically speaking, a Machiavellian *tratto doppio,* by bestowing this territory upon Godfrey. The surrender satisfied the claims which previous possession of the country had given to the Northmen, and also found full employment for the new Count in maintaining his rule. If Godfrey rendered Friezeland a tranquil Imperial Province, well.—If the Frisons could despatch Godfrey, better—But Godfrey succeeded in coercing the natives, and according to the traditions of Friezeland, they, the Frisons, were so completely (though temporarily) reduced, that, in token of subjection, Godfrey compelled every man to go about with a halter round his neck, which was immediately tightened upon the slightest token of disobedience to his power; a significant and instructive myth, insomuch as it explains the principle so generally enabling the few, or the one, to coerce the multitude. Each individual brings home to himself his own chance of danger, and individual fear pulverizes resistance.

§ 23. When Godfrey demanded Friezeland and Gisella, had her beauty charmed him? Gisella was King Lothair's daughter, and sister of Count Hugh the son of Waldrada: of that Hugh who was so determinately opposing the legitimate branches of the family, all inimical to him, all

862—888
883

Count Godfrey gains the mastery of the Frisons.

885
Godfrey and Hugh combine against the Emperor Charles

862—888
——
885
scoffing and scorning him, all agreeing to keep
him out of any share of his father's dominions.
And we doubt not but that the transactions immediately subsequent to the marriage, disclose
the suggestions upon which the Suitor spoke as
well as the Adviser.

Godfrey and Hugh combined : the latter exhorted his brother-in-law, the Dane, to co-operate
with him. If Hugh regained his inheritance, he
would share Lotharingia with Godfrey. Godfrey
should be confirmed in half that kingdom.

Godfrey combining with Hugh of Alsace demands from Charles an encrease of territory.
Godfrey commenced by deputing ambassa-
dors to the Emperor, soliciting additional territory, the whole Rhine-land from Sinzig to Coblentz. Fertile Friezeland abounded with cattle
and crops, grain and flesh-meat, butter and cheese;
but though barn, larder and dairy were well
stored, the cellar was scantily supplied, and therefore he craved a country which (as he alleged)
would supply him with wine—that Rhine-coun-
try where Charlemagne's practical sound sense
and judgment covered the sterile rocks with gar-
lands of green. Godfrey's policy, however, was
perfectly sober ; and the requisition, though it
sounds to us roughly worded, was in substance
justified by the expansive arguments of diplomacy.
He claimed a Danish land : the Rhine-benefices
had been granted to Harold by Louis-le-débonnaire, and his pretensions were warranted by a
sufficient shew of reason. Had the Dane pre-

vailed, he would have established himself in the 862—888
heart of the Empire. Cologne, and all the Ripuarian country between Moselle and Frisia, would 885
have been amalgamated into Godfrey's kingdom;
and Godfrey the husband of Gisella King Lothair's daughter, might, like Rollo, the husband
of Gisella King Charles-le-Simple's daughter,
have founded a flourishing dynasty.

The Emperor Charles was equally clearsighted, Scheme de-
and devised a scheme for ridding himself of the emperor,
enemy. Three were his counsellors, all entering bishop of
heartily into his views—Willibert, Archbishop of &c, for rid-
Cologne, who must have quailed at the very empire of
thought of the Danes fixing themselves within a
morning's march from Cologne—Count Henry,
whose title to the Rhine-benefices would be most
inconveniently disturbed by Danish suzerainty—
and a Count Everard, whom Godfrey had evicted.
—Count Henry took the lead in council. To dispossess Godfrey by force was impracticable. In
Friezeland, protected by his rivers and swamps,
he was unassailable: no army could march thither.
"We must draw him out," quoth Count Henry:
—they therefore spoke fairly to Godfrey's ambassadors, giving him good hopes that his demand
should be granted, and invited him to a conference with the Bishop and Count Henry, who
would offer terms on the Emperor's behalf. Godfrey came unsuspiciously, accompanied by his wife
Gisella. An island at the confluence of the rivers

862—888

885

Godfrey killed by Count Henry.

Rhine and Waal was proposed for the conference. Godfrey was received by a small, but apparently hospitable party—good Bishop Willibert, Count Henry, and Count Everard. The whole day passed in discussion: from humanity or other causes, they did not like to murder Godfrey before the eyes of his wife, so the Bishop helped, and by his intervention Gisella was induced to quit her husband, and leave him with Henry and Everard upon the island. The discussions were renewed between the Northman and the two German nobles. Count Everard complained of the injury he had sustained from Godfrey. Rudely preferred, Everard's complaints were answered angrily by the Dane—Count Everard drew his sword, and cut the unarmed Northman down at one blow: Everard will perhaps appear again performing a similar safe service. Few in number, the German soldiery were well equipped, and they made the matter sure, stabbing Godfrey through and through: others who were dispersed about in the vicinity, dealt similarly with all the Northmen by whom Godfrey had been escorted to the place of slaughter.

Godfrey thus had been successfully removed, yet the work was only half done—the other half remained to be performed. Hugh, Waldrada's son, continued powerful as ever, and when he should know how his friend, ally and brother had perished, would he not become a more inveterate

and dangerous enemy than before? The outlaw 862—888
Prince, sheltered in his forest-country and sup- 885—886
ported by his affectionate retainers, was beyond
the grasp of Charles: further wiles were therefore needed to accomplish the desired end, neatly
and speedily. Ere he could receive the intelligence of Godfrey's assassination, the kind and
friendly promises of Count Henry invited Hugh
to Gondreville, on the Moselle. Count Hugh,
nothing suspicious, repaired to the appointed
place of meeting. There the confiding prince was Hugh of Alsace
seized —"Put out his eyes, Count Henry, when treacher-ously seized
you have him,"—was the command which the and blinded.
Emperor Charles had given. Count Henry most
willingly obeyed the mandate. Hugh's companions, cruelly and shamefully mutilated, also
sustained their doom. Blind Hugh was sent far
away, to the Abbey of St. Gall. After a time
they transferred him to doleful Pruhm in the
Ardennes, and there he was shorn as a monk by
Abbot Regino, who inserts in his chronicle the
narration of these dealings, without affecting any
compunction for his share in the transaction, or
any regret or sorrow for the victims whose fate
he records.

Regino was truthy and honest, he saw no
wrong in such transactions: how could he? nor
should we, had we been in Regino's place; nor
would Regino do worse than we do, were he in
ours. There are fashions in wrong, but wrong

862—888

883—886

abides: the stuff is identical, though make and pattern change. The world's progress gratifies mankind with varieties and modifications of injustice, but the progressing world's injustice remains indestructible. The Danes and those who companied with the Danes were well served—they were beyond the pale of Carlovingian civilization.

885
Danish
warfare
recom-
n ences
more in-
tensely.

§ 24. The Northmen again directed their operations towards Central France through the Seine-country.—Paris stands in the way, and Paris must be gained or subdued.—Like all amphibious creatures, they took most naturally to the water, and therefore they determined, as during previous invasions, to render the Seine their highway. Reinforcements swarmed in from Lotharingia, from Belgium, from the British Islands : the Danes were intoxicated with success, they had measured their strength against their enemies, and they could appreciate that strength. How thoroughly had they overcome the stout Germans on Luneburgh Heath : how had they baffled the craven Franks, tricked them, drained them, pillaged them, disgraced them, defied them !

The Danish battle-axe, gisarme and arbalest, had always been the terror of the foe : the Danes had always been fearless warriors, but threescore years of incessant warfare had disciplined the desperate Berserkers into a skilled soldiery.— Jarls and Vikings now added excellent general-

ship to personal bravery: obsidional devices, 862—888
whether for attack or defence, had become familiar to the Northmen: the Teutonic and Scandi- 885
navian nations were clever carpenters: born in
the forest or the forest-glades, the hatchet was
the first plaything in the hand of the boy. The
Burgundians so fierce in war, who now appear
so awfully mysterious, the spectres of the Nibe-
lungen Lied, used to travel the country, and get
their honest living by working at their timber-
trade. Norsk ingenuity is the admiration of
every traveller at the present day.

Sigurd or Sigfried is the acknowledged leader 885
July 25.
of the enterprize, he alone is honoured by the The Northmen re-
title of King. Rollo acts concurrently though in- occupy
Rouen.
dependently, and reoccupies Rouen.—This movement was made before the main body of the Northmen had come up: the French were therefore
encouraged to resistance. Hard fighting ensued,
both in the advance and about the city. Ragnald,
whom the French chroniclers call Duke of Maine,
while the Northmen exalt him to a higher rank,
"Prince of all France," was the chief French
commander. So imperfect are our historical materials for this period, that it is impracticable to
identify Ragnald, though so distinguished in station. Ragnald endeavoured to play Hastings off '
against Rollo, but did not succeed. He then collected a large army from Burgundy and Neustria,
and prepared for battle; but, on the other hand,

862—888 the French not unfrequently favoured the enemy.
Some dreaded the consequences of resistance.
885 Who could forget the horrors of the cold year?
The events of the former invasion, the corpses
floating in the river, or swinging from the
branches, had left a warning remembrance; and
others gladly placed themselves under Danish
protection. This assimilating process, which had
been going on more or less through all the periods
of the Danish invasions, aided the Northmen, but
885 assisted in extinguishing their nationality. A
Aug.
Ragnald fisherman or boatman, who entered Rollo's ser-
duke of
Maine kill- vice, saved his new master all trouble from the
ed. Rollo
proceeds Duke of Maine: he killed Ragnald, probably by
to Paris
stealth: he ran him through. Ragnald's army
dispersed.—"And now, my men, on to Paris!"
Age nunc, navigemus Parisius—Rollo's words,
which we give in Dudo's Latin, were preserved
traditionally in the family.

The main 　§ 25.　"On to Paris!"—This was the general
fleet and
army of cry amongst the Danes. Sigfried was coming, and
the Danes
advance to Sigfried came. So mighty a fleet had never been
Paris
seen: for two leagues in length the broad river
was covered with Danish craft, great and small,
boats and wherries, barks and barges: their forces
were reckoned at forty thousand.

Pontoise 　Pontoise, strongly and judiciously fortified,
taken.
surrendered by capitulation, without offering any
opposition: the garrison retired to Beauvais—a
transaction raising suspicions of collusion . the

Northmen entered the town, burnt and destroyed 862—888
as usual; and, rejoicing in their success, prepared
to attack Paris. On all previous occasions Paris 885
had been the easiest of conquests: long before
Regner Lodbrok had carried away the big iron
bar of Paris gate, Paris gate stood open to them;
for the inhabitants had no heart to defend their
homes. Counts and Bishops, monks and merchants, landsmen and seamen, had been always
ready to purchase safety by flight or ignominious
submission; but amidst the Empire's decay, an
unexpected element of strength was disclosed.

Old travellers tell us how the matchless Da- Utility of Charles-le-
mascus steel is prepared by burying worn-out Chauve's fortifica-
horseshoes in a damp cellar: the metal's weaker tions of Paris.
portion perishes by oxidation, and the bright
particles are discovered, shining amidst the brown
rust, and in them is concentrated the essence of
the trenchant ore. This Arabian process typifies
a moral process not unfrequently occurring:
misfortunes eliciting virtues or powers unknown
or unused.—The wisdom of Charles-le-Chauve's
plans of fortification now became apparent.
Gaily coloured, and therefore called the Pons
Pictus, his breakwater bridge, stretching across
the river, completely prevented the advance of
the Danish vessels: his castles, particularly the
Grand-Châtelet, having been recently protected
by additional bulwarks and superstructures, could
only be reduced by a regular siege: on every

862—888
885
side was the island carefully defended.   And let us be here permitted to wander into the regions of poetry for the description which most vividly enables us to look down upon the scene.

> Siede Parigi in una gran pianura,
> Nel' ombilico di Francia, anzi nel cuore
> Gli passa la riviera entro le mura,
> E corre e esce in altra parte fuore:
> Ma fa un isola prima, e v' assicura
> De la città una parte, e la migliore;
> L'altre due, (che in tre parti è la gran terra)
> Di fuor' la fossa, e dentro il fiume serra.

> Dovunque intorno il gran muro circonda
> Gran munizioni havea già CARLO fatte;
> Fortificando d' argine ogni sponda,
> Con scanna-fossi dentro e case-matte.
> Onde entra nella terra, onde esce l'onda,
> Grossissime catene aveva tratte,
> Ma fece piu ch'altrove provedere
> Là, dove area più causa di temere.

Yet bridges and towers were only secondary protections and defences: the disintegration of the kingdom was bringing out more.   Chief in command within the city is Eudes, son of Robert-le-Fort, Count of Paris, the future king; and with him his brother Robert, for whom also is a crown in prospect.   We have not the slightest means of conjecturing how and in what manner the sons of Robert-le-Fort had regained their ancestorial importance.   We have an indistinct perception that this city passed to the Capets from Conrad the Guelph—but many of Robert-le-Fort's ho-

The defenders
of Paris,
Eudes and
Robert
Capet, &c.

nours, which upon his death were granted to 862—888
Hugh the Abbot, had not been restored to the
Capet family. 885

In this event-abounding period, the most important pages of French history are unfortunately
lacerated or lost; were they extant, we should
know the battles in which Eudes had so signally
distinguished himself against the Northmen as
to acquire his now pre-eminent fame. Bishop
Gauzeline was the compeer of Eudes in military
valour and skill: by his side, supporting him in
noble rivalry, was his sister's son, Ebles, brother
of Rainulph the second Count of Poitiers. This
Ebles, Abbot of Saint Germain-des-prés, afterwards Abbot of Saint Denis and Chancellor of
the realm, was a sturdy soldier in hand and heart,
an excellent marksman.—Abbot Ebles can kill
seven Danes at one shot, was the saying at Paris,
testifying the opinion entertained of his skill;
which Abbo, the antient poetic historian of the
siege, expresses so ingeniously in his ambiguous
verse, that you may suppose he records the feat,
not as an hypothetical but an actual performance.
Ebles, a favourite personage with the Monkish
Poet, is frequently designated by him as *Martius
Abba*, or *Mavortius Abba*, thereby misleading a
very learned historian into the creation of an
Abbé Mars as an additional defender of Paris.
Rainier Count of Hainault was much distinguished for valour, Eudes Capet pre-eminent above all.

862—868

862

An exceedingly curious narrative of the siege exists in the poem, addressed by the before-mentioned Abbo, the monk of Saint Germains, to his teacher, a great master of verse, from whom, toiling over Virgil, the author learned the art.

Abbo's Poem "de bellis Pari- siacæ m- bis ´

The florid and ample composition, an encomium upon Eudes, commemorating the prowess which conducted him to the throne, narrates the events occurring during the beleaguering of the Capetian Capital : details abound, singularly curious and authentic. Abbo delighted in his toil; yet verse was an ungrateful labour, extorted from an unwilling muse. Perplexed and obscure, his rugged lines are studded by barbarous Hellenisms, many passages almost defying interpretation.

Abbo's poem, notwithstanding its imperfections, is a most remarkable muniment, a textual guide to the historian ; but if we seek a picture possessing life and colour, we must contemplate the siege as idealized by the Bard of chivalry. The lays of the Trouveurs readily transmuted the Danes into the more familiar miscreants, the Saracens, and the achievements of Eudes-le-Grand were bestowed upon the greater Charlemagne. The sonorous *Chansons de Geste* acquired a wider circulation in florid prose, and the *Reali di Francia* and the other tales composing the

Siege of Paris by the Danes, ro- manticized by Ariosto.

Carlovingian cycle, became the most favourite volumes of popular Italian literature. Ariosto adopted the inspiration of these fictions, his renaissance poetry imparting grace and elegance to the rudeness of Gothic romance. Sigfried is adorned by Agramante's plumed casque; and the *Assedio di Parigi*, the most brilliant episode in the Orlando Furioso, may be read with delight as an exalted version of the events which now befel.

862—888
885

The Northmen fully appreciated the difficulties they had to overcome. Paris fortifications, and the front presented by the garrison, opposed formidable, and, as the event proved, insuperable obstacles. The Northmen never wasted their strength, never fought if they could gain their object without fighting, always ready, according to the Italian proverb, to lengthen the lion's skin by the fox's tail. Could the Commanders of the Place be inveigled into a truce, the Seine would be free to the Northmen. Sigfried therefore commenced negotiations. He sought a personal interview with Bishop Gauzeline, endeavouring to obtain the Prelate's assent. The cunning Dane made tempting overtures:—the Bishop and Eudes and the other chieftains, if they acceded, should preserve their dignities and possessions, nay, be the gainers. Sigfried's offers produced no effect: his threats were equally fruitless; and hurling his defiance at the Bishop, the Viking departed.

885
Sigfried demands a free passage up the Seine for the Northmen, and is refused.

§ 26. Mournful was Saint Catherine's morn, when the siege began. Eudes and his brother

885
Nov. 27,
The siege begins.

862—888

885—896

Robert, and Count Rainier, and Abbot Ebles, and Bishop Gauzeline occupied the Grand-Châtelet, the city-castle. Against this Donjon the Northmen directed their first onslaught; and Bishop Gauzeline was wounded. Urged to the utmost fierceness, the Danes, provoked by resistance, continued their attacks against the stubborn walls. Terror spread throughout the city: the assault continued from morn till nightfall, the inhabitants were in the utmost dismay.

Sonar' per gli alti e spaziosi tetti
S' odono gridi e femmil' lamenti.
L' afflitte donne percotendo i petti,
Corron' per casa, pallide e dolenti;

Le campane si sentono a martello
Di spessi colpi, e spaventose tocche.
Si vede molto in questo tempio e in quello,
Alzar' di mano, e dimenar' di bocche.
Se 'l tesoro paresse a Dio si bello
Come a le nostre opinioni sciocche,
Questo era il dì, che 'l Santo Concistoro
Fatto avria in terra ogni sua statua d'oro.

S' odon' rammaricare i vecchi giusti,
Che s' erano serbati in quegli affanni
E nominar' felici i sacri busti,
Composti in terra già molti e molt' anni,
Ma gl' animosi giovani robusti,
Che miran' poco i lor propinqui danni
Sprezzando le ragion' de' più maturi
Di quà, di là, vanno correndo a i muri.

Strenuously had the Parisians laboured in strengthening their defences; yet the additional fortifications of the Grand-Châtelet were not quite completed. Eudes and the Bishop therefore employed themselves throughout the night in directing the needful operations, watching whilst the Northmen caroused. With the dawn, the enemy renewed their attacks, and again sustained a repulse. The siege continued with varied fortunes. Sometimes Paris sustained the greatest strait, whilst at others the dangers diminished : intervals ensued during which the Danes merely observed the city. Yet the assailants and defenders, besiegers and garrison, though their powers might fluctuate, were so equally matched, that during the whole period,—first and last nearly four years,—Paris was never at ease, nor the Northmen neglectful of the object which, ultimately, they were reluctantly compelled to resign.

862—888

886

In the course of the early Spring the Danes were favoured by their favourite element : Hnikkar, the Scandinavian Neptune, the tricksy water-demon, ought to have been the Norskman's tutelary deity. The Seine swelled to a great height, swept away several piers of the Petit-Pont, and opened the stream for the Danish vessels. Indefatigable Bishop Gauzeline repaired the bridge and manned the adjoining tower, entrusted to twelve citizens, or rather members of the merchant Guild. The Northmen endeavoured to burn the painted bridge; but the bishop's activity frustrated their plans : he sunk the Danish fire-

886
Feb. 6,
Great flood
of the
Seine
further
attacks
made by
the Northmen.

R R 2

862—888
886
ships, and the bridge was saved.—The Northmen also attacked the Petit-Pont tower, heaping combustibles against and around the building. The conflagration compelled the selected garrison who defended the bulwark to surrender, the Northmen promising security of life and limb: but the promise given was immediately violated, and the twelve defenders mercilessly slaughtered. Abbo preserves their uncouth names, and Paris has been invited to commemorate their prowess by a national monument.

Bishop Gauzeline's health was beginning to fail: this last calamity disheartened him; he solicited aid from Charles, King and Emperor. The Sovereign was now in trouble: the Eastern parts of Germany were becoming alienated under an inimical influence, and discontent was increasing in the Gauls. Charles however ordered Count Henry, the treacherous betrayer of the Danish Godfrey, to march for the relief of the city. Had the troops or their commander exerted themselves, the Northmen might possibly have been driven away from their positions; but Count Henry and his Germans were cool   Why should they shed their blood in defending the French, for whom they cared not?   Count Henry returned exhausted to Germany without striking a blow.

Count Henry sent by Charles to relieve the city, but fails.

883
Death of Bishop Gauzeline, discouragement of the Parisians.
§ 27. Bishop Gauzeline exerted his strength to the utmost, became more harassed, and died: his death shed great gloom upon the citizens, who

trusted his valour and his prudence. He had 862—888
been endeavouring to treat with the Northmen;
but the expectations of peace were destroyed, and 886
general depression prevailed.

Provisions became scarce within the walls,
the citizens, more and more dispirited. Eudes,
secretly quitting the city, repaired hastily to the
Emperor, earnestly soliciting further aid, lest
Paris should utterly succumb. Charging through
the Danish squadrons who attempted to intercept
him at the gate, he re-entered Paris safely, report-
ing a promised reinforcement. Eight months however elapsed ere the perplexed Emperor could
fulfil the promise, when he despatched Count
Henry again, with more confidence than before.
The army under this ill-omened commander was
fully adequate, it should seem, to effect the military operations with which he was entrusted.
This time Count Henry was active, too active:
the Northmen, entertaining an excusable hatred
against the executioner, if not murderer, of Godfrey, had prepared a snare for him and his troops—
deep ditches covered with hurdles and grass, a
contrivance so stale and common that it should
seem as if the simplest tyro would have been
able to anticipate and frustrate the device. But
astute Count Henry's proficiency in artifice failed
to warn him against other men's stratagems . gallopping round the Danish camp, he and his horse
fell into a pit; and the Danes, rushing out of

886
July, Aug.
Count
Henry
despatched
a second
time: slain
by strata-
gem.

862—888
886—887

their hiding-places, killed him, carrying off shield and sword as trophies—a successful vengeance, dispiriting to the French and Germans, and causing corresponding joy to the Danes.

Revolt in Burgundy.

§ 28. Whilst the Northmen were beleaguering Paris, the Burgundians rebelled, refusing obedience to Charles or assistance to their fellow-subjects, probably instigated by Count Raoul, aspiring to independence. The disaffection of Eastern Germany was sympathetic. Charles, though contending against disloyalty and disabled by encreasing infirmities, acted boldly: he assembled his forces, and prepared wisely for action. He conciliated Eudes, restoring to him such of Robert-le-Fort's domains as had been held by Hugh the Abbot, and appeared in person before Paris with a very large army. The Emperor expected to have been supported by Count Henry. Henry had been slain; nevertheless the Imperial General boldly pitched his tents in the face of the enemy. Winter was drawing on, and both parties ready for a compromise. Charles offered a Danegelt, and moreover he ceded to Sigfried,—the transaction amounting to a cession—the revolted Burgundy, thus employing a foreign enemy to suppress domestic rebellion.

886 Sept. Charles treats with the Danes, and compromises by a subsidy. Siege partially raised.

The Danes made ample use of the opportunity granted to them, not conceiving themselves under any obligation to keep within a prescribed boundary Some continued encamped or quartered near Paris, but large numbers dispersed ^{862—888} themselves over the adjoining districts. The truce was imperfectly observed by the Danes: ^{886—887} the Parisians abstained from positive hostility, but they would not allow the Danish craft to ascend the river, so the Northmen dragged their vessels round : this was thought a wonderful manœuvre. During the movements before Paris, one of their heavy, stout and clumsy boats, the keel hollowed out from a single piece of timber, was swallowed by the silt, and dug up about fifty years since near the Champ-de-Mars.

Beauvais was burned : Rollo helped to kindle 886 Autumn. the fire. Saint-Médard was burned, Sens be-Beauvais, Sens, sieged ; the gigantic, almost cyclopean, Roman &c taken by the walls (yet standing) enabled the inhabitants to Northmen. resist. Yet Bishop Everard thought it expedient to ransom the city. He probably felt that no fortifications could compensate for the astounding pusillanimity of the Frankish Community. Shortly afterwards the Bishop died ; and the Northmen, as on other occasions, considered that the covenant had expired, and spoiled all the adjoining districts of Burgundy.

The Loire and Seine-country was pillaged, Danish operations Rollo amongst the ravagers : Sigfried returned to his fleet in the following spring, resuming his devastations ; but during the autumn he sailed to Friezeland or Holland, where he was killed. The Royal general's death did not derange the

862—888
886—887

operations of the Northmen · possibly Rollo, who returned to Paris during some of these transactions, assumed the command. They continued to watch the city, making occasional hostile demonstrations, until the last penny was paid. The King of France who succeeded Charles had to discharge the balance.

§ 29. Bitterly was the Emperor reviled for his dealings with the Northmen by his subjects and contemporaries. Modern historians repeat the hootings—" *Cet infâme traité*," says one, no less indignantly than if the Emperor Charles were a living legitimate Sovereign; yet, if we endeavour to form a calmer judgment, the transactions are undeserving of such stern reprobation. They may have proved detrimental: they sound disgraceful; nevertheless Charles was justified by precedent, by policy, above all by necessity.

Wise men recommend making a bridge of gold for a flying enemy. It was no new thing which Charles had done. Louis-le-Bégue, Charles-le-Chauve, our Anglo-Saxon kings, our great Alfred, gladly purchased peace from the Pagans by money or more than money,—grants of territory, provinces or Kingdoms. Charles the Emperor abandoned Burgundy to the Danes—and wherefore? —the Burgundians were abandoning him, and he surrendered them to the chastisement of the foeman. He bravely attempted to relieve Paris, though Paris was scarcely his. Paris virtually

belonged to Count Eudes, and Charles must have
had a presentiment of the Capetian aspirations.

The unfairness of these harsh censures is
peculiarly manifested by the feature, that in the
estimates thus formed concerning the conduct of
the unfortunate Emperor, no consideration is
given to the accompanying circumstances.   The
subject is discussed and commented upon as
though Charles could choose.   But he was appalled, and well he might be, by the raging
Saracens, and the advancing Magyars.   Italy was
almost overwhelmed by the Mahometan Hosts—
from the gates of Rome southward, the country
was completely under their power.   They were
committing enormous devastations: awful sensation was produced by the destruction of the most
hallowed sanctuaries, Monte Cassino for example.
The political or moral influence of the Saracens
was even more to be apprehended than their
warlike energy : the Italian nobles and communities often colluded or combined with the Infidels.
This was memorably the case with the Republic
of Amalfi.   Worse than all, they were favoured by
the Prelates ; and Athanasius Bishop of Naples,
supporting them by his alliance, had opened the
way further to the gates of Rome.   The fierce
Magyars were drawing nigh to the Imperial confines.   The united, honest, loyal and hearty co-
operation of Franks and Germans could alone
expel the Northmen.   Experience had shewn that

862—888

886—887
Charles-
le-Gras,
unfairly
censured
for his com-
promise
with the
Danes.

Charles-le-
Gras com-
pelled to
compro-
mise with
the Danes
by the
pressure of
other
enemies

862—888
886—887 such a condition was impossible; therefore weigh-
ing evil against evil, the temporizing plan adopted
by Charles was the best which could be devised.

886—887
Domestic
troubles.
Empress
Richarda
accused of
adultery. § 30. Home and foreign anxieties combined:
a troubled household and domestic dissensions
discredited the monarch, and contributed to destroy the reverence due to his person, and thereby
weaken his sovereign authority. When the spell
of obedience is once broken by contempt, the
power of command departs. Vices, nay even
virtues, incidentally assuming the tinge of mean-
ness or silliness, often damage the earthly divinity
of Royalty proportionably more than crimes. Nero
the fiddler clenched the deposition of Nero the
tyrant. Whilst Henry the Eighth died quietly in
his bed, Charles Stuart's awkward fondlings with
Henrietta Maria at the banquet, contributed almost as effectually as the High Commission Court
or the Star-Chamber in conducting him to the
scaffold through the windows of Whitehall.

Charles was on very bad terms with his
wife, Richarda. Ten years married, their marriage was childless. She was defamed as an
adulteress, Bishop Liutward her reputed paramour. He certainly appears to have been politically untrue. Richarda offered to clear herself
by the ordeal, the battle-trial or the labyrinth
of glowing ploughshares. But the Empress was
not permitted to justify herself; and she retired
to the monastery of Andlau in Alsace, which she

had founded. Charles had other views. He doted 862—888
on Bernard, his concubine's son, for whom he
was most anxious to secure the throne. To pro- 887
mote this earnestly-desired object, Charles ne- Charles labours to secure
gotiated with Pope Hadrian. Rome and Rome's the succession to his
Bishop, and the Roman people, needed the Em- illegitimate son Ber-
peror's protection. The Pontiff was not un- nard.
willing to gratify the father's wishes. Hadrian He is dis-appointed
undertook a journey to France for the purpose by the death of
of sanctioning the proposed scheme of succession, Pope Ha-drian III.
giving such aid as Papal influence might bestow;
but just as he had crossed the Po he died, to the
extreme exultation of the Emperor's ill-wishers,
particularly in Germany, the centre of disaffection.

No human prudence could extricate Charles 887
from his position of peril, the more distressingly Increasing perils of the
painful because there were tantalizing possibilities Empire.
that he might be rescued. He was sliding down
a precipice seeming to offer some narrow ridge
giving stayhold to his feet, or some branch which
might furnish grasphold for his hands; but the
chances kept escaping when he tried them. As
far as birthright extended, the legal or constitutional claims of his own Bernard and the Ca-
rinthian Arnolph were equal. Ansgarda's infant,
if he were the son of Louis-le-Bégue, had disappeared. Could public opinion be made to
support Bernard, the youth might reign; but the
tall, magnificent, winning, bold, skilful Arnolph,

802—888 Duke of Carinthia, securely defended in his castle

837 of Mosaburch, was already considered by the Germans as their Sovereign. Hence their malevolent delight when the Pope's sudden death deprived the Emperor of his support, and frustrated those plans in which, not merely Bernard's elevation to the throne, but even the preservation of his own life, might be involved.

Destruction of principle occasioned by the general conduct of the Carlovingians. All the sins and errors of his ancestors and his own were accumulating upon Charles the Emperor. He had been inviting that retributive justice which imparts such awful unity to the tremendous epic of Carlovingian history. On whom, or upon what institution or upon what laws, human or divine, had any member of the Carlovingian family a right to depend? Their good was rendered reprobate by their evil. They had destroyed the very notion of truth and honour: they had shed blood like water: they had confounded the boundaries of temporal and spiritual authority: they had laid their hands upon the Ark: their empire was founded upon political and social treason. By their examples, their acts, their deeds, they had continually inculcated the lesson, that it was right for a servant to depose his master, a nephew to rise against an uncle, a son to dethrone a father,—for a kinsman to profit by any advantage he might gain over a kinsman by force or by fraud, by deceit or by violence— the adult over the child, the mighty over the feeble,

the cunning over the unwary, and, most odious 862—888
of all, the sound and healthy over the sick and
dying.—When the stalwart Carloman, nerveless, 887
motionless, speechless, fell stricken by the palsy,
Charles had gallopped away from his brother's
bedside, and, seizing the kingdom of Italy, co-
operated in excluding Arnolph:—his own turn
had come now.

§ 31.   The burthensome and loathsome in-
flation of his miserable body increased fearfully.
So swollen that he could not move without assistance, they were forced to lift him in and out of
his chair.   Notwithstanding this enduring physical
affliction, we have seen how he exerted himself
in the functions of government and against the
Northmen   no slackness could be imputed to him,
no neglect, no cowardice, a King in council, a
King in the field; but his maladies were now
gaining upon him so rapidly, that his mind seemed
dulled by the oppression of his frame.   Irksome 887.
to his subjects who were tired of him, those sub- The people
turn against
jects recollecting nothing of the eagerness with the Emperor
which they had courted his authority, a silent but
universal and irresistible conspiracy pullulated
throughout the empire, for the purpose of anticipating his death.   Because he so truly deserved
compassion, the people scorned and despised him.

Arnolph of Carinthia advanced as the most
exalted of the pretenders, yet scarcely yielding
in eagerness to Eudes and Robert, the sons of

862—888
887—888 Robert-le-Fort. Treading close upon Eudes and Robert was the energetic and expectant Berenger, Berenger elbowed by Guido Duke of Spoleto—Raoul of Burgundy and Boso of Provence and Rainulph of Aquitaine, bold, eager and designing, pressing onwards, and the Counts of Armorica and Sancho Mitarra Duke of the Gascons, planning to render themselves independent of the Carlovingian Crown, upon whomsoever it might devolve. The Emperor's manifested intention on behalf of the bastard Bernard, added more point and vigour to the encreasing discontent ; and the Germans, the Saxons, the Thuringians, the Franconians, the Bavarians, the Lombards, the Romans, who had so enthusiastically invoked Kaiser Karl when prosperously floating on the top of the tide, were now most bitterly inimical in the day of misfortune.

887. Nov Charles deposed by the Germans, and Arnolph accepted in his stead § 32. All the Teutonic nations solicited Arnolph to assume the royal authority. Small exertion was required ; and Charles accelerated the crisis by summoning a Diet at Tribur near Mayence, in order to promote the object so earnestly, dearly, anxiously sought, his son Bernard's enthronization. When the Diet was convened, Arnolph, triumphing in the ruddy bloom and brilliancy of health and youthful vigour, presented himself at the head of his army: he had sworn allegiance to his uncle, and if he believed in the doctrines of his age, he perilled his salvation by

the violation of his oath : what mattered ? he was
absolved by the legislature of the realm. Teutons
and Sclavonians, Archbishops, Bishops, Abbots,
Counts, Nobles, Knights, Priests and Laymen, vied
with each other in hailing the Duke of Carinthia
king of Germany. They thronged in to perform
homage, a race who should be foremost :—the old
story . as in the Colmar camp, so in the Tribur
council-chamber, the treachery of the Luegen-
feld acted over again. Ere three days had elapsed, Charles
miserably
all had deserted the bloated, helpless sufferer, not abandoned
merely as a Sovereign, but as a fellow-creature.
Not a human being was left to perform for
Charles the slightest offices which suffering nature requires · he might have starved had not the
Archbishop of Mayence, Liutbert, sent him meat
and drink. These supplies were so scanty and
irregular, that all the cares and anxieties of
Charles were absorbed in the horrid dread lest
he should die of hunger : he begged his victuals
from day to day.

§ 33. All the kingdoms, states, dominions, Arnolph
inaugu-
prelates and powers subjected to the Carlovin- rated at
Ratisbon.
gian domination, concurred in the sentence of
deposition : Arnolph, inaugurated at Ratisbon,
was solemnly acknowledged as king by all Baioaria and Suabia and Franconia and Thuringia :
indeed by all the nations of the German tongue,
and all the Sclavonian dependencies of the Carlovingian Crown.

862—888

888

Charles pitifully besought the new King of Germany to have mercy on him and on poor Bernard, imploring protection for the youth; and the more to move Arnolph, he sent to him the relic, the particle of the true Cross, upon which, as Duke of Carinthia, he had taken the oath of fealty. Arnolph shewed for his uncle some touch of compassion, which cost him nothing: a few inconsiderable demesnes were assigned to the heart-broken, fallen monarch for his sustenance. But when the bounty was granted, king Arnolph knew it could not be needed long:

12 or 13 Jan. 888 Death of Charles-le-Gras Cause of his death uncertain

about two months afterwards Charles was dead, having earned great pity and respect by the contrition he evinced, and the patient bearing of his misfortunes. On the morrow, they buried the body at Reichenau . the monks of Saint Gall, of which House the Emperor Charles was also a benefactor, were accustomed to sing his obit on the day of his funeral, the ides of January. But other dates are given, and the proximate cause of his death is uncertain; whether disease killed him, or sorrow, or poison, or violence, no one can tell. It was believed in France that Charles was strangled by his attendants, tired of the profitless and disagreeable care which nursing the cumbered disgusting beggar required.

Many and excellent talents had been bestowed upon him, but he lost their fruits when living, and posterity has denied him the delusive honours of posthumous renown. The French have erased him from the list of their monarchs . they do not reckon him in. Fame is very truly a breath. Charlemagne's world-wise praise has been permanently sustained by his popular denomination. He was a hero unquestionably; nevertheless "Carolus Magnus," "Karl der Grosse," "Charles-le-Grand," is pre-eminently indebted to his epithet for his vast celebrity. You cannot disconnect the idea from his name; but all the merits of his unfortunate descendant have been obscured by the associations involuntarily annexed to the designation derived from his clumsy corporeal disfigurement.—The world's commiserating contempt is poured out upon "Carolus Crassus," "Karl der Dicke," "Charles-le-Gras."

862—888

888

CHAPTER V.

DISMEMBERMENT OF THE EMPIRE: EUDES AND CHARLES-LE-SIMPLE. ESTABLISHMENT OF ROLLO IN NORMANDY.

888—912.

888—912

Accumulation of misfortunes upon the Carlovingian race.

§ 1. WITH a Charles arose the second dynasty's glory: with a Charles that glory departed. It is a profitable aid to the memory in the teaching of history, when important events coincide with dates rendered distinguishable or remarkable, whether by regular or serial sequences, or by repetitions or by regular combinations of numerals; so that the chronological era assumes a species of concrete identity. Signally is this the case with the thrice-repeated eight, the eight hundred and eighty and eight, which dissolved the Carlovingian Empire.

The mouth speaks the fulness of the heart: hence the similarity of proverbs and proverbial phrases in all languages and at all times, sentiments echoed in various tones, but of one import, passages of one strain, because harmonized by common feelings and universal experience. Hence the deep instruction conveyed in that familiar aphorism often used with irreverent levity or discontent, "misfortunes never come single;" testifying the predetermined consilience of events, when chastisements are specially appointed in anger or in mercy. All things, and all the

relations of matter and spirit, are governed by 888—912
laws; and human punishments, as well as human
rewards, are produced by the convergence of
lines whose first direction proceeds from all eternity: the arrows wing their flight against the
flesh, where they are to stick fast.

History, private or public, everywhere abounds
in such examples; and writers least willing to
acknowledge the Invisible Presence ruling the
affairs of man, are enforced to render the extorted acknowledgment, that the contingencies and
calamities which destroyed the Carlovingian dynasty were beyond calculation. The Carlovingians
were ruined by a glut of miseries. Within twenty
years, Charlemagne's lineage had possessed fifteen
Emperors, Kings and Princes, either ruling on the
throne, or expectant and competent to assume
supreme authority. In the year Eight hundred
and eighty-eight, the old and the young, the ripe
and the immature, were all swept away: some
according to the ordinary course of human life,
but many more by strange diseases, by mean,
trivial, or household accidents, by unexpected,
and as one might say, unreasonable contingencies.
Their good angel had departed from them. One
individual only who could colourably pretend to
be a Carlovingian, now wore a Royal crown:
one whom Charlemagne would have blushed to
acknowledge, the half-caste Sclavonian bastard
ARNOLPH, who had obtained the supremacy of

888—912 GERMANY and all the dominions speaking the German tongue, together with the Sclavonian
888—924 Marches and borders, where he was heartily acknowledged and obeyed, and seeking to extend his sway over the whole empire.

Revolutions of Italy.

§ 2. Not so in ITALY—here Arnolph was neglected or opposed; Apulia and Calabria would have scarcely cared had they passed under the Emir or the Soldan ; and if the wreck of the old Longobard aristocracy desired a Christian king, they would prefer some sovereign more congenial to them than the semi-Sclavonian Ar-

888—924 nolph. Rome, the Roman Senate, the Roman
Berengarius, King. clergy, and the Roman people, exercised their
889—893 suffrage for their own advantage, and according to
Guido, King. their own pleasure. All the interest which Pope Stephen could exert was bestowed upon his adopted son, the bold, active and shrewd GUIDO Count of Spoleto. But in Lombardy and the North, the French interest fostered by the Court of Pavia was preponderating, and the Estates of the kingdom either invited or accepted the grandson of Louis-le-Débonnaire by his daughter Gisella, the "august BERENGER," worthy of the diadem he acquired.

Ere they contested Italy, these two illustrious princes had become good friends, and when the deposition of the unfortunate Charles-le-Gras was impending, they agreed to act in concord and share the spoil: Guido should take France,

and *il Rè Berengario*, the Transalpine Empire. 888—912
Guido entered France, but, as we shall soon see, 889—893
yielded to a more popular rival. Tempted by
opportunity, he broke the compact he had made
with Berenger. A series of adventurous and
varied conflicts arose between the competitors
for Rome and Italy, in which the skill and prowess of the Princes appear as remarkable as the
sufferings inflicted upon the people during the
lengthened frays. Guido assumed the royal title,
whilst Berengarius received the iron crown in
San Michele's Basilica. Great celebrity did *il Rè
Berengario* earn in Italy, his long reign being
full of dramatic vicissitudes. His recollections
are still fresh in Lombardy—go to the Treasury
of Monza : by the side of Queen Theodolinda's
Ciocca, the strange plateau representing the mo-
therly hen encircled by her nestling brood, you
may yet see the Gospel-book deposited by Berengarius in the Sanctuary, when, after his Coronation, he restored the iron crown to the shrine. As
Berengarius left that Gospel-book, so the Book
remains, the crumbling leaves enclosed between
the ivory tablets. These are quaintly carved and
pierced, adorned by the interlacings termed runic
knots, according to conventional archæological 891—893
Guido Em-
phraseology ; but no Scandinavian sculptured peror.
their embossed and graceful foliage : they were
worked by a Celtic hand.

Civil wars ensued, tediously and destructively

888—912 complicated. Pope Stephen, and Rome, and southern Italy supported GUIDO, and he obtained

892—901 the imperial dignity. And having, in imitation of his antient predecessors, appointed his valorous

892—898 son LAMBERT to be his colleague, the latter upon
Lambeit
Emperor. his father's decease received the Imperial name.

ARNOLPH arose as a powerful enemy, and

896—898 repeatedly led his armies into Italy. The King
Arnolph
Emperor. of Germany acquired the Imperial diadem. He reigned with extraordinary splendour; but Lambert refused to resign the Imperial title, and retained a considerable portion of the territory.

Arnolph survived his rival for a few months:

899 a short interregnum ensued. LOUIS,—of whom
Louis of
Provence more hereafter—the son of Hermengarda and
invoked to
Italy. (See Boso, king of Provence, then entered into the
p. 632) conflict, and triumphed for awhile, to his great misfortune. Much affinity subsisted between the Provençals and the more unmixed populations of Italy. In the Provincia Romana, the municipal succession of the cities was uninterrupted, the languages were kindred. Adalbert, the Marquis of Tuscany, suggested to Louis that Italy might be easily conquered. Hermengarda's child, not undegenerate, accepted the hazardous invitation; and from the Lombard Diet and the Roman electors, Louis received the royal and imperial dignities.

899—901
Louis King Expelling the great Berengarius for a time,
of Italy and
Emperor and crowned King and Emperor, LOUIS esta-

blished his court at Verona, where he was re- 888—912
ceived with pretended cordiality and loyalty.
Reigning in full confidence, he disbanded his
troops; when the treacherous Lombards, apparently so contented, surrendered him to Berenga- 905
rius, who avenged himself by inflicting blindness Louis, blinded by
upon his competitor. The horrible operation was Berenga- rius, re-
performed with unusual mildness. Either in con- turns to Provence.
sequence of the executioner's unskilfulness or
mercy, the glowing bason did not entirely destroy
the visual power, and some faint glimmering of
light remained. Rabid dissensions endured seven
and twenty years. At length Berenger obtained 915—924 Berenga-
the pre-eminence—sole Emperor, and during the rius Empe- ror.
twenty-seven years, king, or claiming to be king.
The Magyars overwhelmed Italy, and the country
was reduced to the utmost misery. Berengarius
dallied with Arpad's hordes for the purpose of
protecting himself against the Burgundian Raoul, (See p. 635).
but uselessly and fatally, and he died by an
assassin's hand. Every convulsion in Italy at this
period is of vast historical importance; and the
throbbings of her wounds were felt throughout
Western Christendom.

§ 3. Boso, king of Provence, detested by Provence. Boso dies
the Carlovingians as an usurper, died about the about 887—8.
period when Charles the Emperor was deposed,
leaving his young son, the before-mentioned
Louis. The matron Hermengarda assumed the
regency in behalf of her boy; but this fine

888—924

890
country was persecuted by the Saracens, whose colonizations were even more alarming than their ravages: the sons of Arabia dwelt even amongst the snows of the Mons Jovis, Saint Bernard's kindly Hospice, then a murderous fastness. The Northmen also penetrated into Provence; and during an unsettled period of about two or three years, the country was almost without regular government, until, thanks to Hermengarda's talent, activity and wisdom, —the Provençals delighting in their "glorious Queen"— Louis, or Louis-Boso, was acknowledged as king in the great Council of Valence. Louis commenced prosperously. He acquired great part of the modern *Langue d'Oc*, the counties and dioceses on the Western bank of the Rhone, which he united to his kingdom. He espoused an Eadgiva, daughter of Edward the Elder, king Alfred's grand-daughter; his alliance with a Princess from such a distant land testifies his influence and renown. Possibly Eadgiva was receiving her education at Chelles; and the sagacious Hermengarda may have resorted to the Monastery with which the Merovingian, Anglo-Saxon, and Carlovingian Queens and Princesses were so closely connected, when planning an advantageous marriage for her son. We have related the miserable result of his Italian expedition: Louis, thenceforth called *l'Aveugle*, returned to Vienne, where he reigned unmolested and

Louis' son of Boso acknowledged as King of Provence in the Council of Valence.

(p. 631).

governed prudently. His counsellors and people, 888—912 compassionating his misfortunes, continued faith- 890 ful : he solaced himself by retaining the imperial title, and died in tolerable tranquillity, leaving Louis l'Aveugle one Son, CHARLES-CONSTANTINE, who lost all his died about 928 father's honours and dominions excepting the county of Vienne, afterwards Dauphiné:—the kingdom of Provence passed into other lines.

§ 4. The name of BURGUNDY stands forth prominently in every era of French history. The more recent portions of the Burgundian Burgundy annals, when her sovereigns became the pre- —parti-tions of the antient mier Dukes of Christendom, have received every Kingdom. elucidation which historical talent can bestow; but the anterior periods have continued comparatively disregarded, and the evidences accumulated by Benedictine diligence are left to furnish occupation for equivalent labour. By inheritance or usage, by constitutional acts or usurpations, the antient kingdom of Burgundy was partitioned into several dominations, well-known in their general aspect, but whose territorial boundaries are vaguely defined : subjected to rulers whose contested or conflicting rights offer as many problems as the demarcations of their territories. To the historical difficulties hence arising, must be added the circumstance, which, perplexing to the enquirer in every era of Carlovingian history, becomes here particularly troublesome—the recurrence of the same Christian

862—888 names. All who ruled as Counts in any portion
of antique Burgundia are indiscriminately called
879—880 " Counts of Burgundy;" and there are so many
Raouls and Hughs galloping about the field in
armour of uniform fashion, and bearing the same
patterned coronal on their helmets, that their
identification may baffle the most attentive observer. Or, if we think fit to place the question
in another aspect, the confusions of the times are
reflected in the confusions of the historians.

887—921 The French Chancery had, during the reign
Richard-le-
Justicier's of Charles-le-Chauve, designated the monarch as
country,
afterwards King of "France and Burgundy." Louis-le-Bégue
the modern
"Duchy of assumed the same style; but his authority in and
Burgun-
dy." within Burgundy, was practically intercepted by
those who enjoyed the usufruct of dominion. A
considerable portion had been detached by Boso;
and three Counties had been also erected within
the antient kingdom. Richard-le-Justicier, son
of the astute and intriguing Theodorick, and brother or half-brother of King Boso, governed the
Autunais, the Dijonnais, the Châlonnais and the
Auxois, the Avalonnois and some other Bail-
liages, nearly equivalent to the illustrious Duchy
of modern times, Burgundy Proper—the Burgundy so resplendently glorious in the creative
age of fantastic chivalry.

Richard-le-Justicier's eldest son, RODOLPH or
RAOUL, reserved for a higher destiny, did not
receive any appanage, whereas his brother Hugh-

le-Noir, in the father's lifetime, held that gay and 888—912 fertile and varied territory, afterwards known as the Franche-Comté, the valleys and the lower ranges of the Jura hills.

Transjurane Burgundy, principally consisting 888—912 Transju-rane Bur-gundy erected into a Kingdom by Rodolph or Raoul the Guelph. (See p 236) of modern Helvetia on this side of the Reuss and the passes of the Mons Jovis or the Great Saint-Bernard, constituted the third Burgundian County now held by another RODOLPH or RAOUL,—Rodolph the Guelph, son of the younger Conrad, Count of Auxerre;—he, following Boso's example, assembled his prelates and nobles in the solemnly cheerful valley of Saint-Maurice, and, crowned in the yet existing Basilica, established a new kingdom. Arnolph endeavoured to subjugate this rival; but Raoul strenuously defended his narrow realm of Alps and glaciers, and won and maintained his independence, governing with remarkable wisdom and equity. Rodolph or Raoul the Second, his son, uniting transjurane Burgundy to Provence, founded the Arelatic kingdom.

These revolutions, descending from the Alps, dissevered a large proportion of countries speaking the Romane tongue from the Kingdom of France. The kingdom of Arles subsequently became united to the Empire. Rodolph of Hapsburg lost this kingdom, which insensibly passed under the French supremacy; nevertheless, according to the constitutional theory, the "Count

888—912   of Provence" was to be distinguished from the
"king of France and Navarre," even until the
888—889   Revolution.

388
Rainulph
of Poitiers
attempts to
assume the
Royal title
in Aqui-
taine.

§ 5. RAINULPH the Second, son of the Mar-
quis Bernard, flits before us as King of AQUI-
TAINE, Septimania, and the Spanish marches.
This Rainulph, Count of Poitiers and Abbot of
Saint Hilary, was brother of Ebles Abbot of
Saint Denis, the good marksman, and father of
Ebles the mamzer, also Count of Poitiers; and
Ebles the mamzer was father of *Guillaume Tête
d'étoupe*, the Husband of Rollo's daughter. Rain-
ulph soon abandoned his pretensions; and the
Chroniclers touch so hastily upon Aquitanian
events, that we know next to nothing of the
transactions in which this powerful Suzerain was
engaged.

888—889
Competi-
tors for the
crown of
France,
Arnolph,
Guido and
Eudes
Capet.

§ 6. For FRANCE, or rather for so much of
France as was not held by the King of France
and the Kings or Counts of Provence, Burgundy,
Aquitaine, Gascony or Armorica. three candi-
dates appeared. ARNOLPH, who claimed an undefined supremacy over the whole Carlovingian
Empire, GUIDO Count of Spoleto, and the Count
of Paris, EUDES CAPET.

A fourth competitor, a nobleman, a statesman
and a warrior, might have entered the arena
with far higher pretensions than Arnolph or than
Guido or than Eudes; for, at this period, a lineage
combining the claims of legitimacy and seniority

had suddenly acquired extraordinary prosperity — the lineage descended from Charlemagne's loved son, Pepin king of Italy — noble, royal, imperial VERMANDOIS, Herbert the father now educating Herbert the son, and both successfully amplifying the dominions which they ruled with vigorous talent.

862—912

888—889 House of Verman-dois, Her-bert I. and Herbert II. (See pp 355,356).

Peronne and the Abbey of Saint-Quintin composed the nucleus of their Principality; but, quietly and without contradiction, they had extended their sway over the heart of the kingdom of Soissons; and that antient Soissons, and the rock of Lâon, and Rheims, the prerogative city of the Gauls, were all within the geographical ambit of their territory. In such enclavures as we have named, Vermandois did not possess direct authority. Lâon, for example, had a Count and a Bishop, and was a royal domain.

Nevertheless the influence of the Vermandois potentates permeated these countries; and their hereditary right, their personal importance, and the possession of the localities rendered so venerable by historical and religious traditions,— all, it should seem, ought to have concurred in stimulating these lineal representatives of the Empire's founder to have asserted their claims; but they were matched in conflict by their compeers. "It has been the misfortune of France," observes the contemporary Regino, "that her princes are so equally balanced in wealth, power and ability,—none can obtain a permanent pre-

888—912

883—889

eminence." Rival Burgundy and the rival Capets therefore restrained cautious Vermandois
from contesting the throne. These families,
including the antagonistic house of Flanders,
had already become much allied by intermar-
riages, forming connections which created a unity
of aristocratic feeling, without necessarily en-
suring unity of interest. All were against the
Carlovingians, though dissentient amongst themselves; and, until the establishment of the third

Great in-
fluence of
the House
of Verman-
dois in the
subsequent
revolutions
of France.
dynasty, the history of France becomes virtually
an intricate history of factions,—the Counts of
Vermandois endeavouring to gain the ascendancy, but missing their aim, king-makers, king-
unmakers, king-restorers, king-deposers, but not
enabled to be kings themselves:—Burgundy partially succeeding: the Capets falling, rising, yet
always advancing: Normandy following in the
wake of the Capets, and ultimately obtaining a
station which, though undecorated by the name
of royalty, was invested with full royal power.

§ 7. Three national parties were formed,
each desiring to carry the question their own
way. Fulco, Archbishop of Rheims, Hincmar's
successor, represented and headed the Franks of
the old stock, holding to the constitutional doctrine of Carlovingian legitimacy, but nevertheless considering that the extreme exigencies of
the State enforced the postponement, if not the
rejection, of the infant heir,—" Wo to the land
whose king is a child," — and Fulco therefore

deemed that the common weal imperatively dictated the selection of a mature and competent Sovereign. For this reason Fulco had concurred in the elevation of Charles-le-Gras, the late deposed Emperor. He now wavered between Guido and Arnolph : consanguinity might incline him to the first, but merit decided him in favour of the last. Theodorick of Autun, leader in every revolution since the, death of Charles-le-Chauve, supported Eudes Capet. The Burgundians inclined to the Count of Spoleto; but the Northmen constituted a fourth party, whose presence at this time and turn brought on a speedy practical decision of the question. They encamped in great force at Chezy, threatening Paris, and ravaging various other parts of the country. Who could resist them but Eudes, the triumphant defender of that city which we may henceforth consider as the Capetian Capital?—and his partizans, hastily convening at Compiègne, caused the Count of Paris to be proclaimed and crowned, Walter, Archbishop of Sens, performing the ceremony.

888—912
888—889

888
Mar.–Apr
Eudes Capet proclaimed and crowned at Compiègne.

Guido before he entered France numbered an influential party, but he disgusted the French by his Italian frugality. "That fellow is not fit to reign over us," said the Bishop of Metz, according to the current story, "who would be content to dine for ten farthings." However Guido was proclaimed, and crowned at Langres by Bishop

888
Mar.–Apr.
Guido of Spoleto crowned at Langres, but abandons the contest.

888—912
888

Geilo.   Had he persevered, he might perhaps have maintained himself as King of Burgundy, but disheartened by his unpopularity, Guido abandoned France and returned to Italy, where, in his first campaign, he defeated his late confederate, but now rival, Berenger.

Eudes Capet may be admired as the type of a *preud chevalier* when *preux chevaliers* were none, courteous, honourable and winning: kind, and merciful if he thought that kindness and gentleness would answer, but firm, even harsh, in dealing with his political opponents.   Archbishop Fulco now strenuously endeavoured to aid Arnolph: so also Rodolph, Count-Abbot of Saint Vedast, and Baudouin-le-Chauve.   Arnolph did not hasten to accept the invitation; but Eudes was willing to strengthen his own authority by acknowledging Arnolph's honorary suzerainty; and the King of Germany did not attempt any hostile operations against the Capet.

888
June 24.
Battle of
Montfau-
con Danes
defeated by
Eudes.

Eudes therefore was the more at liberty to do his duty in defending France against the Northmen.   It was for this duty that he had been exalted to the throne.   On Midsummer-day he encountered the Danes at Montfaucon-en-Argonne.   Some suppose that Rollo engaged in this battle.   The Franks reckoned the Capetian squadrons at one thousand, the Danish army at nineteen thousand.   Such colloquial estimates must simply be accepted as rude approximations, vaguely indicating the relative proportions of 888—912 the hostile forces. Eudes, displaying great per- 888 sonal prowess, was nearly cut down by the battle-axe of a Dane with whom he engaged in single combat, but he triumphed equally as a Champion and as a General, and acquired great glory. Eudes put the Northmen to flight seven times, and defeated them nine,—thus was it said or sung :—the passage in the chronicle containing this commendation seems to be a quotation or fragment translated from some popular ballad.

Montfaucon-en-Argonne told much in favour of Eudes. Hitherto he had been but grudgingly acknowledged in Belgic Gaul, where the Vermandois interest prevailed, but now he greatly increased in power. He exercised his prerogatives boldly and broadly. If an Abbey became vacant, King Eudes conferred the preferment upon some tough worthy blade, or kept the good thing himself. Thus did he treat the first which fell in, the Abbey of Saint Denis; and he confiscated the "honours" of his gainsayers whenever he had the power. Baudouin-le-Chauve performed homage. Other Nobles, north of the 888
13 Nov. Loire, tacitly submitted. Arnolph graciously sent Eudes again crowned at Rheims. Eudes a royal crown, with which on Saint Brice's day he was again solemnly inaugurated and proclaimed King. No consecration or further ecclesiastical confirmation seems to have been asked

888—912 or required; and Eudes granted a general am-
nesty.

888—889
Rainulph
of Poitiers
submits to
Eudes.

Aquitaine, however, was still unsettled; and Eudes, the Christmas festivities being over, repaired thither with a small train of Frankish soldiers. Rainulph humbled himself, and resigned his transient crown; but that nominal crown was far less an object of suspicion than the child

Charles-le-
Simple
produced.

whom he had in charge—Charles, the infant son of Ansgarda. How this child of sorrow came under the guardianship of Count Rainulph, we know not, but there he was; and all who saw the boy were struck with his likeness to Louis-le-Bégue his father, that father who had never beheld the babe, destined to humiliation, contempt and misfortune. The little Charles was presented to Eudes, Eudes concealed his vexation; and Rainulph, clearing himself by oath of all accusations, professed himself a liege-man of the Capet.

Neither the submission nor the oath of any of those who had become the homagers of Eudes amounted, however, to more than contrivances for saving appearances; and hardly so much. Amidst all changes, trials, triumphs, vicissitudes and misfortunes, the destructive spirit of untruth continued to possess the Carlovingian Empire with unabated pertinacity. Old England won her national character upon Runnymede; Lombard history dates from the field of Roncaglia; but

the Franks, high or low, clergy and laity, were 888—912
all the representatives of the Luegen-feld. Archbishop Fulco and Baudouin-le-Chauve, and Her- 889
bert of Vermandois, and Pepin of Senlis, and the
Burgundian Richard, and William of Auvergne,
and Rainulph of Poitou, only endured the domination of Eudes till they could rid themselves of
him. Some individuals might be friendly to Eudes
if convenient, but every man considered it his
-paramount duty to consult his own interest by all
means in his power: oaths, promises, and engagements disappeared whenever occasion required.

§ 8. We now revert to the Northmen, 889—891
always keeping in mind the concurrent plague The Danes
of the Magyars, their hordes rapidly approaching resume their attacks.
and bearing down against Germany and Italy,
and the Saracens disporting in the Southern
regions, occupying the Alpine passes, despoiling
pilgrims on their way to Saint Peter's shrine.

Danish detachments continued about Paris,
and they were numerous in the Seine-country,
where Eudes was compelled to leave them undisturbed: the rayon of the Frankish operations
was always very short: Eudes could only prose-
cute a confined and partial warfare. They spread
themselves in all directions. Whilst Eudes was
in Poitou, vast numbers ravaged other parts
of the Loire-country, Burgundy also, and threatened Paris quite as formidably as before. In
these incursions we vaguely discern the form of

888—912
889—891

Rollo; but the narrative is perplexed, and the more difficult to unravel, because at this period there were besides him two or three Rollos afloat, a Rodo or Rollo also called Hunedeus, and a Rotland or Rollo, the son of Oskytel or Ketil: our hero however soon appears more distinctly, and Botho, his faithful friend and the friend of his yet unborn children, joins him. Méaux was besieged by Rollo. Count Theutbert and most of his soldiers, who defended the place valiantly, were slain by the Danish missiles. Upon Count Theutbert's death, Bishop Sigmund took the command. This bold Prelate walled up the gates, enclosing a worse enemy than the Danes—famine. The starved inhabitants surrendered, the Northmen promising to allow them to depart safely; but when they came forth, the Northmen seized them, and burned the city.

888—889
Méaux
besieged
and taken
by the
Danes

889—890
Northmen
again be-
siege
Paris.

The battle of Montfaucon, instead of depressing the Danish audacity, stimulated them to further exertions. Again they presented themselves before Paris. They pitched their tents, and recommenced a regular siege. This may be called the second siege of Paris. But the genius of Charles-le-Chauve kept them off; they could not make way through walls and bridge and bastilles; and after spending their strength in vain, they retreated. So much the worse for the Marne country, Lorraine and Champagne: Troyes had to pay the reckoning for Paris. When they

890
The third
siege of
Paris.

exhausted those fields, they tried their chance at 888—912
Paris for the third time. Eudes immediately
reoccupied his old position, of which the capabi- 890
lities were so well known to him. But he was
frustrated by the universal faithlessness. Eudes, Eudes com-
promises
bold and warlike as he was, could not help fol- by a sub-
sidy.
lowing the Danegeld precedents afforded by his
predecessors. Provisions were scarce, defections
were beginning amongst the Franks. If he continued long within the walls of Paris, his subjects
without, would soon uncrown him. Eudes therefore offered money to the enemy, which they
accepted: Rollo had his share, and, raising the 890
siege, the Danes turned their forces towards the Armorican
Marches
Armorican Marches. invaded by
the Danes.

Alan and Judicael, the two Breton Counts,
were disputing desperately—all the better for the
Northmen. It is very probable that the Channel-
islands were occupied by them. Coutances, near
the coast, had been dreadfully harassed by the
Danes, and the Christian population of maritime
Britanny, or the Côtentin, almost wholly scattered The
Côtentin
or extirpated. The "black book" of Coutances ravaged,
Saint-Lo
tells us that the desolation continued seventy destroyed.
years. Bishop Lista took refuge at Saint-Lo, on
the other side of the river Vire; and, during
centuries, though the Cathedral remained at Coutances, the Chair was removed. The Northmen
besieged Saint-Lo. Want of water compelled
the inhabitants to surrender : the Northmen pro-

888—912
890
mising them their lives, broke the promise, Bishop and inhabitants were slaughtered, and Saint-Lo, then a fine city, levelled with the ground. One very remarkable fragment of a church, decorated with uncouth sculptures, however, still exists, apparently of such remote antiquity that French archæologists suppose *Sainte-Croix* to have been built anterior to this invasion.

Rollo be-
sieges
Bayeux.
Grants a
truce.

Rollo and Botho had previously attacked Bayeux. The exact date of this movement is uncertain; but it was evidently connected with the general plan of the Armorican campaign. The city made a stubborn defence. Botho was captured. Rollo, much regretting the loss of his fellow-warrior, proposed to grant a twelve month's truce if the citizens would release his companion. By the family historian he is called " Count Botho," and very probably was so denominated in the Northern camp, the Danes, like the Barbarians during the Lower Empire, having begun to adopt the phraseology of their adversaries. Rollo lost no advantage by this partial cessation of hostilities, he had full employment in devastating the Seine territories; and having joined in besieging Paris, he presented himself again before Bayeux when the truce had terminated,

Bayeux be-
sieged
again by
Rollo, and
taken.

and attacked the city a second time. Bayeux resisted bravely, but yielded to the Northern force. Stormed, plundered and burnt, hosts of captives were carried away by the victor, amongst

them the little damsel known only by the fond- 838—912
ling appellation of "Popa," the *poupée* or *pop-* 890—891
pet, whom he married according to the Danish
usages, and who gave him a daughter, Gerloc, and
his son and successor Guillaume-Longue-épée.
Count Berenger, the *Poppet's* father, cannot be
distinctly identified, but her brother or half-
brother was Bernard-de-Senlis or Senlis-Verman-
dois.   The union, however rudely commenced,
proved a happy one.   Bernard-de-Senlis took
heartily to Rollo and his family : trusted, and
worthy of trust, he protected not merely the
authority of Rollo's children and grandchildren,
but their lives.   Guillaume-Longue-épée, when
friends and advisers were failing him, turned in
full confidence to this uncle : Bernard-de-Senlis
sheltered the young Richard Sans-peur, the son
of Guillaume-Longue-épée, from the power of the
inimical Louis-d'Outremer and his more inimical
Queen, the wily Gerberga.—Rollo's line would
have failed but for the efficient and ready help
given by Bernard-de-Senlis.

The Breton Counts, when the danger came 890—891
upon them imminently, suspended their mutual Danes partially eva-
cuate Ar-
hostilities, and turned their forces against the moiica.
common enemy; yet they could not learn to act
in concert.   Judicael, without waiting for Alan,
attacked the Danes and was killed : Alan rallied the Bretons, and after much hard fighting,
compelled the Danish forces to retreat.   The

888—912
890—891 Bretons boasted that of fifteen thousand Danes who had entered the country, only four hundred re-embarked. The number so specified may be correct as to some particular detachment, but the Danes, who evacuated the country in three divisions, the first crossing the Seine, the second the Loire and the third sailing away to Lotharingia, were unsubdued; and large numbers remained in the Armorican Marches and their vicinities. When the "Terra Normannorum" began to settle into the character of "Normandy" under Guillaume-Longue-épée, there was no part of the country in which the Danish or Teutonic nationality still continued so decidedly marked as in the tract between the Saint-Lo river, the Vire, and the Olne, the Caen river. Here, more than in any other Norman district, do the names of places bear a Teutonic aspect and echo the Teutonic sound: Bayeux was ultimately the only city in Normandy where the Danish language lingered as a vernacular tongue.

Evreux taken by the Northmen.

§ 9. Victorious Rollo again conjoined the Danish squadrons before Paris, or resumed the siege on his own account. There was a constant flickering of warfare, ever ready to break out into a blaze. According to Rollo's desultory fashion, he marched towards Evreux, evidently contemplating the breaking down of all points of resistance in or surrounding the territory he afterwards ruled. Evreux, Saint Taurin's city, was still prosperous

and opulent; and the well-watered Pagus Ebroi- 888—912
cacensis, afterwards the county of Evreux, still
continuing to be the most fertile tract in Nor- 890—891
mandy. The province had been occasionally
ravaged, but, as yet, the city remained untouched:
possibly some lurking reverence rendered to the
Sanctuaries may have deterred the invaders. But
golden lamps and silver thuribles, shrines and
decked altars, offered temptations which now
overcame such imperfect veneration.

Rollo directed his forces against Evreux. Capture of Evreux.
Bishop Sebard, whose name, except on this
occasion, appears but once in the fragmentary
ecclesiastical annals of antient Neustria, held the
command : the city was taken by storm, pillaged,
and in great part destroyed. Some marvellous
chance enabled Bishop Sebard to escape; and
the monks of Saint-Ouen evaded with their treasures, relics of Saint-Ouen, and Saint-Leufroi,
and Saint-Agofroy his brother, and Saint-Taurin,
which the fugitives deposited in the Abbey of
Saint Germain-des-près at Paris. The Abbey of
Saint Taurin was completely subverted by the
Northmen, and the Abbot of Saint-Germain-des-
près kindly received the wanderers, relics and
all. No Abbot could be a better protector, for
the Abbot was sturdy Robert, Count of Paris.

Dudon de Saint-Quentin relates these incidents *con amore*. Fastidious criticism blames
such monastic loquacity;—yet this is one of the

888—912
890—891
numerous instances in which apparently trivial circumstances tighten the vagueness of chronicle history. Upon Count Robert's request, Charles-le-Simple united Evreux Abbey to Saint-Germain-des-près, in order that the latter establishment might furnish subsistence to the despoiled Evreux monks. Dudon's relation is confirmed by diplomatic testimony; and the Royal charter confutes the gainsayers of the family history. The intensity of the devastations committed at Evreux has been evidenced by the discovery of the fire-destroyed ruins of the antient Carlovingian castle. All the circumjacent country shared the fate of the Cathedral city, and Rollo again harassed Paris.—Many districts purchased forbearance by a Danegelt, yet whole populations, encouraged to resistance, refused their tribute, and Rollo cruized to England.

892—893
Danes pe-
netrate into
central
France
Eudes car-
ries on ope-
rations
against
them.
§ 10.   Central France continued to attract the Danes. They repeatedly endeavoured to establish themselves in these provinces: had they succeeded, they might, like the Romans, have rendered this most defensible territory the nucleus of an Empire. Clermont is indicated as the scene of Rollo's exploits, without any particulars of date or time. If the Pagans failed to fortify themselves amidst Velay and Auvergne's volcanic fastnesses, or were prevented from establishing themselves permanently in the rich and teeming Limagne, this result was due to Eudes

Capet's valour and activity. Notwithstanding the troubles occasioned by disloyal adherents south and north of the Loire, he still held his judicial circuits in Burgundia and Aquitania with the regularity of a Carlovingian King. Périgord and Angoulême and Puy-en-Velay witnessed his *Grands-jours*, when Eudes administered justice in person according to the forms of antient royalty.

888—912
891—893

A soldier, raised to the throne by prowess, Eudes laboured to retain his well-deserved reputation. A favourite of the people in Aquitaine, most of the Aquitanian and southern chieftains, excepting the ambitious Count of Poitiers, again adhered to him, or refrained from opposing his authority. Troops joined King Eudes from Arles and from Orange, from Toulouse and from Nîmes. The Danes concentrated their forces in the river district of Auvergne, between Sioul and Allier. Eudes marshalled his troops at Brioude; invoking Saint Julian's protection, and laying his gifts upon the Altar, he marched onwards. The Danes were universally giving tokens of their intentions, seeking to convert their military occupancy into dominion, and, wherever they could, to establish a Danelaghe.

Consistently with this intent, they attempted to win the positions which would give them fast hold of the country; and the main body of their troops besieged Montpensier, so well known in

The Danes besiege Montpensier. Battle of the Allier.

888—912
801—893

history as the future Orleans-appanage. The castle of Montpensier, now wholly demolished, was situated upon a volcanic hill, and, therefore, from its situation between the rivers, the military key of the country. Here Eudes attacked the Pagans. The Capet encouraged his troops by his talent and valour: he reminded them how the Arverni of old had bravely defended their country against the Romans, earning the respect of their conquerors · why should not they equally signalize themselves against these foul and base barbarians? Such allusions were not displays of misplaced and paltry College erudition, prompted by frigid pedantry, but the utterances of real feeling. Rome lived around them; even now, the Auvergnat peasant points to the vast hill of Gergoye, and tells you how bravely the ramparts, lengthening along the sky-line, were defended against Cæsar.

Murder of Oskytel the Dane.

In the battle of the Allier the Danes were completely defeated, and Oskytel, their commander, the ravager of Croyland, captured.—Provided he would accept baptism, the victors promised to spare his life. Oskytel assented, but he was cruelly and basely slain by Ingo, the standard-bearer of King Eudes, whilst he was emerging from the baptistery. Eudes did not instigate this hideous crime, yet he became an accomplice after the fact, not only pardoning the perpetrator, but bestowing upon him munificent rewards. " It is

impossible to trust a Dane," replied Ingo, " and
therefore I slew him for the good of the country;" a plea of which the validity was admitted
by Ingo's royal master;—read *Saracen* for *Dane*,
and the like would have been done by many a
preud-chevalier.

888—912

891—893

§ 11. North of the Loire the indefatigable
Danes were formidable to all parties: no matter against whom they combated, Eudes or Arnolph. Hastings cheated Rodolph, the Count-
Abbot of Saint Vedast; and their cunning rendered them the more terrible. Very appropriate
was their national ensign, the thievish, rapacious,
artful raven. Lotharingia became the chief scene
of the present campaign. Sigfried and Godfrey,
reinforced by the detachments from Britanny,
renewed their spirited warfare. A great battle
ensued near Trèves. The Germans were discomfited, and the Archbishop of Mayence slain.

Transac-
tions in the
north of
the Gauls.

Arnolph hastened from Baioaria: the Danish kings entrenched themselves nigh Louvaine.
Protected in the rear by the river Dyle, they
selected this position as being best calculated
for defence; but, contrary to their calculations,
the defence proved their destruction. A marked
improvement in the German tactics dates from
Arnolph: he had raised an efficient body of
heavy-armed cavalry, the first appearance of such
a force in mediæval annals. The Northmen,
borne down by the German squadrons, fled: more

891

Battle of
Louvaine,
Danes de-
feated by
Arnolph.

888—912
891—893
perished in the sluggish insidious stream than by spear or sword; and sixteen raven-banners were the victor's trophies. The slaughtered Pagans were reckoned by thousands, and the Germans reported that only one single Christian was killed. Arnolph, like an old Roman Emperor, held an allocution on the battle-field, solemn services were sung, and Arnolph acquired immense renown; yet there did not seem to be a Dane the less in the country. The Northmen occupied Louvaine as long as they thought fit, evacuated Lotharingia when it suited their convenience, and remained in great power about Amiens. All successes gained by the Franks or Germans were countervailed by the general unsteadiness, levity and faithlessness of chieftains and people. Eudes marched from Aquitaine to improve the advantages Arnolph gained; but the nobles of Belgic Gaul determined to desert him. Whilst in the Vermandois territory, Eudes was in peril of being surprised by the Danes: the Vermandois levies, on whom he relied unsuspiciously, either neglected their duty or betrayed him.

Baudouin-le-Chauve quarrels with Eudes.
A particular feud accelerated the impending Revolution. The great Abbeys were the capital prizes. Much difficulty attends the investigation of their history: the ecclesiastical historians, both antient and modern, ashamed of the abusive system which virtually rendered them lay-fees, try to conceal the transactions as far as possible.

Materials are scanty, and a judicious selection 888—912 from the few known facts often leaves you in ignorance of the Abbot's secularity. Saint-Ve- 891—893 dast, like Tynemouth, was a castle as well as an Abbey, the citadel in fact of Arras. Rodolph conducted himself valiantly, and greatly strength- ened the fortifications; but at this critical period he died childless. The notion of property in the secularized Abbeys was becoming more settled and consistent; and examples can now be ad- duced of hereditary succession in such prefer- ments. Upon the death of Rodolph, his kins- man, Baudouin-le-Chauve made suit to Eudes for Saint-Vedast as the heir. Eudes replied he would do what he pleased with his own.—Abbeys were peculiarly the King's own; but if Baudouin would repair to the King, the King would re- turn a gracious answer. The Count of Flanders took offence, and rose in open hostility against the Capet. Archbishop Fulco, despite of his pre- vious vacillations, which he would have justified as arising from a conscientious feeling of duty towards the kingdom, now became the loyal sup- porter of the Carlovingian line. The Vermandois party merely tolerated the Capet domination.

We last found Charles under the care of Rain- Plans for the restora- tion of Charles. ulph: his friends then quietly and secretly sent him to England, where they kept him till the opportunity for investing the heir with his an- cestorial rights should arrive. The young prince,

888—912
891—893

active, intelligent, winning in manners, well-taught, and having profited by his tuition, liberally munificent, with a love of enterprize only restrained by his greater love of ease and pleasure, and endued with all the elements of popularity, was fully ready for action ; and Archbishop Fulco and Herbert and Pepin, the Counts of Vermandois, diligently worked for the royal Heir.

July 892.
Revolt
against
Eudes in
the Ver-
mandois

§ 12. A new and zealous partizan made the first demonstration. Amongst the Franks, the saying, "blood is thicker than water," did not hold. Consanguinity rarely mitigated enmity or averted hostility. Count Walter, nephew of Eudes, drew his sword against Eudes in the great Council of Verberie, and having passed over to the Carlovingian party, surprised the rock of Lâon. Eudes besieged the fortress, compelled Walter to surrender, and then caused the assertor of legitimate royalty to be executed as a criminal. Walter was beheaded, and the Bishop of Lâon refused him Christian burial. Such summary judicial vengeance was rarely exercised. The severity practised by Eudes taught the Vermandois party the reward they might expect, and rendered them more cautious and also more pertinacious.

892
Death of
Rainulph.
Eudes re-
pairs to the
South of
the Loire.

Eudes thus engaged in the North, Rainulph Count of Poitiers died. Rainulph was said to have leagued with Rollo. Eudes, according to

report, had him removed by poison. Whether 888—912
the suspicion could be warranted or not, there 891—893
was a general tendency to assume that persons
of eminence met their death unfairly. Rainulph
was succeeded, though not immediately, by "Ebles
the *mamzer*," whose illegitimacy became a part
of his style.—*Abbot* Ebles, who had so strenuously assisted Eudes in defending Paris, possessed
great power in Poitou, and, with other nobles,
entertained inimical feelings against the Capet.
The Vermandois party craftily contriving to draw
King Eudes away from their part of the country,
exaggerated this discontent, and made him believe that the Poitevins were plotting to deprive
him of kingdom and life. Eudes and his brother
Count Robert, immediately marched to Aquitaine,
and the insurrection was suppressed. A stone
cast from a balista killed the excellent marksman, Abbot Ebles; and the people said, that the
soldier Prelate, so notoriously violating his vows
and calling, well deserved his fate.

Eudes prevailed gloriously, unconscious that Counter-
revolution,
whilst thus triumphing, the son of Louis-le-Bégue restoration
of Charles.
had been conducted to the throne. The Vermandois Counts, Herbert and Pepin, and Fulco Archbishop of Rheims, were unquestionably the efficient organizers of the counter-revolution. During
the time that the Capet was so busily employed
in Aquitaine, the protectors of the Carlovingian
Prince brought him over from England; and the

888—912 nobles of " France," together with Richard-le-
Justicier Count of Burgundy, and Guillaume-le-
893   Pieux Count of Aquitaine, proclaimed him King.
The inauguration ceremonies were cautiously
completed: invested with the purple, and consecrated on the Feast of Saint Agnes, observed
893   thenceforth by Charles as a solemn anniversary,
Jan 28
Feb 2   a pause ensued, probably occupied in discussing
Charles
consecrated the arrangements needed by the new govern-
and crown-
ed.   ment; and, on the feast of the Purification he
received the crown.

The young competitor's elevation, though sudden, could not have been altogether a surprisal.
Eudes and Robert crossed the Loire from Aquitaine into " France," not very hastily, but inter-
posing a due interval, during which expectations
could be encouraged, apprehensions excited, and
private intimations conveyed. All those who had
concurred in recognizing Charles, appeared to
rally loyally and strenuously round their young
893   Sovereign. About Easter, the rival Kings and
April, May.
Eudes gains their armies were in sight of each other, so near
over the ad- that a battle seemed imminent; but, at this junc-
herents of
Charles   ture, hostilities were dexterously avoided. Eudes applied himself to Fulco and the Vermandois
Counts, to Richard-le-Justicier and Guillaume-
le-Pieux, and to all who were mustered under
the Carlovingian eagle. He addressed them
temperately yet boldly. Had they not committed
a great wrong, deserting him, the king of their

choice?—let them return to their willing obe- 888—912
dience, and they should receive a gracious pardon.
—So said, so done: a prompt and hearty response 893—895
was made to the call. Few were the weeks which
had elapsed since Archbishop Fulco, and Count
Herbert, and Count Richard-le-Justicier, and
Count Guillaume-le-Pieux, not coerced, but acting upon their sense of duty, had unanimously
sworn allegiance to the son of Louis-le-Bégue;
and now, as unanimously, they slipped out of
their oaths and abandoned him.

Raised to the throne in early Spring, when 894
July—Sept
Summer came, Charles was a dethroned fugitive; Charles ex-
but trusting to the untrustworthiness of the pelled, but
re-enters
Franks, and to the chances afforded by their the King-
dom.
marvellous versatility, he fled cheerily, and with
good hope of regaining his ground.

Like the diligent husbandman, his preparations
were rewarded in the Autumnal season: by that
time he had gathered a large and imposing force,
re-entered France, and, with so much power, that
a compromise ensued, Capet and Carlovingian
agreeing to divide the kingdom.—Eudes is to rule 894
north of the Loire, Charles southward far as the Compro-
mise be-
Pyrenees, if he can command obedience;—but tween
Eudes and
the agreement was not kept, and indeed not in- Charles;
Eudes to
tended to be so. The treaty took no effect. Had reign north
of the Loire
Eudes and Charles been willing to abide by their Charles
south.
convention, their nobles were not: a worrying
civil war, interspersed with fraudulent truces,

888—912 occupied about three years:—no " great principles" were invoked, no "national interests" sought.

894—895 Important as the results became in their ultimate
consequences, the conflict between Eudes and
Charles, when you approach the fray, dwindles
into a complication of miserable feuds, destitute
of sentiment or grandeur.

Charles re-
ceives in-
vestiture of
France
from Ar-
nolph. § 13. The contest, though protracted, was
unequal—the Capet King, an experienced and
tried warrior, supported by his brother Robert:
Charles, a boy, destitute of any coadjutor upon
whom he could rely.—The skirmishes, scarcely
to be called campaigns, were principally carried
on within the Vermandois territory. Charles,
driven into Rheims and besieged by Count Robert, saw his cause speedily abandoned by his
men; they stole out of the city, but upon favourable terms granted by Robert. The latter did
not seek to drive his adversaries to extremities.
Charles himself was allowed by Robert to depart
in safety, and he visited the Court of King
Arnolph, whose assistance he implored. Arnolph
welcomed the son of Louis-le-Bégue kindly, and
Charles was willing to receive investiture of the
kingdom from him; a great triumph for the
Slavo-Teutonic Senior. Arnolph commanded the
Lotharingians to assist the expelled sovereign;
but Eudes, an able tactitian, prevented Arnolph's
troops from entering the kingdom, and Charles
retreated to Burgundy. Their barbarian enemies

were, as usual, profiting by the civil war :—Mag- 888—912
yars pressing onwards, Northmen gnawing out
the heart of the country. Arnolph, whose cha- 895—897
Eudes and
racter displays much magnificence, was impa- Charles
summoned
tient to justify his ancestry—his aspirations were by Arnolph
to appear
grand ; he was seeking to be Emperor, a real before him
Emperor;—he now attempted to exercise his
authority for the commonweal, and, by producing
concord to diminish the Empire's calamities.
He summoned the two kings of France to appear
before him. Eudes complied : Charles, according
to his recent submission, was bound to obey the
mandate ; but he spurned the subjection he had
sought. Arnolph's mediation therefore failed, and
the contest was renewed with greater pertinacity·

Herbert of Vermandois changed sides again, 896—897
attaching himself to Charles ; others followed his Successes of
Eudes—
example. Eudes never faltered in demonstrating Charles
takes re-
his royal rights. All the power belonging to the fuge in Lo-
tharingia.
Sovereign by the Frankish constitution, over the
possessions, beneficiary or otherwise, of his vassals, Eudes exercised to the fullest extent : ad-
herence to Charles he treated as felony: the
nobles composing the party which supported
Charles, he dispersed ; he picked them out one
by one. Peronne was taken, Saint-Quentin taken,
till at last the Carlists had lost the whole of
their towns and lands. Rheims alone held out
against Eudes, who elsewhere enforced universal
submission, even from Count Herbert ; and

888—912 Charles took refuge under the wing of King
896—897 Arnolph in Lotharingia, where he was protected,
though unsatisfactorily, by Arnolph's son, the
turbulent King Zwentibold.

Vigorous
conduct of
Charles

Despite of all troubles and traverses, the
courage of Charles was unabated: a naturally
vigorous character received an additional support from the buoyancy of youth ; he was
inventive and full of resource : and he determined upon a measure, hazardous, almost desperate, but which the pressure of his position
might suggest or justify. The Northmen were
habitually cruising in the Seine, and the chieftain
now occupying the river was a certain Hunedeus.
This name is of singular sound, it never occurs
before—possibly the reading is corrupt,—but
the sudden apparition of "Hunedeus" is rendered
more remarkable from the circumstance that
others call him Rodo, or even *Rollo*.

Destitute of any adviser whom he could
love or trust, Charles could not fail to discern
that the Frankish prelates and nobles constituting his party, acted, when they did give
him their uncertain support, for their sakes, and
not for his own ; and he formed the scheme
of strengthening himself upon the throne by

Charles en-
deavours to
support
himself by
gaining
over the
Northmen.

an alliance with the Pagan Northmen. Could
he induce the Danes to unite their interest to
the interests of France, he would infuse new
blood, and the kingdom would acquire new

glory. The instinctive prescience, the shadow of 888—912
events cast before, is, in history, the observation
of the causes which conduce to the future event; 897—898
and the policy now attempted by Charles was
afterwards consummated by his compact at Saint
Clair-sur-Epte. "Hunedeus," upon the request
of Charles, was baptized; and the treaties thus
commenced would, had they been perfected, have
then created Normandy. But their operation was
suspended. Archbishop Fulco impeded the transaction to the utmost of his power. The apparent
conversion of the Northmen he counted for nought:
Hunedeus, clad in the neophyte's white garment,
would be as much a Heathen Viking as before:
he upbraided Charles with seeking such detestable aid. If he joined himself to the Pagans,
he would be no better than a Pagan himself—
better not reign at all than reign *sub patrocinio
diaboli*.—Had the Franks ever kept any oath
which they swore on cross, relic, or shrine, the
Archbishop's admonition would have been more
cogent. Charles might have replied that Fulco's
own oath-breakings excused *his* condonation of
Danish unbelievers.

But, under existing circumstances, it was not 897 Charles un-prosperous: interces-sions made to Eudes on his behalf.
practicable for Charles to work out any effectual
or satisfactory results. The Danes spread themselves widely—more dissensions and troubles: a
bitter feud raged between Raoul, Count of Cambrai, Baudouin-le-Chauve's brother, and Herbert

888—912

897—899

of Vermandois; Raoul was killed by Herbert when besieging Saint-Quentin; and the very few partisans whom Charles could muster, seeing that the Carlist cause was desperate, repaired on his behalf to Eudes. They became petitioners on the desolate young king's behalf;—would not the Capet recollect that their Seigneur was son of the Capet's Seigneur?—and they besought that King Eudes would allow unto the young prince some portion of his paternal kingdom. This appeal to the conscience of Eudes was not unavailing. Eudes agreed to the proposed pacification. He received Charles kindly, granted certain appanages to him, promised more, and made friends with Herbert and Baudouin.

899
Jan 1.
Death of
Eudes.

Eudes, brave Eudes, during these transactions was preparing for death.—Scarcely exceeding forty years of age, exertions and anxieties had worn him out. He had long been exceedingly distressed by morbid sleeplessness: this affection caused occasional delirium, and he knew his case was hopeless. At La-Fère-sur-Oise the mortal attack came on. Languishing on his dying bed, he exhorted all who had access to him that they should observe and keep their faith to Charles. Eudes died on the feast of the Circumcision; and the first king of the third dynasty received an honourable sepulture, with his Merovingian and Carlovingian predecessors, in the royal Abbey of Saint-Denis.

§ 14. " Le roi est mort—vive le Roi !" Within three days after Eudes' death, and in that same Abbey of Saint-Denis, Charles was again proclaimed king; and he re-entered upon the full exercise of his royal authority, uncontested, unopposed, hailed by all parties. A joyous hearty constitutional accession :—strange, that whilst the royal authority was becoming weaker in the king's person, the doctrines of royal legitimacy were pronounced more distinctly. Charles now employed a double date in his charters. He reckoned his regnal years from his first coronation, and also from this restoration, or, as the event is sometimes termed in these documents, the *reintegration* of his royal power. Robert Capet, the brother of Eudes, after a short delay, performed a simulated homage to Charles, and accepted a grant, or re-grant of the Duchy of France and County of Paris. Baudouin-le-Chauve, Count Herbert, Richard-le-Justicier and Guillaume-le-Pieux, all acted in the same manner, and again became the king's lieges. The Danes invaded the Vimeux, where they were defeated by king Charles, and his victory was gained by a force comparatively small. They were also beaten in Burgundy by Richard-le-Justicier ; and circumstances fully warranted the expectation of tranquillity.

But the nobles would not allow the mortar to set. Incessant and sanguinary feuds prevailed. Baudouin-le-Chauve continued embittered against

888—912

899
Jan.
Restoration
of Charles

The successes of Charles.

888—912
898 - 900
Seculariza-
tion of ec-
clesiastical
endow-
ments.

the Vermandois family, and he was also most intent upon the object of usurping the great Abbeys
within or adjoining to his dominions. — These
transactions, so often noticed, constitute a main
feature throughout the Carlovingian era; but although constantly presented to us, we scarcely
appreciate their full extent; the ecclesiastical
annalists were grieved at these perversions and
ashamed of them, and they conceal, as far as is
practicable, the fact that so many of the Prelates
who appear in their Fasti are lay-intruders.

898—900
Disputes
between
Baudouin-
le-Chauve
and Abp.
Fulco.

The habitations congregated round Sithiu, or
Saint-Bertin, had now become the flourishing
Burgh of Saint-Omer: Saint-Vedast's Abbey and
the abbatial Castle-garth constituted the most
important quarter of Arras—Arras was identified
with Saint-Vedast. These two tempting Abbeys
had ·long been coveted by Baudouin-le-Chauve.
Many a time and oft were these pieces of preferment assaulted and won and lost. At the present
juncture, Archbishop Fulco held both the Abbeys,
which he administered conscientiously and worthily. At Sithiu he had been much aided by the
moral influence and talent of holy Grimbald—
the Grimbald to whom tradition ascribes the well-
known crypt under Saint Peter's in Oxford; for
he soon found a welcome in England, where we
know him as Bishop of Winchester and King
Alfred's Chancellor. Fulco afforded efficient aid
to Alfred in the restoration of the Anglo-Saxon

Church ; he was wise and pious, and the lament- 888—912
able inconsistencies of his character must be 898—900
ascribed to the political murrain which infected
the whole State.   Fulco's possession thwarted
Baudouin-le-Chauve's views.   Baudouin's vexation provoked him to the utmost against the
clergy: he caused a priest to be publicly whipped,
seized the churches, and rioted in anti-clerical
disorder.   Indeed the Church was in continual
strife with the principalities and powers of the
world : viewed historically, it seems truly marvellous that she did not succumb to her enemies.

The Marquisate of Flanders had been erected
in favour of Baudouin-bras-de-fer, for the purpose
of opposing a barrier against the Danes.   Baudouin-le-Chauve, busy in his quarrel, could ill perform his duty as a Lord-Marcher ; the Danes were
swarming, the Magyars rapidly approaching, and
the reports of their devastation filling France
with terror and confusion.

Charles assembled his army near the Oise, 900
Baudouin
demands
St. Vedast
Abp Fulco
murdered.
convening at the same time a great Council,
for the purpose of considering how he could best
deal with the Northmen.   Baudouin-le-Chauve
attended, but the defence of the country was
the last thing in his mind.   He pleaded before
Charles for the restoration of Saint-Vedast ; the
King being considered as having the complete
prerogative of dealing with these possessions according to his full will and pleasure.   Archbishop

888—912
898—911 Fulco opposed the demand. Herbert of Vermandois supported Fulco, and Grimbald aided Fulco's
cause by his arguments. The dispute, so far as
it was personal, between Archbishop Fulco and
Baudouin-le-Chauve, received a speedy termination The Archbishop went to and from the court
as usual, unprotected and without suspicion. A
band of ruffians, headed by Baudouin's vassals,
Winemar and Wilfrid and Everard, surrounded
the old man, and basely murdered him. Proof
cannot be furnished that Baudouin suggested this
assassination, but he did not evince any disap-
probation of the deed. Much confusion ensued,
yet the Council continued. It should seem that
measures were under discussion for renewing
negotiations with the Northmen. King Charles
chiefly advised with Count Robert Capet, Herbert of Vermandois, Richard-le-Justicier, and
Quarrel in
Council. Manasses Count of Dijon. The counsellors were
divided and factious. Count Manasses spoke dis-
respectfully of Robert Capet—some busy mis-
chief-maker reported the words to Robert, who
mounted his horse and rode off in anger, and
900—911
Singular
chasm in-
the mate-
rials of
French
history. the Council broke up in confusion. The only
Chronicle upon which we can depend, breaks off
as abruptly as the Council, and a chasm of about
ten years ensues, during which we scarcely possess any knowledge whatever of French history.

900—911 § 15. These ten years constituted a period of
trouble and disorder, the Empire continuing to

be cruelly infested by the Northmen; we only 888—912
guess at their devastations by the appearance of
public affairs: some insulated facts scantily en- 900—911
abling us to feel our way until the voice of the
witnesses is again heard.   Charles had been
living "gaily," according to the common phrase .
"dissolutely" would be less euphemistic, but
more true.   A wife or concubine dead or dis- 907
carded had not given him any male issue ; Gisella Charles
is considered to have been her daughter.   Upon Frederuna.
the demand of his Proceres, anxious without
doubt concerning the succession—for he was
now (Vermandois being excluded) the only acknowledged throne-capable representative of
Charlemagne—Charles therefore married: selecting for his consort the noble damsel Frederuna,
sister of Boso, Bishop of Chalons.

The parentage, nay, even the existence of
Gisella, the state-offering to Rollo, has been
treated as an important problem by recent French
historians: they question her identity, her existence, and we are therefore interested in
Frederuna, whom some suppose to have been
Gisella's mother; but hardly any memorials exist
in which this lady is named excepting the recitals
testified by Charles in the Charter under his hand
and seal, whereby he bestows on his Queen a
somewhat scanty dowry, and the notices contained
in certain other charters relating to her pious
foundations—authentic evidence unquestionably,

888—912
900—911 yet meagre and jejune.—Consecrated and crowned at Rheims, Frederuna died about ten years after her marriage, and tradition pointed out her place of interment in the church of Saint-Remi, beneath the great corona-lucis, but undistinguished by any monument.

Herbert of Verman-dois slain— succeeded by Herbert II. (See p. 356.) Amongst the few reminiscences transmitted from this dim period, we learn the death of Herbert of Vermandois. In fair and open warfare had the Seigneur of Peronne and Saint-Quentin slain Raoul of Cambrai, Baudouin-le-Chauve's brother : but a bitter feud arose. Herbert sought peace, Adeliza his daughter was betrothed to Arnoul, Baudouin's son, after him Count of Flanders, historically designated as Arnoul-le-Vieux, and lamentably conspicuous in Norman history ; but no reconciliation ensued: and Count Herbert was massacred at the instigation of Baudouin, implacably avenging his brother's blood.

Herbert the second of Vermandois, who succeeded his father, inherited and enlarged the dominions which imparted so much importance to the disinherited branch of the Carlovingian stem. Power, perverseness and activity, rendered this Herbert a participator in all political troubles so long as he lived. But the Capets were not to be stayed in their orbit ; and Robert Duke of France, espousing Rothaida or Rothilda, dubiously connected with royalty, assumed a station in the realm inferior only to the king.

§ 16.   Rollo returns from England, heading a gathering of warriors and soldiers, more ambitious, more strenuous, more determined than ever before.—Hitherto, renowned as Rollo had been, he did not appear predominant in the Danish host.   Hitherto his fighting men had been accustomed to boast,—We are equal, we know no Seigneur;—but they now deferred the supreme authority to him, a king without a kingdom. Some of his squadron-crews were unquestionably Norskmen from Norway, others Anglo - Danes, Jutes, Englishmen :—whatever may have been the precise proportion of these national constituencies, the French were accustomed to call their language English ; and it is remarkable, that the very scanty vestiges of their dialects preserved in local denominations, and in the single exclamatory phrase which we possess in Rollo's words, are rather Anglo-Teutonic in their sound.

888—912
911
Rollo returns to the Gauls.

The invaders extended themselves southward and northward.   They plundered Aquitaine ; the peasantry of the Gironde coast again pressed their grapes and filled their casks for the benefit of the guzzling Northmen.   The Danish bands on the borders of the Loire received new accessions ; but they prospered principally in the Seine territories, now so worn as to be in many parts completely waste and desolate, inviting a new population—Rouen, the ruined capital of a ruined country.   Their occupation here was now rapidly

Encrease of the Danish settlements

888—912 assuming the aspect of a permanent settlement;
——————— their dominion began to appear lawful. *It is*
911   *nice to cut thongs out of other folks' hides.* The
principles which, according to the ethics of civilization, justify or condemn the modes of exercising territorial acquisitivenes, are divided by
boundary lines exquisitely fine, nay evanescent,
when we attempt to discriminate between the
moral right of the *squatter*, the *colonist*, and the
conqueror.—The Northman was all three combined.

The North-   Whatever violence, fraud or injustice, had
men and
the Ro-   enabled the Northmen to gain possession of the
mane popu-
lation.   Frankish territory, many of their children, being
born of Romane mothers, were naturalized in the
country; and all, more or less, were conforming themselves to the nations amongst whom
they were planted. Christianity made some progress amongst them, they affected the "civil-
ity" and the usages of the Romanized populations. Amidst the tumults of the times, the
ecclesiastical magistracy exerted their powers to
mitigate hostility. Fulco, the murdered bishop
of Rheims, had been succeeded by Hervé, a royal
clerk, a chaplain of the Palace, mild, pious, benign, laborious and learned, and, as Primate of
the Gauls, took earnest thought concerning the
spiritual welfare of the Northmen. Not less
earnest in the good cause was Witto or Guido,
Archbishop of Rouen, an individual otherwise

wholly unknown; the like being the case with
the greater number of the Neustrian and Armorican prelates during this calamitous era The
student opens the conscientious "Gallia Christiana" for information; and he is answered by
the Prelate's name, printed in capitals, mar-
gined by hypothetical dates, and followed by a
line of modest conjecture. Almost all ecclesiastical documents perished during the invasions; and
notwithstanding the labour bestowed by the indefatigable Benedictines in compiling their excellent and, as yet, unrivalled repertory, they are
compelled to acknowledge that even the chronological succession of the ecclesiastical dignitaries
cannot be determined with certainty.

Idolatry—and ethnic usages—the sport or the
festival, the funeral or the marriage, celebrated
with antient rites, or contracted according to
the antient dooms and laws of the Asi, which
though not absolutely idolatrous, fostered idolatry—offered powerful obstacles to Christianity;
but greater practically, were the difficulties occasioned by their adoption of an imperfect Christianity.   Many of the Northmen, having been
baptized and rebaptized, relapsed into their ancient superstitions : many of the Franks also,
familiarized with the Danes, apostatized to their
opinions and customs : cathedral chapters and
monasteries had been in a great measure broken
up or dispersed, and the priesthood driven away

888—912

900—909
Hervé
Arch-
bishop of
Rheims
(900—921),
and Witto,
or Guido,
Archbishop
of Rouen
(892—909),
labour for
the conver-
sion of the
Northmen.

888—912 or slain, save the few demoralized or degraded survivors.

900—909   These distressing perplexities were amongst the accustomed trials of the church. Analogous circumstances had produced analogous effects; they were no new things. Dismissing from consideration the apostolic era, the Church, acting through her organized hierarchy, had constantly and consistently striven against such evils, teaching as she had been taught, and thereby inured to the conflict. Each successive age enriched the treasury of experience : for in each successive age Councils, Popes and Fathers had adjudicated during similar exigencies ; and the missionary saints, their lives and writings, afforded most instructive examples of the course to be pursued.   From

900—905
Archbishop
Hervé's
pastoral
monition.

such materials, Archbishop Hervé, upon the request of Archbishop Guido, compiled a pastoral monition, containing twenty-three Chapters or heads of instruction, which he transmitted to the Prelate of Rouen for his guidance in labouring amongst the rude population of his diocese.

900
Pope John
IX his
advice to
Abp
Hervé

Be mild, be considerate, be sparing of our weaker brethren, had been the advice given by the Supreme Pontiff, whose affectionate counsel guided the archbishop :—no novelties are propounded, no striking facts disclosed, yet the homiletic epistle, by declaring the errors which the teachers had to combat, and the exigencies they were required to meet, conveys a clearer idea

of the Danish mind than the vague Chronicle 888—912
language.

911

§ 17. The Church thus working to procure
peace, Charles was encouraged to resume the
policy, which, under another aspect, Fulco had
so strenuously condemned The long-continued
invasions had rendered the country extremely
miserable : whole districts were thrown out of
cultivation ; and the complaints of the people
excited the King to attempt a remedy for the
prevailing evils.

Rollo ruled in Rouen. Franco, who became Charles
Archbishop after Guido, acknowledged the Dane concludes a truce with
as Senior or Lord, and Charles, the Archbishop Rollo,— discontent of the
mediating, concluded a three months' truce with Counts of Burgundy
Rollo, contemplating, (as evinced by subsequent and Poitou, who attack
events,) a cession of Neustrian territory. Among Rollo when the truce
the Magnates of the Franks, there were, how- expires.
ever, those who considered such pacific overtures
as a national degradation : national pride was
provoked by national weakness ; and, the truce
having expired, Richard-le-Justicier, Count or
Duke of Burgundy, and Ebles the Mamzer, Count
of Poitou, assembling their forces, attacked the
Dane.

Rollo was exceedingly angered. Did the Rollo's ag-
Frenchmen hold him cheap? he would make gressive campaign
them feel his power,—challenged, he accepted
the challenge : he determined to punish the
country, and an exterminating war was renewed.

X X 2

888—912 Rollo marched into Burgundy and plundered
911—912 beyond Sens; his barges also entering the Seine
from the Yonne, and combining with his land-
forces, spread up the country, which they burnt
and ravaged as far as Clermont in the Beauvoisis.
Dudon relates the campaign's details with singular precision. They must have been well recollected in Rollo's family, for we can trace his
route upon the map by and through the towns
and rivers which Dudo enumerates. The desolating host visited Fleury on the Loire, the monastery so venerated in the Anglo-Saxon Church,
bearing Saint Benedict's name, and honoured
by his mortal remains translated from distant
Monte-Cassino : but a compunctious feeling induced Rollo to spare the Sanctuary. These slight
touches enable us to estimate his character ;—
good temper, humanity, and perhaps Christian
instruction already slightly received, or some fear
of supernatural vengeance, contending against the
interests and passions fostered by the vocation of
the conquering pirate.

The Danes then occupied the opposite bank
of the Seine, pillaged Etampes, an ancient and
splendid palace—thence to Villemeux near Dreux,
and threatened Paris.

Chartres,
supported
by the
Frankish
command-
ers, pre-
pares for
defence.
Rendered desperate by their sufferings, the
peasantry assembled tumultuously against the
Danes. Rollo's light cavalry massacred the churls,
and he then occupied the Dunois and the Pays-

Chartrain.—Chartres, impoverished and wasted by the Danish hordes, was governed by bishop Walthelm, the city well fortified, and the inhabit- ants stoutly determined upon resistance. The cathedral contained and yet contains a remark- able relic, a delicate silken web of Byzantine or oriental manufacture, fondly supposed to be the Holy Virgin's garment. The people confiding in her protection, prepared themselves for the peril, whilst Robert duke of France, Richard of Bur- gundy, and Ebles the Mamzer, the three great Frankish commanders, had, upon the approach of the Danes, mustered before the walls. A portion of Rollo's forces encamped upon a hill, the Mont- Levis, north of the city. The remainder of the Danish troops continued stationed in the plain.

On Saturday the twentieth day of July, a day celebrated at Chartres even until the Revolution, the combined Frankish and Burgundian forces gave battle to the Northmen; the townsmen at the same time sallying forth, bearing the relic as their banner. Rollo and his forces were shame- fully routed, smitten, as the legend tells, with cor- poreal blindness. A panic fear assuredly fell upon the heroic commander, a species of mental in- firmity discernible in his descendants: the con- tagious terror unnerved the host. Unpursued, they dispersed and fled without resistance. Six thousand eight hundred Danish corpses were counted on the field, and the name of the *Pré*

888—912

911

20 July, 911.
Battle of Chartres
Panic of Rollo and the North- men.

888—912 *des Reculés,*—just without the *Porte Drouaise,*
911—912 the gate leading to Dreux,—commemorates the
raising of the siege and the delivery of Chartres.

The Danes recover from their panic, and storm the French camp.

Thanks to the imprudence of their enemies, the Danes immediately regained the superiority which they had lost without a cause: the Count of Poitou, Ebles the Mamzer, lagging behind, had not arrived opportunely to take his due share in the conflict. The Franks and Burgundians, glorying in their successes, mocked Ebles and his Poitevins: a foolish quarrel and foolish boastings ensued, and the Poitevins were scornfully told by their rivals in their own camp, that there were Danes enough remaining upon the Mont-Levis to try their metal—they might redeem their honour if they chose. Ebles accepted the challenge; but the Danes, advantaged by their position, repelled the Poitevins with great loss. In the dark of the night, the Northmen, sounding their horns and making a terrible clamour, rushed down the mount and stormed the Frankish camp. Ebles ran away and concealed himself in a fuller's workshop,—his recreancy was derided in popular ballads, which continued current (as it should seem) till the Plantagenet age:

> " *Vers en firent e estraloz*
> *U out assez de vileins moz.*"

and the Danes, the Frankish army being dispersed, rejoined Rollo.

The defeat of the Danes before Chartres, though

worthily deemed a local triumph, was an incident 888—912
without any importance in the general fortunes of
the campaign, except that, on the whole, the out- 911—912
burst of the Mont-Levis encouraged the Northmen.
The Danes pursued their warfare with systematic Charles de-
termines to
pertinacity, the French were pressed harder than negotiate
with Rollo.
ever; all now agreed in the necessity of a pacification: and a negotiation was opened on the
part of King Charles, mainly conducted by Robert
Capet.—Duke Robert was indeed the principal
in these transactions.   Any cession made to the
Danes in Neustria would be at his expence, for
he asserted a superiority, positive, though undefined, over all the dominions between Seine and
Loire, and unless Duke Robert assented, no compact could be concluded.   Many *pour-parlers* and
propositions took place and were exchanged.
On and off, Rollo had been in France during the
greater part of his active life, fighting, negotiating, receiving French money : he knew the country and people well, the terms he should demand
and the propositions he should reject; and he
was resolved to secure a settlement in a territory
where he might establish his future power.

§ 18.   At length the conference took place 911.
The con-
on the left or eastern bank of the shallow gliding ference of
St. Clair-
Epte, Charles occupying the little town of Saint- sur-Epte.
Clair.   On the right or western bank stood Rollo,
assisted and advised by Franco, Archbishop of
Rouen,—he whom the Norman reminiscences

888—912
911—912

confused with Franco Bishop of Liege, the counsellor of Charles-le-Chauve,—and surrounding
and supporting Rollo were the eagerly expectant
groups, chieftains and soldiers, old men, young
men and growing boys, amongst whom the fragments of historical traditions enable us to discern
some few ancestors of Normandy's stalwart aristocracy, the Danish men who had accompanied the
prosperous warrior, sharing his fortunes or his
dangers.

The fol-
lowers of
Rollo.

Numerous were Rollo's kith and kin. The
names of two may be recalled,—*Gerlo*, who held
the County of Blois, and *Huldrich* or *Malahulc*,
the uncle of Rollo.—This Malahulc was the ancestor of a widely-spread noble sept, chief amongst
whom were the renowned Houses of Conches
and Toeny.

Botho, the well-trusted veteran, founded the
opulent family of Tesson. According to popular
etymology, a natural amusement of the human
mind, the Tessons obtained their surname, "the
badger," from their peculiar talent of burrowing
or fixing their claws wherever they could gain
possession: a significant if not a noble epithet.
—"La-Roche-Tesson,"—it was also a common
saying,—"holds one-third of broad Normandy:
one-third of Normandy belongs to La-Roche-
Tesson."

Near to Botho stands *Bernard the Dane:*
supported by his son *Torf;* and eight or more

seignorial towns tell by their present names that 888—912
Torf was their former Lord.   Lofty were the $\overline{}$
banners raised by the Dane Bernard's progeny Bernard
amongst the baronial blazonry of Normandy and the Dane
and his
of England;—the Harcourts displaying their descendants
cheering motto, *Le bon temps viendra;*—and
Beaumont Earl of Mellent and Beaumont Earl
of Warwic, Beaumont Earl of Leicester and Beaumont Earl of Bedford, and Tancreville, and Gour-
nay, Aumalle, Elbeuf, and Eu, and more than we
have room to reckon, all claim Bernard as their
ancestor.

Oslac or *Auslac*, his name misread or eupho-
nized into the form of "Lancelot," consorts with
Bernard.—Oslac's son *Thurstan* assumed the territorial denomination of "Tourstain de Basten-
bourg." From Thurstan came the Seigneurs of
Briquebec, or Birkbeck, and the Counts of Mont-
fort-sur-Rille.

Osfrid was the ancestor of Hugh Lupus, Earl
of Chester. *Riulph*, rich and powerful in Evreux,
became also Count of the Côtentin; and one
more may be recognized, *Osmund*, from whom
descended the family of Osmond-de-Centvilles;
they who give the bearing also appertaining to
the illustrious Seymours,—the *Vol*,—the wings
displayed, the hieroglyphic significantly recalling
the achievement which, preserving the liberty or
life of Rollo's grandchild, has entitled Osmund to
so conspicuous a station in Norman history.

888—912

911—912
911.
"Treaty"
of Saint
Clair-sur-
Epte.

§ 19. The transactions ensuing are usually quoted as constituting the treaty of Saint Clair-sur-Epte, a designation somewhat inappropriate, inasmuch as the term "treaty" conveys the idea of a diplomatic instrument, to which the parties could appeal with certainty. This, however, was not the case. It is the cardinal fact in Norman history, that the Normans, during the period comprehended in the reigns of the first two Dukes or *Seniors*, never employed the art of writing in their political or legal transactions—the State was, in practice, absolutely illiterate—and the particulars of this celebrated compact can only be collected from oral traditions, not reduced into writing until Dudon de Saint-Quentin, the first historian of Normandy, took up the pen, and inscribed the first pages of her history.

The Franks
urgent for
peace.

When Charles concluded his three months' truce with Rollo, we have seen that the Franks were indignant at the compromise; but their pride was brought low, and they thronged upon their monarch to conciliate the dreaded Dane. Archbishop Franco, again mediating between the parties, but more immediately concerned for Rollo, employed all his influence. State-marriages had been long considered as a legitimate mode of advancing the royal interest; and the advisers of Charles urged him to give a daughter in marriage to the Dane, the damsel Gisella. Charles assented, but Rollo did not glow towards the

Princess; he had his own bonne-amie, he cared _{888—912} nothing for Gisella. The old Soldier held out with obstinate tranquillity against the praises _{911—912} bestowed by Archbishop Franco upon Gisella's beauty and procerity, accompanied by a full exposition of the advantages he would derive from the alliance; but the Frankish counsellors ^{Gisella given in} insisted: the Danish chieftains also strongly ^{marriage to Rollo.} supported the proposition:—would not Rollo, through Gisella, become the father of a right royal progeny?—Thus courted and exhorted, Rollo agreed to accept the damsel's hand: his coy assent to the alliance being accompanied by a demand for a competent dowry.

Such a request had, of course, been antici- ^{Offer made by the} pated, yet considerable difficulties arose. When ^{French.} Charles was required to define and complete the covenant which should establish the Dane in Gaul, imparting a legal title to the acquisitions the Northmen had made upon the banks of the Seine, and settling them in the heart of the Frankish kingdom, he became jealous for his own dignity, and would fain have avoided fulfilling his own designs. He therefore endeavoured to restrict the donation to the narrowest bounds, and to part with no more than what he had already lost. Rouen, or the heap of ruins which constituted Rouen, could not be taken from Rollo: who could unlock his grasp? Osker had discovered the city for the Danes, and their suc-

888—912
911—912
cessive occupations and invasions had kept up
their continual claim : the treaty with Charles-
le-Chauve recognized their domination ; Charles
his grandson was willing to declare that the
desolated tracts about the ruined Rouen, un-
stocked by the herdsmen, untilled by the plough,
might belong to Rollo.

But even the French King's counsellors supported Rollo in rejecting this insufficient and
almost affronting offer. Rollo must have wherewithal he and his men can live—if Rollo and
his men do not receive their needs, they must
help themselves, of necessity, by robbing and
reiving. The demand propounded by Rollo was
large and ambiguous : from the banks of the
Epte, whereon they stood, even until the sea.—
To that demand an ample concession was reluctantly yielded, a territory including those districts
of the Duchy afterwards known as *la haute
Normandie*, to wit, the territory of the antient
Caleti, the *Pays de Caux*, together with the
Comté d'Eu and the *Pays de Brai*, between
the Brêle and the Seine—the *Roumois*, or Pagus
Rothomagensis, whose boundaries are the Andelle and the Rille,—and the *Vexin Normand*,
or so much of the Pagus Veliocassinus as is
included between that same Andelle and the
Epte, which, rising near Bolbec, runs by Gisors,
and falls into the Seine between Mantes and
Vernon. There are few countries in which the

Cession
made to
Rollo com-
prehending
the district
known as
" Haute
Norman-
die."

artificial or political demarcations are so neatly 888—912 marked out by rivers and rivulets as Normandy; 911—912 the streams forming convenient natural divisions, which, guiding the aboriginal inhabitants in their settlements, were permanently adopted in the civil and ecclesiastical repartitions of the country. The remainder of the Pagus Veliocassinus, retained by Charles, acquired the name of the *Vexin Français*, and became a source of much trouble between France and Normandy. In the contest to gain or regain this border-land, William the Conqueror received the injury which brought him to the grave.

But the terms of Rollo's asking, from the Epte to the sea, warranted the extension of the Danish dominion to the Atlantic. Charles would have preferred to send Rollo in the opposite direction, and offered him Flanders,— *ut ex ea viveret*—he would provide occupation for his son-in-law as far away as he could. Flanders proper, as we know, was now held by her own sturdy Count, Baudouin-le-Chauve, and Flanders was not the King's to give;—but probably under this familiar and colloquial term, Friezland was the country intended. *Discussions concerning the cession of territory.*

The acute Rollo declined the proposition. Why should he resume his fight against the Frisons to win their swamps and marshes? Frisia was an ill-fated country for the Northmen: none had prospered there. Charles was contented to com- *Britanny granted to Rollo.*

888—912
911—912

promise by conferring another dominion upon Rollo, which the Crown of France had virtually abandoned, Armorica, and whatever other territories such a royal grant might include, or enable Rollo to acquire. The Armorican Marches were already largely in the possession of the Northmen, and whether these Northmen would obey Rollo or not, he was well satisfied to accept whatever authority the grant might convey.

Rollo performs homage to King Charles.

§ 20. The dominion thus determined, Rollo, obeying the directions given by the Frankish counsellors, placed his hands betweeen the hands of the king, and became the King's man; such an act as never had been performed by Rollo's father, or Rollo's grandfather, or Rollo's great-grandfather before him. Therefore from the king he received his investiture—the appointed land to be held *in alodo et in fundo*, and all Britanny: the land from the Epte to the sea. A custom subsisted in the Carlovingian court, that whoever asked or received any boon from royalty, kissed the sovereign's knee or buskin, in token of grateful humility. This mode of obeisance had no relation to "feudalism."—*La bouche et les mains* sufficed; merely as "Senior," the king could require no more; but the ceremony of *adoration* was a very ancient and universal mode of testifying subjection, and was rendered without difficulty by any suppliant for grace and favour. The incident would scarcely require much notice,

were it not for the dogged illiberality which has 888—912
converted the usage into an accusation against
the Bishops, who are charged with having intro- 911—912
duced the practice for the purpose of humiliating
the temporal nobility.

The demand, however, though accustomed, Rollo re-fuses to kiss the King's foot.
affronted Rollo, who indignantly refused—*ne si*
by Got,—was his exclamation.   The Franks in-
sisting upon conformity, Rollo surlily consented
that his proxy should render the worship claimed
for the King, and Charles, as is well known, was
rudely thrown backwards by the Danish soldier.
Norman arrogance,—such as was displayed when
Rollo's descendant, Robert-le-Diable, the conqueror's father, bullied the throne of the Eastern
Emperor,—may perhaps be considered as con-
firming the story; and if it be not true, the
family were proud of an insult fabled to have
been offered to the French sovereign, which
amounts to nearly the same thing.

A remarkable assurance given by Charles The assur-ance given to Rollo by King Charles, Duke Robert, &c.
and his legislature to Rollo, (almost unnoticed
by historians,) completed the cession.— King
Charles and Duke Robert, and the Counts and
the Proceres, the Bishops and the Abbots, promised to be faithful to the Patrician Rollo in
life and limb, and the honour of the realm;
and that the territory, as he held and possessed
the same, should pass to his heirs and descendants from generation to generation for ever;

888—912   and, the transactions concluded, Charles returned
911—912   home, and Duke Robert and Archbishop Franco
remained with Rollo.

Uncertainty as to the extent of the Feudal Suzerainty of the Crown of France.   § 21. Thus was the Dane installed in the "Terra Northmannorum."—What are the evidences declaring the relations subsisting between the Frankish Sovereign and the Norman chief?
Over-loyal jurists have dreamed of letters patent issued by Charles-le-Simple, his great seal pendent *semé de fleurs de lis sans nombre.* Others assert that Rollo accepted the country as a fief, recognizing the sovereignty of the Carlovingian Crown.—
When our first Edward proceeded to claim the rights which, as he alleged, resulted from the Scottish subjection, he produced some muniments from his treasury; but the proofs of the superiority of the English Crown, could not from their nature, be perfected otherwise than by connecting them with the testimony afforded by the chronicles of past times. These were not preserved amongst the records of the realm, and could only be found in ecclesiastical libraries. The English Sovereign therefore addressed his writs to the cathedrals and principal monasteries throughout England, commanding each Dean and chapter, Abbot, Prior and convent, to make search amongst their archives for all matters relating to Scotland, and to transmit the same to the king under their common seals; and the certificates transmitted accordingly, are still extant. Truth

was asked, truth was told, and due diligence em- 888—912
ployed by the plaintiff in the great Scottish cause.

912

Philippe-Auguste, asserting his "feudal-rights"
over Normandy, and pronouncing sentence of forfeiture against John Lackland, did not direct any
such search to be instituted; but we in a manner
have done so; and in other portions of this work
the reader will find extracted every existing text
bearing upon the Norman question, by which
his judgment may be guided. In the present
instance, it is sufficient to state that Charles
construed the cession to "Rollo" and his Counts,
the "Northmen of the Seine," as having been made
pro tutela regni, whereas the same body of Nor- Denial of
the supre-
man Counts, in the time of Rollo's grandson, macy of
France by
Richard Sans-peur, boldly told the Carlovingian the Normans.
Monarch, "Duke Richard governs the Norman
region as a king: he serves neither king nor duke,
and owns no superior under Heaven." Or, adopting the phraseology which gives such poetic
force to the traditionary jurisprudence of the Teutonic races, they asserted that he held Normandy
as a *Sonnen-Lehn*—" from God and the Sun."

§ 22. A confused, but very remarkable narration, compiled soon after the accession of Hugh
Capet, would lead us to suppose that, hostilities
having recommenced between Rollo and the
Franks, the Northmen refused to accept Christianity until their conversion was enforced by
Robert Capet's prowess. It is quite impracticable

888—912 to marshal the evidence satisfactorily. Nor can
912 we dismiss an awkward suspicion, suggested by
the Frankish chronicles, that Rollo, when he
treated at Saint-Clair-sur-Epte, was well known
to Charles as a relapsed Pagan. Dudon de Saint-
Quentin gives us no such hint: but we may
excuse Rollo's descendants if they forgot any
circumstances derogatory to the reputation of
their great ancestor. His history is perplexing
from beginning to end; the fragmentary and
often contradictory statements which furnish
much matter for critical—(and perhaps tediously
unprofitable)—discussion, cannot by any means be
all included in one consistent or coherent narrative. Any how the formal reception of Christianity by Rollo was retarded until the subsequent
year. Robert Duke of France appeared as his
912 sponsor, and, at the font, the name of Robert
Rollo bap-
tized at was given to the Dane. Dudon de Saint-Quentin
Rouen. denominates the hero by his baptismal appellation; and such may have been the courtly style;
but the old Norsk name, the name which had
honoured him in youth and in age, was alone
recognized by the world; the world will ever
know him as Rollo.

Rollo signalized his baptism by donations to
the Church; the Archbishop directed his bounty;
and each of the seven days which elapsed whilst
Rollo-Robert wore the white chrismal vestment
(perhaps not for the first time) the catechumen

displayed some token of his liberality. On the
first day, Notre-Dame of Rouen was compensated
for the territories which the See had lost.—
Saint-Exupere, of Bayeux, smarting under the
wounds the Dane had inflicted, was aided on the
second.—Dilapidated Saint-Taurin, at Evreux, on
the third.—On the fourth, the Celtic Cell, the
rock-sanctuary of Saint Michael, well denominated *in periculo maris*, received a grant, and the
Archangel was adopted as the tutelary patron of
the Northmen.—On the fifth, Saint-Ouen, then
without the city boundary.—On the sixth, Jumièges, where the scared monks crouched in huts
and hovels amidst the walls of the fire-scathed
fabric. —Lastly, on the seventh, royal Saint-Denis
obtained Brenneval, whose field was destined to
become so mournfully memorable in the pages
of Norman history.

§ 23. A formal repartition of the ceded territory ensued, chieftains and soldiery taking or
retaining their shares. The Carlovingian title of
' *Count* was adopted by the Leaders according to the
natural course of events; for, without any effort,
Rollo and the Romanized Danes conformed to the
ethos of the Carlovingian monarchy.   Listening
to tradition, and repeating the only words we can
use in the total absence of any deed or of any
coeval testimony, the lands were divided by the
rope, or according to measurement. Rollo's grandchildren were thus accustomed to describe the

888—912

912
Rollo's
donations
to the Nor-
man
church

888—912

912
Norman measure- ments.

act of their ancestor, "Illam terram suis fidelibus funiculos divisit."—The *reebning*, or mensuration by the rope or line, supplied the technical term of *hrepp* to the glossary of Scandinavian legislation: archæologists have therefore pronounced an opinion that the *Rapes* of Sussex, the divisions ranging from the Channel shore to the *Suthrige* border, were, according to Norwegian fashion, thus plotted out by the Conqueror.

We also find in England, more certainly borrowed from Normandy, the *leucata*, or *lowy*, a circuit averaging a custumary league in diameter, surrounding certain castles or towns, marking out the extent of jurisdiction.—In these examples, the *line* was unquestionably employed; yet the ancient landmarks, such as existed in the Gallo-Roman period, seem to have been rarely disturbed. The Pagus became a Bailliage, or a County, and the ambit of a Villa, a township or a seignory. Except during the heat and fury

Peasantry, not evicted by the Danes.

of conquest, the peasantry, the descendants of the ancient *coloni*, were not evicted by the Danes, but continued to dwell on the land they tilled, as is fully evinced by the preponderance of the Romane dialect.—The conquerors however gave the widest construction to the law of property: air, water and earth, were all to be theirs, fowl, fish, and beast of chase, where the arrow could fly, the dog could draw, or the net could fall— sportsmen, huntsmen, the Danish lords appro-

priated to themselves all woodland and water, 888—912
copse and grove, river, marsh and mere.   Their 912
usurpation of the rights previously enjoyed in
common occasioned in the days of Rollo's great-
grandson a fearful rebellion; and the spirit of
the forest-laws, the pregnant source of misery to
Old England, has perhaps acquired additional
bitterness in our present age; we retain the evil,
whilst our pariahs have lost the compensations
which mitigated mediæval tyranny.

Rollo is said to have introduced an har- "Feudal
monious and perfect system of *feudality*, me- system"
supposedby
thodizing the laws and usages of tenure as they Sismondi,
&c. to have
prevailed elsewhere, and profiting by all the im- been introduced by
provements which experience had suggested.— Rollo—
doubts as
His legislative talent (it is thus supposed) gave to this
opinion.
one origin to all rights of property, imparting
to feudality a regularity hitherto unknown; and
this Province, the most modern in Gaul, became
a model for all others.—

Such are the observations entitled to respect
on account of the authority whence they proceed; and the theory thus enounced is incorporated, so to speak, in the textus receptus of
Norman history; but, however recommended by
simplicity, and conformable to our general prepossessions, the support of any evidence whatever is absolutely wanting.   Not a single Norman deed or muniment, grant or charter, signed
or unsigned, sealed or unsealed, can be found until

888—912 the reign of Richard Sans-peur; and then very
——— rarely—a dearth contrasting singularly with the
912 diplomatic opulence of Anglo-Saxon England. The
lieger-books of the Norman monasteries, anterior
to the reign of William the Bastard, scarcely
contain a document of importance: and, whilst
we possess full information concerning the Anglo-
Saxon tenures of land previous to Duke William's
conquest of our country, we know absolutely
nothing concerning the parallel circumstances of
his own Normandy. The legitimate boundaries
of historical doubt are therefore not over-stepped,
if we consider the invention of the full "*feudal
system*" by Rollo exercising the plenitude of his
power, as a legal fiction in the most extensive
sense of the term. Nay, it remains to be proved
whether any system of Norman tenure had been
matured into consistency by fiscal talent until
after the seventh Duke of Normandy won the
Anglo-Saxon Crown.

Was the
system of
tenures in
Normandy
older than
the Con-
queror?

§ 24. Rollo assimilated himself to the Romane modes of thought, art, and action, in all
the concerns of human life or society. He caused
the dilapidated towns and cities to be rebuilt:
Rouen and her Cathedral demanded his primary
care. Zealous antiquarians, kneeling on the pavement, and closely examining the basement courses
of the northernmost tower, the *Tour de Saint-
Romain*, decide that the masonry belonged to the
original structure. There is a crypt, possibly of

the Roman Christian period, beneath the Church
of Saint-Gervais; and Saint-Ouen displays, as it
is thought, a portion of the Merovingian choir.
With some such few exceptions, all the sacred
edifices were reconstructed by or under the influence of Rollo.

888—912
Rouen
Rollo's en-
largement
of the City
and other
works
therein.

Ancient Rothomagus was refounded by the
city's Danish Lord.   Embankments and trenches
restrained or absorbed the idle waste of waters :
where Rollo found islands he left dry land, the
channels were obliterated ; and the rocks, at whose
foot, when he first entered Rouen, he staid his vessel's course, buried in the causeway.   The *terres-
neuves*, the land regained by the works which
Rollo executed, doubled the size of the renovated
metropolis.   The whole was re-fortified, and the
great castle, afterwards called the Vieux Palais,
erected by Rollo.   Every vestige of this building
has perished; and our curiosity is vainly excited
by the notice that an *Alfred*, whoever he may
have been, gave his name to one of the towers.
Henceforward Rouen grew from age to age : successive sovereigns—Richard-sans-peur, Philippe-
Auguste, Saint-Louis and Philippe-de-Valois,—
enlarged the circuit.   Suburbs and outlying villages were embraced by the expanding walls and
ramparts; and, counting Rollo's as the second,
six new and concentric enceintes during the
ancien regime encreased the flourishing city; the
area which they enclosed being now quadrupled
within the boundary of the existing Octroi.

The Vieux
Palais, Al-
fred's
tower.

888—912

The three
Legends of
Rollo the
lawgiver.

§ 25. The reputation of Rollo the legislator vied with the reputation of Rollo the conqueror; and in the old time, three popular legends peculiarly commemorated his love of justice.

It was a "wise custom" in Normandy, established by Rollo's decree, that whoever sustained or feared to sustain any damage of goods or chattels, life or limb, was entitled to raise the

Legend I, the *Clameur de Haro*.

country by the cry of *haro*, or *harou*, upon which cry all the lieges were bound to join in pursuit of the offender, *Harou ! Ha Raoul !*—justice invoked in Duke Rollo's name. Whoever failed to aid, made fine to the Sovereign; whilst a heavier mulct was consistently inflicted upon the mocker who raised the *clameur de haro* without due and sufficient cause, a disturber of the commonwealth's tranquillity.

Legend II, the *Roumare*.

Strict and severe, yet mild and equitable, was Rollo in the punishment of violence or wrong. In his time, the rivulet of Bapaume which falls into the Seine nearly opposite to Queville, expanded into a Lake or Mere in the centre of a pleasant forest; but Mere and forest have long since vanished amidst the fabrics which cover the country about the prosperous city, or have yielded to the spread of cultivation. Here Rollo was accustomed to take his pleasure, and it chanced that one day, after his sport, he and his companions having sat down to their banquet, the cloth spread upon the grass, the thought came across Rollo's mind that he would measure the effect of his ordinances by exposing 888—912 his people to temptation. Therefore, unclasping his bracelets, the well-known signs of his dignity, he suspended the golden circles to the branch of a tree, to be guarded only by the terror of his name.—When he returned, three years afterwards, there were the bracelets still pendant, untouched, unharmed, glittering in the sun ; and thenceforth was the Mere called the *Roumare*, the Mere of *Rou* or Rollo.

Rollo peculiarly sought to protect the husbandman. In the open field, by night or by day, plough and oxen, fork and harrow, stock and gear, were watched by the law ; if loss were sustained, the Sovereign, taking the neglect upon himself, would indemnify the loser. Now there Legend III, was a certain rustic in the village of Long-paon, of *Long-* who had an ill-conditioned wife, and he knew *paon.* it, who, secreting harness and ploughshare for the purpose in the first instance of teasing her husband, enabled him to receive compensation for the damage he had not sustained.—Wife and husband were hanged ; but, excusing the reader the details of an uncouth story, Rollo's stern decision savours more of harshness than of equity.

§ 26. As cumulative proofs that the ancient Examina- legislation of the Terra Normannorum was purely tion of the oral and traditional, these three legends have three legal their value : they display in some degree the prac- legends. tice, and in a greater degree the spirit of the Northman's law ; but their verity would scarcely

888—912 deserve examination had they not been accepted

The *clameur de Haro*, the English hue and cry. as portions of Rollo's historical character.—The *clameur de Haro* is the English system of hue and cry. The old English exclamation *Harrow!*— our national vernacular *Hurrah!* being only a variation thereof—is identical with the supposed invocation of the Norman chieftain; and the usage, suggested by common sense, prevailed under various modifications throughout the greater part of the *Pays Coutumier* of France.

The legend of the *Roumare*, common to many countries. With respect to the suspended bracelets, Benoit de Saint-More, the Anglo-Norman Trouveur who versified the Latin chronicle, records, though he rejects, the more vulgar notion, that the *Roumare*, the "*Red Mere*," was so called from the good red-wine which sportive Rollo's revelling bravery poured into the blushing waters. But the truth of the anecdote, if any argument were needed, is destroyed by its universality. Travelling from Rouen to Caen, the pilgrim would meet another *Mare-des-anneaux*, and a third at Caen, near the site where Queen Matilda founded her abbey. The tale is echoed in England, Ireland, Denmark, and Lombardy. Alfred, Brian-Boroimhe, Frotho, and Theodoric the Ostrogoth, are all respectively commemorated as having tried the efficacy of their social policy by the same test; the myth being the symbol in which the people embodied their recollections of the confidence reposed in the administration of the laws.

The rustic tragedy of Long-paon has more

individuality. The general principle upon which
the case is grounded conforms to the jurisprudence of the Scandinavians, amongst whom the
members of the community were knitted together by the closest social bonds. The husbandman, if his own hinds failed him, could demand
the gratuitous assistance of his fellow-yeomen in
gathering his harvest : and with solemn earnestness the law proclaimed that the crop open to
the trespasser and unwatched by the master, was
under God's lock, heaven for the roof, though
but the hedge for the wall. The pilferer who
plucked the growing ears from the stalk incurred
a grievous penalty; whilst the rapacious thief who
stole the ripe corn out of the field, binding his
burthen and bearing it into his own barn, forfeited his life and all his fee: and the hard if not
unmerciful judgment of Rollo, is susceptible of
numerous parallels. But it is a dream to accept
the assertion that Rollo instituted a regular code.
—The *Grand Coutumier* is comparatively of
recent date. The customs of Normandy were not
reduced into writing until after the Duchy was
lost to Rollo's progeny.

§ 27. The Pictish language has scarcely disappeared more thoroughly from Scotland, than
the Danish from the Terra Normannorum. What
was the speech of the pirates and the pagans?—
Rollo is speaking English, said the courtiers
of king Charles, when he astounded them by

Side notes:

The *Longpaon* legend—its conformity to Scandinavian jurisprudence

Extinction of the Danish language in Normandy.

888—912 refusing to perform the Court ceremony: but this term might be applied to any Anglo-Danish dialect of Northumbria or East-Anglia, or any other German-sounding language.

912

Of the Northman's speech we possess no example excepting the exclamation of Rollo—no rhyme, no proverb, no legal formula, no magical charm. Let the lexicographer search for any trace of Dansk or Norsk in the Norman French, and how will his search be rewarded? The "Norman of the Normans," Montgomery, could not have quoted a Dansk word : the Norman Jurist can find none in his *Sages Coûtumes*. But language adheres to the soil when the lips which spake are resolved in the dust. Mountains repeat and rivers murmur the voices of nations denationalized or extirpated in their own land. Norman topography, local or provincial, therefore, becomes our only resource : the map discloses the tokens, if tokens they be, of Scandinavianism, wholly absent from the Glossary.—The *Holegate*, or *Houlgat*, at Hermoustier and Granville and Cormelles, and most particularly at Caen, where the road so called passed between the excavated rock ;—the *Dêrnethal* and the *Depedal*,—may respectively be construed into the *Hoehlegasse*, the *Hollowgate*, the *Derndale* and the *Deepdale*, without any difficulty. Places in whose denomination the syllable *del, dale* or *thal* is found to enter, abound in Normandy. There

Vestiges of the Danish language in Norman topography.

are fifty or more *dells, dals* or *tals*, in the 888—912 Bessin.

912

The term so familiar as an affix, the well-known Danish "*Bye*," a dwelling, an abiding place, a word which in other northern forms, or in Norsk, is spelt *boe, bojgd*, or *bygd*, occurs, though variously disguised, in a large proportion of Norman names—*Elbœuf* and *Belbœuf* and *Marbœuf*, and *Bourguebuf*, and *Carquebuf*, and *Tournebue*, are examples.

Names denoting the running water, the *beck, bek* or *bach*, are scattered in good number all over Normandy.—*Beaubec*, and *Briquebec*, and *Caldebec*, and *Foulbec*, and *Houlbec*, the pleasant brook or the birch-fringed brook, or the cool rivulet, or the mud-stained rivulet, or the streamlet in the hollow channel.—*Fisigard* and *Auppegard* and *Epegard*, the Fishyard, and the Applegarth or Appleyard, hardly need a transslation.—*Toft*, somewhat varied into *tot*, is tolerably common: the kingdom of *Yvetot*, Yvo's toft, is an illustrious example; and *bosc* or *busk*, the bush or the wood, abounds.

All these, with many others, are claimed as vestiges of the Northmen's occupancy, plausibly and possibly, yet not certainly—they may be no such. In the detritus of languages, covering the Northern Gauls, the crystals are so rounded and smoothed, that it is very difficult to pronounce with absolute precision on their primitive form;

888—912 and we believe that amongst the Teutonic vocables which may be adduced, the greater majority possess an even chance of belonging to any of the Frankish, Alemannic, Belgic, Anglian or Saxon dialects. At all events, we may expect a due proportion of the latter, seeing that the Saxons of the Bessin, the *Otlingua-Saxonica,* had been established on the channel-coast centuries before the arrival of Rollo. But, in point of fact, the Danish language was never prevalent or strong in Normandy. The Northmen had long been talking themselves into Frenchmen; and in the second generation, the half-caste Northmen, the sons of French wives and French concubines, spoke the Romane-French as their mothers' tongue.

Danish language extinguished by the preponderant influence of the Romane-French language.

Norman chorography, to which we have appealed as the record of Northmanism, displays convincingly the general acceptance of the Romane-French by the Danish settlers. In England, where the Danes did unquestionably retain their language for a lengthened period, they generally compounded their local denominations out of a Danish proper name and a Danish or Anglo-Saxon noun. The *lurdanes* prided themselves in giving their names to their possessions. Asker called his Township *Askarby,* Ketil, *Kettleby;* and Clapa's heim, or *Clapham,* Osgod Clapa's home, is a very familiar example of the practice; but in Normandy, the Danes very often took the opposite

Romano-Danish names of places

direction, compounding their local denominations 888—912 out of a Danish proper name and a Romane noun. —*Gremonville, Tourville, Toufreville, Tancarville, Haqueville, Toustainville,* prove incontestably that *Gormund* and *Torf* and *Thorolf* and *Tancred* and *Haco* and *Thurstan* settled themselves as French nobles in the country.—The gallicized appellations thus bestowed upon their Seigneuries rendered them more kindly; the adoption of the French language conciliating the unpleasant foreign aspect of the Lords, and giving them more gentility.   In the cities, Bayeux only excepted, hardly any language but French was spoken. Forty years after Rollo's establishment, the Danish language struggled for existence.   It was in Nor- Romane-French attains its greatest perfection in Normandy. mandy that the *Langue d'oil* acquired its greatest polish and regularity.   The earliest specimens of the French language, in the proper sense of the term, are now surrendered by the French philologists to the Normans.   The phenomenon of the organs of speech yielding to social or moral influences, and losing the power of repeating certain sounds, was prominently observable amongst the Normans.   No modern French gazette writer could disfigure English names more whimsically than the Domesday Commissioners.—To the last, the Normans never could learn to say "*Lincoln*"— they never could get nearer than "*Nincol*" or "*Nicole.*"

§ 28.   The Normans dismissed all practical

888—912 recollection in their families of their original
Scandinavian ancestry.—Not one of their nobles
912—927 ever thought of deducing his lineage from the
The Nor-
mans, as a Hersers or Jarls or Vikings who occupy so con-
community,
repudiate spicuous a place in Norwegian history, not even
their Scan-
dinavian through the medium of any traditional fable.
character
Roger de Montgomery designated himself, as
" Northmannus Northmannorum ;" but, for all
practical purposes, Roger was a Frenchman of
the Frenchmen, though he might not like to own
it. This ancestorial reminiscence must have resulted from some peculiar fancy : no Montgomery
possessed or transmitted any memorial of his
Norman progenitors.   The very name of Rollo's
father, "*Senex quidam in partibus Daciæ*," was
unknown to Rollo's grandchildren, and if not
known, worse than unknown, neglected.

Foreign   § 29.   When treating of the " Normans," we
talent en-
couraged must always consider the appellation as descrip-
by the Nor-
mans. tive rather than ethnographical, indicative of
political relations rather than of race.   Like
William the Conqueror's army, the hosts of Rollo
were augmented by adventurers from all countries.   Rollo exhibited a remarkable flexibility of
character; he encouraged settlers from all parts
of France and the Gauls and England, and his
successors systematically obeyed the precedent.

Inclination, policy, interest, strengthened the
impulse given by the diffusion of the Romane
speech.   Liberality was the Norman virtue. " Nor-

man talent," or "Norman taste," or Norman art, 888—912
are expressions intelligible and definite, conveying
912—927
clear ideas, substantially true and yet substantially inaccurate. What, for example, do we intend when we speak of Norman architecture?—
Who taught the Norman architect? Ask, when
you contemplate the structures raised by Lanfranc or Anselm—will not the reply conduct you
beyond the Alps, and lead you to Pavia or Aosta?
the cities where these fathers of the Anglo-Norman Church were nurtured, their learning acquired or their taste informed. Amongst the
eminent men who gloriously adorn the Anglo-
Norman annals, perhaps the smallest number
derive their origin from Normandy. Discern-
ment in the choice of talent, and munificence in
rewarding ability, may be truly ascribed to
Rollo's successors: openhanded, openhearted, not
indifferent to birth or lineage, but never allowing
station or origin, nation or language, to ob-
struct the elevation of those whose talent, learning, knowledge or aptitude, gave them their
patent of nobility.

§ 30. Rollo's marriage, so anxiously promoted, Rollo's se-
produced those disappointments which any ex- from Gi-
cept statesmen could have foreseen, or which
statesmen do foresee and do not regard. Grim
wrinkled Rollo—three-score and upwards when
he married her—never lived as a husband with
blooming Gisella; and yet the unjoyful bond was

888—912
912—927

attended with all the discomforts of love and jealousy. Two Knights were despatched by king Charles to his daughter. The Frenchmen gave no notice to the "venerable Patrician" of their arrival, and lodged themselves in Rouen, neglecting or avoiding all opportunities of coming before him. Information was brought to Rollo concerning these questionable emissaries; and the news was so conveyed as to encrease any suspicions which might naturally arise. The knights concealed themselves in Gisella's mansion, were searched for, found, and by Rollo's orders beheaded in the market-place :—and this, except a parenthetical notice of her death, is the last we hear about Gisella.

Rollo's children: careful training of his son, Guillaume Longue-épée.

No children of Rollo are known, excepting those two whom he had by the Vermandois damsel,—a son, Guillaume, and Gerloc, otherwise the Adela, a daughter. — He returned to his bonne-amie, some say he married her according to the rites of the Church, when delivered from Gisella. Rollo's inclination and policy equally concurred in inducing him to rear his boy in such a manner, as to render the future Duke of Normandy a fit companion for the Princes of the Carlovingian Empire. Wise and faithful Botho, now one of the Counts of the Palace, was appointed the child's governor; but he equally continued under his mother's care: he was taught to pride himself upon her illustrious

French descent. The clergy trained him in sound 888—912
learning: the boy loved their society, their
teaching, their life; his earliest, childish wish, 912—927
was to enter a monastery, and he yearned for the
solitude of Jumièges, the cell amidst the ruins.
Gay, cheerful and generous, the personal performance of the works of mercy always constituted
the relaxations of Guillaume Longue-épée.

Bright and varied natural gifts were inhe- Talent in-
rited by Rollo's descendants, adaptability, vigour, herited by
cleverness in every sense, conspicuous even a- of Rollo.
mongst those who tarnished their character by
vice and profligacy. They flourished during an
era when the mental cultivation of the superior
classes of society was sedulously pursued: the
best got the best, and they profited thereby.
Noble and Royal families carefully kept themselves up to the highest standard. Had Rollo
chosen to despise the *clergie* of his age, and
to bring up Guillaume as a mere rough soldier, a half-tamed Berserker, Guillaume's sons
and sons' sons might have grown up untaught.
But the need of a sound education was transmitted to the Dukes of Normandy and Kings
of England as a family doctrine: so long as
Rollo's race subsisted, so long may we discern
their inherent as well as their acquired talents,
conflicting with their vices and failings, and obeying or surmounting the temptations to which
royalty and power are exposed.

888—912
887—899
Arnolph
King of
Germany
and Empe-
ror (See p.
630)

§ 31. In the year when the compact of Saint Clair-sur-Epte was concluded with Rollo, a great revolution was consummated in Germany. The institutions of Charlemagne were completely subverted, and political changes ensued which had an important influence upon the fortunes of France as well as of the "*terra Normannorum*," soon to become Normandy, an integral portion of the French monarchy, and yet a rival. After the battle of Louvaine, Arnolph continued to advance in renown and power, the talent of the statesman being supported by the military organization which the extensive employment of heavy cavalry afforded. Arnolph destroyed the preponderance of the Moravian Slavi, and checked the progress of the Magyars. Some accuse him of having invited them, but at all events his force or policy rescued his dominions from their inroads.

The German nations persevered in their willing allegiance, but Arnolph's dominion was incomplete and unsatisfactory unless he could reign in the capital of Christendom. Two successive expeditions crossed the Alps, the first directed against Guido, Berengarius aiding Arnolph. The German king treated the Italians as rebels; and Count Ambrosio, who had stoutly defended the lofty rock of Bergamo, the Insubrian Pergamum, being taken, was hanged before the walls of the city. Such an execution of a Noble was unparalleled. The second expedition was directed against

Berengarius, his late ally.—All yielded to Arnolph: 888—912 the conqueror entered Rome in triumph. The 892 Roman Senate and Clergy came forth to meet him with standard and banner. The Pontiff Formosus received him on the gradins of St. Peter's Basilica. The imperial consecration was bestowed *more majorum*, Arnolph was hailed as Cæsar and Augustus, and the Roman people took the oath of fealty to their Sovereign. But after Arnolph had quitted Italy, threatening insurrections arose. Arnolph was troubled on every side. His Consort Uta was accused of adultery. She cleared herself by compurgation. Seventy-two witnesses swore to her innocence; but Arnolph's spirit was entirely broken. He died strangely: witchcraft and poison, are said to have been employed against him.

Painful mystery attends his end. The miserable death of Charles-le-Gros was avenged upon his perjured betrayer; and men scarcely dared to whisper that Arnolph sunk under the most horrible bodily affliction with which our nature can be visited—tormented and exhausted by swarming vermin. Arnolph left two children, the illegitimate Zwentibold, who became king of Lotharingia, and *Ludwig das Kind*. Hardly anything is known concerning the events which occurred during the "child's" nominal reign, excepting the dreadful invasion of the Magyars and the bloody Babbenberg feud; alone sufficient to have

899
Arnolph's strange death—his son "Ludwig-das-Kind" succeeds him.

911
Extinction of the Carlovingian line in Germany in the person of "Ludwig-das-Kind."

882–912

912–919

brought the Empire to destruction. Germany reappears as an imperfect federation, composed of five predominant States, Duchies or Nations: Frankenland, obeying the wise and venerable Conrad—The Saxons, proud of their individuality, under Otho, the illustrious Otho, magnanimous and wise—The Bavarians had their Duke Arnolph—The Suabians their Duke Burchard—and lastly Lotharingia, the border-land, where Duke Rainer had acquired a paramount authority. CONRAD THE FRANCONIAN, acknowledged by all the nations except Lotharingia, acquired Germany. Upon his death, the Germans elected HENRY THE FOWLER, the Saxon, son of Otho the Illustrious, and father of Otho the Great: and the race most hated by Charlemagne completed the exclusion of his descendants from Germany and the Empire.

919.
Henry the
Fowler.

NOTES.

NOTES.

For the purpose of facilitating references to the original authorities, I have adopted a plan (partially suggested by Luden s practice, in his excellent History of Germany) which, I believe, will render their consultation easy and interesting, should any of my readers wish to compare the work with the texts upon which it is founded. At the head of each chapter, or at the head of each series of sections, as the case may require, I enumerate, and usually describe, the principal chroniclers, or historians, whom I have adopted for the general substratum of the text : and the dates in the margin of that text will guide the inquirer to the corresponding portion of the chronicles But he must keep in mind, that I have not always adhered precisely to the arrangement of matter exhibited by the original writers, if the clearness or credibility of the narrative has required otherwise When special authorities (i e. authorities not employed for the substratum of the text) supply facts not contained in the principal authorities, or corroborate or impugn them, or when it is needful to direct the attention of the reader to any particular passage in the principal authorities, a reference is given, or the passage is quoted at full length With respect to matters of historical or literary notoriety subsidiary to the main narrative, or introduced as incidental illustrations, I have not thought it needful to increase the bulk of the work by references or quotations

INTRODUCTION.

CHAPTER I.

THE FOURTH MONARCHY

Devolution of Authority from Rome, p 3.

In the History of the Rise and Progress of the English Commonwealth, Chapters x , xi , xvii., xviii., xix., I have fully discussed this subject in all its bearings, except only those specially relating to the German Empire, therein narrating, rather than establishing by argument (for the facts prove themselves), the Roman origination of mediæval royalty, mediæval institutions, and, very particularly, mediæval feudality The last branch of enquiry, however, can only be imperfectly examined, in consequence of the absence of information concerning the territorial institutions of the Byzantine Empire Possibly, documentary evidence may yet exist in the secret archives of some Greek monastery.

My authorities are fully adduced in the work to which I have referred: Allen employed many of them in his Essay upon the Royal Prerogative ; we worked in the same field, concurrently, but without mutual communication, and Hallam adds others, [4, *Theory of Dubos*, Supplemental Notes], corroborating, as I submit, the views I entertain. But I would observe, that the term "theory" cannot be properly applied, as in the heading of his note, to doctrines subsisting both in principle and practice, from the very commencement of every sovereignty constituting the European Commonwealth.

Sismondi incidentally, and Guizot substantially, accept the Romanization of the barbarian sovereigns as an incontestable fact —"Clovis, Childebert, Gontram, Chilpéric, Clotaire travaillent incessamment à se parer des noms, à exercer les droits de l'empire. Ils voudraient distribuer leurs Ducs, leurs Comtes, comme les Empereurs distribuaient leurs consulaires, leurs correcteurs, leurs présidents : ils essaient de rétablir tout ce systeme d'impôts, de recrutement d'administration qui tombe en ruine." (Guizot, 8ᵉᵐᵉ leçon, p 316)

Allen says that the "fiction of a King ruling by Roman rights is not peculiar to England : it is to be found in all the monarchies of Europe, established on the subversion of the Roman Empire However different in other respects, all the governments agree in recognising, as a fundamental principle of their Constitution, that the sovereign power of the Commonwealth resides in the King."

This "phantom," Allen supposes to have been evoked by those powerful necromancers, the clergy and the jurists, to whom he ascribes the enthralment of mediæval society. Sismondi attributes the same potency to them, speaking with even greater acerbity, nor does Guizot entirely discourage the opinion But at no period of Church-history have the priesthood been so little liable to the degrading imputation of sycophancy as during the dark and middle ages : they were bold almost to a fault ; and the very writers who inveigh most against the servility of the clergy, equally reprehend them for their resistance against the Crown. Such doctrines as the clergy held regarding the reverence due to royal authority, were fairly and sincerely deduced from Holy Scripture.

Hallam has an excellent note [196, *Prerogative of English Kings*] upon the confused ratiocination of Allen, concerning the personal king and the ideal king.   But, admitting to the fullest extent the influence of the clergy and jurists in strengthening the Roman prerogatives possessed by the mediæval sovereigns, and transmitted by them to the existing governments, the argument deduced from their co-operation is only a mode of stating the fact, that the two most intellectual and influential classes of society supported the authority with which the Sovereign was invested. The Roman law subsisted traditionally, after the barbarian conquests, throughout the larger portion of the Western Empire. When the erudition and talent of the jurists gave fresh vigour to the civil law, they did not introduce any novelties : they only imparted more method and learning to a living system. With regard to the Germano-Roman Empire, properly so called, whether the actual power of the Emperor was greater or less, whether he were a Frederick the First or a Francis the Last, no one ever doubted but that his authority was, in the strictest sense, a perpetuation of the imperial authority. The supremacy of Cæsar was the first article of the Ghibelline political creed. Dante's profound treatise *de Monarchia* is an admirable exposition of the aspect under which the question was viewed during the great contests between the Tiara and the Crown.

Rome never conquered by the Barbarians, p. 18.

"Il y a, Messieurs, quand au dévélopement de la Papauté en Europe, un fait primitif, *dont on n'a jamais, je crois, tenu assez de compte.* Non seulement Rome était toujours la ville la plus importante de l'Occident... mais Rome eut en Occident un avantage particulier : ce fut de ne jamais demeurer entre les mains des Barbares, Hérules, Goths, Vandales, ou autres. Ils la prirent et la pillèrent plusieurs fois ; ils n'en retinrent jamais long-temps la possession, seule entre toutes les grandes cités occidentales ; et, soit comme liée encore à l'Empire de l'Orient, soit comme indépendante, elle ne passa point définitivement sous le joug Germanique, seule elle resta Romaine après la ruine de l'Empire Romain" (*Hist. de la Civilisation en France*, 27eme leçon, p. 63)

Degradation of Rome, p. 19.

These verses are quoted from Hildebert of Mans, and may be found in the topographical description of Rome given by William of Malmesbury, now best to be consulted in Mr Hardy's convenient and excellent edition (Lib. IV § 351, p. 537)

Adherence to Roman architecture and insignia, p. 21.

Of these feelings, a remarkable instance is afforded by Crescentius, (A.D. 998, 999), whom Gibbon (Chap. XLIX) calls the Brutus of the mediæval Republic. Previous to his elevation he is styled Senator. He not merely rose to the command of the city, but assumed the imperial authority, and, for some brief season, enjoyed the imperial name (*Ademari Cabanensis Hist.* Pertz T. VI p. 130) In this capacity Crescentius issued a remarkable medallion, preserved in the Museo Maffei at Verona, and figured by the owner ; (*Verona Illustrata*, P. III c. 7) Crescentius upon this medallion takes the titles of "Imperator," "Cæsar," "Augustus," and "Pater patriæ ;" but the reverse is even more remarkable. Crescentius is represented on horseback, holding a military allocution, exactly as the same ceremonial is shewn upon the medals of Hadrian and his successors

The medallion is not inelegant. " *Si può conoscere,*" says Maffei, " *ancora da questo metallo come le belle arti in Italia non mancarono mai del tutto, mentre fin dal Secolo del novo cento, veggiamo qui un lavoro il cui disegno e maniera non si può dire dispregevole* "—The circumstance that the medallion is a copy from an ancient medal, shews the earnest endeavour to cling to the ancient imperial type The continued use of the Roman military ensigns, just as they appear on the Trajan and Antonine columns and other ancient monuments, is testified by the procession accompanying the memorable reception of the Emperor Henry IV. by Pope Pascal, A.D 1111, as the account is given in the Chronicle of Monte Casino, Lib. IV c 38. Muratori, *S. S. R. R. Italicarum*, T. IV. p. 515

I have elsewhere spoken upon this subject as connected with the cultivation of Art : (*The Fine Arts in Florence   Quarterly Review,* Vol LXVI. pp 336, 337)

Municipality of Rome, p. 22.

Gibbon's very interesting chapter (XLIX) on this subject, is grounded upon the erroneous assumption that the Roman Senate or Roman Community was *restored* in the twelfth century It is certain, however, that the Roman Senate and the Roman people retained their unbroken national existence, their degradation contrasting strangely with the lofty pretensions which they made. An able account of the Roman municipal constitution has been recently given by Hegel, (*Geschichte der Stadteverfassung von Italien.* Leipsic, 1847). A good deal to the purpose has also been previously collected by Von Raumer (*Geschichte der Hohenstauffen,* Vol. v. 214).

Classical Romances, p. 34.

A full, though not by any means complete enumeration of mediæval classical romances is given by Grasse : (*Die grossen Sagenkreise des Mittelalters.* Dresden, 1842).

The fondness for these themes has been noticed by Warton and others, and indeed the taste is so prominent that no writer on the History of mediæval poetry could neglect the observation. But it has been thought that the selection of such subjects was extraneous to the mediæval ethos, whereas, in fact, they were essential elements thereof.

CHAPTER II.

THE ROMAN LANGUAGE

This chapter has been principally gleaned from the Essays and Dissertations of Muratori and Bonamy, the works of Raynouard, and an excellent note and chapter of Hallam's, (*Middle Ages,* chap. IX pt. 1). But for the most complete, accurate and satisfactory investigation, we are indebted to Mr. Cornewall Lewis : (*Essay on the Origin and Formation of the Romance Languages*). I have availed myself of his assistance as far as was consistent with my plan.

Bodenkos, p 40.

Arnold, however, (*Rom. Hist.* I 525,) seems rather to have put the question as if he expected it would be answeied in the negative If no Celtic root be found, to what language can we resort but to the Teutonic ?

Isarnodor, p. 41.

See the life of Saint Eugendus or Saint Oyan, who was born there "Ortus nempe est haud longè a vico, cui vetusta paganitas ob celebiitatem clausuramque fortissimam superstitiosissimi templi Gallicâ lingua *Isarnodori*, id est *ferrei ostii*, indidit nomen." (*Acta S.S. Ord. S. Benedicti*, T. i. p. 570). The temple was situated in the Jura. It afterwards became the Monastery of *Condate*.

The Suffetes, p. 43.

An account of these Judges, as well as the Hebrew etymology of their name, will be found in Arnold ; (*Rom. Hist* II 548). The existence of their office is evidenced in two very remarkable missives, (Maffei, *Istoria Diplomatica*, p. 78), whereby the cities of Themetria and Thimelgia severally accept Caius Silius Aiiola as their Patron The names subscribed are very remarkable, as shewing the thorough reception in these cities of the antient Punic nationality, notwithstanding the retention of the Latin in public affairs. Did any nation of true Semitic race, except the Jews compelled by their captivity, ever adopt a Japhetian tongue ? The Semitic power of resistance to foreign influence has been remarkably exemplified by the Maltese

Latinitas, p. 45.

See Du Cange Thus Ordericus Vitalis, p. 777, speaks of Pope Urban having promulgated his anathema *in omni Latinitate*.

Romana Rustica, p. 46

On this subject, see Niebuhr's *Lectures*, Lect. xix. Vol ii.

Saint Jerome's scheme of education, p. 50.

Discat Græcorum versuum numerum. Sequatur statim et Latina eruditio : quæ si non ab initio os tenerum composuerit, in peregrinum sonum lingua corrumpitur, et externis vitiis sermo patrius sordidatur. (*Ep. ad Lætam*). But these instructions are only incidental in Saint Jerome's scheme, of which the main purport was to keep the child out of the way of all intercourse with those by whom her manners or morals might be injured.

Proscription of heathen literature, p. 57.

The Apostolical Constitutions, a miscellaneous collection methodized in the third century, and faithful expositors of traditions descending from the Apostolic age, leave no doubt of this principle. The Scripture warranties for the prohibitory Canon are sufficiently obvious, none more cogent than the words of St Paul. Can we imagine that the writer of the first chapter of Romans and the last of Philippians would recommend Ovid's *Metamorphoses* as a profitable study to Hermas, or present Clement with a copy of Aristophanes ?

Τῶν ἐθνικῶν βιβλίων πάντων ἀπέχου. Τί γάρ σοι καὶ ἀλλοτρίοις λόγοις, ἢ νόμοις, ἢ ψευδοπροφήταις, ἅ δὴ καὶ παρατρέπει τῆς πίστεως τοὺς ἐλαφρούς; τί γάρ σοι καὶ λείπει ἐν τῷ νόμῳ τοῦ Θεοῦ, ἵνα ἐπ᾽ ἐκεῖνα τὰ ἐθνόμυνθα ὁρμήσεις; εἴτε γὰρ ἱστορικὰ θέλεις διέρχεσθαι, ἔχεις τὰς βασιλείους, εἴτε σοφιστικὰ καὶ ποιητικὰ, ἔχεις τοὺς προφήτας, τὸν Ἰὼβ, τὸν παροιμιαστήν, ἐν οἷς πάσης ποιήσεως καὶ σοφιστείας πλείονα ἀγχίνοιαν εὑρήσεις, ὅτι Κυρίου τοῦ μόνου σοφοῦ Θεοῦ φθογγαί εἰσιν· εἴτε ἀσματικῶν ὀρέγῃ, ἔχεις τοὺς ψαλμούς· εἴτε ἀρχαιογονίας, ἔχεις τὴν γένεσιν· εἴτε νομίμων καὶ παραγγελιῶν, τὸν ἔνδοξον Κυρίου τοῦ Θεοῦ νόμον Πάντων οὖν τῶν ἀλλοτρίων καὶ διαβολικῶν ἰσχυρῶς ἀπόσχου. (Lib. I Cap. 6.)

Classical Latin inadequate to Christian literature, p. 58.

St Augustine not only exemplifies the imperfection of Classical Latin for Christian instruction, but insists upon the necessity of abandoning classical elegance or correctness : see his treatise *de Doctrina Christiana*, II. 11, 16, 19, 20. IX. 24. The influence of Christianity upon the Teutonic languages has been investigated by Rudolf von Raumer; (*Die Einwerkung des Christenthums auf die althochdeutsche sprache*. Stuttgart. 1845).

Fordun's classification of the Latin Dialects, p. 63.

It will be found in his curious disquisitions upon the laws of King Gaythelos, (*Scotichronicon*, Lib. I. c. 19. Ed. Hearne, p. 34). The digressive excursions of Fordun and his amplificator Bowyer, are instructive portions of these valuable, but neglected writers.

The Oaths of Strasburg, p. 66.

Of the transactions of Verdun and Strasburg I speak fully hereafter, p. 341. I add the oath, in *Roman*—"Pro Deo amur, et pro Christian poblo, et nostro commun salvament, dist di in avant, in quant Deus savir et podir me dunat, si salvrae io cist meon fradre Karlo, et in adiudha, et in cadhuna cosa, si com om per dreit son fradre salvar dist in o quid il mi altresi fazet, et ab Ludher nul plaid nunquam prindrai qui, meon vol, cist meon fradre Karle in damno sit "

Diffusion of the French language, p. 72.

Besides the instructions given in the *Speculum Regale*, or *Kongs-Skugg-Sio*, p 23 (Soroe, 1763), composed in Norway somewhat later than 1250, the extraordinary number of romance poems, including the lays of Marie de France, translated into Norsk, and assuming the national denomination of *Sagas*, affords a most cogent proof of the cultivation of the language When the famous, or infamous Bishop of Ely, Long-champ, was labouring to acquire popularity with the English public, he hired French ministrels "ut de illo canerent in plateis" (*Benedictus Abbas*, p 702.) Upon the complete extinction of the Gothic language by the *Romance* I have observed elsewhere (*The Gothic Laws of Spain. Ed. Rev.* xxx. p. 113).

Latin Language retained in peculiar localities, p. 75.

For the hymn sung round the walls of Modena during the Hungarian invasions, see p. 414. It was first published by Muiatori, *Ant H. Diss.* 40. Another strangely uncouth specimen is the ballad commemorating the liberation of the Emperor Louis II. p. 372. From its tenor, one would suppose that it was not composed at Benevento, though probably in some neighbouring locality With respect to the Lament of Fontenay, which I have inserted in my text, p. 331, the song may be considered as a proof of the continued use of the Latin language amongst the cultivated ranks of society.

July and August, p. 78.

Charlemagne invented the mariner's card. When he came to the throne, the Germanic nomenclature was limited to the four winds, or four quarters of the heavens. He added eight more, adopting the familiar modes of combination, *e. g.* Ost-Suudroni, Suud-ostroni, which have been encreased, till, with the original four, they give us the thirty-two points of the compass, and have thus been perpetuated, to the exclusion, in England and in some parts of France, of any Latinized names. The Franks had partially adopted Latin names for the months of the year, some had Latin names, some Barbaric Charlemagne's Roman ethos did not diminish his personal nationality, nor his affection for the traditions of his forefathers ; and he therefore sought to complete the *Teutonization* of the Calendar. *Wintermanoth, Horning, Lenzenmanoth, Ostarmanoth, Wunnemanoth, Brachmanoth, Heuuemanoth, Aranmanoth, Uuintumanoth, Windumanoth, Herbistmanoth, Heilagmanoth.* The deno-minations he bestowed were well chosen, significant and poetical; but, as Luden truly observes, the Roman Calendar gained the victory. Even an Emperor cannot command language,—his names were rejected in common speech The attempts made by modern purists to revive their usage never succeeded. Luden records, and regrets the failure (*Geschichte des Teutschen Volkes*, Vol. v. p. 210.)

CHAPTER III.

Anglo-Saxon origin claimed for the Norman laws, p. 109.

So affirmed by Rouille, the Coke of Normandy, in his comment upon the Grand-Coutumier (*Coutumier General*, Paris, 1724, Vol. iv p. 1). A copy of Magna Charta, adapted to Normandy, was certainly current in the Duchy. This document, printed by Dachery, does not appear to have been noticed by any of the Norman writers. The Church of Normandy is substituted for the Church of England, and the city of Rouen for the city of London. I am unable to explain this species of phenomenon, which may in some degree be paralleled by the extraordinary manner in which the French employed the Coronation-oath, especially intended for our Anglo-Saxon kings. (*Rise and Progress of the English Commonwealth*, Vol. i. p. 344)

Formation of Chronicles, p. 117.

For the parchment and the plummet see the Monk of Worcester, (*Anglia Sacra*, i p. 469) An extract from the Chronicle of Weissemburg (Pertz, T. v. p. 53) exhibits such memoranda in their genuine form.

DCCCCVI.	Ungarii vastaverunt Saxoniam.
DCCCCVII.	Adelbertus comes decollatus est, iubente Ludovico Rege.
DCCCCVIII.	Liutboldus dux occisus est ab Ungariis.
DCCCCVIIII.	Burghardus dux Thuringorum occisus est ab Ungariis
DCCCCX.	Ludovicus Rex pugnavit cum Ungariis.
DCCCCXI.	Ungarii vastaverunt Franciam.
DCCCCXII.	Ludovicus rex obiit, cui Conradus successit.
DCCCCXIII.	
DCCCCXIIII.	Otto Saxonicus dux obiit.
DCCCCXV.	Ungarii vastando venerunt usque Fuldam.
DCCCCXVI.	
DCCCCXVII.	
DCCCCXVIII.	
DCCCCXVIIII.	Cuonradus Rex obiit, cui Heinricus successit.

The following is equally curious as a specimen of the dateless chronographies :

Annus.   Riderch filius Caradauc obiit.

Annus.   Bellum Guinnetal inter filios Caddugan Goronin et Lewelin et Resum filium Owini et ab eo victi sunt

Annus.   Bellum Pullgudir in quo Trahern rex Norwallie victor fuit. Resus et Hoelus fiater ejus a Trahaiin filio Caraduc occisus est.

Annus   Filius Teudur Resus regnare inchoavit.

Annus.   Menevia a gentilibus vastata est.

The Chronicle from which this extract is made, is annexed, together with other curious miscellaneous matter relating to Wales and the

Marches, to an abridgement of Domesday, amongst the records of the antient receipt of the Exchequer, now in the Public Record Office. The handwriting is of the reign of Edward I After the Norman Conquest the Chronicle acquires more amplitude, and becomes very valuable for the later history of Wales, a history which, in all its branches, has been so apathetically neglected.

BOOK I.

CARLOVINGIAN NORMANDY.

CHAPTER I.

LOUIS-LE-DEBONNAIRE, HIS PREDECESSORS AND SUCCESSORS

A.D. 741—824.

PRINCIPAL AUTHORITIES.

(I) Eginhardt's well-known life of Charlemagne. (II) The Chronicles respectively known by the names of the *Annales Laurissenses*, and the *Annales Einhardi*. Both commence A.D. 741 ; but A.D. 801, the first falls into the second, which concludes A.D 829. This latter chronicle is an enlarged and continued edition of the first; both very sincere, and evidently grounded upon coæval information. This Einhardt, otherwise Eginhart or Aginhardt, has been conjectured, and not without probability, to be Charlemagne s son-in-law. (III.) *Annales Mettenses*, A D 687—930. Originating in the pre-eminently Carlovingian monastery of Saint Arnolph, at Metz (IV) *Chronicon Moissiacense*, A.D. 500—840. The Chronicle of the great Abbey of Moisiac in the Toulousain, rich in facts, not found elsewhere

(v.) The Chronicle usually quoted as the *Annales Fuldenses*, but the production of *five* several writers, as follows: (1) Enhardus, probably a monk in the Abbey of St Boniface at Fulda, is the author of the *first* section Commencing with brief historical notes of the reign of Charlemagne, the annals expand in matter, and terminate A D. 838. The marginal note marking where Enhardus desisted from his task, "*Huc usque Enhardus*," was added by his illustrious continuator, Rudolph of Fulda. (2) No chasm ensues. Rudolph begins the *second* portion by completing the imperfect narrative of the year 838. Rudolph was distinguished in every branch of learning. He is very remarkable as being the only mediæval writer to whom Tacitus was known at first hand

There is every reason to suppose that the Fulda manuscript of Tacitus was then the only subsisting copy, and that it is the codex in Lombard characters now in the Laurentian library. Rudolph rather alludes to Tacitus than quotes him : the passage has occasioned much discussion ; Ritter treats upon the subject in the preface to his recent edition of Tacitus. Rudolph was much in the confidence of Louis-le-Germanique, before whom he was accustomed to preach, being the royal chaplain and confessor. He was Master of the Schools of Fulda. His portion ends A.D. 863; and in the margin of the year, the formula which Rudolph employed to indicate the conclusion of his predecessor's labours, is adopted by his successor, *"huc usque Rudolphus."* Infirmity probably compelled him to desist, for he died in 865, as recorded by his continuator, who adds the following remarkable encomium : " Rudolphus, Fuldensis cœnobii presbyter et monachus, qui apud tocius pene Germaniæ partes doctor egregius floruit hystoriographus et poeta, atque omnium artium nobilissimus auctor habebatur, viii. id. Martii diem ultimum feliciter clausit." (3) According to the most probable opinion, Meginhardus, Rudolph's disciple, continuing his teacher's work, is the author of the *third* portion, ending A D. 882. (4.) From 882 the work was carried on by two writers whose names cannot be ascertained.—A monk of Fulda gives us the *fourth* portion, ending 887 : the confusions of the times probably interrupted him. (5.) The *fifth* portion, also terminating abruptly, and, as we conjecture, for the same reason, A.D. 901, bears internal evidence that the writer lived in Bavaria. He is supposed to have been a monk of Ratisbon These annals are extremely important, as presenting the German version of Carlovingian affairs, and they were very largely employed by subsequent mediæval chroniclers. By Adam of Bremen they are quoted as the "Annales Francorum." Pertz (Vol i.) has published the *Annales Fuldenses* completely and continuously, distinguishing the several portions. The unfortunate plan adopted by Dom Bouquet, who distributes his excerpts in five volumes, ii 1739, v. 1744, vi 1749, vii. 1749, and viii. 1752, quite destroys the character of the annals ; and, whilst his volumes were appearing, must have rendered them nearly useless. Dubos, *e. g.* employed upon the History of France, in the year 1739, would have to provide himself with a Duchesne, or to wait thirteen years for a chronicle which would form an octavo of about 250 pages.

The before-mentioned Chronicles ascend and descend ; but the materials for the particular history of Louis-le-Débonnaire are remarkably authentic and interesting.

(vi) We possess a complete biography of this Sovereign, composed by the anonymous historian, who is commonly quoted by the description of the " Astronomer." The writer notices his conferences with Louis upon the subject of astronomical, or, as we should now term them, astrological phænomena, whence he is supposed to have been versed in the science.

He held, as he informs us in his Preface, an office in the Imperial Palace, and having entered into the service of Louis upon his accession to the Empire, continued with him till his death. The "Astronomer" stood by the King's bedside when he expired. He commences his biography from the birth of Louis at Casseneuil. The events, anterior to his personal knowledge of Louis, he received from Adhemar, *nobilissimus et devotissimus monachus,* who was the same age as the King, and brought up with him —The remainder he tells from his own knowledge.

(VII.) Another biography of Louis-le-Débonnaire, by Theganus, is, so far as it extends, no less important. Theganus or Thegambert, born of a noble family, and distinguished by great talent, was Bishop-coadjutor, or Chorepiscopus, of Trèves. Intimately acquainted with Louis, and sincerely attached to him, Theganus appears to have written the history mainly for the purpose of testifying against the faithlessness of those who persecuted and abandoned the monarch. Theganus carries on the narrative until A.D. 835, and concludes with the following prayer: "Iste est annus vicesimus secundus regni domni Hludowici piissimi imperatoris, quem conservare et protegere diu in hoc sæculo dignetur feliciter commorantem, et post hæc discurrentia tempora perducere concedat ad societatem omnium sanctorum ejus, ille, qui est benedictus in sæcula sæculorum. Amen." Theganus evidently had completed the biography according to his intentions, for he is known to have been living in 844. The work was published after his death by Walafrid Strabo, who divided it into chapters, and prefixed a preface, apologising for the zeal which, as Walafrid hints, had seduced the author into some degree of unfairness.

Throughout this work I have derived much assistance from the historians of the French provinces—Languedoc, and the South of France, (*Histoire Générale de Languedoc,* par Dom Vic et Dom Vaissette, *deux Religieux Bénédictins de la Congregation de Saint Maur,* 5 vols. folio, Paris, 1730—1745).—Britanny, two extensive works, (*Histoire de Bretagne,* par Dom Lobineau, 2 vols. folio, Paris, 1707), and (*Histoire Ecclésiastique et Civile de Bretagne,* par Dom Morice et Dom Talandres, et *Mémoires pour servir de Preuves,* 5 vols. folio, Paris, 1742—1756); improved amplifications of Lobineau, yet not superseding him (see p. 754). —Lorraine, (*Histoire Ecclésiastique et Civile de Lorraine,* par Dom Augustin Calmet, 5 vols. folio, Nancy).—Burgundy, (*Histoire Générale et Particulière de Bourgogne,* par Dom Plancher, 3 vols. folio, Dijon, 1739— 1748).—Provence, (*Chorographie de Provence,* par Honoré Bouche, Aix, 1644); and occasionally from Muratori in his *Annali d'Italia.*

An Austin Friar, Père Anselme, emulating Benedictine diligence, laid the foundation of a work of the highest importance in the study of French history—I mean the *Histoire Généalogique et Chronologique de la Maison royale de France, des Pairs, Grands Officiers de la Couronne et de la Maison du Roi, et des anciens Barons du Royaume.* The third edition, due to the care of Père Ange and Père Simplicien (9 vols folio, Paris, 1727), has been a constant aid to me in deducing the various lineages and successions so also the *Art de Vérifier les Dates* Yet in all cases it has been needful to examine their statements, and occasionally to depart from them.

Marriage and Concubinage, p. 144.

The Teutonic learning upon this subject will be found in Grimm's *Deutsche Rechtsalterthümer*, (Gottingen, 1828) under the head *Ehe.*

Carlovingian Genealogies, p. 148

These may be seen in greater length, with more details as to females and their descendants, and somewhat differently arranged, in Père Anselme's *Histoire.*

The Charta Divisionis, p. 151.

The existing text of the Charta Divisionis, *Recueil des Hist.* T. v. p. 771, is undated, the concurrent testimony however of all the chroniclers leaves no doubt but that the document is the record of the proceedings at Thionville It is divided into twenty chapters · the eighteenth contains the memorable clause, prohibiting the enforcement of monastic vows upon members of the royal family See p. 198.

Pepin, King of Italy, p. 156.

The Frankish historians are silent upon the subject of Pepin's defeat, which constitutes a conspicuous incident in Andrea Dandolo s Chronicle, (Muratori, T. xii.), as well as in the general recollections of Venetian history. See also Daru's *Histoire de Venise*, i c 23. Pepin rebuilt the magnificent Basilica of San' Zeno at Verona, near which he is buried. His sepulchre, without the walls of the Church, shews how carefully the Lombards still avoided the custom of interment within the sacred edifice.

Charlemagne's Entombment, p. 158.

The particulars of this strange and solemn deposition are given in a life of the Monarch, compiled by a monk of Angoulême (*Rec. des Hist.* T. v p. 186) According to the *Deutsche Sagen* (ii p 173), the tomb was opened by the Emperor Otho III when the corpse was beheld as described the nails of the fingers had grown through the leathern gloves The tomb was reverently closed; but in the course of the night, Charlemagne appeared in a dream to Otho, and foretold him that he would die childless and prematurely. The shrines and reliquaries of the Cathedral preserve many of the Babylonian gems which had belonged to the great Emperor

Wetinus, the monk of Reichenau, pp. 162, 165, 166.

The prose narrative by Bishop Heitto, and the versification by Walafrid Strabo, are both given by Mabillon (*Acta SS Ord S Benedicti*, v. pp 265, 283)

For the constitution of the sodality between Saint Gall and Reichenau, A D 850, and the renovation thereof, A D. 945, see Mabillon (*Ann. O S. Ben* xxvi. § 101, and xliv § 87). The further history of the Festival is told by Fleury, *Hist. Ecc.* lix. c. 5

The visions of Fursæus and Drithelm—Feast of All Souls, pp. 163—165.

Both are given by Venerable Bede, whose ecclesiastical history has, thanks to Dr Giles, been rendered a popular volume An account of Fursæus may be found in Alban Butler's *Lives of the Saints*, a work which should always lie on the desk of the historical student, being the most honest and convenient hagiography which has yet appeared. An Anglo-Saxon version of the legend has, by Mr Wright's laudable exertions, been published from a manuscript in the Bodleian Library, (*Reliquiæ Antiquæ*, Vol. i. p. 266) Tracing the course of thought upwards, through the visions of *Alberic* and *Owain Miles*, and the other compositions of a like nature, we have no difficulty in deducing the poetic genealogy of the *Inferno* and the *Purgatorio* to the Milesian Fursæus For the recently-discovered East-Anglian frescoes, representing the probation or punishment of the departed, consult the transactions of the Norfolk Archæological Society.—The *Paradiso* is derived from other sources. A highly poetical outline of a similar cosmology is found in Salomo ben Gabirol's noble hymn, the *Kether Malcuth* (see Sachs, *die Religiose Poesie der Juden in Spanien*, Berlin, 1845).

Adelhard and Wala, p. 168. *Libel Literature*, p. 275—277.

The history of Adelhard and Wala is preserved in the very remarkable compositions of Paschasius Radbertus, which are only found entire in Mabillon's Collection (*Acta S S. Ord. S. Ben.* T. v pp. 306, 444, 453, 521).

To the life of Wala, Radbertus has given the singular, but not unexampled title (St Jerome having done the like) of *Epitaphium*, and Wala being designated throughout by the name of Arsenius, the work acquires the title of *Epitaphium Arsenii*. It is written dramatically : a conversation between various interlocutors, of whom Paschasius is one All the characters are designated by fictitious names The style is tedious and diffuse, but so very characteristic a memorial of the spirit of the times, that, to the historian, no part can be said to be superfluous. The Eclogue, the dialogue between the two Monasteries, is appended to the life of Adelhard —Wala's name is sometimes written Walah, or Wallach.

Desiderata, p. 171.

The circumstances attending her marriage, and the share taken by Bertha in forwarding the match, are found, with more or less particularity, in all the Chronicles; but one only, the monk of St Gall (Lib. II. c 26), says, that Desiderata was *chnica*, and childless. It is the general opinion of Italian topographers, adopted by Mr Hope, that the huge Visconti palace stands on the site of the palace of the Lombard kings.

"*Ludovicus Pius*," p. 181.

The coin upon which he assumes this title is engraved by Père Daniel, (*Hist. de France*, Paris, 1729, T. II. p. 283), and he is so styled by Theganus, writing in his life-time.—This is never the case with the mere familiar or historical epithets, such as *Martel, Balbus*, &c.

Varied talents of Louis-le-Débonnaire. Version of the Scriptures, pp. 179—188.

Theganus, c. ix., has given an ample account of the King's talents, and their cultivation, his affection for learning, and his diligence. Some passages, relating to his astrological knowledge, are found in his Life by the Astronomer His *Conquestio*, his "Complaint" (p. 730), in which he relates the treatment he received from his children, is eloquently touching and impassioned. I have, following other guides, adopted the opinion, that the Cottonian MS (Caligula A.7) contains a portion of the metrical version to which the Latin preface (*Rec des Hist*. T. VI p. 256) belongs.

Imperial Signet, p. 194.

It is figured by Mabillon, *De re Diplomatica*, Tab XXVIII.

Roman de la Rose, p. 201.

The whole passage (v. 9628—9695) contains a spirited view of the progress of society I quote from Méon's Edition, T. II. p. 250. I have rather modernized the orthography.

Volcanic energies, p. 220.

Very recently, the waters which fill the crater of Laach were disturbed, and the fish killed.

Golden globes, p. 221.

I ought to have said golden eagles.

Charta Divisionis, p. 226.

See *Recueil des Historiens*, T. VI 405—7.

Trial and condemnation of King Bernard, p. 230.

For Hermengarda's responsibility in this transaction, see the Chronicle of Andrea the Priest (*Rec. des Hist*. T. VII. p. 680).

Guelphic Dynasties, p. 234.

These Guelphic genealogies are taken principally from the *Origines Guelficæ*, the result of the continued and successive labours of Leibnitz, Eccard, Gruber, and Scheidius, (Hanover, 1750) T. II. Præf. pp. 2—5; and chapters II iii. v. vi.

Bera and Sanila, p. 240.

The circumstances of their combat are minutely described by Ermoldus Nigellus, Lib. III. vv. 550—638.

Bernard of Septimania, p. 242.

See De la Marca, *Histoire de Béarn.*

Expeditions against the Bretons, p. 254.

See Morice, *Hist. de la Bretagne.*

Harold, King of Jutland, p. 256.

In this, as well as in other circumstances relating to the Danes, and particularly as to the identification of the Danish chieftains, I have usually followed Suhm, whose indexes to the first and second volumes of his *Historie af Danmark* (Copenhagen, 1784), afford a sufficient reference with respect to any particular individual. The ceremonies of Harold's investiture are related minutely in Ermoldus Nigellus.

"Ego Ludovicus," p. 262.

The Imperial Constitution, edited from a collation of the four Vatican exemplars, will be found in Baronius, an. 817

Sismondi, in his chapter upon the relations between the Popes and the Emperors (*Républiques Italiennes*, I. c. iii) does not even notice the document.

CHAPTER II.

LOUIS-LE-DEBONNAIRE AND HIS SUCCESSORS, TO THE FINAL DETHRONEMENT OF THE CARLOVINGIAN DYNASTY.

CONCLUSION OF THE REIGN OF LOUIS-LE-DEBONNAIRE.

A. D. 824—840.

§§ 1—17, pp. 264—309.

PRINCIPAL AUTHORITIES.

(I.) The *Annales Einhardi*, (II) *Annales Mettenses*, (III.) *The Chronicon Moissiacense*, (IV.) Enhardus, and (v.) Rudolph of Fulda (*i.e.* the *Annales Fuldenses*), and (VI.) Theganus, continue as authorities in their several proportions. (VII) The Astronomer, connecting all the other

authorities, accompanies us to the end of Louis-le-Débonnaire's life and
reign.—But we receive a great accession from the Chronicle quoted as
the *Annales Bertiniani*, a misleading designation, inasmuch as the work
has no other connexion with St Bertin except through the accident that
the manuscript was discovered in the Abbey Library, whereas the
whole contexture points at other local origins.

The so-called *Annales Bertiniani* (viii.) consist of *three* separate but
consecutive works. (1.) The name of the author of the *first* portion, A.D
830—835, is unknown ; but the writer is supposed to have lived somewhere
in the Ardennes. (2.) The *second*, 835—861, is ascertained, both by external and internal evidence. to be the composition of the celebrated Prudentius, Bishop of Troyes. A Spaniard, his original name being Galindo,
he is considered to have belonged to the family of the Counts of Arragon.
Brought to France at an early age, and educated in the royal palace,
his disputations with Erigena have gained for Prudentius a high station
amongst theological writers But in opposing Gottescalk's doctrines he
incurred the charge of great error, or rather heresy He composed his
Chronicle in the reign, and under the patronage, of Charles-le-Chauve.
(3) The monarch lent his own copy to Archbishop Hincmar, who, in
his turn, began the *third* and last portion, A.D 861, which he opens by
recording the death of his predecessor, who was cut short whilst relating
the annals of the year. And in the same manner as Prudentius was
stopped in his task by death. so was Hincmar, A D 882. Driven from
Rheims by the Northmen (see p. 585), Hincmar died during his flight,
some attending priest or chaplain having probably completed the last
paragraphs. The several portions are properly and critically entitled
and distinguished by Pertz, but not by Dom Bouquet, who breaks them
up according to his fashion.

(ix) Towards the conclusion of the reign, we enter upon the interesting Memoirs of Count Nithardus, undertaken by him, according to the
suggestion of Charles-le-Chauve (pp. 335, 336), amidst the troubles and
wars in which he was engaged, and which he describes with remarkable
fidelity and accuracy. His history is comprised in four Books, the last
of which ends abruptly. in consequence of his being called off into actual
service and killed by the Danes. (x.) The life of Wala is also an authority
of peculiar importance, not only for the facts, but the spirit of the age.

Political application of French History, p. 264.

I allude to Thierry's *Considerations sur l'Histoire de France*, an Essay affording a rapid and lively review of the French constitutional
writers, by whom, as he says, the national memorials have been continually misapplied, for the purpose of truckling to political party. Yet
Thierry is unfair to himself, as well as to his compeers. The various
historico-political theories to which Thierry alludes, and which he ex-

amines, criticises, opposes, or refutes, always with great talent, and often with success, constitute an instructive commentary upon the exertions made by the French to promote the study of their national history. It is the exposition, the doctrinal elucidation of an historical text, which makes it tell· the value thus bestowed is as appreciable by those who oppose the historian's opinions, as by those who adopt them (See *Progress of Historical Enquiry in France, Edin. Review,* April, 1841.)

The young Charles-le-Chauve, p. 270.

See the Poem of Ermoldus Nigellus, Lib iv. vv 419—424.

Veni Creator, p. 273.

This hymn is ascribed to Charlemagne. (See Daniel, *Thesaurus Hymnologicus,* Vol. i p. 213)

Charles-le-Chauve's literary cultivation, p. 273.

No monarch ever deserved the title of a protector of literature more truly ; and no protector of literature ever pursued literature with a more earnest enjoyment of the studies which he encouraged and practised. Charles-le-Chauve peculiarly delighted in history we have seen how Nithard was excited to his work by the King's special direction. At his instigation, Lupus Servatus, generally known as Loup-de-Ferrières, composed a history of the Roman Emperors The composition is lost, but the epistolary dedication exists, in which the author exhorts the monarch to imitate the glorious examples of Trajan and Theodosius. Encouraged by Charles-le-Chauve, Usuardus compiled his martyrology, the foundation of all subsequent works of the same class. Not being satisfied with the existing version of Dionysius the Areopagite, Charles caused another to be made by Erigena. Almost every theological work appearing during his reign was dedicated to him His classical taste is peculiarly displayed in the classical name which he proposed to bestow upon Compiègne. As in the architecture of his Basilica, so in the denomination which Charles gave to his palatial city, did he adopt the ethos of Imperial Rome. " Carolus postquam Imperator effectus est, Ecclesias plures ædificavit in villa Compendio, quam de suo nomine *Carlopolim* appellavit Nam ibi maximam civitatem ædificare proposuit : Ecclesiam sanctorum Cornelii et Cypriani construxit, et in eadem villa in suo Palatio Ecclesiam sanctæ Dei genitricis, quam pretiosissimis reliquiis adornavit. Ibidem etiam obtulit corpus S Cornelii atque S. Cypriani, in quorum adventu composuit Responsorium, *Cives Apostolorum* " (Yperius, *Rec. des Hist.* T. vii p. 270).

Wala taking the lead against Louis-le-Débonnaire, pp. 276, 277.

Wala's vehement conduct as leader of the opposition appears very fully in the Second Book of the *Epitaphium,* chapters i —vi.

Expedition against the Bretons. Nominoë, p. 278.

This expedition constitutes the first incident in the *Annales Bertiniani*. For Nominoë, see Morice, *Hist. de Bretagne.*

Paris, p. 279—282.

The materials shewing the early condition of Paris are diligently collected and elucidated by the Benedictines (*Histoire de la Ville de Paris par les PP. Felibien et Lobineau.* Paris, 1724, 5 vols. folio). The island unquestionably enjoyed a considerable degree of municipal and mercantile importance ; and Bonamy, with his usual acuteness, clearness and knowledge, has made the most of his case, in his *Récherches sur la célébrité et l'étendue de la Ville de Paris avant les ravages des Normands* (Mémoires de l'Acad. des Inscrip. Vol xv.) Nevertheless the whole tenor of French history, anterior to the Capets, displays the secondary rank which Paris then held.

The Luegen-feld, p. 290.

See Luden, v. p. 357. The Siegburg was also called the Siegwaldburg. The antient names are emphatically commemorated by Nithard.

The Complaint of Louis-le-Débonnaire, p 293.

This curious, but almost forgotten document, has been published by Duchesne, T. II. p 336, from the transcript furnished by Petavius,— it bears the following title, *Conquestio Domni Chludowici, Imp. et Aug. piissimi, de crudelitate et defectione et fideiruptione militum suorum, et horrendo scelere filiorum suorum in sui dejectione et depositione patrato.* It is inserted in the history of the translation of the relics of St Sebastian and St George, by Odilo, the monk of St Médard, printed completely by Mabillon (*Acta S. S Ord S. Ben.* VI. p. 387), and partly by Dom Bouquet (*Rec des Hist.* T. VI. p 323.) The basement story of the tower containing the cell in which Louis was imprisoned is still standing. Near the loop-hole window there is an inscription in French verse, in "gothic" characters of the sixteenth century, commemorating his misfortunes, which I believe has been quoted or published as having been inscribed by the royal captive.

Deposition of Louis-le-Débonnaire, p. 295.

This is one of the portions of French history which have not been sufficiently investigated The conduct of the parties concerned should be considered calmly, and without invective. The proceedings were completely revolutionary in the modern sense, grounded upon the assumption that public safety required the deposition of the king. The Articles of the Acta Exauctorationis constitute a formal impeachment. All the documents are collected by Dom Bouquet, T vi. pp 243—251 Agobard's manifesto, or address to the people, is peculiarly remarkable. The limits of this work have prevented me from exhibiting the history of parties undei Louis-le-Débonnaire to the full extent. Archbishop Ebbo behaved with shameful ingratitude, and was subsequently deposed

The seventh partition of the Empire, p. 298.

The Præceptum, or Charter of Division, is only preserved in a fragmentary state, wanting the conclusion (Rec. des Hist. T. vii. p. 411). Baronius refers the document to A D 837 ; but I have adopted the opinion of Luden.

Pepin of Aquitaine, p. 303.

See the Benedictine history of Languedoc, Vol. i. .

The thatched Lodge on the Pfaltz island, p. 309.

The directions given by Louis for the construction of the Lodge, his dying bed, are related by his biographer, the Astronomer. (Rec. des Hist. T. vi. p. 124).

Epitaph of Louis-le Débonnaire, p. 309.

See Rec. des Hist. T. vi. p. 267.

EVENTS FROM THE ACCESSION OF CHARLES-LE-CHAUVE TO THE TREATY OF MERSEN. A. D. 840—847.

§§ 18—32, pp. 309—346.

PRINCIPAL AUTHORITIES.

The events comprehended in this division of the chapter include the first five years of the reign of Charles-le-Chauve. Nithard, the warrior and historian, furnishes the main foundation for the narrative. The other sources have been already indicated.

Alterations in the course of rivers, &c. p. 321.

See Depping (Hist. des Expéditions maritimes des Normands. Paris, 1844, pp. 148, 417).

The Eager of the Seine, p. 323.

The Monk of Fontenelle (or Saint Wandregisil), delineating the site of the monastery, introduces a forcible description of this phenomenon. Du Cange supposes, and probably correctly, that the name Géon is given to the Seine in allusion to the river Gihon in Eden, see also his glossary for *Malmea* I insert the entire passage as affording a view of the Norman landscape in the tenth century Dudon de Saint-Quentin also mentions the *Eager*, in a passage which will be subsequently quoted (p. 740).

"Situs quippe ejusdem Cœnobii hujusmodi feitur esse A tribus enim plagis, id est a Septentrionali, Occidua, atque Australi, montibus arduis ac frugiferis, Bacchique fertilissimis, silvisque est obsitum condensis. Ab Oriente item habet fontem uberrimum, qui ab ortu suæ emanationis per spacia passuum plus minusve mille trecentorum manat: sicque cuisu suo expleto, in alveum Sequanam influit ad meridianam ejusdem Cœnobii plagam. Ab Occidente item ibi fluvius est mirabilis, in Aquilonari ejusdem Cœnobii plagâ ab imo progrediens, atque in meridiana Geon prædicti alvei profunda se demergens. Inter hæc duo mirabilia flumina, prata ejusdem Cœnobii sunt amœna atque irrigua Quia admirabilis Wandregisili atque Veneiandi Patroni nostri solertiâ inutilia quæque ablata vireta, militumque Christi ejusdem Fontinellensis Cœnobii degentium sudoie solo coæquata, eorumdem necessitatibus aptissima sunt reddita. Ab Austro item maximus fluviorum Geon, qui et Sequana, commerciis navium gloriosus, abundantiâ piscium præstantissimus, distans ab eodem Cœnobio passus octingentos. In quo scilicet fluvio ex infinito Oceano sive mari Britannico bini æstus diurno nocturnove tempore sibimet invicem compugnantes occurrunt: ut versâ vice alveus potius retrorsum conveiti quam ad ima videatur fluere. Talique cum impetu tempore malineæ accedunt, ut super millia quinque aut eo amplius et sonitus murmuris ejus humanas repercutiat aures, et aspectibus intuentium ceu farus altissimè lympham ejusdem penetret alvei. Talique impetu per meatus prædictorum duorum fluminum, perque prata illis contigua ceu Nilus Ægyptiacus per spatia passuum plus minusve octingentorum ad murum ejusdem accedunt Cœnobii, finitoque confluctu in Oceanum infusi unde venerant revertuntur" (*Spicilegium Dacherii*, 1659, T. iii. p. 190).

Insular Rouen, p. 323.

Upon this subject see Licquet, *Hist. de la Normandie*, T. i. p. 104, Rouen, 1835, and Pluquet in his note upon the *Roman du Rou*, i. p. 58. Other information bearing upon the subject is afforded in the *Description Géographique et Historique de la Haute Normandie*, Paris, 1740; a very useful work, of which I have much availed myself.

Notker, p. 325.

Cum adhuc juvenculus essem, et melodiæ longissimæ sæpius memoriæ commendatæ instabile corculum aufugerent, cœpi tacitus mecum volvere quonam modo eas potuerim colligaie. Interim vero contigit, ut presbyter quidam de Gemidia, nuper a Nordmannis vastata, veniret ad nos, Antiphonarium suum secum deferens, in quo aliqui versus ad sequentias erant modulati . .ad imitationem tamen eorundem cœpi scribere (Notkeri præfatio in librum sequentiarum. Pezii, *Thesaurus Anecdotorum Novissimus*, T. ɪ p 17.)

Battle of Fontenay, p. 328.

The locality where this great battle was fought has been diligently investigated by the Abbé le Bœuf, who appears to have accurately ascertained the position of the armies   Fontenay is now called Fontenailles ; but I preserve an appellation which has become historical. All the early French or German historians record this mighty conflict, which decided the fortunes of Charlemagne's Empire   Angelbert's rhythm or lament was discovered by the indefatigable Le Bœuf, in a manuscript of nearly coæval date (*Rec. des Hist.* T. vii. p 304). With respect to the custom of Champagne, jurists may have entertained doubts respecting the existence of the privilege, but the legal doubt does not diminish the historical value of the tradition.

Lotharingian Architecture, p. 344.

This is not the place to discuss the age of the buildings in question, nor the origin of their peculiar conformation (see *Ecclesiastical Architecture, Quarterly Rev.* Vol. ʟxxv p. 389), but the uniformity of style prevailing in Lothair's share of the Empire is apparent to the eye of every traveller who, steaming up the Rhine, and crossing the Saint-Gothard, reaches Rome by Pavia   Much remains to be done for the architectural investigation of the Alpine countries and passes   The stone towers of the churches in those regions are probably coæval with the first establishment of Christianity.   The churches themselves are, with very few exceptions, modern : affording a presumption that they were constructed of timber.   The towers have many features in common with those in England, which antiquaries now suppose to belong to the Anglo-Saxon æra   The finest Campanile is that belonging to the Basilica of Saint-Maurice in the Valais

Treaty of Mersen, p. 346.

The Capitular or Treaty of Mersen is given by Dom Bouquet, *Rec. des Hist.* T. vii p 603.   The quotation is from Chap. ɪx.   The tenth and eleventh Chapters direct that negotiations should be opened with the Armoricans for the preservation of peace, and the like with the Northmen—"ut similiter ad Regem Nordmannorum, legati mittantur, qui eum contestentur quod aut pacem servare studebit, aut communitei eos infensos habebit."   Then follow the rescripts made or issued by the three sovereigns, Lothair, Louis and Charles, to their subjects.   In the rescript issued by Louis, he again notices, with some variation of expression, the proposed negotiations with the Armoricans and the Northmen.

The authorities for this synopsis will be found generally in the preceding and subsequent chapters

House of Vermandois. p. 355.

For the genealogy and history of this family, I have, besides the general genealogical works, consulted Collette's special history, (*Mémoires pour servir a l'Histoire de la Province du Vermandois*, 3 vols. 4to. Cambrai, 1777, an ill-digested work, but containing much unused information.

Rollo's Bonne-amie, p. 356.

This celebrated damsel's relationship to Bernard de Senlis is unquestionably proved by Dudon de Saint-Quentin. see p 571.

Partition of Lotharingia. p. 370.

This document has been commented on and explained with great diligence by Dom Calmet (*Hist. de Lorraine*, Vol. I.) Yet much as he has effected, Calmet has only prepared the way for the future historian of Lotharingia. should such an one ever appear. The despair of the antient French compiler of the venerable but historically worthless *Chronique de Saint-Denis*, when he gives up the rendering of the German names into any decent shape as an utter impossibility, is amusing (*Rec. des Hist.* T. VII. p 134).

Louis II. Emperor and King of Italy, p. 371.

A very accurate account of this important reign, wholly passed over by Gibbon as well as by Sismondi, will be found in Muratori's *Annali d'Italia*. In his *Antichità d'Italia, Diss.* 40, he has given the Benevento ballad as a specimen of colloquial Latinity

Death and Funeral of Louis. p 375.

See extracts from Andrea the Presbyter (*Rec. des Hist* Vol. VI. p 203)

Alexander the Great's Charter. p. 379.

This tradition certainly existed in various versions at a very early period: a certified copy of the Macedonian Charter, made A.D. 1289, exists in the Venetian archives. Gallucioli, *Memorie Venete*, Venice, 1795, I. p 173.

Robert-le-Fort. p. 407.

All that we know with any certainty concerning Robert-le-Fort's ancestry is contained in Richerius (Lib. I. c. 5), who, describing the elevation of Eudes, proceeds to state—"*hic patrem habuit ex Equestri ordine, Rothbertum; avum verò paternum Witikinum advenam Germanum.*" The several theories relating to the origin of Robert-le-Fort have been repeatedly discussed in the *Art de Vérifier les Dates*,—in the preface to the tenth volume of the *Recueil des Historiens*,—and more recently by Thierry, Guizot, and Michelet. In the coæval chronicles, Hincmar's brief notice of Robert's joining the Armorican confederacy A.D. 859 (see p. 469) is the first announcement of the great Chieftain in history. The expression employed by Richerius, "ex equestri ordine," must not in any wise be taken as implying nobility of blood: the description simply designates the position which he held. We have not any proof that the early Capets endeavoured to exalt their ancestry, or thought about it: they were well or better content to be included in the ranks of the *new men* who acquired their rank for themselves. The faint voice of tradition always pointed out an ignoble origin; and Dante has only diffused throughout the world the ideas which from the old time had been current in France. Villon's ballad has been long known. Michel, *Chroniques des Ducs de Normandie, par Benoit,* Vol II p. 84, has given an extract of the Chanson de Geste, of which "*Huez Capez qu'on apelle bouchier*" is the hero; and, from a German romance which Michel quotes, it is evident that the history existed in a more complete form.

CHAPTER III.

THE NORTHMEN DURING THE TIMES OF CHARLES-LE-CHAUVE AND ROBERT-LE-FORT TO THE END OF THE REIGN.

A. D. 840—877.

Principal Authorities.

(I.) Prudentius of Troyes continues with us until A D. 861, when he died, worn out by exertion and anxiety, his labours and his life ending together: "vivendi et scribendi finem fecit," says Hincmar, as he takes up the pen to complete the narrative of the transactions of the year (II.) Thus commencing, the Archbishop accompanies us to and beyond the conclusion of Charles-le-Chauve's reign Hincmar always works with an object, directing his labours for the benefit of the State, as we find when we arrive at the troublous times which ensued upon the death of Charles Hincmar inserts many state-documents, writing as one well acquainted with men and motives: and his work must be reckoned as the firmest foundation of French history during the era which it includes (III) The *Annales Mettenses* do not, during this chapter, furnish much in addition to the other chroniclers. (IV.) Rudolph of Fulda becomes very interesting, on account of the decided German feeling which he exhibits, evidencing the antagonism between the French and German nations, and the bitter enmity between the French and German Houses. And from A D. 863 (V.) Meginhardus, the disciple of Rudolph, continues the work in the spirit of his master.

On the German side of the question we receive a valuable accession in a Chronicler, who now appears to us for the first time, (VI) Regino, some-while Abbot of Pruhm. Regino grafts his work upon universal history, commencing with the Incarnation. A brief but respectable summary of Roman history introduces the Carlovingian annals, until the death of the great Emperor. This Carlovingian segment Regino compiled, as he states, from a book in plebeian and rustic Latin, which he reduced into grammatical language. Whether this work was in the *Romana Rustica* or not, we cannot judge. Probably, however, it only exhibited the collo-quial or vulgar inaccuracies characterising the original manuscripts of Gregory of Tours, and effaced by the affectionate but injudicious care of modern editors

The second book of Regino's Chronicle, commencing with the death of Charlemagne, includes, in the earlier periods, much which he learned from tradition. Regino was a diligent collector and a still more diligent observer, noting events as they arose, and telling the reader, as he pro-ceeds, that he bears testimony to the events of his own time ;—one of the many who, at that æra, were writers of memoirs as well as Chroniclers. Regino completed his work A D. 899, when he published it, with a prefa-tory dedication to Adalbero, Bishop of Augsburg, stating the intent with which he had undertaken his labours, and entreating that this Preface may be in nowise omitted by any transcriber whom his work may please. —What Hincmar is for France, Regino is for Germany; and although a primary authority for French affairs in all transactions in Lotharingia or Germany which concern France, his Chronicle is omitted by Dom Bouquet. Pertz reprints it with a carefully corrected text.

(VII.) So far as the breadth of the work extends, the History of the Counts of Anjou, or *Gesta Consulum Andegavensium*, composed by a Monk of Marmoutier, is singularly useful and interesting. Addressed by the author to Henry II, under whose patronage he wrote, the writer deduces the history of the family from Torquatus the Forester, to the time of Geoffrey Plantagenet, embodying all the traditions of the dynasty. This work, of great authenticity and value, is to be found only in Dachery's *Spicilegium*, T. x. A few scraps are given by Dom Bouquet.

(VIII) Towards the conclusion of this chapter, we begin to avail our-selves of Dudon de Saint-Quentin, *De Moribus et Actis Normannorum*, who, when we contemplate Normandy from within, must be reck-oned as the principal source of Norman history during the reigns of Rollo,

Guillaume-Longue-épée, and Richard-Sans-peur (see pp 99, 100, and p. 515). When employing Dudon, I concurrently consult the metrical translation made by Benoit de Saint-Maur, the Norman Trouveur who flourished in the reign of Henry II., which constitutes the first portion of his *Chronique des Ducs de Normandie,* edited by M. Michel from the unique MS. in the British Museum, (Paris, 1836), and included in the magnificent series of historical publications, commenced under Guizot's direction and patronage. Benoit's translation is usually faithful; and when he adds further facts, or traditions, they are always clearly distinguished from his original authority —The *Roman du Rou,* the composition of Robert Wace, the clerk of Caen (edited by Pluquet, Rouen, 1828), departs more widely from the original, but is richer in traditionary history. Dudon, only found in Duchesne's *Normannorum Scriptores Antiqui* (Paris, 1619), has been entirely neglected for his abbreviator, Guillaume de Jumièges, who omits matters of primary importance.

(ix) Langebec and Suhm, in their great collection, *Scriptores rerum Danicarum medii Ævi,* Copenhagen, 1783, T. i pp. 496—561, and T. v pp. 1—232, have excerpted all the passages contained in the Anglo-Saxon, as well as in the French, German, and other Continental historians relating to the conquests and expeditions of the Danes, constituting the whole of their external history to the conclusion of the ninth century. But, as I before observed, the history of the Danes is lame and incomplete, unless taken in connexion with the histories of the countries which they ravaged, or where they settled. Therefore I have in no case considered myself as dispensed from the constant employment of the writers from whom Langebec and Suhm have made their extracts. Very elaborate and judicious notes are added by these Editors, together with genealogical Tables. The work is as nearly perfect as possible, and yet it is incomplete, being maimed in its due proportions by the usual bane of such collections, the exaggerated scrupulosity of the learned Editors. They had a predecessor in the person of Eric Pontoppidan (*Gesta et Vestigia Danorum extra Daniam,* Leipsic, 1740), whose collections became the foundations of theirs. Amongst the extracts from the early historians, Pontoppidan has intercalated many of later date, inscriptions also, and fragments of antient ballads, exceedingly useful, from the collateral information which they afford. These are omitted by Langebec and Suhm, though they might without difficulty have been inserted in the notes ;— and consequently Pontoppidan's work continues to be as needful as before for the Danish historical library.—Suhm's Danish history is a trustworthy digest of all the materials which he and his predecessor assembled.

Zernebog, p. 409.

The deities of Walhalla are well known, the Sclavonian Pantheon is perhaps less familiar. Sir Walter Scott has committed a curious, or perhaps an intentional mistake, by introducing Zernebog as a Teutonic deity. Zernebog was purely Sclavonian The Sclavonian mythology has been developed by Mone (*Geschichte des Heidenthums in Nordlichem Europa* Leipsic, 1822).

" *Landking wilful*," p. 410.

There are various redactions of these verses—one has been published by Hickes; see also *Reliquiæ Antiquæ*, by Wright and Halliwell, Vol I. p. 316; Vol. II. p. 15.   The text I have employed (modernising the orthography) is the most ample   It is contained in a Spelman MS now belonging to Hudson Gurney, Esq

The Magyars, pp. 383—410.

The slight notices of this valiant and unfortunate nation are gathered from the only authentic sources of their primæval history, the *Historia Ducum Hungariæ* of King Bela's Notary or Chancellor, and Johannes de Thurocz, who lived in the time of Matthias Corvinus; both given by Schwandtner (*SS. Rerum Hungaricarum*, Vienna, 1746, Vol I.)   The Chancellor addresses his work to his anonymous " Magister," for the purpose of answering, amongst other questions, "quare populus de terra Scythica egressus, per idioma alienigenarum, *Hungari*, et in sua lingua propria, *Mogeri*, vocantur ?"—Thurocz spells the name with an *o*.—The hymn is from Muratori.

Saracen Invasions and Settlements, p. 416.

Bouche, in his *Histoire de Provence*, Vol. I furnishes us with an interesting, though perhaps somewhat uncritical, account of these settlements in the South of France and the Hautes Alpes

Alterations in the bed and level of the Seine, p. 436.

The great inundation of 1740 suggested to Bonamy an historical dissertation on this subject, which he illustrates by a map (*Mém. de l'Académie des Inscrip.* T. xvii.).   The general street-level of extra-insular Paris has, since the thirteenth century, been raised from four to six feet.   The map shewing the extent flooded in 1740, affords some notion of the spread of the river in the Carlovingian era.   The earliest recorded inundation took place A.D. 583; and it appears from Gregory of Tours, that, in his time, a navigable *Broad* was formed between the city and the church of St Laurent.

Oscelles, p. 450.

Many learned men, besides those whom I have named, were involved in this discussion, affording matter for two *Mémoires* by Bonamy, and one by the Abbé le Bœuf (*Mém de l'Académie des Inscrip.* T. xx).   Such is the cleverness and learning of these writers, that the investigation s interesting.

Charles jealous over his Game, p. 453.

The qualified sporting license to which I allude, is contained in the thirty-second chapter of the Capitular of Kiersy, (see p. 519) by which Louis-le-Bégue was appointed Regent, during his father's absence in Italy It is the only direct restriction upon his authority.

The Litany of Ste Généviève, p. 460

For the continuance of this prayer, see Michel's *Benoit*, Vol. I. p. 35. Till the demolition of the Abbey, the inscription was one of the curiosities shewn to visitors.

Fortifications erected by Charles-le-Chauve, p. 463.

For these, see p. 605, and note.

Brise-Sarthe, p. 491.

The church is near the high road leading from Sablé to Angers. The account of Robert-le-Fort's death appears to have been derived from an eyewitness.

Armorica, pp. 490—500.

Consulting the great *Histoire de Bretagne*, I have condensed these passages from the original authorities. Much of Solomon's history is derived from the Chronicle of Nantes, included by Morice amongst the *Preuves*. Dom Bouquet gives only fragments.

The " New men," p. 501.   *The Plantagenets*, p. 503.

The Monk of Marmoutier exemplifies the policy thus adopted, by the biography of the founder of the Plantagenets

" Iste autem Torquatius sive Tortulfus genuit Tertullum, qui primus ex progenie Andegavensium Comitum per antiquos genealogiæ illorum relatores computatus est: tempore enim Caroli Calvi complures novi atque innobiles, bono et honesto nobilibus potiores, clari et magni effecti sunt. Quos enim appetentes gloriæ militaris conspiciebat, periculis objectare, et per eos fortunam temperare non dubitabat. Erant enim illis diebus homines veteris prosapiæ, multarumque imaginum, qui acta majorum suorum non sua ostentabant: qui cum ad aliquod grave officium mittebantur, aliquem e populo monitorem sui officii sumebant, quibus cum Rex alius imperare jussisset, ipsi sibi alium Imperatorem poscebant. Ideò ex illo globo paucos secum Rex Carolus habebat: novis militaria dona et hæreditates pluribus laboribus et periculis adquisitas benigné præbebat. ᵒ Ex quo genere fuit iste Tertullus, a quo Andegavorum Consulum progenies sumpsit exordium, vir doctus hostem ferire, humi requiescere, inopiam et laborem tolerare, hiemem et æstatem juxta pati, nihil præter turpem famam metuere. Hoc profecto constat, quod Tertullus quidem acer ingenio, fortunam suam et rerum tenuitatem, animi amplitudine supervadens, majora se cupere et aggredi ausus sit. Hæc ergo et similia faciendo nobilitatem sibi et suo generi peperisse refertur." (*Dacherii Spicilegium*, T. x. p. 408)

Gerlo, p. 504.

See *Art de Vérifier les Dates* There are difficulties in chronology concerning these Danish Counts of Blois; but not affecting the main facts.

Imperial Coronation of Charles-le-Chauve, p 507.

Meginhard (*Rec des Hist.* T vii. p 181), relating this transaction, equally displays his classical knowledge and his enmity:—"Quo inde discedente et promissionibus illius credente, ille quæcumque pollicitus est, mentitui, et quanta potuit velocitate Romam profectus est, omnemque Senatum populi Romani more Jugurthino corrupit, sibique sociavit; ita ut etiam Johannes Papa votis ejus annuens, corona capiti ejus imposita, eum Imperatorem et Augustum appellare præcepisset." Qualitei autem regnum illud postea cum suis disposuerit, qualiterve cum thesauris quos tulerat in regnum suum redierit, quantasque cædes et incendia in itinere exercuerit, quia certum non habui latorem, scribere nolui Melius est enim tacere quam falsa loqui"

Duke Boso, p. 507.

A. D 876 "Nonis Januarii Româ exiens, Papiam redit, ubi et placitum suum habuit: et Bosone uxoris suæ fratre Duce ipsius terræ constituto, et corona Ducali ornato, &c." (Hincmar, *Rec. des Hist.* T. vii p 119).

Battle of Andernach, p. 510

It is important to compare the accounts of this battle as given by Archbishop Hincmar, and the monk of Fulda. Hincmar implies that the conduct of Charles-le-Chauve was unduly inimical, whilst the German glories in the defeat of "Sennacherib."

Rollo, p. 513

A.D. 876.—"Nortmanni cum centum circiter navibus magnis, quas nostrates *bargas* vocant, xvi Kalendas Octobris Sequanam introierunt." (Hincmar, *Rec des Hist.* vii 121.)

Dudon de Saint-Quentin, in the passage quoted below, (and which affords a curious notice of the *eager*) dates Rollo's first landing in Normandy in this year So also the Chronicles of Nantes, A D 876, "Rollo Dux Normannorum in Gallias appulit" (*Rec. des Hist.* T. vii p 222, and Asser in his *Life of Alfred.*) All the antient, though subsequent writers, concur Modern French historians have doubted the fact, principally for the reason that in 876 Franco was not Archbishop of Rouen. Hincmar, the contemporary, received his intelligence from the disturbed country, troubled by the invaders: Dudon de Saint-Quentin obtained his intelligence traditionally, and after three generations had elapsed, yet both concur in the main.   We find Fianco, the Archbishop of Tongres, so constantly about Charles-le-Chauve at this period, and so trusted, that no reasonable doubt can subsist but that he was one of the Primores who had been despatched to the Northmen. The French verses are those of Master Wace, partly modernized in orthography.

"Anno igitur octingentesimo septuagesimo sexto ab Incarnatione Domini, nobilis Rollo consultu fidelium suorum libravit vela ventis navigeris, fluminis Scaldi alveum descerens, atque permenso ponto qua Sequana cæruleo gurgite perspicuisque cursibus fluens, oderiferasque excellentium riparum herbas lambens, *fluctuque inflatiore maris sæpe reverberata secundum discrimina lunæ inundantis maris pelago se immutit*, aggrediens navibus Gimeias venit... ..Audientes igitur pauperes homines, inopesque mercatores Rotomo commorantes illiusque regiones habitatores copiosam multitudinem Normannorum adesse Gimegias, venerunt unanimes ad Franconem Episcopum Rothomagensem consulturi quid agerent " (*Dudo de Moribus*, p. 75.)

Rollo's landing at Rouen, p. 517.

See Dudon de Saint-Quentin, p. 76, and the *Roman du Rou*, p. 58.

Capitulars of Kiersy, p. 519.

Upon the construction of the ninth chapter of this Capitular, (*Rec des Hist.* T. vii. p 698), supposed, but erroneously, to have established the hereditary transmission of Fiefs, see *Rise and Progress of the English Commonwealth*, Vol. i. p. 514, Vol. ii. p. cccxcii.   The Regency is appointed by the fifteenth chapter.

Assessment of the Danegeld.   Rollo's Subsidy, p. 519

Two documents are extant directing the levying of this Danegeld, for the benefit of the Northmen *qui erant in Sequana* (*Rec. des Hist* T. vii. p. 697) The first is undated. the second has special reference to the year of Rollo's invasion

---

CHAPTER IV.

FLANDERS, FRANCE, AND THE NORTHMEN, TO THE DETHRONEMENT AND DEATH OF CHARLES-LE-GRAS, AND THE FINAL DISMEMBERMENT OF THE CARLOVINGIAN EMPIRE.

A D. 862—919.   (*Flanders*).
A. D. 862—888.   (*France*).

PRINCIPAL AUTHORITIES.

(1.) Hincmar's Chronicle, increasing in interest as he proceeds, extends to Carloman's accession as sole King of France ; but shortly after-

wards, A.D 882, the work is abruptly stayed by the flight and death of
the venerable Archbishop (see p 585)—(II.) The *Annales Mettenses* continue, becoming more useful by supplying facts relating to Germany not
found elsewhere,—valuable also with respect to the northern invasions —
(III.) *Regino of Pruhm* we also retain, his chronicle being the chief
source of information for Germany generally, and for France also in connexion with Germany   Regino's local position at Pruhm in Lotharingia,
between France and Germany, gave him opportunities of which he fully
availed himself, for obtaining intelligence concerning both countries;
and he seems to have been much in the confidence of Charles-le-Gros —
(IV.) *Meginhardus*, the intelligent continuator of Rodolph of Fulda,
lasts us till A D 882; and (v) and (VI.), his two anonymous continuators
(all quoted as the *Annales Fuldenses*) are full of information, though
their attention is principally directed to Germany

New authorities of great value arise, and aid us in telling the story.
(VII) Abbo's poem, abounding in incidents (p. 608), was commenced immediately after the raising of the first siege of Paris, January, 887. The
first Book, in which the siege is described, was published about 889. We
ascertain this fact from the circumstance, that, towards the conclusion of
the Book, as well as in the preface or dedication to his friend, teacher and
fellow-monk, Goscelme (not the Bishop), he speaks of Eudes Capet as
king.

The research of Duchesne and his predecessors and contemporaries,
whether in France or Germany, brought out nearly the whole stock of
French and German Chroniclers; yet some escaped their diligence. A
Chronicle of great value continued concealed in the Abbey of St Bertin,
till recovered for the world by the unwearied Abbé Le Bœuf—(VIII)
The original manuscript of this Chronicle is considered by the Abbé as
belonging to the tenth century: no title is prefixed, nor is there any
external evidence enabling us to identify the author; but, inasmuch as
the events concerning the Abbey of St Vedast are rather prominent, the
Abbé Le Bœuf conjectured that the composition had originated there,
and he has entitled it *Annales Vedastini*, accordingly   The Abbé Le
Bœuf contributed an excellent analysis of the work to the Académie
des Inscriptions (T XXIV 1756), and having liberally communicated his
transcript to Dom Bouquet, the latter published it in the *Recueil* (T. VIII
pp. 79—94)   Pertz has repeated the text with corrections

Commencing 877, these Annals constitute a new vein of information
They amplify Hincmar where the works are concurrent, and as well during that period as afterwards, supply information which we do not obtain
from other authorities. The Annalist is peculiarly ample with respect to
the troubles which ensued upon Louis le-Bégue's accession. The Danish
transactions of the æra, from Louis-le-Bégue onwards, especially those
occurring in the Seine country, are principally known through the Vedas-

tine annals. Rollo is nowhere mentioned by name; nevertheless great light is thereby thrown upon his history; and by annexing a precise date to a particular incident, *i. e.* the death of Ragnald, Duke of Maine (see p. 746), unnoticed in any other Carlovingian Chronicle, we are enabled, as it were, to haul up Rollo's history into its right place. Details are given of the siege of Paris corresponding closely with Abbo's poetical narrative, yet neither writer copies the other. they write independently: therefore the Annalist and Abbo were both present in or near Paris during the siege, both decidedly espoused the cause of Eudes, both are Capetians These are the circumstances which induce me to ascribe the composition to an inmate of S. Germain-des-Prés; and it would not be an unauthorized conjecture to suppose that the Annalist was Abbo's friend and teacher, Gosceline.

(ix.) For Normandy we continue, as before, to be guided by Dudon, correcting his statements and supplying his deficiencies by comparison with the Frankish Chroniclers, and particularly, as last mentioned, by the *Annales Vedastini*, and for Flanders, we have, besides the general authorities, (x.) the Chronicle of Yperius, (the real Chronicle of Saint Bertin) (Martene *Thesaurus Anecdotorum*, T III), from which Bouquet has given a few extracts, and the writers mentioned in the note below.

Judith Countess of Flanders—her Marriages, p. 528.

Her English marriages belong to English history. For the marriage-ritual, as well as the proceedings against Baldwin and Judith, see Dom Bouquet (T. VII. pp 621, 650) The aid given to the lovers by Louis-le-Bégue is spoken of plainly by Archbishop Hincmar, and in still plainer terms by Yperius, the Chronicler of Saint Bertin (*Rec. des Hist* T. VII. p. 268). St Gregory's decision is accepted as a portion of the antient Canon-law intended for the regulation or restraint of second marriages.

The Foresters of Flanders, p. 530.

For these legends, and several facts connected with Baldwin and Judith, I am indebted to Peter van Oudegherst, as edited by Lesbroussart (Ghent, 1789), and also to the *Chronyke van Vlaenderen* (Bruges, 1727). The description of the country I have endeavoured to extract from Lesbroussart's notes, and from Gheldolf's translation of *Warnkonig* (*Histoire de la Flandres*, Brussels, 1835). There are variations in the lists of the ten Flemish Counties (p. 538); but it is not needful for our present purpose to enter into minute inquiries.

Coronation of Louis-le-Bégue, p. 543.

The Fealties of the Bishops, Lieges, and the "Professio" or Covenant of Louis-le-Bégue, are inserted textually in Hincmar's Chronicle. It is very possible that the instruments were drawn by him (*Rec. des Hist.* T. VIII. p. 27)

Judith, Queen of Louis-le-Bégue, p. 545

She is supposed to have been the sister of Wilfied, Abbot of Flavigni, in Burgundy. Historians denominate her by her epithet of *Adela*, or *Adeliza*, but that her real name was Judith, appears from a chaiter which she granted to the Abbey of Saint Sixtus at Placentia Her genealogy is deduced from Alpaida, great grandmother of Louis-le-Débonnaire (see Père Labbe, *Tab Gen.* p. 577, and Père Anselme, T. i p. 35). The noble Abbey of Chelles or Cala, on the Marne, is about six miles from Paris. The house was founded by Clotilda, and re-endowed by Bathilda (*Gall. Christ.* T. vii. p 558) For the abduction of the Adeliza from the monastery, see the Chronicle of Richard of Poitou (*Rec des Hist* T. ix. p. 21,) and the continuator of Aimoinus, (T. ix. p 137).

Parties or factions supporting or opposing the children of Louis-le-Bégue, p. 554.

The following passage shews how strongly the opinion of the illegitimacy of Ansgarda's children (see p. 548) prevailed :—

" a d 880 Rex Francorum Ludovicus Balbus moritur, uxorem suam ex se giavidam relinquens. De regno ejus Francis varie sentientibus : aliis illud Ludovico et Carlomanno filiis Ludovici Balbi ex concubina debere judicantibus ; aliis Bosoni Provinciæ Regulo ad illud injustè invadendum adsentientibus ; *aliis verò illud regno Germaniæ resociare volentibus ;* nascitur interim ex legitima uxore Ludovici Balbi filius, qui ex nomine avi Karoli, *Karolus* nominatus est Filii tamen Ludovici Balbi ex concubina, Ludovicus et Carlomannus dicti, interim regnum Francorum inter se dividentes, regnant annis quatuor, et Bosonem semper persecuti sunt." (Sigeberti Gemblacensis Chron. *Rec. des Hist.* T. viii p. 308)

Regrets occasioned by the division of the Empire, p. 555.

For a strong expression of these feelings, as they arose upon the division of the Empire, and which after the death of Louis-le-Débonnaire unquestionably greatly assisted in facilitating the election of Charles-le-Gros, see the complaints of Florus the Deacon (*Rec. des Hist.* T. vii p. 315). They are also testified in the above-quoted passage of Sigebertus.

King Boso, p 560.

The documents relating to King Boso's election are given by Bouche (*Hist. Gén. de Provence,* Tom. i. p 758—769). His ample history of King Boso is one of the best portions of the work. See also the *Histoire de Languedoc.* Bouche preserves the remarkable portrait of King Boso. In Boso's capital all his monuments and memorials have been destroyed. After a careful search in the fine cathedral of Vienne, I could find no trace of his epitaph, said to have existed till within the last thirty years The antient fortifications, however, so valiantly defended by Hermengarda, on behalf of her husband, are very perfect. The noble Roman remains which still adorn Vienne, shew how thoroughly the city bore a Roman aspect

Caroletto, p. 566.

This affectionate name was given to him when he first appeared in Italy, A D 875 " Ludovicus misit filium suum, quem homines cœperunt *Caroletum* nominare"—(Andreæ Presbyteri Chron. *Rec des Hist* T. vii. p 206)

Death of Louis the Saxon's child, p. 571.

"(Annales Mettenses, 882.) Puerulus de fenestra cecidit, et confractis cervicibus statim exspiravit. Quæ non tantum immatura, quantum inhonesta mors non solum regi et reginæ, verum etiam omni domo regiæ maximum luctum ingessit." It is somewhat difficult to assign a precise meaning to the epithet *inhonesta.*—A friend, to whom I owe many obligations, observes :—"inhonesta seems to me to mean, *a death not fit for a gentleman*, a phrase conceived in the same feeling that made Achilles chafe at the thought of being drowned by the combined efforts of the Xanthus and Simois, and Æneas weep in the near prospect of shipwreck "

Battle of Saulcourt, p. 575.

Isembard, the traitor, was Patron of Centulla, or Saint-Riquier, *Advocatus* or *Defensor*, in the old phraseology. Hence the battle of Saulcourt constitutes an important event in the history of the Abbey. Popular songs in the Romance language, sung about the streets, commemorated Isembard's treachery. It is evidently to such ballads, and not to the Teutonic rhythm, that Hariulphus refers in his Chronicle (see *Rec des Hist* T vii. p. 275 ; also *Hist. Ancienne et Moderne d'Abbeville*, par Louandre, Abbeville, 1834, and Depping). The *Ludwigs-Lied* was first discovered by Mabillon in the Abbey of St Amand, and constitutes an important monument in the history of German poetry, as well as of the German language (See *Antient German and Northern Poetry, Edinburgh Review*, Vol xxvi. 1816.) When I wrote that Essay, I could only use the imperfect text in Schilther's *Thesaurus* ; but the original MS. has since been recovered, and the text given with accuracy. (*Elnonensia, Monumens des Langues Romane et Tudesque*, par Fallersleben et Willelms. Gand 1837, and, from this publication, by Depping) The lay is spirited and bold ; and the dialect evidently shews that it was composed in the countries on the Eastern side of the Rhine.

The Roman Camp of Estreuns, p. 577.

The Camp at Etrun is described by the Abbé de Fontenu, who contributed to the *Académie des Inscriptions* (Tom. x) a very curious series of memoirs upon the so-called Camps of Cæsar, the generic name given in France to every antient entrenchment. This denomination affords a remarkable proof of the preponderance which the Romans obtained over the national mind · very few are the local traditions in the Gauls which do not speak of Rome. This Camp of Etrun is in Artois: there is another Etrun, also with a Roman camp, in Hainault, at the confluence of the Scheldt and the Sausat. It is a curious coincidence, or rather a further proof of Roman military skill in the choice of their positions, that, during the march, when Marshal Villars occupied the Roman Camp upon the Scarpe, the Duke of Marlborough also encamped within the Roman entrenchments in Hainault (See Piganiol de la Force, *Description de la France*, Paris, 1754, T IV. p. 432.)

Death of Louis III , p. 580.

The annalist of St Vedast gives the narrative which I have adopted, and the great grief which ensued : "unde ægrotare cœpit, et delatus apud Sanctum Dionysium, Nonis Augusti defunctus, magnum dolorem Francis reliquit, sepultusque est in Ecclesia Sancti Dionysii " Hincmar is silent as to the cause of the King's death. The continuator of Aimoinus, rejected by Dom Bouquet's text, but from whom an extract is given in a note (T. VIII p. 36), adds : "vir plenus omnibus immunditiis et vanitatibus."

Arnolph's Oath, p. 583.

All these transactions are fully and accurately told by Luden, Vol. VI. Book xiii. c 12.

Death of Carloman, p. 591.

See Ann. Vedast (*Rec des Hist*) T. VIII. p 94. This appears to be the most accurate account.

Free Friezeland, p. 595.

I have attempted a short investigation of the history of this most interesting country, to which I must here refer. (*Antient Laws and Constitutions of the Frisons, Edinb Review*, Vol. XXII 1819.)

Rollo's re-occupation of Rouen—Death of Ragnald, Duke of Maine, pp. 603, 604.

In Dudon de Saint-Quentin, after the landing of Rollo, the narrative is continuously pursued without a date The notice in the Vedastine Annals of Duke Ragnald's death, with a specific date, month, and year, is one of the coincidences which enable us to chronologize Rollo's history.

"Ragnoldus vero Comes, congregato majore exercitu priore, iterum conatur eos invadere Noitmanni autem se conglobantes strictim accubitaverunt se, ut parvissima putaretur summa corum. Illico Ragnoldus init bellum, suæ sorti non profuturum. Daci verò per aciem Ragnoldi inconvulse pergentes, prosternebant duris verberibus plures Videns autem Ragnoldus suos deficere, cœpit celeri cursu fugere Cui quidam piscator Sequanæ attributus Rolloni, obviavit ei, teloque transverberatum occidit. Ragnoldidæ suum Seniorem videntes mortuum, fugam torquentes nimium equos expetiverunt Tunc Rollo persequens eos multos occidit, pluresque captos ad naves deduxit Convocatisque fidelibus suis dixit : Age, nunc navigemus Parisius, civesque qui prælia fugerunt requiramus." (*Dudo de Moribus*, p 77)

"885. Mense itaque Julio, viii Kal. Augusti, Normanni Rotomagum civitatem ingressi cum omni exercitu, Francique eos usque in dictum locum insecuti sunt : et quia necdum eorum naves advenerant, cum navibus in Sequana repertis fluvium transeunt, et sedem sibi firmare non desistunt. Inter hæc, omnes, qui morabantur in Neustria atque Burgundia, adunantur, et, collecto exercitu, adveniunt quasi debellaturi Nortmannos. Sed ut congiedi debuerunt, contigit ruere Ragnoldum Ducem Cinomannicum cum paucis : et hinc rediere omnes ad loca sua cum magna tristitia : nil actum utile.

Tunc Nortmanni sævire cœperunt . ...Franci parant se ad resistendum : non in bello, sed munitiones construunt. Castrum statuunt super fluvium Hisam in loco qui dicitur ad Pontem Hisaræ . Parisius civitatem Gauzlinus Episcopus munit Nortmanni vero dictum igne cremaverunt Castrum, diripientes omnia inibi reperta Hac Nortmanni patrata victoria valde elati Parisius adeunt." (Annales Vedastini, *Rec. des Hist.* T. viii p 84.)

"*Parisius* sine flexu interdum pro ipsa Parisiorum urbe usurpatur" (Ducange) In the earlier writers, *Parisius* is the more common appellation.

Charles-le-Chauve's Fortifications of Paris, p. 605.

In describing the defences of Paris, I have followed Bonamy (*Mém. de l'Académie des Inscrip.* T. xvii. pp. 289—295), comparing his essay with Felibien. It is certain that before Charles-le-Chauve erected his fortifications, the Northmen entered Paris at pleasure ; and equally certain that Paris was afterwards able to offer a stout resistance. For the adoption of the Carlovingian cycle of Romance by the Italians, see Panizzi's excellent Introduction to the *Orlando Innamorato*. I have adopted Ariosto as an historian of the Siege of Paris ; for, once read, it is impossible to dismiss the magnificent animation of his pictures from one's mind.

The Danish Boat, p. 615.

Dug up in 1806, and described by Mongez, (*Mém. de l'Institut Inscriptions et Belles Lettres*, **T.** v.).

CHAPTER V.

DISMEMBERMENT OF THE EMPIRE EUDES AND CHARLES-
LE-SIMPLE. ESTABLISHMENT OF ROLLO IN NORMANDY.

A.D. 888—912.

PRINCIPAL AUTHORITIES.

(I) Abbo, having concluded the siege of Paris, becomes, in the second
Book of his Poem, the historical panegyrist of King Eudes. Allowing
for this avowed object, the story is told faithfully, though obscured
by the perplexities of his verse. There are some few chronological difficulties, yet not greater than might have occurred if he had written in
prose The third Book of Abbo, devoted to St. Germain's miracles,
remains unpublished, though probably containing historical information.

(II.) Regino continues, as before mentioned, till A D 906. His continuator, mainly devoted to German affairs,is, at the commencement, somewhat meagre (III.) Not so the continuators of Rudolph, in the *Annales
Fuldenses*, from whom we collect the most useful information concerning
German history : they also enter largely and satisfactorily into the affairs
of France. (IV.) The history of Eudes, and a considerable portion of the
reign of Charles-le-Simple, would scarcely be known but for the *Vedastine
Annals*. Rich and satisfactory, they increase in interest as they advance,
till they bring us to the edge of the singular chasm, A D 900, which
disappoints us during the most eventful æra in French history.

Yet we now begin to receive instruction from (V.) Frodoardus Remensis, singularly distinguished by his learning, not less so by the excellence
of his character, brought into intercourse with the principal personages of
his age, and furnished with materials of which he fully availed himself
for the historian's task The Cathedral archives were entrusted to his
care; from these sources, and his own knowledge, Frodoardus composed
the history of the Church of Rheims, deduced to his own time. In the
fourth Book, the influential position maintained by the Archbishops
conducts their biographer and historian amply into politics and dissensions. Archbishop Fulco was a prime mover in the political events and
revolutions by which Charles-le-Simple was exalted or depressed, sometimes supporting the young monarch, sometimes opposing him ; and the
quarrels and dissensions between the Archbishops and the Counts of
Flanders and the Vermandois render them very important personages in
the general affairs of Northern Gaul.

In the Ecclesiastical history, these transactions, however, hold only
a subordinate place; for Frodoardus, a very able historian, had well considered the relative proportions of the ecclesiastical and secular materials;
and the matters which he excluded from his *Historia Remensis* he re-

served for his (VI.) Chronicle, the most valuable of its æra. Beginning with a fragment of the year A D. 877, a chasm immediately occurs until A D 919, so the *Chronicon Frodoardi* cannot avail us in the present chapter of our history ; though we shall find it of the greatest use hereafter

The Chronicles of Eckhard, Abbot of Urangen, and Trithemius, Abbot of Hirschau, respectively contain extracts from a Chronicler not employed by any other mediæval compilers. Eckhard flourished in the twelfth century, Trithemius in the fifteenth ; but no intermediate writer has the passages ; and from the time of Trithemius, until very recently, all traces of the source were lost. Richerius, a monk of Saint Remi, well known by various theological and poetical compositions, whom Trithemius quotes as his authority, was an individual enjoying considerable literary eminence. Yet the Manuscript from which Trithemius made his extracts disappeared ; and, though much enquired after by the learned, all attempts to recover it were fruitless. "Il est étrange," say the Benedictine authors of the *Histoire Littéraire de la France* (T. VI p. 504), "qu'un ouvrage aussi intéressant pour notre nation, qui existait au moins à la fin du quinzième siécle, ait été tellement négligé qu'on ne le voit plus paraitre nulle part"

The indefatigable research of Pertz has been happily aided by a species of fox-hound instinct, enabling him to scent out that game which, unearthed by previous sportsmen, still lurks in or between the close covers of public libraries. Thus he discerned at Brussels, for the use of the British archæologist, the long-lost Poem of Guido of Amiens, describing the Conqueror's siege of London The same combination of luck and diligence guided his eye and hand to the Chronicle of Richerius, in the Cathedral library at Bamberg. Apart from its historical value, this Manuscript is very interesting : the Codex is the author's holograph, passages altered, inserted, corrected, expunged ; yet Richerius probably considered it only as a draft, inasmuch as the last vellum page contains notes for the continuation of the Chronicle, for chapters which Richerius never completed. Death probably stayed the writer's hand The work, thus left imperfect, and never published by the author, was not multiplied by transcribers ; and the original, known only to Eckhard and Trithemius, was laid by and forgotten, till brought to light by the fortunate diligence of Pertz. His literary modesty is as praiseworthy as his acuteness. Instead of parading his discovery, he included the Chronicle of Richerius (VII) in his great collection, Vol. VI. working upon it, as might be expected, with the utmost care A fac-simile, which he has added, shews the original state of the manuscript in a manner which never could have been effected by printing-types. In such cases, fac-similes of manuscripts are much more than mere specimens of palæography : they are essential elements for the critical knowledge of history. The Chronicle has been reprinted by the Société Historique

(Paris, 1840)   The work, consisting of four Books, opens with the
accession of Eudes, and concludes just before the death of Hugh Capet
From the dethronement of Charles-le-Simple, Richerius becomes a primary authority.   The earlier portion gives us valuable and authentic
information concerning Eudes, and much respecting Rollo; but the first
book of Richerius, like the last fragments, must be considered rather as a
collection of historical notes than as a connected history.   There is no
attempt at chronology; and Richerius has so evidently confounded *our*
Rollo with another Danish chieftain bearing the same name, that I have
not attempted to reconcile him with the other authorities.

(VIII.) The transactions relating to the settlement of Normandy
depend mainly upon Dudon de Saint-Quentin   Whatever inaccuracies
there may be in the form or arrangement of his narrative, I do not see
any just reason for distrusting his general accuracy   In fact, unless we
accept Dudon, such as he is, we must abandon the history of the first
three Norman sovereigns.

Berenger and Guido, p. 628.

Gibbon and Sismondi have elided these monarchs, whose reigns constitute a most stirring era.   A general reference may be made to Muratori
The Monza relics are known to most travellers.

Louis, King of Provence, p. 632.

See, besides the history of Languedoc, Bouche, *Hist. Générale de Provence*, T. I. pp. 775—784.

Richard-le-Justicier, Transjurane Burgundy, p. 634.

See the Benedictine *Histoire de Bourgogne*

Vermandois, p. 638.

See Collette.

Guido's parsimony, p. 639.

" Metensis vero Episcopus, dum cibaria ei multa secundum Francorum
consuetudinem ministraret, hujusmodi responsa a Dapifero suscepit :—Si
equum saltem mihi dederis, faciam ut tertia obsonii hujus parte sit Rex
Wido contentus.   Quod Episcopus audiens, Non decet, inquit, talem
super nos regnare Regem, qui decem dragmis vile sibi obsonium præpa-
rat "   (Luitprandi Hist. *Rec. des Hist*. T. VIII. p 131.)

Battle of Montfaucon, pp. 640—644.

Montfaucon-en-Argonne is a small town or hamlet in the Rethelois,
on the banks of the Meuse.

Méaux besieged by the Danes, pp. 644, 646.

"A.D. 888. Normanni Meldis Civitatem obsidione vallant," *Ann.
Vedast. Rec des Hist*. T. VIII p. 87   The account of the siege follows.

This account enables ùs to date the undated narrative of Dudo, p 87. By some historians Meldis has been confounded with Melun or even Mellent.

Ravages of the Côtentin and St Lo, pp. 645, 616.

See *Gall. Christ* T. x p. 857, which contains the extract from the famous Black book of Coutances, stating that divine service was intermitted for seventy-three years, in consequence of the Danish ravages. The names of the Bishops of Lisieux are wanting from A D. 876 to 990.

Popa, or the Poppet, p. 647.

For the capture and abduction of the damsel, see Dudon, p. 77, whom all other Chroniclers have copied, or abridged, or misrepresented. That Bernard de Senlis was the uncle of her son Guillaume-Longue-Epée, is proved by the respective declarations of Guillaume and of Bernard. Dudon, pp 95 and 118

Storming of Evreux, p. 648.

Besides the Chronicles, and the matter in the *Gallia Christiana*, I have also employed Le Brasseur (*Histoire Civile et Ecclésiastique du Comté d'Evreux*, Paris, 1722).

Battle of the Allier, pp. 650, 651.

It is only from *Richerius*, Lib I c 7—11, that we collect the details of Eudes' campaign in Auvergne, and the histories of Osketyl and Ingo. All that concerns Eudes is clear and consecutive; but I suspect some unrectifiable confusion as to Ingo.

Hunedeus, p. 662.

" A.D. 895—896 Per idem tempus iterum Normanni cum Duce eorum, Hunedeo nomine, et quinque barchis iterum Sequanam ingressi · et dum Rex ad alia intendit, magnum sibi et regno malum accrescere facit . Normanni vero jam multiplicati paucis ante Nativitatem diebus Hisam ingressi, Cauciaco sedem sibi, nullo resistente, firmant " (*Ann. Vedast*)

" 895 Northmanni iterum cum Duce eorum, qui Rollo dictus est nomine, rursus Sequanam ingressi, jam multiplicati ante Nativitatem Domini Hisam ingressi," &c (*Chronicon de Gestis Normannorum in Francia*. Duchesne, *Hist. Franc. S. S.* T. II p. 530). In this Chronicle Duchesne employed two manuscripts; one reads *Rodo*, the other *Rollo* The *Recueil des Historiens* does not at all remove the necessity of consulting Duchesne.

" 896—897 Posthac Normanni usque Mosam in prædam exierunt, nullo sibi resistente. A præda verò illis revertentibus occurrit Regis exercitus: sed nil profecerunt. Verum Nortmanni ad naves reversi, timentes multitudinem exercitûs ne obsiderentur, in Sequanam redierunt: ibique tota demorantes æstate prædas agebant, nullo sibi resistente   Karolus vero Hunedeum ad se deductum Cluninio Monasterio eum de sacro fonte suscepit." (*Ann Vedast*)

"896   Carolus Rex Hunedeum Regem Northmannorum baptizari fecit, eumque de sacro fonte suscepit " (Sigebertus Gemblacensis, *Rec. des Hist* T. viii. p 310)

Archbishop Fulco's Objurgations, p. 663.

See Fiodoard, (*Hist. Remensis*, Lib iv. cap 6).

The Quarrel in Council, p. 668.

It is with this incident that the Vedastine Annals suddenly terminate, as if the pen had been stuck out of the writer's hand during the dissensions.

Frederuna, p. 669.

Her dowry, Corbigny and Pontyon, is granted by Charter, dated at Attigny, 907, "anno xv regnante Domno (*i.e.* Domino) Karolo gloriosissimo Rege, redintegrante decimo" (*Rec. des Hist*. T. ix p. 504). In this Charter he styles her "quædam nobili prosapia puella," whom he takes in marriage by the advice of his counsellors. Another Charter, granted in favour of the Church of Saint Remi, in which he notices her coronation, is dated "anno xxv regnante Karolo Rege gloriosissimo, redintegrante xx, largiore verò hæreditate indepta vi " (p. 530.)

Archbishop Hervé's Pastoral, p. 674.

This will be found, together with the letter of Pope John IX , in Dom Bessin's collection of the Norman Councils, (*Concilia Rothomagensis Provinciæ*, Rouen, 1717). Were any proof required that it is most inexpedient to sever the civil and ecclesiastical memorials of the mediæval era, it would be afforded by the circumstance that these important documents are excluded from the *Recueil des Historiens*

Battle of Chartres, p. 676.

This event occupies a prominent position in French history. I consider Dudon de Saint-Quentin as the main source of my narrative (pp 80, 81), engrafting, as far as is practicable, his account upon the brief chronicles of Anjou, (Dom Bouquet, T viii. p. 252), the fragment of French history, p. 302 ; *Hugo Floriacensis*, p 318 ; and Benoit's metrical paraphrase vv. 5169—6004. The notice of the satirical songs by which Ebles of Poitou was defamed, is found only in Benoit. There is much uncertainty as to the exact date of the battle, but I have adopted the most probable , rejecting also those incidents which do not appear trustworthy. For the *Pré des Reculés*, see Michel's *Benoit*, Vol i p 271.

The Followers of Rollo, p. 680

I have ventured to assemble all the Danes who are in any wise recorded as founders of Norman families The concluding Book (VIII) of Guillaume de Jumièges, enlarged and continued by another monk of the same monastery, contains many important genealogical notices : some are scattered in Ordericus Vitalis ; and Duchesne's genealogies, appended to his editions of these Historians (*S. S. Hist. Norm.* pp. 1069—1104) have paginal references to the passages upon which they are grounded — Four folio volumes, richly adorned by armorial bearings, have been devoted to the descendants of Bernard the Dane, by the industrious gratitude of Giles André de la Roque, (*Hist Généalogique de la Maison de Harcourt*, Paris, 1662).—Some families, and in particular La Roche Tesson, are amply illustrated by M. Vaultier (*Recherches Historiques sur l'Ancien Pays de Cinglais, Mémoires de la Société des Antiquaires de Normandie*, 2ᵉ Serie, T. IV. pp. 1—293). The Crespin family are said to be descended from Rollo by a daughter, Crispine.

Pluquet (*Roman du Rou*, Vol. I. p. 152) has a notice concerning the family of Osmond de Cent-villes — "présentement Ducs et Pairs de France " So also Goubé (*Hist de la Normandie*, Rouen, 1815, Vol. I. p 91). Roger de Montgomery styles himself *Normannus Normannorum*, but unfortunately he and all his contemporaries forgot to tell us the name of his ancestor. Ademar of Chavanes says (*Rec des Hist.* VIII. p. 232) that Rollo's followers accepted him as King

Cession made to Rollo, p. 684.

The Frankish Proceres, in urging the marriage and the cession, held out as an inducement the homage which Rollo would render ·—"Rollo, Dux Northmannorum tibi amoris et amicitiæ inextricabilis, quinetiam servitii pactum Si dederis filiam tuam, ut ei dixisti, conjugem, terramque maritimam in sempiternam per progenies progenierum possessionem, manus suas se subjugando tibi dabit fidelitatis gratiâ, tuumque servitium incessanter explebit." (Dudo, pp. 82, 83.)

Archbishop Franco makes a most energetic claim on behalf of his patron : " .. non conciliabitur tibi, nisi terram quam daturus es, in sacramento Christianæ religionis juraveris, tu et Archipræsules et Episcopi, Comites et Abbates totius regni, ut teneat ipse et successores ejus ipsam terram ab Eptæ fluviolo ad mare usque, quasi fundum et allodium in sempiternum."

Duke Robert and the Prelates and Proceres equally so : " Tunc Flandrensem terram, ut ex ea viveret, voluit Rex ei dare : sed ille noluit præ paludium impeditione recipere. Itaque spondet Rex ei Britanniam dare, quæ erat in confinio promissæ terræ." (Dudo, p. 83.)

Frodoardus (*Hist. Rem.* Lib. IV c 24) does not make any mention of the King, but connects the transaction with the baptism of the Danes after the battle of Chartres : "fidem Christi suscipere receperunt, conces-

sis sibi maritimis quibusdam pagis, cum Rotomagensi quam pene dele-
verant urbe, et aliis eidem subjectis "

The exact extent of the cession made by Charles-le-Simple has been
much debated by Licquet and others.

For all matters relating to the antient geography of the Duchy, we
are exceedingly indebted to the labours of the late Honourable Thomas
Stapleton, whose introductions to the great Rolls of the Exchequer of Normandy, as published by the Society of Antiquaries, (1840—1844), condense
and almost exhaust all the information upon the subject, whilst his map
brings every particular before the eye. Maps executed with such clearness and accuracy afford great aid to the study of mediæval history. Mr
Stapleton's map is the most satisfactory specimen of this class hitherto
produced at home or abroad.

Superiority of Britanny, p. 686.

" Emit namque Rex Francorum Karolus pacem atque amicitiam a
Rollone primo Duce Normannorum, ac posteriorum parente, natam suam
Gislam in matrimonium, et Britanniam in servitium perpetuum ei tradens
Exoraverunt id fœdus Franci, non valentes amplius resistere Gallico ense
Danicæ securi. Exinde Comites Britannici e jugo Normannicæ domi-
nationis cervicem omninò solvere nunquam valuerunt, etsi multotiens id
conati, tota vi obluctando " (*Guil Pict.* p. 191.) It seems as if Guillaume
de Poitou, the commencement of whose history is lost, had somewhat
more information than we now possess.

All these Norman transactions will also be found bearing upon the
mouvance of Britanny, that is to say, they elucidate the antient feudal
dependence of Britanny, one of the most vexed questions in French constitutional history : a practical question also, for the French Legists
argued that certain important privileges exercised by the Crown after the
final reunion of the province by the marriage of the last heiress, Claude,
daughter of the Duchess Anne with Francis the First, were to be decided
thereby. A discussion, therefore, which, upon its first aspect, appears to
be ranked only amongst the dullest, or, as some would consider, the most
useless labour of archæology,—for, if thoroughly sifted and debated, it
must be taken up from Clovis and a good while beyond—acquires a
living interest from its connexion with the rights and franchises of the
most independent and sensitive member of the French monarchy under
Louis-le-Grand.

Historical literature profited greatly by this same discussion —The
States of Britanny, in order to sustain their pretensions in the least
offensive manner, sought the historical advocacy of the congregation of
Saint Maur. Dom Lobineau undertook the task, actuated equally by
national zeal and antiquarian enthusiasm, and the result was one huge
folio of text and another huge folio of *preuves*, chronicles and legends,

and a selection from fifteen thousand deeds and charters, constituting an invaluable treasury of information

Such was the production of the Benedictine Réligieux.—A courtly Historiograper, his opponent, celebrated for the facility with which he was accustomed to release himself from the encumbrance of authentic evidence,—*grand merci, mon siége est fait!*—took up the gauntlet, and vindicated the authority of the Louvre in a neat duodecimo. This was one of the cases in which an acute and clever superficial writer has the means of triumphing over laborious and conscientious erudition. The Benedictine replied modestly, but ineffectually. If the cause of "Dom Lobineau *versus* the Abbé Vertot" had been brought before the Académie des Inscriptions, there can be little doubt but that judgment would have been given for the defendant.—Abbé Vertot, however, though in the right, was as angry as if he had been in the wrong, and, meanly seeking revenge, he obtained a *lettre-de-cachet* against his adversary. The wisdom and moderation of the great D'Aguisseau alone saved the historian of Britanny from close, and perhaps life-long imprisonment; but such was the dread inspired by the Bastille, that, on the Breton side, the controversy was completely silenced.

Rollo's Homage, p. 686.

"—Francorum coactus verbis, manus suas misit inter manus Regis, quod nunquam pater ejus, et avus, atque proavus cuiquam fecit Dedit itaque filiam suam, Gislam nomine, uxorem illi Duci, terramque determinatam in alodo et in fundo, a flumine Eptæ usque ad mare, totamque Britanniam de qua posset vivere." (Dudo, p. 83).

Rollo's refusal to kiss the King's foot, p. 687.

"Cumque sui Comites illum ammonerent ut pedem regis in acceptionem tanti muneris oscularetur, lingua Anglica respondit, *Ne se, bi Goth*"—(Chron. S. Martini Turon. *Rec. des Hist* viii p 316.)

Assurance given to Rollo by the Franks, p. 687.

"Cæterum, Karolus Rex, Duxque Rotbertus, Comitesque et Proceres, Præsules et Abbates, juraverunt sacramento Catholicæ fidei Patricio Rolloni vitam suam, et membra et honorem totius Regni, insuper terram denominatam, quatinus ipsam teneret et possideret hæredibusque traderet; et per curricula cunctorum annorum successio nepotum in progenies progenierum haberet et excoleret." (Dudo, p 84)

Charles-le-Simple's construction of his Grant, p. 688.

In a grant to the Abbey of Saint Germain-des-prés he excepts that portion of the lands of the Abbey of the Croix Saint-Ouen — "quam annuimus Nortmannis Sequanensibus, videlicet Rolloni suisque comitibus, pro tutela Regni." (*Rec. des Hist.* T. ix p 536)

Supremacy of France denied, p. 689.

Hugh the Great joins the Norman Proceres in declaring, when Louis d'Outremer threatens to invade young Richard's Duchy—"Tenet sicuti Rex Monarchiam Northmannicæ regionis —Richardus nec Regi nec Duci militat, nec ulli nisi Deo obsequium præstat." (Dudo, p. 128.)

Was not Rollo a relapsed Pagan? p 690.

Richerius presents us with the adventures of a Rollo, the son of Catillus, or Kctyl, who is stated to have been conquered by Duke Robert, which cannot in any wise be brought into conformity with Dudon de Saint-Quentin. Nevertheless, the narrative of Richerius (Lib. I. chapters 29, 33, 50), combined with the probability that Hunedeus is to be identified with Rollo, raises the suspicion of Rollo's relapse, which, though we may not urge its acceptance as a fact, cannot be excluded from Rollo's history.

Legends of Rollo the Lawgiver, p. 696.

See Dudon de Saint-Quentin (p 85), Guillaume de Jumièges, Lib II. c. 20; Wace, v. 1942—1984; and Benoit de Saint-Maur (v. 7145—7469). For the doctrines of Scandinavian jurisprudence to which I have here alluded, I may refer to an Essay written years ago (*Antient Laws of the Scandinavians, Edinb. Rev.* xxxiv 1820).

Vestiges of the Danish Language in Norman topography, p. 700.

Depping, in his note or excursus, *Des Noms Topographiques d'origine étrangère en Normandie,* has thoroughly investigated this subject. See also De la Rue, (*Hist. de la Ville de Caen,* Caen, Vol. I. p. 56)

Rollo and Gisella, p. 706.

It is Licquet, who in his history of Normandy rejects the whole of this history of Gisella's marriage. Depping takes the reasonable side of the question.

Arnolph's Death, p. 709.

" ..   . profectusque in propria, turpissima valetudine expiravit. Minutis quippe vermibus, quos pedunculos aiunt, vehementer afflictus, spiritum reddidit." (Luitprandi Hist. *Rec. des Hist.* T VIII. p 133.)

I.

One Volume, 12mo,

A New History of the Anglo-Saxons.

II.

Two Volumes, Quarto,

The Rise and Progress of the English Commonwealth;

Containing the Anglo-Saxon Policy, and the Institutions arising out of Laws and Usages which prevailed before the Conquest.

III.

Four Volumes, Folio,

The Parliamentary Writs and Writs of Military Summons,

Together with the Records and Muniments relating to the Suit and Service due and performed to the King's High Court of Parliament and the Councils of the Realm.

IV.

Two Volumes, Royal Octavo,

Rotuli Curiæ Regis,

Or the Rolls and Records of the Court held before the King's Justices, from the 6th Richard I. to 1st John; with Historical Introductions.

V

Three Volumes, Royal Octavo, with Plates,

The Ancient Calendars and Inventories of the Treasury of Her Majesty's Exchequer;

Together with other Documents illustrating the History of that Repository. With Historical Introductions and Illustrations

VI.

One Volume, Royal Octavo,

Scotland.

Documents, hitherto inedited, illustrating the ancient History of Scotland, and the Relations between the Crowns of Scotland and England , now first printed from the Originals, with an Historical Analysis thereof.

VII.

One Volume Octavo,

An Essay upon the Original Authority of the King's Council.

Explanatory of the Nature of the Ancient Parliamentary Petitions as Materials for the Constitutional History of England.

VIII.

One Volume 12mo,

Truths and Fictions of the Middle Ages: The Merchant and the Friar.

IX.

In Octavo,

Observations upon the Principles to be adopted in the Establishment of New Municipalities.

X.

In Octavo,

Parliamentary Reform;

Or the Ancient Legal Right (anterior to the Reform Act) of the Dormant Parliamentary Boroughs.

XI.

In Octavo,

Parliamentary Reform;

Or the Means of reconciling Parliamentary Reform to the Interests and Opinions of the different orders of the Community.

STANDARD BOOKS

PUBLISHED BY

JOHN W. PARKER & SON, WEST STRAND,

LONDON.

History of Normandy and of England By Sir FRANCIS PALGRAVE. Vol I Octavo 21s.

History of the Whig Ministry of 1830 By J ARTHUR ROEBUCK, M P Vols I & II —to the Passing of the Reform Bill Octavo

Principles of Political Economy By J STUART MILL Second Edition Two Volumes Octavo 30s

Essays on Unsettled Questions of Political Economy. By the same Author 6s. 6d.

System of Logic By the same Author Third and Cheaper Edition Two Volumes Octavo 25s

Discourse on the Studies of the University of Cambridge By ADAM SEDGWICK, M A , Woodwardian Professor Fifth Edition With Preliminary Dissertation and Supplement. (770 pages) 12s

On the Influence of Authority in Matters of Opinion By G CORNEWALL LEWIS, M P. Octavo. 10s. 6d.

Elements of Logic. By R WHATELY, D D , Archbishop of Dublin With all the Author's Additions Small Octavo, 4s 6d Library Edition, 10s 6d

Elements of Rhetoric By the same Author With all the Author's Additions Small Octavo, 4s 6d. Library Edition, 10s. 6d

Introductory Lectures on Political Economy. By the same Author 8s

History of the Inductive Sciences By W WHEWELL, D D , F.R S , Master of Trinity College, Cambridge Second Edition, revised Three Vols £2 2s

Philosophy of the Inductive Sciences. By the same Author Second Edition, revised Two Volumes Octavo 30s

Indications of the Creator—Theological Extracts from the History and the Philosophy of the Inductive Sciences By the same Author Second Edition 5s 6d

Elements of Morality, including Polity By the same Author Second and Cheaper Edition Two Volumes. 15s

History of the Royal Society, compiled from Original Authentic Documents By C R. WELD, Assistant-Secretary of the Royal Society Two Volumes Octavo 30s

Lectures on the Principles and Practice of Physic. By T WATSON, M D Third Edition Two Volumes Octavo 34s

Cycle of Celestial Objects By Captain W H SMYTH, R N ,F R S., Foreign Secretary of the Royal Society. Two Vols I Prolegomena, II The Bedford Catalogue. Octavo, with Illustrations £2 2s

Manual of Chemistry By W. T BRANDE, F R S , Professor of Chemistry in the Royal Institution Sixth Edition, much enlarged, and embodying all Recent Discoveries Two large Volumes £2 5s

Dictionary of the Materia Medica and Pharmacy By the same Author Octavo 15s

Principles of Mechanism By R. WILLIS, M A , F R S , Professor of Natural Philosophy, Cambridge 15s

Mechanics applied to the Arts By H MOSELEY, M A , F R S , one of Her Majesty's Inspectors of Schools 6s 6d

Lectures on Astronomy By the same Author. Third Edition 5s 6d.

Elements of Meteorology. By the late Professor DANIELL. With Plates Two Volumes Octavo 32s

On the Nature of Thunderstorms, and on the means of Protecting Churches and other Buildings, and Shipping, against the Destructive Effects of Lightning By SIR W SNOW HARRIS, F R S Octavo, with Illustrations 10s 6d

Physiological Anatomy and Physiology of Man By Dr TODD and W. BOWMAN, F R S With numerous Illustrations Part III , 7s Volume I , 15s

Connexion of Natural and Divine Truth By BADEN POWELL, M A , F R S , Professor of Geometry, Oxford 9s

Undulatory Theory as applied to the Dispersion of Light. By the same Author Octavo With a coloured Chart of the Prismatic Spectra 9s

Mathematical Tracts   By G. BID-
DELL AIRY, M.A, F R S, Astronomer
Royal   I Lunar and Planetary Theories
—II Figure of the Earth —III Precession
and Nutation —IV Calculus of Variations
—V. Undulatory Theory of Optics, and
Theory of Polarization   Octavo. Third
Edition 15s.

The Philosophy of Living. By HER-
BERT MAYO, M D, formerly Surgeon to the
Middlesex Hospital   Third and Cheaper
Edition, with Additions   5s

Management of the Organs of Di-
gestion in Health and in Disease   By the
same Author   Second Edition. 6s 6d

Lunacy and Lunatic Life, with Hints
on the Personal Care and Management of
those afflicted with Derangement. 3s 6d

Lectures on the German Mineral
Waters   the Result of a Professional In-
vestigation of their respective Merits in the
Cure of certain Chronic Diseases   By S
SUTRO, M D, Senior Physician of the
German Hospital.

Spasm, Languor, and Palsy   By J.
A WILSON, M D, Physician to St George's
Hospital 7s

Gout, Chronic Rheumatism, and In-
flammation of the Joints   By ROBERT
BENTLEY TODD, M D, F R S, Physician
of King's College Hospital 7s 6d

Minerals and their Uses   By J R.
JACKSON, F R S. With coloured Frontis-
piece 7s 6d.

Lectures on Dental Physiology and
Surgery. By J TOMES, F R S, Surgeon-
Dentist to the Middlesex Hospital. Octavo
With 100 Illustrations. 12s

Instructions in the Use and Management of Artificial Teeth. By the same
Author   With Illustrations. 3s 6d

Practical Geology and Mineralogy,
and the Chemistry of Metals. By JOSHUA
TRIMMER, F G S   Octavo, with Two Hundred Illustrations 12s

Practical Chemistry for Farmers and
Landowners   By the same Author   5s

Practical Geodesy, comprising Chain
Surveying, the Use of Surveying Instruments Levelling, Trigonometrical, Mining,
and Maritime Surveying   By BUTLER
WILLIAMS, C E   New Edition, with
Chapters on Estate, Parochial, and Rail-
road Surveying With Illustrations 12s 6d

Manual for Teaching Model-Draw-
ing, with a Popular View of Perspective.
By the same Author   (Under the Sanction
of the Committee of Council on Education)
Octavo, with shaded Engravings 15s

Instructions in Drawing. Abridged
from the above   3s

Chemistry of the Crystal Palace   a
Popular Account of the Chemical Pro-
perties of the Chief Materials employed
in its Construction   By T GRIFFITHS, late
Professor of Chemistry in St. Bartholo-
mew's Hospital 5s

Chemistry of the four Ancient Elements   By the same Author   With numerous Illustrations   Second Edition 4s 6d

Recreations in Chemistry. By the
same Author   Second Edition, with numerous Illustrations, much enlarged   5s

Recreations in Physical Geography;
or, the Earth as It Is   By Miss R. M
ZORNLIN   Third Edition   6s

World of Waters; or, Recreations
in Hydrology.   By the same Author.
Second Edition   6s

Recreations in Geology. By the
same Author   Second Edition. 4s 6d

Recreations in Astronomy. By Rev.
L TOMLINSON, M A. Third Edition 4s 6d

Young Italy   By A. BAILLIE COCH-
RANE, M P   Post 8vo   10s 6d.

Wales   The Social, Moral, and Religious Condition of the People, considered
especially with reference to Education. By
Sir THOMAS PHILLIPS   Octavo. 14s

Journal of Summer Time in the
Country   By Rev R A WILLMOTT
Second Edition 5s

Schiller's Complete Poems, including all his early suppressed Pieces, together
with the Poems introduced in his Dramatic
Works, attempted in English   By EDGAR
ALFRED BOWRING. 6s.

Correspondence of Sir Isaac Newton
and Professor Cotes, and other unpublished
Letters and Papers of Newton. Edited,
with Synoptical View of Newton's Life, by
J EDLESTON, M A, Fel Trin Col. Cambridge   With Portrait. Octavo 10s.

Shipwrecks of the Royal Navy. Compiled principally from Official Documents
in the Admiralty By WILLIAM O S GILLY.
With a Preface by W S GILLY, D D,
Canon of Durham   Second Edition. 7s 6d.

Danger of Superficial Knowledge
A Lecture   By J D FORBES, F R S, Professor of Natural Philosophy, Edinburgh 2s

The Introductory Lectures delivered at Queen's College, London, by

W S. BENNETT	REV T JACKSON
DR BEOLCHI	REV C KINGSLEY
PROF BERNAYS	PROF MAURICE.
PROF BRASSEUR	REV C G NICOLAY
REV. S CLARK	PROF O'BRIEN
PROF HALL.	REV A B STRETTELL
JOHN HULLAH.	HENRY WARREN.

Foolscap Octavo. 5s

The Saint's Tragedy, the true Story of Elizabeth of Hungary By C. KINGSLEY, Rector of Eversley. With Preface, by Professor MAURICE Cheaper Edition

Yeast a Problem Reprinted, with Additions and Alterations, from *Fraser's Magazine* 5s.

The Professor's Wife a Tale from the German of Auerbach. 3s 6d

Chance and Choice or, the Education of Circumstances Two Tales —I The Young Governess — II. Claudine de Soligny 7s 6d.

Anschar: a Story of the North. By RICHARD JOHN KING 7s.

Brampton Rectory or, the Lesson of Life Second Edition. 8s 6d.

Compton Merivale another Leaf from the Lesson of Life By the Author of *Brampton Rectory*. 8s. 6d

John Sterling's Essays and Tales Edited, with a Sketch of the Author's Life, by Archdeacon HARE Two volumes, with Portrait. 21s

The City of God; a Vision of the Past, the Present, and the Future By E RUDGE, Rector of Bratton. 8s 6d

Chronicles of the Seasons; or, the Progress of the Year being a Course of Daily Instruction and Amusement, selected from the Popular Details of the Natural History, Science, Art, Antiquities, and Biography of our Father-land In Four Books, 3s 6d each.

The Merchant and the Friar, or, Truths and Fictions of the Middle Ages By Sir F. PALGRAVE Second Edition. 3s.

Tales and Stories from History. By AGNES STRICKLAND Cheaper Edition. One Volume

Woman's Mission. Thirteenth Edition 2s

The Little Bracken Burners A Tale By LADY CALLCOTT Third Edition 1s. 6d

Sister Mary's Tales on Natural History Seventh Edition, with numerous Woodcuts 1s 6d

Natural Philosophy for Beginners Third Edition, with 143 Woodcuts 2s

Popular Poems, selected by ELIZABETH PARKER Third Edition

Easy Poetry for Children. Third Edition 1s

Introduction to English Composition By Rev J EDWARDS Fifth Edition. 2s

Bible Biography By E FARR. Second Edition. 4s

Abbott's Reader a Series of Familiar Pieces in Prose and Verse, calculated to produce a Moral Influence on the Hearts and Lives of Young Persons Fifth Edition 3s

History of the Christian Church. By the late Professor BURTON, of Oxford. Eighth and Cheaper Edition 5s

Outlines of Sacred History Twelfth and Cheaper Edition 2s 6d

History of the Church of England. By T VOWLER SHORT, D D , Bishop of St Asaph Fifth Edition Octavo 16s

Burnet's History of the Reformation, abridged Edited, with Additions, by G. E CORRIE, B D , Norrisian Professor of Divinity, and Master of Jesus College, Cambridge 10s 6d

History of the English Reformation By F C MASSINGBERD, M A , Rector of South Ormsby Second Edition 6s

History of Popery; the Origin, Growth, and Progress of the Papal Power , its Political Influence, and Effects on the Progress of Civilization 9s 6d

The Anglo-Saxon Church, its History, Revenues, and General Character By H SOAMES, M A , Chancellor of St Paul's Cathedral Third Edition 10s. 6d

Elizabethan Religious History By the same Author. Octavo 16s.

Ullmann's Gregory of Nazianzum A Contribution to the Ecclesiastical History of the Fourth Century Translated by G V Cox, M A 6s

Neander's Julian the Apostate and his Generation an Historical Picture. Translated by G V. Cox, M A 3s 6d.

Dahlmann's Life of Herodotus, drawn out from his Book With Notes Translated by G V Cox, M A 5s.

Student's Manual of Ancient History By W Cooke Taylor, LL D Fifth Edition 10s 6d

Student's Manual of Modern History. By the same Author Fifth Edition, with New Supplementary Chapter 10s. 6d.

History of Mohammedanism. Cheaper Edition By the same Author 4s

Crusaders; Scenes, Events, and Characters from the Times of the Crusades By T. Keightley 7s.

Historical Sketch of the British Army By G R Gleig, M A, Chaplain General to the Forces 3s 6d

Family History of England By the same Author With numerous Illustrations Three Volumes 6s. 6d each

School History of England, abridged from Gleig's Family History of England, with copious Chronology, List of Contemporary Sovereigns, and Questions 6s.

Familiar History of Birds. By E. Stanley, D D, Bishop of Norwich Fifth Edition, with numerous Illustrations 5s.

Memoir of Edward Copleston, D D, Bishop of Llandaff, with Selections from his Diary and Correspondence, &c By W J Copleston, M A, Rector of Cromhall

Life of Archbishop Usher, with an Account of his Writings By C R Elrington, D D, Regius Professor of Divinity, Dublin Portrait Octavo 12s

Life of Archbishop Sancroft By the late Dr D'Oyly Octavo 9s

Memoirs of the Life, Character, and Writings of Bishop Butler By T Bartlett, M A, Rector of Kingstone Octavo, 12s, with a Portrait

Lives of Eminent Christians By R B Hone, M A, Archdeacon of Worcester. New Edition. Four Volumes 4s 6d each

Bishop Jeremy Taylor, his Predecessors, Contemporaries, and Successors By Rev R A Willmott Second Edition 5s.

Lives of English Sacred Poets By the same Author. Two Vols 4s 6d each

Life and Services of Lord Harris By the Right Hon S R Lushington Second Edition, 6s 6d

Notes on the Parables By R. Chenevix Trench, B D Examining Chaplain to the Lord Bishop of Oxford Fourth Edition Octavo 12s

Notes on the Miracles. By the same Author Third Edition 12s

Literature of the Church of England, exhibited in Specimens of the Writings of Eminent Divines, with Memoirs of their Lives, and Sketches of the Times in which they lived By R Cattermole, B D Two Volumes. Octavo 25s

Essays on Peculiarities of the Christian Religion By R Whately, D D, Archbishop of Dublin Cheaper Edition 7s 6d

Essays on Difficulties in the Writings of the Apostle Paul By the same Author Cheaper Edition 8s

Essays on the Errors of Romanism having their Origin in Human Nature Cheaper Edition By the same Author 7s 6d

Essays on Dangers to Christian Faith from the Teaching or the Conduct of its Professors By the same Author. 10s.

Mission of the Comforter By J. C. Hare M A, Archdeacon of Lewes Second Edition Octavo 12s

The Victory of Faith By the same Author. Second Edition 6s.

Parish Sermons. By the same Author Two Series Octavo 12s each

The Church a Family· Sermons on the Occasional Services of the Prayer-Book By F D Maurice, M A, Professor of Divinity in King's College 4s. 6d

The Prayer Book; specially considered as a Protection against Romanism By the same Author 5s 6d.

The Lord's Prayer Nine Sermons By the same Author Third Edition 2s 6d.

The Religions of the World, and their Relations to Christianity By the same Author Cheaper Edition 5s

Lectures on the Epistle to the Hebrews, with a Review of Newman's Theory of Development By the same Author Octavo. 7s 6d

Christmas Day, and other Sermons By the same Author Octavo 10s 6d

Lectures on the Characters of our
Lord's Apostles　By a Country Pastor
3s 6d

Lectures on the Scripture Revelations respecting Good and Evil Angels. By
the same Author　3s 6d

View of the Scripture Revelations
respecting a Future State　Sixth Edition.
By the same Author　5s.

Twenty-five Village Sermons. By
C. KINGSLEY, Jun , Rector of Eversley　5s

Churchman's Theological Dictionary.
By R. EDEN, M A , Chaplain to the Bishop
of Norwich. Second Edition. 5s.

The Gospel-Narrative according to
the Authorized Text, without Repetition
or Omission　With a Continuous Exposition, Marginal Proofs in full, and Notes
By JOHN FORSTER, M A , Her Majesty's
Chaplain of the Savoy　Fourth Edition,
12s , larger paper, 16s.

Statutes relating to the Ecclesiastical and Eleemosynary Institutions of England, Wales, Ireland, India, and the Colonies , with Decisions　By A J STEPHENS,
M A , F.R S　Two large Volumes, with
copious Indices, £3 3s

Exposition of the Thirty-Nine
Articles, Historical and Doctrinal. By E.
H BROWNE, M A , Prebendary of Exeter,
formerly Vice-Principal of Lampeter Col-
lege　The First Volume Octavo 10s 6d
To be completed in Two Volumes.

The Churchman's Guide; an Index
of Sermons and other Works, arranged
according to their subjects　By JOHN
FORSTER, M A. Octavo. 7s

Manual of Christian Antiquities
By J E RIDDLE, M A , Bampton Lecturer,
Oxford　Second Edition　18s

Luther and his Times　By the same
Author　5s

Churchman's Guide to the Use of
the English Liturgy. By the same Author.
3s 6d

First Sundays at Church　By the
same Author　Fifth Edition　3s 6d

The Early Christians　By the Rev
W PRIDDEN, M A　Fourth Edition　4s.

The Book of the Fathers, and the
Spirit of their Writings　9s 6d.

*Edited for the Syndics of the Cambridge
University Press*

De Obligatione Conscientiæ Prælec-
tiones Decem Oxonii in Schola Theologica
Habitæ　A Roberto Sanderson, S Theo-
logiæ Ibidem Professore Regio　With
English Notes, including an abridged
Translation, by W WHEWELL, D D ,
Master of Trinity College　Octavo　9s

The Homilies, with various Readings,
and the Quotations from the Fathers given
at length in the Original Languages　Edited
by G E. CORRIE, B D , Master of Jesus
College, and Norrisian Professor of Divinity
Octavo. 10s 6d

Pearson on the Creed. Revised and
Corrected by TEMPLE CHEVALLIER, B D.,
Professor of Mathematics, Durham. Octavo.
12s

⁎ In this edition the folio of 1669 has been
taken as the principal model of the text,
being the latest edition to which Bishop
Pearson made any additions or alterations,
and the quotations from the Fathers have
been verified throughout　The passages
from the Rabbinical writings and Chaldee
paraphrases have also been carefully col-
lated

Twysden's Historical Vindication of
the Church of England in point of Schism
Edited, with the Author's MS Corrections,
by Professor CORRIE　7s 6d

Archbishop Usher's Answer to a
Jesuit, with other Tracts on Popery.
Octavo　13s 6d

Lectures on Divinity, delivered in
the University of Cambridge　By JOHN
HEY, D D　Third Edition. Two Volumes
Octavo　30s

Wilson's Illustration of the Method
of Explaining the New Testament　Edited
by THOMAS TURTON, D D , Lord Bishop of
Ely　Octavo　8s.

The Church of St Patrick, an Inquiry into the Independence of the Ancient
Church of Ireland　By W. G. TODD, A B
4s

Civil History of the Jews, from
Joshua to Hadrian　By Rev O COCKAYNE,
M A , King's College, London. Second
Edition, with Maps　4s. 6d

Cudworth on Freewill, now first
Edited, with Notes, by J. ALLEN, M A ,
Archdeacon of Salop. 3s

Manual of the Antiquities of the
Christian Church　By Dr GUERICKE,
Professor of Theology at Halle　Trans-
lated and Adapted to the Use of the English
Church, by A J W MORRISON, B A ,
Master of Grammar School, Truro　Fools-
cap octavo　5s 6d

Garrick's Mode of Reading the Liturgy With Notes, and a Discourse on Public Reading. By R CULL Octavo 5s 6d

Ordo Sæclorum; a Treatise on the Chronology of the Holy Scriptures. By H Browne, M A., Canon of Chichester. Octavo 20s

Observations on Dr Wiseman's Reply to Dr Turton's Roman Catholic Doctrine of the Eucharist Considered By THOMAS TURTON, D D , Regius Professor of Divinity in the University of Cambridge, now Bishop of Ely Octavo 4s 6d.

James's Treatise on the Corruptions of Scripture, Councils, and Fathers, by the Prelates, Pastors, and Pillars of the Church of Rome, for the Maintenance of Popery Revised and Corrected by J E. Cox, M A , Vicar of St. Helen's, Bishopsgate Octavo 12s

Fullwood's Roma Ruit The Pillars of Rome Broken · wherein all the several Pleas for the Pope's Authority in England, with all the material Defences of them, are Revised and Answered A New Edition, by C HARDWICK, M A., Fellow of St Catharine's Hall, Cambridge Octavo 10s 6d

The Scriptural Character of the English Church considered With Notes By DERWENT COLERIDGE, M A., Principal of St Mark's College. Octavo 12s 6d

College Lectures on Ecclesiastical History By W BATES, B D, Fellow of Christ's College, Cambridge. Second Edition. 6s 6d

College Lectures on Christian Antiquities, and the Ritual By the same Author 9s.

Hints for an Improved Translation of the New Testament. By J SCHOLE-FIELD, M A , Professor of Greek, Cambridge Third Edition, with Appendix incorporated 3s 6d.

Choral Service of the United Church of England and Ireland, being an Inquiry into the Liturgical System of the Cathedral and Collegiate Foundations of the Anglican Communion. By J JEBB, M A , Rector of Peterstow Octavo. 16s

Rituale Anglo-Catholicum; or, the Testimony of the Catholic Church to the Book of Common Prayer, as exhibited in Quotations from the Ancient Fathers, Councils, Liturgies, and Rituals By H. BAILEY, B D , Warden of St Augustine's College, Canterbury Octavo 15s

Sermons preached before the University of Oxford By C A OGILVIE, D D , Canon of Christ Church Octavo 5s.

Lectures on the Prophecies, proving the Divine Origin of Christianity. By A M'CAUL, D D , Professor of Divinity in King's College, London Octavo 7s 6d

Two Series of Discourses I On Christian Humiliation II On the City of God By C H TERROT, D D , Bishop of Edinburgh. Octavo 7s 6d

College Chapel Sermons. By W. WHEWELL, D D., Master of Trinity College, Cambridge.

The Liturgy as it is, illustrated in a Series of Practical Sermons By H HOWARTH, B D , Rector of St George, Hanover Square Second Edition 4s. 6d

Sermons By J O W. HAWEIS, M A , Morning Preacher at the Magdalen Hospital 5s. 6d.

Practical Sermons, by Dignitaries and other Clergymen Edited by J C CROSTHWAITE, M A , Rector of St Mary-at-Hill Three Volumes Octavo 7s each.

Short Sermons for Children, illustrative of the Catechism and Liturgy By the Rev. C A JOHNS, B A. 3s 6d

The Calling of a Medical Student; Four Sermons preached at King's College, London. By E H PLUMPTRE, M A , Chaplain and Divinity Lecturer. 1s 6d

Butler's Three Sermons on Human Nature, and Dissertation on Virtue. With Preface and Syllabus, by W WHEWELL, D D Second Edition 3s 6d

Butler's Six Sermons on Moral Subjects With Preface and Syllabus, by Dr WHEWELL 3s 6d.

Village Lectures on the Liturgy By W PALIN, Rector of Stifford 3s 6d

The Holy City; Historical, Topographical, and Antiquarian Notices of Jerusalem By G WILLIAMS, B D , Fellow of King's College, Cambridge Second Edition, with numerous Illustrations and Additions, and a Plan of Jerusalem, from the Ordnance Survey Two large Volumes £2 5s

** The Plan is published separately, with a Memoir, 9s , or Mounted on Rollers, 18s

History of the Holy Sepulchre. By Professor WILLIS. Reprinted from Williams's Holy City With Illustrations 9s

Notes on German Churches. By W. WHEWELL, D D , Master of Trinity College, Cambridge Third Edition. 12s

Handbook for New Zealand. Recent Information, compiled for the Use of Intending Colonists. 6s.

View of the Art of Colonization. By E GIBBON WAKEFIELD. Octavo 12s.

Travels in the Track of the Ten Thousand Greeks, a Geographical and Descriptive Account of the Expedition of Cyrus, as related by Xenophon. By W. F. AINSWORTH, F R G S. 7s 6d

Travels and Researches in Asia Minor, Mesopotamia, Chaldea, and Armenia By the same Author Two Vols , with Illustrations. 24s.

Auvergne, Piedmont, and Savoy· a Summer Ramble By C R WELD 8s 6d

Wanderings in the Republics of Western America By GEORGE BYAM With Illustrations 7s 6d

Wild Life in the Interior of Central America. By the same Author 5s.

Hesperos, or, Travels in the West. Two Volumes By Mrs HOUSTOUN 14s

Commentary on the Cuneiform Inscriptions of Babylonia and Assyria. By Lieut -Colonel RAWLINSON. Octavo 3s

Port Phillip in 1849 By Dr. CLUTTERBUCK, Nine Years Resident in the Colony With a Map 3s

Charters of the Old English Colonies in America With Introduction and Notes. By S LUCAS, M A 4s 6d

Canterbury Papers Nos. I. to VIII 6d. each, in a wrapper, 4s , or, by post, 4s 6d

Hints on Church Colonization By J C WYNTER, M A , Rector of Gatton. 6d.

Captain Cook's Voyages; with Accounts of Pitcairn's Island, and the Mutiny of the Bounty. Fourth Edition 2s 6d

Christopher Columbus; his Life, Voyages, and Discovery of the New World Third Edition 2s 6d.

Mungo Park, his Life and Travels, with an Account of his Death, and of later Discoveries Third Edition. 2s 6d

Humboldt's Travels and Discoveries in America. Second Edition 2s 6d.

GERMAN WORKS FOR LEARNERS,

By PROFESSOR BERNAYS, of King's College, London

German Grammar. 5s.

German Exercises, adapted to the Grammar, with Notes , and Specimens of German Handwriting 5s 6d

German Examples, forming a Key to the Exercises. 3s.

German Reader, with Translations and Notes 5s.

German Poetry for Beginners 4s.

German Historical Anthology. 5s.

German Poetical Anthology. 7s.

GERMAN CLASSICS,

With Introduction, and English Notes, by PROFESSOR BERNAYS, of King's College

Schiller's Maid of Orleans 2s.

Schiller's William Tell. 2s.

CLASSICAL TEXTS,

Carefully Revised by C. BADHAM, M A , PROFESSOR BROWNE, of King's College, W HAIG BROWN, M A , DR DONALDSON, of Bury, DR MAJOR, of King's College, PROFESSOR PILLANS, of Edinburgh, &c &c

CICERO de SENECTUTE 1s
CICERO de AMICITIA 1s
CICERO de OFFICIIS 2s
CICERO pro PLANCIO 1s
CICERO pro MILONE 1s
CICERO pro MURÆNA 1s
CICERONIS ORATIO PHILIPPICA SECUNDA 1s
TACITI GERMANIA 1s
TACITI AGRICOLA 1s
EXCERPTA ex TACITI ANNALIBUS 2s 6d
CÆSAR de BELLO GALLICO I to IV 1s 6d
VIRGILII GEORGICA. 1s. 6d
OVIDII FASTI. 2s
HORATII SATIRÆ 1s
HORATII CARMINA 1s 6d
HORATII ARS POETICA 6d
TERENTII ANDRIA 1s
PLATONIS PHÆDO. 2s
PLATONIS MENEXENUS 1s
PLATONIS PHÆDRUS 1s 6d.
EXCERPTA ex ARRIANO 2s 6d
SOPHOCLIS PHILOCTETES, with English Notes. 2s
SOPHOCLIS ŒDIPUS TYRANNUS, with English Notes 2s 6d
EURIPIDIS BACCHÆ 1s
ÆSCHYLI EUMENIDES 1s
PLUTARCH'S LIVES of SOLON, PERICLES, and PHILOPŒMEN 2s

Arundines Cami, sive Musarum Cantabrigiensium Lusus Canori, collegit atque edidit HENRICUS DRURY, M.A   Third Edition   12s.

The New Cratylus, Contributions towards a more Accurate Knowledge of the Greek Language   By J W DONALDSON, D D , Head Master of King Edward the Sixth's School, Bury St Edmunds   Second Edition, Octavo, much enlarged   18s

Agamemnon of Æschylus, the Text, with a Translation into English Verse, and Notes   By J CONINGTON, M A , Fellow of University College, Oxford   7s 6d

Æschylus translated into English Verse   With Notes, Life of Æschylus, and a Discourse on Greek Tragedy   By J STUART BLACKIE, Professor of Latin in Marischal College, Aberdeen   Two Volumes. 16s

Phædrus, Lysis, and Protagoras of Plato   Translated by J WRIGHT, M A , Master of Sutton Coldfield School.   4s. 6d.

Homeric Ballads   the Text, with Metrical Translations and Notes   By the late Dr MAGINN   6s

Tacitus, the Complete Works, with a Commentary, Life of Tacitus, Indices, and Notes.   Edited by Professor RITTER, of Bonn   Four Volumes   Octavo.   28s

Aristophanis Comœdiæ Vndecim, cum Notis et Indice Historice, edidit HVBERTVS A HOLDEN, A M   Coll Trin Cant Socius. Octavo   15s

Aulularia and Menæchmei of Plautus, with Notes by J HILDYARD, B D , Fellow of Christ's Coll , Camb   7s 6d each

Antigone of Sophocles, in Greek and English, with Notes   By J W DONALDSON, D D , Head Master of Bury School   9s.

Pindar s Epinician Odes, and the Fragments of his Lost Compositions, revised and explained; with copious Notes and Indices   By Dr DONALDSON   16s

Becker's Gallus , or, Roman Scenes of the Time of Augustus, with Notes and Excursus   Translated by F. METCALFE, M A   Second Edition   12s

Becker's Charicles , or, Illustrations of the Private Life of the Ancient Greeks. Translated by F. METCALFE, M A   12s

Speeches of Demosthenes against Aphobus and Onetor, Translated, with Explanatory Notes, by C RANN KENNEDY, M A , Fellow of Trin Coll , Camb   9s

Selection from the Greek Verses of Shrewsbury School, with an Account of the Iambic Metre and Style of Greek Tragedy, and Exercises in Greek Tragic Senarii.   By B H KENNEDY, D D , Head Master of Shrewsbury School   8s

Select Private Orations of Demosthenes   with English Notes   By the Rev C T PENROSE, M A , Head Master of Sherborne School.   5s.

Frogs of Aristophanes; with English Notes   By the Rev H P COOKESLEY   7s

Classical Examination Papers of King's College, London   By R. W BROWNE, M A , Professor of Classical Literature in King's College   6s

Fables of Babrius   Edited by G C. LEWIS, M.A.   5s 6d

Cambridge Greek and English Testament   Edited by J SCHOLEFIELD, M A , Professor of Greek in the University   Third Edition.   7s. 6d.

Sacred Latin Poetry ; with Notes and Introduction   By R C TRENCH, B D   7s , or 14s bound in antique calf

Commentary on the Book of the Acts of the Apostles   By W G HUMPHRY, B D , Examining Chaplain to the Lord Bishop of London   Octavo   7s

Greek Text of the Acts of the Apostles , with English Notes   By H. ROBINSON, D D   8s

New Hebrew Lexicon   Hebrew and English, arranged according to the permanent letters in each word   English and Hebrew   With a Hebrew Grammar, Vocabulary, and Analysis of the Book of Genesis   Also, a Chaldee Grammar, Lexicon, and Analysis of the Old Testament   By T JARRETT, M A , Professor of Arabic, Cambridge   Octavo.   21s

Guide to the Hebrew Student.   By H H BERNARD, Teacher of Hebrew, Cambridge   10s 6d

The Psalms in Hebrew, with Critical, Exegetical, and Philological Commentary   By G PHILLIPS, B D , Fellow and Tutor of Queen's College, Cambridge   Two Volumes   32s

Elements of Syriac Grammar   By G PHILLIPS, B D.   Second Edition .   10s

Practical Arabic Grammar .   By DUNCAN STEWART   Octavo   1 s

Ingram Content Group UK Ltd.
Milton Keynes UK
UKHW050341300323
419267UK00028B/104

9 781017 440140